PIERS TREHANE

INDEX HORTENSIS

VOLUME 1: PERENNIALS

including

Border Plants, Herbs, Bulbous Plants,
Non-woody Alpines, Aquatic Plants,
Outdoor Ferns and Ornamental Grasses

A modern nomenclator for botanists,
horticulturalists, plantsmen,
and the serious gardener

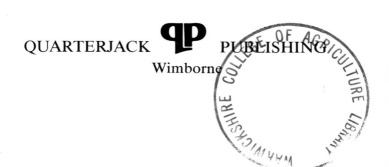

QUARTERJACK **QP** PUBLISHING

Wimborne

Published by Quarterjack Publishing
Hampreston Manor, Wimborne, Dorset BH21 7LX

Trade distribution through Prism Press Book Publishers Ltd
2 South Street, Bridport, Dorset DT6 3NQ

© R.P. Trehane 1989
First published 1989

Printed and bound in Great Britain by William Clowes Ltd
Beccles, Suffolk NR34 9QE

Typeset by Maggie Spooner Typesetting
Imperial Works, Block C, Perren Street, London NW5 3ED

Cover by Terry Whitworth
Illustration by Don Grant

ISBN 0 948117 00 1

CONTENTS

INTRODUCTION

The wealth of plants that we use to decorate our surroundings today is truly breathtaking. From earliest times, man has brought those plants he considered useful or attractive close to hand so that he might enjoy their virtues without having to travel inconvenient distances.

The spread of civilisations throughout the millennia has enriched different cultures with newer and stranger plants. The discovery of new lands, conquest of its peoples, and exploration of new territory has enabled the plant hunter to adorn his homeland with the spoils of new vegetation.

In the garden too, man has found new plants that have inspired him to develop the science of horticulture. From all walks of life, the gardener has emerged as one who has enriched the local landscape with his perception of beauty and maintenance of excellence.

The botanist has also evolved as a result of man's never-ending quest for knowledge and understanding of life. Originating as natural historians, today's botanists are highly skilled scientists with powerful research tools at hand, and with a long legacy of writings to draw upon to help them fit together the jig-saw of evolution.

While the lay gardener has named his favourite plants with a plethora of names in every different language and dialect, the botanist, in a reflection of his organised mind, has developed an orderly method of naming our plants. These names confound the restraints of national frontiers and cultures. The simple system refined by Linnaeus and his followers after 1753 AD consists of two words in a Latinised language that is so convenient that this binomial system is used as the basis for the International Code of Botanical Nomenclature. Its adoption by scientists throughout the civilised world has been instrumental in achieving better communication within the scientific community.

Only a very small proportion of the world's flora has been adopted by mankind for cultivation. From these natural jewels, new plants with an increased appeal continue to be developed, often with the result that the parent plants are no longer considered worthy of the limited space in and around our homes. It was in an effort to bring order into the chaos of names for our own creations that the International Code of Nomenclature of Cultivated Plants was introduced.

It is in this spirit of uniformity that Index Hortensis has been developed. Many individual plants are distributed under many different names — often with incorrect spelling, and this adds to the general confusion. Often the botanists are blamed for changing names. This is unfair to a noble profession. The truth of the matter is that, under the botanical codes, there is only one name permissable as being correct for each plant. The botanist, as part of diligent and excellent research, may have unearthed information that demonstrates that a hitherto well known name has been used incorrectly. Why should he be the butt of other people's ignorance?

Name changes also occur as a result of an alteration in botanical opinion. If, as a result of years of research, some brilliant mind working in a botanic garden or herbarium deduces that one of our favoured plants ought to be "shifted" into a different taxonomic position, who is the lay person to complain? Scientists of all disciplines are, by nature, critical of each other's work, and if such taxonomic revision is found acceptable by fellow workers, that review has passed the test.

While botanists disseminate their results amongst themselves in their own journals, their discoveries and ideas find few media through which to communicate to the "outside world". Academics no longer edit the popular gardening journals, and it is largely left to specialist societies to keep their membership informed about developments and changes in taxonomy and nomenclature.

It is no wonder that plant naming is confused. Is it fair to accuse the nurseryman of neglect in this direction if he is too busy trying to make a living to concern himself with matters of an academic nature?

The truth is that there has not been a single, easily available reference work that all can refer to in trying to name a plant properly. Index Hortensis attempts to provide just that in three convenient volumes. This first volume has the emphasis on perennial plants; woody plants and indoor plants will each be featured in two separate volumes.

This volume of the Index consists of an assembly of the plant names I have found in some 2,800 nursery catalogues from Northern Europe over the years 1984-1987. Any other names arise from corrected synonymy. A few names from later lists have also been incorporated during the course of later revisional work.

I have retained those plant names listed by nurseries that have ceased to trade since the plants concerned hopefully remain extant. It is important to remember that the Index does not try to cover all plants in cultivation. The basic information is taken from nursery catalogues, not from garden lists.

The list of amalgamated names has then been compared with modern floras, monographs, and other botanic literature with adjustments made so that the list might reflect modern taxonomic thought. Often, I have found conflicting botanical views on a number of matters and, after careful study, have inflicted my judgement in a rather pragmatic way to resolve a debatable issue. To some extent therefore, Index Hortensis takes a personal view when matters of opinion are required.

I have used rather modern concepts of plant families, rather than stick to the older ideas which have formed the basis for the arrangement of herbaria for so long. I detect a growing usage amongst writers and taxonomists for this modernist view as it more closely follows present-day thinking about the arrangement of plant groups.

Index Hortensis should be used as a nomenclator for today's plants. Many would like to have descriptions provided in the same volume, but such a mammoth task must remain the work of others. We live in fortunate days; more and more excellent monographs are being issued by a variety of publishing houses, floristic work flourishes, and some immense publishing projects of truly encyclopedic dimensions are being planned. By the time the next edition of this volume appears, it will be possible to look-up most current plants in up-to-date, easily available references. I make no apologies for the references I cite in this first edition. Generally, I have chosen works of excellence that have had, or should have had, a wide distribution within the gardening and horticultural public. I have deliberately excluded a comprehensive bibliography from this issue, since to do so would add a further seventy pages to an almost unwieldy volume. I plan to issue a separate bibliography at a later date for those who may be interested.

Whilst remaining a useful tool for the horticultural taxonomist, the Index is primarily designed to be used by the lay person. I have therefore refrained from using too many technical words although I have included some that would be invaluable to the gardener. For the same reasons I have spelled out the names of validating authorities in full and have not used the standard abbreviations that are familiar to botanists. I have given the date of publication to give a historical perspective to plant naming. A later edition might also specify the place of publication if there is a significant demand for this information. A few taxa do not have botanical authorities shown and are prefixed by an asterisk; such names are currently in use, although I have yet to determine whether they have taxonomic or nomenclatural validity.

A few other taxa have an incomplete botanical authority. The describer of the original name is given in round brackets in the usual way but an exclamation mark follows. This indicates that I am fairly certain that the taxon has yet to be validly transferred to the taxonomic position shown. I stress that I do not seek to generate flocks of new combinations or to offer controversial taxonomic opinion but that this has been done to re-locate a few taxa which have been "left behind" during revision. Further research will need to be carried out before validating these *nomina nuda*.

In this first edition of volume one, I have placed the emphasis on sorting out the nomenclature of nature's own plants. The problems surrounding legitimate use of cultivar names are rather awesome since such work can only be done properly after analysis of every catalogue and horticultural text ever written. Such a herculean task is likely to send anyone taking it on to an early grave and yet the gathering of the information required to establish the original valid publication of names must be done at some time. The work already done on selected groups of plants by International Registration Authorities is impressive, but to survey "everything else" presents an enormous challenge for tomorrow's researchers.

Compilation of this work has taken several years and even as I write, it becomes somewhat out of date: I have found another two hundred plant names since I ceased adding new names to this volume! A second edition will appear in due course which will show the newer introductions and reflect the continuing changes in taxonomic opinion. In the meantime I proffer a simple plea. If you know of errors in this text, or have any special knowledge, especially with regard to cultivar names, please write to me, giving some reference that I can refer to. The elusive goal of perfection can only be achieved with the aid of positive criticism. The negative cries that a manual of this sort is bound to generate lead only to further confusion and will do nothing to improve the image of either botany or horticulture.

Piers Trehane
Hampreston Manor
Wimborne, Dorset BH21 7LX

January 1989

ACKNOWLEDGEMENTS

The enormous task of collecting the information for this book and sorting out the hundreds of nomenclatural problems would not have been possible without a great deal of assistance from many people. The help, guidance and friendship that I have received has been both invaluable and inspirational. I cannot possibly give full credit to Legion in these pages. To the hundreds of nurserymen who have fed me catalogues and information, and the many gardeners and plantsmen who have told me enthusiastic stories about the plants they love, I express simple but sincere thanks.

There are some who have done me special service in my hopeless quest for perfection. I am indebted to Jim Archibald, Duncan Donald (Chelsea Physic Garden), Brian Halliwell and Brian Mathew (both at the Royal Botanic Gardens, Kew) and especially Graham Thomas for examining an early draft of plant names in great detail and for their invaluable comments, criticism and suggestions.

Others who have taken a critical look at parts of the text include, alphabetically: John Akeroyd (*Polygonaceae*), Chris Brickell (*Galanthus*), Martin Cheek (*Malvaceae*), Tom Cope (*Poaceae*), Jill Cowley (*Zingiberaceae*), Kate Donald (*Narcissus taxonomy*), Christopher Grey-Wilson (*Cyclamen*), Diana Grenfell (*Hosta*), Chris Humphries (*Anthemideae*), Sally Kington (*Narcissus cultivars*), Dick Kitchingman (*Hemerocallis*), Sabina Knees (*Apiaceae*), Alan Leslie (*Dianthus, Delphinium, Lilium*), Brian Mathew (*Helleborus, Iris and all things bulbous!*), Victoria Matthews (*Lilium, Tulipa*), David McClintock (*Cyperaceae*), Alison Paul (*Ferns*), Martin Rickard (*Fern cultivars*), Martyn Rix (*Fritillaria*), Norman Robson (*Hypericum*), Professor William Stearn (*Allium*), David Sutton (*Antirrhineae*) and Max Walters (*Alchemilla and Caryophyllaceae in part*). While respecting their comments, I should state that, in some cases, the criticisms and opinions so generously offered have not been necessarily adopted in the final text. Responsibility for omissions and errors in the Index lie squarely on my shoulders.

Nicola Round, Christine Ellwood and Malcolm Beasley in the understaffed Botany Library of the British Museum (Natural History) have been of enormous help to me in my researches as has Brent Elliott and his able assistants Barbara Collecott and Ruth Howell at the impressive Lindley Library in Vincent Square. I thank them, and the librarians at The Royal Botanic Gardens, Kew for their humour and patience over the years.

I pay particular tribute to Chris Brickell, Duncan Donald, Graham Thomas and Max Walters for their encouragement and permission to use kind words in the prospectus for this publication. I trust their faith in this work is not diminished.

Amongst the many others who deserve credit for the production of the book, I single out Colin Spooner and Julian King at Prism Press for many years of help and advice, Alan Solomon and his assistants at S & S Enterprises, Chesham, who miraculously recovered all the information when my computer failed me, and Maggie Spooner who typeset this book and who probably never wants to see another latin word ever again.

Finally I thank all members of my family who must have wondered what I have been doing these past years, but who have continued to support my body and soul even in difficult times.

HOW TO USE THE INDEX

The Index is arranged alphabetically by genus. Those names accepted as correct are shown in **bold text** and any synonyms found to be in current use are in *italics*.

For hybrid species, the epithet is preceded by the letter x and if the parentage is known, this is given in alphabetical order. The few hybrid genera are treated in the same way, exrept that parentage is shown after the specific epithets concerned.

After each botanical epithet the author citation for the name is shown along with the year of publication.

Family names adopted in the Index are shown within square brackets opposite the generic name.

Some larger genera have been further classified by Section or by other such taxonomic device to enable the reader to recognise similarities within groups of taxa. The conventions adopted vary within different genera.

Taxa below species rank are listed alphabetically and not in taxonomic order since this reflects the conventions used by nursery catalogues.

Cultivar names appear in single quotation marks '. . . .'. The raiser or introducer may be given in square brackets [. . . .] afterwards. Normally, just the raiser's name is given but the introducer or second party may be credited by preceding his name with "via". Any date given is the earliest date found and may be shown prefixed with a "c" or a "pre-" to demonstrate an approximation or that the plant is known to have been in cultivation before the evidenced date.

Those cultivar names known to be registered by an International Registration Authority are indicated by a "®". This has not been done for *Gladiolus*, *Paeonia* or *Narcissus* cultivars since at the time of going to press, this information had yet to be confirmed.

A full list of codes used in the Index is given on page 63, and a list of abbreviations on page 64.

REFERENCES CITED IN THE INDEX

Monographic accounts are featured under generic names. Other works of reference are indicated on the right-hand margin as being useful sources of further information, particularly for cultural notes and identification.

Future editions of this volume will incorporate newer works which are known to be in preparation. For the time being, the following works are well known, and are often carried by public libraries.

"The European Garden Flora". Written by botanists for gardeners, this imaginative project gives excellent general descriptions of our garden plants down to species rank. So far, just two volumes have appeared and the remainder seem to be on the way. The nomenclature does not always agree with that in this Index, so beware! There are useful keys for identification, but no illustrations. The whole project suffers from being over-priced for all but the keenest gardener, but good libraries would be foolish not to carry a set.

"Perennial Garden Plants". Certainly the most important book on its subject in recent years, written in characteristic style by one of our foremost plantsmen, Graham Stuart Thomas. This work has done more to stimulate the resurgent interest in perennials than any other in modern times with its enthusiastic descriptions and astute observations on plant associations.

"Collector's Alpines" by Royton E. Heath remains the standard text on alpine plants.

"The Bulb Book" by Martyn Rix and Roger Phillips is a first-rate photographic guide to over 800 hardy bulbs and a truly invaluable aid to identification.

"The Smaller Bulbs". Written by Brian Mathew, one of our foremost botanists from Kew, this is set to become the standard text on its subject. There are excellent descriptions and illustrations and cultural notes based on the author's personal observations.

"The Dictionary of Garden Plants in Colour". The classic illustrated guide to the full range of garden plants by Roy Hay and Patrick Synge. This book was the first of its kind and is on everyone's bookshelf. Although in need of revision, the photographs remain very useful for rudimentary identification.

The Reader's Digest **"Encyclopaedia of Garden Plants and Flowers"** is another widely distributed book of great value. A first-class set of contributors ensure a quality up-to-date text with good cultural advice and illustrations. Now into a fourth edition.

All the above titles are in print and available from good bookshops carrying a comprehensive range of gardening books.

PLANT TAXONOMY AND NOMENCLATURE

The science of classification is called **taxonomy**, derived from the word **taxon** (plural **taxa**) meaning a unit of classification. Someone placing taxa in order by the process of classification is called a **taxonomist**.

With around 330,000 green plant species recognisable as being distinct from each other, it is vital that the botanist has a workable system of classification to help him identify plant material. The system employed uses a number of descending **ranks**, each with its own set of characteristics so that the taxonomist can determine where a plant should be placed in the general scheme.

Having established where a plant belongs in this hierarchy, the botanist must then decide how to name it. Study of the systems and methods of naming is covered by the term **nomenclature** and for botanists, the rules and regulations are laid down in the International Code of Botanical Nomenclature (Botanical Code or ICBN). It is important to remember that the practice of nomenclature comes after decisions of taxonomy.

Plant (and animal) species are named using a **binomial** made by combining a **generic epithet** with a **specific epithet**. The first book to include binomials for all plant species described was the 1753 edition of *Species Plantarum* by Linnaeus and for this reason 1753 is taken as the starting date for modern botanical nomenclature. Users of this Index will observe how often Linnaeus 1753 appears after a generic or specific epithet in the text, — an indication of how many of today's garden plants were around in the first half of the 18th century.

Binomials are as **illegitimate** as common names are unless they are **validly published**. To be validly published nowadays, a name must obey the rules of the ICBN, be accompanied by a diagnosis in Latin or by reference to a previously published valid diagnosis, have its nomenclatural **type** specified, and have its rank stated.

The diagnosis specifies the details of a plant which make it distinct from another. The type is the preserved specimen or drawing from which the original author made his diagnosis. Thus, in drawing up a description of a plant, the author has one specimen in mind to which anything else must be matched in the process of **determination** or identification. There are special provisions for designating replacement types if the original is lost or destroyed.

Campanula glomerata Linnaeus 1753 refers to the specimen described and named by Linnaeus in that year. Use of the author citation is an important part of the name when more than one author has used the same epithet for quite different plants.

Author citations may appear in a number of forms. *Sparaxis pulcherrima* Hooker f. 1866 is now known as *Dierama pulcherrimum* (Hooker f.) Baker 1877 since in 1877, Baker transferred the species first described by Hooker junior in 1866 to the new genus. This form of citation is also used when taxonomic rank is altered. *Saxifraga rosacea* ssp. *hartii* (D. A. Webb) D. A. Webb 1987 was originally described by Webb as *Saxifraga hartii* but in later work he changed his mind and placed it as a subspecies of another. The author of the original name or **basionym** is placed in round brackets.

Two other styles of author citation are commonly used. Where a name has been coined by one person but the ensuing description made by someone else, the word "ex" separates the authorities, the validating authority appearing last. Sometimes an author has described a plant in someone else's work, in which case the authorities are separated by the word "in", the validating authority appearing first.

NAMING OUR GARDEN PLANTS

While the rules of nomenclature of nature's own plants are laid down in the ICBN, cultivar names are governed by the provisions in the International Code of Nomenclature of Cultivated Plants (Cultivated Code or ICNCP).

The international term *cultivar* is derived from the words *cul*tivated *var*iety, and is quite different from the botanical term *varietas*. A cultivar denotes a clearly recognisable cultivated plant which, when reproduced, retains those recognisable characteristics.

Cultivars therefore, are either the result of deliberate crosses, or selections of plants found in the wild or in the garden, and maintained by mankind.

In this Index, the differentiation is made between widely-occuring natural variants of a species and collected oddities which have been brought into cultivation. The former, if validly described, have usually been given a Latinised name, while the latter carry cultivar names. Some validly described plants are treated here as cultivars if their original description was based upon a garden or one-off native plant as has so often happened in North American and Japanese botanical literature.

All words in a cultivar name begin with a capital letter and are either prefixed with "cv" or are enclosed in single quotation marks. Double quotation marks must never be used for cultivar names.

The rules of the Cultivated Code took effect from January 1st 1959. On or after that date, all new cultivar names must be fancy names, that is, not in Latin form. Since that date for example, it is not permissable to name plants 'Alba', 'Plena', 'Rosea' or 'Variegata'. Imaginary cultivars could, however, have names like 'Wimborne Red'. 'Hampreston White' or 'Trehane's Variegated', provided that the plants were distinct and that such names had never been used before for plants within the same group. Names should be of one or two words, never more than three.

Names in a Latin style published before 1959 are not changed unless transferred to a different genus in which case the gender might have to be altered to match the generic name.

Cultivar names must now not begin with an abbreviation, except for the abbreviation "Mrs." in English or the equivalent foreign form of address for married women. Title words such as Colonel, Reverend and Saint must be spelled in full.

International Registration Authorities (IRAs) have been set up under the ICNCP for a number of plant genera or groups. This has provided great stability for such large genera as *Delphinium, Dianthus, Gladiolus Hemerocallis, Hosta, Iris, Narcissus, Paeonia, Sempervivum* and *Tulipa*. Raisers or introducers of new plants covered by IRAs should always register the name along with details of distinguishing features, breeding and other aspects of interest. Registration costs very little and is often free of charge, certificates usually being issued to registrants. A list of current IRAs for plant groups in this volume is given on pages 18-21.

Copies of the current (1980) ICNCP are available from RHS Enterprises Ltd, Wisley Garden, Woking, Surrey GU23 6QB at £6.95 + £2.00 post and packing.

PLANT FAMILIES

It may seem slightly irrelevant to include a circumspection of families in a nomenclator such as Index Hortensis, but since so many nursery lists include this information, incorporation is essential. Of all the higher taxa, the family taxon is the most useful to the gardener. An unfamiliar plant name becomes less mysterious if the reader can associate it with other plants he knows.

For dicotyledons, the Index follows Professor Cronquist's *"An integrated system of classification of flowering plants"* (1981). Monocotyledon families are as described in *"The families of the monocotyledons"* by Dahlgren, Clifford and Yeo (1985), but adjusted to follow the pragmatic interpretation used in the arrangement of the herbarium at the Royal Botanic Gardens, Kew.

Fern families are designated according to the arrangement in *"A Checklist of European Pteridophytes"* by Derrick, Jermy and Paul in Sommerfeltia 6 (1987) which reflects the arrangement of the cryptogram herbarium at the British Museum (Natural History).

An alphabetic synopsis of families with included genera is given on pages 51-62.

HERB NAMES

A noticeable feature of British horticulture is the enormous number of herb nurseries: there seem to be more in England than in the rest of Europe put together. Examination of nursery lists shows that herbalists are not generally concerned with questions of nomenclature. The preferred use of vernacular names by most such nurseries may suit the cook, medicine man or dyer, but surely the precision of a botanical name should be included in all such nursery catalogues. For the more enlightened herbalist, a review of the names used in the trade may be found on pages 42-51, cross-referenced to the nomenclature adopted in the Index. This list is in need of further refinement, and the compiler would be glad to receive comments of a constructive nature.

KEEPING UP TO DATE

Apart from by attending shows and by being a member of a worthy society, the best way to keep up to date with changes in the plant world is by subscribing to worthwhile journals. There are a number of lightweight popular magazines directed at the leisure industry of gardening, but in the United Kingdom there are very few publications with more serious content. Listed here are four publications that the compiler considers indispensable to the keener gardener and plantsman. Subscription to all four in 1989 would cost just £1.45 per week. Institutions and overseas subscribers should check for special rates.

"The Garden" is the monthly journal of the Royal Horticultural Society. The annual standard subscription of £14.00, entitles members to entry to Wisley (and other gardens) and to the Westminster shows as well as receipt of this high quality publication. Few societies show such good value for money and receipt of the journal alone more than justifies the cost of membership. The address for the RHS is given on page 27.

"The Plantsman" is a quarterly magazine for all dedicated gardeners wishing to learn more about plants and how to grow them. Articles are of the highest standard and yet are not over-technical. This invaluable publication is published in association with the RHS and is available from Home and Law Publishing Ltd, Greater London House, Hampstead Road, London NW1 7QQ. The current annual subscription of £12.00 is remarkably good value.

"The Kew Magazine" Published for the Bentham-Moxton Trust at The Royal Botanic Gardens, Kew by Basil Blackwell Ltd., 108 Cowley Road, Oxford OX4 1JF to whom subscriptions (£27.50 per annum for individuals) should be sent. The magazine has a long and dignified history all of its own but the current editors have succeeded in bridging the gap between professional botanists and horticulturists and gardeners. Four parts of this beautifully produced magazine are issued yearly.

"Hortus" is the most recent and welcome addition to the bookshelf. Privately published four times a year, it contains in-depth articles by some of the best writers around today. The emphasis is certainly on the more decorative aspects of gardening as opposed to botany and much of content features garden history, travel and plant people. This wonderful read is available by subscription £22.00 per annum) from Hortus, The Neuadd, Rhyader, Powys LD6 5HH.

WHERE TO FIND THE PLANTS

The demonstration and botanic gardens listed on pages 22 to 24 hold a massive range of labelled plants between them. National Collections (pages 28 to 41) are often available to view by prior arrangement with their owners and some of these collections may have a selection of plants for sale. National Trust gardens and other private gardens open under the National Gardens Scheme also often have less common plants available for sale.

Garden centres usually only carry a small range of stock bought in from nurseries according to season, so unless you are lucky enough to live near a major retail nursery, you will have difficulty finding less usual plants.

The only handy directory currently available is **"The Plant Finder"** published annually since 1987 by Headmain Ltd, Lakeside, Gaines Road, Whitbourne, Worcestershire WR6 5RD for the Hardy Plant Society. This is an extremely useful publication containing about 27,000 plant names, including Trees, Shrubs, Climbers, Chrysanthemums and Dahlias, and showing the whereabouts of some UK nurseries listing them. The nomenclature given does not always match that in this Index so beware!

Another very useful book is the **"Guide to Specialist Nurseries and Garden Suppliers of Britain and Ireland"**, an impressive publication by Garden Art Press Ltd., Northiam, East Sussex TN31 6NH which, as the name suggests, has details of nurseries stocking specific groups of plants.

"Trehane's Plantfinder", details about which were first published in 1986 and which will list the whereabouts of extant plants in Index Hortensis, will be published eventually. This work in three occasional volumes of about 2,000 pages each, and of the size of 'Who's Who', will cover known European sources of garden plants.

In the meantime, membership of, and participation in a specialist plant society such as those listed on pages 25 to 27 will keep you in touch with what is happening in horticulture. Some of the societies are regional, others national with local branches. They all arrange shows during the year and most have regular newsletters, journals or year books packed with information. Dialogue with friends in such societies is the surest way to locate the less usual plant.

A certain way to see, and often acquire, new plants is by attending the regular shows at the Royal Horticultural Society in Vincent Square, London, where visitors may buy plants from trade exhibitors on a cash-and-carry basis. New and neglected plants put up for award are shown, and many smaller specialist societies mount keen competitions amongst their membership which never fail to be of great interest to all plantsmen.

THE NATIONAL COUNCIL FOR CONSERVATION OF PLANTS AND GARDENS

One of the most exciting developments in horticulture over the past ten years has been the enormous success of NCCPG. Founded in 1979 following a conference sponsored by the Royal Horticultural Society, it now has some 5,000 members spread across the British Isles. Membership is divided into autonomous regional groups with varying geographical spread, each group actively engaged in locating and surveying important gardens and plant collections. Finding and saving scarce plants has been a major achievement as has been the creation of National Collections where groups of similar plants are gathered together under caring hands to be perpetuated for posterity.

The aims of NCCPG are:

A. To encourage the conservation of uncommon plants which are valuable because of their historic, aesthetic, scientific or educational value by propagating and distributing them as widely as possible.
B. To list plants held in important collections and gardens.
C. To encourage the widest possible cultivation of uncommon and endangered plants by arranging conferences, exhibitions, discussions and visits to gardens, specialist plant collections and nurseries.
D. To encourage the reintroduction and distribution of uncommon and endangered plants.
E. To establish and support National Collections of specified genera, part genera and other defined collections of plants, for the enjoyment and information of the public and the benefit of science.

The setting up of a network of National Collections was not a new idea, it being first promoted after the Second World War by the Ministry of Agriculture which recognised the importance of having well documented reference collections of economically important plants in scientific institutions. The idea was short-lived and the only collection surviving is that for Tulip species at Cambridge Botanic Garden.

The great success of present-day collections lies largely with the enthusiasm of the modern gardener and horticulturist. As commercial pressures exert themselves on the nursery trade, it has been left more and more to the individual to keep, cherish, propagate and ultimately distribute plants at risk from extinction. Many of the plants kept in these reserves will be either the treasures of tomorrow or the parents of new generations of garden delights.

Of the 467 current National Collections, those 240 dealing with plants relevant to this volume of Index Hortensis are listed on pages 28 to 41.

If you have a specific interest in a group of plants, why not apply to become a collection holder? The procedure for application is quite simple, and although collections are maintained and developed mainly at the holder's expense, valuable assistance with research and acquisition of plants from botanic gardens and elsewhere is often provided by the Secretariat.

Everybody interested in our garden heritage should join their local NCCPG group. Membership is not expensive, and the rewards are tremendous. To discover your local group contact, or for any further information about NCCPG, write, enclosing a stamped addressed envelope to: The General Secretary, NCCPG, Wisley Garden, Woking, Surrey, GU23 6QB, or telephone 0483 224234 during office hours.

INTERNATIONAL REGISTRATION AUTHORITIES
FOR CULTIVAR NAMES

(Only for those genera or groups pertaining to this volume)

Allium, see Hyacinthus, etc

ALOE:
> The South African Aloe Breeders Association, attn.: Mr. A. J. Bezuidenhout, P.O. Box 59904, Karen Park, 0118, Pretoria, Republic of South Africa.

Alstroemeria, see Hyacinthus, etc
X Amarcrinum, see Amaryllidaceae
X Amarine, see Amaryllidaceae
X Amarygia, see Amaryllidaceae

AMARYLLIDACEAE: excluding *Hemerocallis* and *Narcissus*:
> The American Plant Life Society, attn.: Mr. James M Weinstock, 10331 Independence, Chatsworth, California 91311, U.S.A.

Amaryllis, see Amaryllidaceae
Amaryllis, see Hyacinthus, etc.
Anemone, see Hyacinthus, etc.
Anomatheca, see Hyacinthus, etc.

ARACEAE:
> International Aroid Society, attn.: Mr. John Banta, Route 2, Box 144, Alva, Florida 33920, U. S. A.

Babiana, see Hyacinthus, etc.
Brodiaea, see Hyacinthus, etc.

BROMELIACEAE:
> The Bromeliad Society Inc., attn.: Mr Joseph F Carrone Jr., 305 North Woodlawn Avenue, Metairies, Louisiana 70001, U.S.A.

Brunsvigia, see Amaryllidaceae
Bulbocodium, see Hyacinthus, etc.
Calochortus, see Hyacinthus, etc.
Camassia, see Hyacinthus, etc.
Canna, see Hyacinthus, etc.
Chionodoxa, see Hyacinthus, etc.
Chlidanthus, see Amaryllidaceae

CHRYSANTHEMUMS, perennials only:
> National Chrysanthemum Society, attn.: Mr. H. B. Locke, National Chrysanthemum Society, 2 Lucas House, Craven Road, Rugby. Warwickshire CV21 3JQ, U. K.

Clivia, see Amaryllidaceae
Colchicum, see Hyacinthus, etc.
Corydalis, see Hyacinthus, etc.
Crinum, see Amaryllidaceae
Crocosmia, see Hyacinthus, etc.
Crocus, see Hyacinthus, etc.
Cyclamen, see Hyacinthus, etc.
Cyrtanthus, see Amaryllidaceae

DAHLIA:
The Royal Horticultural Society. attn.: Mr. David Pycraft, Royal Horticultural Society's Garden, Wisley, Woking, Surrey GU23 6QB, U. K.

DELPHINIUM, perennials only:
The Royal Horticultural Society, attn.: Dr. Alan C. Leslie, Royal Horticultural Society's Garden, Wisley, Woking, Surrey GU23 6QB, U. K.

DIANTHUS:
The Royal Horticultural Society, attn.: Dr. Alan C. Leslie, Royal Horticultural Society's Garden, Wisley, Woking, Surrey GU23 6QB, U.K.

Dichelostemma, see Hyacinthus, etc.
Eranthis, see Hyacinthus, etc.
Eremurus, see Hyacinthus, etc.
Erythronium, see Hyacinthus, etc.
Eucomis, see Hyacinthus, etc.
Eucharis, see Amaryllidaceae
Eustephia, see Amaryllidaceae
*Ferraria,*see Hyacinthus, etc.
Freesia, see Hyacinthus, etc,
Fritillaria, see Hyacinthus, etc.
Galanthus, see Amaryllidaceae
Galtonia, see Hyacinthus,etc.

GLADIOLUS:
North American Gladiolus Council, attn.: Mr. Samuel N. Fisher, 11345 Moreno Avenue, Lakeside, California 92040, U.S.A.

Gladiolus (primary hybrids), see Hyacinthus, etc.
Gloriosa, see Hyacinthus, etc.
Habranthus, see Amaryllidaceae
Haemanthus, see Amaryllidaceae

HARDY HERBACEOUS PERENNIALS, apart from those genera for which IRA's have been appointed:
Internationale Stauden-Union (ISU) (International Hardy Plant Union); att.: Dr. Josef Sieber, Mur-Str. 22, D-8050 Freising, Federal Republic of Germany.

HEMEROCALLIS:
American Hemerocallis Society, attn.: Mr. W. E. Munroe, 2244 Cloverdale Avenue, Baton Rouge, Louisiana 70808, U.S.A.

Hermodactylis, see Hyacinthus, etc.
Hesperantha, see Hyacinthus, etc.
Homeria, see Hyacinthus, etc.

HOSTA:
American Hosta Society, attn.: Mr. Mervin C. Eisel, University of Minnesota Landscape Arboretum, 3675 Arboretum Drive, Chanhassen, Minnesota 55317, U.S.A.

BRITISH REGISTRARS: Ann & Roger Bowden, Cleave House, Sticklepath, Okehampton, Devon, EX20 2NN

Hyacinthella, see Hyacinthus, etc.
Hyacinthoides, see Hyacinthus, etc.

HYACINTHUS, and other BULBOUS and TUBEROUS-ROOTED PLANTS, excluding *Tulipa*, *Dahlia*, *Lilium* and *Narcissus*:
Royal General Bulbgrowers' Society, attn.: Ing. J. R. Stuurman, P. O.Box 175, 2180 AD Hillegom, Netherlands.

Hymenocallis, see Amaryllidaceae
Ipheion, see Hyacinthus, etc.

IRIS, excluding bulbous *Iris*:
American Iris Society, att: Mrs. Kathleen Kay Nelson, P.O. Box 37613, Omaha, Nebraska 68137, U.S.A.

BRITISH REGISTRAR: Mrs J. Peirson, 35 Middle Road, Higher Denham, Bucks, UB9 5EG

Iris (bulbous), see Hyacinthus, etc.
Ixia, see Hyacinthus, etc.
Ixiolirion, see Hyacinthus, etc.
Jovibarba, see Sempervivum
Lachenalia, see Hyacinthus, etc.
Lepeyrousia, see Hyacinthus, etc.
Leucojum, see Amaryllidaceae

LILIUM:
The Royal Horticultural Society, attn.: Dr. Alan C. Leslie, Royal Horticultural Society's Garden, Wisley, Woking, Surrey GU23 6QB, U. K.

Lycoris, see Hyacinthus,etc.
Moraea, see Hyacinthus, etc.
Muscari, see Hyacinthus, etc.

NARCISSUS:
The Royal Horticultural Society, attn.: Mrs Sally Kington, The Royal Horticultural Society, P. O. Box 313, Vincent Square, London SW1P 2PE, U.K.

Nerine, see Amaryllidaceae
Odontostomum, see Amaryllidaceae
Ornithogalum, see Hyacinthus, etc.
Oxalis, see Hyacinthus, etc.

PAEONIA:
American Peony Society, attn.: Mrs. Greta M. Kessenich, 250 Interlachen Road, Hopkins, Minnesota 55343, U.S.A.

Panacratium, see Amaryllidaceae

PENSTEMON:
American Penstemon Society, attn.: Mr. Mark McDonough, 4725-119th Avenue SE, Bellevue, Washington 98006, U.S.A.

Phaedranassa, see Amaryllidaceae

PHORMIUM:
> Royal New Zealand Institute of Horticulture, attn.: Mr. L. J. Metcalf, c/o Parks & Recreation Dept., Invercargill City Council, P. O. Box 58, Invercargill, New Zealand.

Polianthes, see Amaryllidaceae
Puschkinia, see Hyacinthus, etc.
Ranunculus (bulbous), see Hyacinthus, etc.
Rhodophiala, see Amaryllidaceae
*Rosularia,*see Sempervivum
Sauromatum, see Hyacinthus, etc.
Scadoxus, see Amaryllidaceae
*Scilla,*see Hyacinthus, etc.

SEMPERVIVUM, including *JOVIBARBA* and *ROSULARIA*:
> The Sempervivum Society, attn.: Mr. Peter J. Mitchell, 11 Wingle Tye Road, Burgess Hill, West Sussex RH15 9HR, U. K.

Sparaxis, see Hyacinthus, etc.
Sprekelia, see Amaryllidaceae
*Sternbergia,*see Amaryllidaceae
Streptanthera, see Hyacinthus, etc.
Tecophilaea, see Amaryllidaceae
Tigridia, see Hyacinthus, etc.
Triteleia, see Hyacinthus, etc.
Tritonia, see Hyacinthus, etc.

TULIPA:
> Royal General Bulbgrowers' Society, attn.: Ing. J. R. Stuurman, P.O. Box 175, 2180 AD Hillegom, Netherlands.

Veltheimia, see Hyacinthus, etc.
Zantedeschia, see Hyacinthus, etc.
Zephyranthes, see Amaryllidaceae
*Zigadenus,*see Hyacinthus, etc.

BOTANIC GARDENS

The following Botanic and Demonstration Gardens
are known to be open to the public.

*The information was checked prior to going to press but potential visitors are advised to
ensure there has been no alteration to opening times or entrance charges.*

BATH BOTANICAL GARDENS
Royal Victoria Park, Marlborough Lane, BATH, Avon, BA22 2NQ
Tel: (0225) 24728 (Nurseries)
Open: Dawn to Dusk, Every Day. Charge: Free

BIRMINGHAM BOTANICAL GARDENS
Westbourne Road, Edgbaston, BIRMINGHAM, B15 3TR
Tel: 021-454 1860
Open: Monday - Saturday, 9.00am - 8.00pm or Dusk
Sunday, 10.00am - 8.00pm or Dusk
Closed: Christmas Day
Charges: £1.70 Adults (£2.00 on Sundays), 85p Children daily

BRISTOL UNIVERSITY BOTANIC GARDENS
Bracken Hill, North Road, Leigh Woods, BRISTOL, BS8 3PL
Tel: (0272) 733682
Open: Monday - Friday, 8.30am - 5.00pm (Members only on Saturdays & Sundays)
Closed: Bank Holidays (open to Members) Charge: Free

CAMBRIDGE UNIVERSITY BOTANIC GARDEN
Cory Lodge, Bateman Street, CAMBRIDGE, CB2 1JS
Tel:(0223) 336265
Open: Monday - Saturday, 8.00am - 6.00pm or Dusk
Members only on Sundays
Charge: Free

CHELSEA PHYSIC GARDEN
66 Royal Hospital Road, LONDON, SW3
Tel: 01-352 5646
Open: Mid-April - Mid-October, 2.00pm - 5.00pm
Charges: £2.00 Adults, £1.00 Children, Students & UB40s

CRUICKSHANK BOTANIC GARDEN
University of Aberdeen, St. Machar Drive, ABERDEEN, AB9 2UD
Tel: 0224-272000 ext. 2704
Open: Monday - Friday,9.00am - 4.30pm.
Saturdays & Sundays, May - September, 2.00pm - 5.00pm
Charge: Free

DAWYCK BOTANIC GARDENS
Stobo, Tweddale, Peebleshire EH45 9JU
Tel: (07216) 254
Open: 10.00am - 5.00pm, April 1st - October 26th
Charges: 60p Adults, 30p OAPs & Children

DUNDEE UNIVERSITY BOTANIC GARDEN
516 Perth Road, DUNDEE, DD2 1LW
Entrance in Riverside Drive
Tel: (0382) 66939
Open: March - October, 10.00am - 4.30pm
Closed: Sundays
Charge: Collection Box

DURHAM UNIVERSITY BOTANIC GARDEN
University of Durham, Hollingside Lane, DURHAM, DH1 3TN
Tel: 091-374 2671
Open: Daily, 9am - 4pm, (Visitor's Centre closes later). Charge: Free

FLETCHER MOSS BOTANICAL GARDENS
Millgate Lane, Didsbury, MANCHESTER, M20 8SD
Tel: 061-434 1877
Open: Monday - Friday, 7.45am - Dusk
Saturday & Sunday, 9.00am - Dusk
Charge: Free

GLASGOW BOTANIC GARDENS
Great Western Road, GLASGOW, G12 0UE
Tel: 041-334 2422
Open: Daily, 7.00am - Dusk. Charge: Free

HARLOW CAR GARDENS
(*The Garden of the Northern Horticultural Society*)
Crag Lane, HARROGATE, North Yorkshire, HG3 1QB
Tel: (0423) 65418
Open: Daily, 9.00am - 7.30pm or Dusk, if earlier.
Charges: Non Members; £2.00 Adults, £1.50 OAPs, Children Free

HUME'S SOUTH LONDON BOTANICAL INSTITUTE BOTANIC GARDEN
323 Norwood Road, LONDON, SE24 9AQ
Tel: 01-674 5787
Open: Mondays are best, telephone first. Charge: Free

LEICESTER UNIVERSITY BOTANIC GARDEN
Stoughton Drive South, Oadby, LEICESTER, LE2 2NA
Tel: (0533) 717725
Open: Monday - Friday, 10.00am - 5.00pm
Closed: Bank Holidays. Charge: Free

LIVERPOOL UNIVERSITY BOTANIC GARDEN
Ness, Neston, SOUTH WIRRAL, L64 4AY
Tel: 051-336 2135
Open: Daily, 9.00am - Dusk
Closed: Christmas Day
Charges: Expected to be (1989) £1.80 for Adults £1.00 OAPs & Children
Reduced rates in Winter months

LOGAN BOTANIC GARDEN
Port Logan, STRANRAER, DG9 9ND
Tel: 077-686 231
Open: 10.00am - 5.00pm, April 1st - October 26th
Charges: 60p Adults, 30p OAPs & Children

OXFORD UNIVERSITY BOTANIC GARDEN
Rose Lane, OXFORD, OX1 4AX
Tel: (0865) 242737
Open: March - October
Monday - Saturday, 8.30am - 5.00pm
Sunday, 9.00am - 5.00pm
October - March
Monday - Saturday, 9.00am - 4.30pm
Sunday, 10.00am - 4.30pm
Closed: Christmas Day & Good Friday
Charge: Free

THE ROYAL BOTANIC GARDEN, EDINBURGH
Inverleith Row, EDINBURGH, EH3 5LR
Tel: 031-552 7171
Open: Monday - Saturday, 9.00am - Dusk
Sunday, 11.00am - Dusk
Closed: Christmas Day & New Year's Day
Charge: Free

THE ROYAL BOTANIC GARDENS, KEW
Kew, RICHMOND, Surrey, TW9 3AB
Tel: 01-9401171
Open: Daily, 9.30am - Dusk
Closed: Christmas Day & New Year's Day
Charges: (1988) 50p Adults, Children Free

SHEFFIELD BOTANICAL GARDEN
Clarkehouse Road, SHEFFIELD, South Yorkshire, S10 2LN
Tel: (0742) 671115
Open: Monday - Friday, 7.30am - Dusk
Saturday & Sunday, 10.00am - Dusk
Charge: Free

SOUTHAMPTON UNIVERSITY BOTANIC GARDEN
Biology Department, Building 44, University of Southampton,
SOUTHAMPTON, SO9 5NH
Tel: (0703) 595000 ext. 2444
Open: Monday - Friday, 9.00am - 5.00pm.
Closed: Christmas Week, Easter Week & Bank Holidays
Charge: Free

ST. ANDREWS BOTANIC GARDEN
The Canongate, ST ANDREWS, Fife, KY16 8RP
Open: April, Daily, 10.00am - 4.00pm
May - September,Daily, 10.00am - 7.00pm
October, 10.00am - 4.00pm
November - March, Monday - Friday, 10.00am - 4.00pm
Charge: Unknown

UNIVERSITY COLLEGE OF SWANSEA BOTANIC GARDEN
Singleton Park, SWANSEA, SA2 8PP
Tel: (0792) 295386
Open: Monday - Thursday 9.00am - 4.30pm
Friday 9.00am - 4.00pm
Closed: Saturdays & Sundays, Christmas Eve - about January 2nd.
Charge: Free

WAKEHURST PLACE
Ardingly, HAYWARDS HEATH, West Sussex, RH17 6TN
Tel: (0444) 892701
Open: Daily,
10.00am - 4.00pm/5.00pm (Winter)
10.00am - 7.00pm (Summer)
Closed: Christmas Day & New Year's Day
Charges: £1.50 Adults, 60p Children

WISLEY GARDEN
(*The Garden of the Royal Horticultural Society*)
Wisley, WOKING, Surrey, GU23 6QB
Tel: (0483) 224234
Open: 10.00am to Dusk or 7.00pm
Closed: Sundays, except to Members & Christmas Day
Charges: £2.50 Adults, £1.00 Children 6-14 years

SPECIALIST SOCIETIES

This list of Societies and other Associations covers plant groups covered in this volume. The names and addresses given under each is the contact or spokesman that one should use to gain further information. Most societies have special interest or regional groups that the contact person can put you in touch with.

ALPINE GARDEN SOCIETY
Hon. Secretary: Mr E. M. Upward,
Lye End Link, St. Johns,
Woking, Surrey, GU21 1SW
Tel: (04862) 69327

BOTANICAL SOCIETY OF THE BRITISH ISLES
c/o Dept.of Botany,
British Museum (Natural History),
Cromwell Road,
London, SW7 5BD
Tel: 01-589 6323

BRITISH BROMELIAD SOCIETY
Hon. Secretary: Mr R. J. Lucibell,
7 Fontayne Avenue,
Romford, Essex, RM13 7TH
Tel: (04027) 54620

BRITISH CACTUS & SUCCULENT SOCIETY
Hon. Publicity Officer: Miss W. E. Dunn,
43 Dewer Drive,
Sheffield, S7 2GR
Tel: (0742) 361649

BRITISH & EUROPEAN GERANIUM SOCIETY
Hon. Secretary: Mrs D. P. Codling,
56 Shrigley Road, Higher Poynton,
Cheshire, SK12 1TF
Tel: (0625) 873056

BRITISH GLADIOLUS SOCIETY
Chairman: Mr Arthur Smith,
3 Baddeley Drive, Wigston,
Leicester, LE8 1BF
Tel: (0533) 811075

BRITISH HOSTA & HEMEROCALLIS SOCIETY
Hon. Secretary: Mr Roger Bowden,
Cleave Path, Sticklepath,
Oakhampton, Devon EX20 2NN
Tel: (083784) 0481

BRITISH IRIS SOCIETY
Hon. Secretary: Mr P.R. Maynard,
43 Sea Lane, Goring-by-Sea,
Worthing, West Sussex BN12 4QD
Tel: (0903) 41993

BRITISH NATIONAL CARNATION SOCIETY
Hon. General Secretary:
Mrs P.E. Dimond,
3 Canberra Close, Hornchurch,
Essex RM12 5TR
Tel: (04024) 41786

BRITISH PELARGONIUM AND GERANIUM SOCIETY
Hon. Secretary: Mrs J. Taylor,
23 Beech Crescent, Kidlington,
Oxford, OX5 1DW
Tel: (08675) 5063

BRITISH PTERIDOLOGICAL SOCIETY
c/o Dept. of Botany,
British Museum (Natural History),
Cromwell Road, London, SW7 5BD
Tel: 01-589 6323

CORNISH GARDEN SOCIETY
Hon. Secretary: Mr L. Abbott,
Top Meadow, St Germans Road,
Callington, Cornwall, PL17 7EN
Tel: (0579) 82159

COTTAGE GARDEN SOCIETY
Hon. Correspondence Secretary:
Pat Taylor,
Old Hall Cottage, Pump Lane,
Churton, Chester CH3 6LR

CYCLAMEN SOCIETY
Hon. Secretary: Mr P.J.M. Moore,
Tile Barn House, Standen Street,
Iden Green, Benenden,
Kent TN17 4LB
Tel: (0580) 240221

DAFFODIL SOCIETY
Hon. Secretary: Mr D. Barnes,
32 Montgomery Avenue,
Sheffield S7 1NZ
Tel: (0742) 550559

DELPHINIUM SOCIETY
*Hon. Secretary:*Mr V. A. Labati,
143 Victoria Road, Horley,
Surrey, RH6 7AS
Tel: (0293) 782145

GARDEN HISTORY SOCIETY
Hon. Membership Secretary:
Mrs Anne Richard,
5 The Knoll, Hereford HR1 1RU

HARDY PLANT SOCIETY
Hon. General Secretary:
Mrs Jean Sambrook,
Garden Cottage, 214 Ruxley Lane,
West Ewell, Surrey, KT17 9EU
Tel: (0272) 872067

HEBE SOCIETY
Hon. Secretary: Mr G. Scoble,
7 Friars Stile Road, Richmond,
Surrey, TW10 6NH
Tel: 01-940 3819

HERB SOCIETY
77 Great Peter Street,
London, SW1P 2EZ
Tel:01-222 3634

INTERNATIONAL ASCLEPIAD SOCIETY
Hon. Secretary: Mr L. Delderfield,
136 Chanctonbury Road,
Burgess Hill,
West Sussex RH15 9HA
Tel: (04446) 3579

IRISH GARDEN PLANT SOCIETY
Reg Maxwell,
241 Cavehill Road, Belfast 15,
Northern Ireland

LAKELAND HORTICULTURAL SOCIETY
Hon. Membership Secretary:
Mr S. Leader
Gill Syke, Troutbeck, Windermere,
Cumbria LA23 1PE
Tel: (05394) 33622

LILY GROUP
Hon. Membership Secretary:
Dr A. F. Hayward,
Rosemary Cottage, Lowbands,
Redmarley,
Gloucestershire, GL9 3NG
Tel: (045284) 661

MIDLAND GERANIUM, GLASSHOUSE AND GARDEN SOCIETY
Hon. Secretary: Miss J. Y. Baynham,
179 Poplar Avenue, Edgebaston,
Birmingham B17 8EJ
Tel: 021-429 1947

NATIONAL AURICULA AND PRIMULA SOCIETY (Midlands)
Hon. Secretary: Mr B. H. Goalby,
99 Sommerfield Road,
Bloxwich, Walsall,
West Midlands WS3 2EG
Tel: (0922) 400992

NATIONAL AURICULA AND PRIMULA SOCIETY (Northern)
Hon. Secretary: Mr D. G. Hadfield,
146 Queens Road, Cheadle Hulme,
Cheshire, SK8 5HY
Tel: 061-485 6371

NATIONAL AURICULA AND PRIMULA SOCIETY (Southern)
Hon. Secretary: Mr L. E. Wigley,
67 Warnham Court Road,
Carshalton Beeches,
Surrey SM5 3ND

NATIONAL CHRYSANTHEMUM SOCIETY
General Secretary: Mr H. B. Locke,
2 Lucas House, Craven Road, Rugby,
Warwickshire CV21 3JQ
Tel: (0788) 69039

NATIONAL COUNCIL FOR THE CONSERVATION OF PLANTS AND GARDENS
General Secretary: R.A.W. Lowe
c/o The Royal Horticultural Society,
Wisley Garden, Wisley, Woking,
Surrey GU23 6QB
Tel: (0483) 224234

NATIONAL DAHLIA SOCIETY
General Secretary: A. G. Winkless,
8 Station Road, Kirby Muxloe,
Leicester, LE9 9EJ
Tel: (0533) 387717

NATIONAL VIOLA AND PANSY SOCIETY
Hon. Secretary: Mrs A. Jackson
42 Harleston Road, Great Barr,
Birmingham B44 8RR
Tel: 021 382 1604

NORTHERN HORTICULTURAL SOCIETY
Harlow Car Gardens,
Crag Lane, Harrogate,
North Yorkshire, HG3 1QB
Tel: (0423) 65418

ROYAL HORTICULTURAL SOCIETY
80 Vincent Square,
London,SW1P 2PE
Tel: 01-834 4333

**ROYAL HORTICULTURAL SOCIETY
OF IRELAND**
Thomas Prior House, Merrion Road,
Dublin 4, Eire
Tel: (0001) 684358

SEMPERVIVUM SOCIETY
Hon.Secretary: P.J. Mitchell,
11 Wingle Tye Road, Burgess Hill,
West Sussex, RH15 9HR
Tel: (04446) 6848

SCOTTISH ROCK GARDEN CLUB
Hon. Secretary: Dr. Evelyn Stevens,
The Linns, Sheriffmuir, Dunblane,
Perthshire FK15 0LP
Tel: (0786) 822295

**SOCIETY FOR THE HISTORY OF
NATURAL HISTORY**
c/o The British Museum (Natural
History),
Cromwell Road,
London SW7 5BD
Tel: 01-589 6323

TRADESCANT TRUST
Museum of Garden History,
St. Mary-at-Lambeth,
Lambeth Palace Road,
London SE1 7JU
Tel: 01-373 4030 (between 6pm-9am)
& 01-261 1891 (between 11am-2.30pm)

NCCPG NATIONAL COLLECTIONS

Only those collections relevant to plants in this Volume of **Index Hortensis**
are included here.

*Further information may be obtained from NCCPG, c/o Wisley Garden, Woking,
Surrey GU23 6QB but please enclose return postage.*

ACANTHUS
Mr L Butler
Wagtail Cottage
3 Woolley Green
Bradford-on-Avon
Wiltshire BA15 1TY

ACHILLEA
Ms J Thorn
'Gardening from Which?' Trials
Garden
Capel Manor
Waltham Cross
Hertfordshire EN7 5HR

ACONITUM
Mr R B Rutherford
University of Aberdeen
Cruickshank Botanic Garden
St. Machar Drive
Aberdeen
Grampian AB9 2UD

ADIANTUM
Mr S J Youd
The National Trust
Tatton Park
Knutsford
Cheshire WA16 6QN

AGAPANTHUS
Devon NCCPG Group
c/o Mr N Lucas
Torbay Health Authority
Lawes Bridge
Torquay
Devon TQ2 7AA

AJUGA
Mr N B Junker
Junkers Tree & Landscape Services
Lower Mead
West Hatch
Taunton
Somerset

ALCHEMILLA
Mr P Orriss
University Botanic Garden
Cambridge
Cambridgeshire CB2 1JF

ALLIUM
Mrs P K Davies
6 Blenheim Road
Caversham
Reading
Berkshire RG4 7RS

ANEMONE: "Japanese" cvs
Miss M McKendrick
Hadlow College of Agriculture
& Horticulture
Hadlow
Tonbridge
Kent TN11 0AL

Mr D G Barker
Stone Pine
Hyde Lane
Chelmsford
Essex CM3 4LJ

Dr J W Burwell
47 Locks Road
Locks Heath
Southampton
Hampshire SO3 6NS

ANEMONE: *A.nemorosa* cvs
Mr P Cotton
The National Trust
Cliveden
Taplow
Maidenhead
Berkshire SL6 0JB

ANTHERICUM
Mr R Grounds & Mrs D Grenfell
Apple Court
Hordle Lane
Lymington
Hampshire SO41 0HU

AQUILEGIA
Mr J Drake
Hardwicke House
Fen Ditton
Cambridge
Cambridgeshire CB5 8TF

ARABIS
Mr J A Maddox
Luton Parks Division
Wardown Park Offices
Old Bedford Road
Luton
Bedfordshire LU27HA

ARACEAE (*excluding Arisaema & Zantedeschia*)
Mrs E Honnor
14 Homefield Close
Creech St. Michael
Taunton
Somerset TA3 5QR

ARGYRANTHEMUM
Mr R V Cheek
Somerset College of Agriculture
& Horticulture
Cannington
Bridgewater
Somerset TA5 2LS

ARISAEMA
Mr R A Hammond
The Magnolias
18 St. Johns Avenue
Brentwood
Essex CM14 5DF

ARTEMESIA
Mr C C Williams
Emmings Farm Herbs
Elton
Newnham-on-Severn
Gloucestershire GL14 1JL

Dr J Twibell
Avenue Farm Cottage
31 Smith Street
Elsworth
Cambridge
Cambridgeshire CB3 8HY

ASPHODELUS & ASPHODELINE
East Anglian Garden Society
c/o Mr R J A Leeds
Chestnuts
Whelp Street
Preston St. Mary
Sudbury
Suffolk CO10 9NL

ASPLENIUM: *A.scolopendrium*
Mr M Hutcheson
The National Trust
Sizergh Castle
Kendal
Cumbria LA8 8AE

Mr G Garnall
Wigan College of Technology
PO BOX 53
Parsons Walk
Wigan
Greater Manchester WN1 1RS

ASTER: Michaelmas Daisies
Miss I Allen & Miss J Huish
Belmont House
Tyntesfield
Wraxall
Bristol
Avon BS19 1NR

Mr J Kirby
Leeds City Council
Temple Newsam Park
Leeds
West Yorkshire LS15 0AD

ASTER: *A. cordifolius, A. dumosus, A. ericoides, A. novi-belgii & A. novae-angliae* cvs
Mr P Picton
Old Court Nurseries Ltd
Colwall
Malvern
Worcestershire WR13 6QE

ASTER: *A.ericoides & A. amellus* cvs
Ms S Cook
Upton House
Edgehill
Banbury
Oxfordshire OX15 6HT

ASTILBE
Lord Harewood
Harewood House Gardens
Harewood
Leeds
West Yorkshire LS17 9LF

Mr H Noblett
Lakeland Horticultural Society
Riseholm
Stainton
Penrith
Cumbria CA11 0ET

Dr J Smart
Marwood Hill
Barnstaple
Devon EX31 4EB

ASTRANTIA
Mrs S Bond
Goldbrook Plants
Hoxne
Eye
Suffolk IP21 5AN

ATHYRIUM
Mr J D Bond
Crown Estate Office
The Great Park
Windsor
Berkshire SL4 2HT

AUBRETIA
Mr R J Gornall
University of Leicester
Dept of Botany
University Road
Leicester
Leicestershire LE1 7RH

Mr J A Maddox
Luton Parks Division
Wardown Park Offices
Old Bedford Road
Luton
Bedfordshire LU2 7HA

BELLIS: *B. perennis* **cvs**
Mrs J Andrews
Crossways
Shrewley
Warwick
Warwickshire CV35 7AU

BERGENIA: Species & primary hybrids
(*excluding cvs*)
Mr. P Orriss
University Botanic Garden
Cambridge
Cambridgeshire CB2 1BY

BERGENIA: cvs
Mr J Hobson
Cambridge City Council
Mandela House
4 Regent Street
Cambridge
Cambridgeshire CB2 1BY

Mr C D Hallsworth
21 Mount Pleasant Road
South Woodham Ferrers
Essex CM3 5PA

CALAMINTHA
Mrs L Williams
Marle Place Plants
Brenchley
Tonbridge
Kent TN12 7HS

CALCEOLARIA
Mr J A Maddox
Luton Parks Division
Wardown Park Offices
Old Bedford Road
Luton
Bedfordshire LU2 7HA

CALTHA
Mr & Mrs J E Hudson
The Mill
21 Mill Lane
Cannington
Bridgewater
Somerset TA5 2HB

CAMASSIA
Mr R Grounds & Mrs D Grenfell
Apple Court
Hordle Lane
Lymington
Hampshire SO41 0HU

CAMPANULA
Mr P Lewis
19 Padlock Road
West Wratting
Cambridge
Cambridgeshire CB1 5LS

CAUTLEYA
Mr E Needham
Derow
Kelliwith
Feock
Truro
Cornwall TR3 6QZ

CENTAUREA
Mrs H Hiley
25 Little Woodcote Estate
Wallington
Surrey SM5 4AU

CHRYSANTHEMUM see:
DENDRANTHEMA & LEUCANTHEMUM

CIMICIFUGA
Mr J Ravenscroft
Bridgemere Nurseries Ltd.
Bridgemere
Nantwich
Cheshire CW5 7QB

CLEMATIS
Treasures of Tenby Ltd.
Burford House
Tenbury Wells
Worcestershire WR15 8HQ

Mr R Evison
The Guernsey Clematis Nursery Ltd.
Dormarie Vineries
Les Sauvagees
St Sampson
Guernsey C I

COLCHICUM
Mr E Bullock
The National Trust
Felbrigg Hall
Cromer
Norfolk NR11 8PR

The Curator
The Royal Horticultural Society
Wisley Garden
Woking
Surrey GU23 6QB

CONVALLARIA
Mr P Cotton
The National Trust
Cliveden
Maidenhead
Berkshire SL6 0JB

COREOPSIS
The Hardy Plant Society
Nottingham Branch
c/o Mr J Widdison
17 Stanley Drive
Beeston
Nottingham
Nottinghamshire NG9 3JY

CORTADERIA
Mr J A Maddox
Luton Parks Division
Wardown Park Offices
Old Bedford Road
Luton
Bedfordshire LU2 7HA

CROCOSMIA
Mr M P Borlase
The National Trust
Lanhydrock
Bodmin
Cornwall PL30 5AD

CROCUS (*excluding C. chrysanthus*
& C. vernus cvs)
Mr R Cobb
Aurelia
188 Bramcote Lane
Wollaton
Nottingham
Nottinghamshire NG8 2QN

CROCUS: *C. chrysanthus* **cvs**
Mr & Mrs R A Grout
5 Rockley Avenue
Radcliffe-on-Trent
Nottinghamshire NG12 1AR

CYCLAMEN
The Cyclamen Society
c/o Mr A Aird
134 Lots Road
London SW10 0RJ

CYCLAMEN: *C. coum* **cvs**
Mr R Poulett
Nurses Cottage
North Mundham
Chichester
Sussex PO20 6JY

CYSTOPTERIS
Mr M Hutcheson
The National Trust
Sizergh Castle
Kendal
Cumbria LA8 8AE

DELPHINIUM
Mr G Kirby
Leeds City Council
Temple Newsam Park
Leeds
West Yorkshire LS15 0AD

DELPHINIUM: *D.elatum*
& *D. x belladonna* **cvs**
Mr G Alway
The Coach House
The Old Vicarage
Hillesley
Wotton-under-Edge
Gloucestershire

DENDRANTHEMA: Rubellum cvs
Mr B Wallis
3 Church Street
Buckden
Huntingdon
Cambridgeshire PE18 9TE

DENDRANTHEMA: Korean & Pompon cvs
Mr M Stone
Little Mynthurst Farm
Norwood Hill
Horley
Surrey RH16 0HR

DIANELLA
Mr & Mrs H F J Read
Vicar's Mead
East Budleigh
Devon EX9 7DA

DIANTHUS: Border Pinks
Mr J Gingell
Ramparts Nursery
Bakers Lane
Braiswick
Colchester
Essex CO4 5BD

Mr & Mrs S Farquhar
Old Inn Cottage
Piddington
Bicester
Oxfordshire OX6 0PY

DIANTHUS: Malmaison Carnations
Mr D Maclean
The National Trust for Scotland
Crathes Castle
Banchory
Kincardineshire AB3 3QJ

DIANTHUS: Old Garden Pinks
Mrs S Hughes
Kingstone Cottage
Weston under Penyard
Ross-on-Wye
Herefordshire HR9 7NX

DICENTRA
Mr R A Brook
Betula
Marsh Lane
Bolton Percy
York
North Yorkshire YO57BA

DIGITALIS
Mr T A Baker
Rookery Nurseries
Atworth
Melksham
Wiltshire SN12 8NU

Mrs N G Jardine
167 Leamington Road
Coventry
West Midlands CV3 6GT

DIMORPHOTHECA
Mr P H Keen
Somerset College of Agriculture
& Horticulture
Cannington
Bridgewater
Somerset TA5 2LS

DODECATHEON
Mr & Mrs S M Wills
The Manor House
Walton in Gordano
Clevedon
Avon BS21 7AN

Mr T Wiltshire
Pencarn
Gonvena
Wadebridge
Cornwall PL27 6DL

DORONICUM
Mr B Simpson
Seamill Teachers Centre
West Kilbride
Ayreshire KA23 9NJ

DRYOPTERIS
The Northern Horticultural Society
Harlow Car Gardens
Harrogate
North Yorkshire HG3 1QB

Mr C D & Mr C J Fraser-Jenkins
Newcastle House
Bridgend
Mid Glamorgan CF31 4HD

Mr M Hutcheson
The National Trust
Sizergh Castle, Kendal
Cumbria LA8 8AE

ECHINOPS
Mr F R Shorten
Cambridge College of Agriculture
& Horticulture
Newcommon Bridge
Wisbech
Cambridgeshire PE13 2SJ

EPIMEDIUM
The Curator
The Royal Horticultural Society
Wisley Garden
Woking
Surrey GU23 6QB

Mr D G Barker
Stone Pine
Hyde Lane
Chelmsford
Essex CM3 4LJ

Mrs M Owen
Parsons Pleasure
Acton Burnell
Shrewsbury
Shropshire SY7 7HQ

ERIGERON
Mr P Heaton
Brachenbury
Coombe
Wotton-under-Edge
Gloucestershire GL12 7NF

ERODIUM
Mrs M Addyman
Rivendell
Porters Headland
Pickering
North Yorkshire YO18 8AG

ERYNGIUM
Mr J Lamont
Lancashire College of Agriculture
& Horticulture
Myerscough Hall
Bilsborrow
Preston
Lancashire PR3 0RY

ERYTHRONIUM
Mr D MacAlpine
Suntrap Horticultural and Gardening
Advice Centre
(Oatridge Agricultural College)
43 Gogarbank
Edinburgh
Lothian EH12 9BY

EUPHORBIA
Mr T Walker
Oxford Botanic Garden
Rose Lane
Oxford
Oxfordshire OX1 4AX

Mrs S Sage
Abbey Dore Court Gardens
Hereford
Herefordshire HR2 0AD

FERNS: Hardy
Mr J D Bond
Crown Estate Office
The Great Park
Windsor
Berkshire SL4 2HT

FRITILLARIA: Species
Mr P Orriss
University Botanic Garden
Cambridge
Cambridgeshire CB2 1JF

FRITILLARIA: *F. imperialis* cvs
Mr J Hobson
Cambridge City Council
Mandela House
4 Regent Street
Cambridge
Cambridgeshire CB2 1BY

GALANTHUS
The Curator
The Royal Horticultural Society
Wisley Garden
Woking
Surrey GU23 6QB

GENTIANA
Mr N Prichard
University of Aberdeen
Cruickshank Botanic Garden
St. Machar Drive
Aberdeen
Grampian AB9 2UD

GERANIUM
Mr A Norton
Margery Fish Plant Nursery
East Lambrook Manor
South Petherton
Somerset TA13 5HL

GERANIUM: Species and primary hybrids
Mr P Orriss
University Botanic Garden
Cambridge
Cambridgeshire CB2 1JF

GERANIUM: cvs
Mr J Hobson
Cambridge City Council
Mandela House
4 Regent Street
Cambridge
Cambridgeshire CB2 1BY

GEUM
Mrs A Mallett
Lurley Manor
Tiverton
Devon EX16 9QS

HEDYCHIUM
Mr E Needham
Derow
Killiwich
Feock
Truro
Cornwall TR3 6QZ

HELENIUM
Mr A R Busby
16 Kirby Corner Road
Canley
Coventry
West Midlands CV4 8GD

HELENIUM (*continued*)
The Hardy Plant Society
Nottingham Branch
c/o Mr J Widdison
17 Stanley Drive
Beeston
Nottingham
Nottinghamshire NG9 3JY

HELIANTHELLA
The Hardy Plant Society
Nottingham Branch
c/o Mr J Widdison
17 Stanley Drive
Beeston
Nottingham
Nottinghamshire NG9 3JY

HELIANTHEMUM: *H. nummularium* **cvs**
Mr R J Broughton
Hampshire College of Agriculture
Sparsholt
Winchester
Hampshire SO21 2NF

HELIANTHUS
The Hardy Plant Society
Nottingham Branch
c/o Mr J Widdison
17 Stanley Drive
Beeston
Nottingham
Nottinghamshire NG9 3JY

HELICHRYSUM: Alpine
Mr R Stuckey
38 Phillips Avenue
Exmouth
Devon EX8 3HZ

HELIOPSIS
The Hardy Plant Society
Nottingham Branch
c/o Mr J Widdison
17 Stanley Drive
Beeston
Nottingham
Nottinghamshire NG9 3JY

HELLEBORUS
Mr D MacAlpine
Suntrap Horticultural and Gardening
Advice Centre
(Oatridge Agricultural College)
Edinburgh
Lothian EH12 9BY

Hampshire NCCPG Group
c/o Mr J Wood
Lower House
Whiteparish
Salisbury
Hampshire SP5 2SL

HEMEROCALLIS
Mr Joyce
Borough of Epsom & Ewell
Parks Dept
Ewell Court House
Epsom
Surrey KT19 0DZ

Mr T Exley
Leeds City Council
19 Wellington Street
Leeds
West Yorkshire LS1 4DG

Mrs Valerie Hole
The National Trust
Antony House
Torpoint
Cornwall PL11 2QA

HEPATICA
Mr M Bishop
Dreycott
3 Woodlands End
Glenholt
Plymouth
Devon PL6 7RE

Mr M D Myers
Fairview
Smelthouses
Summerbridge
Harrogate
North Yorkshire HG3 4DH

HESPERIS
Dr R J Gornall
University of Leicester
Department of Botany
University Road
Leicester
Leicestershire LE1 7RH

HEUCHERA
Mrs M Ramsdale
Winkfield
Swan Hill Road
Colyford
Colyton
Honiton
Devon EX13 6QJ

HOSTA
The Curator
The Royal Horticultural Society
Wisley Garden
Woking
Surrey GU23 6QB

HOSTA (*continued*)
Lord Harewood
Harewood House Gardens
Harewood
Leeds
West Yorkshire LS17 9LF

Lt Col & Mrs H Jordan
Kittoch Mill
Carmunnock
Lanarkshire G76 9BJ

HOSTA: Large-leaved cvs
Mr T Exley
Leeds City Council
19 Wellington Street
Leeds
West Yorkshire LS1 4DG

HOSTA: Small-leaved cvs
Mr R Grounds & Mrs D Grenfell
Apple Court
Hordle Lane
Lymington
Hampshire SO41 0HU

HYACINTHUS: *H. orientalis* cvs
Mr P R Swindells
Wycliffe Hall Botanical Gardens
Wycliffe Hall
Barnard Castle
Co Durham DL12 9TS

HYPERICUM
The Northern Horticultural Society
Harlow Car Gardens
Harrogate
North Yorkshire HG3 1QB

IRIS
Dr S L Jury
Dept of Botany
University of Reading
Whiteknights
Reading
Berkshire RG6 2AS

IRIS: *I. sibirica* cvs
Shropshire NCCPG Group
c/o Mrs J Hewitt
Haygarth
Cleeton-St-Mary
Cleobury Mortimer
Kidderminster
Worcestershire DY14 0QU

IRIS: *I. unguicularis* cvs
Mrs A Ala
Hall Farm
Wetheroak Hill
Alvechurch
Birmingham
West Midlands B48 7EG

Mr R Nutt
Great Barfield
Bradenham
High Wycombe
Buckinghamshire HP14 4HD

IRIS: Tall Bearded & Award of Merit cvs
Mr G Stebbings
Lee Valley Regional Park Authority
Myddelton House
Bulls Cross
Enfield
Middlesex EN2 9HG

IRIS: Series *spuriae*
Mr S Anderton
Stable Cottage
Belsay Hall
Belsay
Newcastle-upon-Tyne
Northumberland NE20 0DX

**IRIS: Series *laevigatae* (*excluding
I. ensata* cvs)**
Mrs S Bond
Goldbrook Plants
Hoxne
Eye
Suffolk IP21 5AN

KNIPHOFIA
Mr A Goddard
Barton Manor
Whippingham
East Cowes
Isle of Wight PO23 6LB

Mr C R Sanders
Bridgemere Nurseries Ltd.
Bridgemere
Nantwich
Cheshire CW5 7QB

LAMIUM (& GALEOBDOLEN)
Mr J Sharman
Church Lane Farm
Cottenham
Cambridge
Cambridgeshire CB4 4SN

LEUCANTHEMUM
Ayrshire & Arran NCCPG Group
c/o Lady Hagart-Alexander
Kingencleuch House
Mauchline
Ayrshire KA5 5JL

LEUCOJUM
Mr R D Nutt
Great Barfield
Bradenham
High Wycombe
Buckinghamshire HP14 4HD

LEWISIA
Mr P Baulk
Ashwood Nurseries and Aquatics
Greensforge
Kingswinford
West Midlands DY6 0AE

Mrs K Dryden
Berries
30 Sheering Lower Road
Sawbridgeworth
Hertfordshire CM21 9LF

Mr D Tattersfield
The National Trust for Scotland
Branklyn Garden
Dundee Road
Perth
Tayside PH2 7BB

LIBERTIA
Mr & Mrs H F J Read
Vicar's Mead
East Budleigh
Devon EX9 7DA

LIGULARIA
Hardy Plant Society (North-
Western Branch)
c/o Mrs E Fisher
20 Park Street
Skipton
North Yorkshire BD23 1NS

LINUM
Mrs P Taylor
17 Bartelotts Road
Slough
Berkshire

LIRIOPE
Mr & Mrs H F J Read
Vicar's Mead
East Budleigh
Devon EX9 7DA

LOBELIA: *L. x speciosa* etc.
Mrs A Stevens
Ivy Cottage
Ansty
Dorchester
Dorset DT2 7PX

LUPINUS: Russell Lupins
Mrs P Edwards
Swallow Hayes
Rectory Road
Albrighton
Wolverhampton
West Midlands WV7 3EP

LYCHNIS
Mr P Sargent
Hinchley Wood First & Middle School
Claygate Lane
Esher
Surrey KT10 0AQ

MECONOPSIS
Mr J M Hirst
Durham Agricultural College
Houghall
Durham
Co Durham DH1 3SG

MENTHA: Culinary Mints
Mr R Lunn
Herbs in Stock
Whites Hill
Stock
Ingatestone
Essex CM4 9QR

MERTENSIA
Mr R Rutherford
University of Aberdeen
Cruickshank Botanic Garden
St. Machar Drive
Aberdeen
Grampian AB9 2UD

MONARDA
Mr C J Skinner
Leeds Castle Foundation
Leeds Castle
Maidstone
Kent ME17 1PL

MUSCARI
Miss J Robinson
Chequers
Boxford
Suffolk CO6 5DT

NARCISSUS
Mr C McVicker
University of Ulster
Cromore Road
Coleraine
Co Londonderry
Northern Ireland BT52 1SA

Mr M Harwood
Hope Cottage
Halebourne Lane
Chobham
Surrey GU24 8SL

NARCISSUS: Alec Grey miniatures
Broadleigh Gardens
Bishops Hull
Taunton
Somerset TA4 1AE

NARCISSUS: Brodie cvs
Mr B Cockburn
The National Trust for Scotland
Brodie Castle
Forres
Grampian IV36 0TE

NEPETA
Mr C Skinner
Leeds Castle Foundation
Leeds Castle
Maidstone
Kent ME17 1PL

NERINE
Mr C A Norris
Nerine Nurseries
Welland
Malvern
Worcestershire WR13 8LN

NYMPHAEA
Mr P R Swindells
Wycliffe Hall Botanical Gardens
Wycliffe Hall
Barnard Castle
Co Durham DL12 9TS

OENOTHERA
Mr J N d'Arcy
The Old Vicarage
Edington
Westbury
Wiltshire

OMPHALODES
Mr N Prichard
University of Aberdeen
Cruickshank Botanic Garden
St. Machar Drive
Aberdeen
Grampian AB9 2UD

OPHIOPOGON
Mr & Mrs H F J Read
Vicar's Mead
East Budleigh
Devon EX9 7DA

ORIGANUM
Mr D & Mrs R Titterington
Iden Croft Herbs
Staplehurst
Kent TN12 0DH

OSMUNDA
Mr M Hutcheson
The National Trust
Sizergh Castle
Kendal
Cumbria LA8 8AE

Mr A R Busby
16 Kirby Corner Road
Canley
Coventry
West Midlands CV4 8GD

OSTEOSPERMUM
Mr R V Cheek
Somerset College of Agriculture
& Horticulture
Cannington
Bridgewater
Somerset TA5 2LS

OURISIA
Mr P Clough
The National Trust for Scotland
Inverewe Garden
Poolewe
Achnasheen
Rossshire IV22 2LQ

PAEONIA: Species & primary hybrids
Mr P Nicholls
The National Trust
Hidcote Manor Garden
Hidcote Bartrim
Chipping Campden
Gloucestershire GL55 6LR

PAEONIA: Cvs pre 1900
Gloucestershire NCCPG Group
c/o Mrs M Baber
Green Cottage
Redhill Lane
Lydney
Gloucestershire GL15 6BS

PAPAVER: *P. orientale* **cvs**
Mr M Hitchon
West of Scotland Agricultural College
Horticulture & Beekeeping dept.
Auchincruive
Ayr
Ayreshire KA6 5AE

PARADISEA
Mr R Grounds & Mrs D Grenfell
Apple Court
Hordle Lane
Lymington
Hampshire SO41 0HU

PARAHEBE
Mr G Hutchins
County Park Nursery
Essex Gardens
Hornchurch
Essex RM11 3BU

PARAQUILEGIA see **AQUILEGIA**

PENSTEMON: Herbaceous types
Mr R Adams
Dorset College of Agriculture
Kingston Maurward
Dorchester
Dorset DT2 8PY

Mr W R Hean
The National Trust for Scotland
Threave School of Gardening
Castle Douglas
Dumfries & Galloway DG7 1RX

PENSTEMON: Large-flowered cvs
Mr M Snowden
The National Trust
Rowallane House
Saintfield
Ballynaminch
Co Down
Northern Ireland BT24 7LH

PHLOX: Border types
Mr T Exley
Leeds City Council
19 Wellington Street
Leeds
West Yorkshire LS1 4DG

PHORMIUM
Mr R V Cheek
Somerset College of Agriculture
& Horticulture
Cannington
Bridgewater
Somerset TA5 2LS

PLATYCODON
Mr J Ritchie
Hoo House
Gloucester Road
Tewkesbury
Gloucestershire GL20 7DA

PLEIONE
Mr I Butterfield
Butterfields Nursery
Harvest Hill
Bourne End
Buckinghamshire SL8 5JJ

POLYGONATUM
Hardy Plant Society (North-
Western Group)
c/o Mrs E Fisher
20 Park Street
Skipton
North Yorkshire BD23 1NS

Mr & Mrs K Beckett
Bramley Cottage
Stanhoe
King's Lynn
Norfolk PE31 8QF

POLYGONUM etc.
Mr J R L Carter
Rowden Gardens
Brentnor
Tavistock
Devon PL19 0NG

POLYPODIUM
The Northern Horticultural Society
Harlow Car Gardens
Harrogate
North Yorkshire HG3 1QB

POTENTILLA: Perennial types
Mr M C Swash
Longfield Nursery
Oreton
Cleobury Mortimer
Shropshire DY14 0TJ

PRIMULA: *P. allionii* cvs
Mr J Main
East Gate House
7b Inverleith Row
Edinburgh
Lothian EH3 5LP

PRIMULA: *P. marginata* cvs
Mr M D Myers
Fairview
Smellhouses
Summerbridge
Harrogate
North Yorkshire HG3 4DH

PRIMULA: Alpine Auriculas
Mr T Exley
Leeds City Council
19 Wellington Street
Leeds
West Yorkshire LS1 4DG

PRIMULA: Border Auriculas
Mr G Nicolle
Rising Sun Cottage
Nolton Haven
Haverford West
Dyfed SA62 3NN

PRIMULA: Double Auriculas
Mr D W Salt
Donington House
Main Road
Wrangle
Boston
Lincolnshire PE22 9AT

PRIMULA: Sections *Candelabra & Sikkimensis*
Newick Park Enterprises
Newick
East Sussex BN8 4SB

PRIMULA: European species
Mr & Mrs C Quest-Ritson
Corsley Mill
Corsley
Warminster
Wiltshire BA12 7QA

PRIMULA: Section *Vernales*
Mr J W Martin
The Orchard
Longford
Market Drayton
Shropshire TF9 3PW

Mrs B N Shaw
Tan Cottage
West Lane
Cononly
Nr Keighley
North Yorkshire BD20 8NL

Mrs P Gossage
Oakenlea
West Coker Hill
Yeovil
Somerset BA22 9DG

PULMONARIA
The Curator
The Royal Horticultural Society
Wisley Garden
Woking
Surrey GU23 6QB

Mr G Garnall
Wigan College of Technology
PO BOX 53
Parsons Walk
Wigan
Greater Manchester WN1 1RS

PYRETHRUM see: **TANACETUM**

RANUNCULUS: *R. ficaria*
Mr R D Nutt
Great Barfield
Bradenham
High Wycombe
Buckinghamshire HP14 4HD

RHEUM: Species & cvs
The Northern Horticultural Society
Harlow Car Gardens
Harrogate
North Yorkshire HG3 1QB

RODGERSIA
Mr & Mrs Pope
Laundry Cottage
Hadspen House
Castle Cary
Somerset BA5 7NG

ROHDEA: *R. japonica*
Mr R Grounds & Mrs D Grenfell
Apple Court
Hordle Lane
Lymington
Hampshire SO41 0HU

ROSCOEA
Mr E Needham
Derow
Killiwich
Feock
Truro
Cornwall TR3 6QZ

SALVIA
Mr & Mrs P Vlasto
Wyke End
20 Belle Vue Road
Weymouth
Dorset DT9 8RY

Mr S Torode
Dyffryn Gardens
St Nicholas
Cardiff
South Glamorgan CF5 6SU

SALVIA: Tender
Mr R Adams
Dorset College of Agriculture
Kingston Maurward
Dorchester
Dorset DT2 8PY

SAXIFRAGA: European species & primary hybrids
Mr P Orriss
University Botanic Garden
Cambridge
Cambridgeshire CB2 1JF

SAXAFRAGA: Section *Porophyllum*
Mrs M R Spiller
Waterperry Horticultural Centre
Wheatley
Oxfordshire OX9 1LZ

SCABIOSA
Mrs S J Parrett
Dinkling Green Farm
Whitewell
Clithero
Lancashire

SCABIOSA: *S. caucasica* **cvs**
Mr R J Allan
The National Trust
Hardwick Hall
Doe Lea
Chesterfield
Derbyshire S44 5QJ

SCHIZOSTYLIS
Mr F Shepherd
Bosbigal
Old Carnon Hill
Carnon Downs
Truro
Cornwall TR3 6LF

P A Ketley
Duchy College of Agriculture
and Horticulture
Cornwall Centre for Further Education
Pool
Redruth
Cornwall TR15 3RD

SEDUM
Mrs S F Sage
Abbey Dore Court Gardens
Hereford
Herefordshire HR2 0AD

Mr R Stephenson
55 Beverley Drive
Choppington
Northumberland NE62 5YA

***SEMIAQUILEGIA* see AQUILEGIA**

SIDALCEA
Mrs M Ramsdale
Winkfield
Swan Hill Road
Colyford
Colyton
Honiton
Devon EX13 6QJ

SISYRINCHIUM
Mrs R Heaton
11 Keyberry Mill
Newton Abbot
Devon TQ12 1DW

SYMPHYTUM
Mrs I Strachan
Banner Lodge
9 Newbattle Terrace
Edinburgh
Lothian EH10 4RU

TANACETUM: Garden Pyrethrums
Mr G W Goddard
25 Mornington Road
Chingford
London E4 7DT

Mr M Drye
Lamport Hall Trust
Lamport Hall
Northampton
Northamptonshire NN6 9HB

THALICTRUM
Mr & Mrs G Buchanan-Dunlop
Broughton Place
Broughton
Biggar
Lanarkshire ML12 6JH

Mr J Ravenscroft
Bridgemere Nurseries Ltd.
Bridgemere
Nantwich
Cheshire CW5 7QB

THYMUS
Mr & Mrs F Huntington
Quantock Herbs
Hethersett
Cothelstone
Taunton
Somerset TD4 3DP

Mr K A White
Hexham Herbs
Tecket Cottage
Simonburn
Hexham
Northumberland HR48 3AH

TRICYRTIS
Hardy Plant Society (North-
Western Branch)
c/o Mrs E Fisher
The Old Sawmill
Castle Woods
Skipton
North Yorkshire

TRILLIUM
Mr A Page
38 Shaftesbury Avenue
Chandlers Ford
Eastleigh
Hampshire SO5 3BS

TROLLIUS
Mrs A Stevens
Ivy Cottage
Ansty
Dorchester
Dorset DT2 7PX

TROPAOLEUM
Mr & Mrs G Buchanan-Dunlop
Broughton House
Broughton
Biggar
Lanarkshire ML12 6HJ

TULBAGHIA
Mr S Benham
Gardens Cottage
Knightshayes Court
Tiverton
Devon EX16 7RQ

TULIPA: Species & primary hybrids
(*excluding cvs*)
Mr P Orriss
University Botanic Garden
Cambridge
Cambridgeshire CB2 1JF

TULIPA: Florists' & other old cvs
Mr D Bromley
Moortown
Ercall
Telford
Shropshire TF6 6JE

VERATRUM
Surrey NCCPG Group
c/o Mrs E Degenhardt
7 Lower Road
Fetcham
Leatherhead
Surrey KT22 9EL

VERBENA
Mr J May
The National Trust for Scotland
Greenbank Garden
Clarkston
Glasgow
Strathclyde G76 8RB

VERONICA: Section *Spicata*
Mr & Mrs J Foulsham
Kings Head House
Itchel Lane
Crondall
Farnham
Surrey GU10 5PR

VINCA
Mr J Sharman
Church Lane Farm
Cottenham
Cambridge
Cambridgeshire CB4 4SN

VIOLA: Violas & Violettas
Mr R G M Cawthorne
Lower Daltons Nursery
Swanley Village
Swanley
Kent BR8 7NU

Mr T Exley
Leeds City Council
19 Wellington Street
Leeds
West Yorkshire LS1 4DG

VIOLA: *V. odorata* cvs
Mrs Y S Matthews
Cornwall
(full address from NCCPG Secretariat)

WATSONIA
Mr A Goddard
Barton Manor
Whippingham
East Cowes
Isle of Wight PO32 6LB

WOODWARDIA
Mr R Grounds & Mrs D Grenfell
Apple Court
Hordle Lane
Lymington
Hampshire SO41 0HU

YUCCA
Mr R V Cheek
Somerset College of Agriculture
& Horticulture
Cannington
Bridgewater
Somerset TA5 2LS

ENGLISH HERB NAMES

A survey of vernacular culinary, medicinal and dyer's herb names found in British nursery lists and cross-referenced to the nomenclature adopted in INDEX HORTENSIS

[A] = Annual,   [B] = Biennial,   [S] = Shrubby

(Some Trees & Shrubs not included in Volume 1 have been included for the sake of completion)

Aaron's Rod ....**Verbascum thapsus**
Abcess Root ....**Polemonium reptans**
Absinthe..**Artemisia absinthium**
Aconite ....**Aconitum nepellus**
Agrimony ....**Agrimonia eupatoria**
— Hemp......................................**Eupatorium cannabinum**
Alecost ....**Tanacetum balsamita**
All-good ....**Chenopodium bonus-henricus**
Alexanders ....**Smyrnium olusatrum** [B]
Alkenet ....**Anchusa officinalis** [B]
Angelica ....**Angelica archangelica**
— Wild ....**Angelica sylvestris**
Anise ....**Pimpinella anisum** [A]
Aniseed ....**Pimpinella anisum** [A]
Arnica ....**Arnica montana**
Asarabacca ....**Asarum europaeum**
Avens, Wood ....**Geum urbanum**

Balm...**Melissa officinalis**
— Bee ....**Melissa officinalis**
— Canary Island ....**Cedronella triphylla** [S]
— Gentle......................................**Melissa officinalis**
— Lemon ....**Melissa officinalis**
— Mint ....**Melissa officinalis**
— Sweet.......................................**Melissa officinalis**
Balm of Gilead ....**Cedronella triphylla** [S]
Balomony ....**Chelone glabra**
Balsam Herb ....**Tanacetum balsamita**
Balsam Rub ....**Melissa officinalis**
Baneberry ....**Actaea spicata**
Basil..**Ocimum basilicum** [A]
— Bush ....**Ocimum minimum** [A]
— Sweet ....**Ocimum basilicum** [A]
Bay ....**Laurus nobilis** [VOL.2]

Bear's Breech ....**Acanthus mollis**
Bergamot ....**Monarda didyma**
— Wild ....**Monarda fistulosa**
Betony ....**Stachys officinalis**
Birthwort ....**Aristolochia clematitis**
Bistort ....**Persicaria bistorta**
Blue-eyed Grass ....**Sisyrinchium bermudianum**
Bogbean ....**Menyanthes trifoliata**
Boneset ....**Symphytum officinale**
Borage ....**Borago officinalis** [A]
Brooklime...**Veronica beccabunga**
Bouncing Bet ....**Saponaria officinalis**
Broom, Dyer's..............................**Genista tinctoria** [VOL.2]
Brotherwort.......................................**Thymus vulgaris** [S]
Bruisewort..**Symphytum officinale**
Bryony, White ....**Bryonia cretica** ssp.**dioica**
Bugle ....**Ajuga reptans**
Burdock..**Arctium lappa** [B]
Burnet, Salad....................................**Sanguisorba minor**
Burnet Saxifrage ....**Pimpinella saxifraga**
Burning Bush ....**Dictamnus albus**
Butterfly Weed....................................**Asclepias tuberosa**

Calamint..**Calamintha grandiflora**
— Lesser...**Calamintha nepeta**
Camphor Plant ....**Tanacetum balsamita**
Caper Spurge....................................**Euphorbia lathyrus** [B]
Caraway ....**Carum carvi** [B]
Carosella ....**Foeniculum vulgare** var. **dulce**
Carpenter's Square ....**Scrophularia nodosa**
Catmint, Garden ....**Nepeta x faassenii**
— Wild ....**Nepeta cataria**
Catnep (Catnip).....................................**Nepeta cataria**
— Lemon ....**Nepeta cataria** 'Citriodora'
Catsfoot ....**Antennaria dioica**
Celandine, Greater ....**Chelidonium majus**
— Lesser ....**Ranunculus ficaria**
Celery, Wild ....**Apium graveolens** [B]
Chamomile, Dyer's.............................**Anthemis tinctoria**
— Roman ....**Chamaemelum nobile**
— Lawn ....**Chamaemelum nobile** 'Treneague'
Chaste Tree ....**Vitex agnus-castus** [VOL.2]
Cheese Rennet....................................**Galium verum**
Chervil ....**Anthriscus cerefolium** [A]
— Fern-leaved ....**Myrrhis odorata**
— Giant ....**Myrrhis odorata**
— Sweet ....**Myrrhis odorata**
Chervin ....**Sium sisarum**

Chicory .... **Cichorium intybus**
Chinese Artichoke .... **Stachys affinis**
Chives .... **Allium schoenoprasum**
— Chinese .... **Allium tuberosum**
— Giant .... **Allium schoenoprasum** ssp. **sibiricum**
— Garlic .... **Allium tuberosum**
Church Steeples .... **Agrimonia eupatoria**
Christmas Rose .... **Helleborus foetidus**
Clary.. **Salvia sclarea** [B]
Clover, Red..................................... **Trifolium pratense**
Cohosh, Black .... **Cimicifuga racemosa**
— Siberian .... **Cimicifuga foetida**
— White .... **Actaea pachypoda**
Colt's Foot .... **Tussilago farfara**
Columbine .... **Aquilegia vulgaris**
— Alpine.................................... **Aquilegia alpina**
Comfrey..................................... **Symphytum officinale**
— Caucasian .... **Symphytum caucasicum**
— Russian .... **Symphytum x uplandicum**
— Dwarf.................................... **Symphytum ibericum**
Coneflower..................................... **Echinacea purpurea**
Coriander.................................... **Coriandrum sativum** [A]
Cornsalad .... **Valerianella locusta** [A]
Costmary .... **Tanacetum balsamita**
Cotton Thistle............................ **Onopordum acanthium** [B]
Cowslip .... **Primula veris**
Creeping Jenny............................. **Lysimachia nummularia**
Cumin...................................... **Cuminum cyminium** [A]
Cupid's Dart .... **Catananche caerulea**
Curry Plant................................. **Helichrysum italicum** [S]

Dandelion .... **Taraxacum officinale**
Deadly Nightshade .... **Atropa belladonna**
Dewcup .... **Alchemilla mollis**
Dill .... **Anethum graveolens** [A]
Dropwort................................... **Filipendula vulgaris**

Elder .... **Sambucus nigra** [VOL.2]
Elecampane .... **Inula helenium**
Evening Primrose, Common .... **Oenothera biennis** [B]

Fennel .... **Foeniculum vulgare**
— Bronze .... **Foeniculum vulgare 'Purpurascens'**
— Finocchio........................ **Foeniculum vulgare** var. **dulce**
— Florence .... **Foeniculum vulgare** var. **dulce**
— Sweet...................... **Foeniculum vulgare** var. **dulce**
Feverfew.................................... **Tanacetum parthenium**
— Annual .... **Matricaria recutita** [A]

Figwort, Common or Knotted .... **Scrophularia nodosa**
— Variegated .... **Scrophularia auriculata 'Variegata'**
— Water .... **Scrophularia auriculata**
Finocchio .... **Foeniculum vulgare** var. **dulce**
Flax, Perennial .... **Linum perenne**
Foxglove.. **Digitalis purpurea**
— Woolly .... **Digitalis lanata**
— Yellow .... **Digitalis lutea**

Garlic... **Allium sativum**
— Black .... **Allium scordoprasum**
— Giant .... **Allium scordoprasum**
— Wood .... **Allium ursinum**
Gayfeather .... **Liatris spicata**
Gentian, Yellow .... **Gentiana lutea**
Ginger .... **Zingiber officinale**
— Green.. **Artemisia absinthium**
Gladdon .... **Iris foetidissima**
Gladwyn .... **Iris foetidissima**
Goat's Rue .... **Galega officinalis**
Goldenrod .... **Solidago virgaurea**
Golden Seal .... **Hydrastis canadensis**
Good-King-Henry .... **Chenopodium bonus-henricus**
Gravelroot   **Eupatorium purpureum**
Ground-ivy....................................... **Glechoma hederacea**
Gypsywort .... **Lycopus europaeus**

Heartsease .... **Viola tricolor**
Hellebore, Black .... **Helleborus niger**
— Stinking .... **Helleborus foetidus**
Hemlock .... **Conium maculatum** [B]
Henbane .... **Hyoscyamus niger** [B]
Herb Bennet .... **Geum urbanum**
Herb Patience.................................... **Rumex alpinus**
Herb Robert .... **Geranium robertianum**
Holy Herb .... **Verbena officinalis**
Hop.. **Humulus lupulus**
Horehound, Black .... **Ballota nigra**
— Stinking... **Ballota nigra**
— White .... **Marrubium vulgare**
Horseradish...................................... **Armoracia rusticana**
Hound's Tongue .... **Cynoglossum officinale**
Houseleek .... **Sempervivum tectorum**
Hyssop .... **Hyssopus officinalis**
— Anise....................................... **Agastache anethiodora**
— Hedge.. **Gratiola officinalis**
— Rock.................... **Hyssopus officinalis** ssp. **aristatus**
Indian Physic.................................... **Gillenia trifoliata**

Indigo, Dyer's.................................**Baptisia tinctoria**
— False ....**Baptisia tinctoria**

Jacob's Ladder ....**Polemonium caeruleum**
Joe Pye Weed................................**Eupatorium purpureum**
Joseph and Mary ....**Pulmonaria officinalis**

Knitbone.....................................**Symphytum officinalis**

Lad's Love...................................**Artemisia abrotanum** [S]
Lady's Bedstraw ....**Galium verum**
Lady's Mantle ....**Alchemilla** *species*
Lady's Maid ....**Artemisia chamaemelifolia** [S]
Lavender.................................**Lavandula** *species* [VOL.2]
— Cotton ....**Santolina chamaecyparissus** [VOL.2]
Life Everlasting..............................**Antennaria dioica**
Lily-of-the-valley ....**Convallaria majalis**
Lion's Foot ....**Alchemilla xanthochlora**
Lobelia, Great................................**Lobelia siphilitica**
Lovage ....**Levisticum officinalis**
— Scots ....**Ligusticum scoticum**
Lungwort ....**Pulmonaria officinalis**

Mace, English ....**Achillea decolorans**
Madder ....**Rubia tinctoria**
Maiden's Ruin ....**Artemisia abrotanum** [S]
Male Fern...................................**Dryopteris filix-mas**
Mandrake, American....................**Podophyllum peltatum**
— English ....**Bryonia cretica** ssp. **dioica**
— European ....**Mandragora officinarum**
— Himalayan ....**Podophyllum hexandrum**
Marjoram..**Origanum vulgare**
— Annual...............................**Origanum marjorana** [A]
— Compact.....................**Origanum vulgare 'Compactum'**
— Golden ....**Origanum onites 'Aureum'** [S]
— Golden Curled ....**Origanum onites 'Aureo-crispum'** [S]
— Gold-tipped ....**Origanum onites 'Variegatum'** [S]
— Knotted ....**Origanum majorana** [A]
— Pot...................................**Origanum onites** [S]
— Sweet ....**Origanum majorana** [A]
— Wild..**Origanum vulgare**
— Winter...........................**Origanum vulgare** ssp. **hirtum**
Marsh Mallow ....**Althaea officinalis**
Marsh Marigold...............................**Caltha palustris**
Meadowsweet ....**Filipendula ulmaria**
Meadow Pimpernel ....**Sanguisorba minor**
Meadow Saffron ....**Colchicum autumnale**
Melilot.................................**Melilotus officinalis** [B]

Mercury (in part) ....**Chenopodium bonus-henricus**
Mint, Apple.............................**Mentha suaveolens**
— Bergamot ....**Mentha x piperita nm.citrata**
— Bowles' ....**Mentha x villosa nm. alopecuroides**
— Buddleja ....**Mentha longifolia**
— Common.................................**Mentha spicata**
— Corn ....**Mentha arvensis [A]**
— Corsican...............................**Mentha requienii**
— Creeping ....**Mentha gattefossii**
— Curly ....**Mentha** *species* **'Crispa'**
— Eau de Cologne ....**Mentha x piperita nm. citrata**
— Garden ....**Mentha spicata**
— Ginger ....**Mentha x gentilis**
— Horse p.p............................**Mentha longifolia**
— Horse p.p. ....**Mentha x villosonervata**
— Lamb ....**Mentha spicata**
— Lemon ....**Mentha x piperita nm. citrata**
— Mountain ....**Pycnanthemum pilosum**
— Orange ....**Mentha x piperita nm. citrata**
— Pea ....**Mentha spicata**
— Pennyroyal ....**Mentha pulegium**
— Pineapple ....**Mentha suaveolens 'Variegata'**
— Raripila ....**Menthax smithiana**
— Round-leaved...........................**Mentha suaveolens**
— Scotch ....**Mentha x gentilis**
— Slender ....**Mentha x gentilis**
— Tall ....**Mentha niliaca**
— Water.................................**Mentha aquatica**
Monkshood ....**Aconitum napellus**
Motherwort.............................**Leonurus cardiaca**
Mountain Tobacco ....**Arnica montana**
Mugwort................................**Artemisia vulgaris**
Mullein................................**Verbascum thapsus**
Musk Mallow ....**Malva moschata**
Myrtle ....**Myrtus communis [VOL.2]**
— Small-leaved ....**Myrtus tarentina [VOL.2]**

Old Lady.....................**Artemisia campestris ssp. borealis [S]**
Old Man ....**Artemisia abrotanum [S]**
Old Warrior ....**Artemisia pontica**
Onion, Garden ....**Allium cepa**
— Everlasting....................**Allium cepa 'Perutile'**
— Ever-ready ....**Allium cepa 'Perutile'**
— Tree ....**Allium cepa 'Proliferum'**
— Welsh ....**Allium fistulosum**
Oregano, European ....**Origanum vulgare**
— True ....**Lippia graveolens [VOL.2]**

Orris . . . . **Iris florentina**
Oxlip . . . . **Primula elatior**

Parsley, Garden . . . . **Petroselinum crispum** [B]
— Curled . . . . **Petroselinum crispum** [B]
— French . . . . **Petroselinum crispum** [B]
— Hamburg . . . . **Petroselinum crispum 'Tuberosum'** [B]
— Japanese . . . . **Cryptotaenia canadensis**
— Turnip-rooted . . . . **Petroselinum crispum 'Tuberosum'** [B]
Pasque Flower. . . . . **Pulsatilla vulgaris**
Pellitory-of-the-Wall . . . . **Parietaria judaica**
Pennyroyal . . . . **Mentha pulegium**
Peppermint, Black . . . . **Mentha x piperita nm. piperita**
— White . . . . **Mentha x piperita nm. officinalis**
Pilewort. . . . . **Ranunculus ficaria**
Pink, Clove . . . . **Dianthus caryophyllus**
— Cheddar . . . . **Dianthus gratianopolitanus**
— Maiden . . . . **Dianthus deltoides**
Plant's Physician . . . . **Chamaemelum nobile**
Pleurisy Root . . . . **Asclepias tuberosa**
Pokeroot . . . . **Phytolacca americana**
Pot Marigold. . . . . **Calendula officinalis** [A]
Primrose . . . . **Primula vulgaris**
Purple Loosestrife. . . . . **Lythrum salicaria**
Pyrethrum, Garden. . . . . **Tanacetum coccineum**

Rampion . . . . **Campanula rapunculus** [B]
Ransoms. . . . . **Allium ursinum**
Raripila . . . . **Mentha x smithiana**
Rhubarb, Culinary . . . . **Rheum officinale**
Rosemary . . . . **Rosmarinus officinalis** [VOL.2]
Rue . . . . **Ruta graveolens** [VOL.2]
— Goat's . . . . **Galega officinalis**
Rupturewort. . . . . **Herniaria glabra**
Rushleek . . . . **Allium schoenoprasum**

Saffron Crocus . . . . **Crocus sativus**
Saffron Thistle. . . . . **Carthamus tinctorius** [A]
Sage . . . . **Salvia officinalis** [S]
— Clary . . . . **Salvia sclarea** [B]
— Jerusalem . . . . **Phlomis fruticosa**
— Pineapple. . . . . **Salvia rutilans** [S]
— Russian . . . . **Perovskia atriplicifolia** [S]
Sainfoin . . . . **Onobrychis viciifolia**
St. John's Girdle . . . . **Artemisia abrotanum** [S]
St. Patrick's Cabbage . . . . **Sempervivum tectorum**
Sampler's Joy . . . . **Verbena officinalis**

Sanicle . . . . **Sanicula europaea**
Savory, Creeping . . . . **Satureja spicigera**
— Prostrate . . . . **Satureja spicigera**
— Summer . . . . **Satureja hortensis** [A]
— Purple . . . . **Satureja coerulea**
— Winter. . . . . **Satureja montana** [S]
Scabious, Field . . . . **Knautia arvensis**
Scented Mayweed. . . . . **Matricaria recutita** [A]
Scotch Thistle. . . . . **Onopordum acanthium** [B]
Sea Holly . . . . **Eryngium maritimum**
Sea Kale . . . . **Crambe maritima**
Self-heal . . . . **Prunella vulgaris**
Silkweed . . . . **Asclepias syriaca**
Skirret . . . . **Sium sisarum**
Skullcap . . . . **Scutelleria galericulata**
— Virginian . . . . **Scutelleria laterifolia**
Sneezewort . . . . **Achillea ptarmica**
Soapwort . . . . **Saponaria officinalis**
Soldiers and Sailors . . . . **Pulmonaria officinalis**
Solomon's Seal . . . . **Polygonatum x hybridum**
Sorrel, Broadleaf. . . . . **Rumex rugosus**
— Buckler-leaved . . . . **Rumex scutatus**
— Common . . . . **Rumex acetosa**
— French . . . . **Rumex scutatus**
— Garden . . . . **Rumex rugosus**
Southernwood . . . . **Artemisia abrotanum** [S]
Spearmint . . . . **Mentha spicata**
Star of Bethlehem . . . . **Ornithogalum umbellatum**
Stinking Iris . . . . **Iris foetidissima**
Strawberry, Alpine. . . . . **Fragaria vesca 'Semperflorens'**
— Wild. . . . . **Fragaria vesca**
Stonecrop . . . . **Sedum acre**
Sweet Cicely. . . . . **Myrrhis odorata**
Sweet Fern . . . . **Myrrhis odorata**
Sweet Flag. . . . . **Acorus calamus**
Sweet Rocket . . . . **Hesperis matronalis**

Tansy . . . . **Tanacetum vulgare**
Tarragon . . . . **Artemisia dracunculus**
— French . . . . **Artemisia dracunculus 'Sativa'**
— Russian . . . . **Artemisia dracunculus 'Inodora'**
Teasel . . . . **Dipsacus fullonum** [B]
— Dyer's . . . . **Dipsacus fullonum** [B]
Thistle, Cotton . . . . **Onopordum acanthium** [B]
— Saffron . . . . **Carthamus tinctorius** [A]
— Scotch . . . . **Onopordum acanthium** [A]
Thrift. . . . . **Armeria maritima**

Thyme, Basil ....**Acinos arvensis** [A]
— Caraway ....**Thymus herba-barona**
— Creeping.......................................**Thymus serpyllum**
— Garden...**Thymus vulgaris**
— Lemon.....................................**Thymus x citriodorus**
— Mother's.......................................**Thymus vulgaris**
Toadflax, Common ....**Linaria vulgaris**
Tormentil ....**Potentilla erecta**
Tree Lupin ....**Lupinus arboreus**
Tree Onion...............................**Allium cepa 'Proliferum'**

Valerian, Common ....**Valeriana officinalis**
Verbena, Lemon ....**Aloysia triphylla** [VOL.2]
Vervain ....**Verbena officinalis**
Violet, Sweet ....**Viola odorata**
— Tufted or Horned ....**Viola cornuta**
Viper's Bugloss ....**Echium vulgare**
Virginian Skullcap ....**Scutellaria laterifolia**
Virginian Poke Weed ....**Phytolacca americana**

Wall Germander........................**Teucrium chamaedrys** [S]
Wall Pepper ....**Sedum acre**
Weld, Dyer's ....**Reseda luteola**
Wild Wallflower...................................**Cheiranthus cheiri**
Wintergreen ....**Gaultheria procumbens** [VOL.2]
Winter Heliotrope ....**Petasites fragrans**
Woad...**Isatis tinctoria** [B]
Woodruff, Sweet ....**Galium odoratum**
— Dyer's ....**Asperula tinctoria**
Woodsage....................................**Teucrium scorodonia** [S]
Wormwood ....**Artemisia absinthium**
— Roman..**Artemisia pontica**
— White ....**Artemisia lactiflora**

Yarrow ....**Achillea millefolium**
— Woolly ....**Achillea tomentosum**
Yellow Flag ....**Iris pseudacorus**
Yellow Purslane...........................**Portulaca oleracea** [A]

THE FAMILIES OF PLANTS

An alphabetic synopsis of family names adopted in the index with a summary of the genera assigned to them. A generic name followed by '=' indicates that the whole genus is considered synonymous with another. Taxa listed within genera followed by 'vide' have been referred to the genus or genera shown, but this does not mean that the entire genus has been sunk into the genus indicated. Tribal groupings have only been given in members of the *Asteraceae* and *Poaceae* for interest and to demonstrate the wide range of diversity in these families.

ACANTHACEAE
Acanthus
Strobilanthes

ADIANTACEAE   [FERNS]
Adiantum
Cheilanthes
Cryptogramma

AGAVACEAE
Agave
Beschorneria
Furcraea
Hesperaloe
Yucca

AIZOACEAE
Delosperma
Drosanthemum
Lampranthus
Malephora
Mesembryanthemum

ALISMATACEAE
Alisma
Baldellia
Caldesia
Luronium
Sagittaria

ALLIACEAE (LILIACEAE)
Agapanthus
Allium
Beauverdia = Ipheion
Brodiaea
Caloscordum
Dichelostemma
Ipheion
Leucocoryne
Nectaroscordum
Nothoscordum
Triteleia
Tulbaghia

ALOEACEAE (*LILIACEAE*)
Aloe

ALSTROEMERIACEAE (*LILIACEAE*)
Alstroemeria

AMARYLLIDACEAE
X Amacrinum
X Amarine
X Amarygia
Amaryllis
Anoiganthus = Cyrtanthus
X Brunsdonna = X Amarygia
Brunsvigia
Chlidanthus
Clivia
Corbularia = Narcissus
X Crinodonna = X Amacrinum
Crinum
Cyrtanthus
Elisena = Hymenocallis
Eucharis
Eustephia
Galanthus
Habranthus
Haemanthus
Hippeastrum
Hymenocallis
Ismene = Hymenocallis
Leucojum
Lycoris
Narcissus
Nerine
Odontostomum
Pancratium
Phaedranassa
Polianthes
Rhodophiala
Scadoxus
Sprekelia
Sternbergia
Tapeinanthus = Narcissus
Tecophilaea
Vallota = Cyrtanthus
Zephyranthes

ANTHERICACEAE (*LILIACEAE*)
  Anthericum
  Arthropodium
  Bottionea = Trichopetalum
  Herpolirion
  Trichopetalum

APHYLLANTHACEAE (*LILIACEAE*)
  Aphyllanthes

APIACEAE (*UMBELLIFERAE*)
  Aciphylla
  Aegopodium
  Anethum
  Angelica
  Anisotome
  Anthriscus
  Apium
  Astrantia
  Athamanta
  Azorella
  Bolax = Azorella
  Bupleurum
  Carum
  Chaerophyllum
  Conium
  Coriandrum
  Cryptotaenia
  Cuminum
  Eryngium
  Ferula
  Foeniculum
  Hacquetia
  Heracleum
  Hydrocotyle
  Levisticum
  Ligusticum
  Meum
  Myrrhis
  Petroselinum
  Peucedanum
  Pimpinella
  Pleurospermum
  Sanicula
  Selinum
  Seseli
  Sium
  Smyrnium

APOCYNACEAE
  Amsonia
  Rhazya
  Vinca

APONOGETONACEAE
  Aponogeton

ARACEAE
  Acorus
  Amorphophallus
  Arisaema
  Arisarum
  Arum
  Biarum
  Calla
  Colocasia
  Dracunculus
  Eminium
  Helicodiceros = Dracunculus
  Lysichiton
  Orontium
  Peltandra
  Pinellia
  Pistia
  Sauromatum
  Spathiphyllum
  Spathyema
  Symplocarpus = Spathyema
  Xanthosoma
  Zantedeschia

ARALIACEAE
  Aralia

ARISTOLOCHIACEAE
  Aristolochia
  Asarum

ASCLEPIADACEAE
  Asclepias
  Ceropegia
  Cynanchum
  Oxypetalum vide Tweedia
  Tweedia

ASPARAGACEAE (*LILIACEAE*)
  Asparagus

ASPHODELACEAE (*LILIACEAE*)
  Asphodeline
  Asphodelus
  Bulbine
  Bulbinella
  Eremurus
  Kniphofia
  Paradisea
  Tritoma = Kniphofia

ASPLENIACEAE   [FERNS]
  Asplenium
  Ceterach
  Phyllitis = Asplenium

ASTELIACEAE (*LILIACEAE*)
  Astelia

ASTERACEAE (*COMPOSITAE*)
  Anthemideae
  Achillea
  Allardia
  Anacyclus
  Anthemis

ASTERACEAE (*continued*)
- Arctanthemum
- Argyranthemum
- Artemisia
- *Balsamita* = Tanacetum
- Chamaemelum
- *Chamomilla* = Matricaria
- Chrysanthemopsis
- Chrysanthemum
- Cotula
- Dendranthema
- Leptinella
- Leucanthemella
- Leucanthemopsis
- Leucanthemum
- Matricaria
- Nipponanthemum
- *Pyrethrum* = Tanacetum
- Seriphidium
- *Spathipappus* = Tanacetum
- Tanacetum
- Tripleurospermum
- *Waldheimia* = Allardia

Arctotideae
- Gazania
- Haplocarpha
- X Venidio-Arctotis

Astereae
- Aster
- Bellis
- Bellium
- Boltonia
- Brachycome
- Celmisia
- Chrysopsis
- Corethrogyne
- Erigeron
- Felicia
- Grindelia
- Haastia
- Haplopappus
- Lagenophora
- Solidago
- X Solidaster
- Townsendia

Calenduleae
- Calendula
- *Dimorphotheca* vide Osteospermum
- Osteospermum

Cardueae
- Arctium
- Carduncellus
- Carlina
- Carthamus
- Centaurea
- Cirsium
- Cnicus
- Cynara
- Echinops
- Galactites
- Jurinea

- Leuzea
- Onopordum
- Serratula
- Silybum

Cichorieae
- Agoseris
- Andryala
- Catananche
- Cichorium
- Crepis
- Hieracium
- Lactuca
- Taraxacum
- Tolpis
- Tragopogon
- *Troximum* = Agoseris
- Urospermum

Eupatorieae
- Eupatorium
- Liatris

Helenieae
- Actinella
- Eriophyllum
- Gaillardia
- Helenium
- Hymenoxys

Heliantheae
- Actinomeris
- Bidens
- Chrysogonum
- Coreopsis
- Cosmos
- Dahlia
- Echinacea
- Helianthella
- Helianthus
- Heliopsis
- *Ridan* = Actinomeris
- Rudbeckia
- Silphium
- *Verbesina* vide Actinomeris

Inuleae
- Anaphalis
- Antennaria
- Asteriscus
- Buphthalmum
- Calocephalus
- Craspedia
- *Gnaphalium* vide Helichrysum
- Helichrysum
- Helipterum
- Inula
- Jasonia
- Leontopodium
- Leucogenes
- X Leucoraoulia
- Raoulia
- Telekia

Mutisieae
- Nassauvia
- Perezia

ASTERACEAE (*continued*)
  Senecioneae
    Arnica
    Cremanthodium
    Doronicum
    Hertia = Othonnopsis
    Homogyne
    Ligularia
    Othonnopsis
    Petasites
    Senecio
    Tussilago
  Vernonieae
    Stokesia
    Vernonia

AZOLLACEAE   [WATER FERNS]
    Azolla

BALSAMINACEAE
    Impatiens

BASELLACEAE
    Boussingaultia

BEGONIACEAE
    Begonia

BERBERIDACEAE
    Achlys
    Bongardia
    Caulophyllum
    Diphylleia
    Epimedium
    Gymnospermium
    Jeffersonia
    Leontice vide Gymnospermium
    Plagiorhegma = Jeffersonia
    Podophyllum
    Vancouveria

BIGNONIACEAE
    Amphicome
    Incarvillea

BLECHNACEAE   [FERNS]
    Blechnum
    Doodia
    Lomaria = Blechnum
    Woodwardia

BORAGINACEAE
    Alkanna
    Anchusa
    Arnebia
    Borago
    Brunnera
    Buglossoides = Lithospermum
    Cerinthe
    Cynoglossum
    Echiodes = Arnebia
    Echium

Eritrichium
Lindelofia
Lithodora
Lithospermum
Mertensia
Moltkia
Myosotidium
Myosotis
Omphalodes
Onosma
Pentaglottis
Plumbago
Pulmonaria
Symphytum
Trachystemon

BRASSICACEAE (*CRUCIFERAE*)
    Aethionema
    Alyssoides
    Alyssum
    Anastatica
    Arabis
    Armoracia
    Aubrieta
    Barbarea
    Cardamine
    Cheiranthus
    Cochlearia vide Armoracia
    Crambe
    Degenia
    Dentaria = Cardamine
    Draba
    Erysimum
    Eunomia = Aethionema
    Hesperis
    Hugueninia
    Hutchinsia
    Iberis
    Ionopsidium
    Isatis
    Lepidium
    Lesquerella
    Lobularia
    Lunaria
    Matthiola
    Megacarpaea
    Morisia
    Pachyphragma
    Petrocallis
    Physaria
    Ptilotrichum
    Schivereckia
    Smelowskia
    Thlaspi
    Vesicaria = Alyssoides

BROMELIACEAE
    Billbergia
    Fascicularia
    Ochagavia
    Puya

BUTOMACEAE
Butomus

CACTACEAE
Opuntia

CALLITRICHACEAE
Callitriche

CAMPANULACEAE
Adenophora
Asyneuma
Azorina
Campanula
Codonopsis
Cyanthus
Edraianthus
Hypsela
Isotoma
Jasione
Lobelia
Ostrowskia
Petromarula
Physoplexis
Phyteuma
Platycodon
Pratia
Symphyandra
Trachelium
Wahlenbergia

CANNABIDACEAE
Humulus

CANNACEAE
Canna

CAPRIFOLIACEAE
Linnaea
Triosteum

CARYOPHYLLACEAE
Acanthophyllum
Agrostemma
Arenaria
Cerastium
Colobanthus
Dianthus
Gypsophila
Heliosperma = Silene
Herniaria
Lychnis
Melandrium = Silene
Minuartia
Moehringia
Paronychia
Petrocoptis
Petrorhagia
Pteranthus
Sagina
Saponaria

Scleranthus
Silene
Tunica = Petrorhagia
Viscaria = Lychnis

CERATOPHYLLACEAE
Ceratophyllum

CHENOPODIACEAE
Chenopodium

CISTACEAE
Helianthemum
Tuberaria

CLUSIACEAE (*GUTTIFERAE*)
Hypericum

COLCHICACEAE (*LILIACEAE*)
Bulbocodium
Colchicum
Gloriosa
Merendera
Sandersonia

COMMELINACEAE
Commelina
Tradescantia

COMPOSITAE = **ASTERACEAE**

CONVALLARIACEAE (*LILIACEAE*)
Aspidistra
Clintonia
Convallaria
Disporum
Liriope
Maianthemum
Oaksiella = Uvularia
Ophiopogon
Polygonatum
Reineckia
Smilacina = Maianthemum
Speirantha
Streptopus
Tricyrtis
Uvularia

CONVOLVULACEAE
Calystegia
Convolvulus
Pharbitis

CORNACEAE
Cornus

CRASSULACEAE
Chiastophyllum
Cotyledon vide Rosularia
& Chiastophyllum
Crassula

CRASSULACEAE (*continued*)
   Jovibarba
   Orostachys
   Rhodiola = Sedum
   Rosularia
   Sedum
   Sempervivella
   Sempervivum
   Tillaea = Crassula
   Umbilicus

CRUCIFERAE = **BRASSICACEAE**

CUCURBITACEAE
   Bryonia

CYATHEACEAE   [FERNS]
   Cyathea
   Dicksonia

CYPERACEAE
   Carex
   Cladium
   Cyperus
   Eleocharis
   Eriophorum
   Gahnia
   Oreobolus
   Schoenus
   Scirpus
   Uncinia

DAVALLIACEAE   [FERNS]
   Davallia

DENNSTAEDTIACEAE   [FERNS]
   Dennstaedtia
   Hypolepis
   Paesia
   Pteridium

DIOSCOREACEAE
   Dioscorea

DIAPENSIACEAE
   Galax
   Schizocodon = Shortia
   Shortia

DIPSACACEAE
   Cephalaria
   Dipsacus
   Galax
   Knautia
   Pterocephalus
   Scabiosa
   Succisa

DRYOPTERIDACEAE   [FERNS]
   Arachniodes
   Cyrtomium
   Dryopteris

   Polystichopsis = Arachniodes
   Polystichum

EQUISETACEAE   [HORSETAILS]
   Equisetum

EUPHORBIACEAE
   Euphorbia

FABACEAE (*LEGUMINOSAE*)
   Anthyllis
   Astragalus
   Baptisia
   Coronilla
   Dorycnium
   Erinacea
   Galega
   Hedysarum
   Hippocrepis
   Lathyrus
   Lotus
   Lupinus
   Melilotus
   Onobrychis
   Ononis
   Oxytropis
   Parochetus
   Thermopsis
   Trifolium
   Vicia

FONTINALACEAE   [MOSSES]
   Fontinalis

FRANKENIACEAE
   Frankenia

FUMARIACEAE
   Adlumia
   Corydalis
   Dicentra
   Pteridophyllum

GENTIANACEAE
   Centaurium
   Crawfurdia
   Erythraea = Centaurium
   Gentiana
   Gentianella
   Gentianopsis
   Swertia

GERANIACEAE
   Erodium
   Geranium
   Pelargonium

GESNERIACEAE
   Briggsia
   Conandron
   Haberlea

GESNERIACEAE (*continued*)
Jankaea
Ramonda
Rehmannia
Sinningia

GLOBULARIACEAE
Globularia

GOODENIACEAE
Goodenia
Selliera

GRAMINEAE = **POACEAE**

GUNNERACEAE
Gunnera

GUTTIFERAE = **CLUSIACEAE**

HAEMODORACEAE
Anigozanthos
Wachendorfia

HALORIDAGACEAE
Myriophyllum

HEMEROCALLIDACEAE (*LILIACEAE*)
Hemerocallis

HIPPURIDACEAE
Hippuris

HOSTACEAE (*LILIACEAE*)
Hosta

HYACINTHACEAE (*LILIACEAE*)
Albuca
Bellevalia
Brimeura
Camassia
Chionodoxa
X Chionoscilla
Endymion = Hyacinthoides
Eucomis
Galtonia
Hyacinthella
Hyacinthoides
Hyacinthus
Lachenalia
Ledebouria
Leopoldia
Muscari
Muscarimia
Ornithogalum
Polyxena
Pseudomuscari
Puschkinia
Scilla
Urginea
Veltheimia

HYDRANGEACEAE
Deinanthe
Kirengeshoma

HYDROCHARITACEAE
Egeria
Elodea
Hydrilla
Hydrocharis
Lagarosiphon
Stratiotes

HYDROPHYLLACEAE
Hesperochiron
Phacelia
Romanzoffia

HYPOXIDACEAE
Rhodohypoxis

IRIDACEAE
Acidanthera = Gladiolus
Anomatheca
Antholyza
Aristea
Babiana
Belamcanda
Chasmanthe
Crocosmia
Crocus
Curtonus = Crocosmia
Cypella
Dierama
Dietes
Diplarrhena
Ferraria
Freesia
Gelasine
Gladiolus
Gynandriris
Hermodactylus
Hesperantha
Homeria
Homoglossum
Iris
Ixia
Lapeirousia vide Anomatheca
Libertia
Montbretia = Crocosmia
Moraea
Orthrosanthus
Romulea
Schizostylis
Sisyrinchium
Solenomelus
Sparaxis
Synnotia
Tigridia
Tritonia
Watsonia

IXIOLIRIACEAE (*AMARYLLIDACEAE*)
Ixiolirion

JUNCACEAE
Juncus
Luzula

LABIATAE = **LAMIACEAE**

LAMIACEAE (*LABIATAE*)
Acinos
Agastache
Ajuga
Ballota
Betonica = Stachys
Calamintha
Cedronella
Dracocephalum
Elsholtzia
Galeobdolon
Glechoma
Horminium
Hyssopus
Lamiastrum = Galeobdolon
Lamium
Leonurus
Lycopus
Marrubium
Meehania
Melissa
Melittis
Mentha
Micromeria
Monarda
Nepeta
Ocimum
Origanum
Perovskia
Phlomis
Physostegia
Preslia = Mentha
Prunella
Pycnanthemum
Salvia
Satureja
Scutellaria
Sphacele
Stachys
Teucrium
Thymus

LEGUMINOSAE = **FABACEAE**

LEMNACEAE
Lemna
Spirodela

LILIACEAE
Calochortus
Cardiocrinum

Erythronium
Fritillaria
Gagea
Korolkowia = Fritillaria
Lilium
Lloydia
Nomocharis
Notholirion
Tulipa

LIMNANTHACEAE
Limnanthemum

LINACEAE
Linum

LYTHRACEAE
Cuphea
Lythrum

MALVACEAE
Alcaea
Altheae
Callirhoe
Kitaibela
Lavatera
Malva
Malvastrum
Sidalcea
Sphaeralcea

MARSILEACEAE   [FERNS]
Marsilea
Pilularia

MELANTHIACEAE (*LILIACEAE*)
Aletris
Chamaelirium
Chionographis
Heloniopsis
Stenanthium
Veratrum
Xerophyllum
Zigadenus

MENYANTHACEAE
Limnanthemum = Nymphoides
Menyanthes
Nymphoides
Villarsia vide Menyanthes
& Nymphoides

MORINACEAE
Morina

NELUMBONACEAE
Nelumbo

NYCTAGINACEAE
Mirabilis

NYMPHAEACEAE
  Nuphar
  Nymphaea

ONAGRACEAE
  Chamaenerion
  Epilobium
  Gaura
  Isnardia = Ludwigia
  Ludwigia
  Oenothera
  Zauschneria

ORCHIDACEAE
  Aceras
  Anacamptis
  Aplectrum
  Barlia
  Bletilla
  Calanthe
  Calypso
  Cephalanthera
  Corybas
  Cypripedium
  Dactylorhiza
  Epipactis
  Goodyera
  Gymnadenia
  Habenaria
  Himantoglossum
  Listera
  Neotinea
  Ophrys
  Orchis
  Pecteilis vide Habenaria
  Plantanthera
  Pleione
  Pterostylis
  Serapias
  Spiranthes

OSMUNDACEAE   [FERNS]
  Osmunda

OXALIDACEAE
  Oxalis

PAEONIACEAE
  Glaucidium
  Paeonia

PAPAVERACEAE
  Bocconia vide Macleaya
  Chelidonium
  Eomecon
  Glaucium
  Hylomecon
  Macleaya
  Meconopsis
  Papaver
  Romneya

  Sanguinaria
  Stylophorum

PHILESIACEAE (*LILIACEAE*)
  Luzuriaga

PHORMIACEAE (*LILIACEAE*)
  Dianella
  Phormium
  Xeronema

PHYTOLACCACEAE
  Phytolacca

PLANTAGINACEAE
  Littorella
  Plantago

PLUMBAGINACEAE
  Acantholimon
  Armeria
  Ceratostigma
  Dictyolimon
  Goniolimon
  Limonium
  Statice = Goniolimon & Limonium

POACEAE (*GRAMINEAE*)
  Andropogoneae
    Andropogon
    Chrysopogon vide Sorghastrum
    Erianthus = Saccharum
    Imperata vide Miscanthus
    Miscanthus
    Saccharum
    Sorghastrum
    Spodiopogon
    Themeda
  Arundineae
    Arundo
    Chionochloa
    Cortaderia
    Gynerium vide Cortaderia
    Hakonechloa
    Molinia
    Phragmites
  Aveneae
    Alopecurus
    Anthoxanthum
    Apera
    Arrhenatherum
    Avena vide Helictotrichon
    Calamagrostis
    Deschampsia
    Helictotrichon
    Holcus
    Koeleria
    Mibora
    Phalaris
  Bromeae
    Bromus

POACEAE (*GRAMINEAE*)
  Centotheceae
    Chasmanthium
  Cynodonteae
    Bouteloua
    Chondrosum
    Spartina
  Eragrostideae
    Eragrostis
    Muhlenbergia
    Uniola vide Chasmanthium
  Meliceae
    Glyceria
    Melica
  Nardeae
    Nardus
  Oryzeae
    Zizania
  Paniceae
    Cenchrus
    Panicum
    Pennisetum
  Poeae
    Briza
    Dactylis
    Festuca
    Poa
    Sesleria
  Stipeae
    Achnatherum = Stipa
    Lasiogrostis = Stipa
    Milium
    Stipa
  Triticeae
    Agropyron
    Elymus
    Hystrix
    Leymus

POLEMONIACEAE
    Phlox
    Polemonium

POLYGONACEAE
    Aconogonum = Persicaria
    Bistorta = Persicaria
    Eriogonum
    Fallopia
    Fagopyrum
    Oxyria
    Persicaria
    Polygonum
    Reynoutria = Fallopia
    Rheum
    Rumex
    Tovara = Persicaria

POLYPODIACEAE   [FERNS]
    Polypodium

PONTEDERIACEAE
    Eichhornia
    Pontederia

PORTULACACEAE
    Calandrinia
    Calyptridium
    Claytonia
    Lewisia
    Montia
    Neopaxia
    Portulaca
    Spraguea = Calyptridium
    Talinum

POTAMOGETONACEAE
    Potamogeton

PRIMULACEAE
    Anagallis
    Androsace
    Cortusa
    Cyclamen
    Dionysia
    Dodecatheon
    Douglasia
    Hottonia
    Lysimachia
    Omphalogramma
    Primula
    Soldanella
    Vitaliana

RANUNCULACEAE
    Aconitum
    Actaea
    Adonis
    Anemone
    Anemonella
    Anemonopsis
    Aquilegia
    Callianthemum
    Caltha
    Cimicifuga
    Clematis
    Coptis
    Delphinium
    Eranthis
    Helleborus
    Hepatica
    Hydrastis
    Isopyrum
    Paraquilegia
    Pulsatilla
    Ranunculus
    Semiaquilegia
    Thalictrum
    Trollius

RESEDACEAE
    Reseda

ROSACEAE
Acaena
Agrimonia
Alchemilla
Aphanes
Aruncus
Comarum = Potentilla
Dryas
Duchesnea
Filipendula
Fragaria
Geum
Gillenia
Kelseya
Luetkea
Petrophyton
Potentilla
Poterium = Sanguisorba
Sanguisorba
Sibbaldia
Sibbaldiopsis
Spiraea vide Filipendula
Waldsteinia

RUBIACEAE
Asperula
Bouvardia
Crucianella vide Phuopsis
Galium
Houstonia
Mitchella
Nertera
Phuopsis
Rubia

RUTACEAE
Boenninghausenia
Boronia
Dictamnus

SALVINIACEAE   [WATER FERNS]
Salvinia

SAURURACEAE
Anemopsis
Houttuynia
Saururus

SAXIFRAGACEAE
Acerophyllum
Astilbe
Astilboides
Bergenia
Boykinia
Chrysosplenium
Darmera
Elmera
Francoa
Heuchera
X Heucherella
Lithophragma
Mitella

Parnassia
Peltiphyllum = Darmera
Peltoboykinia
Rodgersia
Saxifraga
Tanakaea
Telesonix
Tellima
Tiarella
Tolmiea

SCROPHULARIACEAE
Alonsoa
Antirrhinum
Asarina
Calceolaria
Celsia = Verbascum
X Celsioverbascum = Verbascum
Chaenorhinum
Chelone
Cymbalaria
Diascia
Digitalis
Diplacus = Mimulus
Erinus
Freylinia
Gratiola
Hemiphragma
Jovellana
Lagotis
Linaria
Lophospermum
Maurandya
Mazus
Mimulus
Ourisia
Paederota
Parahebe
Penstemon
Phygelius
Pygmaea
Rhodochiton
Scrophularia
Synthyris
Verbascum
Veronica
Veronicastrum
Wulfenia

SELAGINELLACEAE   [FERNS]
Selaginella

SOLANACEAE
Atropa
Datura
Hyoscyamus
Jaborosa
Mandragora
Nierembergia
Physalis
Scopolia

SPARGANIACEAE
Sparganium

STYLIDIACEAE
Stylidium

TACCACEAE
Tacca

THELYPTERIDACEAE   [FERNS]
Lastrea = Oreopteris & Thelypteris
Oreopteris
Phegopteris
Thelypteris

THYMELAEACEAE
Pimelea

TRAPACEAE
Trapa

TRILLIACEAE (*LILIACEAE*)
Scoliopus
Trillium

TROPAEOLACEAE
Tropaeoleum

TYPHACEAE
Typha

UMBELLIFERAE = **APIACEAE**

URTICACEAE
Helxine = Soleirolia
Parietaria
Soleirolia

VALERIANACEAE
Centranthus
Kentranthus = Centranthus
Patrinia
Valeriana
Valerianella

VERBENACEAE
Glandularia = Verbena
Lippia vide Phyla
Phyla
Verbena

VIOLACEAE
Viola

WOODSIACEAE   [FERNS]
Athyrium
Cystopteris
Diplazium
Gymnocarpium
Matteuccia
Onoclea
Woodsia

ZINGIBERACEAE
Cautleya
Hedychium
Roscoea
Zingiber

INFORMATION CODES USED
IN THE INDEX

At left margin:

A — Annual

B — Biennial

C — Climber

S — Shrubby

H — Refer to Herb list

N — Native or Naturalised in Britain as per *'Flora of the British Isles'* 3rd Edition, Clapham, Tutin & Moore (1987)

‡ — Illustrated in W. Keble Martin's *'New Concise British Flora'*

L — Recommended for Landscape use by the Joint Liaison Committee on Plant Supplies

At right margin:

Further information can be found in:

M   A **m**onograph specified under the generic heading

EGF *'The European Garden Flora'* S.M. Walters et al., Volumes 1 & 2 to date (1986) & (1984)

PGP *'Perennial Garden Plants'* Graham Stuart Thomas, 2nd Edition (1982)

CA   *'Collectors' Alpines'* Royton E. Heath, 2nd Edition (1981)

BB   *The Bulb Book'* Martyn Rix and Roger Phillips, (1981)

SB   *'The Smaller Bulbs'* Brian Mathew, (1987)

DGP *'The Dictionary of Garden Plants in Colour'* Roy Hay & Patrick M. Synge (1969)

RD   *'Encyclopaedia of Garden Plants and Flowers'* **R**eader's **D**igest, 4th Edition (1987)

Emboldened codes indicate useful illustrations

STANDARD ABBREVIATIONS USED
IN 'INDEX HORTENSIS'

(Not all have been used in this Volume)

al.	*alii*:	**others**
c.	*circa*:	**about**
cit.	*citatus*:	**cited**
comb.	*combinatio*:	**combination**
cons.	*conservandus*:	**to be kept**
cult.	*cultus*:	**cultivated**
cv.	*cultivarietas*:	**cultivar**
etc.	*et cetera*:	**and the rest**
e.g.	*exempli gratia*:	**by way of example, for example**
em.	*emendatus*:	**emended**
err. typogr.	*errore typographico*:	**by a printing mistake**
f.	(after a personal noun) *filius*:	**son**
f.	(before an epithet) *forma*:	**form**
hort.	*hortorum*:	**of gardens**; *hortulanorum*: **of gardeners**
i.e.	*id est*:	**that is**
ign.	*ignotus*:	**unknown**
in litt.	*in litteris*:	**in correspondence**
ined.	*ineditus*:	**unpublished**
inq.	*inquilinus*:	**naturalised**
i.q.	*idem quod*:	**the same as**
nm.	*nothomorpha*:	**nothomorph**
no.	*numero*:	**number**
nom.	*nomen*:	**name**
nom. ambig.	*nomen ambiguum*:	**ambiguous name**
nom. confus.	*nomen confusum*:	**confused name**
nom. cons.	*nomen conservandum*:	**name conserved in ICBN**
nom. illeg.	*nomen illegitimum*:	**illegitimate name**
nom. nud.	*nomen nudem*:	**name unaccompanied by a description**
nom. obsc.	*nomen obscurum*:	**obscure name**
nom. rejic.	*nomen rejiciendum*:	**name rejected in ICBN**
nom. superfl.	*nomen superfluum*:	**name superfluous when published**
nov.	*novus*:	**new**
p.p.	*pro parte*:	**partly, in part**
q.e.	*quod est*:	**which is**
q.v.	*quod vide*:	**which see**
sens.	*sensu*:	**in the sense of**
seq.	*sequens*:	**following**
sp.	*species*:	**species**
sphalm.	*sphalmate*:	**by mistake, mistakenly**
ssp.	*subspecies*:	**subspecies**
syn.	*synonymon*:	**synonym**
var.	*varietas*:	**variety**
vol.	*volumen*:	**volume**
viz.	*videlicet*:	**namely**

ACAENA Mutis ex Linnaeus 1771   [*Rosaceae*]
  adscendens Vahl 1805 (*A. affinis*)
  affinis Hooker f. 1845 = **A. adscendens**
  anserinifolia (Forster & Forster f.) Druce 1917 = **A. sanguisorbae**
  anserinifolia hort., non (Forster & Forster f.) Druce = **A. novae-zealandiae**
L **'Blue Haze'** (A. 'Pewter')
  buchananii Hooker f. 1864   RD
  caesiiglauca (Bitter) Bergmans 1939 (*A. coerulea* hort., *A. glauca* hort.) RD
  coerulea hort. = **A. caesiiglauca**
S **glabra** Buchan 1872
  glauca hort. non Buchan = **A. caesiiglauca**
  glaucophylla Bitter 1910 = **A. magellanica**
  'Greencourt Hybrid'
N **inermis** Hooker f. 1852 (*A. microphylla inermis*)
N **laevigata** Aiton f. 1810
N **magellanica** Vahl 1805 (*A. glaucophylla*)
L **microphylla** Hooker f. 1852   RD
      'Copper Carpet' = **A. microphylla 'Kupferteppich'**
      'Glauca' = **A. caesiiglauca**
      inermis (Hooker f.) hort. = **A. inermis**
      'Kupferteppich' ('Copper Carpet')   RD
SN **novae-zealandiae** Kirk 1871
N **ovalifolia** Ruiz & Pavon 1798
  pallida (Kirk) Allan 1961
  'Pewter' = **A. 'Blue Haze'**
  pinnatifida Ruiz & Pavon 1798 non Lindley 1829
  platyacantha Spegazzini 1897
  pumila Vahl 1805
  'Purple Carpet' = **A. microphylla 'Kupferteppich'**
  saccaticupula Bitter 1911
N **sanguisorbae** Vahl 1805 (*A. anserinifolia* (Forster & Forster f.) Druce)
S **splendens** Hooker & Arnot 1833

ACANTHOLIMON Boissier 1846 nom. cons.   [*Plumbaginaceae*]
  acerosum (Willldenow) Boissier 1846
      var. **brachystachyum** Boissier 1879 (*A. pinardii*)
  'Albanicum'
  androsaceum (Jaubert & Spach) Boissier 1879 = **A. ulicinum**
  armenum Boissier & Huet 1859
  aulieatense Czerniakowska 1923 (*A. gramineum*)
  avenaceum Bunge 1872
  caryophyllaceum Boissier 1846
  confertiflorum Bokhari 1970
  echinus Boissier 1879 = **A. ulicinum**
  glumaceum (Jaubert & Spach) Boissier 1846
  gramineum Korovin 1923 = **A. aulietense**
  hohenackeri (Jaubert & Spach) Boissier 1846   CA
  kotschyi (Jaubert & Spach) Boissier 1846
  lepturoides (Jaubert & Spach) Boissier 1846
  libanoticum Boissier 1848   CA
  lycopodioides Boissier 1848
  melananthum Boissier 1846
  olivieri (Jabert & Spach) Boissier 1846   CA
  pinardii Boissier 1846 = **A. acerosum** var. **brachystachyum**
  ulicinum (Willdenow & Schultes) Boissier 1848 (*A. androsaceum, A. echinus*) CA
      var. **creticum** (Boissier) Bokhavi & Edmondson   CA
  venustum Boissier 1846   CA

ACANTHOPHYLLUM C. A. Meyer 1831   [*Caryophyllaceae*]
  glandulosum Bunge & Boissier 1867
  grandiflorum Stocks 1852

ACANTHUS Linnaeus 1753   *[Acanthaceae]*
    balcanicus Heywood & Richardson 1972 = **A. hungaricus**
    caroli-alexandri Haussknecht 1887   PGP
    dioscoridis Willdenow 1800   PGP
        var. **perringii** (Siehe) E. Hossain 1982
    hungaricus (Borbas) Baenitz 1896 (*A. balcanicus, A. longifolius*)   PGP-RD
    longifolius Host 1831 non Poiret 1810 = **A. hungaricus**
HNL   **mollis** Linnaeus 1753   PGP-DGP-**RD**
        Latifolius Agg.   PGP
L   **spinosus** Linnaeus 1753   PGP-**DGP-RD**
        Spinosissimus Agg.   PGP

ACERAS R. Brown 1813   *[Orchidaceae]*
N‡   **anthropophorum** (Linnaeus) R. Brown 1813   EGF2-CA

ACERIPHYLLUM Engelmann 1890   *[Saxifragaceae]*
    rossii (Oliver) Englemann 1890

ACHILLEA Linnaeus 1753   *[Asteraceae (Compositae)]*
    abrotanoides (Visiani) Visiani 1847
    aegyptiaca Smith 1838 non Linnaeus = **A. taygetea**
    ageratifolia (Smith) Boissier 1875
        ssp. **aizoon** (Grisebach) Heimerl 1884 (*A. aizoon, Anthemis aizoon* hort.)
        ssp. *serbica* (Nyman) Heimerl 1884 = **A. serbica**
        'Hans Simon'
    aizoon Grisebach 1844 = **A. ageratifolia** ssp. **aizoon**
    ambigua Heimerl 1884 = **A. erba-rotta** ssp. **ambigua**
    'Ambigua' Sündermann 1906 nom. illegit. (*A. ageratifolia* x *A. umbellata*)
    'Apfelbute' (*A. millefolium* x A. 'Taygetea')   [W. Kikillus]
    'Apple Blossom' = **A. 'Apfelbute'**
    argentea Lamarck 1783 = **Tanacetum argenteum**
    atrata Linnaeus 1753
        ssp. **clusiana** (Tausch) Heimerl
    aurea Lamarck 1783 nom. illegit. = **A. chrysocoma**
    barbeyana Heldreich & Heimerl 1884
    brachyphylla Boissier & Hausknecht 1875
    canescens Formanek 1909
    chrysocoma Frivaldsky 1835 (*A. aurea*)   RD
        'Grandiflora'
    clavennae Linnaeus 1753 (*A. argentea*)   RD
        ssp. **integrifolia**
    clypeolata Smith 1806   RD
    'Clypeolata' Hort. non Smith nom. illegit.   PGP-**DGP**
    compacta Lamarck 1783 non Willdenow 1803 (*A. sericea*)
L   **'Coronation Gold'** (*A. cypeolata* x *A. filipendulina*)   [Pole]   PGP-**DGP-RD**
H   **decolorans** Schrader 1809 (*A. serrata*)   PGP
        'W. B. Child'
    depressa Janka 1873 (*A. pseudopectinata*)
    erba-rotta Allioni 1773 (*A. herba-rota* hort.)
        ssp. **ambigua** (Heimerl) I. B. K. Richardson 1976 (*A. ambigua*)
        ssp. **moschata** (Wulfen) I. B. K. Richardson 1976 (*A. moschata*)
        ssp. **rupestris** (Porta) I. B. K. Richardson 1976 (*A. rupestris*)
    eupatorium Marshall von Bieberstein 1798 = **A. filipendulina**
    'Fanal' (*A. millefolium* x A. 'Taygetea')   [W. Kikillus]
    filipendulina Lamarck 1783 (*A. eupatorium*)   PGP-DGP-RD
        'Altgold'
        'Cloth of Gold'   RD
        'Gold Plate'   PGP-DGP
        'Neugold'
        'Parker's Variety'   PGP-DGP

'**Sonnengold**'
fraasii Schultz-Bip 1855
grandifolia Frivaldsky 1836   PGP
'Great Expectations' = **A. 'Hoffnung'**
x grisebachii Sündermann 1906 (*A. ageratifolia* ssp. *aizoon* x *A. ageratifolia*)
'**Heidi**' (*A. millefolium* x A. 'Taygetea')   [W. Kikillus]
herba-rota hort. = **A. erba-rotta**
'**Hoffnung**' (*A. millefolium* x A. 'Taygetea')   [W. Kikillus]
holosericea Smith 1813
x huteri Sündermann 1906 (*A. ageratifolia* x *A. rupestris*)
integrifolia hort. = **A. clavennae** ssp. **integrifolia**
x jaborneggii Halacsy 1877 (*A. clavennae* x *A. erba-rotta* ssp. *moschata*)
x kellereri Sündermann 1906 (*A. clypeolata* x *A. ageratifolia* ssp. *aizoon*)   RD
x kolbiana Sündermann 1906 (*A. clavennae* x *A. umbellata*)
    '**Weston**'
'**Lachsschönheit**' (*A. millefolium* x A. 'Taygetea')
leptophylla Marshall von Bieberstein 1808
x lewisii Ingwersen (*A. clavennae* x *A. tomentosa*)
    '**King Edward**'   RD
HN‡L **millefolium** Linnaeus 1753   PGP-DGP
    var. **borealis** (Bongard) !
L   '**Cerise Queen**'   PGP-DGP-**RD**
    '**Fire King**'   PGP-**DGP**
    '**Kelwayi**'   [Kelway]   RD
    '**Kirschkönigin**'
    '**Landsdorferglut**'
    '**Lavender Beauty**'
    '**Lilac Beauty**'
    '**Paprika**'
    '**Purpureum**'
    '**Red Beauty**'   PGP
    '**Rosea**'
    '**Sammetriese**'   [K. Foerster]   PGP
    '**Wesersandstein**'
    '**White Beauty**'
L '**Moonshine**' (*A. clypeolata* x A. 'Taygetea')   [A. Bloom]   PGP-**DGP**-RD
monocephala Boissier & Balansa 1856
moschata Wulfen 1877 = **A. erba-rotta** ssp. **moschata**
x obristii Sündermann 1906 (*A. rupestris* x *A. umbellata*)
nana Linnaeus 1753
neilreichii Kerner 1871 = **A. nobilis** ssp. **neilreichii**
nobilis Linnaeus 1753
    ssp. **neilreichii** (Kerner) Formanek 1892 (*A. neilreichii*)
odorata Linnaeus 1759
'Peter Davis' = **Tanacetum herderi**
x portae Sündermann 1906 (*A. clavennae* x *A. rupestris*)
*x prichardii
pseudopectinata Janka 1872 = **A. depressa**
HN‡ **ptarmica** Linnaeus 1753   PGP-DGP-RD
    '**Ballerina**'
L   '**Boule de Neige**' ('Schneeball', 'The Pearl')   PGP-**DGP**-RD
    '**Nana Compacta**'   [K. Foerster 1953]
    '**Perry's White**'   [M. Perry]   PGP-DGP-RD
    'Schneeball' = **A. ptarmica 'Boule de Neige'**
    'The Pearl' = **A. ptarmica 'Boule de Neige'**
    '**Unschuld**'   [E. Benary]
pyrenaica Sibthorp ex Godron 1851
rupestris Porta 1882 non Huter ex Beck 1882 = **A. erba-rotta** ssp. **rupestris**
'Salmon Beauty' = **A. 'Lachsschönheit'**
'**Schwefelblüte**' ('Flowers of Sulphur')   [G. Arends 1935]   PGP-**DGP**

'**Schwellenburg**' (*A. fillipendulina* x ?)   [Bachmann]
serbica Nyman 1879 (*A. ageratifolia* var. *serbica*)
sericea Janka 1859 = **A. compacta**
serrata Smith 1807 = **A. decolorans**
setacea Waldstein & Kitaibel 1801
taygetea Boissier & Heldreich 1849 (*A. aegyptiaca* Smith)   RD
'**Taygetea**' Hort. non Boissier & Heldreich nom. illegit.   PGP
'The Beacon' = **A. 'Fanal'**
HN **tomentosa** Linnaeus 1753   RD
    '**Aurea**' ('Maynard's Gold')
    'Maynard's Gold' = **A. tomentosa 'Aurea'**
'**Trautmanii**' (*A. pyrenaica* x *A. tomentosa*)
umbellata Smith 1813
    '**Alba**'
    '**Mariesii**'
vermicularis Trinius 1818
x wilczekii Sündermann 1906 (*A. ageratifolia* x *A. lingulata*)   RD

ACHLYS de Candolle 1821   [*Berberidaceae*]
triphylla (Smith) de Candolle 1821
    var. **japonica** (Maximowicz) Ito 1887

ACHNATHERUM Palisot de Beauvois 1812   [*Poaceae (Gramineae)*]
*****brachytricha**
calamagrostis (Linnaeus) Palisot de Beauvois 1812 = **Stipa calamagrostis**
splendens (Trinius) Nevski 1937 = **Stipa splendens**

ACIDANTHERA Hochstetter 1844   [*Iridaceae*]
bicolor Hochstetter 1844 = **Gladiolus callianthus**
murielae Hoog nom. invalid = **Gladiolus callianthus**

ACINOS Miller 1754   [*Lamiaceae (Labiatae)*]
alpinus (Linnaeus) Moench 1794 (*Calamintha alpina*)
    ssp. **meridionalis** (Nyman) P. W. Ball 1972
HAN‡ **arvensis** (Lamarck) Dandy 1946 (*A. thymoides*)
corsicus (Persoon) Getliffe 1972 (*Micromeria corsica*)   CA
thymoides Moench 1794 = **A. arvensis**

ACIPHYLLA Forster 1776   [*Apiaceae (Umbelliferae)*]
aurea W. R. B. Oliver 1956
congesta Cheeseman 1915
crenulata J. B. Armstrong 1879
dobsonii Hooker f. 1864
ferox W. R. B. Oliver 1956
glaucescens W. R. B. Oliver 1956
hectori Buchan 1882
lecomtei J. W. Dawson 1979
monroi Hooker f. 1855
montana J. F. Armstrong 1872
pinnatifida Petrie 1911
procumbens F. Mueller ex Bentham 1867
scott-thomsonii Cockayne & Allan 1927   PGP
similis Cheeseman 1913
simplex Petrie 1890
spedenii Cheeseman 1913
squarrosa Forster & Forster f. 1776   PGP
subflabellata W. R. B. Oliver 1956

ACONITUM Linnaeus 1753   [*Ranunculaceae*]
anglicum Stapf 1926   PGP

x cammarum Linnaeus 1762 em. Fries (*A. napellus* x *A. variegatum*, etc)
    var. **bicolor** (Schultes) Bergmans   PGP-RD
      'Caeruleum'
      'Doppelgänger'
      'Grandiflorum Album'
      'Franz Marc'
      'Nachthimmel'
      'Sternennacht'
carmichaelii Debeaux 1879 (*A. fischeri*)   PGP-DGP-RD
      'Arendsii'   PGP
    var. **wilsonii** (Stapf) Munz   RD
    var. **wilsonii 'Barker's Variety'**   PGP-DGP-RD
    var. **wilsonii 'Kelmscott'**   PGP-RD
chasmanthum Stapf 1903
compactum Reichenbach 1819
      'Album'
      'Carneum'   PGP
coreanum Leveille 1909
fischeri hort. non Reichenbach 1823 = **A. carmichaelii**
henryi E. Pritz ex Diels
      'Spark's Variety'   PGP-DGP-RD
koreanum hort. = **A. coreanum**
lamarckii Reichenbach 1825 (*A. pyrenaicum*)
lycoctonum Linnaeus 1753   DGP
HN‡ **napellus** Linnaeus 1753
  nepellus Agg.   DGP-**RD**
      'Album' = **A. compactum 'Album'**
      'Bergfürst'
      'Blue Sceptre' = **A. tauricum 'Blue Sceptre'**
      'Bressingham Spire' = **A. tauricum 'Bressingham Spire'**
      'Carneum' = **A. compactum 'Carneum'**
      'Gletschereis'
      'Grandiflorum Album'
      'Newry Blue'   PGP-**DGP**-RD
      'Roseum' = **A. compactum 'Carneum'**
orientale Miller 1768   PGP
pyrenaicum Linnaeus 1753 p.p. nom. confus. = **A. lamarckii**
septentrionale Koelle 1786   RD
      'Ivorine'   PGP-RD
tauricum Wulfen 1788
L   **'Blue Sceptre'**   PGP-DGP
L   **'Bressingham Blue'**   PGP-DGP-RD
violaceum Jacquemont ex Stapf 1905
volubile Pallas ex Koelle 1786   PGP-**BB**
N **vulparia** Reichenbech 1819   PGP
wilsonii Stapf 1903 = **A. carmichaelii** var. **wilsonii**

ACONOGONUM (Meissner) Reichenbach 1837   [*Polygonaceae*]
    campanulatum (Hooker f.) Hara 1966 = **Persicaria campanulata**
    molle (D. Don) Hara 1966 = **Persicaria molle**
    polymorphum (Ledebour) Nakai 1922 = **Persicaria polymorpha**
    polystachyum (Wallich ex Meissner) K. Haraldson 1978 = **Persicaria polystachya**
    sericeum (Pallas) Hara 1966 = **Persicaria sericea**
    weyrichii (F. Schmidt) Hara 1966 = **Persicaria weyrichii**

ACORUS Linnaeus 1753   [*Araceae*]
HN‡ **calamus** Linnaeus 1753   EGF2.
      'Variegatus'   PGP
    gramineus Solander 1789   EGF2.
      'Argenteostriatus'   PGP

var. **pusillus** Engelmann
'Variegatus'
x intermedius Hort. (*A. calamus* x *A. gramineus*)

ACTAEA Linnaeus 1753 [*Ranunculaceae*]
  alba (Linnaeus) Miller 1768 = **A. pachypoda** (N. USA)
  alba hort. non (Linnaeus) Miller = **A. spicata** (Eurasia)
  asiatica Hara 1939 (*A. spicata* 'Nigra')   RD
  erythrocarpa Fischer 1835 = **A. spicata** ssp. **erythrocarpa**
  pachypoda S. Elliot 1816   PGP-RD
  rubra (Aiton) Willdenow 1809 = **A. spicata** ssp. **rubra**
HN‡L **spicata** Linnaeus 1753 (*A. spicata* 'Alba')   PGP-RD
    'Alba' = **A. spicata**
    ssp. **erythrocarpa** (Fischer) Hulten 1971 (*A. erythrocarpa*)
    'Nigra' = **A. asiatica**
    ssp. **rubra** (Aiton) Hulten 1971 (*A. rubra*)   PGP-**RD**

ACTINELLA Nuttall 1818 [*Asteraceae (Compositae)*]
  acaulis Nuttall 1818
  scaposa Nuttall 1841

ACTINOMERIS Nuttall 1818 nom. cons. [*Asteraceae (Compositae)*]
  alternifola (Linnaeus) de Candolle 1836 (*Ridan alternifolius, Verbesina alternifolia*)

ADENOPHORA Fischer 1823 [*Campanulaceae*]
  bulleyana Diels 1912   PGP
  communis Fischer 1823 = **A. lilifolia**
  confusa Nannfeldt 1936 (*A. farreri* hort.)
  denticulata Fischer 1823 (*A. tricuspidata*)
  farreri hort. = **A. confusa**
  lamarckii Fischer 1823
  latifolia hort. non Fischer 1823 = **A. pereskieaefolia**
  lilifolia (Linnaeus) Ledebour ex A. de Candolle 1830 (*A. communis, A. suaveolens*)
  megalantha Diels 1912
  moiwana Nakai 1922 = **A. pereskiaefolia** var. **heterotricha**
  nikoensis Franchet & Savatier 1875
  ornata Diels 1912
  palustris Komarov
  pereskiaefolia G. Don 1830 (*A. latifolia* hort.)
    var. **heterotricha** (Nakai) Hara (*A. moiwana*)
  polymorpha Ledebour
  potaninii Korshinsky 1894
  remotiflora (Siebold & Zuccarini) Miquel 1866
  sinensis A. de Candolle 1830
  stricta Miquel 1866
  suaveolens Reichenbach = **A. lilifolia**
  takedai Makino 1906
  tashiroi (Makino & Nakai) Makino & Nakai 1911   PGP
  tricuspidata A. de Candolle 1830 = **A. denticulata**
  triphylla (Thunberg) A. de Candolle 1830
    var. **hakusanensis** (Nakai) Kitamura 1936

ADIANTUM Linnaeus 1753 [*Adiantaceae*]
N **capillus-veneris** Linnaeus 1753   EGF.1-**RD**
  hispidulum Swartz 1801   EGF.1
  x marisii Moore 1885 (*A. aethiopicum* ? x *A. capillus-veneris*)
  pedatum Linnaeus 1753   EGF.1-PGP-**RD**
    var. **aleuticum** Ruprecht   EGF.1-PGP-RD
    'Aleuticum' hort. = **A. pedatum** var. **subpumilum**
    Asiatic form

'**Imbricatum**'　　　　　　　　　　　　　　　　　　　　　PGP
'**Japonicum**'　　　　　　　　　　　　　　　　　　　　　　PGP-RD
'**Laciniatum**'
'Minus' ('Minor') = **A. pedatum** var. **subpumilum**
'**Miss Sharples**'
　　var. **subpumilum** W. H. Wagner ('Aleuticum' hort., 'Minus', 'Minor')
venustum D. Don. 1825　　　　　　　　　　　　　　　EGF.1-PGP-**RD**
　　'Don's Form' = **A. venustum**

ADLUMIA Rafinesque 1808　　　　　　　　　　　[*Fumariaceae*]
BC　　**fungosa** (Aiton) Greene 1888　　　　　　　　　　　PGP

ADONIS Linnaeus 1753　　　　　　　　　　　　[*Ranunculaceae*]
　　amurensis Regel 1861　　　　　　　　　　　　PGP-**DGP**-RD
　　　'**Fukujukai**'
　　　'**Plena**'　　　　　　　　　　　　　　　　　　　　RD
　　pyrenaica de Candolle 1815　　　　　　　　　　　PGP
N　　**vernalis** Linnaeus 1753　　　　　　　　　　　　PGP-**RD**
　　volgensis Steven 1817　　　　　　　　　　　　　PGP

AEGOPODIUM Linnaeus 1753　　　　　[*Apiaceae (Umbelliferae)*]
N‡　　**podagraria** Linnaeus 1753
　　　'**Variegatum**'

AETHIONEMA R. Brown 1812　　　　　　[*Brassicaceae (Cruciferae)*]
　　armenum Boissier 1842　　　　　　　　　　　　CA
　　　'**Mavis Holmes**'
L　　'**Warley Rose**'　　　[E. Willmott c1910]　　　CA-**DGP**-RD
　　　'**Warley Ruber**'　　　　　　　　　　　　　　　CA
　　cardiophyllum Boissier & Heldreich 1849 = **A. cordatum**
　　cordatum (Desfontaines) Boissier 1867 (*A. cardiophyllum*)
　　coridifolium de Candolle 1821 (*A. jucundum* hort.)
　　creticum Boissier & Heldreich 1845 = **A. saxatile** ssp. **creticum**
　　diastrophis Bunge 1841
　　gracile de Candolle 1821 = **A. saxatile**
　　graecum Boissier & Spruner 1846 = **A. saxatile** ssp. **graecum**
　　grandiflorum Boissier & Hohenacker 1849 (*A. kotschyi* hort., *A. pulchellum*) CA-**RD**
　　iberideum (Boissier) Boissier 1867 (*A. theodorum*)　　RD
　　jucundum hort. = **A. coridifolium**
　　kotschyi hort. = **A. grandiflorum**
S　　**oppositifolium** (Persoon) Hedge 1965 (*Eunomia oppositifolia*)　　CA
　　ovalifolium (de Candolle) Boissier 1856 = **A. saxatile** ssp. **creticum**
　　pulchellum Boissier & Huet 1856 = **A. grandiflorum**
　　rotundifolium (C. A.Meyer) Boissier 1867
　　saxatile (Linnaeus) R. Brown 1812
　　　ssp. **creticum** (Boissier & Heldreich) Andersson et al. 1983 (*A. creticum, A.*
　　　　　　　　　　　　　　　　　　　　　　　　　　　ovalifolium)
　　　ssp. **graecum** (Boissier & Spruner) Hayek 1925 (*A. graecum*)
　　schistosum (Boissier & Kotschy) Kotschy 1856　　　CA
　　　'**Dixcroft Variety**'
　　stylosum de Candolle 1821
　　theodorum hort. = **A. iberideum**
　　trinervium (de Candolle) Boissier 1867

AGAPANTHUS L'Heritier 1788　　　　　　　[*Alliaceae (Liliaceae)*]
　　africanus (Linnaeus) Hoffmannsegg 1824 (*A. umbellatus*)　　EGF.1-DGP
　　　'**Albus**'
　　campanulatus F. M. Leighton 1934　　　　　EGF.1-PGP-RD
　　　'**Albus**'
　　　ssp. **patens** (F. M. Leighton) F. M. Leighton 1965 (*A. patens*)　　EGF.1-PGP

L   **Headbourne Hybrids**   [L. Palmer] (A. Palmer Hybrids)   EGF.1-PGP-**DGP**
　　inapertus Beauverd 1910 (*A. weillighii* hort.)   EGF.1-PGP
　　　ssp. **pendulus** (L. Bolus) F. M. Leighton 1965   EGF.1-PGP
　　Palmer Hybrids = **A. Headbourne Hybrids**
　　orientalis F. M. Leighton 1939 = **A. praecox** ssp. **orientalis**
　　praecox Willdenow 1809   EGF.1-PGP
　　　ssp. **orientalis** (F. M. Leighton) F. M. Leighton 1965 (*A. orientalis, A.*
　　　　　　　　　　　　　　　　　　　umbellatus hort.)   EGF.1-PGP
　　　ssp. **orientalis** 'Albus'
　　patens F. M. Leighton 1936 = **A. campanulatus** ssp. **patens**
　　pendulus L. Bolus 1923 = **A. inapertus** ssp. **pendulus**
　　umbellatus L'Heritier 1788 = **A. africanus**
　　umbellatus hort. non L'Heritier 1788 = **A. praecox** ssp. **orientalis**
　　weillighii hort. = **A. inapertus**

NAMED CULTIVARS

　　　'Albidus'
　　　'Ardernei'   PGP
　　　'Baby Blue'
　　　'Ben Hope'
　　　'Blue Giant'   PGP
　　　'Blue Moon'   PGP
　　　'Blue Ribbon'
　　　'Blue Star'
　　　'Blue Triumphator'
　　　'Bressingham Blue'   [A. Bloom]
　　　'Bressingham White'   [A. Bloom]
　　　'Donau'
　　　'Hydon Mist'
　　　'Golden Rule'
　　　'Intermedia'
　　　'Isis'   [A. Bloom]   PGP-**RD**
　　　'Kobald'
　　　'Lady Moore'
　　　'Loch Hope'   PGP
　　　'Norman Hadden'
　　　'Maximus Albus'   PGP
　　　'Peter Pan'
　　　'Profusion'
　　　'Sapphire'
　　　'Zella Thomas'

AGASTACHE Clayton ex Gronov 1762   [*Lamiaceae (Labiatae)*]
　　anethiodora (Nuttall) Britton 1898 = **A. foeniculum**
　　anisata (Bentham) hort. = **A. foeniculum**
H   **foeniculum** (Pursh) Kuntze 1898 (*A. anethiodora, A. anisata* hort.)   PGP
　　mexicana (Kunth) Epling 1945   PGP
　　　'Rosea'

AGAVE Linnaeus 1753   [*Agavaceae*]
　　americana Linnaeus 1753   EGF.1-PGP-RD
　　　'Marginata'   **RD**
　　parryi Englemann 1878   EGF.1
　　utahensis Englemann 1878   EGF.1

AGOSERIS Rafinesque 1833   [*Asteraceae (Compositae)*]
　　cuspidata (Pursh) D. Dietrich 1847 (*Troximon cuspidatum*)
　　glauca (Pursh) Rafinesque 1833 (*Troximon glaucum*)

AGRIMONIA Linnaeus 1753 [Rosaceae]
HN‡   **eupatoria** Linnaeus 1753

AGROPYRON Gaertner 1770 [Poaceae (Gramineae)]
  cristatum (Linnaeus) Gaertner 1770
    var. **imbricatum** (Marshall von Bieberstein) G. Beck 1890
    var. **puberulum** Boissier 1853 (A. puberulum)
  magellanicum (Desvaux) Hackel 1900 = **Elymus magellanicus**
  puberulum (Boissier) Prokudin 1938 = **A. cristatum** var. **puberulum**

AGROSTEMMA Linnaeus 1753 [Caryophyllaceae]
  coronaria Linnaeus 1753 = **Lychnis coronaria**
AN‡   **githago** Linnaeus 1753
  tomentosum hort. = **Lychnis coronaria**   DGP

AJUGA Linnaeus 1753 [Lamiaceae (Labiatae)]
  alpina Linnaeus 1767 = **A. genevensis**
  'Brockbankii' (A. genevensis x A. pyramidalis)
N‡   **chamaepitys** (Linnaeus) Schreber 1773
    ssp. **chia** (Schreber) Arcangeli 1882
  chia Schreber 1773 = **A. chamaepitys** ssp. **chia**
N‡   **genevensis** Linnaeus 1753 (A. alpina)
    'Brockbankii' = **A. 'Brockbankii'**
    'Robusta'
    'Tottenham'
  orientalis Linnaeus 1753
  ovalifolia Bureau & Franchet 1891
  piskoi Degen & Baldacci 1896
N‡   **pyramidalis** Linnaeus 1753   **DGP-RD**
    'Metallica Crispa'
HN‡L   **reptans** Linnaeus 1753   DGP-RD
    'Alba'
    'Argentea' = **A. reptans 'Variegata'**
L   **'Atropurpurea'** ('Purpurea')   DGP-RD
    'Braunherz'
L   **'Burgundy Glow'**
    'Catlin's Giant'
    'Cristata'
    'Delight'
    'Jungle Beauty'
    'Multicolor' ('Rainbow', 'Tricolor')   **DGP-RD**
    'Palisander'
    'Purple Torch'
    'Purpurea' = **A. reptans 'Atropurpurea'**
    'Rainbow' = **A. reptans 'Multicolor'**
    'Riesmove'
    'Rosea'
    'Pink Elf'
    'Rosakerze' ('Pink Candle')
    'Teppichrosa' ('Pink Carpet')
    'Tricolor' = **A. reptans 'Multicolor'**
L   **'Variegata'** ('Argentea')   DGP-RD
  tenorii C. Presl 1822

ALBUCA Linnaeus 1762 [Hyacinthaceae (Liliaceae)]
  angolense Welwitsch 1858
  canadensis (Linnaeus) F. M. Leighton 1948   EGF.1
  humilis Baker 1895   EGF.1-SB
  'Karoo Yellow'

nelsonii N. E. Brown 1880   EGF.1
shawii Baker 1874
'The Giant'

ALCEA Linnaeus 1753   [*Malvaceae*]
   ficifolia Linnaeus 1753   RD
N   **rosea** Linnaeus 1753 (*Althaea rosea*)   PGP-**DGP-RD**
      Chater's Double Hybrids   DGP-RD
      'Flore Pleno' ('Pleniflora')
      'Nigra'
      'Pleniflora' = **A. rosea 'Flore Pleno'**
      'Summer Carnival'   RD
      'Suttons' Single Brilliant'
      'Trophy'   RD

ALCHEMILLA Linnaeus 1753   [*Rosaceae*]
   abyssinica Fresius 1837
   alpestris hort, non F. W. Schmidt 1794 = **A. glabra**
N‡   **alpina** Linnaeus 1753
   alpina hort. non Linnaeus = **A. conjuncta**
   asterophylla Tausch ex Buser 1891 = **A. plicatula**
N‡   **conjuncta** Babington 1842 (*A. alpina* hort. p.p.)   RD
   compactilis Juzepczuk 1934
   ellenbeckii Engler 1906
   epipsila Juzepczuk 1934
   erythropoda Juzepczuk 1934
   faeroensis (Lange) Buser 1894
   fissa Günther & Schummel 1819
N‡   **glabra** Neygenfind 1821 (*A. alpestris* hort.)
   glomerulans Buser 1893
   hageniae T. C. E. Fries 1923
   *hookeri nom. dub.
   hoppeana (Reichenbach) Dalla Torre 1882
   lapeyrousii Buser 1893
HNL   **mollis** (Buser) Rothmaler 1934 (*A. vulgaris* hort. p.p. non Linnaeus 1753)
                PGP-**DGP-RD**

      'Grandiflora' nom. dub.
      'Robusta' nom. dub.
      'Variegata'
   pentaphyllea Linnaeus 1753
   plicatula Gandoger 1883 (*A. asterophylla*)
   pyrenaica Dufour 1821
   sericata Reichenbach ex Buser 1846
   splendens Christ ex Favrat 1889
   vulgaris hort., non Linnaeus 1753 = **A. mollis, A. xanthochlora**
HN   **xanthochlora** Rothmaler 1937 (*A. vulgaris* hort. p.p., non Linnaeus 1753)

ALETRIS Linnaeus 1753   [*Melanthiaceae (Liliaceae)*]
   farinosa Linnaeus 1753   EGF.1

ALISMA Linnaeus 1753   [*Alismataceae*]
   parviflorum Pursh ex Rafinesque 1840   EGF.1
N‡L   **plantago-aquaticum** Linnaeus 1753   EGF.1
   natans Linnaeus 1753 = **Luronium natans**
   ranunculoides Linnaeus 1753 = **Baldellia ranunculoides**

ALKANNA Tausch 1824   [*Boraginaceae*]
   aucherana A. de Candolle 1846
   incana Boissier 1844
   orientalis (Linnaeus) Boissier 1844
   tinctoria (Linnaeus) Tausch 1824   PGP

ALLARDIA Decaisne 1847   *[Asteraceae (Compositae)]*
S   **tomentosa** Decaisne 1847 (*Waldheimia tomentosa*)

ALLIUM Linnaeus 1753   *[Alliaceae (Liliaceae)]*
    acuminatum Hooker 1839 (*A. murrayanum*)   EGF.1-SB
    aflatunense B. Fedtschenko 1904   EGF.1-PGP-**DGP-RD**
    aflatunense hort., non B. Fedtschenko = **A. stipitatum**
       'Purple Sensation' = **A. 'Purple Sensation'**
    akaka S. Gmelin ex Roemer & Schultes f. 1830   EGF.1-**BB-SB**
    albopilosum C. H. Wright 1903 = **A. christophii**
    amabile Stapf 1931 = **A. mairei** var. **amabile**
    amplectens Torrey 1857
    atropurpureum Waldstein & Kitaibel 1802   EGF.1-**BB**
    atroviolaceum Boissier 1846
    auctum Omelczuk 1962
    azureum Ledebour 1830 non Bunge 1852 = **A. caeruleum**
    beesianum W. W. Smith 1914   EGF.1-PGP-SB-**DGP**-RD
       'Album'
    bidwelliae S. Watson 1879 = **A. campanulatum**
    borszczowii Regel 1875
    bulgaricum (Janka) Prodan 1923 = **Nectaroscordum siculum** ssp. **bulgaricum**
    caeruleum Pallas 1773 (*A. azureum*)   EGF.1-PGP-**BB**-RD
    caesium Schrenk 1844   EGF.1
    callimischon Link 1835   EGF.1-SB
       ssp. **callimischon**   EGF.1-**BB**
       ssp. **haemostictum** Stearn 1978   EGF.1-**BB**-SB
    campanulatum S. Watson 1879 (*A. bidwelliae*)   EGF.1
    canescens hort. = **A. senescens**
N   **carinatum** Linnaeus 1753   EGF.1-SB
       ssp. **pulchellum** (G. Don) Bonnier & Layens 1894 (*A. cirrhosum, A.*
                 pulchellum)   EGF.1-PGP-SB-**DGP**
       ssp. **pulchellum** 'Album'   PGP
HN **cepa** Linnaeus 1753   EGF.1-RD
H   'Perutile' Stearn 1942   EGF.1
H   'Proliferum'
    cernuum Roth 1789   EGF.1-PGP-**BB**-SB-**DGP**
       var. **neomexicanum** (Rydberg) Macbride 1918
    christophii Trautvetter 1884 (*A. albopilosum*)   EGF.1-PGP-**BB**-SB-**DGP-RD**
    cirrhosum Vandelli 1771 non Raeuschel 1797 = **A. carinatum** ssp. **pulchellum**
    condensatum Turczaninow 1855
    cowanii Lindley 1823 = **A. neapolitanum** 'Cowanii'
    cyaneum Regel 1875   EGF.1-CA-**BB**-SB-RD
       var. *brachystemon* Regel 1882 = **A. sikkimense**
    cyathophorum Bureau & Franchet 1891   EGF.1
       var. **farreri** (Stearn) Stearn   EGF.1-PGP-**BB**-SB
    dichlamydeum Greene 1888   EGF.1
    dioscoridis hort. non Smith 1806 = **Nectaroscordum siculum** ssp. **bulgaricum**
    drummondii Regel 1875 (*A. nuttallii*)   EGF.1
    elatum Regel 1884 = **A. macleanii**
    farreri Stearn 1930 = **A. cyathophorum** var. **farreri**
HN **fistulosum** Linnaeus 1753   EGF.1-RD
    flavum Linnaeus 1753   EGF.1-**BB**-SB-**DGP**
       'Blue Leaf'
       var. **minus** Boissier 1882   **BB**
    geyeri S. Watson 1879   EGF.1
    giganteum Regel 1883   EGF.1-PGP-**BB**-SB-DGP-**RD**
    glaucum Schrader 1814 = **A. senescens** ssp. **glaucum**
    globosum Marshall von Bieberstein ex Redoute 1807
    globosum Boissier 1884 = **A. saxatile**

govanianum Wallich ex Baker 1874 = **A. humile**
griffithianum Boissier 1859
gulczense B. Fedtschenko 1906
humile Kunth 1843 (*A. govanianum*)
huteri hort. = **A. senescens** ssp. **huteri**
hymenorhizum Ledebour 1830   EGF.1
insubricum Boissier & Reuter 1854   EGF.1-**BB**
jajlae Vvedensky 1934 = **A. scorodoprasum** ssp. **jajlae**
kansuense Regel 1889 = **A. sikkimense**
karataviense Regel 1875   EGF.1-**BB**-SB-**DGP**
macleanii Baker 1883 (*A. elatum*)   EGF.1-PGP-**BB**
macranthum Baker 1874   EGF.1-PGP
macrostemon Bunge 1833
mairei Leveille 1909 (*A. yunnanense*)   EGF.1-SB
     var. **amabile** (Stapf) !   CA-**BB**-SB
moly Linnaeus 1753   EGF.1-**BB**-SB-**DGP**-RD
     'Jeannine'
montanum F. W. Schmidt 1794, non Schrank = **A. senescens** ssp. **glaucum**
multibulbosum Jacquin 1773 = **A. nigrum**
murrayanum Regel 1873 = **A. acuminatum**
narcissiflorum Villars 1779 (*A. pedemontanum*)   EGF.1-CA-**BB**-SB-**DGP**-RD
neapolitanum Cyrillo 1788   EGF.1-PGP-**BB**-RD
     'Cowanii' (*A. cowanii*)
nigrum Linnaeus 1762 (*A. multibulbosum*)   EGF.1-**BB**
nutans Linnaeus 1753   EGF.1-**BB**
nuttallii S. Watson 1879 = **A. drummondii**
obliquum Linnaeus 1753   EGF.1-**BB**
odorum hort. non Linnaeus 1767 = **A.**ramosum p.p., **A** tuberosum p.p.
olympicum Boissier 1853
oreophilum C. A. Meyer 1831 (*A. ostrowskianum*)   EGF.1-**BB**-SB-**DGP**-RD
     'Zwanenburg'   [van Tubergen 1954]   SB-DGP
orientale Boissier 1853
oschaninii B. Fedtschenko 1906
ostrowskianum Regel 1881 = **A. oreophilum**
paniculatum Linnaeus 1759   EGF.1-**BB**
N   **paradoxum** (Marshall von Bieberstein) G. Don 1827   EGF.1-**BB**
     var. **normale** Stearn 1987   EGF.1
pedemontanum Willdenow 1799 = **A. narcissiflorum**
peninsulare Lemmon ex Greene 1888   EGF.1
pskemense B. Fedtschenko 1905
pulchellum G. Don 1827 nom. illegit = **A. carinatum** ssp. **pulchellum**
     'Purple Sensation'   [J. Bijl 1963]
pyrenaicum Costa & Vayreda 1877   RD
ramosum Linnaeus 1753, non Jacquin 1781 (*A. odorum* hort. p.p.)   EGF.1-**BB**
ramosum Jacquin 1781 non Linnaeus 1753 = **A. obliquum**
rosenbachianum Regel 1884   EGF.1-PGP-SB-DGP-RD
     'Album'
N   **roseum** Linnaeus 1753   EGF.1-**BB**
HN   **sativum** Linnaeus 1753   EGF.1
saxatile Marshall von Bieberstein 1798
HN‡   **schoenoprasum** Linnaeus 1753   EGF.1-PGP-**BB**-**DGP**-RD
     'Forescate'
H   ssp. **sibiricum** (Linnaeus) Celak
schubertii Zuccarini 1843   EGF.1-PGP-**BB**-RD
H‡   **scorodoprasum** Linnaeus 1753   EGF.1
     ssp. **jajlae** (Vvedensky) Stearn 1978   **BB**
senescens Linnaeus 1753 (*A. canescans* hort.)   EGF.1-PGP-SB
     var. **glaucum** (Schrader) !
     *var. **huteri**
     ssp. **montanum** (Fries) Holub 1970 (*A. montanum*)   EGF.1-SB

'Roseum'
siculum Ucria 1793 = **Nectaroscordum siculum** ssp. **siculum**
sikkimense Baker 1874 (*A. cyaneum* var. *brachystemon, A. kansuense, A.*
　　　　　　　　　　　　　　　tibeticum)　　　　　　　　　　　　　EGF.1-CA-SB
N　**sphaerocephalon** Linnaeus 1753　　　　　　　　　　　EGF.1-PGP-**BB**
splendens Willdenow ex Roemer & Schultes f. 1830 = **A. stellerianum**
stamineum Boissier 1859　　　　　　　　　　　　　　　　**BB**
stellatum Ker-Gawler 1813　　　　　　　　　　　　　　　EGF.1
stellerianum Willdenow 1799 (*A. splendens*)
　　*var. **kurilense**
stipitatum Regel 1881 (*A. aflatunense* hort., non B. Fedtschenko)　　EGF.1-PGP
　　'Album'
stracheyi Baker 1874
subhirsutum Linnaeus 1753　　　　　　　　　　　　　　EGF.1-**BB**
thunbergii G. Don 1827
　　'Nanum'
tibeticum Rendle 1906 = **A. sikkimense**
N‡　**triquetrum** Linnaeus 1753　　　　　　　EGF.1-**BB**-SB-**DGP**-RD
H　**tuberosum** Rottler ex Sprengel 1825 (*A. odorum* hort.,p.p.)　EGF.1-PGP-**BB**
unifolium Kellogg 1863　　　　　　　　　　　　　　EGF.1-PGP-**BB**-SB
HN‡L　**ursinum** Linnaeus 1753　　　　　　　　　　　　　　EGF.1-**BB**
victorialis Linnaeus 1753　　　　　　　　　　　　　　EGF.1-PGP
virgunculae Maekawa & Kitamura 1952　　　　　　　　EGF.1-SB
walliachianum hort. = **A. wallichii**
wallichii Kunth 1843　　　　　　　　　　　　　　　　EGF.1-PGP
yunnanense Diels 1912 = **A. mairei**
zebdanense Boissier & Nöe 1859　　　　　　　　　　　EGF.1-**BB**

ALOE Linnaeus 1753　　　　　　　　　　　　[*Aloeaceae (Liliaceae)*]
aristata Haworth 1825　　　　　　　　　　　　　　EGF.1-PGP-RD
variegata Linnaeus 1753　　　　　　　　　　　　　　　　RD

ALONSOA Ruiz & Pavon 1798　　　　　　　　　[*Scrophulariaceae*]
warscewiczii Regel 1854　　　　　　　　　　　　　　　　RD

ALOPECURUS Linnaeus 1753　　　　　　　　　[*Poaceae (Gramineae)*]
gerardii (Allioni) Villars 1785
lanatus Smith 1806
N‡　**pratensis** Linnaeus 1753　　　　　　　　　　　　　　EGF.2
　　'Aureus' ('Aureo-variegatus')　　　　　　　　　　　　　PGP

ALSTROEMERIA Linnaeus 1762　　　　　[*Alstroemeriaceae (Liliaceae)*]
angustifolia Herbert 1837 = **A. ligtu** var. **angustifolia**
aurantiaca D. Don 1843 = **A. aurea**
aurea Graham 1833 (*A. aurantiaca*)　　　　　　　　　EGF.1-**RD**
　　'Dover Orange'　®　[Clark pre-1935]　　　　　　　PGP-RD
　　'Dover Yellow' nom. dub.
　　'Lutea'　®　　　　　　　　　　　　　　　　　　PGP-RD
　　'Moerheim Gem' nom. dub.
　　'Moerheim Orange'　®　[Moerheim 1946]　　　　　PGP-RD
　　'Orange King'　®　[Jac. Ruiter pre-1930]
brasiliensis Sprengel 1825　　　　　　　　　　　　　　EGF.1
chiloensis Philippi 1857
haemantha Ruiz & Pavon 1802　　　　　　　　　　　　EGF.1-PGP
hookeri Loddiges 1827　　　　　　　　　　　　　　　EGF.1-PGP
kingii Philippi 1873 = **A. versicolor**
L　**ligtu** Linnaeus 1762　　　　　　　　　　　　　　EGF.1-PGP-RD
　　var. **angustifolia** (Herbert) Anon (*A. angustifolia*)　　EGF.1-PGP

Ligtu Hybrids (*A. haemantha* x *A. ligtu* var. *angustifolia*)   EGF.1-RD
pelegrina Linnaeus 1762   EGF.1-PGP
    'Alba'   ®   [pre-1894]   EGF.1-PGP
    'Rosea'   ®
pulchella Linnaeus f. 1781 = **A. psittacina**
psittacina Lehmann (*A. pulchella*)   PGP
pygmaea Herbert 1837   EGF.1
versicolor Ruiz & Pavon 1802 (*A. kingii*)
violacea Philippi 1860   EGF.1-PGP

NAMED CULTIVARS

    'Afterglow'   ®   [Parigo via Wültinghoff 1969]   PGP
    'Ballerina'   ®   [Parigo via Wültinghoff 1959]   PGP
    Butterfly Hybrids
    'Charm'   ®   [Parigo via Wültinghoff 1960]   PGP
    'Jubilee'   ®   [M. C. van Staaveren 1970]
    'Orchid' = **A. 'Walter Fleming'**
    'Parigo's Charm' = **A. 'Charm'**
    'Purple Joy'   [Cor van Duyn]
    'Regina'   ®   [M. C. van Staaveren 1973]
    'Rosy Wings'   [Cor van Duyn]   PGP
    'Sonata'   ®   [Parigo via Wültinghoff 1961]
    'Sovereign'   [Cor van Duyn]
    'Sunny Way'   [Cor van Duyn]
    'Sweetheart'   [Cor van Duyn]
    'Walter Fleming'   ®   [W.A.Constable] ('Orchid')   EGF.1-PGP

ALTHAEA Linnaeus 1753   [*Malvaceae*]
    cannabina Linnaeus 1753   PGP
    ficifolia (Linnaeus) Cavanilles 1786 = **Alcea ficifolia**
HN‡ **officinalis** Linnaeus 1753
    rosea (Linnaeus) Cavanilles 1786 = **Alcea rosea**
    rugosa hort. = **A. rugoso-stellulata**
    rugoso-stellulata Czeczott 1932

ALYSSOIDES Adanson 1763   [*Brassicaceae (Cruciferae)*]
    graecum (Reuter) Javorka 1923 = **A. utriculatum** var. **graecum**
    utriculatum (Linnaeus) Medicus 1789 (*Vesicaria utriculata*)   PGP
        var. **graecum** (Reuter) Javorka (*A. graecum*)

ALYSSUM Linnaeus 1753   [*Brassicaceae (Cruciferae)*]
    argenteum hort. non Vitman 1790 = **A. murale**
    cuneifolium Tenore 1811
    idaeum Boissier & Heldreich 1849   CA
    markgrafii O. E. Schulz 1926
    mildeanum Podpera 1902 = **A. stribrnyi**
    moellendorfianum Ascherson ex G. Beck 1887
    montanum Linnaeus 1753   CA-RD
        'Berggold' ('Mountain Gold')
        'Mountain Gold' = **A. montanum 'Berggold'**
    murale Waldstein & Kitaibel 1798 (*A. argenteum* hort.)
N   **saxatile** Linnaeus 1753 (*A. petraeum, Aurinia saxatalis*)   DGP-**RD**
L   **'Citrinum'**   **DGP-RD**
        'Compactum'   RD
        'Dudley Nevill'   [D. Nevill c1930]   DGP-RD
        'Dudley Nevill Variegated'
        'Flore Pleno'   DGP-RD
        'Gold Ball' = **A. saxatile 'Goldkugel'**

       'Gold Dust'
       'Goldkugel' ('Gold Ball')
       'Griechenland'
       'Nanum'
       'Roseum'
       'Silver Queen'
       'Variegatum'

S   **serpyllifolium** Desfontaines 1798   CA-RD
     spinosum Linnaeus 1753 = **Ptilotrichum spinosum**
     stribrnyi Velenovsky 1891 (*A. mildeanum*)
S   **tortuosum** Willdenow 1800   CA
S   **troodi** Boissier ex Boissier 1888
     wulfenianum Bernhardi 1813

X AMARCRINUM Coutts 1925   [*Amaryllidaceae*]
    memoria-corsii (Ragioneri) H. E. Moore 1975 (*Amaryllis belladonna* x *Crinum moorei*)

X AMARINE Sealy 1968   [*Amaryllidaceae*]
    tubergenii Sealy 1968 (*Amaryllis belladonna* x *Nerine*)   PGP
        '**Zwanenburg**'   PGP

X AMARYGIA Ciferri & Giacomini 1950   [*Amaryllidaceae*]
    parkeri (W. Watson) H. E. Moore 1975 (*Amaryllis belladonna* x *Brunsvigia josephinae*)
        'Alba'

AMARYLLIS Linnaeus 1753   [*Amaryllidaceae*]
    belladonna Linnaeus 1753   EGF.1-PGP-**BB-DGP-RD**
        '**Barberton**'   [van Tubergen]   PGP
        '**Beacon**'   PGP
        '**Cape Town**'   [van Tubergen]   PGP
        '**Hathor**'   [H. B. Bradley 1911]   PGP-RD
        '**Jagersfontein**'   [van Tubergen]   PGP
        '**Johannesburg**'   [van Tubergen]   PGP
        '**Kimberley**'
        '**Major**'
        'Parkeri' = **X Amarygia parkeri**
        '**Purpurea**'   PGP
        'Purpurea Major' = **A. 'Major'**
        '**Rosea**'   PGP
        '**Spectabilis**'   PGP

AMORPHOPHALLUS Blume ex Decaisne 1835   [*Araceae*]
    rivieri Durieu ex Riviere 1869

AMPHICOME Royle 1835   [*Bignoniaceae*]
    arguta Royle 1835 (*Incarvillea arguta*)
    emodi Royle ex Lindley 1838 (*Incarvillea emodi*)

AMSONIA Walter 1788   [*Apocynaceae*]
    angustifolia (Aiton) Michaux 1803 = **A. ciliata**
    ciliata Walter 1788 (*A. angustifolia*)
    illustris Woodson 1929
    orientalis Decaisne 1803 = **Rhazya orientalis**
    tabernaemontana Walter 1788   PGP
        var. **salicifolia** (Pursh) Woodson 1928   **DGP**

ANACAMPTIS L C M Richard 1818   [*Orchidaceae*]
N‡   **pyramidalis** (Linnaeus) L. C. M. Richard 1818 (*Orchis pyramidalis*)   EGF.2-CA

ANACYCLUS Linnaeus 1753   [*Asteraceae (Compositae)*]
  depressus Ball 1873 = **A. pyrethrum** var. **depressus**
  pyrethrum (Linnaeus) Link 1822
      var. **depressus** (Ball) Maire 1934 (*A. depressus*)   CA-**DGP-RD**

ANAGALLIS Linnaeus 1753   [*Primulaceae*]
AN‡   **arvensis** Linnaeus 1753   **RD**
      var. **caerulea** (Linnaeus) Govan 1765   RD
      var. **latifolia** (Linnaeus) Lange
  collina Schousboe 1800 = **A. monellii**
  linifolia Linnaeus 1762 = **A. monellii**
  monellii Linnaeus 1753 (*A. collina, A. linifolia*)   **DGP-RD**
      'Sunrise'
N‡   **tenella** (Linnaeus) Linnaeus 1774   RD
      'Studland'   **RD**

ANAPHALIS de Candolle 1838   [*Asteraceae (Compositae)*]
  cinnamomea de Candolle 1838 = **A. margaritacea**
  *gromulata
N   **margaritacea** (Linnaeus) Bentham & Hooker f. 1873 (*A. cinnamomea, H. yedoensis*)
                                                      PGP-DGP-RD
      'New Snow'
      var. **yedoensis** (Franchet & Savier) Ohwi   **DGP-RD**
  nubigena (Wallich) de Candolle 1837   PGP-**DGP**-RD
L   **triplinervis** (Sims) Sims ex C. B. Clarke 1876   PGP-**DGP**-RD
      'Silberregen'   [H. Klose 1974]
      'Sommerschnee' ('Summer Snow')   [H. Klose 1973]
      'Summer Snow' = **H. triplinervis 'Sommerschnee'**
  yedoensis (Franchet & Savatier) Maximowicz 1881 = **H. margaritacea** var. **yedoensis**

ANASTATICA Linnaeus 1753   [*Brassicaceae (Cruciferae)*]
A   **hierochuntica** Linnaeus 1753

ANCHUSA Linnaeus 1753   [*Boraginaceae*]
  angustissima C. Koch 1849 = **A. leptophylla** ssp. **incana**
  angustifolia Linnaeus 1753 = **A. officinalis**
  azurea Miller 1768 (*A. italica*)   PGP-DGP-RD
      'Dropmore'   PGP-**RD**
      'Feltham Pride'
      'Little John'   PGP
L   'Loddon Royalist'   PGP-**DGP**-RD
      'Morning Glory'   DGP-RD
      'Opal'   PGP-RD
      'Pride of Dover'
  caespitosa Lamarck 1785   CA
  caespitosa hort. non Lamarck = **A. leptophylla** ssp. **incana**
  italica Retzius 1779 = **A. azurea**
  leptophylla Roemer & Schultz 1819
      ssp. **incana** (Ledebour) Chamberlain 1977 (*A. angustissima, A. caespitosa* hort.)
                                                           RD
  mysotidiflora Lehmann 1818 = **Brunnera macrophylla**
H   **officinalis** Linnaeus 1753 (*A. angustifolia*)
  sempervirens Linnaeus 1753 = **Pentaglottis sempervirens**

ANDROPOGON Linnaeus 1753   [*Poaceae (Gramineae)*]
  gerardii Vitman 1792   EGF.2
  scoparius Michaux 1803

ANDROSACE Linnaeus 1753   [*Primulaceae*]

M - SMITH, G.F., & LOWE, D.B.,:   *'Androsaces'* Alpine Garden Society Guide 1977

albana Steven 1812   M-CA
alpina (Linnaeus) Lamarck 1778 (*A. tirolensis*)   M-**CA**-RD
x aretioides Kerner 1875 non Heer ex Duby 1844 (*A. alpina* x *A. obtusifolia*) M-CA
brevis (Hegetsch) Cesati 1844   M
carnea Linnaeus 1753   M-CA-RD
  'Alba'
  ssp. **brigantiaca** (Jordan & Fourreau) I. K. Ferguson 1971   M-CA
  ssp. **carnea**   M
  var. *halleri* Linnaeus = **A. carnea** ssp. **rosea**
  ssp. **laggeri** (Huet) Nyman 1881 (*A. laggeri*)   M-CA
  ssp. *reverchonii* Jordan = **A. carnea** ssp. **carnea**
  ssp. **rosea** (Jordan & Fourreau) Rouy 1908 (*A. carnea* var. *halleri*) M-CA
  'Val d'Eyne'
A **chaixii** Grenier & Godron 1853   M-CA
chamaejasme (Wulfen) Host 1787   M-CA-**RD**
  ssp. **lehmanniana** (Sprengel) Hulten 1968   M
ciliata de Candolle 1805   M-**CA**
cylindrica de Candolle 1805   M-CA
cylindrica de Candolle x **A. hirtella** Dufour   CA
delavayi Franchet 1895   M
A **filiformis** Retzius 1781   M
foliosa Duby 1844   M
globifera Duby 1844   M
halleri Jordan & Fourreau non Linnaeus 1753 = **A. carnea** ssp. **rosea**
hausmannii Leybold 1852   M-CA
hedraeantha Grisebach 1944   M
  'Alba'
x heeri Hegetschweiler ex Hausmann 1854 (*A. alpina* x *A. helvetica*) M-CA
  'Alba'
helvetica (Linnaeus) Allioni 1785 (*A. imbricata*)   M-**CA**-**DGP**-RD
hirtella Dufour 1856   M-**CA**
hookeriana Klatt 1863   M
x hybrida Kerner 1854 (*A. helvetica* x *A. pubescens*)   M
imbricata Lamarck 1805 = **A. helvetica**
jacquemontii (Duby) hort. = **A. villosa** var. **jacquemontii**
lactea Linnaeus 1753   M-CA
laevigata (A. Gray) Wendelbo 1961 = **Douglasia laevigata**
lanuginosa Wallich 1824   M-**DGP**-**RD**
  'Leichtlinii'   RD
lehmannii Wallich ex Duby 1844   M
  'Alba'
  'Rosea'
limprichtii Pax & Hoffmann 1921 = **A. sarmentosa** var. **watkinsii**
mathildae Levier 1877   M-CA
microphylla hort. = **A. mucronifolia**
mollis Handel-Mazzetti 1931 = **A. sarmentosa** var. **yunnanense**
montana (A. Gray) Wendelbo 1961 = **Douglasia montana**
mucronifolia Watt 1884 (*A. microphylla* hort.)   M
mucronifolia hort., non Watt = **A. sempervivoides**
muscoidea Duby 1844   M-CA
  f. **longiscapa** (Knuth) Handel-Mazzetti 1931   M
nivalis (Lindley) Wendelbo 1961 = **Douglasia nivalis**
obtusifolia Allioni 1785   M
primuloides Duby 1844   M
primuloides hort., non Duby = **A. sarmentosa**
pubescens de Candolle 1808   M-CA
pyrenaica Lamarck 1792   M-CA-**DGP**-RD
reverchonii (Jordan) hort. = **A. carnea** ssp. **carnea**
rotundifolia Hardwicke 1799   M
  'Elegans'

L	**sarmentosa** Wallich 1824	M-**DGP**-RD
	'Brilliant'	
	'Chumbyi'	M-DGP-RD
	'Galmont's Variety' = **A. sarmentosa 'Salmon's Variety'**	
	'Mollis' = **A. sarmentosa** var. **yunnanense**	
	var. *primuloides* (Duby) hort. = **A. primuloides**	
	'Salmon's Variety' [C. E. Salmon]	M-**RD**
	'Sherriffii'	
	var. **watkinsii** Hooker f. 1882 (*A. limprichtii*)	**CA**-DGP
	var. **yunnanense** Knuth 1905 (*A. mollis*)	M-DGP-RD
	sempervivoides Jacquemont 1844	M-**RD**
	sherriffii hort. = **A. sarmentosa 'Sherriffii'**	
	strigillosa Franchet 1885	M
	taurica Ovczinnikov 1952 = **A. villosa**	
	tirolensis F. Wettstein 1919 = **A. alpina**	
	vandellii (Turra) Chiovenda 1919	M-**RD**
	villosa Linnaeus 1753	M-CA-DGP-**RD**
	var. **arachnoidea** (Schott, Nyman & Kotschy) Knuth 1905	M-CA-**DGP**
	var. **arachnoidea 'Superba'**	
	var. **jacquemontii** Duby 1844	M-**DGP**
	var. **jacquemontii 'Rosea'**	
	'Taurica' hort, non Ovczinnikov 1952	
	vitaliana (Linnaeus) Lapeyrouse 1813 = **Vitaliana primuliflora**	
	watkinsii (Hooker) hort. = **A. sarmentosa** var. **watkinsii**	
	wulfeniana Sieber ex Koch 1838	M-**CA**

	ANDRYALA Linnaeus 1753	[*Asteraceae (Compositae)*]
S	**agardhii** Haenseler ex de Candolle 1838	**CA**
	lanata Linnaeus 1788 = **Hieracium lanatum**	

	ANEMONE Linnaeus 1753	[*Ranunculaceae*]
	altaica Fischer & C. A. Meyer 1830	**BB**
	'Alba' = **A. altaica**	
N	**apennina** Linnaeus 1753	CA-**BB**-SB
	'Alba'	
	'Petrovac'	
	asiaticus hort. = **Ranunculus asiaticus**	
	baicalensis Turczaninow ex Ledebour 1841	
	baldensis Linnaeus 1767	CA
	biflora de Candolle 1824	**BB**-SB
N	**blanda** Schott & Kotschy 1854	CA-**BB**-SB-DGP-**RD**
	var. **alba** Leichtlin 1890	
	'Atrocoerulea' = **A. blanda 'Ingramii'**	
	'Blue Mist'	
	'Blue Pearl' ® [J. Bijl van Duyvenbode]	
	'Bridesmaid' ® [van Tubergen pre-1949]	
	'Charmer' ® [van Tubergen pre-1957]	SB
	'Ingramii' ® [E. A. Bowles pre-1938] ('Atrocoerulea')	CA-**BB**-SB-**DGP**
	'Pink Star' ® [J. Bijl van Duyvenbode pre-1958]	SB
	'Radar' ® [van Tubergen 1950]	**BB**-SB-DGP
	Rainbow Hybrids	
	'Rosea' ® [E. A. Bowles]	CA
	var. **scythinica** Jenkinson 1892	CA-SB-DGP
	'Violet Star' ®	SB
	'White Splendour' ® [van Tubergen 1950]	**BB**-SB
	bucharica (Regel) Finlayson ex Gagnepagne 1804	**BB**-SB
	canadensis Linnaeus 1768	PGP
	caroliniana Walter 1788	
	caucasica Willdenow ex Ruprecht 1869	SB
N	**coronaria** Linnaeus 1753	**BB**-SB-DGP

'Admiral'   ®   [van Tubergen pre-1927]   DGP-RD
'de Caen'   ®   PGP-**RD**
'Governer'   ®   [van Tubergen]   DGP-RD
'Hollandia' ®   [pre-1927]
'Lord Lieutenant'   ®   [van Tubergen pre-1927]   RD
'Mr. Fokker' ®   DGP
'St. Brigid' ®   [Lawrenson c1870]   PGP-**RD**
'Sylphide'   ®   DGP
'The Bride' ®   [via Krelage 1870]   DGP
crinita Juzepczuk 1937
cylindrica A. Gray 1836
davidii Franchet 1885
drummondii S. Watson 1880   CA
elongata D. Don 1825
eranthoides Regel 1884   **BB**-SB
flaccida F. Schmidt 1868
x fulgens Gay 1824 (*A. hortensis* x *A. pavonina*)   PGP-CA-SB-DGP-**RD**
    'Aldborohensis'
    'Annulata'
    'Annulata Grandiflora'   ®
    'Multipetala'   ®
    'St. Bavo'   ®   [van Tubergen pre-1920]   PGP-**DGP**
globosa (Torrey & A. Gray) Nuttall 1841 = **A. multifida** var. **globosa**
gortschakowii Karelin & Kirilow 1842   **BB**-SB
hortensis Linnaeus 1753   SB
hupehensis (Lemoine) Lemoine 1910   PGP-DGP-RD
    var. japonica (Thunberg) Bowles & Stearn 1947   PGP
    'Praecox'   [Arends 1935]
    'September Charm'   [Bristol Nurseries 1932]   PGP-RD
    'Splendens'   PGP
x hybrida Paxton 1849 non Keil (*A. japonica* hort. non (Thunberg) Bowles & Stearn)
                                                                PGP
    'Alba'
    'Bowles' Pink'
    'Bressingham Glow'   [A. Bloom]   PGP
    'Charmeuse'
    'Elegans' = **A. x hybrida** Paxton
    'Coupe d'Argent'
    'Frau Marie Manshardt'
    'Geante des Blanches' ('White Queen')   PGP-RD
    'Hadspen Abundance'
    'Honorine Jobert'   [1858]   PGP-DGP-RD
    'Königin Charlotte' ('Queen Charlotte')   [1898]   PGP-**RD**
    'Krimhilde'   [1909]   PGP-DGP
    'Lady Gilmour'
    'Lorelei'   PGP-RD
    'Luise Uhink'   PGP
    'Margarete'   PGP-DGP
    'Max Vogel'   RD
    'Montrose'   [1899]   PGP
    'Pamina'
    'Praecox' = **A. hupehensis** 'Praecox'
    'Prince Henry' = **A. x hybrida** 'Prinz Heinrich'
    'Prinz Heinrich' ('Prince Henry')   [1902]   PGP
    'Rosea'
    'Rosenschale'   [H. Hagemann 1978]
    'Rotkäppchen'
    'Splendens' = **A. hupehensis** 'Splendens'
    'Stuttgard'
    'Superba' = **A. tomentosa** 'Superba'

'Whirlwind' ('Wirbewind')   [1887]   PGP
'White Queen' = **A. x hybrida 'Geante des Blanches'**
'Wirbewind' = **A. x hybrida 'Whirlwind'**
x intermedia Winkler ex Pritzel 1841 non G. Don = **A. x lipsiensis**
japonica hort. non (Thunberg) Siebold & Zuccarini 1835 = **A. x hybrida
keiskeana** Ito ex Maximowicz 1888
x lesseri Wehrhahn 1932 (*A. multifida* x *A. sylvestris*)   PGP-**DGP**-**RD**
leveillei Ulbrich in Engler
x lipsiensis G. Beck 1890 (*A. nemorosa* x *A. ranunculoides*) (*A. x intermedia,
                              A. x seemenii*)   PGP-**BB**-SB
      'Pallida'
magellanica Hort. ex Wehrahn 1932   CA
multifida Poiret 1810 non Standley 1931
      var. **globosa** Torrey & A. Gray 1838 (*A. globosa*)
      'Major'
narcissiflora Linnaeus 1753   PGP-**DGP**-**RD**
nemorosa Linnaeus 1753   PGP-CA-**BB**-SB-DGP-RD
      'Alba'
      'Alba Plena'
      'Allenii' ®   [J. Allen 1907]   PGP-CA-**BB**-SB-**DGP**
      'Atrocaerulea'
      'Blue Beauty'   ®   [van Tubergen]
      'Blue Bonnet'   ®   [T. Smith]   PGP
      'Blue Queen'   [J. Allen]
      'Bowles' Purple'   SB
      'Bracteata'   PGP-**BB**
      'Bracteata Plena' nom. dub.
      'Caerulea' = **A. nemorosa 'Robinsoniana'**
      'Celestial'
      'Currie's Pink'
      'Flore Pleno'
      'Grandiflora'   BB
      'Green Fingers'
      'Hannah Gubbay'
      'Hilda'   [U. Toubol]   SB
      'Lady Doneraile'
      'Leeds' Variety'   PGP-SB
      'Lismore Blue'   PGP
      'Lismore Pink'   PGP
      'Lychette'
      'Monstrosa'
      'Monte Bondone'
      'Pallida' = **A. 'Pallida'**
      'Pentre Pink'   [P. Christian]
      'Purity'
      'Robinsoniana' ('Caerulea')   PGP-**BB**-SB-DGP-**RD**
      'Rosea'   PGP-SB
      'Royal Blue'   ®   [van Tubergen pre-1915]   SB-DGP
      'Tinney's Double'   [G. A. Mundey]
      'Vestal'   PGP-**BB**-RD
      'Virescens'
      'Wilks' Giant' ('Wilks' White')   PGP
nobilis (Garsault) hort. non Jordan = **Hepatica nobilis**
obtusiloba D. Don 1825
      'Alba'
palmata Linnaeus 1753
pavonina Lamarck 1783   PGP-**BB**-SB-**DGP**
      'Barr Salmon'
petiolulosa Juzepczuk 1937   **BB**-**SB**
polyanthes D. Don 1825
pseudoaltaica Hara 1939

pulsatilla Linnaeus 1753 = **Pulsatilla vulgaris**
quinquefolia Linnaeus 1753
raddeana Regel 1861
N   **ranunculoides** Linnaeus 1753   PGP-**BB**-SB
    'Flore Plena'   PGP
    'Semi-Plena'
    'Superba'   PGP
    ssp. **wockeana** (Ascherson & Graebner) Hegi 1912   **BB**
rivularis Buchanan-Hamilton ex de Candolle 1817   PGP-DGP
rupicola Cambessedes 1835   CA
x seemenii Camus 1898 nom. nud. = **A. x lipsiensis**
sylvestris Linnaeus 1753   PGP
    'Spring Beauty'
tomentosa (Maximowicz) P'ei 1933 (*A. vitifolia* hort., *A. vitifolia* 'Robustissima')
                                                                       PGP
transsylvanica (Fuss) Heuffel 1858 = **Hepatica transsylvanica**
trifolia Linnaeus 1753   SB
tschernjaewii Regel 1884   **BB**-SB
vitifolia Buchanan-Hamilton ex de Candolle 1817   PGP
    'Alba Dura'
    'Robustissima' = **A. tomentosa**
    'Superba'
vitifolia hort. non Buchanan-Hamilton ex de Candolle = **A. tomentosa**
wockeana Ascherson & Graebner = **A. ranunculoides** ssp. **wockeana**

ANEMONELLA Spach 1839   [*Ranunculaceae*]
    thalictroides (Linnaeus) Spach 1839   CA
      'Rosea'

ANEMONOPSIS Siebold & Zuccarini 1846   [*Ranunculaceae*]
    macrophylla Seibold & Zuccarini 1846   **PGP**

ANEMOPSIS Hooker f. 1838   [*Saururaceae*]
    californica (Nuttall) Hooker f. & Arnott 1841

ANETHUM Linnaeus 1753   [*Apiaceae (Umbelliferae)*]
AHN   **graveolens** Linnaeus 1753

ANGELICA Linnaeus 1753   [*Apiaceae (Umbelliferae)*]
HN   **archangelica** Linnaeus 1753   PGP
    montana Brotero 1804 = **A. sylvestris**
HN‡   **sylvestris** Linnaeus 1753 (*A. montana*)

ANIGOZANTHOS Labillardiere 1798   [*Haemodoraceae*]
    coccinea Paxton 1794
    flavida A. de Candolle 1807   EGF.1-PGP

ANISOTOME Hooker f. 1844   [*Apiaceae (Umbelliferae)*]
    imbricata (Hooker f.) Cockayne 1921

ANOIGANTHUS Baker 1878   [*Amaryllidaceae*]
    luteus Baker 1878 = **Cyrtanthus brevifolius**

ANOMATHECA Ker-Gawler 1805   [*Iridaceae*]
    cruenta Lindley 1830 = **A. laxa**
    laxa (Thunberg) Goldblatt 1971 (*A. cruenta, Lapeirousia laxa*)   EGF.1-CA-SB
      'Alba'   CA
    viridis (Aiton) Goldblatt 1971 (*Lapeirousia viridis*)   EGF.1

ANTENNARIA Gaertner 1791   [*Asteraceae (Compositae)*]
    anaphaloides Rydberg 1900

aprica Greene 1898 = **A. parvifolia**
HNL **dioica** (Linnaeus) Gaertner 1791   RD
    var. **hyperborea** (D. Don) de Candolle (*A. dioica* 'Tomentosa')
      'Minima'   RD
      'Nyewood'   RD
    var. *rosea* D. Eaton ex Cockerell 1889 = **A. rosea**
      'Rubra' nom. dub.
      'Rubra Plena' nom. dub.
      'Tomentosa' = **A. dioica** var. **hyperborea**
    microphylla Rydberg 1897
    parvifolia Nuttall 1841 (*A. aprica*)   RD
      var. *rosea* Greene 1897 nom. nud. = **A. rosea**
    plantaginifolia (Linnaeus) Richards 1823
    rosea Greene 1898   RD
      'Plena'

ANTHEMIS Linnaeus 1753   *[Asteraceae (Compositae)]*
  aizoon Grisebach 1843 = **Achillea ageratifolia** ssp. **aizoon**
  biebersteiniana (Adams) K. Koch 1851 = **A. marschalliana**
  carpatica Waldstein & Kitaibel 1803 = **A. cretica** ssp. **carpatica**
    petraea hort. = **A. cretica** ssp. **carpatica**
  cretica Linnaeus 1753 (*A. montana*)
    ssp. **carpatica** (Willdenow) Grierson 1975
L   ssp. **cupaniana** (Nyman) ! (A. cupaniana)   PGP-**DGP**-RD
    ssp. **pontica** (Willdenow) Grierson 1975
  cupaniana Todaro ex Nyman 1879 = **A. cretica** ssp. **cupaniana**
  marschalliana Willdenow 1803 (*A. biebersteiniana, A. rudolphiana* hort.)
  montana Linnaeus 1763 = **A. cretica**
  nobilis Linnaeus 1753 = **Chamaemelum nobile**
  pedunculata Desfontaines 1799
    'Tuberculata' = **A. tuberculata**
  punctata Vahl 1791
    ssp. *cupaniana* (Todaro ex Nyman) R. Fernandes 1975 = **A. cretica** ssp. **cupaniana**
  rudolphiana Adams 1805 = **A. marschalliana**
  sancti-johannis Turrill 1926   PGP-**DGP**-RD
HN‡ **tinctoria** Linnaeus 1753   PGP-DGP-RD

    A. TINCTORIA HYBRIDS

    'Beauty of Grallagh' = **A. 'Grallagh Glory'**
L   **'E.C. Buxton'**   [E. C. Buxton]   PGP-DGP-RD
    'Grallagh Glory' [B. Poë 1946]   PGP-**DGP**-RD
    'Grallagh Gold' [B. Poë 1951]   PGP-**DGP**-RD
    'Kelway's Variety' [Kelway]
    'Perry's Variety' [A. Perry]   **DGP**
    'Wargrave'   PGP-**DGP**-RD
  tuberculata Boissier 1838
  zyghia Woronow 1917

ANTHERICUM Linnaeus 1753   *[Anthericaceae (Liliaceae)]*
  baeticum (Boissier) Boissier 1842
  liliago Linnaeus 1753   EGF.1-PGP-**DGP**-RD
    'Major'
  plumosum Ruiz & Pavon 1802 = **Trichopetalum plumosum**
  ramosum Linnaeus 1753   EGF.1-PGP-RD

ANTHOLYZA Linnaeus 1753   *[Iridaceae]*
  floribunda Salisbury 1812 = **Chasmanthe floribunda**
  paniculata Klatt 1868 = **Crocosmia paniculata**
  ringens Linnaeus 1753

ANTHOXANTHUM Linnaeus 1753   [*Poaceae (Gramineae)*]
N‡L **odoratum** Linnaeus 1753

ANTHRISCUS Persoon 1805   [*Apiaceae (Umbelliferae)*]
AH **cerefolium** (Linnaeus) Hoffmann 1814

ANTHYLLIS Linnaeus 1753   [*Fabiaceae (Leguminosae)*]
S **hermanniae** Linnaeus 1753
    'Minor'
    montana Linnaeus 1753   CA
      'Carminea'
      'Rubra'   CA
N‡L **vulneraria** Linnaeus 1753
      ssp. **alpestris** (Kitaibel & Schultes) Ascherson & Graebner 1908
      'Coccinea'
      'Compacta'
      'Minor'
      ssp. **polyphylla** (de Candolle) Nyman 1878
      'Purpurea'

ANTIRRHINUM Linnaeus 1753   [*Scrophulariaceae*]
    asarina Linnaeus 1753 = **Asarina procumbens**
    glutinosum Boissier & Reuter 1852, non (Hoffmanns & Link) Brotero 1827 =
                                                              A. hispanicum
    hispanicum Chavannes 1833 (*A. glutinosum* Boissier & Reuter 1852)
      'Album'
      'Boughton House'
      'Roseum'
      'Taff's White'
N **majus** Linnaeus 1753   DGP-**RD**
    maurandioides A. Gray 1868
S **molle** Linnaeus 1753
S **pulverulentum** Lazaro 1900
S **sempervirens** Lapeyrouse 1795
    siculum Miller 1768

APERA Adanson 1763   [*Poaceae (Gramineae)*]
    arundinacea Hooker f. 1853

APHANES Linnaeus 1753   [*Rosaceae*]
AN‡ **arvensis** Linnaeus 1753

APHYLLANTHES Linnaeus 1753   [*Aphyllanthaceae (Liliaceae)*]
    monspeliensis Linnaeus 1753   EGF.1-CA

APIUM Linnaeus 1753   [*Apiaceae (Umbelliferae)*]
BHN‡ **graveolens** Linnaeus 1753
N‡ **nodiflorum** (Linnaeus) Lagasca 1821
N‡ **repens** (Jacquin) Lagasca 1821

APLECTRUM (Nuttall) Torrey 1826   [*Orchidaceae*]
    hyemale (Muhlenberg) Torrey 1826   EGF.2

APONOGETON Linnaeus f. 1781   [*Aponogetonaceae*]
    desertorum Zeyher ex Steudel (*A. krausseanus*)
NL **distachyos** Linnaeus f. 1781   EGF.1-**RD**
    krausseanus Hochstetter ex Engler 1882 = **A. desertorum**

AQUILEGIA Linnaeus 1753   [*Ranunculaceae*]
 akitensis Huth 1897 = **A. flabellata**
  var. *pumila* Huth 1987 = **A. flabellata** var. **pumila**
H **alpina** Linnaeus 1753   PGP-RD
  'Alba'
  'Blue Spurs'
  'Superba'
 amaliae Heldreich ex Boissier 1854 = **A. ottonis** ssp. **amaliae**
 atrata Koch 1830   RD
 aurea Janka 1872   CA
 'Baikalensis'
 barnebyi Munz 1949
 bertolonii Schott 1853 (*A. reuteri*)   **CA-RD**
  'Blue Berry'
 brevistyla Hooker 1829
 buergeriana Siebold & Zuccarini 1845
 californica Hartwiss 1854 non A. Gray 1868 = **A. formosa** var. **truncata**
 canadensis Linnaeus 1753   PGP-CA-RD
  var. **australis** (Small) Munz 1946
  'Nana' nom. dub.
 cazorlensis Heywood 1954
N **chrysantha** A. Gray 1873   PGP
  var. **hinckleyana** (Munz) E. J. Lott 1985 (*A. hinckleyana*)
  'Yellow Queen'
 clematiflora hort. = **A. Clematiflora Hybrids**
N **coerulea** James 1823   RD
  'Crimson Star'   PGP-DGP-RD
  *var. **daileyae**
  var. **ochroleuca** Hooker 1864
 *coronato
 discolor Levier & Leresche 1879   **CA-RD**
 einseleana F. Schultes 1848   CA
 elegantula Greene 1899   CA
 ecalcarata Maximowicz 1889 = **Semiaquilegia ecalcarata**
 eximia Van Houtte ex Planchon 1857 non Borbas 1882
 flabellata Siebold & Zuccarini 1846 (*A. akitensis*)   PGP-CA-RD
  'Alba'   CA
  'Nana' = **A. flabellata** var. **pumila**
  var. **pumila** (Huth) Kudo (*A. akitensis* var. *pumila*, *A. japonica*)   **CA-RD**
  var. **pumila** 'Alba'   PGP-CA-RD
  var. **pumila** 'Kurilensis'
  var. **pumila** 'Ministar'
  var. **pumila** 'Rosea'
 flavescens S. Watson 1871
N **formosa** Fischer 1824   PGP
  var. **truncata** (Fischer & C. A.Meyer) Baker 1878 (*A. californica*)
 fragrans Bentham
 glandulosa Fischer ex Link 1822
  var. **jucunda** (Fischer & Ave-Lallemant) Baker 1878
 glauca Lindley 1840 (*A. nivalis*)
 grata F. Maly ex Zimmeter 1875
 hinckleyana Munz 1946 = **A. chrysantha** var. **hinckleyana**
 kurilensis hort. = **A. flabellata** var. **pumila** 'Kurilensis'
 japonica Nakai & Hara 1935 = **A. flabellata** var. **pumila**
 jonesii Parry 1874   CA
 jonesii Parry x **A. saximontana** Robinson
 longissima A. Gray ex S. Watson 1881   PGP-DGP-**RD**
 microphylla (Korshinsky) Ikonnikov 1971
 nevadensis Boissier & Reuter 1854 = **A. vulgaris** ssp. **nevadensis**
 nigricans Baumgarten 1816

nivalis Falconer ex Baker 1878 = **A. glauca**
olympica Boissier 1841
ottonis Orphanides & Boissier 1854
    ssp. **amaliae** (Orphanides ex Boissier) Strid 1986 (*A. amaliae*)
oxysepala Trautvetter & C. A. Meyer 1856
pubiflora Wallich ex Royle 1834
N **pyrenaica** de Candolle 1815   CA
reuteri Boissier 1854 = **A. bertolonii**
saximontana Rydberg ex Robinson 1895   CA
scopulorum Tidestrom 1910   CA-RD
schockleyi Eastwood 1905
sibirica Lamarck 1785
skinneri Hooker 1842   PGP
stellata hort. = **A. vulgaris Spurless Form**
thalictrifolia Schott & Kotschy 1853   CA
transsilvanica Schur 1853
triternata Payson 1918   CA
viridiflora Pallas 1783   CA
HN‡ **vulgaris** Linnaeus 1753   PGP-DGP-RD
    'Alba' = **A. vulgaris 'Nivea'**
    'Adelaide Addison'
    'Anne Calder'
    'Double Pink Cottage'
    'Double Red Cottage'
    'Flore Pleno' ('Double Purple')
    'Gisela Powell'
    'Millicent Bowden'
    'Munstead White' = **A. vulgaris 'Nivea'**
    ssp. **nevadensis** (Boissier & Reuter) T. E. Diaz Gonzales 1984 (*A. nevadensis*)
    'Nivea' (A. 'Munstead White')   PGP
    'Nora Barlow'
    'Patricia Zavros'
    'Rev. E. Baty'
    Scented Form
    'Tom Fairhurst'
    'Variegated'

HYBRID GROUPS & CULTIVARS

    'Belhaven Blue Spurless'
    'Biedermeier'   PGP-RD
    'Blue Star'
    'Blue Spurs'
    'Bowles' Variety'
    'Celestial Blue'
    Clematiflora Hybrids (Spurless Hybrids)
    'Clematiflora Alba'
    'Clematiflora Rosea'
    'Clematiflora Rubra'
    'Dragonfly'
    Dunkelblaue Riesen
    'Edelweiss'
    'Giant White' = **A. 'Clematiflora Alba'**
    Harbutt's Hybrids   [K. Harbutt]
    'Haylodgensis' (*A. caerulea* x *A. flabellata*)
    'Helenae'
    'Hensol Harebell' (*A. alpina* x *A. vulgaris*)   [C. Elliott]   PGP
    'Himmelblau'
    'Koralle'
    'Kristall'

Langdon's Rainbow Hybrids
Lowdham Hybrids
'Maxistar'
L   **McKana Hybrids**   PGP-DGP-RD
'Miss Coventry'
Mrs Scott Elliott Hybrids   PGP-DGP-RD
Music Series Hybrids
'Olympia'
'Pikei' (*A. formosa* x *A. longissima*)
'Rotstern'
'Schneekonigin' ('Snow Queen')   PGP-DGP
'Snow Queen' = **'Schneekonigin'**
Spurless = **A. Clematidiflora Hybrids**
'Stuartii' (*A. glutinosa* x *A. olympica*)

ARABIS Linnaeus 1753   [*Brassicaceae (Cruciferae)*]
albida Steven 1808 = **A. caucasica**
N‡   **alpina** Linnaeus 1753
'Coccinea'
'Flore Pleno'
'Rosea'
'Snowdrop'
'Variegata'
androsacea Fenzl 1842   CA
blepharophylla Hooker & Arnott 1841   CA
'Alba'
'Frülingszauber' ('Spring Charm')
'Spring Charm' = **A. blepharophylla 'Frülingszauber'**
breweri S. Watson 1876
bryoides Boissier 1842   **CA**
*imbricata
*olympica
carduchorum Boissier 1867 (*Draba gigas*)   CA
NL   **caucasica** Schlechtendal 1813 (*A. albida*)   DGP-RD
'Albo-plena' = **A. caucasica 'Plena'**
'Bakkely'
'Compinkie'
'Corfe Castle'
'Georg Arends'   [G. Arends]
'Hedi'   [H. Götz 1981]
'Kirschrot'
'La Fraicheur'
'Monte Rosa'   [Pötschke/Walther]
'Nana' nom. dub.
'Pink Pearl'
'Plena'   [Keyne 1896]   **DGP-RD**
'Rosabella'   DGP
'Rosea'
'Rose Frost'
'Rosenquartz'
'Rubin'
'Schneehaube' ('Snowcap')   [E. Benary 1935]
'Snowcap' = **A. caucasica 'Schneehaube'**
'Snowdrop'
'Snowflake'
'Sulphurea'
'Superba'
'Variegata'
collina Tenore 1810 (*A. muralis, A. rosea*)
ferdinandi-coburgii J. Kellerer & Sündermann 1904   RD

'Aureo-variegata'
'Old Gold'
'Variegata'
halleri Linnaeus 1753
jacquinii G. Beck 1884 = **A. soyeri** ssp. **jacquinii**
japonica (A. Gray) A. Gray 1858 = **A. stelleri** var. **japonica**
x kellereri Sündermann 1925 (*A. bryoides* x *A. ferdinandi-coburgii*)   CA
x landaueri Sündermann 1925 (*A. bellidifolia* x *A. ferdinandi-coburgii*)
muralis Bertolini 1806 nom. illegit. = **A. collina**
procurrens Waldstein & Kitaibel 1863
    'Filigran'
    'Schneeteppich'   [H. Klose 1971]
    'Variegata'
pumila Jacquin 1775
rosea de Candolle 1821 = **A. collina**
soyeri Reuter & Huet 1853
    ssp. **jacquinii** (G. Beck) B. M. G. Jones 1964
stelleri de Candolle 1821
    var. **japonica** (A. Gray) F. Schmidt (*A. japonica*)
*x sturii
x suendermannii J. Kellerer & Sündermann 1925 (*A. ferdinandi-coburgii* x *A. procurrens*)
vochinensis Sprengel 1813
x wilczeckii Sündermann 1925 (*A. bryoides* x *A. carduchorum*)

ARACHNIODES Blume 1828   [*Dryopteridaceae*]
    aristata (Forster) Tindale 1961   EGF.1
        'Variegata'
    nipponica (Rosenstock) Ohwi 1962 (*Polystichopsis nipponica*)

ARALIA Linnaeus 1753   [*Araliaceae*]
    cachemirica Decaisne 1841   PGP
    californica S. Watson 1876
    racemosa Linnaeus 1753   PGP

ARCTANTHEMUM (Tzvelev) Tzvelev 1985
    arcticum (Linnaeus) Tzvelev 1985 (*Chrysanthemum arcticum, Dendranthema arcticum*)
        'Roseum'   [Berggarten-Herrenhausen]
        'Schwefelglanz'   [G. Arends]

ARCTIUM Linnaeus 1753   [*Asteraceae (Compositae)*]
HN‡   **lappa** Linnaeus 1753 (*A. officinalis* hort.)
    officinalis hort. = **A. lappa**

ARENARIA Linnaeus 1753   [*Caryophyllaceae*]
N   **balearica** Linnaeus 1768   RD
    caespitosa Ehrhart 1790 = **Minuartia verna** ssp. **caespitosa**
    capillaris Poiret 1804
    cretica Sprengel 1825
    gracilis Waldstein & Kitaibel 1812
    grandiflora Linnaeus 1759   RD
    imbricata Marshall von Bieberstein 1808 = **Minuartia imbricata**
    laricifolia Linnaeus 1753 = **Minuartia laricifolia**
    ledebouriana Fenzl 1843
    lithops Heywood & McNeil 1962
    longifolia Marshall von Bieberstein 1808
N   **montana** Linnaeus 1755   RD
    nevadensis Boissier & Reuter 1853
N‡   **norvegica** Gunnerus 1772
    pinifolia Marshall von Bieberstein 1808 = **Minuartia circassica**
    procera Sprengel 1808

ssp. **glabra** (F. N. Williams) J. Holub 1956
pulvinata Edgeworth & Hooker f. 1874
purpurascens Ramond ex de Candolle 1805   CA-RD
   'Elliott's Variety'   [J. Elliott]   RD
rigida Marshall von Bieberstein 1808
sajanensis Willdenow ex Schlecht 1813 = **Minuartia biflora**
tetraquetra Linnaeus 1753   CA
   var. **granatensis** Boissier
tmolea Boissier 1843

ARGYRANTHEMUM Schultz-Bip 1844   [*Asteraceae (Compositae)*]
s   **foeniculaceum** (Willdenow) Webb & Schultz-Bip 1844 (*Chrysanthemum foeniculaceum*)
   'Albo Pleno' nom. dub.
s   **frutescens** (Linnaeus) Schultz-Bip 1844 (*Chrysanthemum frutescens*)   PGP
gracile Schultz-Bip 1844
ochroleuca Webb ex Schultz-Bip 1844 = **A. maderense**
maderense (D. Don) C. J. Humphries 1976 (*A. ochroleuca*)

HYBRID CULTIVARS

   'Brontes'
   'Chelsea Girl'
   'Coronation'   PGP
   'Edelweiss'
   'Etoile d'Or'
   'Jamaica Primrose' ('Jamaica Yellow')   PGP
   'Jamaica Yellow' = **A. frutescens 'Jamaica Primrose'**
   'Lemon Treasure'
   'Leyton Treasure'
   'Margaret Lynch'   [M. Lynch]
   'Mary Wooton'   PGP
   'Mrs. Sanders'
   'Nevada Cream'
   'Overbecks'
   'Powder Puff'
   'Quinta White'
   'Rollason's Red'
   'Royal Haze'
   'Snowflake'
   'Soleile d'Or'
   'Vancouver'
   'Wellwood Park'

ARISAEMA C. Martius 1831   [*Araceae*]
amurense Maximowicz 1859
candidissimum W. W. Smith 1917   EGF.2-PGP-**BB**-SB-DGP-RD
consanguineum Schott 1859   EGF.2-PGP-SB
costatum (Wallich) C. Martius ex Schott & Endlichter 1832   SB
dracontium (Linnaeus) Schott 1832   EGF.2-PGP
flavum (Forsskal) Schott 1860   SB
griffithii Schott 1856   EGF.2-**BB**-SB
helleborifolium Schott 1856 = **A. tortuosum**
japonicum Blume 1836 = **A. serratum**
jacquemontii Blume 1836   **BB**-SB
kiushianum Makino 1918   SB
nepenthoides (Wallich) C. Martius in Schott 1832
ochraceum Schott 1859
ringens (Thunberg) Schott 1832   EGF.2-PGP-**BB**-SB
serratum (Thunberg) Schott 1832 (*A. japonicum*)   EGF.2-SB
sikokianum Franchet & Savatier 1878   EGF.2-PGP-**BB**-**SB**

speciosum (Wallich) C. Martius in Schott 1832   EGF.2-PGP-**BB**-SB
thunbergii Blume 1836
   ssp. **urashima** (Hara) Ohashi & J. Murata 1980
tortuosum (Wallich) Schott 1832 (*A. helleborifolium*)   **BB**-SB
triphyllum (Linnaeus) Torrey 1843   EGF.2-PGP-**BB**-SB
urashima Hara 1935 = **A. thunbergii** ssp. **urashima**
utile Hooker f. ex Schott 1860   SB
yamatense (Nakai) Nakai 1929
   var. **sugimotoi** (Nakai) Kitamura

ARISARUM Targioni-Tozzetti 1810   [*Araceae*]
proboscideum (Linnaeus) Savi 1816   EGF.2-**BB**-SB
vulgare Targioni-Tozzetti 1810   EGF.2-**BB**-**SB**

ARISTEA Solander ex Aiton 1789   [*Iridaceae*]
ecklonii Baker 1877   EGF.1-PGP
major Andrews 1801   EGF.1

ARISTOLOCHIA Linnaeus 1753   [*Aristolochiaceae*]
argentina Grisebach 1874
HN‡ **clematitis** Linnaeus 1753   PGP
lindneri A. Berger 1927
longa Linnaeus 1753
pistolochia Linnaeus 1753
sempervirens Linnaeus 1753

ARMERIA (de Candolle) Willdenow 1809   [*Plumbaginaceae*]
N **alliacea** (Cavanilles) Hoffmannsegg & Link 1813 (*A. plantaginea*)   PGP
   'Bees' Ruby' (*A. alliacea* x *A. maritima*)   PGP-RD
cephalotes Boissier 1848 = **A. pseudoarmeria**
cespitosa (Cavanilles) Boissier 1848 = **A. juniperifolia**
corsica hort. = **A. leucocephala 'Corsica'**
Formosa Hybrids (*A. alliacea* x *A. leucocephala* 'Corsica')
girardii (Bernis) Litardiere 1955
   'Alba'
juniperifolia (Vahl) Hoffmannsegg & Link 1813 (*A. caespitosa*)   CA-DGP-RD
   'Alba'
   'Ardenholme'
   'Beechwood'
   'Bevan's Variety'   [R. Bevan pre-1946]   CA-**DGP**-**RD**
   Dark Form
   'Rubra'
   'Six Hills'
   'Suendermannii'
   'Variabilis'
S **leucocephala** Salzmann ex Koch 1823   PGP
   'Corsica' (*A. corsica* hort.)
HN‡ **maritima** (Miller) Willdenow 1809   DGP-RD
   'Alba'   RD
   'Alba Minor'
   'Birch Pink'
   'Bloodstone'
   'Dusseldorf Pride' = **A. maritima 'Düsseldorfer Stolz'**
   'Düsseldorfer Stolz'   [Nosbüsch 1957]('Dusseldorf Pride')
   'Frülingszauber'
   'Glory of Holland'
   'Laucheana'
   'Ornament'
   'Pride' = **A. maritima 'Düsseldorfer Stolz'**
   'Rosea Compacta'

'**Rotfeuer**'   [M. Baltin]
'**Ruby Glow**'
'**Schöne von Fellbach**'
ssp. **sibirica** (Turczaninow ex Boissier) Nyman
'**Splendens**'
'**Splendens Alba**'
L   '**Vindictive**'   [via C. Elliot]   **DGP**-RD
plantaginea Willdenow 1809 = **A. alliacea**
N   **pseudarmeria** (Murray) Mansfield 1939 (*A. cephalotes*)
pungens (Link) Hoffmannsegg & Link 1813
setacea Delile & Nyman 1881   CA
***tweedyi**
welwitschii Boissier 1848

ARMORACIA Gilibert 1782   [*Brassicaceae (Cruciferae)*]
HN   **rusticana** (Lamarck) Gaertner, Meyer & Scherbius 1800 (*Cochlearia armoracia*)
                                                              PGP

ARNEBIA Forsskal 1775   [*Boraginaceae*]
echioides A. de Candolle 1846 = **A. pulchra**
pulchra (Willdenow ex Roemer & Schultes) Edmonson 1977 (*A. echioides, Echioides
                                        longiflorum*)   **RD**

ARNICA Linnaeus 1753   [*Asteraceae (Compositae)*]
alpina (Linnaeus) Olin & Ladau 1799 non Salisbury = **A. angustifolia**
angustifolia Vahl 1816 (*A. alpina* (Linnaeus) Olin & Ladau)
chamissonis Lessing 1831
longifolia D. Eaton 1871
mollis Hooker 1834
H   **montana** Linnaeus 1753   PGP-CA
sachalinensis (Regel) S. F. Gray 1883

ARRHENATHERUM Palisot de Beavois 1812   [*Poaceae (Gramineae)*]
N‡   **elatius** (Linnaeus) Presl 1819   EGF.2
ssp. **bulbosum** (Willdenow) Hylander 1953
ssp. **bulbosum** '**Variegatum**'

ARTEMISIA Linnaeus 1753   [*Asteraceae (Compositae)*]
HSN   **abrotanum** Linnaeus 1753   PGP-**RD**
HN‡   **absinthium** Linnaeus 1753   PGP-DGP-RD
'**Lambrook Giant**'   PGP
L   '**Lambrook Silver**'   PGP-**DGP**
alba Turra 1764 (*A. camphorata*)
albula Wooton = **A. ludoviciana** var. **albula**
arborescens Linnaeus 1763   PGP-**DGP**
'**Faith Raven**'   PGP
'Powis Castle' = **A. 'Powis Castle**'
armeniaca Lamarck 1783   PGP
assoana Wilkomm 1865
borealis Pallas 1791 = **A. campestris** ssp. **borealis**
brachyloba Franchet 1883
brachyphylla Kitamura 1936 = **A. splendens** var. **brachyphylla**
SN‡   **campestris** Linnaeus 1753
H   ssp. **borealis** (Pallas) H. M. Hall & Clements 1923
camphorata Villars 1779 = **A. alba**
'**Canescens**'   PGP
caucasica Willdenow 1803 (*A. lanata, A. pedemontana*)   CA
HS   **chamaemelifolia** Villars 1779
discolor Douglas ex Besser 1836 = **A. ludoviciana** var. **incompta**
dracunculoides Pursh 1814 = **A. dracunculus**

H   **dracunculus** Linnaeus 1753 (*A. dracunculoides*)
H   **'Inodora'**
H   **'Sativa'**
     eriantha Tenore 1831 (*A. villarsii*)
     filifolia Torrey 1827
     frigida Willdenow 1804
     genipi Weber 1775
     glacialis Linnaeus 1763   CA
     gnaphalodes Nuttall 1818 = **A. ludoviciana**
     granatensis Boissier 1833
HL   **lactiflora** Wallich ex de Candolle 1830   PGP-**DGP-RD**
     'Variegata'
     lanata Willdenow 1823 non Lamarck 1783 = **A. caucasica**
     laxa (Lamarck) Fritsch 1893 = **A. mutellina**
     ludoviciana Nuttall 1818 (*A. gnaphalodes, A. purshiana*)   PGP-**RD**
         var. **albula** (Wooton) Shinners (*A. albula*)
         var. **incompta** (Nuttall) Cronquist 1955 (*A. discolor, A vulgaris* ssp. *discolor*)
         var. **latiloba** Nuttall 1841   PGP
L   **'Silver Queen'**   PGP
     maritima Linnaeus 1753 = **Seriphidium maritimum**
     michauxiana Besser 1833 = **A. ludoviciana** var. **incompta**
     mutellina Villars 1779 non S.G. Gmelin (*A. laxa, A. umbelliformis*)   CA
     nitida Bertoloni 1832
     nutans Willdenow 1800 = **Seriphidium nutans**
     palmeri A. Gray 1876 = **Seriphidium palmeri**
     pedemontana Balbis 1810 = **A. caucasica**
HN   **pontica** Linnaeus 1753   PGP
     'Powis Castle' (*A. absinthium*? x *A. arborescens*?)   [A. J. Hancock c1978] PGP-RD
     purshiana Besser 1834 = **A. ludoviciana**
     rothrockii A. Gray 1876 = **Seriphidium rothrockii**
     rupestris Linnaeus 1753 (*A. viridiflora*)
     schmidtiana Maximowicz 1872   **RD**
        'Nana' = **A. schmidtiana**
     splendens Willdenow 1803
        var. **brachyphylla** (Kitamura) Kitamura (*A. brachyphylla*)
N   **stelleriana** Besser 1834   PGP-**RD**
      'Boughton Silver' = **A. stelleriana 'Mori's Form'**
      'Mori's Form' ('Boughton Silver', 'Prostrata')   PGP
      'Prostrata' = **A. stelleriana 'Mori's Form'**
     tridentata Nuttall 1841 = **Seriphidium tridentatum**
     umbelliformis Lamarck 1783 = **A. mutellina**
     *****versicolor**
     villarsii Grenier & Godron 1850 = **A. eriantha**
     viridiflora Ledebour 1823 = **A. rupestris**
HN‡ **vulgaris** Linnaeus 1753
        ssp. *discolor* Hall & Clements 1923 = **A. ludoviciana** var. **incompta**
     'Variegata'

ARTHROPODIUM R. Brown 1822   *[Anthericaceae (Liliaceae)]*
     candidum Raoul 1844   EGF.1-CA
        Bronze Form
        'Maculatum'
        'Purpureum'
     cirrhatum (Foster f.) R. Brown 1822   EGF.1-PGP
     milleflorum (de Candolle) Macbride 1918   EGF.1

ARUM Linnaeus 1753   *[Araceae]*
     conophalloides Kotschy ex Schott 1860   **BB**
     cornutum hort. = **Sauromatum venosum**

	corsicum Loiseleur 1807 = **A. pictum**	
	creticum Boissier 1854	EGF.2-PGP-**BB**-SB-**DGP**
	dioscoridis Smith 1813	EGF.2-PGP-**BB**-SB
	var. **smithii** Engler 1879	SB
	hygrophilum Boissier 1854	EGF.2
N‡	**italicum** Miller 1768	EGF.2-PGP-**BB**-RD
	ssp. **albispathum** (Steven) Prime 1978	**BB**
	ssp. **byzantinum** (Blume) Nyman 1882	**BB**
	ssp. **italicum**	**BB**
	'Marmoratum' = **A. italicum 'Pictum'**	
	ssp. **neglectum** (Townsend) Prime 1961	**BB**
L	**'Pictum'** Hort. non Linnaeus f.	PGP-**BB**-SB-**DGP**-RD
N‡	**maculatum** Linnaeus 1753	EGF.2-SB
	f. **flavescens** (Melzev ex Janchen) H. Riedl 1979	
	'Pleddel'	
	nickellii Schott 1860	
	nigrum Schott 1857 = **A. petteri**	
	orientale Marshall von Bieberstein 1808	EGF.2-PGP
	ssp. **alpinum** (Schott & Kotschy) H. Riedl 1979	
	palaestinum Boissier 1854	EGF.2-**BB**
	petteri Schott 1856 (*A. nigrum*)	SB
	pictum Linnaeus f. 1781 (*A. corsicum*)	EGF.2-PGP-SB
	***stevensii**	

ARUNCUS Linnaeus 1758		*[Rosaceae]*
	aethusifolius (Leveille) Nakai 1912	
L	**dioicus** (Walter) Fernald 1939 (*A. silvester, Spiraea aruncus*)	PGP-**DGP**-RD
	var. **astilboides** (Maximowicz) Hara 1933	PGP
L	**'Kneiffii'**	PGP-RD
	***maculatum**	
	parvulus Komarov 1950	
	'Dagalet' (*Astilbe x crispa* 'Dagalet' Hort. in err.)	
	'Plumosus Glasnevin' = **A. dioicus**	
	silvester Kostel 1844 nom. nudum = **A. dioicus**	
	***sinensis**	
	'Zweiweltenkind' [Foerster 1960]	

ARUNDO Linnaeus 1753		*[Poaceae (Gramineae)]*
	donax Linnaeus 1753	EGF.2-PGP
	var. **variegata** Vilmorin 1863	PGP
	pliniana Turra 1765	
	plinii Turra 1765 non C. A. Meyer & Braun 1823 = **A. pliniana**	

ASARINA Miller 1768		*[Scrophulariaceae]*
	hispanica (Boissier & Reuter) hort. = **Antirrhinum hispanicum**	
N	**procumbens** Miller 1768 (*Antirrhinum asarina*)	

ASARUM Linnaeus 1753		*[Aristolochiaceae]*
	canadense Linnaeus 1753	
	caudatum Lindley 1831	RD
HN‡L	**europaeum** Linnaeus 1753	RD
	hartwegii S. Watson 1875	
	lemmonii S. Watson 1879	
	megacalyx Maekawa 1934	
	nipponicum Maekawa 1932	
	shuttleworthii Britton & Baker 1898	
	tamaense Makino 1931	

ASCLEPIAS Linnaeus 1753		*[Asclepiadaceae]*
	cornuti Decaisne 1844 = **A. syriaca**	
	curassavica Linnaeus 1753	RD

incarnata Linnaeus 1753
speciosa Torrey 1826   PGP
H   **syriaca** Linnaeus 1753 (*A. cornuti*)
H   **tuberosa** Linnaeus 1753   PGP
    'Rosea'

ASPARAGUS Linnaeus 1753   [*Asparagaceae (Liliaceae)*]
densiflorus (Kunth) Jessop 1966   EGF.1
    'Gwebe'
    'Mazeppa Bay'
laricinus Burchell 1822   EGF.1
N‡   **officinalis** Linnaeus 1753   EGF.1-PGP-RD
    var. **pseudoscaber** Ascherson & Graebner   EGF.1
    var. **pseudoscaber 'Spitzenschleier'**   PGP
tenuifolius Lamarck 1783   EGF.1-PGP
tenuifolius hort p.p., non Lamarck = **A. officinalis**   ·

ASPERULA Linnaeus 1753   [*Rubiaceae*]
arcadiensis Sims 1820   CA
aristata Linnaeus f. 1781
    ssp. *longiflora* (Waldstein & Kitaibel) Hayek 1930 = **A. aristata** ssp. **scabra**
    ssp. **scabra** (J. & C. Presl) Nyman 1879 (*A. aristata* ssp. *longiflora*)
    ssp. **thessala** (Boissier & Heldreich) Hayek 1930 (*A. nitida* ssp. *puberula*)
caespitosa hort. = **A. lilaciflora**
gussonii Boissier 1849
hirta Ramond 1800   CA
lilaciflora Boissier 1843 (*A. caespitosa*)   RD
nitida Smith 1806   CA
    *ssp. **puberula** = **A. aristata** ssp. **thessala**
odorata Linnaeus 1753 = **Galium odoratum**
sintinensis Halacsy 1890 non Ascherson 1883 = **A. aristata** ssp. **thessala**
suberosa Smith 1806   **CA-DGP-RD**
H   **tinctoria** Linnaeus 1753

ASPHODELINE Reichenbach 1830   [*Asphodelaceae (Liliaceae)*]
liburnica (Scopoli) Reichenbach 1830   EGF.1
L   **lutea** (Linnaeus) Reichenbach 1830 (*Asphodelus luteus*)   EGF.1
subalpina (Grenier & Godron) hort. = **Asphodelus albus**

ASPHODELUS Linnaeus 1753   [*Asphodelaceae (Liliaceae)*]
acaulis Desfontaines 1798   EGF.1-CA
albus Miller 1768 (*A. subalpinus*)   EGF.1
bento-rainhae P. Silva 1956
cerasiferus J. Gay 1857 = **A. ramosus**
A   **fistulosus** Linnaeus 1753   EGF.1
lusitanicus Coutinho 1890
luteus Linnaeus 1753 = **Asphodeline lutea**
ramosus Linnaeus 1753 (*A. cerasiferus*)   **PGP**
subalpinus Grenier & Godron 1855 = **A. alba**

ASPIDISTRA Ker-Gawler 1823   [*Convallariaceae (Liliaceae)*]
elatior Blume 1834 (*A. lurida* hort.)   EGF.1-RD
    'Variegata'   EGF.1-PGP-**RD**
lurida Ker-Gawler 1822   EGF.1-PGP
lurida hort. non Ker-Gawler = **A. elatior**

ASPLENIUM Linnaeus 1753   [*Aspleniaceae*]
N   **adiantum-nigrum** Linnaeus 1753   EGF.1-**RD**
bulbiferum Forster f. 1786   EGF.1-DGP-RD
N   **ceterach** Linnaeus 1753 (*Ceterach officinarum*)   PGP

	dareoides Desvaux 1811	
	fontanum (Linnaeus) Bernhardi 1799	EGF.1
	foriesiacum (Le Grand) Christ 1900 = **A. foreziense**	
	foreziense Le Grand 1885 (*A. foriesiacum*)	
N	**marinum** Linnaeus 1753	EGF.1
	platyneuron (Linnaeus) Oakes 1879	
N	**ruta-muraria** Linnaeus 1753	EGF.1
NL	**scolopendrium** Linnaeus 1753 (*Phyllitis scolopendrium*)	EGF.1-PGP-RD

     'Alto'
     'Angustatum' ('Angustifolium')
     'Angustifolium = **A. scolopendrium 'Angustatum'**
     'Crenatum'
     'Crispum'   PGP-RD
     'Crispum fimbriatium'
     'Crispum nobile'
     'Crispum sagittatum'
     'Cristatum'   RD
     'Digitatum'
     'Fisilis Monkmanii' nom. dub.
     'Laceratum'
     'Laceratum Kaye's Variety'
     'Marginatum'
     'Marginatum irregulare'
     'Muricatum'
     'Ramo-cristatum'
     'Sagittatum cristatum'
     'Stagshorn Variety'
     'Treble'
     'Undulatum'

N	**septentrionale** (Linnaeus) Hoffmann 1795	
N	**trichomanes** Linnaeus 1753	EGF.1-PGP-RD

     'Cristatum'   RD
     'Incisum'
     'Ramosum'

N	**viride** Hudson 1762	EGF.1

ASTELIA Banks & Solander ex R. Brown 1810   [*Asteliaceae (Liliaceae)*]
     chathamica (Skottsberg) L. B. Moore 1965 = **A. nervosa** var. **chathamica**
     fragrans Colenso 1883
     grandis Hooker f. ex Kirk 1872
     montana (Kirk) Cockayne 1908 = **A. nervosa**
     nervosa Hooker f. 1853 (*A. montana*)   EGF.1-PGP
       var. **chathamica** Skottsberg 1934 (*A. chathamica*)
       'Silver Spear'
     nivicola Cockayne ex Cheeseman 1925   EGF.1
       'Gem' ('Red Gem')
       'Red Gem' = **A. nivicola 'Gem'**
     petriei Cockayne 1899   EGF.1-PGP

ASTER Linnaeus 1753   [*Asteraceae (Compositae)*]
     acris Linnaeus 1762 = **A. sedifolius**
     ageratoides Turczaninow 1837
       'Vesoensis'
     x alpellus hort. (*A. alpinus* x *A. amellus*)
       'Triumph'   [van der Schoot]
     alpigenus (Torrey & A. Gray) A. Gray 1872 (*A. pulchellus* D. Eaton)
       ssp. **andersonii** (A. Gray) Onno 1932 (*A. andersonii*)
     alpinus Linnaeus 1753   CA-**DGP**-RD
       'Abendschein'
       'Albus'   CA-RD

'Beechwood'   DGP-RD
'Dark Beauty' = **A. alpinus 'Dunkle Schöne'**
'Dunkle Schöne' ('Dark Beauty')
'Happy End'
'Roseus'
'Trimix'
'Wargrave Variety'
'Wunder'   **RD**

N **amellus** Linnaeus 1753   PGP-DGP-RD
'Blue King'
'Blütendecke'
'Breslau'
L 'Brilliant'
'Butzemann'
'Dr. Otto Petschek'
'Hermann Löns'
'Glücksfund'
'Gnome' = **A. amellus 'Kobald'**
L 'King George'   PGP-**DGP-RD**
'Kobald' ('Gnome')
'Kugelstrauss'
'Lac de Geneve'
'Lady Hindlip'   PGP-RD
'Lise'
'Mignon'
'Mira'
'Moerheim Gem'   PGP
'Mrs. Ralph Woods'   PGP
'Nocturne'   PGP-RD
'Oktoberkind'
'Peach Blossom'
'Pink Pearl'
'Pink Zenith'
'Praecox Junifreude'
'Praecox Sommergrüss'
'Rosa Erfüllung'
'Rot Feuer' ('Red Fire')
'Rudolph Goethe'   PGP-**DGP-RD**
'Santa Anita'
'Sonia'   PGP-DGP-RD
'Sonora'
'Sternkugel'
'Ultramarine'   PGP
L 'Veilchenkönigin' ('Violet Queen')   PGP
'Weltenfrieden'

andersonii A. Gray 1868 (*A. alpinus* ssp. *andersonii*)
asperulus Wallich ex Nees 1818 non Torrey & A. Gray 1841
asper Nees 1818
aureus D. Don 1825 non O. Kuntze 1891 = **Solidago aurea**
belliadistrum (Linnaeus) Scopoli 1769   CA
capensis Lessing 1832 = **Felicia amelloides**
carolinianus Walter 1788 (*A. scandens*)
'Coombe Fishacre' (*A. lateriflorus* x ?)   [Archer-Hind]
cordifolius Linnaeus 1753   PGP
'Aldeboran'
'Elegans'
'Ideal'   PGP
'Little Carlow'
'Little Dorrit'
'Photograph'

'Silver Queen'
'Silver Spray'   PGP
'Sweet Lavender'
corymbosus Aiton 1789 = **A. divaricatus**
divaricatus Linnaeus 1753 (*A. corymbosus*)   PGP
x dumosus hort., non Linnaeus 1753
   'Alice Haslem'
   'Audrey'   DGP-RD
   'Autumn Princess'
   'Blue Baby'
   'Blue Bouquet'
   'Blue Lagoon'
   'Blue Orb'
   'Chatterbox'
   'Cecily'
   'Countess of Dudley'
   'Court Herald'
   'Cristina'
   'Dandy'   RD
   'Daphne'
   'Diana'
   'Ernie Moss'
   'Gulliver'
   'Heather'
   'Hebe'
   'Heinz Richard'
   'Herbstfreude'
   'Herbstgruss von Bresserhof'
   'Herbstpurzel'
   'Jean'
   'Jenny'   **DGP**
   'Kassel'
   'Kristina'   RD
   'Lady-in-Blue'   RD
   'Lilac Time'
   'Little Blue Beauty'
   'Little Pink Beauty'   **RD**
   'Little Pink Pyramid'
   'Little Red Boy'
   'Little Treasure'
   'Lucy'
   'Margaret Rose'
   'Marjorie'
   'Miss Muffet'
   'Mittelmeer'
   'Mrs H. Maddocks'
   'Nancy'
   'Nesthäkchen'
   'Newton Pink'
   'Niobe'
   'Pacific Amarant'
   'Peter Harrison'
   'Peter Pan'
   'Pink Lace'
   'Professor Anton Kippenberg'   **RD**
   'Purple Dome'
   'Queen of Sheba'
   'Red Boy'
   'Red Robin'
   'Remembrance'

'Rosamund'
'Rose Bonnet'
'Rosebud'
'Rosenwichtel'
'Rozika'
'Schneekissen' ('Snow Cushion')
'Silberblaukissen'
'Silberteppich'
'Snowsprite'   **DGP**-RD
'Snow Cushion' = **A. dumosus 'Schneekissen'**
'Starlight'   RD
'Terry's Pride'
'Trixie'
'Victor'
'Violet Queen'
'Wachsenburg'
ericoides Linnaeus 1753   PGP-RD
'Blue Star'   PGP-RD
'Blue Wonder'
'Brimstone'   PGP
'Cinderella'
'Delight'   RD
'Enchantress'
'Erlkönig'
'Esther'
'Golden Spray'   PGP
'Herbstmyrte'
'Hon. Edith Gibbs'
'Hon. Vicary Gibbs'
'Lovely'
'Maidenhood'
'Monte Cassino'
'Perfection'
'Pink Cloud'   PGP
'Ringdove'   PGP-RD
'Schneegitter'
'Schneetanne'
'Rosy Veil'
'Vimmer's Delight'
'White Heather'   PGP
'Yvette Richardson'
falconeri (C. B. Clarke) Hutchinson 1910
farreri W. W. Smith & Jeffrey 1916
flaccidus Bunge 1835
framfieldii hort. = **A. amellus 'Framfieldii'**
x frikartii Frikart ex hort. (*A. amellus* x *A. thomsonii*)   PGP-**DGP**-RD
'Flora's Delight'   [A. Bloom]
'Jungfrau'   [Frikart]   PGP
'Mönch'   [Frickart]   PGP
'Wunder von Stäfa'   PGP
himalaicus C. B. Clarke 1876   CA
horizontalis hort. = **A. lateriflorus 'Horizontalis'**
hybridus luteus Arends ex hort. = **X Solidaster luteus**
laevis Linnaeus 1753
'Albus'
lateriflorus (Linnaeus) Britton 1889   PGP
'Horizontalis' (*A. horizontalis* hort.)   PGP
likiangensis Franchet 1896   CA
linosyris (Linnaeus) Bernhardi 1800   PGP-**DGP**-RD
'Goldilocks' = **A. linosyris**

macrophyllus Linnaeus 1763   PGP
    'Albus'
natalensis (Walpers) Harvey 1865 = **Felicia rosulata**
N **novae-angliae** Linnaeus 1753   PG-DGP-RD
    'Andenken an Alma Pötschke'   [Pötschke]   **RD**
    'Andenken an Paul Gerber'
    'Autumn Snow' = **A. novae-angliae 'Herbstschnee'**
    'Barr's Blue'
    'Barr's Pink'   DGP-**RD**
    'Barr's Violet'
    'Guinton Menzies'
L   'Harrington's Pink'   PGP-DGP-RD
    'Herbstschnee' ('Autumn Snow')
    'Lye End Beauty'   PGP-RD
    'Lye End Companion'
    'Mrs S. T. Wright'
    'Mrs Winder' = **A. novae-angliae 'Mrs S. T. Wright'**
    'Purple Cloud'
    'Red Cloud'
    'Rosa Sieger'   [K. Foerster via H. Hagemann]
    'Rubinschatz'   [K. Foerster]
    'Rudelsburg'   [Pötschke]
    'September Ruby'   **DGP**-RD
    'Treasure'
    'W. Bowman'
NL **novi-belgii** Linnaeus 1753   PGP-DGP
    'Ada Ballard'   **DGP**
    'Albanian'
    'Alderman Vokes'
    'Alex Norman'
    'Algar's Pride'
    'Alpenglow'
    'Amethyst'
    'Anita Ballard'
    'Anita Webb'
    'Antwerp Pearl'
    'Arctic'
    'Ashwick'
    'Autumn Beauty'
    'Autumn Days'
    'Autumn Rose'
    'Baby Climax'
    'Beechwood Beacon'
    'Beechwood Charm'
    'Beechwood Lady'
    'Beechwood Rival'
    'Beechwood Supreme'
    'Belmont Blue'
    'Berunderung'
    'Blandie'
    'Blarney'
    'Blauglut'
    'Blaue Nachhut'
    'Blue Danube'
    'Blue Eyes'
    'Blue Gem'
    'Blue Gown'   PGP
    'Blue Jacket'
    'Blue Patrol'
    'Blue Plume'

'Blue Radiance'
'Blue Whirl'
'Bonanza'
'Bonningdale Blue'
'Bonningdale White'
'Borealis'
'Bridesmaid'
'Bridget'
'Brightest and Best'
'Brigitte'
'Cameo'
'Camerton'
'Candelabra'
'Carlingcot'
'Carnival'   **RD**
'Catherine Chiswell'
'Charmwood'
'Chelwood'
'Chequers'   RD
'Chilcompton'
'Choristers'
'Cliff Lewis'
'Climax'   PGP
'Cloudy Blue'
'Colonel Durham'
'Colin Bailey'
'Coombe Delight'
'Coombe Gladys'
'Coombe Joy'
'Coombe Margaret'
'Coombe Pink'
'Coombe Radiance'
'Coombe Rosemary'   RD
'Coombe Ronald'
'Coombe Queen'
'Coombe Violet'
'Crimson Brocade'
'Crimson Velvet'
'Dauerblau'
'Davey's True Blue'
'Dazzler'
'Desert Song'
'Destiny'
'Diana Watts'
'D. M. Harrison'
'Dorothy Chiswell'
'Dorothy Bailey'
'Dunkerton'
'Dusty Maid'
'Dymbro'
'Early Melbourne Red'
'Elizabeth'
'Elizabeth Bright'
'Elsie Dale'
'Elta'
'Emma'
'Erica'
'Ernest Ballard'   **DGP**
'Eva'
'Eventide'

'Faith'
'Fair Trial'
'Fair Lady'
'Farringdon'
'Felicity'
'Festival'
'Fellowship'   RD
'Flair'
'Flamingo'
'F. M. Simpson'
'Fontaine'
'Frank Watts'
'Freda Ballard'   RD
'Fuldatal'
'Gayborder Beauty'
'Gayborder Blue'
'Gayborder Rapture'
'Gayborder Rose'
'Gayborder Royal'
'Gayborder Spire'
'Gayborder Splendour'
'Glorious'
'Goblin Coombe'
'Goliath'
'Grey Lady'
'Guardsman'
'Gurney Slade'
'Guy Ballard'
'Happiness'
'Harrison's Blue'
'Helen'
'Helen Ballard'
'Hey Day'
'Hilda Ballard'
'Irene'
'Janet McMullen'
'Janet Watts'
'Janice Stephenson'
'Jean Gyte'
'Jezabel'
'Jollity'
'Julia'
'Juliet'
'Just So'
'Karen'
'Karminkugel'
'King of the Belgians'
'King's College'
'Kilmersdon'
'Lady Frances'   RD
'Lady Paget'
'Lassie'
'Lavender Dream'
'Leona'
'Leuchtfeuer'
'Lisa Dawn'
'Little Boy Blue'
'Little Pink Lady'
'Lucille'
'Mabel Reeves'

'Madge Cato'
'Maid of Athens'
'Malvern Castle'
'Malvern Queen'
'Mammoth'
'Margaret Murray'
'Margaret Bennett'
'Marie Ballard'   RD
'Mars'
'Mary'
'May Louise'
'Melbourne'
'Melbourne Belle'
'Melbourne Glory'
'Melbourne Lad'
'Melbourne Magnet'
'Melbourne Mauve'
'Melbourne Sparkler'
'Michelle'
'Minster'
'Miranda'
'Mistress Ford'
'Mistress Quickly'
'Moderator'
'Monkton Coombe'
'Mount Everest'
'Mrs J. Sangster'
'Mrs Leo Hunter'
'My Smokey'
'Newton Pink'
'Nightfall'
'Norman Thornley'
'Norton Fayre'
'Nursteed Charm'
'Oktoberdawn'
'Olga Keith'
'Orchid Pink'
'Orlando'
'Owen Tudor'
'Owen Wells'
'Pamela'
'Patricia Ballard'   RD
'Peace'
'Peaceful'
'Peerless'
'Penelope'
'Pensford'
'Percy Thrower'
'Perry's White'
'Petunia'
'Picture'
'Pink Buttons'
'Pink Cascade'
'Pink Lace'
'Pink Perfection'
'Pink Profusion'
'Pitcott'
'Plenty'
'Powder Puff'
'Pride of Colwall'

'Princess Marie Louise'
'Priory Blush'
'Priory Maid'
'Prosperity'
'Prunella'
'Purple Emperor'
'Queen Mary'
'Queen of Colwall'
'Rachel Ballard'
'Raspberries and Cream'
'Raspberry Ripple'
'Real Pleasure'
'Rebecca'
'Red Cloud'
'Red Greetings'
'Red King'
'Red Sunset'
'Rembrandt'
'Rev. V. Dale'
'Richness'
'Robert'
'Robin Adair'
'Rose Bouquet'
'Rosebud'
'Rosenhügel'
'Rosie Nutt'
'Royal Blue'
'Royal Ruby'   RD
'Royal Velvet'   RD
'Royal Violet'
'Royalty'
'Ruby Glow'
'Rufus'
'Sailing Light'
'Sailor Boy'
'Sandford's Purple'
'Sarah Ballard'
'Saturn'
'Schöne von Dietlikon'
'Schoolgirl'
'Sheena'
'Silver Mist'
'Sir Edward Elgar'
'Snow Drift'
'Sonata'
'Sophia'
'Sputnik'
'Steinebrück'
'Stella Lewis'
'St. Egwin'
'Stirling Silver'
'Strawberries and Cream'
'Sunset'
'Sussex Violet'
'Symbol'
'Tapestry'
'Taplow Spire'
'The Archbishop'
'The Bishop'
'The Cardinal'   RD

	'The Dean'	
	'The Rector'	
	'The Sexton'	
	'The Urchin'	
	'Thundercloud'	
	'Timberley'	
	'Timsbury'	
	'Tony'	
	'Tosca'	
	'Tovarich'	
	'True Blue'	
	'Twinkle'	
	'Vice Regal'	
	'Violet Lady'	
	'Walkden's Pink'	
	'Weisse Wunder'	
	'White Climax'	
	'White Cloud'	
	'White Heather'	
	'White Ladies'	RD
	'White Swan'	
	'White Wings'	
	'Wickwar Crimson'	
	'Winford'	
	'Winsome Winnie'	
	'Winston S. Churchill'	**DGP-RD**
	'Wonder of Colwall'	
N	**paniculatus** Lamarck 1783	PGP
	'Edwin Beckett'	
	pappei Harvey 1865 = **Felicia amoena**	
	petiolatus Harvey 1865 = **Felicia petiolata**	
	pilosus Willdenow 1803	
	var. **demotus** (*A. tradescantii* hort.)	PGP
	ptarmicoides (Nees) Torrey & A. Gray 1841	
	'Major'	
	pulchellus D. Eaton 1871 non Willdenow 1803 = **A. alpigenus**	
	pyrenaeus Desfontaines ex de Candolle 1805	
	'Lutetia' [Cayeux 1912]	
	radula Lessing 1831	
	rotundifolius Thunberg 1800 = **Felicia amelloides**	
	scandens Jacquin f. ex Sprengel 1826 = **A. carolinianus**	
N	**sedifolius** Linnaeus 1753 (*A. acris*)	PGP-**DGP**-**RD**
	'Nanus'	PGP-**DGP**-RD
	'Roseus'	
	spectabilis Aiton 1789	PGP-**DGP**
	subcaeruleus S. Moore 1901 = **A. tongolensis**	
	'Summer Greetings'	
	thomsonii C. B. Clarke 1876	PGP-DGP-RD
	'Nanus' hort. = **A. sedifolius 'Nanus'**	
	tibeticus Hooker f. 1881	RD
	tongolensis Franchet 1896 (*A. subcaeruleus*)	PGP
	'Berggarten' [P. Peltzer 1953]	PGP
	'Berggartenzwerg'	
	'Lavender Star'	
	'Leuchtenburg' ('Shining Mountain') [Pötschke]	
	'Napsbury' (*A. yunnanensis* 'Napsbury')	PGP-DGP-RD
	'Shining Mountain' = **A. tongolensis 'Leuchtenburg'**	
	'Sternschnuppe'	
	'Wartburgstern'	
	tradescantii Linnaeus 1753 non Torrey & A. Gray 1841	

tradescantii hort. non Linnaeus = **A. pilosus** var. **demotus**
turbinellus Lindley 1835   PGP
   'Roseus'
umbellatus Miller 1768   PGP
vimineus Lamarck 1783
   'Delight'
   'Lovely'
   'Ptarmicoides'
yunnanensis Franchet 1896   CA-DGP-RD
   'Napsbury' = **A. tongolensis 'Napsbury'**

ASTERISCUS Miller 1754   [*Asteraceae (Compositae)*]
   maritimus (Linnaeus) Lessing 1832

ASTILBE Buchanan-Hamilton ex D. Don 1825   [*Saxifragaceae*]
   x arendsii Arends 1908   **DGP**-RD
      'Amethyst'   [G. Arends 1920]   PGP
      'Anita Pfeifer'   [G. Arends 1930]
      'Bergkristall'   [G. Arends 1920]   PGP
      'Brautschleier'   [G. Arends 1929] ('Bridal Veil')   PGP
      'Bridal Veil' = **A. x arendsii 'Brautschleier'**
      'Cattleya'   [G. Arends 1953]   PGP
      'Ceres'   [G. Arends 1909]   PGP
      'Diamant'   [G. Arends 1920]
      'Else Schluck'   [G. Arends 1930]
      'Erica'   [G. Arends 1940]   PGP
L   **'Fanal'**   [G. Arends 1933]   PGP-**DGP**-RD
      'Feuer'   [G. Arends 1940] ('Fire')   PGP-RD
      'Fire' = **A. x arendsii 'Feuer'**
      'Gertrud Brix'   [G. Arends 1930]
      'Gloria'   [G. Arends 1913]
      'Glut'   [G. Arends 1952] ('Glow')   PGP
      'Glow' = **A. x arendsii 'Glut'**
      'Granat'   [G. Arends 1920]   DGP
      'Grete Püngel'   [G. Arends 1924]
      'Hyacinth' = **A. x arendsii 'Hyazinth'**
      'Hyazinth'   [G. Arends 1920] ('Hyacinth')   **DGP-RD**
      'Lilli Goos'   [G. Arends 1930]   PGP
      'Pink Pearl' = **A. x arendsii 'Rosa Perle'**
      'Rosa Perle'   [G. Arends 1910] ('Pink Pearl')
      'Spinell'   [G. Arends 1955]   PGP
L   **'Venus'**   [G. Arends 1910]
      'Weisse Gloria'   [G. Arends 1924] ('White Gloria')   PGP-RD
      'White Gloria' = **A. x arendsii 'Weisse Gloria'**
   astilboides (Maximowicz) Lemoine 1882
   chinensis (Maximowicz) Franchet & Savatier 1875   **DGP**
      var. **davidii** Franchet & Savatier 1875 (*A. davidii*)   PGP-DGP-RD
      var. **taquetii** (Leveille) Vilmorin (*A. taquetii*)   PGP
      var. **taquetii 'Purpurkerze'**
      var. **taquetii 'Purpurlanze'**
L   var. **taquetii 'Superba'**   [G. Arends 1923]

   A. CHINENSIS GROUP HYBRIDS

      'Finale'   [G. Arends 1952]
      'Intermezzo'   [G. Arends 1957]
L   **'Pumila'**   [G. Arends 1932]   PGP-CA-RD
      'Rosea' nom. dub.
      'Serenade'   [G. Arends 1954]   PGP
      'Spätsommer'   [Weinreich]

'Veronica Klose'   [H. Klose 1983]
congesta (H. Boissieu) Nakai 1922
x crispa (Arends) Bergmans 1924   CA-RD
    'Dagalet' = **Aruncus parvulus 'Dagalet'**
    'Liliput'   [G. Arends 1927]
    'Perkeo'   [G. Arends 1930]
    'Peter Pan'   RD
davidii (Franchet & Savatier) Henry 1902 = **A. chinensis** var. **davidii**
glaberrima Nakai 1922   RD
    'Saxatilis'   CA
    saxosa hort. = **A. 'Saxosa'**
grandis Stapf ex Wilson 1905   PGP
x hybrida Hort ex Ievinya & Lusinya 1975
    'America'   [B. Ruys]
    'Betsy Cuperus'   [B. Ruys 1917]   **PGP**
    'Bonanza'   [Marx]

L   **'Bressingham Beauty'**   [A. Bloom]   RD
    'Bressingham Giant'   [A. Bloom]
    'Carminea'   [E. Lemoine 1907]
    'Drayton Glory'
    'Etna'   [B. Ruys]
    'Gloria Purpurea'   [B. Ruys 1921]
    'Jo Ophurst'   [B. Ruys 1916]   PGP
    'Lady Digby'
    'Orestad'
    'Red Light' = **A. x hybrida 'Rotlicht'**
    'Robinson's Pink'
    'Rosenschleier'   [Spijker]
    'Rotlicht'   [E. Pagels] ('Red Light')
    'Salland'   [B. Ruys 1913]   PGP
    'Salmon Queen'
    'Spartan'
    'Snowdrift'
    'Tamarix'   [B. Ruys]
    'White Queen'
    'William Reeves'
japonica (Morren & Decaisne) A. Gray 1841

A. JAPONICA GROUP HYBRIDS

    'Bonn'   [G. Arends 1930]
    'Bremen'   [G. Arends 1929]
    'Cologne' = **A. 'Köln'**
L   **'Deutschland'**   [G. Arends 1920]   **DGP**-RD
    'Düsseldorf'   [G. Arends 1936]
    'Emden'   [G. Arends 1920]
    'Europa'   [G. Arends 1930]   PGP
    'Federsee'   [P. Theoboldt 1939]   RD
    'Irrlicht'   [P. Theoboldt 1939]
    'Koblenz'   [G. Arends 1938]   PGP
    'Köln'   [G. Arends 1930] ('Cologne')
    'Mainz'   [G. Arends 1952]
    'Möve'   [G. Arends 1920]
    'Montgomery'   [Kooy 1949]
    'Obergärtner Jürgans'   [H. Hesse 1954]
    'Red Sentinal'   [H. den Ouden 1947]   PGP-RD
    'Rheinland'   [G. Arends 1920]
    'Washington'
    'W E Gladstone'   [G. Arends]
rivularis Buchanan-Hamilton ex D. Don 1825   PGP
    'Grandiflora'

x rosea van Waveren & Kruyff 1902
    'Peach Blossom'   [van Waveren & Kruyff 1902]
    'Queen Alexandra'   [van Waveren & Kruyff 1902]
'Saxosa' (*A. glaberrima* 'Saxatilis' x *A. simplicifolia*)
simplicifolia Makino 1893   CA-RD

A. SIMPLICIFOLIA GROUP HYBRIDS

    'Alba'   [G. Arends 1923]
    'Aphrodite'   [E. Pagels 1958]
    'Atrorosea'   [G. Arends 1934]   PGP
L   **'Bronce Elegans'**   [G. Arends 1956]('Bronze Elegance')   PGP
    'Carnea'   [G. Arends 1923]
    'Dunkellachs'   [G. Arends 1940]   PGP
    'Inshriach Pink'   [J. Drake]
    'Peter Barrow'   [P. Barrow via W. E. Th. Ingwersen Ltd]
    'Praecox'   [G. Arends 1934]
    'Praecox Alba'   [G. Arends 1952]   PGP
    'Rosea'   [G. Arends 1923]
L   **'Sprite'**   PGP
    'Willy Buchanan'
taquetii (Leveille) Koidzumi 1936 = **A. chinensis** var. **taquetii**
thunbergii (Siebold & Zuccarini) Miquel 1867   PGP
    var. *congesta* H. Boissieu = **A. congesta**
    var. *taquetii* Leveille = **A. chinensis** var. **taquetii**

A. THUNBERGII GROUP HYBRIDS

    'Moerheimii'   [B. Ruys 1909]
    'Ostrich Plume' = **A. thunbergii** '**Straussenfeder**'
    'Professor Van der Wielen'   [B. Ruys 1917]   PGP
    'Straussenfeder'   [G. Arends 1952] ('Ostrich Plume')   **PGP**

ASTILBOIDES (Hemsley) Engler 1919   [*Saxifragaceae*]
L   **tabularis** (Hemsley) Engler 1919 (*Rodgersia tabularis*)   **PGP-DGP**-RD

ASTRAGALUS Linnaeus 1753   [*Fabiaceae (Leguminosae)*]
S   **angustifolius** Lamarck 1783   CA
SN‡ **glycyphyllos** Linnaeus 1753
S   **monspessulanus** Linnaeus 1753   CA

ASTRANTIA Linnaeus 1753   [*Apiaceae (Umbelliferae)*]
   carniolica Jacquin 1778   RD
   helleborifolia Salisbury 1877 = **A. maxima**
N‡L **major** Linnaeus 1753   PGP-**RD**
    'Alba'
    ssp. **involucrata** Koch   PGP
    ssp. **involucrata 'Barrister'**
    ssp. *involucrata* 'Margery Fish' = **A. major** ssp. **involucrata 'Shaggy'**
    ssp. **involucrata 'Shaggy'** ('Margery Fish')   PGP
    'Rosea'
    'Rosensymphonie'
    'Rubra'   PGP-RD
    'Sunningdale Variegated'   PGP
    'Variegata' = **A. major 'Sunningdale Vareiegated'**
   maxima Pallas 1793 (*A. helleborifolia*)   PGP-**DGP**-RD
    'Alba' nom. dub.

ASYNEUMA Grisebach & Schenk 1852   [*Campanulaceae*]
   linifolium (Boissier & Heldreich) Bornmueller 1921

ssp. **eximium** (Reichenbach f.) Damboldt 1970
pulvinatum P. H. Davis 1949   CA

ATHAMANTA Linnaeus 1753   [*Apiaceae (Umbelliferae)*]
    cretensis Linnaeus 1753
    haynaldii Borbas & Uechtritz 1877 = **A. turbith**
    matthioli Wulfen 1786 = **A. turbith**
    turbith (Linnaeus) Brotero 1804 (*A. haynaldii, A. matthioli*)   PGP

ATHYRIUM Roth 1799   [*Woodsiaceae*]
    alpestre (Hoppe) Rylands ex T. Moore 1860 = **A. distentifolium**
    crenatum (Sommerfield) Ruprecht 1844 = **Diplazium sibiricum**
N   **distentifolium** Tausch ex Opitz 1820 (*A. alpestre*)   EGF.1
        '**Kupferstiel**'
NL   **filix-femina** (Linnaeus) Roth 1799   EGF.1-PGP-RD
        '**Angustatum cristatum**'
        '**Angustatum cruciatum**'
        '**Bornholmiense**'
        '**Congestum cristatum**'
        '**Corymbiferum**'
        '**Crispum**'
        '**Crispum grandiceps**'
        '**Crispum grandiceps Kaye**'
        '**Cristatum**'
        '**Cristulatum**'
        '**Cruciatum grandiceps**'
        '**Fieldiae**'
        '**Frizelliae**'
        '**Frizelliae capitatum**'
        '**Frizelliae cristatum**'
        '**Glomeratum**'
        'Minor' = **A. filix-femina 'Minutissimum'**
        '**Minutissimum**' ('Minor')   PGP
        '**Multifidum**'
        '**Percristatum**'   PGP
        '**Plumosum**'   PGP-**RD**
        '**Plumosum cristatum**'
        '**Plumosum Druery**'
        '**Plumosum percristatum**'
        '**Plumosum superbum Druery**'
        '**Proteoides**'
        '**Rotstiel**'
        '**Setigerum cristatum**'
        '**Todeoides**'
        '**Vernoniae**'
        '**Vernoniae cristatum**'
        '**Victoriae**'   RD
    goeringianum hort. = **A. niponicum**
    iseanum Rosenstock 1913
    iseanum hort. non Rosenstock = **A. niponicum**
    niponicum (Mettenius) Hance 1873 (*A. goeringianum* hort.)   EGF.1
        'Metalicum' = **A. niponicum 'Pictum'**
        '**Pictum**' ('Metallicum')   PGP-**RD**
    palustre Serigawa
    thelypteroides (Michaux) Desvaux 1827
    vidalii (Franchet & Savatier) Nakai 1925   PGP

ATROPA Linnaeus 1753   [*Solanaceae*]
HN‡ **belladonna** Linnaeus 1753

AUBRIETA de Candolle 1821   [*Brassicaceae (Cruciferae)*]
  canescens (Boissier) Bornmueller
  x cultorum Bergmans 1924 (*A. deltoidea* hort. non (Linnaeus) de Candolle 1821)
                                                           DGP-**RD**

      'Alida Vahli'
      'April Joy'
      'Argentea'
      'Argenteo-variegata' ('Silver Queen')
      'Asthead Purple'
      'Astolat'
      'Astolat Double'
      'Aurea'   RD
      'Aureo-variegata' ('Golden King')
      'Barker's Double'   **DGP**-RD
      'Barker's Violet'
      'Belisha Beacon'
      'Blaumeise'
      'Blue Beauty'
      'Blue Cascade'
      'Blue Emperor'   [Gebr. Verboom 1936]
      'Blue King'
      'Bob Sanders'
      'Bonfire'
      'Bordeaux'   [Baltin]
      'Bougainvillea'
      'Bressingham Pink'   [A. Bloom 1953]   DGP
      'Bressingham Red'   [A. Bloom]
      'Bridesmaid'
      'Bright Eyes'
      'Britannia'
      'Burgundy'
      'Carnival' = **A. 'Hartswood Purple'**
      Cascade Hybrids
      'Church Knowle'
      'Clio'
      'Coronation Purple'
      'Crimson Bedder'
      'Crimson Queen'
      'Daybreak'
      'Dream'
L   'Dr. Mules'   [Clibrans 1895]   DGP-RD
      'Dr. Mules Variegated'
      'Drayton'
      'Elsa Lancaster'
      Eversley Hybrids
      'Feurkönigen'
      'Feuervogel'   [Kayser & Siebert]
      'Frühlingszauber'
      'Gloriosa'
      'Godstone'   RD
      'Golden King' = **A. x cultorum 'Aureo-variegata'**
      'Graeca Superba'
      'Greencourt Purple'
      'Gurgedyke'   RD
      'Hamburger Stadtpark'
      'Hartswood Purple'   [P. Barrow] ('Carnival')
      'Hendersonii'
      'Henslow Purple'
      'Hubert'
      'Ina den Ouden'

'Joan Allen'
'Joy'
'J. S. Barker'
'Kelmscott Claret'
'Kelmscott Wonder'
'Lavender'
'Lavender Gem'
'Laurence Medholme'
'Leichtlinii'
'Lilac Cascade'
'Little Gem'
'Lloyd Edwards' = **A. x cultorum 'Mrs Lloyd Edwards'**
'Lockvogel'   [Kayser & Siebert]
'Lodge Grave'
'Macrostyla'
'Magician'   DGP-RD
'Mars'
'Mary Poppins'
'Maureen Meadholme'
'Maurice Prichard'
'Meadholme Mine'
'Meadholme Violet'
'Michael Meadholme'
'Moerheim'
'Mrs Lloyd Edwards'
'Mrs Rodewald'
'Munkholm'
'Nana Variegata' (A. 'Variegata Nana')
'Neuling'   [Rohrmoser 1936]
'Novalis Blue'   [E. Benary]
'Oakington Lavender'
'Pennine Jewel'
'Pennine Pride'
'Pink Gem'
'Prichard's A 1'   [Prichard]
'Purple Cascade'
'Purple Robe'
'Purple Splendour'
'Red Carnival'
L   'Red Carpet'   [c1973]
'Red Cascade'
'Red Dyke'
'Riverslea'   [Prichard]   RD
'Rodhaette'
'Rosanna Miles'
'Rosea'
'Rosea Splendens'
'Rose Cascade'
'Rosenteppich'
'Rotkäppchen'   [Baltin 1956]
'Schloss Eckberg'   [Matzner 1930]
'Schofield's Double'
'Schofield's Purple'
'Silberrand'   [E. Pagels]
'Silver Queen' = **A. 'Argenteo-variegata'**
L   'Studland'
'Triumphant'
'Valder'
'Variegata'   RD
variegata 'Golden King' = **A. x cultorum 'Aureo-variegata'**

variegata 'Nana' = **A. x cultorum 'Nana Variegata'**
variegata 'Silver Queen' = **A. x cultorum 'Argenteo-variegata'**
'Vesuv'   [G. Arends] ('Vesuvius')
'Vindictive'
'Wanda'
'Whitewell Gem'
'Wisley'
'Wolfsburg'   [Baltin]
N   **deltoidea** (Linnaeus) de Candolle 1821
    'Tauricola'   [Einführung Leichtlin c1889]   RD
deltoidea hort. = **A. x cultorum**

AURINIA Desvaux 1813   [*Brassicaceae (Cruciferae)*]
saxatilis (Linnaeus) Desvaux 1813 = **Alyssum saxatile**

AVENA Linnaeus 1753   [*Poaceae (Gramineae)*]
candida hort. = **Helictotrichon sempervirens**

AZOLLA Lamarck 1783   [*Azollaceae*]
caroliniana Willdenow 1810 = **A. filiculoides**
filiculoides Lamarck 1783 (*A. caroliniana*)   EGF.1

AZORELLA Lamarck 1783   [*Apiaceae (Umbelliferae)*]
trifurcata (Gaertner) Persoon 1805 (*Bolax glebaria*)   CA
    'Nana'
umbellata Grisebach 1854

AZORINA Feer 1890   [*Campanulaceae*]
S   **vidalii** (H. C.Watson) Feer 1890 (*Campanula vidalli*)

BABIANA Ker-Gawler 1802   [*Iridaceae*]
ambigua (Roemer & Schultes) Lewis 1939
rubrocyanea (Jacquin) Ker-Gawler 1805   EGF.1-CA
stricta (Aiton) Ker-Gawler 1803   EGF.1-CA
    'Blue Beauty'   ®
    'Lady Carey'   ®
    'Purple Sensation'   ®   [van Tubergen 1970]
    'White King'   ®
    'Zwanenburg Glory'   ®   [van Tubergen]

BALDELLIA Parlatore 1854   [*Alismataceae*]
N‡   **ranunculoides** (Linnaeus) Parlatore 1854 (*Alisma ranunculoides*)   EGF.1

BALLOTA Linnaeus 1753   [*Lamiaceae (Labiatae)*]
S   **acetabulosa** (Linnaeus) Bentham 1834   RD
S   **frutescens** (Linnaeus) J. Woods 1880
HN‡   **nigra** Linnaeus 1753
    'Variegata'
pseudodictamnus (Linnaeus) Bentham 1834   PGP-**DGP**-RD

BALSAMITA Miller 1754   [*Asteraceae (Compositae)*]
major Desfontaines 1792 = **Tanacetum balsamita**
vulgaris Willdenow 1803 = **Tanacetum balsamita**

BAPTISIA Ventenat 1806   [*Fabiaceae (Leguminosae)*]
L   **australis** (Linnaeus) R. Brown 1811   PGP-**DGP**-RD
    'Exaltata'
exaltata Sweet 1829 = **B. australis 'Exaltata'**
tinctoria (Linnaeus) R. Brown 1811   PGP

BARBAREA R. Brown 1812   [*Brassicaceae (Cruciferae)*]
N‡   **vulgaris** R. Brown 1812
      'Variegata'

BARLIA Parlatore 1858   [*Orchidaceae*]
    robertiana(Loiseleur) W. Greuter 1967 (*Himantoglossum longibracteatum*) EGF.2

BEAUVERDIA Herter 1943 = **IPHEION** Rafinesque 1837

BEGONIA Linnaeus 1753   [*Begoniaceae*]
    bertinii Legros. 1894
    evansiana Andrews 1810 = **B. grandis**
    grandis Dryander 1791 (*B. evansiana*)   PGP-SB
        'Alba'   PGP
        'Maria'
        'Simsii'
    sutherlandii Hooker f. 1868   PGP

BELAMCANDA Adanson 1763   [*Iridaceae*]
    chinensis (Linnaeus) de Candolle 1805   EGF.1-PGP

BELLEVALIA Lapeyrouse 1808   [*Hyacinthaceae (Liliaceae)*]
    atroviolacea Regel 1884   EGF.1-**BB**-SB
    caucasica Grisebach 1844 = **Muscari caucasicum**
    dubia (Gussone) Reichenbach 1830   EGF.1-**BB**
    forniculata (Fomin) Deloney 1922-3   SB
    paradoxa (Fischer & C. A. Meyer) Boissier 1882 (*Muscari paradoxa*)   SD-RD
    pycnantha (C. Koch) Losina-Losinskaya 1935   EGF.1-**BB**-SB
    romana (Linnaeus) Reichenbach 1830 (*Hyacinthus romanus*)   EGF.1-**BB**
    sarmatica (Pallas ex Georgi) Woronow 1927   **BB**
    trifoliata (Tenore) Kunth 1843   **BB**

BELLIS Linnaeus 1753   [*Asteraceae (Compositae)*]
    caerulescens hort., non Cosson ex Ball = **B. rotundifolia 'Caerulescens'**
N‡   **perennis** Linnaeus 1753   DGP-**RD**
        'Alba Plena'
        'Alice'
        'Brilliant'
        'China Pink'
        'Dresden China'   RD
        'Hen and Chickens' = **B. perennis 'Prolifera'**
        'Miss Mason'
        'Monstrosa'   DGP-**RD**
        'Parkinson's White'
        'Pomponette'   **DGP**-RD
        'Prolifera'
        'Purpurmantel'
        'Robert'
        'Rob Roy'
        'Staffordshire Pink'
    rotundifolia (Desfontaines) Boissier & Reuter 1852
        'Caerulescens' (*B. caerulescens* hort.)
    sylvestris Cyrillo 1792

BELLIUM Linnaeus 1771   [*Asteraceae (Compositae)*]
    bellidioides Linnaeus 1771
    crassifolium Moris 1827
    minutum (Linnaeus) Linnaeus 1767   CA

BERGENIA Moench 1794   *[Saxifragaceae]*
   acanthifolia hort. = **B. x spathulata**
   ciliata (Haworth) Sternberg 1831   PGP
      f. **ligulata** (Wallich) Yeo 1966 (*B. ligulata*)   PGP
      f. **ligulata** 'Superba'
   cordifolia (Haworth) Sternberg 1831   PGP-**RD**
     'Ostenholz'
L   'Purpurea'   PGP-**RD**
     'Robusta'
   crassifolia (Linnaeus) Fritsch 1889   PGP-**RD**
     'Autumn Red'
     'Orbicularis' = **B. x schmidtii**
     var. **pacifica** (Komarov) Nekrasova 1917
     'Purpurea'
   delavayi (Franchet) Engler 1891 = **B. purpurascens** var. **delavayi**
   hissarica Boriss 1954
   ligulata (Wallich) Engler 1868 = **B. ciliata** f. **ligulata**
   x media (Haworth) Engler 1891 (*B. cordifolia* x *B. crassifolia*)
   ornata Stein ex Guillaumin 1928 = **B. x schmidtii**
   pacifica Komarov 1911 = **B. crassifolia** var. **pacifica**
   purpurascens (Hooker f. & Thomson) Engler 1868   DGP-**RD**
     var. **delavayi** (Franchet) Engler & Irmsch 1912 (*B. delavayi*)   DGP
   x schmidtii (Regel) Silva-Tarouca 1910 (*B. ciliata* x *B. crassifolia*)
     'Ernst Schmidt'   PGP
   x smithii Engler ex Engler & Irmsch 1919 (*B. cordifolia* x *B. purpurascens*) PGP
   x spathulata Nagels ex Guillaumin 1930 (*B. ciliata* x *B. stracheyi*)
   stracheyi (Hooker f. & Thomson) Engler 1868   PGP-**RD**
     'Afghanica'
     'Alba'
     'Belvedere'

HYBRID CULTIVARS

     'Abendglocken'   [Arends 1971] (B. 'Evening Bells')   PGP
L   **'Abendglut'**   [Arends 1950] (B. 'Evening Glow')   RD
     'Admiral'   [R. Eskuche]
     'Baby Doll'   [zur Linden]
     'Bach'   [E. Smith c1972]
L   **'Ballawley'**   [Ballawley Park pre-1950] (B. 'Delbees')   PGP-**RD**
     'Ballawley Guardsman'
     Ballawley Hybrids
     'Beethoven'   [E. Smith c1972]
     'Bizet'   [J. C. Archibald c1976]
     'Borodin'   [J. C. Archibald c1980]
     'Brahms'   [E. Smith c1972]
     'Bressingham Bountiful'   [Pugsley via A. Bloom 1972]   PGP
     'Bressingham Salmon'   [A. Bloom]
     'Bressingham White'   [A. Bloom]
     'Britten'   [J. C. Archibald c1977]
     'Dawn' = **B. 'Morgenröte'**
     'Delbees' = **B. 'Ballawley'**
     'Distinction'   [T. Smith 1889]   PGP
     'Ernst Schmidt' = **B. x schmidtii 'Ernst Schmidt'**
     'Evening Bells' = **B. 'Abendglocken'**
     'Evening Glow' = **B. 'Abendglut'**
     'Glockenturm'   [R. Eskuche] (B. 'Bell Tower')
     'Illusion'   [H. Klose 1983]
     'Lambrook' = **B. 'Margery Fish'**
     'Margery Fish'   [Pugsley] ('Lambrook')   PGP
     'Milesii'

'Morgenröte'   [G. Arends 1950] (B. 'Dawn')   PGP
'Oeschberg'
'Opal'
'Perfect'
'Pinneberg'   [W. Kikillus]
'Profusion'   [T. Smith c1880]   PGP
'Progress'   [T. Smith 1889]
'Pugsley's Pink'   [Pugsley]
'Pugsley's Purple'   [Pugsley]   PGP
'Purpurglocken'   [G. Arends 1971] (B. 'Purple Bells')   PGP
'Purpurkönig' (B. 'Purple King')
'Rath Blau'
'Rosea'
'Rosette'   [VEB Bornim]
'Rosi Klose'   [H. Klose 1982]
'Rotblum'
'Schneeglocke'   [H. Klose 1983]
'Schneekissen'   [K. Foerster]
'Schneekönigin'   [K. Foerster]
L   **'Silberlicht'**   [G. Arends 1950] (B. 'Silver Light')   PGP-**RD**
   'Silver Light' = **B. 'Silberlicht'**
   Snowblush Hybrids   [The Plantsmen c1975]
L   **'Sunningdale'**   [Sunningdale Nurseries 1964]   PGP
'Sunshade'   [via Barr & Sons 1902]
'Sunshine'
'Traum'   [H. Klose 1983]
'Vorfrühling'   [H. Klose 1977]
'Walter Kienli'
'White Dwarf'
Winter Fire Hybrids   [The Plantsmen c1975]
'Wintermärchen'

BESCHORNERIA Kunth 1850   *[Agavaceae]*
   yuccoides Hooker 1860   EGF.1-**PGP-DGP**

BETONICA Linnaeus 1753   *[Lamiaceae (Labiatae)]*
   grandiflora Willdenow 1800 = **Stachys macrantha**
   nivea Stevens 1812 = **Stachys discolor**
   officinalis Linnaeus 1753 = **Stachys officinalis**

BIARUM Schott 1832   *[Araceae]*
   bovei Blume 1836   SB
   carduchorum (Schott) Engler 1879   SB
   davisii Turrill 1939   **BB-SB**
   eximium (Schott & Kotschy) Engler 1879   EGF.2-SB
   kotschyi (Schott) B. Mathew & H. Riedl 1980
   tenuifolium (Linnaeus) Schott 1832   EGF.2-**BB**-SB
      var. **zeleborii** (Schott) Engler 1879

BIDENS Linnaeus 1753   *[Asteraceae (Compositae)]*
   atrosanguinea (Hooker) Ortgies 1861 = **Cosmos atrosanguineus**
   dahlioides Watson 1891 = **Cosmos diversifolius**
   ferulaefolia (Jacquin) de Candolle 1836
N‡L   **tripartita** Linnaeus 1753

BILLBERGIA Thunberg 1821   *[Bromeliaceae]*
   nutans Wendland f. 1869   EGF.2-**DGP-RD**

BISTORTA Scopoli 1754   *[Polygonaceae]*
   affinis (D. Don) Greene 1904 = **Persicaria affinis**

amplexicaulis (D. Don) Greene 1904 = **Persicaria amplexicaulis**
emodi (Meissner) Hara 1966 = **Persicaria emodi**
major S. F. Gray = **Persicaria bistorta**
macrophylla (D. Don) Sojak 1974 = **Persicaria macrophylla**
milletii Leveille 1913 = **Persicaria milletii**
tenuicaulis (Bisset & Moore) Nakai 1922 = **Persicaria tenuicaulis**
vacciniifolia (Wallich ex Meissner) Green 1904 = **Persicaria vaccinifolia**
vivipara (Linnaeus) S. F. Gray 1821 = **Persicaria vivipara**

BLECHNUM Linnaeus 1753   [*Blechnaceae*]
    alpinum (R. Brown) Mettenius 1856 = **B. penna-marina** ssp. **alpinum**
N   **chilense** (Kaulfuss) Mettenius 1856   PGP
    magellanicum (Desvaux) Mettenius 1856 (*B. tabulare* hort.)   EGF.1
N   **penna-marina** (Poiret) Kuhn 1868   EGF.1-PGP
      ssp. **alpinum** R. Brown (B. alpinum, Lomaria alpina)
      'Cristata'
NL   **spicant** (Linnaeus) Roth 1794   EGF.1-PGP
      'Caespitosa'
    tabulare hort. non (Thunberg) Kuhn = **B. magellanicum**

BLETILLA Reichenbach f. 1851   [*Orchidaceae*]
  striata (Thunberg) Reichenbach f. 1851   EGF.2-PGP-**DGP-RD**
    'Alba'
    'Albo-striata'
    'Marginata'

BOCCONIA Linnaeus 1753   [*Papaveraceae*]
  cordata Willdenow 1799 = **Macleaya cordata**

BOENNINGHAUSENIA Reichenbach ex Meissner 1828   [*Rutaceae*]
S   **albiflora** (Hooker) Reichenbach ex Meissner 1826

BOLAX Commerson ex Jussieu 1789   [*Apiaceae (Umbelliferae)*]
  glebaria Commerson ex Lamarck 1789 = **Azorella trifurcata**

BOLTONIA L'Heritier 1789   [*Asteraceae (Compositae)*]
  asteroides (Linnaeus) L'Heritier 1789   PGP
    var. **latisquama** (A. Gray) Cronquist 1947   PGP

BONGARDIA C. A. Meyer 1831   [*Berberidaceae*]
  chrysogonum (Linnaeus) Spach 1839   **BB-SB**

BORAGO Linnaeus 1753   [*Boraginaceae*]
  laxiflora (de Candolle) Fischer 1808 = **B. pygmaea**
AHN   **officinalis** Linnaeus 1753
  pygmaea (de Candolle) Chater & W. Greuter 1972 (*B. laxiflora*)   PGP

BORONIA Smith 1798   [*Rutaceae*]
  megastigma Nees ex Bartling 1845

BOTTIONEA Colla 1834   [*Anthericaceae (Liliaceae)*]
  plumosa (Ruiz & Pavon) hort. = **Trichopetalum plumosum**

BOUSSINGAULTIA Humboldt, Bonpland & Kunth 1825   [*Basellaceae*]
  baselloides Humboldt, Bonpland & Kunth 1825

BOUTELOUA Lagasca 1805 nom. cons.   [*Poaceae (Gramineae)*]
  curtipendula (Michaux) Torrey 1848 (*B. racemosa*)   EGF.2
  gracilis (Humbolt, Bonpland & Kunth) Lagasca ex Steudel 1840 = **Chondrosum**
                               gracile

oligostachya (Nuttall) Torrey ex A. Gray 1865 = **Chondrosum gracile**
racemosa Lagasca 1805 = **B. curtipendula**

BOUVARDIA Salisbury 1805   [*Rubiaceae*]
    glaberrima Englemann 1848
    ternifolia Schlecht 1853

BOYKINIA Nuttall 1834 non. cons.   [*Saxifragaceae*]
    aconitifolia Nuttall 1834   PGP
    jamesii (Torrey) Engler 1890 = **Telesonix jamesii**
    tellimoides (Torrey) Engler 1919 (*Peltoboykinia tellimoides*)   PGP

BRACHYCOME Cassini 1825   [*Asteraceae (Compositae)*]
    microcarpa F. Mueller 1858
    nivalis F. Mueller 1855
        'Alpina'
    rigidula (de Candolle) G. L. Davis 1948
    scapiformis de Candolle 1836

BRIGGSIA Craib 1920   [*Gesneriaceae*]
    aurantiaca B. L. Burtt 1955
    chienii Chun 1946
    musicola (Diels) Craib 1920   CA

BRIMEURA Salisbury 1866   [*Hyacinthaceae (Liliaceae)*]
    amethystina (Linnaeus) Chouard 1930 (*Hyacinthus amethystinus*)
                                     CA-**BB**-SB-**DGP**-RD
        'Alba' ® [G. A. Arnott 1887]   CA-RD

BRIZA Linnaeus 1753   [*Poaceae (Gramineae)*]
N‡L **media** Linnaeus 1753   EGF.2-PGP-RD
    subaristata Lamarck 1791

BRODIAEA Smith 1811   [*Alliaceae (Liliaceae)*]
    laxa (Bentham) S. Watson 1879 = **Triteleia laxa**
    terrestris (Britton) Kellogg 1895   EGF.1-SB
    tubergenii hort. = **Triteleia x tubergenii**

BROMUS Linnaeus 1753   [*Poaceae (Gramineae)*]
N‡ **ramosus** Hudson 1762 non Linnaeus 1767

BRUNNERA Steven 1851   [*Boraginaceae*]
L **macrophylla** (Adanson) I. M. Johnston 1924 (*Anchusa myosotidiflora*)   PGP-**DGP**
        'Blaukuppel'
        'Dawson's White' [D.Dawson]
        'Eric's Cream' = **B. macrophylla 'Hadspen Cream'**
        'Hadspen Cream' ('Eric's Cream') [E. Smith]   PGP
        'Langtrees' [Dr. Rogerson]   PGP
L   **'Variegata'**   PGP

X BRUNSDONNA van Tubergen ex Worsley 1905 = **X AMARYGIA**

BRUNSVIGIA Heister 1755   [*Amaryllidaceae*]
    josephinae (Redoute) Ker-Gawler 1817

BRYONIA Linnaeus 1753   [*Cucurbitaceae*]
C **cretica** Linnaeus 1753
CHN‡   ssp. **dioica** (Jacquin) Tutin 1968

BUGLOSSOIDES Moench 1794   [*Boraginaceae*]
    purpureocaerulea (Linnaeus) I. M. Johnston 1953 = **Lithospermum purpureocaeruleum**

BULBINE Wolf 1776   *[Asphodelaceae (Liliaceae)]*
   bulbosa (Brown) Haworth 1821   EGF.1-PGP
   caulescens Linnaeus ex Steudel 1821   EGF.1

BULBINELLA Kunth 1843   *[Asphodelaceae (Liliaceae)]*
   hookeri (Colenso ex Hooker) Cheeseman 1906   EGF.1-PGP

BULBOCODIUM Linnaeus 1753   *[Colchicaceae (Liliaceae)]*
   vernum Linnaeus 1753 (*Colchicum vernum*)   EGF.1-CA-**BB**-SB

BUPHTHALMUM Linnaeus 1753   *[Asteraceae (Compositae)]*
   salicifolium Linnaeus 1753 (*Inula* 'Golden Beauty')   PGP-**DGP**
   speciosissimum Linnaeus 1753 = **Telekia speciosissima**
   speciosum Schreber = **Telekia speciosa**

BUPLEURUM Linnaeus 1753   *[Apiaceae (Umbelliferae)]*
   angulosum Linnaeus 1753
   ranunculoides Linnaeus 1753

BUTOMUS Linnaeus 1753   *[Butomaceae]*
N‡L   **umbellatus** Linnaeus 1753   EGF.1-**DGP**

CALAMAGROSTIS Adanson 1763   *[Poaceae (Gramineae)]*
   x acutiflora (Schrader) de Candolle 1815 (*C. arundinacea* x *C. epigejos*)   PGP
     'Karl Foerster'   [K. Foerster 1959]   PGP
   emodensis Grisebach 1868
   lasiagrostis hort. = **Stipa calamagrostis**
   varia (Schrader) Host 1809

CALAMINTHA Miller 1754   *[Lamiaceae (Labiatae)]*
   alpina (Linnaeus) Lamarck 1779 = **Acinos alpinus**
   cretica (Linnaeus) Lamarck 1778
HN   **grandiflora** (Linnaeus) Moench 1794 (*Satureja grandiflora*)   PGP
     'Variegata'
HN‡   **nepeta** (Linnaeus) Savi 1798 (*C. nepetoides*)   **DGP**
   nepetoides Jordan 1846 = **C. nepeta**

CALANDRINIA Humboldt, Bonpland & Kunth 1823 nom. cons.   *[Portulacaceae]*
   caespitosa Gillies ex Arnott 1831
   gilliesii Hooker & Arnott 1833 (*C. umbellata*)   **DGP**-RD
   grandiflora Lindley 1828
   umbellata Hooker & Arnott 1833 = **C. gilliesii**

CALANTHE R. Brown 1821   *[Orchidaceae]*
   aristulifera Reichenbach f. 1878
   bicolor Lindley 1838 = **C. discolor** var. **bicolor**
   discolor Lindley 1838   EGF.2-PGP
      var. **bicolor** (Lindley) Makino (*C. bicolor*)
      f. *sieboldii* (Decaisne ex Regel) Ohwi = **C. striata**
   nipponica Makino
   reflexa Maximowicz 1873   EGF.2
   sieboldii Decaisne ex Regel 1868 = **C. striata**
   striata (Swartz) R. Brown 1821 (*C. sieboldii*)   EGF.2-PGP
   tricarinata Lindley 1833   EGF.2-PGP

CALCEOLARIA Linnaeus 1771   *[Scrophulariaceae]*
   acutifolia Witasek 1906   CA
   arachnoidea Graham 1828   CA
   biflora Ruiz & Pavon 1798   CA-RD
   *bigibbulosa

'Camden Hero'
chelidonioides Humboldt, Bonpland & Kunth 1818
  'Humilis'
corymbosa Ruiz & Pavon 1798
crenatiflora Cavanilles 1799
darwinii Bentham   CA-DGP-RD
falklandica (S. Moore) Kränzlin 1907
fothergillii Solander in Aiton 1789   CA
integrifolia Murr   DGP-RD
  'Angustifolia' (Ruiz & Pavon) hort.   DGP
  'John Innes' (*C. biflora* x *C. polyrrhiza*)   RD
  'Kentish Hero' (*C. integrifolia* x ?)
A   **mexicana** Bentham 1840   RD
polyrrhiza Cavanilles 1799   CA-RD
tenella Poeppig & Endlicher 1845   CA-RD
uniflora Ruiz & Pavon 1798
  'Walter Shrimpton' (*C. darwinii* x *C. fothergillii*)

CALDESIA Parlatore 1858   [*Alismataceae*]
  parnassifolia (Linnaeus) Parlatore 1858

CALENDULA Linnaeus 1753   [*Asteraceae (Compositae)*]
AN   **officinalis** Linnaeus 1753   DGP-RD
  'Hen and Chickens' = **C. officinalis 'Prolifera'**
  'Prolifera' ('Hen and Chickens')

CALLA Linnaeus 1753   [*Araceae*]
  aethiopica Linnaeus 1753 = **Zantedeschia aethiopica**
L   **palustris** Linnaeus 1753   EGF.2

CALLIANTHEMUM C. A.Meyer 1830   [*Ranunculaceae*]
  anemonoides Endlicher ex Heynhold 1841 = **C. rutifolium**
coriandrifolium Reichenbach 1830
kernerianum Freyn ex Kerner 1888   CA
rutifolium C. A. Meyer 1830 (*C. anemonoides*)   CA

CALLIRHOE Nuttall 1821   [*Malvaceae*]
  involucrata A. Gray 1849

CALLITRICHE Linnaeus 1753   [*Callitrichaceae*]
  autumnalis Linnaeus non Michaux, non Pollich = **C. hermaphroditica**
N‡   **hermaphroditica** Linnaeus 1753 (*C. autumnalis* Linnaeus)
N‡L   **palustris** Linnaeus 1753 (*C. verna*)
N‡   **stagnalis** Scopoli
  verna Linnaeus 1755 = **C. palustris**
  vernalis Kuetz

CALOCEPHALUS R. Brown 1817   [*Asteraceae (Compositae)*]
S   *brownii* (Cassini) F. Mueller 1859 = **Leucophtya brownii**

CALOCHORTUS Pursh 1814   [*Liliaceae*]
albus Douglas ex Bentham 1834   EGF.1-CA-**BB**-SB
amabilis Purdy 1901   EGF.1-CA-**BB**-SB
amoenus Greene 1890   EGF.1-CA-**BB**-SB
coeruleus (Kellogg) S. Watson 1879   EGF.1-CA-**BB**-SB
*****cratencola**
gunnisonii S. Watson 1871   EGF.1-SB
luteus Douglas ex Lindley 1833   EGF.1-**BB**-SB
lyallii Baker 1974
macrocarpus Douglas 1828   EGF.1-**SB**

monophyllus (Lindley) Lemaire 1917   EGF.1-CA-**BB**-SB
nuttallii Torrey & A. Gray 1854   **BB**-SB
palmeri S. Watson 1879
pulchellus Douglas ex Bentham 1834   EGF.1-CA-**BB**-SB
uniflorus Hooker & Arnott 1841   EGF.1-CA-SB-**DGP**
venustus Douglas ex Bentham 1834   EGF.1-**BB**-SB
*****volubile**
weedii Wood 1868   EGF.1-SB

CALOSCORDUM Herbert 1844   [*Alliaceae (Liliaceae)*]
    neriniflorum Herbert 1844 (*Nothoscordum neriniflorum*)   EGF.1-**BB**-SB

CALTHA Linnaeus1753   [*Ranunculaceae*]
    asarifolia de Candolle 1818 = **C. palustris** ssp. **asarifolia**
    biflora de Candolle 1818 = **C. leptosepala** ssp. **howellii**
    chelidonii Greene 1899 (*C. uniflora*)
    introloba F.Mueller 1855
    leptosepala de Candolle 1818 (*C. rotundifolia*)   PGP-RD
      ssp. **howellii** (Huth) Smit 1973 (*C. biflora*)
    minor Miller 1768 = **C. palustris** var. **minor**
HN‡L **palustris** Linnaeus 1753   PGP-DGP
      ssp. **asarifolia** (de Candolle) Hulten 1944 (*C. asarifolia*)
      var. **alba** (Cambessedes) Hooker f. & Thomson 1855   PGP-DGP-**RD**
L   **'Plena'** ('Multiplex') [pre-1819]   PGP-**DGP**-**RD**
      'Marilyn' [S. J. Grubb 1986]
N   var. **minor** (Miller) de Candolle 1818 (*C. minor*)   PGP
      'Monstrosa Plena' [pre-1819]
      'Multiplex' = **C. palustris 'Plena'**
      Newlake Hybrids [S. J. Grubb]
      var. **polypetala** (Hochstetter ex Laurent) Huth 1892 (*C. polypetala*)   PGP-RD
      var. **polypetala 'Honeydew'** [S. J. Grubb 1986]
N   var.**radicans** (Forster f.) Beck 1886 (*C. radicans*)
      'Susan' [S. J.Grubb 1986]
      'Tyermanii' [c1880]   PGP
    polypetala Hochstetter ex Laurent 1845 = **C. palustris** var. **polypetala**
    radicans Forster f. 1807 = **C. palustris** var. **radicans**
    rotundifolia Greene 1899 = **C. leptosepala**
    scaposa Hooker f. & Thomson 1855
    uniflora Rydberg 1900 = **C. chelidonii**

CALYPSO Salisbury 1806   [*Orchidaceae*]
    bulbosa (Linnaeus) Oakes 1842   EGF.2

CALYPTRIDIUM Nuttall ex Torrey & A. Gray 1838   [*Portulacaceae*]
    umbellatum (Torrey) Greene 1886 (*Spraguea umbellata*)

CALYSTEGIA R. Brown 1810   [*Convolvulaceae*]
C **silvatica** (Kitaibel) Grisebach 1844
C **tuguriorum** (Forster f.) R. Brown ex Hooker f. 1854

CAMASSIA Lindley 1832   [*Hyacinthaceae (Liliaceae)*]
    cusickii S. Watson 1887   EGF.1PGP-**DGP**-RD
     'Zwanenburg' ®   [van Tubergen 1969]
    esculenta Lindley 1832 = **C. quamash**
    leichtlinii (Baker) S. Watson 1885   EGF.1-RD
     'Alba'
     'Caerulea' ®   [Canon Ellacombe]   **RD**
     'Drocken's Blue'
     'Plena'   PGP
     'Semi-plena' ®   [van Tubergen]
     var. **suksdorfii** (Greenman) C. L. Hitchcock 1969   PGP

var. **suksdorfii** 'Alba'
quamash (Pursh) E. Greene 1894 (*C. esculenta*)   EGF.1-PGP-**DGP**-RD
   'Orion' ® [van Meeuwen pre-1913]   PGP
   'San Juan'
scilloides (Rafinesque) Cory 1936   EGF.1-RD

CAMPANULA Linnaeus 1753   [*Campanulaceae*]
  'Abundance' (*C. carpatica* x *C. rotundifolia*)
  alaskana Leichtlin ex Beddome 1907 = **C. rotundifolia** var. **alaskana**
NL **alliariifolia** Wildenow 1798   PGP-**RD**
   'Ivory Bells' = **C. alliariifolia**
  allionii Villars 1786 = **C. alpestris**
  alpestris Allioni 1773 (*C. allionii*)   CA-**RD**
   'Alba'   CA
   'Grandiflora'   CA
   'Rosea'
  alpina Jacquin 1762   CA
  arvatica Lagasca 1805   CA-RD
   'Alba'   CA-**RD**
  'Avalon' (*C. carpatica* var. *turbinata* x *C. raineri*)
  aucheri A. de Candolle 1839   CA-**RD**
  barbata Linnaeus 1759   CA-**RD**
   'Alba'   CA
  bellidifolia Adam 1805
  betulifolia C. Koch 1850 (*C. finitima*)   CA
  'Birch Hybrid' (*C. portenschlagiana* x *C. poscharskyana*)   [Ingwersen]
  bononiensis Linnaeus 1753   PGP
  bornmuelleri Nabelek 1926
  'Burghaltii' (*C. latifolia* x *C. punctata* ?)   PGP-**DGP**-RD
  calaminthifolia Grisebach 1843 = **C. orphanidea**
  carnica Schiede ex Mertens & Koch 1826 (*C. linifolia*)
  carpatica Jacquin 1770   PGP-**DGP**-RD
   'Alba'
   'Alba Nana' = **C. carpatica** var. **turbinata 'Alba'**
   'Bees' Variety'
   'Blaue Clips' ('Blue Clips')   [Benary]
   'Blaumeise' ('Blue Mouse')   [K. Foerster 1956]
   'Blue Clips' = **C. carpatica 'Blaue Clips'**
   'Blue Moonlight'   [A. Bloom]   RD
   'Blue Mouse' = **C. carpatica 'Blaumeise'**
   'Bressingham White'   [A. Bloom]   RD
   'Chewton Joy'   [Prichard]   **RD**
   'Coerulea'
   'Convexity'
   'Ditton Blue'
   'Gawen'
   'Hannah' = **C. carpatica** var. **turbinata 'Hannah'**
   'Harvest Moon'
   'Isabel'   [Prichard]
   'Jewel' = **C. carpatica** var. **turbinata 'Jewel'**
   'Jingle Bells'
   'Karl Foerster' = **C. carpatica** var. **turbinata 'Karl Foerster'**
   'Karpatenkrone'   [K. Foerster 1949]
   'Kobaltglocke'   [J. Lintner]
   'Lavender'
   'Loddon Belle'   [Thos. Carlile Ltd]
   'Maureen Haddon'   [A. Bloom]
   'Queen of Somerville'
   'Riverslea'   [Prichard]
   'Snowsprite' = **C. carpatica** var. **turbinata 'Snowsprite'**

'Spechtmeise'   [K. Foerster]
var. **turbinata** (Schott, Nyman & Kotschy) Nicholson (*C. turbinata*)   RD
var. **turbinata** 'Alba'
var. **turbinata** 'Georg Arends'   [G. Arends]
var. **turbinata** 'Craven Bells'
var. **turbinata** 'Grandiflora'
var. **turbinata** 'Hannah'   RD
var. **turbinata** 'Jewel'
var. **turbinata** 'Karl Foerster'   [Foerster]
var. **turbinata** 'Pallida'
var. **turbinata** 'Pam'
var. **turbinata** 'Snowsprite'   [A. Bloom]   RD
var. **turbinata** 'Wheatley Violet'   RD
'Violetta'
'Weisse Clips' ('White Clips')   [E. Benary]
'White Star'
'Zwergmöve'   [K. Foerster]
cashmeriana Royle 1835
cenisia Linnaeus 1763   CA
cephalenica Feer 1890 = **C. garganica** ssp. **cephalenica**
cochleariifolia Lamarck 1785 (*C. pusilla*)   DGP-RD
'Alba'   **DGP-RD**
'Blue Tit'   [A. Bloom]
'Cambridge Blue'   [A. Bloom]
'Elizabeth Oliver'   RD
'Flore Pleno'
'Miranda'   [R. Farrer]
'Miss Willmott'
'Oakington Blue'   [A. Bloom]
'Patience Bell'
'Sefinental'
'Silver Chimes'
'Temple Bells'
'Tubby'
'Warleyensis' = **C. x haylodgensis** 'Warley White'
collina Marshall von Bieberstein 1808 non Sims 1806
'Constellation'   [A. Bloom]
coriacea P. H. Davis 1962
'Covadonga'
davisii Turrill 1956
elatines Linnaeus 1759   CA
var. *fenestrellata* (Feer) Fiori = **C. fenestrellata**
var. *garganica* (Tenore) Fiori = **C. garganica**
elatinoides Moretti 1822
'Elizabeth Paine'
eriocarpa Marshall von Bieberstein 1808 = **C. latifolia**
'E. K. Toogood'
ephesia Boissier 1875
excisa Schleicher & Murith 1810   RD
fenestrellata Feer 1890 (*C. elatines* var. *fenestrellata*)
finitima Fomin 1905 = **C. betulifolia**
formanekiana Degen & Doerfler 1899   CA
fragilis Cyrillo 1788   CA
garganica Tenore 1827 (*C. elatines* var. *garganica*)   **DGP-RD**
'Aurea' = **C. garganica** 'Dickson's Gold'
'Blue Diamond'
ssp. **cephalenica** (Feer) Hayek 1930
'Dickson's Gold' ('Aurea')
'Erinus Major'
'W. H. Paine'   RD

N‡ **glomerata** Linnaeus 1753   PGP-DGP-**RD**
    *var. **acaulis**   RD
    'Alba'   DGP-RD
    'Alba Plena'
    'Crown of Snow' = **C. glomerata 'Schneekrone'**
    var. **dahurica** Fischer   PGP-DGP-RD
    'Joan Elliott'   PGP
    'Nana Alba' nom. dub.
    'Purple Pixie'   [A. Bloom]   PGP
    'Schneehäschen'   [H. Klose 1962]
    'Schneekissen' ('Snow Cushion')
    'Schneekrone' ('Crown of Snow')   [E. Benary]   PGP
    'Snow Cushion' = **C. glomerata 'Schneekissen'**
L   **'Superba'**   [G. Arends]   PGP-**DGP**
    'White Barn'   [B. Chatto]
   grandis Fischer & Mayer 1838 = **C. persicifolia** ssp. **sessiliflora**
   'Hallii' (*C. cochlearifolia* 'Alba' x *C. portenschlagiana*)   RD
   hawkinsiana Haussknecht & Heldreich 1887
   x **haylodgensis** hort. (*C. carpatica* x *C. cochlearifolia*)
    'Alba'
    'Plena'
    'Warley White' (*C. x warleyense* hort.)
   hercegovina Degen & Fiala 1984
    'Nana'   CA
   heterophylla Linnaeus 1753
   incurva Aucher ex A. de Candolle 1839
   isophylla Moretti 1824   **DGP-RD**
    'Alba'   DGP-RD
    'Mayi'   DGP-RD
   'Joe Elliott' (*C. morettiana* x *C. raineri*)   [J. Elliott 1979]
   kemulariae Fomin 1937
   kolenatiana Meyer & Ruprecht
N   **lactiflora** Marshall von Bieberstein 1808   PGP-DGP-RD
    'Alba'   DGP
L   **'Loddon Anna'**   [Thos. Carlile Ltd. pre-1952]   PGP-**DGP**-RD
    'Pouffe'   [A. Bloom]   PGP-RD
L   **'Prichard's Variety'**   [Prichard]   PGP-**RD**
    'Superba'   PGP
    'White Pouffe'
   lasiocarpa Chamisso 1829   CA
    'Alba'
N‡L **latifolia** Linnaeus 1753   PGP-DGP-**RD**
    'Alba'   **DGP**-RD
    'Brantwood'   PGP-DGP-RD
    'Gloaming'   [A. Bloom]   PGP-RD
    var. **macrantha** (Fischer ex Hornemann) A. de Candolle 1839   PGP
    var. **macrantha 'Alba'**
    'White Ladies'   [A. Bloom]
   latiloba A. de Candolle 1839 = **C. persicifolia** ssp. **sessiliflora**
   linifolia Scopoli 1769 non Schrank = **C. carnica**
   'Lynchmere' (*C. elatines* x *C. rotundifolia*)
   macrantha (Fischer ex Hornemann) hort. = **C. latifolia** var. **macrantha**
   mirabilis Albov 1895   CA
   'Mist Maiden'
   mollis Linnaeus 1762 (*C. velutina*)
    'Gibraltarica'
    'Molly Pinsent'
   morettiana Reichenbach 1826   CA-RD
    'Alba'   CA
   muralis Portenschlag-Ledermayer ex A. de Candolle 1830 = **C. portenschlagiana**

nitida Solander in Aiton 1810 = **C. persicifolia 'Planiflora'**
nobilis Lindley 1846 = **C. punctata**
'Norman Grove' (*C. isophylla* x *C. stansfieldii*)
ochroleuca Kemularia-Natadze 1941
olympica Boissier 1844
oreadum Boissier & Heldreich 1856
orphanidea Boissier (*C. calaminthifolia*)   CA
ossetica Marshall von Bieberstein 1819 = **Symphyandra ossetica**

N‡   **patula** Linnaeus 1753
N   **persicifolia** Linnaeus 1753   PGP-DGP-RD
      'Alba'   PGP
      'Alba Plena'
      'Blue Belle'   PGP-**DGP**
      'Carillon'
      'Coerulea Coronaria'
      'Cup and Saucer' = **C. persicifolia**
      'Cup and Saucer White' = **C. persicifolia 'Alba'**
      'Fleur de Neige'   PGP
      'Flore Pleno'
      'Grandiflora'
      'Grandiflora Alba'
      'Grandiflora Coerulea'
      'Hampstead White'
      'Loddon Petal'   [Thos. Carlile Ltd.]
      'Loddon Sarah'   [Thos. Carlile Ltd.]
      'Moerheimii'   PGP
      'Planiflora' (*C. nitida*)   CA-RD
      'Planiflora Alba'   CA-**RD**
      'Pride of Exmouth'
      'Sarah'
      ssp. **sessiliflora** (K. Koch) Velenovsky ex W. Greuter & Burdet 1982 (*C. latiloba*)
                                                              PGP-**RD**
          ssp. **sessiliflora 'Alba'**   PGP-RD
          ssp. **sessiliflora 'Hidcote Amethyst'** ('Hidcote Pink')   PGP
L   ssp. **sessiliflora 'Highcliffe'**   [Prichard]   PGP
          ssp. **sessiliflora 'Percy Piper'**   [A. Bloom]   PGP-RD
          'Telham Beauty'   PGP-**DGP**
      petraea Linnaeus 1759
      petrophila Ruprecht 1867
      pilosa Pallas ex Roemer & Schultes 1820   CA
          var. **dasyantha** (Marshall von Bieberstein) !   CA
          'Major'
          'Superba'
      planiflora hort. = **C. persicifolia 'Planifolia'**
L   **portenschlagiana** Schultes 1819 (*C. muralis*)   DGP-RD
          'Bavarica'
          'Major'
          'Resholt Variety'
L   **poscharskyana** Degen 1908   RD
          'Blauranke'   [Kayser & Siebert] ('Blue Gown')
          'Blue Gown' = **C. poscharskyana 'Blauranke'**
          'E. H. Frost'
          'Erich G. Arends'   [G. Arends]
          'Glandore'
          'Lilacina'
          'Lisduggan Variety'
          'Rosea'
          'Stella'   [G. Arends 1945]
          'Super Star'
          'Werner G. Arends'   [G. Arends]

'Pseudo-raineri' (*C. carpatica* x *C. raineri*)
pulla Linnaeus 1753 — RD
x pulloides hort. (*C. carpatica* var. *turbinata* x *C. pulla*) — RD
    'G. F. Wilson'
punctata Lamarck 1785 (*C. nobilis*) — PGP
    'Alba'
    'Nana Alba'
    'Rosea'
    'Rubra'
pusilla Haenke 1788 = **C. cochlearifolia**
pyramidalis Linnaeus 1753 — PGP-RD
    'Alba'
    'Aureo-variegata'
raddeana Trautvetter 1866 — RD
raineri Perpenti 1817 — CA
N‡   **rapunculoides** Linnaeus 1753 — PGP
HBN‡ **rapunculus** Linnaeus 1753
rhomboidalis Linnaeus 1753
N‡L **rotundifolia** Linnaeus 1753 — RD
    var. **alaskana** (Leichtlin ex Beddome) ! (*C. alaskana*)
    'Olympica'
rupestris Smith 1806 — CA
sarmatica Ker-Gawler 1817 — PGP
sartorii Boissier & Spruner 1875
saxifraga Marshall von Bieberstein 1808 — CA
scheuchzeri Villars 1779
'Stansfieldii' (*C. carpatica* var. *turbinata* x *C. waldsteiniana*) — RD
takesimana Nakai 1922 — PGP
teucrioides Boissier 1844
thrysoides Linnaeus 1753
    ssp. **carniolica** (Sündermann) Podl 1964
tommasiniana Koch 1852
topaliana Beauverd 1937
N‡   **trachelium** Linnaeus 1753 — PGP
    'Alba' — PGP
    'Albo Plena' — PGP
    'Bernice' — PGP
tridentata Schreber 1766 — CA
turbinata Schott, Nyman & Kotschy 1854 = **C. carpatica** var. **turbinata**
'Tymonsii' (*C. carpatica* x *C. pyramidalis*)
'Van Houttei' (*C. latifolia* x *C. punctata* ?) — PGP
velutina Desfontaines 1798 = **C. mollis**
versicolor Smith 1806 — PGP
vidalii H. C. Watson 1844 = **Azorina vidalii**
waldsteiniana Schultes 1819
x *warleyense* hort. = **C. x haylodgensis** 'Warley White'
x wockei Sündermann (*C. tommasiniana* x *C. waldsteiniana*)
    'Puck'
'Yvonne'
zoysii Wulfen 1789 — CA-**DGP**-**RD**

CANNA Linnaeus 1753 — [*Cannaceae*]
x generalis L. H. Bailey 1930 — RD
    'America' ®   [C. Sprenger 1893] — PGP-RD
    'Bonfire' ® — RD
    'Brilliant' ®   [A. Crozy]
    'Champol' ®   [Bruant 1905]
    'City of Portland' ®
    'Di Bartolo' ® — RD
    'En Avant' ®   [Vilmorin-Andrieux 1914]

'Evening Star' ®   RD
'Feuerzauber' ®   [W. Pfitzer 1922]('Fire Magic')
'Fire Magic' = C. 'Feuerzauber'
'Gold Dream'
'Golden Lucifer'
'Ingeborg' ®   [W. Pfitzer 1916]
'La Boheme' ®   [Wayside Gardens]
'Liebesglut' ®   PGP
'Lucifer' ®   [H. Faiss pre-1968]   **RD**
'King Humbert' = C. 'Roi Humbert'
'Orchid' ®
'Picasso'
'Pfitzer's Primrose Yellow' ®   [W. Pfitzer]('Primrose Yellow')
'President' ®   [U.S 1923]   RD
'President Carnot' ®   [A. Crozy 1889]
'Primrose Yellow' = C. 'Pfitzer's Primrose Yellow'
'Richard Wallace' ®   [W. Pfitzer 1902]   PGP
'Roi Humbert' ®   [C. Sprenger 1902]('King Humbert')   PGP
'Tirol' ®   [W. Pfitzer 1930]
'Verdi' ®   [L. Kapiteyn]
'Wyoming' ®   [A. Wintzer 1906]   PGP-RD
'Yellow Humbert' ®
indica Linnaeus 1753   EGF.2-PGP
iridiflora Ruiz & Pavon 1820   EGF.2-PGP

CARDAMINE Linnaeus 1753   [*Brassicaceae (Cruciferae)*]
   asarifolia Linnaeus 1753
   asarifolia hort. non Linnaeus = **Pachyphragma macrophylla**
N‡ **bulbifera** (Linnaeus) Crantz 1769 (*Dentaria bulbifera*)
   diphylla Wood 1870 (*Dentaria diphylla*)
   enneaphyllos (Linnaeus) Crantz 1769   RD
   heptaphylla (Villars) O. E. Schulz 1939 (*C. pinnata, Dentaria pinnata*)   PGP
   kitaibelii Becherer 1934 (*C. polyphylla* (Waldstein & Kitaibel) O. E.Schulz)
   latifolia Vahl 1791 non Lejeune 1813 = **C. raphanifolia**
   pentaphyllos(Linnaeus)Crantz 1769(*Dentaria digitata, D. pentaphyllos*)   RD
   pinnata (Lamarck) R. Brown 1812 = **C. heptaphylla**
   polyphylla (Walstein & Kitaibel) O. E. Schulz 1939 non D. Don 1825 =
                                      C. kitaibelii
N‡L **pratensis** Linnaeus 1753   PGP-RD
      'Flore Pleno'   **RD**
N   **raphanifolia** Pourret 1788 (*C. latifolia*)   PGP
N   **trifolia** Linnaeus 1753   RD

CARDIOCRINUM (Endlicher) Lindley 1846   [*Liliaceae*]

M - SYNGE, P.M., *'Lilies'* B.T. Batsford Ltd, London, 1980

   cathayanum (Wilson) Stearn 1948   M-EGF.1-PGP
   cordatum (Thunberg) Makino 1913   M-EGF.1-PGP-RD
   giganteum(Wallich) Makino 1913 (*Lilium giganteum*)   M-EGF.1-PGP-**BB**-DGP-**RD**
     var. **yunnanense** (Leichtlin ex Elwes) Stearn 1948   **M**-EGF.1-PGP-**BB**-DGP-RD
   japonicum hort. = **C. cordatum**

CARDUNCELLUS Adanson 1763   [*Asteraceae (Compositae)*]
   mitissimus (Linnaeus) de Candolle 1805
   multifidus Lojacono-Pojero 1891
   rhaponticoides Cosson & Durieu ex Pomel 1860

CAREX Linnaeus 1753   [*Cyperaceae*]
N‡ **acuta** Linnaeus 1753 (*C. gracilis*)

'**Aureovariegata**'
alba Scopoli 1772

N‡ **atrata** Linnaeus 1753
baldensis Linnaeus 1756   EGF.2
barrattii Torrey ex Schweinitz 1841 (*C. flacca* Carey ex Boott)
berggrenii Petrie 1886
   Bronze form
   Glaucous form
   Narrow-leaved form
boottiana Hooker & Arnott 1841 (*C. oahuensis* var. *boottiana*)
brunnea Thunberg 1784
   '**Variegata**'
buchananii Berggren 1880   EGF.2-RD
   '**Viridis**' nom. dub.
colensoi Boott 1853
comans Berggren 1887   EGF.2-RD
   Brown form
   Pale Green form
conica Boott 1856
   '**Hime Kansuge**'
   '**Variegata**'

N‡ **digitata** Linnaeus 1753
dipascea Berggren 1878
dissita Solander & Boott 1853

N‡ **elata** Allioni 1785 (*C. stricta* Goodenough)   EGF.2-RD
   '**Aurea**'   **PGP**-RD
   '**Knightshayes**' nom. dub.
   '**Limelight**' stat. dub.
firma Host 1797   EGF.2
   '**Variegata**'
flacca Carey ex Boott 1858 = **C. barrattii**

N‡ **flacca** Schreber 1771 (*C. glauca*)
flagellifera Colenso 1884   RD
fortunei hort. = **C. morrowii** Boott
fraseri Andrews 1811   EGF.2-PGP
glauca Scopoli 1772= **C. flacca** Schreber
gracilis Curtis 1783 = **C. acuta**
grayi Carey 1847

N‡ **humilis** Leysser 1761
japonica Fischer ex Boott 1845 = **C. morrowii**
kaloides Petrie 1881

N‡ **montana** Linnaeus 1753
morrowii Boott 1856 (*C. fortunei, C. japonica* Fischer ex Boott)   EGF.2-RD
   Fisher's Form
   '**Variegata**'   [pre-1856]   **PG**-RD
morrowii hort. non Boott
   'Evergold' = **C. oshimensis** '**Evergold**'
muskinguemensis Schweinitz 1824
   '**Wachtposten**'

N‡ **nigra** (Linnaeus) Reichard 1778 non Trevisan 1853
oahuensis Hildebrand 1888
   var. *boottiana* (Hooker & Arnott) Kükenthal 1909 = **C. boottiana**
oederi Retzius 1779 = **C. pilulifera**

N‡ **ornithopoda** Willdenow 1805   RD
   '**Variegata**'   RD
oshimensis Nakai 1914

L   '**Evergold**'   RD

N‡ **panicea** Linnaeus 1753

N‡L **pendula** Hudson 1762   EGF.2-PGP-RD
petriei Cheeseman 1884

N‡   **pilulifera** Linnaeus 1753
      'Tinney's Princess'   [G. A. Mundey via A. Bloom]
    plantaginea Lamarck 1789
N‡   **pseudocyperus** Linnaeus 1753   EGF.2
N‡   **riparia** Curtis 1783   EGF.2
      'Aurea'
      'Aureo-variegata'
      'Variegata'   PGP
    scaposa C. B. Clarke 1887
    secta Boott 1853
    sempervirens Villars 1787
    siderostica Hance 1873
      'Variegata'
    stricta Goodenough 1794 non Lamarck 1789 = **C. elata**
N‡   **sylvatica** Hudson 1762
    testacea Solander ex Boott 1853
    trifida Cavanilles 1799   PGP
    umbrosa Host 1801
    uncifolia Cheeseman 1884

CARLINA Linnaeus 1753   *[Asteraceae (Compositae)]*
    acanthifolia Allioni 1785
      ssp. **cynara** (Pourret ex Duby) Rouy 1903
    acaulis Linnaeus 1753
      ssp. **simplex** (Waldstein & Kitaibel) Nyman 1879 (*C. caulescens*)
      Bronze Form
      'Splendens'
    caulescens Linnaeus 1753 or (Lamarck) Gaudin = **C. acaulis** ssp. **simplex**

CARTHAMUS Linnaeus 1753   *[Asteraceae (Compositae)]*
AHN   **tinctorius** Linnaeus 1753

CARUM Linnaeus 1753   *[Apiaceae (Umbelliferae)]*
HN‡   **carvi** Linnaeus 1753   **RD**

CATANANCHE Linnaeus 1753   *[Asteraceae (Compositae)]*
HL   **caerulea** Linnaeus 1753   PGP-**DGP**-RD
      'Alba'
      'Bicolor'   PGP-RD
      'Major'   PGP-**RD**
      'Wisley'

CAULOPHYLLUM Michaux 1803   *[Berberidaceae]*
    thalictroides (Linnaeus) Michaux 1803   PGP

CAUTLEYA (Bentham) Royle ex Baker 1890   *[Zingiberaceae]*
    gracilis (Smith) Dandy 1932 (*C. lutea*)   EGF.2-PGP
    lutea Royle 1840 = **C. gracilis**
    spicata (Smith) Baker 1890   EGF.2PGP
      'Robusta'   PGP-**DGP**-RD

CEDRONELLA Moench 1794   *[Lamiaceae (Labiatae)]*
    canariensis Webb & Berthelot 1845 = **C. triphylla**
S   **mexicana** Bentham 1834
SH   **triphylla** Moench 1794 (*C. canariensis*)

CELMISIA Cassini 1825   *[Asteraceae (Compositae)]*
S   **argentea** Kirk 1899   **CA**
    asteliifolia Hooker f. 1844
    bellidioides Hooker f. 1864

coriacea (Forster f.) Hooker f. 1844   PGP-CA-**PGP**
dallii Buchan 1882
gracilenta Hooker f. 1844
S   **hectori** Hooker f. 1864
Inshriach Hybrids
S   **ramulosa** Hooker f. 1867
    var. **tuberculata** Simpson & Thomson 1942
walkeri Kirk 1877
*****webbii**

CELSIA Linnaeus 1753   [*Scrophulariaceae*]
acaulis Bory de Saint-Vincent & Chaubard 1832 = **Verbascum acaule**
roripifolium Halaczy 1890 = **Verbascum roripifolium**

X CELSIOVERBASCUM Reichenbach f. & Huber-Morath 1960   [*Scrophulariaceae*]
'Golden Wings' = **Verbascum 'Golden Wings'**

CENCHRUS Linnaeus 1753   [*Poaceae (Gramineae)*]
ciliaris Linnaeus 1771 (*Pennisetum incomptum*)   EGF.2

CENTAUREA Linnaeus 1753   [*Asteraceae (Compositae)*]
argentea Linnaeus 1753
axillaris Willdenow 1803 non. illegit. = **C. triumfetti**
bella Trautvetter 1866
cana Waldstein & Kitaibel 1805 = **C. triumfetti** ssp. **cana**
candissima Lamarck 1785 = **C. putiolia**
chilensis Bertolini ex Hooker & Arnold 1841
cineraria Linnaeus 1753 (*C. gymnocarpa*)   RD
    'Colchester White'
dealbata Willdenow 1803   PGP-RD
    'Steenbergii'   PGP-**DGP**
glastifolia (Linnaeus) Cassini 1829   PGP
gymnocarpa Moris & de Notaris 1839 = **C. cineraria**
hypoleuca de Candolle 1838   PGP-**RD**
L   **'John Coutts'**   PGP-**DGP**-RD
macrocephala Mussin-Puschkin ex Willdenow 1803   PGP-**RD**
NL **montana** Linnaeus 1753   PGP-DGP-RD
    'Alba'   PGP-DGP-RD
    'Carnea' ('Rosea')   PGP-RD
    'Grandiflora'
    'Parham Variety'   PGP-**DGP**
    'Rosea' = **C. montana 'Carnea'**
    'Violetta'   RD
N‡L **nigra** Linnaeus 1753
pulcherrima Willdenow 1803
pulchra de Candolle 1838   PGP-RD
'Pulchra Major'   PGP
*****putiolia** (*C. candissima*)
ruthenica Lamarck 1785   PGP-RD
rutifolia Smith 1840 non Boissier 1875
N‡ **scabiosa** Linnaeus 1753
simplicicaulis Boissier & Huet 1856   PGP-RD
stricta Waldstein & Kitaibel 1805 = **C. triumfetti** ssp. **stricta**
triumfetti Allioni 1773 (*C. axillaris*)
    ssp. **cana** (Waldstein & Kitaibel) Dostal 1931 (*C. cana*)
    ssp. **cana 'Rosea'**
    ssp. **stricta** (Waldstein & Kitaibel) Dostal 1931 (*C. stricta*)   PGP
    ssp. **stricta 'Alba'**
uniflora Linnaeus 1767
    ssp. **nervosa** (Willdenow) Bonnier & Leyens 1894

CENTAURIUM Hill 1756   [*Gentianaceae*]
    chloodes (Brotero) Sampaio 1913 (*Erythraea chloodes*)
N‡L **erythraea** Rafinesque 1800
N‡   **scilloides** (Linnaeus f.) Sampaio 1913 (*Erythraea diffusa*)   CA

CENTRANTHUS Necker ex de Candolle 1805   [*Valerianaceae*]
NL   **ruber** (Linnaeus) de Candolle 1805   PGP-**DGP-RD**
          'Albus'   DGP-DR
          'Coccineus'

CEPHALANTHERA L. C. M. Richard 1818   [*Orchidaceae*]
N‡   **rubra** (Linnaeus) L. C. M. Richard 1818   EGF.2

CEPHALARIA Schrader ex Roemer & Schultes 1818   [*Dipsacaceae*]
    alpina (Linnaeus) Roemer & Schultes 1818 (*Scabiosa alpina*)
        'Nana'
NL   **gigantea** (Ledebour) Bobrov 1932 (*Scabiosa gigantea, S. tatarica*)   PGP

CERASTIUM Linnaeus 1753   [*Caryophyllaceae*]
N‡   **alpinum** Linnaeus 1753   RD
        ssp. **lanatum** (Lamarck) Ascherson & Graebner 1917   RD
N‡   **arvense** Linnaeus 1753
          'Compactum'
          banaticum (Rochel) Heuffel 1856
N   **biebersteinii** de Candolle 1822   RD
    columnae Tenore 1831 = **C. tomentosum** var. **columnae**
    lanatum Lamarck 1785 = **C. alpinum** ssp. **lanatum**
NL   **tomentosum** Linnaeus 1753   RD
        var. **columnae** (Tenore) Arcangeli (*C. columnae*)
        'Nanum'
        'Silberteppich' ('Silver Carpet')
        'Silver Carpet' = **C. tomentosum 'Silberteppich'**
        'Yo Yo'

CERATOPHYLLUM Linnaeus 1753   [*Ceratophyllaceae*]
NL   **demersum** Linnaeus 1753

CERATOSTIGMA Bunge 1835   [*Plumbaginaceae*]
S   **griffithii** C. B. Clarke 1882   PGP-RD
    larpentae hort. = **C. plumbaginoides**
SL   **plumbaginoides** Bunge 1835 (*C. larpentae, Plumbago larpentae*)   PGP-**DGP**-RD
S   **willmottianum** Stapf 1914   PGP-**DGP**-RD

CERINTHE Linnaeus 1753   [*Boraginaceae*]
    alpina Visiani 1872 = **C. glabra**
    glabra Miller (*C. alpina*)

CEROPEGIA Linnaeus 1753   [*Asclepiadaceae*]
    woodii Schlechter 1894

CETERACH Lamarck & de Candolle 1805 nom. cons.   [*Aspleniaceae*]
    officinarum de Candolle 1805 = **Asplenium ceterach**

CHAENORHINUM (de Candolle) Reichenbach 1828   [*Scrophulariaceae*]
    glareosum (Boissier) Willkomm 1886
N   **origanifolium** (Linnaeus) Kostelzky 1844 (*Linaria origanifolia*)   CA

CHAEROPHYLLUM Linnaeus 1753   [*Apiaceae (Umbelliferae)*]
    hirsutum Linnaeus 1753
        'Roseum'

CHAMAELIRIUM Willdenow 1808   *[Melanthiaceae (Liliaceae)]*
   luteum (Linnaeus) A. Gray 1848
                                           EGF.1-PGP

CHAMAEMELUM Miller 1754   *[Asteraceae (Compositae)]*
HN‡   **nobile** (Linnaeus) Allioni 1785 (*Anthemis nobilis*)
      'Flore Pleno'   RD
H   'Treneague'   [via D. Sewart]
                                         RD

CHAMAENERION Adanson 1763   *[Onagraceae]*
N‡   **angustifolium** (Linnaeus) Scopoli 1771 (*Epilobium angustifolium*)
      'Album'   PGP
                                         PGP

CHAMOMILLA S. F. Gray 1821   *[Asteraceae (Compositae)]*
   aurea (Loefling) Gay ex Cosson & Kralik 1854 = **Matricaria aurea**
   recutita (Linnaeus) Rauschert 1974 = **Matricaria recutita**

CHASMANTHE Ker-Gawler ex N. E. Brown 1932   *[Iridaceae]*
   aethiopica (Linnaeus) N. E. Brown 1932   EGF.1-PGP
   floribunda (Salisbury) N. E. Brown 1932   EGF.1
      var. **duckettii** Lewis

CHASMANTHIUM Link 1827   *[Poaceae (Gramineae)]*
   latifolium (Michaux) Yates 1966 (*Uniola latifolia*)
                                       EGF.2

CHEILANTHES Swartz 1806 nom. cons.   *[Adiantaceae]*
   argentea (Gmelin) Kunze 1850   EGF.1
   eatonii Baker 1867
   fragrans (Linnaeus) Swartz 1806 = **C. pteridioides**
   pteridioides (Reichard) C. Christensen 1905 (*C. fragrans*)   EGF.1

CHEIRANTHUS Linnaeus 1753   *[Brassicaceae (Cruciferae)]*
HN   **cheiri** Linnaeus 1753   **DGP**-RD
      'Bloody Warrior'
      'Harpur Crewe'
   *x kewensis (*C. cheiri* x *Erysimum mutabile*)   **DGP**
      'Variegatus'
   linifolius Persoon 1806 = **Erysimum linifolium**
   mutabilis Broussonet ex Sprengel 1825 = **Erysimum mutabile**

   HYBRID CULTIVARS
   See under: **ERYSIMUM HYBRID CULTIVARS**

CHELIDONIUM Linnaeus 1753   *[Papaveraceae]*
HN‡   **majus** Linnaeus 1753
      var. **laciniatum** (Miller) Syme
      'Flore Pleno'
                                         PGP

CHELONE Linnaeus 1753   *[Scrophulariaceae]*
   barbata Cavanilles 1795 = **Penstemon barbatus**
H   **glabra** Linnaeus 1753
   lyonii Pursh 1814
   obliqua Linnaeus 1767   RD
      'Alba'   PGP-**RD**
      'Praecox Nana'
                                         PGP

CHENOPODIUM Linnaeus 1753   *[Chenopodiaceae]*
HN‡   **bonus-henricus** Linnaeus 1753
      'Variegatum'

CHIASTOPHYLLUM Staph ex A. Berger 1930   [*Crassulaceae*]
   oppositifolium (Ledebour) A. Berger 1930 (*Cotyledon oppositifolium*)   **DGP**

CHIONOCHLOA Zotov 1963   [*Poaceae (Gramineae)*]
   conspicua (Forster f.) Zotov 1963   EGF.2-PGP
   rubra Zotov 1963

CHIONODOXA Boissier 1844   [*Hyacinthaceae (Liliaceae)*]
   albescens (Speta) Rix 1981   EGF.1-**BB**-SB
   cretica Boissier & Heldreich 1853 = **C. nana**
   gigantea Whittall 1899 = **C. luciliae** Boissier
   luciliae Boissier 1844 (*C. gigantea*)   CA-**BB**-SB-RD
      'Alba'   CA-**SB**
   luciliae hort., non Boissier = **C. siehei**
   nana (Schultes & Schultes f.) Boissier & Heldreich 1853 (*C. cretica*) EGF.1-CA-**BB**-SB
   sardensis Whittall ex Barr & Sugden 1883   EGF.1-CA-**BB**-SB-**DGP**-RD
   siehei Stapf 1925 (*C. luciliae* hort., *C. tmolusii*)   EGF.1
      'Alba'   ®   [Barr & Sons pre-1897]
      'Pink Giant' ®   [Nic. Roozen Lz. 1942]   EGF.1-**DGP**
      'Rosea'
      'Zwanenburg' ®   [van Tubergen]
   tmolusii Whittall 1889 = **C. siehei**

CHIONOGRAPHIS Maximowicz 1867   [*Melanthiaceae (Liliaceae)*]
   japonica Maximowicz 1867

X CHIONOSCILLA J. Allen ex Nicholson 1897   [*Hyacinthaceae (Liliaceae)*]
   allenii Nicholson 1897 (*Chionodoxa siehei* x *Scilla bifolia*)   EGF.1-**BB**-SB

CHLIDANTHUS Herbert 1821   [*Amaryllidaceae*]
   fragrans Herbert 1821   EGF.1

CHONDROSUM Desvaux 1810   [*Poaceae (Gramineae)*]
   gracile Humbolt, Bonpland & Kunth 1816 (*Bouteloua gracilis, B. oligostachya*)
                                        EGF.2-PGP

CHRYSANTHEMOPSIS (Maire) Wilcox & Humphries in press
                                   [*Asteraceae (Compositae)*]
   atlanticum (Maire) Wilcox, Bremer & Humphries in press
                              (*Leucanthemum atlanticum*)
   catananche (Ball) Wilcox, Bremer & Humphries in press
                             (*Leucanthemum catananche*)
   gayanum (Cosson & Durieu) Wilcox, Bremer & Humphries in press
                          (*Leucanthemum gayanum, L. mawii*)
   hosmariense (Ball) Wilcox, Bremer & Humphries in press (*Chrysanthemum
         hosmariense, Leucanthemum hosmariense*)   **CA-RD**
   maresii (Cosson) Wilcox, Bremer & Humphries in press (*Chrysanthemum maresii
                             Leucanthemum maresii*

CHRYSANTHEMUM Linnaeus 1753   [*Asteraceae (Compositae)*]
   alpinum Linnaeus 1753 = **Leucanthemopsis alpina**
   arcticum Linnaeus 1753 = **Arctanthemum arcticum**
   arcticum hort., non Linnaeus = **Dendranthema yezoense**
   argenteum Willdenow 1803 = **Tanacetum argenteum**
   atratum Linnaeus 1753 = **Leucanthemum atratum**
   balsamita Linnaeus 1763 = **Tanacetum balsamita**
   cinerariifolium (Trevisan) Vissier 1847 = **Tanacetum cinerariifolium**
   clusii (Fischer ex Reichenbach) Handel Mazzetti 1903 = **Tanacetum corymbosum**
                                        ssp. **clusii**
   coccineum Willdenow 1803 = **Tanacetum coccineum**

coreanum Nakai 1922 = **Dendranthema koreanum**
corymbosum Linnaeus 1753 = **Tanacetum corymbosum**
dahurica hort. = **Tanacetum dahurica**
densum (Labilliardiere) Steudel 1821 = **Tanacetum densum**
erubescens Stapf 1933 = **Dendranthema zawadskii** var. latilobum
foeniculaceum (Willdenow) Desfontaines 1829 = **Argyranthemum foeniculaceum**
frutescens Linnaeus 1753 = **Argyranthemum frutescens**
haradjanii K. H. Rechinger 1950 = **Tanacetum haradjanii**
indicum Linnaeus 1753 = **Dendranthema indicum**
x koreanum hort. = **Dendranthema x koreana**
leucanthemum Linnaeus 1753 = **Leucanthemum vulgare**
macrophyllum Walstein & Kitaibel 1802 = **Tanacetum macrophyllum**
maresii Ball 1873 = **Chrysanthemopsis maresii**
    var. *hosmariense* Ball 1873 = **Chrysanthemopsis hosmariense**
mawii Hooker f. 1872 = **Chrysanthemopsis gayanum**
maximum Ramond 1800 = **Leucanthemum maximum**
millefoliatum Linnaeus 1767 = **Tanacetum abrotanifolium**
nipponicum Franchet ex Dammann 1895 = **Nipponanthemum nipponicum**
parthenium (Linnaeus) Bernhardi 1800 = **Tanacetum parthenium**
ptarmiciflorum Puschkin ex Willdenow 1803 = **Tanacetum ptarmiciflorum**
roseum Adam 1805 = **Tanacetum coccineum**
x rubellum Sealy 1938 = **Dendranthema zawadskii Hybrids**
AN‡   **segetum** Linnaeus 1753   DGP
serotinum Linnaeus 1753 = **Leucanthemella serotina**
tanacetum Visiani 1847 = **Tanacetum vulgare**
uliginosum Persoon 1806 = **Leucanthemella serotina**
weyrichii (Maximowicz) Miyabe 1915 = **Dendranthema weyrichii**
yezoense Maekawa 1921 = **Dendranthema yezoense**
zawadskii Herbich 1831 = **Dendranthema zawadskii**

CHRYSOGONUM Linnaeus 1753   *[Asteraceae (Compositae)]*
    virginianum Linnaeus 1753
                                                                        DGP

CHRYSOPOGON Trinius 1822 nom. cons.   *[Poaceae (Gramineae)]*
    nutans (Linnaeus) Bentham 1881 = **Sorghastrum nutans**

CHRYSOPSIS (Nuttall) Elliott 1824 nom. cons.   *[Asteraceae (Compositae)]*
    villosa (Pursh) Nuttall ex de Candolle 1836

CHRYSOSPLENIUM Linnaeus 1753   *[Saxifragaceae]*
N‡   **alternifolium** Linnaeus 1753
    americanum Schwein 1832
    davidianum Decaisne ex Maximowicz 1877
    glaciale Fuss 1866 = **C. oppositifolium** ssp. **glaciale**
N‡L   **oppositifolium** Linnaeus 1753
        ssp. **glaciale** (Fuss) ! (*C. glaciale*)
        ssp. **rosulare** (Schott ex Maximowicz) ! (*C. rosulare*)
    rosulare Schott & Maximowicz 1877 = **C. oppositifolium** ssp. **rosulare**
    tetrandum (N. Lund) T. Fries 1858

CICHORIUM Linnaeus 1753   *[Asteraceae (Compositae)]*
HN‡   **intybus** Linnaeus 1753   PGP-RD
        'Album'
        'Roseum'
    spinosum Linnaeus 1753

CIMICIFUGA Wernisch 1763   *[Ranunculaceae]*
    acerina (Siebold & Zuccarini) T. Tanaka 1925 (*C. japonica* var. *acerina*)
        'Compacta'
    americana Michaux 1803
                                                                        RD

    cordifolia Pursh 1814 = **C. racemosa** var. **cordifolia**
    dahurica (Turczaninow ex Fischer & C. A. Meyer) Maximowicz 1859   PGP-RD
    elata Nuttall 1838
H   **foetida** Linnaeus 1767   **PGP-RD**
        intermedia hort. = **C. simplex**
        ramosa (Nuttall) hort. = **C. ramosa**
    japonica (Thunberg) Sprengel 1825   RD
        var. *acerina* (Siebold & Zuccarini) hort. = **C. acerina**
        'Frau Hermes'
HL   **racemosa** (Linnaeus) Nuttall 1818   **PGP-DGP-RD**
        var. **cordifolia** (Pursh) A. Gray 1895 (*C. cordifolia*)   PGP
        'Variegatum'
    ramosa Nuttall 1818   PGP-DG
        'Atropurpurea'
    simplex Wormskiöld ex de Candolle 1824   PGP-RD
        'Armleuchter' = **C. simplex 'White Pearl'**
        'Braunlaub'   PGP
        'Elstead Variety'   **PGP**-RD
        'White Pearl' ('Armleuchter')   PGP-**RD**

CIRSIUM Miller 1754   *[Asteraceae (Compositae)]*
    falconeri (Hooker f.) Petrak 1911
    heterophyllum (Linnaeus) Hill 1768 = **C. helenioides**
N‡   **helenioides** (Linnaeus) Hill 1768
    japonicum de Candolle 1830
        'Rose Beauty'
    rivulare (Jacquin) Allioni 1789   PGP-DGP
        'Atropurpureum'   PGP-**DGP**

CLADIUM R. Brown 1756   *[Cyperaceae]*
    germanicum (Linnaeus) Pohl 1809 = **C. mariscus**
    mariscus (Linnaeus) Pohl 1809

CLAYTONIA Linnaeus 1753   *[Portulacaceae]*
    australasica Hooker f. 1840 = **Neopaxia australasica**
    megarhiza (A. Gray) Parry ex S. Watson 1878
        var. **nivalis** (English) C. L. Hitchcock 1964
    sibirica Linnaeus 1753 = **Montia sibirica**
N   **virginica** Linnaeus 1753

CLEMATIS Linnaeus 1753   *[Ranunculaceae]*
    x aromatica Lenne & C. Koch 1855 (*C. flammula* x *C. integrifolia*)
    x bonstedtii hort. (*C. heracleifolia* 'Davidiana' x *C. stans*)
        'Campanile'   PGP
        'Cote d'Azur'   PGP
        'Crepuscule'   PGP
        'Gentianoides' = **C. gentianoides**
        'Jaggard'
        'Wyevale'   PGP-DGP
    davidiana Decaisne ex Verlot 1867 = **C. heracleifolia 'Davidiana'**
    douglasii Hooker 1829   PGP
        var. **scottiae** (Porter) Coulter 1885 (*C. scottiae*)
        var. **scottiae 'Rosea'**
    'Durandii' (*C. integrifolia* x *C. x jackmanii*)   PGP
    'Edward Prichard' (*C. heracleifolia* x *C. recta*)   PGP
    x eriostemon Decaisne 1852 (*C. integrifolia* x *C. viticella*)   PGP
L   **'Hendersonii'**   PGP-DGP
    gentianoides de Candolle 1817
N   **heracleifolia** de Candolle 1817   PGP-DGP
        'Davidiana' (Decaisne ex Velot) hort.   PGP-**DGP**

N   **integrifolia** Linnaeus 1753
      'Olgae'   PGP-DGP
      x jouiniana C. K. Schneider 1904 (*C. heracleifolia* 'Davidiana' x *C. vitalba*) PGP

          'Mrs. Robert Brydon'   PGP-**DGP**
          'Praecox'
          *****marmoraria**
          olgae hort. = **C. integrifolia 'Olgae'**
NL   **recta** Linnaeus 1753
          'Grandiflora'   PGP-**DGP**
          'Purpurea'
          scottiae Porter 1874 = **C. douglasii** var. **scottiae**
      stans Siebold & Zuccarini 1846
      tosaensis Makino 1897
N   **viticella** Linnaeus 1753

CLINTONIA Rafinesque 1832   *[Convallariaceae (Liliaceae)]*
      andrewsiana Torrey 1857   EGF.1-PGP
      borealis (Aiton) Rafinesque 1832   EGF.1-PGP
      umbellulata (Michaux) Torrey 1843   EGF.1-PGP
      uniflora (Schultes) Kunth 1850   EGF.1

CLIVIA Lindley 1828   *[Amaryllidaceae]*
      miniata (Hooker) Regel 1864   EGF.1-**DGP**-RD

CNICUS Linnaeus 1753   *[Asteraceae (Compositae)]*
N   **benedictus** Linnaeus 1753
      casabonae (Linnaeus) Roth = **Ptilostemon casabonae**

COCHLEARIA Linnaeus 1753   *[Brassicaceae (Cruciferae)]*
      armoracia Linnaeus 1753 = **Armoracia rusticana**

CODONOPSIS Wallich 1824   *[Campanulaceae]*
      bulleyana Forrest & Diels 1912
      cardiophylla Diels ex Komarov 1908   PGP
      clematidea (Schrenk) Clarke 1881   PGP-**RD**
C   **convolvulacea** Kurz 1873 (*C. vinciflora*)   PGP-**BB**-RD
          'Alba'
          var. *forrestii* (Diels) hort. = **C. forrestii**
          'Summer Snow'
      forrestii Diels 1912
      handeliana Nannfeldt 1936   BB
      meleagris Diels 1912
      ovata Bentham 1836   CA
      purpurea Wallich 1824   PGP-CA-**DGP**-**RD**
      subsimplex Hooker f. & Thomson 1858
      tangshen Oliver 1891
      vinciflora Komarov 1908 = **C. convolvulacea**
      viridiflora Maximowicx 1881

COLCHICUM Linnaeus 1753   *[Colchicaceae (Liliaceae)]*
      agrippinum Baker 1879   EGF.1-CA-**BB**-SB-**RD**
      alpinum de Candolle 1815   EGF.1-**BB**-SB
      atropurpureum Stearn 1934   EGF.1-SB
HN‡   **autumnale** Linnaeus 1753   EGF.1-**BB**-SB-**DGP**-RD
          'Album' ®   CA-**BB**
          'Alboplenum' ®   [Pre-1872]   EGF.1
          'Atropurpureum' ®   [via van Tubergen]
          'Plenum' ® ('Roseum Plenum')   EGF.1-**RD**
          'Roseum Plenum' = **A. autumnale 'Plenum'**

baytopiorum Brickell 1983   EGF.1-SB
bifolium Freyn & Sintensis 1896 = **C. szovitsii**
bivonae Gussone 1821 (*C. bowlesianum, C. sibthorpii*)   EGF.1-**BB**-SB-RD
boissieri Orphanides 1874   EGF.1-**BB**
bornmuelleri Freyn 1889 (*C. speciosum* var. *bornmuelleri*)   EGF.1-**BB**-SB-RD
bowlesianum B. L. Burtt 1951 = **C. bivonae**
burttii Meikle 1976   EGF.1-SB
byzantinum Ker-Gawler 1807   EGF.1-**BB**-SB-**RD**
   'Album'
cilicicum (Boissier) Dammer 1898   EGF.1-CA-**BB**-SB-**DGP**
corsicum Baker 1879   EGF.1-CA-**BB**-SB
cupanii Gussone 1827   EGF.1-**BB**-**SB**
giganteum Leichtlin ex Arnott 1902   EGF.1-SB
hungaricum Janka 1882   EGF.1-CA-**BB**-SB
illyricum hort., non Frivaldsky   **C. speciosum**
kesselringii Regel 1884   EGF.1-**BB**-SB
kotschyi Boissier 1853   EGF.1-**BB**-SB
laetum Steven 1829   EGF.1-**BB**-SB
lingulatum Boissier & Spruner 1844   EGF.1-SB
lusitanicum Brotero 1827   EGF.1-**BB**-SB
luteum Baker 1874   EGF.1-CA-**BB**-**SB**-RD
macrophyllum B. L. Burtt 1951   EGF.1-**BB**-**SB**
micranthum Boissier 1882   EGF.1-SB
nivale Boissier & Huet ex Stefanoff 1926 = **C. szovitsii**
pannonicum Grisebach & Schrenk 1852
parlatoris Orphanides 1876   EGF.1-SB
parnassicumn Sartori, Orphanides & Heldreich in Boissier 1859   EGF.1-SB
sibthorpii Baker 1879 = **C. bivonae**
speciosum Steven 1829   EGF.1-CA-**BB**-SB-**DGP**-RD
   'Album' ®   [Backhouse of York pre-1933]   CA-**BB**-**DGP**-**RD**
   'Atrorubens' ®   [Backhouse of York pre-1933]
   var. *bornmuelleri* (Freyn) Bergmans = **C. bornmuelleri**
   'Maximum'
szovitsii Fischer & C. A. Meyer (*C. bifolium, C. nivale*)   EGF.1-**BB**-SB
tenorii Parlatore 1858   EGF.1-**BB**-SB
triphyllum Kunze 1846   EGF.1-CA-SB
turcicum Janka 1873   EGF.1-SB
umbrosum Steven 1829   EGF.1-SB
variegatum Linnaeus 1753   EGF.1-CA-**BB**-SB
vernum (Linnaeus) Ker-Gawler 1807 = **Bulbocodium vernum**

HYBRID CULTIVARS

   'Antares'
   'Autumn Herald'
   'Autumn Queen' ®   [Zocher & Co pre-1926] ('Prinses Astrid')   RD
   'Beaconsfield'
   'Conquest'   **BB**
   'Daendels' ®   [Zocher & Co.]
   'Darwin'
   'Dick Trotter'
   'E. A. Bowles'
   'Giant' ®   [Zocher & Co. pre-1931]   **BB-DGP-RD**
   'Huxley' ®   [R. O. Backhouse c1950]
   'Lilac Bedder' ®   [P. Visser Czn. 1974]
   'Lilac Wonder' ®   [Zocher & Co pre-1926]   DGP-RD
   'Little Woods'
   'Nancy Lindsay'
   'Pink Goblet'
   'Prinses Astrid' = **A. 'Autumn Queen'**
   'Rosy Dawn' ®   [Barr & Sons pre-1972]

'Violet Queen'   ®   [Zocher & Co]   RD
'Waterlily'   ®   [Zocher & Co pre-1927]   DGP-RD
'William Dykes'

COLOBANTHUS Bartling 1830   [*Caryophyllaceae*]
    canaliculatus Kirk 1895
    hookeri Cheeseman 1921
    muscoides Hooker f. 1844

COLOCASIA Schott 1832   [*Araceae*]
    antiquorum Schott 1867 = **C. esculenta** var. **antiquorum**
    esculenta (Linnaeus) Schott 1832
        var. **antiquorum** (Schott) Hubbard & Rehder (*C. antiquorum*)   EGF.2
        'Fontanesia'

COMARUM Linnaeus 1753   [*Rosaceae*]
    palustre Linnaeus 1753 = **Potentilla palustris**
    salesovianum (Stephan) Ascherson & Graebner 1905 = **Potentilla salesoviana**

COMMELINA Linnaeus 1753   [*Commelinaceae*]
    coelestis Willdenow 1809 = **C. tuberosa**
    dianthifolia Delile   EGF.2
    tuberosa Linnaeus 1753 (*C. coelestis*)   EGF.2-PGP

CONANDRON Siebold & Zuccarini 1843   [*Gesneriaceae*]
    ramondioides Siebold & Zuccarini 1843   CA

CONIUM Linnaeus 1753
BHN‡ **maculatum** Linnaeus 1753   [*Apiaceae (Umbelliferae)*]

CONVALLARIA Linnaeus 1753   [*Convallariaceae (Liliaceae)*]
    keiskei Miquel 1867
HN‡ **majalis** Linnaeus 1753   EGF.1-PGP-**RD**
        'Albistriata' ('Striata', 'Variegata')   EGF.1-PGP-RD
        'Berlin Giant'
        'Flore Pleno'   EGF.1-RD
        'Fortin's Giant'   PGP-RD
        'Grandiflorum'
        'Haddon Hall'
        'Hardwick Hall'   PGP
        'Prolificans'   EGF.1-PGP
        var. **rosea** Reichenbach non Ledebour 1829   EGF.1-PGP-RD
        'Striata' = **P. majalis 'Albistriata'**
        'Variegata' = **P. majalis 'Albistriata'**

CONVOLVULUS Linnaeus 1753   [*Convolvulaceae*]
    althaeoides Linnaeus 1753   PGP-**DGP**-**RD**
    boissieri Steudel (*C. nitidus* Boissier)   CA
    cantabricus Linnaeus 1753   CA
S   **cneorum** Linnaeus 1753   PGP-CA-**DGP**-**RD**
    elegantissimus Miller 1768(*C. tenuissimus*)
    lineatus Linnaeus 1759
    mauritanicus Boissier 1841 = **C. sabatius**   CA
    nitidus Boissier 1838 non Desvaux 1792 = **C. boissieri**
    sabatius Viviani 1824 (*C. mauritanicus*)
    suendermannii hort. non Bornmüller = **C. lineatus**   PGP-**DGP**-RD
    tenuissimus Smith 1806 = **C. elegantissimus**

COPTIS Salisbury 1807
    laciniata A. Gray 1887   [*Ranunculaceae*]

japonica Makino 1899 = **C. orientalis**
orientalis Maximowicz 1868 (*C. japonica*)
quinquefolia Miquel 1867
trifoliata (Makino) Makino 1914

CORBULARIA Salisbury 1812   [*Amaryllidaceae*]
   bulbocodium (Linnaeus) Haworth = **Narcissus bulbocodium**
   monophylla Durieu 1846 = **Narcissus cantabricus** ssp. **monophyllus**

COREOPSIS Linnaeus 1753   [*Asteraceae (Compositae)*]
   auriculata Linnaeus 1753
      'Superba'   PGP
   grandiflora Hogg ex Sweet 1825-7   PGP-DGP-**RD**
      'Astolat'
      'Badengold'   [Legeland]   PGP-DGP-RD
      'Domino'
      'Louis d'Or'
      'Mayfield Giant'   PGP-RD
      'Ruby Throat'
      'Schnittgold'
      'Sonnenkind'
      'Sunburst'   PGP
      'Sun Child'
      'Sunnyboy'
      'Sunray'   [Fleuroselect 1980]
      'Tetragold'
   lanceolata Linnaeus 1753
      'Baby Gold'
      'Baby Sun'
      'Golden Gain'
      'Goldfink'   [Pötschke via Walther 1960]   **DGP**-RD
      'Goldteppich'
      'Lichtstad'
      'Rotkehlchen'   [Pötschke via Walther 1960]
      'Sterntaler'   [Pötschke via Walther 1962]
   palmata Nuttall 1818
   rosea Nuttall 1818
   tripteris Linnaeus 1753
L   **verticillata** Linnaeus 1753   PGP-DGP-**RD**
      'Grandiflora'   [H. Hesse]   PGP-**DGP**
      'Moonbeam'
      'Zagreb'   [Polak]   RD

CORETHROGYNE de Candolle 1836   [*Asteraceae (Compositae)*]
S   **californica** de Candolle 1836 (*C. caespitosa*)   CA
   caespitosa Greene 1878 = **C. californica**

CORIANDRUM Linnaeus 1753   [*Apiaceae (Umbelliferae)*]
AHN   **sativum** Linnaeus 1753

CORNUS Linnaeus 1753   [*Cornaceae*]
   canadensis Linnaeus 1753   **DGP-RD**

CORONILLA Linnaeus 1753   [*Fabaceae (Leguminosae)*]
   cappadocica Willdenow 1802 = **C. orientalis**
S   **minima** Linnaeus 1753
S   **orientalis** Miller 1768 (*C. cappadocica*)
N   **varia** Linnaeus 1753

CORTADERIA Stapf 1897 nom. cons.   *[Poaceae (Gramineae)]*
   argentea (Nees) Stapf 1897 = **C. selloana**
   dioica (Sprengel) Spegazzini 1902
   jubata (Lemaire) Stapf 1898   EGF.2
   richardii (Endlicher) Zotov 1963 (*C. selloana* 'Toetoe')   EGF.2-**PGP**-RD
N **selloana** (Schultes & Schultes f.) Ascherson & Graebner 1855 non Rolfe 1890
                   (C. argentea)   EGF.2-PGP-**DGP**-**RD**
     'Aureo-lineata' (C. 'Gold Band')   PGP
     'Gold Band' = **C. selloana 'Aureo-lineata'**
L   **'Pumila'**
L   **'Rendatleri'**   **PGP**-RD
     'Roi des Roses'   **PGP**-RD
     'Silver Comet'   PGP
L   **'Sunningdale Silver'**   [Sunningdale Nurseries]   PGP-RD
     'Toetoe' = **C. richardii**

CORTUSA Linnaeus 1753   *[Primulaceae]*
   brotheri Pax ex Lipsky 1900 = **C. matthioli** ssp. **brotheri**
   matthioli Linnaeus 1753   PGP-RD
     'Alba'   RD
     ssp. **brotheri** (Pax ex Lipsky) ! (*C. brotheri*)
     ssp. **pekinensis** (A. Richter) Kitagawa 1966   RD

CORYBAS Salisbury 1805   *[Orchidaceae]*
   fimbriatus (R. Brown) Reichenbach f. 1871

CORYDALIS Ventenat 1803 nom. cons.   *[Fumariaceae]*
   alpestris Meyer 1831   SB
   ambigua Chamisso & Schlecht 1826   SB
   angustifolia (Marshall von Bieberstein) de Candolle 1821   SB
   bracteata (Stephan ex Willdenow) Persoon 1806   **SB**
N **bulbosa** (Linnaeus) de Candolle 1821 (*C. cava*)   PGP-**BB**-SB-RD
     'Alba'
   cashmeriana Royle 1833   CA-**BB**-**SB**-**DGP**-**RD**
   caucasica de Candolle 1821   **BB**-SB
     var. **albiflora** de Candolle 1821   **BB**-SB
   cava (Linnaeus) Schweigger & Koerte 1811 = **C. bulbosa**
   cheilanthifolia Hemsley 1892   RD
   chionophylla Czerniakowska ex Czerniakowska 1930   SB
   darwasica Regel ex Prain 1896   SB
   decipiens Schott, Nyman & Kotschy 1854   SB
   decumbens (Thunberg) Persoon 1806   SB
   diphylla Wallich 1826 = **C. rutifolia**
   firouzii Wendelbo 1976   SB
   glauca (Curtis) Pursh 1814 = **C. sempervirens**
   glaucescens Regel 1870   **BB**-SB
   intermedia (Linnaeus) Merat 1812   SB
   ledebouriana Karelin & Kirilow 1842   **BB**-**SB**
   lineariloba Siebold & Zuccarini 1843   SB
N‡ **lutea** (Linnaeus) de Candolle 1805   PGP-**RD**
     'Alba'
   nobilis (Linnaeus) Persoon 1807   PGP
   ochroleuca Koch 1831   PGP
     'Alba' = **C. ochroleuca**
   persica Chamisso & Schlecht 1826   SB
   popovii Nevski ex M. Popov 1934   **BB**-**SB**
   pumila (Host) Reichenbach 1832   CA-SB
   rutifolia (Smith) de Candolle 1821 (*C. diphylla*)   **BB**-SB
   schanginii (Pallas) B. Fedtschenko 1904   SB
A **sempervirens** (Linnaeus) Persoon 1807 (*C. glauca*)

N   **solida** (Linnaeus) Swartz 1817 (*C. transsylvanica* hort.)   PGP-CA-**BB**-SB-**DGP**
    'George Baker'   SB
    transsylvanica hort. = **C. solida**
    wilsonii N. E. Brown 1903

COSMOS Cavanilles 1791   [*Asteraceae (Compositae)*]
    atrosanguineus (Hooker) Ortgies 1881 (*Bidens atrosanguinea*)   PGP
    diversifolius Otto 1838 (*Bidens dahlioides*)

COTULA Linnaeus 1753   [*Asteraceae (Compositae)*]
    atrata Hooker f. 1864 = **Leptinella atrata**
    var. *dendyi* (Cockayne) Cheeseman 1925 = **Leptinella dendyi**
N   **coronopifolia** Linnaeus 1753
    dendyi Cockayne 1915 = **Leptinella dendyi**
    dioica (Hooker f.) Hooker f. 1864 = **Leptinella dioca**
    goyenii Petrie 1886 = **Leptinella goyenii**
    linearifolia Cheeseman 1883 = **Leptinella pyrethrifolia** var. **linearifolia**
    pectinata Hooker f. 1864 = **Leptinella pectinata**
    perpusilla Hooker f. 1864
    potentillina (F. Mueller) Druce 1917 = **Leptinella potentillina**
    pyrethrifolia Hooker f. 1864 = **Leptinella pyrethrifolia**
    reptans Bentham 1867 = **Leptinella scariosa**
    rotundata (Cheeseman) Lloyd 1972 = **Leptinella rotundata**
    scariosa (Cassini) Franchet 1889 = **Leptinella scariosa**
    sericea (Kirk) Cockayne & Allan 1927 = **Leptinella pectinata** var. **sericea**
    squalida (Hooker f.) Hooker f. 1864 = **Leptinella squalida**
    traillii Kirk 1899 = **Leptinella trailii**

COTYLEDON Linnaeus 1753   [*Crassulaceae*]
    chrysantha (Boissier & Heldreich) Bornmueller 1914 = **Rosularia pallida**
    oppositifolia Ledebour ex Nordmann 1837 = **Chiastophyllum oppositifolium**
    simplicifolia hort. ex Gard. Chron. 1931 = **Chiastophyllum oppositifolium**

CRAMBE Linnaeus 1753   [*Brassicaceae (Cruciferae)*]
L   **cordifolia** Steven 1812   PGP-**DGP**-RD
    koktebelica (Junge) Busch 1908   PGP
HN‡L   **maritima** Linnaeus 1753   PGP-RD
    orientalis Linnaeus 1753   PGP

CRASPEDIA Forster f. 1786   [*Asteraceae (Compositae)*]
    glauca (Labillardiere) Sprengel 1826 (*C. richea*)
    incana Allan 1961
    lanata (Hooker f.) Allan 1961
    richea Cassini = **C. glauca**
    uniflora Forster f. 1786

CRASSULA Linnaeus 1753   [*Crassulaceae*]
    bolusii Hooker f. 1887 = **C. cooperi**
    cooperi Regel 1874 (*C. bolusii*)   RD
N   **helmsii** Kirk 1858 (*C. recurva, Tillaea recurva*)
    'Ken Aslet'
    milfordae R. S. Byles 1957   CA-RD
    recurva N. E. Brown 1890 = **C. helmsii**
S   **sarcocaulis** Ecklon & Zeyher 1837   CA-**DGP**-RD
    'Alba'
    sediformis hort. non Schweinfurth = **C. milfordae**

CRAWFURDIA Wallich 1824   [*Gentianaceae*]
    japonica Siebold & Zuccarini 1846 (*Gentiana jesoana*)
    'Alba'

CREMANTHODIUM Bentham 1873   *[Asteraceae (Compositae)]*
    arnicoides (de Candolle ex Royle) Good 1929
    delavayi (Franchet) Leveille 1915
    oblongatum C.B. Clarke 1876
    reniforme (de Candolle) Bentham 1873

CREPIS Linnaeus 1753   *[Asteraceae (Compositae)]*
    aurea (Linnaeus) Cassini 1822   RD
    incana Smith 1813 (*C. rosea* hort.)   **RD**
    rosea hort. = **C. incana**

X CRINODONNA Anon = **X AMARCRINUM**

CRINUM Linnaeus 1753   *[Amaryllidaceae]*
    bulbispermum (Burman f.) Milne-Redhead & Schweickerdt 1939 (*C. capense*)
                           EGF.1-**PGP**-**BB**-RD
    moorei Hooker f. 1874   EGF.1-**PGP**-**BB**-RD
L   **x powellii** Baker 1888 (*C. bulbispermum* x *C. moorei*)   PGP-**BB**-**DGP**-**RD**
        'Album'   [pre-1888]   PGP-DGP
        'Krelagei'   [Krelage pre-1919]   PGP-DGP

CROCOSMIA Planchon 1851   *[Iridaceae]*
    aurea (Pappe ex Hooker) Planchon 1851   EGF.1-PGP-RD
    x crocosmiiflora (Lemoine ex Burbridge & Dean) N. E. Brown 1932 (*C. aurea* x
                               C. pottsii)   EGF.1-**PGP**-DGP-RD
    masonorum (L. Bolus) N. E. Brown 1932   EGF.1-**PGP**-DGP-**RD**
        'Firebird'
L   **paniculata** (Klatt) Goldblatt 1971 (*Antholyza paniculata, Curtonus paniculatus*)
                                  EGF.1-PGP
        'Major'
    pottsii (MacNab ex Baker) N. E. Brown 1932   EGF.1-**PGP**-RD
    rosea hort. = **Tritonia disticha** ssp. **rubrolucens**

    HYBRID CULTIVARS

    'A. E. Amos' ®   [J. E. Fitt]   PGP
    'Aurore' ®   [J. E. Fitt 1924]   PGP
    'Bressingham Blaze'   [A. Bloom]   PGP-RD
    'Carmin Brilliant' ®   [V. Lemoine]   PGP
    'Citronella' ®   [J. E. Fitt]   DGP
    'Dixter Flame'   [C. Lloyd]
    'E. A. Bowles'
    'Emberglow'   [A. Bloom]   PGP-RD
L   **'Emily McKenzie'** ®   [K. McKenzie 1954]   **PGP**
    'Fire King' ®   [E. H. Krelage]
    'George Davidson' ®   [E. Davidson pre-1902]
    'Golden Glory'   PGP
    'His Majesty' ®   [J. E. Fitt c1919]   PGP-DGP
    'Honey Angels' = **C. 'Citronella'**
L   **'Jackanapes'**   PGP-**DGP**-RD
    'James Coey' ®   [J. E. Fitt c1921]   PGP
    'Lady Hamilton'   [c1907]   PGP
    'Lady Wilson' ®   [J. E. Fitt pre-1930]   PGP
L   **'Lucifer'**   [A. Bloom]
    'Lutea' nom. dub.
    'Mars'
    'Meteore' ®   [V. Lemoine 1887]
    'Mount Stewart' nom. dub.
    'Mount Usher'
    'Mrs. Geoffrey Howard'   PGP

'Orange Flame'
'Queen Alexandra' ®   [J. E. Fitt pre-1925]   PGP
'Queen of Spain'   [1916]   **PGP**
'Red King' ®
'Sir Matthew Wilson' ®   [J. E. Fitt c1928]   PGP
'Solfatare' [Pre-1897]   **PGP-RD**
'Spitfire' [A. Bloom]   PGP-RD
'Sprowston Glory'   PGP
'Star of the East' ®   [G. Davidson pre-1913]   PGP-DGP
'Tigridie' ®   [V. Lemoine 1891]   PGP
'Vesuvius' ®   [W. Pfitzer 1907]   PGP
'Vulcan' [A. Bloom]   RD
'Walburton Red'   [D. R. Tristram]   PGP
'Walburton Yellow'   [D. R. Tristram]   PGP

CROCUS Linnaeus 1753   [*Iridaceae*]

M - MATHEW, BRIAN: *The Crocus* B. T. Batsford Ltd., London, 1982

abantensis T. Baytop & B. Mathew 1975   **M**-SB
adamii Gay 1832 = **C. biflorus** ssp. **adamii**
adanensis T. Baytop & B. Mathew 1975   **M**-SB
aerius Herbert 1847 (*C. biliottii*)   **M**-**BB**-SB
aitchisonii hort. = **C. speciosus** var. **aitchisonii**
alatavicus Semenov & Regel 1868   **M**-**BB**-**SB**
albiflorus Kitaibel ex Schultes 1814 = **C. vernus** ssp. **albiflorus**
ancyrensis (Herbert) Maw 1881   M-EGF.1-**BB**-SB-**RD**
    'Golden Bunch' = **C. ancyrensis**
angustifolius Weston 1771 (*C.susianus, C.* 'Cloth of Gold')
                                             M-EGF.1-CA-**BB**-SB-DGP-**RD**
    'Minor' Paxton ®   M
antalyensis B. Mathew 1972   **M**-**BB**-SB
asturicus Herbert 1843 = **C. serotinus** ssp. **salzmannii**
asumaniae B. Mathew & T. Baytop 1979   **M**-SB
aureus Smith 1806 non E. D. Clarke 1812 = **C. flavus** ssp. **flavus**
balsanae Gay ex Baker 1873 = **C. olivieri** ssp. **balsanae**
banaticus Gay 1831 (*C. byzantinus*)   M-EGF.1-CA-**BB**-**SB**-RD
banaticus Heuffel 1835 non Gay = **C. vernus** ssp. **vernus**
    'Albus' = **C. vernus** ssp. **albiflorus**
baytopiorum B. Mathew 1974   **M**-**BB**-SB
biflorus Miller 1768   M-EGF.1-CA-**BB**-SB-RD
    ssp. **adamii** (Gay) B. Mathew 1982 (*C. adamii*)   **M**-SB-RD
    ssp. **alexandri** (Nicic ex Velenovsky) B. Mathew 1982   M-EGF.1-SB
    var. *argenteus* Sabine 1830 = **C. biflorus** ssp. **biflorus**
    ssp. **biflorus**   **M**-EGF.1
    ssp. **crewei** (Hooker f.) B. Mathew 1982   M-SB
    ssp. **isauricus** (Siehe ex Bowles) B. Mathew 1982   M-SB
    ssp. **melantherus** (Boissier & Orphanides) B. Mathew 1982 M-EGF.1-SB
    ssp. **nubigena** (Herbert) B. Mathew 1982   **M**-SB
    var. *parkinsonii* Sabine 1830 = **C. biflorus** ssp. **biflorus**
    ssp. **pseudonubigena** B. Mathew 1982   M-SB
    ssp. **pulchricolor** (Herbert) B. Mathew 1982   **M**-EGF.1-SB
    ssp. **tauri** (Maw) B. Mathew 1982   M-SB
    ssp. **weldenii** (Hoppe & Fünkranz) B. Mathew 1982   M-EGF.1-SB-**RD**
    ssp. **weldenii** 'Albus' ®   [pre-1939]   RD
    ssp. **weldenii** 'Fairy' ®   [van Tubergen pre-1956]
biliottii Maw 1881 = **C. aerius**
boryi Gay 1831   M-EGF.1-CA-**BB**-SB
byzantinus Herbert 1841 = **C. banaticus**
cambessedesii Gay 1831   **M**-SB

cancellatus Herbert 1841 — M-EGF.1-**BB**-SB
   ssp. **cancellatus** — M-EGF.1-**BB**
   var. *cilicicus* Maw 1881 = **C. cancellatus** ssp. **cancellatus**
   ssp. **damascenus** (Herbert) B. Mathew 1982
   ssp. **lycius** B. Mathew 1982 — **M**-SB
   ssp. **mazziaricus** (Herbert) B. Mathew 1982 — **M**-SB
   ssp. **pamphylicus** B. Mathew 1982 — M-EGF.1-**BB**-SB
candidus Clarke 1812 — **M**-SB
   var. *subflavus* hort. = **C. olivieri** ssp. **olivieri** — M-CA-**BB**-SB-RD
cartwrightianus Herbert 1843
   'Albus' = **C. hadriaticus** — M-EGF.1-RD
cashmirianus Royle 1836 = **C. sativus**
chrysanthus (Herbert) Herbert 1843 — M-EGF.1-**CA**-**BB**-DGP-RD
   'Advance' ®   [G. H. Hageman pre-1953] — EGF.1-**BB**-RD
   'Ard Schenk' ®   [C. M. Berbee]
   'Blue Bird' ®   [G. H. Hageman pre-1954] — EGF.1-**BB**-RD
   'Blue Pearl' ®   [G. H. Hageman pre-1950] — EGF.1-**BB**-DGP-RD
   'Blue Peter' ®   [van Tubergen pre-1965]
   'Canary Bird' ®   [van Tubergen]
   'Cream Beauty' ®   [G. H. Hageman pre-1943] — **BB**-DGP
   'Dorothy' ®   [Barr & Sons]
   'E. A. Bowles' ®   [van Tubergen pre-1931] — CA-**DGP**-RD
   'E. P. Bowles' ®   [van Tubergen 1965]
   'Eye-catcher' ®   [P. B. van Eeden 1971]
   var. *fuscotinctus* Baker
   'Gipsy Girl' ®   [G. H. Hageman 1960] — M
   'Goldilocks' ®   [Barr & Sons 1950] — BB
   'Jeannine' ®   [van Tubergen 1973] — DGP-RD
   'Ladykiller' ®   [G. H. Hageman pre-1953] — EGF.1-**DGP**-RD
   'Mariette' ®   [van Tubergen 1956]
   'Miss Vain'
   'Moonlight' ®   [E. A. Bowles via van Tubergen pre-1924] — CA
   'Prins Claus' ®   [C. M. Berbee 1959]
   'Prinses Beatrix' ®   [G. H. Hageman 1953] — RD
   'Saturnus' ®   [G. H. Hageman pre-1967] — BB
   'Skyline' ®   [P. B. van Eeden 1972]
   'Snowbunting' ®   [E. A. Bowles pre-1939] — BB-RD
   'Snow White' ®   [G. H. Hageman pre-1953]
   'Spring Pearl' ®   [P. B. van Eeden 1972]
   'Uschak Orange'
   'Warley' ®   [van Tubergen pre-1905] — DGP
   'White Vain'
   'Zenith' ®   [P. B. van Eeeden 1971]
   'Zwanenburg Bronze' ®   [van Tubergen pre-1938] — BB-RD
chrysobelonicus Herbert = **C. hadriaticus**
'Cloth of Gold' = **C. angustifolius**
'Cloth of Silver' = **C. versicolor** 'Picturatus'
clusii Gay 1831 = **C. serotinus** ssp. **clusii**
corsicus Vanucci 1878 — M-EGF.1-CA-**BB**-SB-DGP-RD
cvijicii Kosanin 1926 — **M**-SB
dalmaticus Visiani 1842 — M-EGF.1-**BB**-SB-RD
danfordiae Maw 1881 — **M**-BB-SB
etruscus Parlatore 1858 — M-EGF.1-CA-**BB**-SB-**DGP**-RD
   'Zwanenburg' ®   [van Tubergen pre-1939] — RD
flavus Weston 1771 — M-EGF.1-SB
   ssp. **flavus** (*C. aureus*) — **M**-DGP-**RD**
   'Golden Yellow' ('Dutch Yellow', 'Mammoth', 'Yellow Giant')   [Old cv.]
   — EGF.1-**BB**-DGP-RD
fleischeri Gay 1831 — M-EGF.1-**CA**-**BB**-SB-RD
fontenayi Reuter ex Nyman 1882 = **C. laevigatus**

gargaricus Herbert 1841   **M**-**BB**-SB
'Golden Bunch' = **C. anacyrensis 'Golden Bunch'**
goulimyi Turrill 1955   **M**-EGF.1-**BB**-SB-RD
'Albus' = **C. niveus**
niveus hort. = **C. niveus**
graveolens Boissier & Reuter ex Boissier 1882   **M**-**BB**-SB
hadriaticus Herbert 1845   **M**-EGF.1-CA-**BB**-SB
var. *chrysobelonicus* Herbert = **C. hadriaticus**
'Tom Blanchard'
hermoneus Kotschy ex Maw 1881   **M**-SB
heuffelianus Herbert 1847 = **C. vernus** ssp. **vernus** var. **heuffelianus**
imperati Tenore 1826   **M**-CA-**BB**-SB-**DGP**-RD
'de Jager'   ®   [P. de Jager & Sons]
karduchorum Kotschy 1881   **M**-**BB**-SB
karduchorum hort. non Kotschy = **C. kotschyi** ssp. **kotschyi** var. **leucostigma**
korolkowii Regel ex Maw 1880   **M**-EGF.1-**BB**-RD
kotschyanus K. Koch 1853   **M**-EGF.1-CA-SB-DGP-RD
ssp. **cappadocicus** B. Mathew 1980   **M**-**BB**-SB
ssp. **hakkariensis** B. Mathew 1980   M-**BB**-SB
ssp. **kotschyanus** (*C. zonatus*)   **M**
ssp. **kotschyanus** var. **leucopharynx** B. L. Burtt 1952   EGF.1-**BB**-SB
ssp. **suworowianus** (K. Koch) B. Mathew 1980 (*C. suworowianus*)   **M**-**BB**-SB
laevigatus Bory & Chaubard 1832 (*C. fontenayi* Reuter)
                                              M-EGF.1-CA-**BB**-SB-**DGP**-RD
leichtlinii (D. Dewar) Bowles 1924   **M**-CA-SB
leucostigma (Maw) hort. = **C. vernus** ssp. **vernus** var. **leucostigma**
longiflorus Rafinesque 1810   **M**-EGF.1-CA-**BB**-SB-RD
malyi Visiani 1871   **M**-CA-**BB**-SB
medius Balbis 1810   **M**-EGF.1-CA-**BB**-SB-**RD**
michelsonii B. Fedtschenko 1932   **M**-**BB**-SB
minimus de Candolle 1805   **M**-EGF.1-CA-**BB**-SB-**DGP**-RD
nevadensis Amo 1871   **M**-**BB**-SB
niveus Bowles 1900   **M**-EGF.1-**BB**-SB-RD
N   **nudiflorus** Smith in Sowerby & Smith 1789   **M**-EGF.1-**BB**-SB-**DGP**
ochroleucus Boissier & Gaillardot 1859   **M**-EGF.1-CA-**BB**-SB-RD
olivieri Gay 1831   **M**-EGF.1-**BB**-SB-RD
ssp. **balansae** (Gay ex Baker) B. Mathew 1973 (*C. balsanae*)
                                               M-EGF.1-CA-**BB**-SB-RD
ssp. **balansae 'Zwanenburg'**   ®   [van Tubergen]
ssp. **istanbulensis** B. Mathew 1982   M-SB
ssp. **olivieri** (*C. suterianus*)   **M**-EGF.1-**CA**-RD
oreocreticus B. L. Burtt 1949   **M**-SB
pallasii Goldbach 1817   **M**-**BB**-SB
ssp. **turcicus** B. Mathew 1977   M-SB
pestalozzae Boissier 1853   **M**-CA-**BB**-SB
'Albus'
'Caeruleus' Barr   M
pulchellus Herbert 1841   **M**-EGF.1-CA-**BB**-SB-DGP-RD
'Sylvia Cobb'
'Zephyr'   ®   [van Tubergen]
reticulatus Steven ex Adams 1805   **M**-CA-**BB**-SB
'Albus'
ssp. **hittiticus** (T. Baytop & B. Mathew) B. Mathew 1982   M-SB
robertianus C. D. Brickell 1973   **M**-**BB**-SB
salzmannii Gay 1831 = **C. serotinus** ssp. **salzmannii**
HN   **sativus** Linnaeus 1753   **M**-EGF.1-**BB**-SB-DGP-RD
var. *cashmirianus* Royle = **C. sativus**
scardicus Kosanin 1926   **M**-CA-**BB**-SB
scepusiensis (Rehm & Woloszczak) Borbas 1919 = **C. vernus** ssp. **vernus** var.
                                                              scepusiensis

scharojanii Ruprecht 1868   **M-BB**-SB
serotinus Salisbury 1806   M-EGF.1-CA--SB
   ssp. **clusii** (Gay) B. Mathew 1977 (*C. clusii*)   M-EGF.1-CA-SB
   ssp. **salzmannii** (Gay) B. Mathew 1977 (*C. asturicus, C. salzmannii*)
       M-EGF.1-CA-**BB**-SB-RD
sieberi Gay 1831   M-EGF.1-CA-**BB**-SB-**DGP**-**RD**
   'Albus' ®   [E. A. Bowles pre-1937] ('Bowles' White)
   ssp. **atticus** (Boissier & Orphanides) B. Mathew 1982   M-EGF.1-SB-RD
   'Bowles' White' = **C. sieberi 'Albus'**
   'Firefly' ®   [M. Thoolen 1956]
   var. *heterochromus* Halacsy = **C. sieberi** ssp. **sieberi**
   'Hubert Edelsten' ®   [H. Mc. D. Edelsten pre-1924]   EGF.1-RD
   ssp. **sieberi**   **M**-EGF.1-**BB**-DGP
   ssp. **sublimis** (Herbert) B. Mathew 1982   **M**-EGF.1-SB
   ssp. **sublimis** f. **tricolor** B. L. Burtt   M-EGF.1-**SB**-DGP
   'Violet Queen' ®   [G. H. Hageman pre-1955]   DGP-RD
speciosus Marshall von Bieberstein 1800   **M**-EGF.1-CA-**BB**-SB-**DGP**-**RD**
   var. **aitchisonii** Bowles   M-RD
   'Albus' ®   [van Tubergen c1913]   EGF.1-RD
   'Artabir' ®   [van Tubergen 1896]   RD
   'Cassiope' ®   [van Tubergen]
   'Conqueror' ®
   'Globosus' ®
   ssp. **ilgazensis** B. Mathew 1982   M-SB
   'Oxonian' ®   [Barr & Sons pre-1945]   **DGP**
   'Pollux' ®   [van Tubergen pre-1938]
   'R. D. Trotter'
   ssp. **xantholaimos** B. Mathew 1982   M-SB
x stellaris Haworth 1812 (*C. angustifolius* x *C. flavus*)   M-SB
susianus Ker-Gawler 1813 = **C. angustifolius**
suterianus Herbert 1845 = **C. olivieri** ssp. **olivieri**
suworowianus K. Koch 1848 = **C. kotschyanus** ssp. **suworowianus**
thomasii Tenore 1826   **M**-SB
tommasinianus Herbert 1847   **M**-EGF.1-**BB**-SB-**DGP**-**RD**
   'Albus'
   'Barr's Purple' ®   [Barr & Sons]   DGP-RD
   'Bobbo' ®
   'Eric Smith'
   var. **pictus** Bowles   M
   var. **roseus** Bowles   M
   'Ruby Giant' ®   [Roozen-Kramer 1956]
   'Taplow Ruby' ®   [Barr & Sons]   DGP
   'Vanguard' ®   [van Tubergen 1934]   RD
   'Whitewell Purple' ®   [J. Jacob pre-1933]   **DGP-RD**
tournefortii Gay 1831   **M**-EGF.1-CA-**BB**-**SB**
vallicola Herbert 1845   **M**-**BB**-SB
veluchensis Herbert 1845   **M**-**BB**-SB
N‡ **vernus** Hill 1765   M-EGF.1-CA-**BB**-SB-DGP
   ssp. **albiflorus** (Kitaibel ex Schultes) Ascherson & Graebner 1906
       M-EGF.1-CA-**BB**-SB
   'Early Perfection' ®   [W. J. Eldering 1925]
   'Enchantress' ®   [W. J. Eldering 1924]
   'Flower Record' ®
   'Golden Yellow' = **C. flavus 'Golden Yellow'**
   'Graecus' ®   [via M. Leichtlin]
   'Grand Maitre' ®   [W. J. Eldering 1924]
   'Haarlem Gem' ®   [van Tubergen pre-1944]   DGP
   var. *heuffelianus* (Herbert) Beck = **C. vernus** ssp. **vernus** var. **heuffelianus**
   'Jeanne d'Arc' ®   [W. J. Eldering 1943]   RD
   'Kathleen Parlow' ®   [G. H. van Waveren 1905]   **DGP**

'King of the Blues'
'King of the Striped'   ®   [W. J. Eldering 1880]
'King of the Whites'   **BB**
'Large Yellow' = **C. flavus 'Golden Yellow'**
var. *leucostigma* Maw 1886 = **C. vernus** ssp. **vernus** var. **leucostigma**
'Little Dorrit'   ®   [W. J. Eldering 1943]   **BB**-RD
'Mammoth' = **C. flavus 'Golden Yellow'**
'Paulus Potter'   ®   [c1920]
'Peter Pan'   ®   [W. J. Eldering 1943]
'Pickwick'   ®   [W. J. Eldering pre-1950]   **BB**-DGP-RD
'Purpureus Grandiflorus'   ®   [c1870]   **DGP**-RD
'Queen of the Blues'   ®   [W. F. van Waveren 1916]   DGP-RD
'Remembrance'   ®   [W. J. Eldering 1925]   **BB**
var. *scepusiensis* Rehm & Woloszczak = **C. vernus** ssp. **vernus** var. **scepusiensis**
'Sky Blue'   ®   [W. J. Eldering 1925]
'Snowstorm'   ®   [W. J. Eldering 1925]   **DGP**
'Striped Beauty'   ®   [W. J. Eldering 1925]   DGP-RD
ssp. **vernus**   **M**-EGF.1-**BB**
ssp. **vernus** var. **heuffelianus** (Herbert) ! (*C. heuffelianus*)   **M**-CA-SB
ssp. **vernus** var. **leucostigma** (Maw) ! (*C. leucostigma*)   **BB**
ssp. **vernus** var. **scepusiensis** (Rehm & Woloszczak) ! (*C. scepusiensis*)
'Victor Hugo'   ®   [W. J. Eldering 1943]
'Yellow Giant' = **C. flavus 'Golden Yellow'**
versicolor Ker-Gawler 1808   **M**-EGF.1-CA-**BB**-SB-RD
   'Picturatus'   ®   [pre-1909] (C. 'Cloth of Silver')   EGF.1-RD
vitellinus Wahlenberg 1826   **M**-CA-**BB**-SB
   'November Flame'
zonatus Gay ex Klatt 1865 = **C. kotschyanus** ssp. **kotschyanus**

CRUCIANELLA Linnaeus 1753   [*Rubiaceae*]
   stylosa Trinius 1818 = **Phuopsis stylosa**

CRYPTOGRAMMA R. Brown ex Richardson 1823   [*Adiantaceae*]
N   **crispa** (Linnaeus) R. Brown 1842   EGF.1-PGP

CRYPTOTAENIA de Candolle 1829   [*Apiaceae (Umbelliferae)*]
H   **canadensis** (Linnaeus) de Candolle 1829 (*C. japonica*)
   japonica Hasskarl 1885 = **C. canadensis**

CUMINUM Linnaeus 1753   [*Apiaceae (Umbelliferae)*]
A   **cyminum** Linnaeus 1753

CUPHEA P. Brown 1756   [*Lythraceae*]
   cyanea Mocino & Sesse 1828
   ignea de Candolle 1849
      'Variegata'

CURTONUS N. E. Brown 1932   [*Iridaceae*]
   paniculatus (Klatt) N. E. Brown 1932 = **Crocosmia paniculata**

CYANANTHUS Wallich ex Bentham 1835   [*Campanulaceae*]
   integer Wallich 1830 nom nudum = **C. microphyllus**
   lobatus Wallich ex Bentham 1835   CA-**DGP**-RD
      'Albus'   CA-**RD**
      'Dark Beauty'
      'Gigantea'
      'Inshriach Blue'
      'Sherriff's Variety' = **C. sherriffii**
   microphyllus Edgeworth 1846 (*C. integer*)   CA-**DGP-RD**
   sherriffii Cowan 1938   CA-RD

CYATHEA J. E. Smith 1793   [*Cyatheaceae*]
    cooperi (Hooker ex F. Mueller) Domin 1929
                                              EGF.1
    dealbata (Forster f.) Swartz 1801   EGF.1
    medullaris (Forster f.) Swartz 1801   EGF.1

CYCLAMEN Linnaeus 1753
                                                     [*Primulaceae*]

M - GREY-WILSON, C.,: *'The Genus Cyclamen'* A Kew Monograph 1988

    abchasicum (Medvedev ex Kusnezov) Kolak 1948 = **C. coum** ssp. **caucasicum**
    africanum Boissier & Reuter 1852   M-CA-**BB**-SB
    alpinum hort. = **C. trichopteranthum**
    x atkinsii T. Moore 1852 = **C. coum 'Atkinsii'**
    balearicum Willkomm 1875   **M**-CA-**BB**-SB-**RD**
    caucasicum (K. Koch) Willdenow ex Boissier 1875 = **C. coum** ssp. **caucasicum**
    cilicium Boissier & Heldreich 1843   M-CA-**BB**-SB-**DGP**-RD
        'Album'   **M**
        var. *alpinum* hort. = **C. intaminatum**
        var. *intaminatum* Meikle 1978 = **C. intaminatum**
    coum Miller 1768 (*C. orbiculatum*)   **M**-CA-**BB**-**DGP**-**RD**
        var. *abchasicum* Medvedev ex Kusnezov 1902 = **C. coum** ssp. **caucasicum**
        'Album'   **M**
        'Atkinsii'   M-SB-**RD**
        ssp. **caucasicum** (K. Koch) Schwartz 1955 (*C. caucasicum, C. coum* var.
                 abchasicum, C. ibericum, C. vernum)   M-**BB**-SB
        'Elegans'
        'Nymans'
        'Pewter Leaf'   **M**
        'Roseum'   **M**
        'Tilebarn Elizabeth'   [P. Moore]   **M**
    creticum (Doerfler) Hildebrand 1906   **M**-CA-**BB**-SB
        'Tilebarn Spoa'   [P. Moore]
    cyprium Kotschy 1865   M-CA-**BB**-SB
    europaeum Linnaeus 1753 ex hort. nom. confus. = **C. purpurascens**
    fatrense Halda & Sojak 1971 = **C. purpurascens**
    graecum Link 1834   M-CA-**BB**-SB-RD
        'Album'
N‡   **hederifolium** Aiton 1789 (*C. neapolitanum*)   **M**-CA-**BB**-SB-**DGP**-RD
        'Album'   **M**-CA-RD
        'Bowles' Apollo'
        'Perlenteppich'   **M**
        'Rosenteppich'   **M**
        Scented form
        Silver-leafed form
    ibericum T. Moore 1852 = **C. coum** ssp. **caucasicum**
    intaminatum (Meikle) Grey-Wilson 1988 (*C. cilicium* var. *intaminatum*) **M**-**BB**-SB
        Silver-leafed form
    libanoticum Hildebrand 1898   **M**-CA-**BB**-SB-**DGP**-RD
    mirabile Hildebrand 1906   **M**-**BB**-SB
    neapolitanum Tenore 1813 = **C. hederifolium**
    orbiculatum Miller 1768 = **C. coum**
    parviflorum Pobedimova 1946   **M**-**BB**-SB
    persicum Miller 1768   **M**-**BB**-SB-**DGP**-RD
        'Tilebarn Karpathos'   [P. Moore]
    pseudibericum Hildebrand 1901   **M**-**BB**-SB-**DGP**
        'Roseum'
    purpurascens Miller 1768 (*C. europaeum, C. fatrense*)   **M**-CA-**BB**-SB-**DGP**-RD
        'Auslese'
        'Limone'
    repandum Smith 1806   **M**-CA-**BB**-SB-**DGP**-RD

'Album'
    ssp. **peloponnesiacum** Grey-Wilson 1988 (*C. repandum* 'Pelops')   **M**-SB
    Red form
    ssp. **rhodense** (Meikle) Grey-Wilson 1988   **M**-**BB**-SB
rohlfsianum Ascherson 1897   **M**-CA-**BB**-SB
trochopteranthum O. Schwarz 1975 (*C. alpinum* hort.)   **M**-**BB**-SB
vernum Sweet 1823 = **C. coum** ssp. **caucasicum**

CYMBALARIA Hill 1756   [*Scrophulariaceae*]
    aequitriloba (Viviani) A. Chevalier 1937 (*Linaria aequitriloba*)   CA
      'Alba'
    hepaticifolia (Poiret) Wettstein 1891 (*Linaria hepaticifolia*)
      'Alba'
N‡   **muralis** P. Gaertner, B. Meyer & Scherbius 1800 (*Linaria cymbalaria*)   RD
      'Alba'
      'Globosa (*Linaria cymbalaria* var. *globosa*)
      'Nana'
      'Nana Alba'
N   **pallida** (Tenore) Wettstein 1891 (*Linaria pallida*)
    pilosa (Jacquin) Grande 1914 (*Linaria pilosa*)

CYNANCHUM Linnaeus 1753   [*Asclepiadaceae*]
    purpurescens Morren & Decaisne 1836

CYNARA Linnaeus 1753   [*Asteraceae (Compositae)*]
HL   **cardunculus** Linnaeus 1753   PGP
    hystrix Ball 1873   PGP
H   **scolymus** Linnaeus 1753   PGP
      'Brittany Belle'
      'Glauca'
      'Purple Globe'
      'Vert de Lyon'

CYNOGLOSSUM Linnaeus 1753   [*Boraginaceae*]
    amabile Staph & Drummond 1906   RD
    lanceolatum Forsskal 1775
    nervosum Bentham & Hooker 1883   PGP-**DGP**-RD
HN‡   **officinale** Linnaeus 1753

CYPELLA Herbert 1826   [*Iridaceae*]
    herbertii (Lindley) Herbert 1826 (*Moraea herbertii*)   EGF.1-**BB**-SB
    plumbea (Herbert) Lindley 1838 (*Ferraria coelestina*)

CYPERUS Linnaeus 1753   [*Cyperaceae*]
    alternifolius Linnaeus 1767   PGP-RD
    alternifolius hort. p.p., non Linnaeus = **C. involucratus**
    eragrostis Lamarck 1791 (*C. vegetus*)   EGF.2-RD
    esculentus Linnaeus 1753   EGF.2
    involucratus Rottboell 1772 (*C. alternifolius* hort p.p.)   EGF.2-DGP
N‡L   **longus** Linnaeus 1753   EGF.2-PGP-RD
    rotundus Linnaeus 1753
    ustulatus A. Richard 1832
    vegetus Willdenow 1797 = **C. eragrostis**

CYPRIPEDIUM Linnaeus 1753   [*Orchidaceae*]
    acaule Aiton 1789   EGF.2-PGP-CA-RD
    arietinum R. Brown 1813   EGF.2-PGP-CA
N‡   **calceolus** Linnaeus 1753   EGF.2-PGP-CA-**DGP**-RD

var. **parviflorum** (Salisbury) Fernald 1946 (*C. parviflorum*) EGF.2-PGP
var. **pubescens** (Willdenow) Correll (*C. pubescens*) EGF.2-PGP-CA
cordigerum D. Don 1825 EGF.2-CA
debile Reichenbach f. 1874 EGF.2-CA
himalaicum Hemsley 1892 EGF.2
guttatum Swartz 1800 (*C. yatebeanum*) EGF.2-PGP
japonicum Thunberg 1784 EGF.2-PGP-CA
macranthum Swartz 1800 EGF.2-CA
  f. **rebunense** (Kudo) Ohwi
parviflorum Salisbury 1791 = **C. calceolus** var. **parviflorum**
pubescens Willdenow 1805 = **C. calceolus** var. **pubescens**
reginae Walter 1788 (*C. spectabile*) EGF.2-PGP-CA-DGP-**RD**
spectabile Salisbury 1791 = **C. reginae**
yatebeanum Makino 1899 = **C. guttatum**

CYRTANTHUS Aiton 1789 [*Amaryllidaceae*]
  brachyscyphus Baker 1888 (*C. parviflorus*)
  brevifolius Harvey 1863 (*Anoiganthus luteus*) SB
  carneus Lindley 1831
  x contractus N. E. Brown 1921 (*C. brachyscyphus* x *C. mackenii*)
  epiphyticus J. M. Wood 1913
  eucallus R. A. Dyer
  falcatus R. A. Dyer 1939
  fergusoniae L. Bolus 1931
  galpinii Baker 1892
  guthriae L. Bolus 1921
  herrei (Leighton) R. A. Dyer 1959
  inaqualis O'Brien 1905
  labiatus R. A. Dyer 1980
  mackenii Hooker f. 1869 EGF.1-SB
    var. **cooperi** SB
  macowanii Baker 1875 EGF.1-SB
  montanus R. A. Dyer 1977
  obliquus (Linnaeus f.) Aiton 1789 EGF.1
  parviflorus Baker 1891 = **C. brachyscyphus**
  purpureus (Aiton) Herbert ex Traub 1963 (*Vallota purpurea, V. speciosa*)
    PGP-EGF.1-SB
  'Albus' EGF.1
  Red Ember Hybrids
  sanguineus (Linnaeus f.) Hooker 1860 EGF.1
  smithianus Herbert 1840
  'Sunrise'

CYRTOMIUM C. Presl 1836 [*Dryopteridaceae*]
N **falcatum** (Linnaeus f.) C. Presl 1836 EGF.1-PGP-**RD**
    'Rochfordianum' RD
  fortunei J. Smith 1866 EGF.1
  lonchitoides (Christ) Christ 1902
  macrophyllum (Makino) Tagawa 1934

CYSTOPTERIS Berhardi 1805 nom. cons. [*Woodsiaceae*]
  bulbifera (Linnaeus) Bernhardi 1806 PGP
N **dickieana** Sim 1848 EGF.1
N **fragilis** (Linnaeus) Bernhardi 1806 EGF.1-PGP
    'Cristata'
  regia (Linnaeus) Desvaux 1827 EGF.1

DACTYLIS Linnaeus 1753 [*Poaceae (Gramineae)*]
  glomerata Linnaeus 1753 EGF.2
    var. **variegata** C. L. Hitchcock 1935 PGP

DACTYLORHIZA Necker ex Nevski 1937   [*Orchidaceae*]
    elata (Poiret) Soo 1962   EGF.2-PGP
    foliosa (Solander ex Vermoesen) Soo 1962 (*D. maderensis*)   EGF.2-PGP-CA-**DGP**
N‡ **fuchsii** (Druce) Soo 1962 (*D. maculata* ssp. *fuschii*)   EGF.2
N‡ **incarnata** (Linnaeus) Soo 1962   EGF.2
N‡ **maculata** (Linnaeus) Soo 1962   EGF.2
        ssp. *fuchsii* (Druce) Hylander = **D. fuchsii**
    maderensis hort. = **D. foliosa**
N‡ **majalis** (Reichenbach f.) Hunt & Summerhayes 1965   EGF.2
        ssp. **praetermissa** (Druce) Moresby, Moore & Soo 1978
    romana (Sebatius & Mauri) Soo 1962 = **D. sulphurea** ssp. **pseudosambucina**
    sambucina (Linnaeus) Soo 1962   EGF.2
    sulphurea (Link) Soo 1962
        ssp. **pseudosambucina** (Tenore) Franco 1978 (*D. romana*)

DAHLIA Cavanilles 1791   [*Asteraceae (Compositae)*]
    merckii Lehmann 1839   PGP

DARMERA Voss 1899   [*Saxifragaceae*]
L **peltata** (Torrey) Voss 1899 (*Peltiphyllum peltatum*)   **PGP-DGP**
    'Nana'   PGP

DATURA Linnaeus 1753   [*Solanaceae*]
S **inioxia** Miller 1768 (*D. meteloides*)   RD
S **metel** Linnaeus 1753 non Miller 1756   RD
    meteloides (de Candolle) Dunal 1849 = **D. inioxia**
AN **stramonium** Linnaeus 1753

DAVALLIA Smith 1793   [*Davalliaceae*]
    mariesii Moore ex Baker 1891   EGF.1-PGP-**RD**

DEGENIA Hayek 1910   [*Brassicaceae (Cruciferae)*]
    velebitica (Degen) Hayek 1910

DEINANTHE Maximowicz 1867   [*Hydrangeaceae*]
    bifida Maximowicz 1867   PGP-CA
    caerulea Stapf 1911   **PGP**-CA

DELOSPERMA N. E. Brown 1925   [*Aizoaceae*]
    aberdeenense (L. Bolus) L. Bolus 1928
    asperulum (Salm-Dyck) L. Bolus 1950
    'Basutoland'
    brunnthaleri (A. Berger) Swantes ex Jacobsen & Sukkel 1933
    caespitosum L. Bolus 1930
    cooperi (Hooker f.) L. Bolus 1927 (*Mesembryanthemum cooperi*)
    lineare L. Bolus 1928 (*Mesembryanthemum othona*)
    lydenburgense L. Bolus 1958
    nubigenum hort. non (Schlechter) L. Bolus 1960 = **D. lineare** p.p. & **Malephora lutea** p.p.
    sutherlandii (Hooker f.) N. E. Brown 1925 (*Mesembryanthemum sutherlandii*)

DELPHINIUM Linnaeus 1753   [*Ranunculaceae*]
L **x belladonna** (Kelway) Bergmans 1924 (*D. elatum* x *D. grandiflorum* ?)
                                          PGP-DGP-RD
        'Andenken an August Koenemann' = **D. x belladonna 'Wendy'**
        'Blue Bees' ®   [Bees' Nursery]   DGP-RD
        'Capri' ®   [Ruys 1910]
        'Cassa Blanca'
        'Cliveden Beauty' ®   [via Barr 1918]
        'Horatius' ®   [Koppius 1925]

'Lamartine' ®   [Lemoine 1903]   RD
'Moerheimii' ®   [Ruys 1906]   DGP-RD
'Orion' ®   [Koppius 1923]
'Piccolo'   [Weinreich 1972]
'Sommerfrische' ®   [H. Klose 1982]
'Völkerfrieden' ®   [Späth - Hillrich 1942]
'Wendy' ®   [Goos & Koenemann 1928]   DGP-RD
brunonianum Royle 1834   PGP
californicum Torrey & A. Gray 1838
cardinale Hooker 1855   PGP-RD
carduchorum Chowdhuri & P. H. Davis 1958
carolinianum Walter 1788
cashmirianum Royle 1839   PGP
caucasicum C. A. Meyer 1849 = **D. elatum**
N **elatum** Linnaeus 1753 (*D. caucasicum*)   PGP-RD
glandulosum Boissier & Huet 1856
grandiflorum Linnaeus 1753 (*D. chinense*)   PGP-RD
'Azure Fairy' ®   [via Thompson & Morgan 1912]
'Blauer Zwerg' ®   [Foerster 1929]
'Blue Butterfly'
'White Butterfly' nom. illegit.   PGP
menziesii de Candolle 1818
muscosum Exell & Hillcoat 1953
nudicaule Torrey & A. Gray 1838   PGP-RD
przewaldskii Huth 1895
B **requienii** de Candolle 1815   PGP
x ruysii Hort. ex Möllers 1934 (*D. elatum* x *D. nudicaule*)
'Pink Sensation' ®('Rosa Überraschung')   [Ruys 1930]   PGP-DGP-RD
'Rosa Überraschung' = **D. x ruysii 'Pink Sensation'**
semibarbatum Bienert ex Boissier 1867 (*D. zalil*)   PGP
speciosum Marshall von Bieberstein 1808
tatsienense Franchet 1893   PGP-RD
'Album'
virescens Nuttall 1818
zalil Aitchison 1888 = **D. semibarbatum**

L   HYBRID CULTIVARS   PGP-DGP

'Abendleuchten'   [Kuhlwein pre-1985]
'Abgesang'   [Foerster 1967]
'Agnes Brooks' ®   [Bishop 1946]
'Alice Artindale' ®   [Artindale 1936]
'Alpenbote'
'Amorspeer'
'Anne Page' ®   [Bishop 1950]
'Annie'
'Antares' ®   [Edwards 1979]
'Apollo' ®   [Blackmore & Langdon 1973]
'Ariel'   [Foerster 1967]
'Atholl' ®   [McGlashan 1981]
'Azurriense'   [Foerster 1949]
'Azurzwerg'   [Foerster pre-1985]
'Baby Doll' ®   [Blackmore & Langdon 1966]
'Bellamosum'
'Berghimmel' ®   [Foerster 1920]
'Blaustrahl' ®   [Klose 1982]
'Blauwal'   [Foerster 1957]
'Blue Dawn' ®   [Blackmore & Langdon 1960]
'Blue Jade' ®   [Blackmore & Langdon 1960]   RD
'Blue Nile' ®   [Blackmore & Langdon pre-1962]   DGP-RD

'Blue Tit'   ®   [Blackmore & Langdon 1960]   **DGP**
'Blue Triumphator'   ®   [Ruys 1948]
'Bridesmaid'   ®   [Blackmore & Langdon 1938]
'Browne's Lavender'   ®   [Browne 1975]
'Bruce'   [McGlashan 1977]
'Butterball'   ®   [Blackmore & Langdon pre-1969]   **DGP-RD**
'Cambria'   ®   [Samuel 1921]
'Can-Can'   ®   [McGlashan 1986]
'Carl Topping'   [Blackmore & Langdon]
'Cassius'   ®   [Blackmore & Langdon 1976]
'Ceylon'   ®   [Bishop 1959]
'Charles F Langdon'   ®   [Blackmore & Langdon 1945]
'Charles Gregory Broan'   ®   [Broan 1967]
'Chelsea Star'   ®   [Blackmore & Langdon 1975]
'Cherry Pie'
'Cherub'   ®   [Kelway 1889]
'Cinderella'   ®   [Bishop 1953]   **RD**
'Circe'   ®   [Parrett]
'Clack's Choice'   ®   [Broan 1980]
'Claire'   ®   [Edwards 1984]
'Clifford Lass'   ®   [Woodfield Bros. 1987]
'Clifford Pink'   ®   [Woodfield Bros. 1984]
'Clifford Sky'   [Woodfield Bros.]
'Conspicua'   ®   [Blackmore & Langdon 1917]
'Corinth'   ®   [Latty 1977]
'Cream Cracker'   ®   [Harding 1976]
'Cressida'   ®   [Blackmore & Langdon 1965]   **RD**
'Crown Jewel'   ®   [Blackmore & Langdon 1977]
'Cristella'   ®   [Blackmore & Langdon 1960]
'Cupid'   ®   [Blackmore & Langdon 1965]
'Daily Express'   ®   [Parrett 1949]
'Dairymaid'   ®   [Parrett 1960]
'Dämmerung'   [Foerster pre-1985]
'Demavand'   ®   [Parrett 1970-71]
'Dolly Bird'
'Dora Larkan'   ®   [Rowe 1982]
'Duchess of Portland'   ®   [Blackmore & Langdon 1933]
'Elmfreude'
'Elmhimmel'
'Emily Hawkins'   ®   [Bassett 1980]
'Emir'   ®   [Blackmore & Langdon 1960]
'Eva Gower'   ®   [Bishop 1941]
'Fanfare'   ®   [Blackmore & Langdon 1960]   **RD**
'Father Thames'   ®   [Bishop 1946]
'Faust'   ®   [Blackmore & Langdon 1960]
'Fenella'   ®   [Blackmore & Langdon 1964]
'Fernzunder'   ®   [Foerster 1931]
'Finsteraarhon'   [Foerster 1937]
'Florestan'   ®   [Latty 1969]
'Frank's Blue'
'Frühschein'   [Foerster 1955]
'F W Smith'   ®   [Smith 1919]
'Garden Party'
'Gewitternacht'
'Gillian Dallas'   ®   [Blackmore & Langdon 1972]
'Gletscherwasser'   ®   [Foerster 1929]
'Gordon Forsyth'   ®   [Blackmore & Langdon 1969]   **RD**
'Gossamer'   ®   [Cowan 1972]
'Great Scot'   ®   [Blackmore & Langdon 1960]
'Grünberg'   [Klose 1972]

'Guy Langdon' ®   [Blackmore & Langdon 1960]   RD
'Harmony' ®   [Bishop 1961]
'Harvest Moon' ®   [Bishop 1947]
'H G Mills' ®   [Bakers' Nurs. 1966]
'Hilda Lucas' ®   [Lucas pre-1961]
'Honey Bee' ®   [McGlashan 1986]
'Icecap' ®   [Blackmore & Langdon 1966]   RD
'Iona' ®   [Cowan 1973]
'Janet Wort' ®   [Wort 1948]
'Joyce Roffey' ®   [Lucas 1966]
'Jubelruf' [Foerster 1956]
'Judy Knight' ®   [Knight 1956]
'Junior' [Neis 1966]
'Kathleen Cooke' ®   [Cooke 1982]
'Kestrel' ®   [Milton 1979]
'Kirchenfenster'
'Kleine Nachtmusik' ®   [Foerster 1936]
'Klingsor'
'Lady Eleanor' ®   [Blackmore & Langdon 1930]
'Lady Guinevere' ®   [Blackmore & Langdon 1931]
'Langdon's Royal Flush' ®   [Blackmore & Langdon 1986]
'Lanzenträger' ®   [Kayser & Siebert 1964]
'Leonora' ®   [Latty 1969]
'Lilian Bassett' ®   [Bassett 1984]
'Loch Leven' ®   [Cowan 1969]
'Loch Lomond' ®   [Cowan 1979]
'Loch Katrine' ®   [Cowan 1969]
'Loch Maree' ®   [Cowan 1968]
'Loch Morar' ®   [Cowan 1972]
'Loch Ness' ®   [Cowan 1965]
'Loch Nevis' ®   [Cowan 1967]   RD
'Loch Torridon' ®   [Cowan 1975]
'Lord Butler' ®   [Blackmore & Langdon 1968]
'Magic Moment'
'Marie Broan' ®   [Broan 1966]
'Mary Loake' ®   [Loake 1966]
'Merrie England' ®   [Bishop 1953]
'Merlin' ®   [Foerster 1929]
'Michael Ayres' ®   [Blackmore & Langdon 1965]
'Mighty Atom' ®   [Blackmore & Langdon 1968]   RD
'Min' ®   [McGlashan 1986]
'Minnelied'
'Molly Buchanan' ®   [Blackmore & Langdon 1960]
'Moonbeam' ®   [Blackmore & Langdon 1961]
'Morgentau' [Foerster pre-1985]
'Morning Cloud'
'Mozart' ®   [Hewitt 1930]
'Mrs Newton Lees' ®   [Blackmore & Langdon 1928]
'Nachtwache' [Foerster pre-1985]
'Neptun' [Weinreich pre-1986]
'Nicholas Loake' ®   [Broan 1977]
'Nicholas Woodfield'
'Nimrod' ®   [Blackmore & Langdon]
'Nobility'
'Oberon' ®   [Blackmore & Langdon 1939]
'Olive Poppleton' ®   [Poppleton 1972]
'Oliver'
'Our Deb'
'Ouvertüre' [Foerster 1936]
'Panda' ®   [Parrett 1972]

'**Parzival**'   ®   [Lindner 1931]
'**Patricia, Lady Hambleden**'   ®   [Blackmore & Langdon 1966]
'**Peace**'   ®   [Bakers' Nurs. 1962]
'**Pericles**'   ®   [via Regel & Kesselring 1910]
'**Perlmutterbaum**'   ®   [Foerster 1931]
'**Pink Ruffles**'
'Pink Sensation' = **D. x ruysii 'Pink Sensation'**
'**Polar Beauty**'
'**Polarnacht**'   ®   [Klose 1983]
'**Polly**'   ®   [Latty 1971]
'**Purple Ruffles**'   ®   [Blackmore & Langdon 1960]
'**Purple Triumph**'   ®   [Blackmore & Langdon 1960]
'**Radiance**'   ®   [Blackmore & Langdon 1961]
'**Rona**'   ®   [Cowan 1973]
'Rosa Überaschung' = **D. x ruysii 'Pink Sensation'**
'**Rosenquarz**'   [Foerster pre-1985]
'**Rosemary Brock**'   ®   [Bassett 1984]
'**Rosemary Langdon**'   ®   [Blackmore & Langdon 1966]
'**Rosina**'   ®   [Latty 1971]
'Royal Flush' = **D. 'Langdon's Royal Flush'**
'**Royal Show**'
'**Royal Wedding**'   RD
'**Ruby**'   ®   [Bakers' Nurs. 1925]
'**Sabrina**'   ®   [Blackmore & Langdon 1960]
'**Sabu**'   ®   [Blackmore & Langdon pre-1962]
'**Samantha**'   ®   [McGlashan 1985]
'**Sandpiper**'   ®   [Latty 1977]
'**Sarabande**'   ®   [Latty 1976]
'**Sarah Edwards**'   ®   [Edwards 1985]
'**Savrola**'   ®   [Blackmore & Langdon 1960]
'**Schildknappe**'   ®   [Foerster 1936]
'**Schloss Wilhelmshöhe**'   ®   [Klose 1977]
'**Sentinel**'   ®   [Blackmore & Langdon 1960]
'**Shimmer**'   ®   [Blackmore & Langdon 1970]
'**Silver Jubilee**'   ®   [Blackmore & Langdon 1977]
'**Silver Moon**'   ®   [Blackmore & Langdon 1960]
'**Skyline**'   ®   [Blackmore & Langdon 1970]
'**Snowdon**'   ®   [Latty 1971]
'**Solomon**'   ®   [Parrett 1961]
'**Sommernachtstraum**'   ®   [Keiser & Siebert 1960]
'**Sommerwind**'   ®   [Kayser & Siebert 1969]
'**South Seas**'   ®   [Blackmore & Langdon 1960]
'**Spindrift**'   ®   [Cowan 1971]   RD
'**Stardust**'   ®   [Blackmore & Langdon 1965]
'**Sternennacht**'   [Foerster pre-1985]
'**Strawberry Fair**'   ®   [Blackmore & Langdon 1967]   RD
'**Summer Haze**'
'**Summer Wine**'   ®   [Latty 1971]
'**Sungleam**'   ®   [Blackmore & Langdon]
'**Susan Langdon**'   ®   [Blackmore & Langdon 1966]
'**Swan Lake**'   ®   [Bishop 1953]   **DGP**
'**Taj Mahal**'   ®   [Parrett 1961]
'**Tempelgang**'   ®   [Foerster 1936]
'**Tessa**'   ®   [Blackmore & Langdon 1936]
'**Thelma Rowe**'   ®   [Rowe 1982]
'**Thundercloud**'
'**Tiddles**'   ®   [Blackmore & Langdon 1969]
'**Tiny Tim**'   ®   [Blackmore & Langdon 1972]
'**Traumulus**'   ®   [Foerster 1931]

'Tropennacht' ®   [Foerster 1931]
'Turkish Delight' ®   [Blackmore & Langdon 1967]
'Vespers' ®   [Blackmore & Langdon]
'Waldenburg' ®   [Klose 1975]
'Wheatear'
'White Knight' ®   [Mills 1933]
'William Richards' ®   [via Bees' Nurs. 1946]
'Zauberfeote'   [Foerster 1955]

HYBRID GROUPS

'Astolat'   [Reinelt]   RD
Bishops' Hybrids
'Black Knight'   [Reinelt]   RD
Blackmore & Langdon Hybrids
'Blue Fountains'   [Gould]
'Blue Bird'   [Reinelt]
'Blue Jay'   [Reinelt]   RD
'Blue Springs'
'Blue Heaven'   [Gould]
'Cameliard'   [Reinelt]   RD
'Connecticut Yankee'   [Steichen]
'Galahad'   [Reinelt]   RD
'Great Expectations'   [Sahin]   RD
'Guinevere'   [Reinelt]
'Ivory Towers'   [Sahin]   RD
'King Arthur'   [Reinelt]
'Lancelot'   [Reinelt]
'Moody Blues'   [Sahin]   RD
'Ordensritter'
'Percival'   [Reinelt]
'Rosy Future'   [Sahin]   RD
'Royal Lilacs'   [Sahin]
'Snow White'
'Summer Skies'   [Reinelt]
'Tafelrunde'
'Ultra Violets'   [Sahin]
'Weisser Herkules'

DENDRANTHEMA (de Candolle) Desmoulins 1860   [*Asteraceae (Compositae)*]
  arcticum (Linnaeus) Tzvelev 1961 = **Arctanthemum arcticum**
  indicum hort., non (Linnaeus) Desmoulins 1859 (*Chrysanthemum indicum* hort.)

GARDEN 'CHRYSANTHEMUMS'

'Anastasia'
'Bronze Elegance'   PGP
'Dr. Tom Parr'
'Emperor of China' ('Old Cottage Pink')   PGP
'Mei-Kyo'
'Mei-Kyo Bronze Elegance' = **D. 'Bronze Elegance'**   PGP
'Old Cottage Pink' = **D. 'Emperor of China'**
'Spoon'

x koreanum hort. (*Chrysanthemum x koreanum*)   PGP

'KOREAN CHRYSANTHEMUMS'

'Aline'
'Anne'
'Apollo'   PGP

'Barbara'
'Belle'
'Brightness'
'Bronce Schweizerland'
'Bronze Elite'
'Brown Eyes'
'Citrus'
'Columbine'
'Copper Nob'
'Debbie'
'Doris'
'Edegard'
'Edelweiss'
'Felbacher Wein'
'Gartenmeister Vegelahn'
'Goldmarianne'
'Hazel'
'Helen'
'Irene'
'Isabella'
'Isabellrosa'
'Kupfergoldstern'
'Lemon Tench'
'L'Innocence'
'Little Dorrit'
'Marion'
'Martha'
'Mary'
'Mauve Gem'
'Moira'
'Moonlight'
'Orange Wonder'
'Ordenstern'
'Primrose Anemone'
'Princess'
'Ruby Mound'
'Schneewolke'
'Schweizerland'
'Sheila'
'Shining Light'
'Starlet'
'Sunspider'
'Tickled Pink'
'Virginia'
'Wedding Sunshine'
'White Gem'
'White Gloss'
'Yellow Starlet'

weyrichii (Maximowicz) Tzvelev 1961 (*Chrysanthemum weyrichii*)   RD
yezoense (Maekawa) D. J. N. Hind 1988 (*Chrysanthemum yesoense*)   PGP
zawadskii (Herbich) Tzvelev 1961 (*Chrysanthemum zawadskii*)   PGP
    var. **latilobum** (*Chrysanthemum erubescens, C. rubellum*)   PGP-RD

'RUBELLUM' CULTIVARS

'Clara Curtis'   PGP-RD
'Lady Clara'
'Duchess of Edinburgh'   PGP-RD
'Lachskönigin'

'Mary Stoker'
'Paul Boissier'   RD

DENNSTAEDTIA Bernhardi 1801
    punctiloba (Michaux) Moore 1857   [*Dennstaedtiaceae*]
                                                            EGF.1-PGP

DENTARIA Linnaeus 1753
    bulbifera Linnaeus 1753 = **Cardamine bulbifera**   [*Brassicaceae (Cruciferae)*]
    digitata Lamarck 1786 = **Cardamine pentaphllos**
    diphylla Michaux 1803 = **Cardamine diphylla**
    pinnata Lamarck 1786 = **Cardamine heptaphylla**

DESCHAMPSIA Palisot de Beauvois 1812   [*Poaceae (Gramineae)*]
N‡L   **cespitosa** (Linnaeus) Palisot de Beauvois 1812   EGF.2-PGP
        'Bronzeschleier'   [K. Foerster 1961]   PGP
        'Fairy's Joke'
        'Goldgehänge'   [K. Partsch]
        'Goldschleier'   [K. Partsch]
        'Goldstaub'
        'Tardiflora'   [K. Foerster 1961]
        'Tauträger'
        'Waldschatt'   [Kayser & Siebert]
N‡L   **flexuosa** (Linnaeus) Trinius 1836   EGF.2-PGP

DIANELLA Lamarck 1786   [*Phormiaceae (Liliaceae)*]
    caerulea Sims 1801   EGF.1-PGP
    intermedia Endlicher 1833   EGF.1
        'Variegata'
    nigra Colenso 1884   EGF.1
    tasmanica Hooker f. 1858   EGF.1-PGP

DIANTHUS Linnaeus 1753   [*Caryophyllaceae*]
    Allwoodii Agg. hort. (*D. caryophyllus* x *D. plumarius*)
        Alpinus Agg. hort. (*D. Allwoodii* x *D. alpinus, D. gratianopolitanus* etc.)
    alpester Balbis 1802 = **D. furcatus**
    alpestris hort. = **D. monspessulanus**
    alpinus Linnaeus 1753   CA-**DGP**-RD
        'Albus'   CA-RD
        'Cherry Beauty'
        'Joan's Blood' ®   [J Elliott pre-1975]   RD
        'Millstream Salmon'   [via Siskiyou Rare Plant Nursery pre-1985]
        'Venus'
    amurensis Jacques 1862
    anatolicus Boissier 1843
    arenarius Linnaeus 1753   CA-RD
    x arvernensis Rouy & Foucard (*D. monspessulanus* x *D. seguieri*)   RD
        'Albus'
        'Major'
    arpadianus Ade & Bornmueller 1934
    atrorubens Allioni 1785
    banaticus Heuffel ex Grisebach & Schrenk 1852 = **D. giganteus** ssp. **banaticus**
    bebius Visiani ex Reichenbach = **D. petreus**
    x boydii hort. = **D. 'Boydii'**
    brachyanthus Boissier 1839 = **D. subacaulis**
    caesius Smith 1794 = **D. gratianopolitanus**
    callizonus Schott & Kotschy 1851   CA
    campestris Marshall von Bieberstein 1808
N   **carthusianorum** Linnaeus 1753   PGP-RD
        var. **humilis**
N‡   **caryophyllus** Linnaeus 1753   PGP-DGP-RD

corymbosus Smith 1809 (*D. grisebachii*)
crinitus Smith 1794
cruentus Grisebach 1843
degenii Baldacca 1899

HN‡ **deltoides** Linnaeus 1753   **DGP-RD**
    'Albus'   RD
    'Bright Eyes'
    'Brilliancy'   [via K. R. Jelitto pre-1982]
    'Brilliant' ®   [pre-1952]   DGP-RD
    'Broughty Blaze' ®   [pre-1980]
    'E A Bowles' ®   [pre-1952]
    'Erectus' ®   [Allwood pre-1933]
    'Flashing Light' = **D. deltoides 'Leuchtfunk'**
    'Heideblut'
    'Hilltop Star'
    'Leuchtfunk' ®   [E Benary 1962]('Flashing Light')   RD
    'Plenus' ®
    'Roseus' ®
    'Samos' ®   [pre-1978]
    'Steriker' ®   [V M S Finnis pre-1964]   DGP
    'Vampir' ®   [ex France pre-1972]
    'Wisley Variety' ®   [pre-1950]   RD
erinaceus Boissier 1843
    var. **alpinus** Boissier 1843
freynii Vandas 1890   CA
    'Joe Elliott'
frigidus Zuccarini 1824 = **D. sylvestris**
furcatus Balbis 1802 (*D. alpester*)
    'Lereschei'
gelidus Schott, Nyman & Kotschy 1854 = **D. glacialis** ssp. **gelidus**
giganteus D'Urville 1822
    ssp. **banaticus** (Heuffel) Tutin 1963
glacialis Haenke 1789   CA
    ssp. **gelidus** (Schott, Nyman & Kotschy) Tutin 1963
gracilis Smith 1809
    degenii (Baldacca) hort. = **D. degenii**
    simulans (Stojanov & Stefani) hort.= **D. simulans**
graniticus Jordan 1849

HN‡ **gratianopolitanus** Villiers 1789 (*D. caesius*)   **DGP-RD**
    'Arvernensis' = **D. x arvernensis**
    'Baker's Variety' ®   [pre-1932]
    'Bodensee'
    'Compactus' = **D. gratianopolitanus 'Compactus Eydangeri'**
    'Compactus Eydangeri' ®   [pre-1980]
    'Double Cheddar' ®   RD
    'Feuerhexe' ®   [Kayser ® Siebert pre-1957]
    'Flore Pleno' = **D. gratianopolitanus 'Double Cheddar'**
    'Emmen'
    'Graukissen'
    'Icombe Hybrid' ®   [S Hayward pre-1952]
    'Jutta' ®   [E Knecht pre-1985]
    'Major' = **D. x arvernensis 'Major'**
    'Nagelfluh'
    'Pink Jewel' ®   [pre-1981]
    'Purpurstjerne' ®   [Norges LandbrushogskQle 1956]
    'Rotkäppchen' ®   [H H Jürgl 1960]
    'Rubin' ®   [E Knecht pre-1985]
    'Scaynes Hill' ®   [L H Cox pre-1932]
    'Tiny Rubies'   [via Mannings Heather Farm pre-1984]
grisebachii Boissier 1853 = **D. corymbosus**

haematocalyx Boissier & Heldreich 1853   CA-**RD**
    'Albus'
    alpinus hort. = **D. haematocalyx** ssp. **pindicola**
    ssp. **pindicola** (Vierhapper) Hayek 1924 (*D. pindicola*)   CA-RD
hungaricus Persoon 1805
japonicus Thunberg 1784
    'Albus'
knappii (Pantocsek) Ascherson & Kanitz ex Borbas 1877   PGP-RD
x lemsii hort. = **D. 'Lemsii'**
lereschii hort. = **D. furcatus 'Lereschei'**
lumnitzeri Wiesbaur 1886
microlepis Boissier 1843   CA
    'Albus'
    var. **musalae** Velenovsky
minutiflorus (Borbas) Halacsy 1900
monspessulanus Linnaeus 1759 (*D. alpestris* hort.)
    ssp. **sternbergii** (Schlectendal ex Seringe) Hegi 1911 (*D. sternbergii*)
myrtinervis Grisebach 1853
nardiformis Janka 1873
neglectus Loiseleur 1809 p. p. = **D. pavonius**
nitidus Waldstein & Kitaibel 1806
noeanus Boissier 1853 = **D. petraeus** ssp. **noeanus**
orientalis Adams 1805
    'Albus'
pavonius Tausch 1839 (D. neglectus p.p.)   **CA-DGP**-RD
    'Albus'
    '**Nancy Lindsay**'   ®   [Miss N Lindsay pre-1959]
petraeus Waldstein & Kitaibel 1808 (*D. bebius, D. suendermannii*)
    ssp. **noeanus** (Boissier) Tutin 1963 (*D. noeanus*)   CA-RD
pindicola Vierhapper = **D. haematocalyx**
pinifolius Smith 1809
HN‡   **plumarius** Linnaeus 1753   PGP-RD
    '**Albiflorus**' (D. tatrae)
    ssp. **blandus** (Reichenbach) Hayek 1924
    '**Praecox**'
praecox Willdenow ex Sprengel 1825
pungens Linnaeus 1771
repens Willdenow 1799
x roysii hort. = **D. 'Roysii'**
scardicus Wettstein 1892
seguieri Villiers 1786
serotinus Waldstein & Kitaibel 1804
simulans Stojanov & Stefani   CA
speculifolius Schur 1866
squarrosus Marshall von Bieberstein 1808
    '**Nanus**' nom dub.
stefanoffii Eig 1937 (*D. strictus*)
sternbergii Schlechtendal ex Seringe 1824 = **D. monspessulanus** ssp. **sternbergii**
strictus Smith 1809 = **D. stefanoffii**
strictus hort. non Solander = **D. petraeus**
    var. *bebius* (Visiani) hort. = **D. petraeus**
    var. *brachyanthus* (Boissier) Boissier = **D. minutiflorus**
subacaulis Viliars 1789
    '**Rosa Zwerg**' nom. dub.
suendermannii Bornmueller = **D. petraeus**
N   **superbus** Linnaeus 1755   RD
    '**Autumnalis**'
sylvestris Wulfen 1786 (*D. frigidus*)
    Dwarf Form
    ssp. **tergestinus** (Reichenbach) Hayek 1924 (*D. tergestinus*)

'Uniflorus' nom. dub.
*ssp. **vaginatus**
tatrae Borbas 1891 = **D. plumarius 'Albiflorus'**
tergestinus (Reichenbach) Kerner = **D. sylvestris** ssp. **tergestinus**
*weyrichii
xylorrizus Boissier & Heldreich 1849

HYBRID CULTIVARS

CLASSIFICATION:

1   **"Pinks"**
2   **"Border Carnations"**
3   **"Perpetual-flowering Carnations"**

2   **'A A Sanders'**   ®   [F W Goodfellow pre-1947]
1   **'Achievement'**   ®   [Allwood pre-1959]
3   **'Adante'**   ®   [M Lek & Zn 1981]
3   **'Admiral Crompton'**   ®   [C Short 1978]
2   **'Admiration'**   ®   [Douglas 1954]
2   **'Afton Water'**   ®   [Douglas 1934]
1   **'Albatross'**   [via Southcombe Gardens Plant Nursery pre-1983]
3   **'Albissola'**   ®   [N Baratta 1976]
2   **'Aldridge Yellow'**   ®   [F W Goodfellow pre-1951]   RD
3   **'Alec Sparkes'**   ®   [F Hicks pre-1964]
1   **'Alder House'**   ®   [Holden Clough Nursery pre-1953]
1   **'Aldersey Rose'**   ®   [Aldersey Gardens pre-1962]
2   **'Alfred Galbally'**   ®   [J Galbally 1977]
2   **'Alfriston'**   ®   [J Galbally pre-1972]
1   **'Alice'**   ®   [Allwood 1930]
3   **'Alice'**   ®   [G Nobbio 1964]   RD
2   **'Alice Forbes Improved'**   ®   [G D Murray 1926]
1   **'Allen's Ballerina'**   ®   [D S Thomas 1982]
1   **'Allen's Huntsman'**   ®   [D S Thomas]
1   **'Allen's Maria'**   ®   [D S Thomas]
1   **'Alloway Star'**   ®   [pre-1966]
1   **'Allspice'**   ®   [Old Cv]
1   **'Allspice Sport'**   [via Kingstone Cottage Plants pre-1985]
3   **'Allwood's Crimson'**   ®   [Allwood 1946]
1   **'Alyson'**   ®   [Allwood pre-1967]
1   **'Amarinth'**   ®   [T J Wood 1979]
1   **'Andrew'**   ®   [Allwood]
3   **'Angel Wings'**   ®   [W W Thomson Co 1974]
1   **'Annabelle'**   ®   [T Carlile Ltd pre-1957]
1   **'Anna Wyatt'**   ®   [C Wyatt 1978]
2   **'Anne Jones'**   ®   [J Wandless 1976]
3   **'Anne Marie'**   ®   [P Kooij & Zn 1969]
3   **'Ann Woodfield'**   ®   [Woodfield Bros 1980]
1   **'Anthony'**   ®   [P A Fenn 1967]
2   **'Apollo'**   ®   [Hayward pre-1972]
3   **'Apricot Sue'**   ®   [T E Bradshaw 1972]
1   **'Argus'**   ®   [Old cv]
3   **'Arevalo'**   [P Kooij & Sons pre-1982]
1   **'Ariel'**   ®   [E Ladhams pre-1937]   CA
1   **'Arthur'**   ®   [Allwood 1920]
2   **'Arthur Leslie'**   ®   [S O Stroud 1969]
    'Arthur Sim' = **D. 'Sir Arthur Sim'**
3   **'Arvalo'**   [P Kooij & Sons pre-1982]
    'Arvernensis' = **D. x arvernensis**
1   **'Asnelliken'**   ®   [Norges LandbrukshQgskole pre-1932] (D 'Nordstern')

3   'Astor'   ®   [S B Talee 1975]
1   'Augusta Godskesen'   ®   [Larsen pre-1981]
2   'Aurora'   ®   [Douglas 1949]
2   'Autumn Glory'   ®   [L A Lowe 1948]
2   'Autumn Tints'   ®   [Douglas 1933]
    'Auvergne' = D. x arvernensis
1   'Avoca Purple'   ®   [Old Cv] (D. 'Laced Avoca')
1   'Baby Treasure'   ®   [Mrs D Underwood 1959]
1   'Badenia'   ®   [E Knecht pre-1985]
3   'Bailey's Amarillo'   ®   [S Bailey 1969]
3   'Bailey's Apricot'   ®   [S Bailey 1951]
3   'Bailey's Splendour'   ®   [S Bailey 1958]   RD
    'Baker's Variety' = D. gratianopolitanus 'Baker's Variety'
1   'Ballerina' = D. 'Allen's Ballerina'
3   'Ballerina'   ®   [Allwood pre-1964]   DGP
1   'Barker's Beauty'
1   'Barleyfield Rose'   [via Hartside Nursery pre-1984]
3   'Barlo'
    'Barsemi' = D. 'Yasmina'
1   'Bat's Double Red'   ®   [T Bat 1700s]   PGP
2   'Beauty of Cambridge'   ®   [R H Bath pre-1929]
1   'Beauty of Healey'   ®   [W Grindrod 1800s]
1   'Becka Falls'   ®   [C Wyatt 1977]
2   'Belle of Bookham'   ®   [Douglas 1937]
1   'Benjamin Barker'
2   'Ben Wyvis'   ®   [Douglas 1957]
3   'Beryl Giles'   ®   [Woodfield Bros 1980]
1   'Betty Buckle'
2   'Betty Day'   ®   [W Thorburn pre-1945]
1   'Betty Norton'   ®   [G Winter pre-1929]
1   'Betty Webber'   [S Bailey Ltd 1982]
3   'Bibby's Cerise'   ®   [J M & R Bibby 1957]
2   'Bijou Clove'   ®   [Douglas 1956]
1   'Binsey Red'
1   'Blauigel'   ®   [Penzler 1957]
1   'Blaureif'   ®   [K Foerster 1936]
1   'Blue Hills'   ®   [pre-1966]
1   'Bobby'   ®   [Allwood 1980]
3   'Bobby'
2   'Bobby Ames'   ®   [R J McGilloway pre-1968]
1   'Bombadier'   ®   [S T Byatt pre-1983]   CA-RD
3   'Bonnie Charlie'   ®   [Allwood 1953]
2   'Bookham Beau'   ®   [Douglas 1927]
2   'Bookham Fancy'   ®   [Douglas 1952]
2   'Bookham Grand'   ®   [Douglas 1945]
2   'Bookham Heroine'   ®   [Douglas 1951]
2   'Bookham Lad'   ®   [Douglas 1950]
2   'Bookham Lass'   ®   [Douglas 1931]
2   'Bookham Perfume'   ®   [Douglas 1939]
2   'Bookham Prince'   ®   [Douglas 1951]
2   'Bookham Sprite'   ®   [Douglas 1956]
3   'Borello'   [G Nobbio pre-1982]
1   'Bovey Belle'   ®   [C Wyatt 1973]
1   'Boydii'   ®   [W B Boyd pre-1918]   CA
1   'Bransgore'   ®   [D Lowndes pre-1939]
1   'Bridal Veil'   ®   [Old Cv]
1   'Bridesmaid'   ®   [Douglas 1965]
1   'Brigadier'   ®   [S T Byatt pre-1965]
1   'Brilliance'   ®   [P A Fenn 1975]
    'Brilliant' = D. deltoides 'Brilliant'

1	**'Cockenzie Pink'** ® [c1720]		
3	**'Cocomo Sim'** ® [Gray pre-1957]		RD
	'Common Pink' = **D. plumarius**		
	'Compactus Eydangeri' = **D. gratianopolitanus 'Compactus Eydangeri'**		
1	**'Constance'** ® [Allwood pre-1955]		
1	**'Constance Finnis'** ® [C S Finnis pre-1969] (D. 'Farnham Rose')		
2	**'Consul'** ® [R H Bath 1934]		RD
2	**'Copperhead'** ® [Douglas 1951]		
3	**'Cordoba'** [P Kooij & Zn 1982]		
1	**'Cornish Snow'** [via Ramparts Nursery pre-1984]		
1	**'Coste Budde'** ® [V M S Finnis 1978]		
2	**'Countess of Lonsdale'** ® [J L Gibson 1925]		
1	**'Cranborne Seedling'** [via Kingstone Cottage Plants pre-1985]		
1	**'Cranmere Pool'** ® [C Wyatt 1981]		
3	**'Cream Sue'** ® [W Jeggo 1979]		
1	**'Crimson Ace'** ® [Lidabruce Nurseries pre-1967]		
1	**'Crimson Treasure'** ® [Mrs D Underwood 1967]		
2	**'Crimson Velvet'** ® [S O Stroud pre-1968]		
3	**'Crompton King'** ® [C Short 1978]		
3	**'Crompton Queen'** ® [C Short 1978]		
1	**'Crossways'** ® [via MacPenny pre-1949]		
3	**'Crowley's Pink Sim'** ® [Crowley Bros 1950]		RD
	'Crowley's Sim' = **D. 'Crowley's Pink Sim'**		
2	**'Crusader'** ® [Douglas 1950]		
1	**'Dad's Favourite'** ® [1700s ?]		PGP-RD
2	**'Dainty'** ® [Allwood 1934]		
2	**'Dainty Clove'** ® [Douglas 1945]		
2	**'Dainty Lady'** ® [Douglas 1929]		
2	**'Daisy Hill Scarlet'** ® [T Smith pre-1898]		
1	**'Damask Superb'** ® [Old Cv]		
3	**'Dannebrog Sim'** ® [Fog-Nisson Inc pre-1959]		
1	**'Daphne'** ® [Allwood pre-1934]		RD
1	**'Dartington Double'** [via Ramparts Nursery pre-1984]		
1	**'Dartmoor Forest'** ® [C Wyatt 1978]		
1	**'David'** ® [Allwood pre-1970]		
2	**'David Saunders'** ® [J Galbally 1977]		
2	**'Dawn'** ® [Douglas 1938]		
1	**'Debutante'** ® [Allwood 1966]		
3	**'Deep Purple'** ® [Homer Hill ? 1959]		
1	**'Denis'** ® [Allwood pre-1958]		
2	**'Desert Song'** ® [Douglas 1935]		
1	**'Desmond'** ® [Mrs D Underwood 1978]		
1	**'Dewdrop'** ® [Allwood pre-1932]		
1	**'Diademe'** ® [Hendriksen pre-1981]		
1	**'Diamant'** ® [A Voight pre-1895]		
1	**'Diana'** ® [Allwood pre-1961]		
1	**'Diane'** ® [Allwood 1964]		RD
3	**'Diane Marie'** ® [J Vernon 1977]		
2	**'Dicker Clove'** ® [J Galbally 1970]		
2	**'Diplomat'** ® [Allwood pre-1934]		
2	**'Doctor Archie Cameron'** ® [Douglas 1931]		
1	**'Donizetti'** ® [R V Prichard pre-1922]		
1	**'Doris'** ® [Allwood pre-1954]		DGP-RD
3	**'Doris Allwood'** ® [Allwood pre-1930]		
1	**'Doris Elite'** ® [Allwood 1978]		
2	**'Doris Galbally'** ® [J Galbally pre-1973]		
1	**'Doris Majestic'** ® [Allwood pre-1980]		
	'Doris Ruby' = **D. 'Houndspool Ruby'**		
1	**'Doris Supreme'** ® [Allwood 1978]		
2	**'Dot Charke'** ® [W Thorburn pre-1947]		

L

'Double Cheddar' = **D. gratianopolitanus 'Double Cheddar'**
2   **'Douglas Fancy'** ®   [Douglas 1937]
2   **'Downs Cerise'** ®   [Allwood pre-1945]
2   **'Downs Glory'** ®   [Allwood pre-1938]
2   **'Downs Souvenir'** ®   [Allwood pre-1946]
2   **'Downs Unique'** ®   [Allwood pre-1951]
2   **'Dryad'** ®   [Douglas 1961]
1   **'Dubarry'** ®   [A Bloom pre-1930]
1   **'Duchess of Fife'** ®   [E Ladhams pre-1940]
3   **'Duchess of Roxburghe'** ®   [J Riddell 1968]
1   **'Dusky'** ®   [Allwood 1945]
3   **'Dusty Rose'** ®   [A N Pierson Co 1961]
3   **'Dusty Sim'** ®   [Millroad Grange 1950]
'E A Bowles' = **D. deltoides 'E A Bowles'**
1   **'Earl of Essex'** ®   [1800s]
2   **'Ebor II'** ®   [S O Stroud 1972]
2   **'Edenside Glory'** ®   [Douglas 1942]
2   **'Edenside Scarlet'** ®   [Douglas 1958]
2   **'Edenside White'**   [Douglas 1933]
1   **'Edna'** ®   [Allwood pre-1958]
1   **'Edward'** ®   [Allwood 1944]
3   **'Edward Allwwod'** ®   [Allwood 1950]
1   **'Eileen'** ®   [Allwood 1927]
2   **'Eileen Neal'** ®   [J Galbally 1977]
2   **'Eileen O'Connor'** ®   [J Galbally 1977]
2   **'E J Baldry'** ®   [Douglas 1947]
1   **'Elizabeth'** ®   [Allwood pre-1922]
1   **'Elizabeth Jane'** ®   [Mrs D Underwood 1957]
'Ember Rose' = **D. 'Le Reve'**
1   **'Emile Pare'** ®   [A Pare 1840]
3   **'Emir'** ®   [A E Jeffs 1947]
1   'Emperor' = **D. 'Bat's Double Red'**
1   **'Enid Anderson'** ®   [1900s]   PGP
'Erectus' = **D. deltoides 'Erectus'**
3   **'Ernesto'** ®   [R Brea pre-1981]
2   **'Erycina'** ®   [S O Stroud 1969]
3   **'Esmeralda'**   [P Kooij & Zn 1982]
3   **'Esperance Sim'** ®   [H G Boerlage pre-1957]
1   **'Esther'** ®   [Allwood 1925]
2   **'Eudoxia'** ®   [Douglas 1958]
2   **'Eva Humphries'** ®   [J H Humphries pre-1946]   RD
1   **'Eve'** ®   [Allwood pre-1969]
3   **'Evita'**   [G Nobbio 1981]
1   **'Excelsior'** ®(D. 'Pink Mrs Sinkins')   RD
2   **'Exquisite'** ®   [Douglas 1942]
1   **'Fair Folly'** ®   [1600s]
1   **'Fanal'** ®   [pre-1974]
2   **'Fancy Monarch'** ®   [Allwood pre-1943]
'Farnham Rose' = **D. 'Constance Finnis'**
2   **'Fascination'** ®   [Allwood 1948]
2   **'Fellowship'** ®   [Douglas 1963]
2   **'Fenbow Nutmeg Clove'** ®   [J Fenbow pre-1652]
1   **'Fettes Mount'** ®   [Potts pre-1928]
'Feuerhexe' = **D. gratianopolitanus 'Feuerhexe'**
2   **'Fiery Cross'** ®   [Douglas 1949]   **DGP-RD**
1   **'Fimbriata'**
2   **'Fingo Clove'** ®   [Douglas 1927]
1   **'Fiona'** ®   [Allwood pre-1971]
2   **'Firefly'** ®   [Allwood pre-1938]
2   **'First Lady'** ®   [C H Fielder 1978]

1 **'Flame'** ® [Lindabruce Nurseries c1955]
3 **'Flame Sim'** ® [D R Braun Floral Co 1961]
2 **'Flanders'** ® [J Galbally pre-1974]
'Flashing Light' = **D. deltoides 'Leuchtfunk'**
1 **'Fleur'** ® [Allwood pre-1971]
3 **'Flor Mayo'** [? ex Italy c1972]
2 **'Forest Glow'** ® [S Bailey 1973]
2 **'Forest Sprite'** ® [S Bailey pre-1972]
2 **'Forest Treasure'** ® [S Bailey pre-1968]
2 **'Forest Violet'** ® [S Bailey 1969]
1 **'Fortuna'** ® [Allwood pre-1945]
1 **'Fountains Abbey'** ® [1500s]
1 **'Fragrance'**
3 **'Fragrant Ann'** ® [J A M Neil 1953]   DGP-RD
1 **'Fragrant Lace'** ® [H Jaynes 1966]
3 **'Fragrant Rose'** ® [S Bailey pre-1963]
1 **'Frances Isabel'** ® [H V Calvert 1972]
2 **'Frances Sellars'** ® [Lindabruce Nurseries pre-1947]
1 **'Frank's Frilly'** [J & E Parker-Jervis 1984]
2 **'Franny'**
1 **'Freckles'** ® [C H Fielder 1948]
1 **'Freda'** ® [Allwood pre-1924]   RD
3 **'Freddy'**
2 **'Freeland Crimson Clove'** ® [S O Stroud pre-1970]
2 **'Friar Tuck'** ® [Douglas 1937]
'Fringed Pink' = **D. superbus**
1 **'Frosty Fire'** ® [T Huber 1978]
1 **'Fusilier'** ® [S T Byatt pre-1955]
1 **'Gaiety'** ® [Lindabruce Nurseries c1955]
1 **'Galilee'**
2 **'Ganeymede'** ® [Fellowes pre-1851]
1 **'Garland'** ® [via A Bloom pre-1950]
2 **'Gaydena'** ® [N J Simister pre-1966]
3 **'Gay Paree'** ® [Woodfield Bros 1976]
1 **'Gemma's Beauty'**
3 **'George Allwood'** ® [Allwood pre-1939]
3 **'George Vernon'** ® [J Vernon 1977]
3 **'George William'** ® [Woodfield Bros 1981]
3 **'George Woodfield'** ® [Woodfield Bros 1980]
1 **'Gingham Gown'** ® [R J Kaye pre-1964]
2 **'Gipsy Clove'** ® [Douglas 1952]
3 **'G J Sim'** ® [c1945]
1 **'Glenda'** ® [Allwood pre-1972]
1 **'Gloriosa'** ® [1700s]
1 **'Glorious'** ® [Lindabruce Nurseries pre-1957]
1 **'Glory'** ® [pre-1923]
1 **'Glory Lyonnaise'** ® [Old Cv]
1 **'Goblin'** ® [Allwood pre-1941]
2 **'Golden Cross'** ® [J Galbally pre-1972]
3 **'Golden Rain'** ® [Solvik pre-1955]
2 **'Goverton'** ® [Douglas 1965]
1 **'Grace Mather'** ® [G Mather 1960]
2 **'Grace How'** [E J Dungey 1980]
3 **'Granada'** [N Baratta 1981]
1 **'Grandad'** [S Bailey Ltd 1983]
1 **'Gran's Favourite'** ® [Mrs D Underwood]
1 **'Gravetye Gem'** ® [W E Th Ingwersen Ltd pre-1960]
3 **'Green Mist'**
1 **'Grenadier'** ® [S T Byatt pre-1963]
2 **'Grey Dove'** ® [J Galbally pre-1974]

1	**'Grome'** [via Ramparts Nurseries pre-1984]		
3	**'Gus Royalette'** ® [G Nilsson pre-1974]		
	'G W Vernon' = **D. 'George Vernon'**		
2	**'Hadrian'** ® [Douglas 1926]		
2	**'Hannah Louise'** ® [J Galbally pre-1974]		
2	**'Happiness'** ® [Allwood pre-1935]		
1	**'Hardwicke's Pink'** [G D Hardwicke pre-1984]		
1	**'Harlequin'** ® [Allwood 1958]		
2	**'Harmony'** ® [Allwood pre-1934]		RD
3	**'Harvest Moon'** ® [J H Hill 1951]		RD
	'Haytor' = **D. 'Haytor White'**		
1	**'Haytor Rock'** ® [C Wyatt 1979]		
1	**'Haytor White'** ® [C Wyatt 1971] (D. 'Haytor')		
1	**'Hazel'**		
2	**'Hazel Ruth'** ® [J Galbally 1977]		
1	**'Heidi'** ® [C Frickart 1959]		
3	**'Heldenbrau'** ® [F T Gillies 1980]		
1	**'Helen'** ® [Allwood pre-1948]		RD
2	**'Helen Keates'** ® [J Galbally 1979]		
2	**'Helen McGovern'** ® [A Fulton pre-1960]		
2	**'Helen Simister'** ® [N J Simister 1971]		
3	**'Helen Wood'**		
1	**'Helga'** ® [Allwood 1961]		
1	**'Henry of Essex'** ® [Ramparts Nursery 1982]		
1	**Herbert's Pinks**		
1	**'Hidcote'** ® [L Johnson pre-1964]		
1	**'Highland Chieftain'** ® [Reginald Kaye Ltd 1980]		
1	**'Highland Fraser'** ® [P S Hayward c1930]		PGP
1	**'Highland Gem'** ® [P S Hayward pre-1930]		
1	**Highland Hybrids**		
1	'Highland King' = **D. 'Highland Chieftain'**		
1	**'Highland Queen'** ® [pre-1952]		PGP
1	**'Hollycroft Fragrance'** ® [Hollycroft Nurseries pre-1979]		
1	**'Hollycroft Rose'** ® [Hollycroft Nurseries pre-1979]		
3	**'Hollywood Sim'** ® [Hollywood Greenhouses 1956]		**DGP**
1	**'Honor's Cerise'**		
1	**'Hope'** ® [Allwood 1946]		
2	**'Horsa'** ® [Douglas 1945]		
1	**'Houndspool Cheryl'** ® [J Whetman 1980] (D 'Cheryl')		
1	**'Houndspool Ruby'** ® [J Whetman 1977] (D 'Ruby Doris', D. 'Ruby')		
1	**'Houstan House'** ® [Old Cv]		
2	**'Howard Hitchcock'** ® [J Galbally 1977]		
	'Huntsman' = **D. 'Allen's Huntsman'**		
1	**'Ian'** ® [Allwood 1938]		RD
2	**'Ibis'** ® [Douglas 1948]		
1	**'Iceberg'** ® [C H Fielder 1950]		
3	**'Ice Cap'** ® [Wood pre-1964]		
	'Icombe Hybrid' = **D. gratianopolitanus 'Icombe Hybrid'**		
	'Ideal' = **D. 'Show Ideal'**		
2	**'Imber'** ® [Douglas 1964]		
2	**'Imperial Clove'** ® [Douglas 1941]		**DGP**-RD
1	**'Ina'** [ex Canada pre-1983]		
1	**'Inchmery'** ® [1700s]		PG-RD
1	**'Ine'** ® [Hendriksen pre-1964]		
1	**'Inglestone'** ® [G Osmond pre-1939]		
1	**'Inshriach Dazzler'** ® [J Drake pre-1979]		
1	**'Inshriach Startler'** [via Jack Drake pre-1983]		
1	**'Ipswich Crimson'** ® [pre-1951]		
1	**'Ipswich Pink'** ® [pre-1951]		
2	**'Irene Della-Torre'** ® [J Galbally 1977]		

1   'Irish Pink' ®   [Old Cv]
2   'Isabel McCartney' ®   [A Fulton 1974]
2   'Isobel Templeton' ®   [M Kennedy 1948]
3   'Jack Wood' ®   [C Short 1980]
3   'Jack's Lass' ®   [C Short & J Wood 1985]
1   'Jacqueline' ®   [Allwood pre-1946]
3   'Jacqueline Ann' ®   [Woodfield Bros 1970]
1   'Jane Austen' ®   [pre-1939]
1   'Jane Bowen' ®   [D H Bowen 1983]
1   'Janet' ®   [Douglas 1927]
1   'Janet Walker' ®   [J. Elliott pre-1955]
2   'Jean Knight' ®   [R H Knight 1974]
1   'Jenny Wyatt' ®   [C Wyatt c1983]
1   'Jester' ®   [C H Herbert 1930]
3   'J M Bibby' ®   [R Bibby 1957]
3   'Joanne' ®   [T E Bradshaw 1974]
    'Joan's Blood' = **D. alpinus 'Joan's Blood'**
3   'Joe Vernon' ®   [C Short 1983]
1   'John Ball' ®   [McLean 1800s]
1   'John Gray' ®   [pre-1960]
2   'John Malcolm' ®   [Hayward 1938]
2   'John Wood' ®   [R A Wood pre-1969]
3   'Joker' ®   [J & A Alderden 1949]
1   'Joy' ®   [Allwood pre-1965]
1   'Judy' ®   [Allwood pre-1946]
1   'Julian' ®   [Mrs D Underwood 1969]
3   'Jupiter' ®   [Yoder Bros 1951]   CA
    'Jutta' = **D. gratianopolitanus 'Jutta'**
1   'Kathleen' ®   [McLean pre-1867]
2   'Kathleen Hitchcock' ®   [J Galbally pre-1973]
1   'Katy'   [via Ramparts Nursery pre-1983]
2   'Katy' ®   [J Moore 1975]
1   'Kesteven Chamonix' ®   [A E Robinson 1971]
1   'Kestor' ®   [C Wyatt 1979]
3   'Kobusa'   [N Baretta pre-1984] (D. 'Pierrot')
    'Kokomo Sim' = **D. 'Cocomo Sim'**
3   'Koranja'   [P Kooij & Zn pre-1978]
1   'La Bourboule' ®   [pre-1952]
1   'La Bourboule Alba' ®   [Six Hills Nursery pre-1952]
    'Laced Avoca' = **D. 'Avoca Purple'**
1   'Laced Hero Improved' ®   [Allwood 1951]
1   'Laced Joy' ®   [Allwood 1947]
1   'Laced Monarch' ®   [Allwood 1972]
    'Laced Prudence' = **D. 'Prudence'**
1   'Laced Romeo' ®   [Allwood 1963]
1   'Laced Treasure' ®   [Allwood 1981]
3   'Laddie Sim' ®   [E C Greiger 1957]   RD
1   'Lady Diana'   [R Kaye pre-1982]
1   'Lady Granville' ®   [c1840]
1   'Lady Salisbury' ®   [S E Webb pre-1980]
2   'Lancing Lady' ®   [Lindabruce Nurseries pre-1947]
1   'Lancing Lass' ®   [Lindabruce Nurseries 1949]
2   'Lancing Monarch' ®   [Lindabruce Nurseries pre-1960]
1   'Laura' ®   [Allwood pre-1952]
2   'Lavender Clove' ®   [L A Lowe 1932]
3   'Lavender Lady' ®   [A Hoffman 1965]   RD
1   'Leader' ®   [C H Fielder 1946]
2   'Leiden' ®   [S Bailey 1956]
1   'Lemsii'   [via Southcombe Gardens Plant Nursery pre-1983]   RD
3   'Lena' ®   [L Hakansson pre-1968]

3	'Le Reve' ®	[Bay State Carnations 1963] (D. 'Ember Rose')	
2	'Leslie Rennison' ®	[R Thain pre-1942]	
1	'Letitia Wyatt' ®	[C Wyatt 1981]	
	'Leuchtfunk' = **D. deltoides 'Leuchtfunk'**		
2	'Lilac Clove' ®	[Douglas 1932]	
1	'Lilian' ®	[Allwood pre-1953]	DGP
2	'Lily Lesurf' ®	[J Galbally pre-1970]	
1	'Linda' ®	[Allwood pre-1970]	
3	'Linda' ®	[Homer Hill 1959]	
1	'Little Beauty'		
1	'Little Jock' ®	[J Gray pre-1930]	CA-RD
1	Little Jock Hybrids ®	[pre-1952]	
	'Little Old Lady' = **D. 'Chelsea Pink'**		
3	'Lochinvar Louise' ®	[pre-1974]	
3	'Lolita'	[Avonmore Nurseries pre-1976]	
1	'London Brocade' ®	[F R McQuown pre-1961]	
1	'London Delight' ®	[F R McQuown pre-1960]	
1	'London Glow' ®	[F R McQuown pre-1944]	
1	'London Lovely' ®	[F R McQuown 1944]	
1	'London Poppet' ®	[F R McQuown 1946]	RD
3	'Lonzelou'		
	'Lord Chatham' = **D. 'Raby Castle'**		
2	'Lord Grey' ®	[Douglas 1946]	
2	'Lord Nuffield' ®	[S O Stroud 1966]	
1	'Loveliness' ®	[Allwood pre-1926]	
	'Loveliness Alba' = **D. 'White Loveliness'**		
2	'Lucy Bertram' ®	[Douglas 1941]	
2	'Lustre' ®	[Allwood 1959]	DGP
3	'Lynda Jardine' ®	[J Vernon 1977]	
1	'Madame Durbury Mauve'		
1	'Madonna' ®	[Old Cv]	
1	'Maggie' ®	[Hendriksen pre-1981]	
	'Maiden Pink' = **D. deltoides**		
2	'Maisie Neal' ®	[J Galbally 1977]	
3	'Maj Britt' ®	[W W Thomson Co 1971]	
3	'Malva' ®	[G Nobbio pre-1973]	
1	'Mandy' ®	[Allwood 1959]	
1	'Mandy's Choice' ®	[J Radcliffe 1970]	
	'Manningtree Pink' = **D. 'Sir Cedric Morris'**		
3	'Manon' ®	[G Nobbio 1972]	
3	'Marchioness of Headfort' ®	[J Boyle pre-1930]	
3	'Marchioness of Salisbury' ®	[Woodfield Bros 1979]	
1	'Margaret Curtis' ®	[G Winter 1929]	
1	'Margaret Lyle'	[via Hartside Nursery pre-1984]	
	'Maria' = **D. 'Allen's Maria'**		
3	'Marina' ®	[C Evangelisti pre-1978]	
1	'Mark' ®	[Allwood pre-1957]	
1	'Mars' ®	[Allwood pre-1934]	CA
1	'Marshwood Mystery' ®	[Three Counties Nurseries 1982]	
2	'Mary Livinstone' ®	[Douglas 1934]	
2	'Mary Murray' ®	[G D Murray pre-1920]	
2	'Mary Simister' ®	[N J Simister 1968]	
2	'Master Stuart' ®	[S Bailey pre-1956]	
2	'Matador'	[Lindabruce Nurseries pre-1960]	
2	'Maudie Hinds' ®	[J Galbally pre-1971]	
2	'Maureen Saunders' ®	[J Galbally 1972]	
1	'Maurice Prichard' ®	[R V Prichard pre-1949]	
2	'Maybole' ®	[Douglas 1957]	
1	'May Jones' ®	[N Overington 1976]	
1	'Maythorne'		

3	'Melanie Charles'		
2	'Mendip Hills' ®	[S J Cook pre-1954]	
3	'Mercury'		
2	'Merlin Clove' ®	[Douglas 1928]	**RD**
1	'Messines Pink' ®	[ex France pre-1933]	
1	'Messines White' ®	[pre-1951]	
2	'Michael Saunders' ®	[J Galbally 1972]	
1	'Milley'	[Milley Nursery c1972]	

'Millstream Salmon' = **D. alpinus 'Millstream Salmon'**

1	'Miss Sinkins' ®	[via Allwood pre-1949]	
1	'Monica Wyatt' ®	[C Wyatt 1981]	

'Montrose Pink' = **D. 'Cockenzie Pink'**

3	'Monty's Pink' ®	[Allwood pre-1953]	
1	'Mrs Blarney's Old Pink' ®	[Old Cv]	

'Mrs Clark' = **D. 'Nellie Clark'**

1	'Mrs Dunlop's Old Pink' ®	[ex Scotland]	
2	'Mrs Edmund Charrington' ®	[G D Murray 1922]	
1	'Mrs Holt' ®	[pre-1962]	
1	'Mrs Jackson'	[via McMurtrie]	
1	'Mrs MacBride'	[via McMurtrie]	
2	'Mrs Perkins' ®	[S O Stroud pre-1971]	
1	'Mrs Pilkington' ®	[Pilkington pre-1971]	
1	'Mrs R Gibbs'		
1	'Mrs Sinkins' ®	[J Sinkins 1868]	PGP-**RD**
1	'Murray's Laced Pink' ®	[1800s]	
3	'Murcia'	[P Kooij & Zn 1985]	
1	'Murton'	[via Kingstone Cottage Plants pre-1985]	
1	'Musgrave's Pink' ®	[c1730] (D. 'Charles Musgrave')	**RD**
1	'Nan Bailey'	[S Bailey Ltd pre-1985]	

L (margin mark for 'Mrs Sinkins')

'Nancy Lindsay' = **D. pavonius 'Nancy Lindsay'**

1	'Napoleon III' ®	[A Pare 1840]	
2	'Nautilus' ®	[Douglas 1949]	
1	'Nellie Clark' ®	[F Clark pre-1946] (D. 'Mrs Clark')	
3	'Neptune' ®	[Yoder Bros 1951]	

'Nieves' = **D. 'Sorolla'**

3	'Nina' ®	[C Englemann 1929]	
1	'N M Goodall'		

'Nordstern' = **D. 'Asnelliken'**

2	'Norman Hayward'	[Hayward 1946]	
3	'Northland' ®	[W Sim 1939]	
1	'Norwich Glow' ®	[P Fenn 1980]	
1	'Norwich Pride' ®	[P Fenn 1982]	
1	'Nyewood's Cream' ®	[? E S Lytte pre-1944]	
2	'Oaken Belle' ®	[H Smart pre-1969]	
2	'Oaken Fragrance' ®	[H Smart 1974]	
2	'Oaken Grey' ®	[H Smart pre-1969]	
2	'Oakfield Clove' ®	[L A Lowe 1932]	
1	'Oakington' ®	[A Bloom c1930] (D. 'Oakington Hybrid')	

'Oakington Hybrid' = **D. 'Oakington'**

1	'Oakwood Bill Ballinger' ®	[S Hall 1985]	
1	'Oakwood Dainty' ®	[S Hall 1985]	

'Old Clove' = **D. 'Old Crimson Clove'**

2	'Old Crimson Clove' ®	[1500s] (D. 'Old Clove', D. 'Old Red Clove')	

PGP

1	'Old Dutch Pink' ®	[1600s]	
1	'Old Fringed Pink' ®	[1600s]	
1	'Old Fringed White' ®	[1600s]	

'Old Red Clove' = **D. 'Old Crimson Clove'**

1	'Old Velvet' ®	[Old Cv]	
1	'Oliver' ®	[Allwood pre-1972]	

2	**'Orange Maid'** ®	[Lindabruce Nurseries pre-1964]	
2	**'Orange Tawny'** ®	[J Galbally pre-1974]	
3	**'Orange Telstar'** ®	[P Kooij & Zn 1974]	
3	**'Orchid Beauty'** ®	[S Littlefield & W Wyman 1949]	
2	**'Orton Glory'** ®	[N J Simister pre-1965]	
2	**'Oscar'** ®	[C H Fielder 1970]	
2	**'Osprey'** ®	[Douglas 1945]	
1	**'Paddington'** ®	[T Hogg 1800s]	
1	**'Painted Beauty'** ®	[Old cv]	
	'Painted Lady' = **D. 'Pink Damask'**		
1	**'Paisley Gem'** ®	[J Macree c1798]	
3	**'Pallas'** ®	[A Nonin pre-1904]	
2	**'Pat Phoenix'** ®	[S O Stroud pre-1968]	
2	**'Patricia'** ®	[J Hayward pre-1966]	
1	**'Paul'** ®	[Allwood pre-1970]	
1	**'Peach'**	[Lindabruce Nurseries 1959]	
2	**'Perfect Clove'** ®	[Douglas 1942]	**RD**
3	**'Persian Pink'** ®	[Woodside Nurseries 1964]	
2	**'Peter Adamson'** ®	[S O Stroud pre-1967]	
2	**'Peter Wood'** ®	[J Galbally 1977]	
1	**'Petticoat Lace'**	[J Hayward]	
1	**'Petula'** ®	[P A Fenn 1968]	
1	**'Pheasant's Eye'** ®	[pre-1671]	
2	**'Philip Archer'** ®	[S O Stroud 1972]	
1	**'Picture'** ®	[Lindabruce Nurseries pre-1962]	
1	**'Pike's Pink'** ®	[J Pike pre-1965]	
1	**'Pink Baby'**		
3	**'Pink Barbi'** ®	[W W Thomson Co pre-1977]	
2	**'Pink Bizarre'** ®	[Allwood pre-1943]	
1	**'Pink Bouquet'** ®	[Mrs D Underwood 1958]	
	'Pink Calypso' = **D. 'Truly Yours'**		
1	**'Pink Damask'** ®	[Reginald Kaye Ltd 1980]	
3	**'Pink Dusty Sim'** ®	[A C Maier 1960]	
3	**'Pink Fragrant Ann'** ®	[J A M Neil 1971]	
3	**'Pink Ice'** ®	[Gohn's Greenhouses 1960]	
	'Pink Jewel' = **D. gratianopolitanus 'Pink Jewel'**		
3	**'Pink Mist Sim'** ®	[Woodside Nurseries 1970]	
1	**'Pink Mrs Sinkins'** ®	[C Turner pre-1908]	
2	**'Pink Pearl'** ®	[Allwood pre-1945]	
1	**'Pixie'** ®	[East Lodge Gardens 1964]	
1	**'Pluto'** ®	[Allwood 1959]	
3	**'Portrait Barbi'** ®	[Siri Bros Greenhouses pre-1979]	
2	**'Portsdown Clove'** ®	[Haywards Carnations c1955]	
2	**'Portsdown Fancy'** ®	[Haywards Carnations pre-1970]	
2	**'Portsdown Lass'** ®	[Haywards Carnations pre-1972]	
2	**'Portsdown Perfume'** ®	[Haywards Carnations 1960]	
2	**'Portsdown Sunset'** ®	[Haywards Carnations 1950]	
1	**'Pretty Lady'**		
1	**'Prichard's Variety'**		
1	**'Pride of Ayrshire'** ®	[Old Cv]	
1	**'Prince Charming'** ®	[via Lowndes pre-1951]	
1	**'Priory Pink'** ®	[Old Cv]	
1	**'Prudence'** ®	[Allwood pre-1953]	**RD**
1	**'Pummelchen'** ®	[Kayser & Siebert pre-1985]	
1	**'Purley King'** ®	[E A Tickle pre-1974]	
3	**'Purple Frosted'** ®	[Holley c1962]	**RD**
2	**'Purple Gem'** ®	[Loudoun Nurseries pre-1965]	
1	**'Purple Treasure'** ®	[Mrs D Underwood 1967]	
	'Purpurstjerne' = **D. gratianopolitanus 'Purpurstjerne'**		
1	**'Queen of Hearts'** ®	[Goldsmith Seeds Inc pre-1976]	

1   'Queen of Sheba'   ®   [1600s]
3   'Queen's Reward'   ®   [C Short 1981]
3   'Quito'   [G Nobbio 1981]
2   'Raby Castle'   ®   [pre-1780] (D. 'Lord Chatham')   PGP
1   'Rachel'
1   'Raeden Pink'   ®   [1800s]
3   'Raggio di Sole'   ®   [G Nobbio 1973]
3   'Raspberry Ice'   ®   [Sim Carnation Co 1951]
1   'Raspberry Ripple'   [via J Marshall pre-1985]
1   'Red and White'
3   'Red Baron'   ®   [W W Thomson Co 1971]
3   'Red Diamond'   ®   [F J Hellberg 1964]
3   'Red-Edged Skyline'   ®   [S Bailey 1962]
1   'Red Emperor'   ®   [pre-1952]
1   'Red Laced'
3   'Red Lena'   [L Hakansson pre-1982]
1   'Red Penny'   ®   [pre-1962]
2   'Renoir'   ®   [Allwood pre-1956]
1   'Revell's Lady Wharncliffe'
2   'Riccardo'   ®   [J Galbally 1977]
1   'Richard Gibbs'   ®   [via A e-1935]
2   'Richard Hough'   ®   [F W Goodfellow pre-1954]
2   'Richard Pollak'   ®   [J Galbally pre-1973]
1   'Robert'   ®   [Allwood 1914]
3   'Robert Allwood'   ®   [Allwood 1931]
2   'Robert Baden-Powell'   ®   [Haywards Carnations 1976]
2   'Robert Douglas'   ®   [Douglas 1958]
2   'Robin Thain'   ®   [R Thain pre-1940]
2   'Robert Smith'   ®   [Loudon Nurseries pre-1957]   DGP
    'Rosa Zwerg' = D. subacaulis 'Rosa Zwerg'
1   'Rosealie'   ®   [Lindabruce Nurseries]
2   'Rose Bradwardine'   ®   [Douglas 1933]
1   'Rose de Mai'   ®   [c1820]
2   'Rosemary'   ®   [Douglas 1959]
1   'Rose Joy'   ®   [T A Percival 1983]
    'Rosenfelder' = D. gratianopolitanus 'Rosenfelder'
3   'Rose Perfection'   ®   [S Bailey 1971]
    'Rotkäppchen' = D. gratianopolitanus 'Rotkäppchen'
3   'Royal Scot'   ®   [Woodfield Bros pre-1980]
1   'Royalty'   ®   [Lindabruce Nurseries 1965]
1   'Roysii'   ®   [pre-1928]
3   'Rozenoord's Yellow'   ®   [C Buys 1956]
    'Rubin' = D 'Knecht's Rubin'
    'Ruby' = D. 'Houndspool Ruby'
    'Ruby Doris' = D. 'Houndspool Ruby'
1   'Ruth'   ®   [Allwood pre-1933]
1   'St Nicholas'   ®   [Old Cv]
3   'Sacha'   [via S Bailey Ltd pre-1982]
3   'Safari'   ®   [W D Holley 1963]
2   'Salmon Clove'   ®   [Douglas 1919]   DGP
3   'Salmon Fragrant Ann'   ®   [J A M Neil 1971]
2   'Salmon Queen'   ®   [Douglas 1962]
1   'Sam Barlow'   ®   [1800s]
    'Samos' = D. deltoides 'Samos'
1   'Sandra'   ®   [Allwood pre-1965]
2   'Sandra Neal'   ®   [J Galbally pre-1972]
3   'Sanremo'   [N Baratta 1982]
2   'Santa Claus'   ®   [Phillips & Taylor 1907]
2   'Sappho'   ®   [F W Burstall pre-1932]
3   'Saturn'   ®   [Yoder Bros 1951]

3	'Scania' ®	[L Haannson 1955]	
1	'Scarlet 79' ®	[C Wyatt pre-1979]	
2	'Scarlet Fragrance' ®	[Allwood pre-1950]	
3	'Scarlet Miniqueen' ®	[W W Thomson Co 1971]	

'Scaynes Hill' = **D. gratianopolitanus** 'Scaynes Hill'

2	'Sean Hitchcock' ®	[J Galbally 1977]	
2	'Selborne' ®	[Douglas 1947]	
2	'Shaston' ®	[D Gamlin pre-1969]	
2	'Shaston Delight' ®	[D Gamlin pre-1969]	
2	'Shaston Scarletta' ®	[D Gamlin pre-1969]	
2	'Shaston Superstar' ®	[D Gamlin pre-1969]	
2	'Shaston Supreme' ®	[D Gamlin pre-1969]	
3	'Sheila Short' ®	[C Short 1983]	
2	'Sheila Weir' ®	[H Lakeman pre-1955]	
3	'Shocking Pink Sim' ®	[G P Barr 1955]	
1	'Show Aristocrat' ®	[Allwood pre-1945]	
1	'Show Beauty' ®	[Allwood pre-1939]	DGP-RD
1	'Show Bride' ®	[Allwood pre-1953]	
1	'Show Charming' ®	[Allwood pre-1955]	
1	'Show Daintiness' ®	[Allwood pre-1956]	
1	'Show Distinction' ®	[Allwood pre-1953]	
1	'Show Emblem' ®	[Allwood pre-1966]	
1	'Show Enchantress' ®	[Allwood pre-1946]	DGP
1	'Show Glory' ®	[Allwood 1948]	
1	'Show Ideal' ®	[Allwood 1945]	DGP
1	'Show Magnificence' ®	[Allwood pre-1969]	
1	'Show Paragon' ®	[Allwood pre-1954]	
1	'Show Pearl' ®	[Allwood pre-1948]	DGP
1	'Show Portrait' ®	[Allwood pre-1950]	
1	'Show Satin' ®	[Allwood pre-1960]	
2	'Shrimp' ®	[via W T Benefield & Sons pre-1911]	
3	'Sir Arthur Sim' ®	[S A Peterson 1956] (D. 'Arthur Sim')	DGP-RD

'Sir Cedric Morris' = **D.** 'Cedric's Oldest'

1	'Sir David Scott' ®	[via Valerie Finnis 1600s]	
2	'Snow Clove' ®	[Douglas 1928]	
1	'Snowflake' ®	[Allwood 1960]	
1	'Snowshill Fringed' ®	[ex France]	
1	'Solomon' ®	[Old Cv]	
1	'Sops-in-Wine' ®	[Old Cv]	
3	'Sorolla'	[D Mansuino] (D. 'Nieves')	
1	'Southmead' ®	[G K Mooney pre-1966]	
2	'Spangle' ®	[Douglas 1938]	
1	'Spark' ®	[pre-1925]	
1	'Spencer Bickham' ®	[R Veitch c1900]	RD
2	'Spindrift'	[Douglas 1961]	
3	'Spotlight' ®	[ex USA 1931]	
2	'Sprite' ®	[F W Goodfellow pre-1948]	
1	'Squeeks' ®	[A G Weeks pre-1965]	
2	'Stanley Stroud' ®	[S O Stroud 1972]	
1	'Startler' ®	[P A Fenn 1974]	RD

'Steriker' = **D. deltoides** 'Steriker'

3	'Storm' ®	[Avonmore Nurseries pre-1967]	RD
2	'Strathspey' ®	[Douglas 1956]	
1	'Strawberries and Cream' ®	[C Wyatt 1981]	
2	'Strawberry Fayre' ®	[W Muir 1960s]	
2	'Sunray' ®	[Douglas 1953]	
2	'Sunstar' ®	[F W Goodfellow pre-1950]	
2	'Surrey Clove' ®	[Douglas 1936]	
1	'Susan' ®	[Allwood 1917]	
1	'Susanah'	[Allwod]	

2   **'Susan Humphries'**   ®   [J H Humphries 1972]
1   **'Swanlake'**   ®   [Lindabruce Nurseries pre-1957]
1   **'Swansdown'**
1   **'Sweetheart Abbey'**   ®   [Old Cv]
2   **'Sweet Sue'**   ®   [S O Stroud pre-1964]
1   **'Syston Beauty'**   [via D Stuart pre-1983]
2   **'Taff Glow'**   ®   [T Brotherton 1978]
2   **'Taff Snow'**   ®   [T Brotherton 1981]
2   **'Taffy'**   ®   [T Brotherton 1978] (D. 'Taff Vale')
    'Taff Vale' = **D. 'Taffy'**
2   **'Tamsin Fifield'**   ®   [J Galbally 1977]
3   **'Tangerine Sim'**   ®   [C H Mann 1956]
3   **'Tango Bambi'**   [G Nobbio pre-1982]
1   **'Taunton'**   ®   [via Southcombe Gardens Plant Nursery pre-1983]
3   **'Telstar'**   ®   [Newberry Greenhouses Ltd 1963]
3   **'Teresa'**   [via R Shemi Ltd pre-1983]
1   **'Terry Sutcliffe'**   [via Kingstone Cottage Plants pre-1985]
3   **'Tetra'**   ®   [A G Rait pre-1965]
2   **'Teviotdale'**   ®   [Douglas 1927]
1   **'Thomas'**   ®   [Allwood pre-1931]   PGP
2   **'Thomas Lee'**   ®   [F W Goodfellow pre-1948]   RD
3   **'Tigre'**   ®   [G Nobbio 1974]
1   **'Timothy'**   ®   [Allwood pre-1956]   DGP-RD
    'Tiny Rubies' = **D. gratianopolitanus 'Tiny Rubies'**
1   **'Toledo'**   ®   [R P Tolley 1972]
3   **'Toledo'**   ®   [W D Holley 1972]
1   **'Tom Welborn'**   [via Ramparts Nursery pre-1983]
3   **'Tony'**   ®   [W W Thomson Co 1971]
2   **'Tony Cutler'**   ®   [E F Cutler 1948]
3   **'Topsy'**   ®   [J H Hill & Co 1919]
3   **'Tracy Short'**   ®   [C Short 1981]
1   **'Treasure'**   ®   [Lindabruce Nurseries pre-1971]
1   **'Trevor'**   ®   [Allwood pre-1968]
2   **'Trojan Clove'**   ®   [Douglas 1957]
3   **'Truly Yours'**   ®   [H P Piers 1971] (D. 'Pink Calypso')
2   **'Uncle Teddy'**   ®   [J Galbally 1970]
1   **'Unique'**   ®   [1600s]
3   **'Uranus'**   ®   [via R Poulter & Sons pre-1927]
1   **'Ursula Le Grove'**   ®   [C O Moreton]
1   **'Valda Wyatt'**   ®   [C Wyatt 1977]
3   **'Valencia'**   [P Kooij & Zn 1982]
    'Vampir' = **D. deltoides 'Vampir'**
1   **'Vanda'**   ®   [Allwood 1980]
3   **'Vera Woodfield'**   ®   [Woodfield Bros 1981]
1   **'Victoria'**
2   **'Violet Carson'**   ®   [S O Stroud 1967]
2   **'Violet Clove'**   ®   [Douglas 1957]
1   **'Waithman's Beauty'**   ®   [R Kaye pre-1967]
1   **'Waithman's Jubilee'**   [R Kaye pre-1982]
1   **'W A Musgrave'**
    'Warden Hybrid' = **D 'Welwyn'**
2   **'Warrior'**   ®   [Lindabruce Nurseries 1949]   DGP
2   **'Water Nymph'**   ®   [F W Goodfellow pre-1950]
3   **'Webby'**   ®   [F Webster 1973]
1   **'Weetwood Double'**   ®   [H E Bawden 1983]
1   **'Welcome'**   ®   [Lindabruce Nurseries pre-1958]
1   **'Welland'**   ®   [R Kaye pre-1966]
1   **'Wells Next The Sea'**
1   **'Welwyn'**   ®   [via MacPenny pre-1955] (D. 'Warden Hybrid')
1   **'Whatfield Anona'**   ®   [J Schofield 1980]

1	**'Whatfield Gem'** ®	[J Schofield 1970]	
1	**'Whatfield Joy'** ®	[J Schofield 1969]	
1	**'Whatfield Mini'** ®	[J Schofield 1979]	
1	**'Whatfield Pom-Pom'** ®	[J Schofield 1979]	
1	**'Whatfield Seedling'** ®	[J Schofield 1983]	
1	**'Whatfield Wisp'** ®	[J Schofield 1983]	
2	**'W H Brooks'** ®	[Douglas 1929]	
1	**'White Bouquet'**		
3	**'White Calypso'** ®	[S B Talee pre-1973]	
2	**'Whitecliff'** ®	[F W Goodfellow 1961]	
1	**'Whitehills'** ®	[pre-1962]	

L

1	**'White Ladies'** ®	[Old Cv]	PGP-RD
1	**'White Loveliness'** ®	[Allwood 1928]	
3	**'White Royalette'** ®	[Siri Bros 1963]	
3	**'White Sim Improved'** ®	[Hilverda BV 1950s]	
2	**'Whitesmith'** ®	[J Galbally pre-1972]	
1	**'Widecombe Fair'** ®	[C Wyatt 1974]	
1	**'William Brownhill'** ®	[W Brownhill 1700s]	
2	**'William Newell'** ®	[F W Goodfellow pre-1946]	
1	**'William of Essex'** ®	[Ramparts Nursery 1982]	
3	**'William Sim'** ®	[Sim Carnation Co 1939]	DGP-RD
2	**'Winnie Lesurf'** ®	[J Galbally 1979]	
1	**'Winsome'** ®	[C H Fielder 1947]	
	'Wisley Variety' = **D. deltoides 'Wisley Variety'**		
1	**'Wisp'** ®	[Allwood pre-1941]	
3	**'Woodfield Apricot'** ®	[Woodfield Bros 1982]	
3	**'Yasmina'**	[ex France c1970] (D. 'Barsemi')	
3	**'Yellow Dusty Sim'** ®	[J Gunther c1956]	RD
2	**'Yorkshireman'** ®	[Miss R Goodfellow pre-1960]	
3	**'Zamora'**	[P Kooij & Zn pre-1982]	
2	**'Zebra'** ®	[Douglas 1928]	DGP-RD
2	**'Zephyr'** ®	[Douglas 1933]	

DIASCIA Link & Otto 1820   [*Scrophulariaceae*]
   aliciae Hiern 1904 = **D. racemulosa**
   barberae Hooker f. 1871   PGP-**DGP**-RD
   cordata N. E. Brown 1895   RD
      'Elegans' = **D. vigilis**
   elegans hort. = **D. vigilis**
   felthamii hort. = **D. fetcaniensis**
   fetcaniensis Hilliard & B. L. Burtt 1984 (*D. felthamii*)
   flanaganii Hiern 1904 = **D. stachyoides**
   integerrima E. Meyer ex Bentham 1836 (*D. moltenensis*)
   lilacina Hilliard & B. L. Burtt 1983
   megathura Hilliard & B. L. Burtt 1983
   moltenensis Hiern 1904 = **D. integerrima**
A **racemulosa** Bentham 1836 (*D. aliciae*)
   rigescens E. Meyer ex Bentham 1836   PGP-**RD**
   'Ruby Field' (*D. cordata* x *D. barbarae*)   [J. Kelly c1971]   RD
   stachyoides Schleichter ex Hiern 1904 (*D. flanaganii*)
   vigilis Hilliard & B. L. Burtt 1983 (*D. elegans* hort.)

DICENTRA Bernhardi 1833 nom. cons.   [*Fumariaceae*]
   candensis (Goldie) Walpers 1842   SB
   cucullaria (Linnaeus) Bernhardi 1833   CA-**SB**-RD
   eximia (Ker-Gawler) Torrey 1843   **PGP**-DGP-**RD**
      'Alba'   **DGP**-RD
   formosa (Andrews) Walpers 1842   **PGP**-SB-DGP-RD
L   **'Adrian Bloom'**   [Bloom]   PGP
      'Alba'
      'Baccharal'

'Bountiful'
'Langtrees' ('Pearl Drops')   PGP-**DGP**
'Luxuriant'   PGP
ssp. **oregona** (Eastwood) Munz 1959 (*D. oregona*)   **PGP**-CA
'Paramount'   PGP
'Pearl Drops' = **D. formosa 'Langtrees'**
'Silver Smith'   PGP
'Spring Morning'   RD
'Stuart Boothman'   [S. Boothman]
macrantha Oliver 1890   **PGP**
oregona Eastwood 1931 = **D. formosa** ssp. **oregona**
pauciflora S. Watson 1880   SB
peregrina (J. Rudolph) Makino 1908 (*D. pusilla*)   CA-SB-**DGP**
'Alba'
pusilla Siebold & Zuccarini 1843 = **D. peregrina**
^NL spectabilis (Linnaeus) Lemaire 1847   **PGP**-SB-**DGP**-RD
'Alba'   DGP-RD

DICHELOSTEMMA Kunth 1843   [*Alliaceae (Liliaceae)*]
congestum (Smith) Kunth 1843   EGF.1-**SB**
ida-maia (Wood) E. Greene 1894   EGF.1-**BB**-SB-**DGP**
pulchellum (Salisbury) Heller 1906   EGF.1-**BB**-SB

DICKSONIA L'Heritier 1789   [*Cyatheaceae*]
^N antarctica Labillardiere 1806   EGF.1-PGP
fibrosa Colenso 1846   EGF.1
squarrosa (Foster f.) Swartz 1806   EGF.1

DICTAMNUS Linnaeus 1753   [*Rutaceae*]
^H albus Linnaeus 1753 (*D. fraxinella*)   PGP-DGP-RD
var. **caucasicus** (Fischer & Meyer) Rouy (*D. caucasicus*)   PGP
^L 'Purpureus'   PGP-**DGP**-RD
caucasicus (Fischer & Meyer) Fischer & Grossheim 1832 = **D. albus** var.
                                                                       caucasicus
fraxinella Persoon 1805 = **D. albus**

DICTYOLIMON K. H. Rechinger 1974   [*Plumbaginaceae*]
macrorrhabdos (Boissier) K. H. Rechinger 1974 (*Statice macrorrhabdos*)

DIERAMA C. Koch 1861   [*Iridaceae*]
cooperi N. E. Brown 1929
pendulum (Linnaeus f.) Baker 1877 (*Sparaxis pendula*)   EGF.1-RD
var. **pumilum** Baker 1877 (D. 'Hermia')   RD
var. **pumilum** 'Puck'   PGP
^L pulcherrimum (Hooker f.) Baker 1877 (*Sparaxis pulcherrima*) EGF.1-PGP-**DGP**-RD
Blackbird Hybrids
'Hermia' = **D. pendulum** var. **pumilum**
'Miranda'
'Nanum'
'Peregrine'
'Slieve Donard'
pumilum (Baker) N. E. Brown 1929 = **D. pendulum** var. **pumilum**

DIETES Salisbury 1812 nom. cons.   [*Iridaceae*]
grandiflora N. E. Brown 1928   EGF.1
iridoides (Linnaeus) Sweet 1830 (*Moraea iridoides*)   EGF.1-PGP
'Johnsonii'   EGF.1

DIGITALIS Linnaeus 1753   [*Scrophulariaceae*]
ambigua Murray 1770 = **D. grandiflora**

	ciliata Trautvetter 1866	
	davisiana Heywood 1949	
	dubia Rodriguez 1874	
	ferruginea Linnaeus 1753	PGP-RD
	'**Gigantea**' nom. dub.	
	ssp. **schischkinii** (Ivanov) Werner 1960 (*D. schischkinii*)	
L	**grandiflora** Miller 1768 (*D. ambigua, D. ochroleuca*)	**PGP**-RD
	'**Dropmore Yellow**'	
	laevigata Waldstein & Kitaibel 1805	
HN	**lanata** Ehrhardt 1792	PGP
	ssp. **leucophaea** (Smith) Werner 1960	
H	**lutea** Linnaeus 1753	PGP-RD
	x mertonensis Buxton & C. Darlington 1931 (*D. grandiflora* x *D. purpurea*)	
		PGP-RD
S	**obscura** Linnaeus 1763	
	ochroleuca Jacquin 1773 = **D. grandiflora**	
	parviflora Jacquin 1770	PGP
HN‡L	**purpurea** Linnaeus 1753	PGP-DGP-**RD**
	'**Alba**'	
	var. **amandiana** (Sampaio) Werner 1960	
	Apricot Hybrids = **D. purpurea** '**Sutton's Apricot**'	
	Excelsior Hybrids	**DGP**-RD
	Foxy Hybrids	**DGP**-RD
	Gelbelanze Hybriden	
	'**Gloxiniflora**'	
	ssp. **heywoodii** P. & M. Silva 1959	
	'**Rosea**'	
	'**Sutton's Apricot**'	
	schischkinii Ivanina 1946 = **D. ferruginea** ssp. **schischkinii**	
	viridiflora Lindley 1821	

DIMORPHOTHECA Vaillant ex Moench 1794 nom. cons.	[*Asteraceae (Compositae)*]
ecklonis A. de Candolle 1837 = **Osteospermum ecklonis**	
jucunda E. Phillips 1936 = **Osteospermum jucundum**	

DIONYSIA Fenzl 1843	[*Primulaceae*]
archibaldii Wendelbo 1967	
aretioides (Lehmann) Boissier 1846	**DGP**
'**Paul Furse**' [J. C. Archibald 1969]	**CA**
'**Phyllis Carter**' [J. Kelly c1970]	
bryoides Boissier & Buhse 1860	**CA**
curviflora Bunge 1871	CA
involucrata Zaprjagaev 1936	
janthina Bornmueller & Winkler 1899	
janthina hort. non Bornmueller & Winkler = **D. curviflora**	
michauxii (Duby) Boissier 1846	**CA**
revoluta Boissier 1846	
ssp. **canescens** (Boissier) Wendelbo 1961	
tapetodes Bunge 1871	
'**Peter Edwards**'	
teucrioides P. H. Davis & Wendelbo 1961	

DIOSCOREA Linnaeus 1753	[*Dioscoreaceae*]
balcanica Kosanin 1914	EGF.1

DIPHYLLEIA Michaux 1803	[*Berberidaceae*]
cymosa Michaux 1814	PGP

DIPLACUS Nuttall 1838	[*Scrophulariaceae*]
glutinosus Nuttall 1838 = **Mimulus aurantiacus**	
puniceus Nuttall 1838 = **Mimulus puniceus**	

DIPLARRHENA Labillardiere 1788   *[Iridaceae]*
   latifolia Bentham 1873   EGF.1
   moraea Labillardiere 1788   EGF.1-PGP
   'Minor' = **D. latifolia**

DIPLAZIUM Swartz 1801   *[Woodsiaceae]*
   sibiricum (Turczaninow ex Kunze) Kurata 1961 (*Athyrium crenatum*)

DIPSACUS Linnaeus 1753   *[Dipsacaceae]*
BHN‡L **fullonum** Linnaeus 1753
B   **laciniatus** Linnaeus 1753
   sylvestris Hudson 1763 = **D. fullonum**

DISPORUM Salisbury ex D.Don 1825   *[Convallariaceae (Liliaceae)]*
   cantoniense (Loureiro) Merrill 1919 (*D. pullum*)   EGF.1-PGP
   hookeri (Torrey) Nicholson 1884   EGF.1
     var. **oreganum** (S. Watson) Q. Jones 1906   EGF.1-PGP
   lanuginosum (Michaux) Nicholson 1884   EGF.1
   maculatum (A. Gray) Britton 1888
   oreganum (S. Watson) J. Howell 1902 = **D. hookeri** var. **oreganum**
   pullum Salisbury 1812 nom. nud. = **D. cantoniense**
   sessile (Thunberg) D. Don 1825   EGF.1-PGP
     'Variegatum'   EGF.1-PGP
     var. **yakushimense**
   smilacinum A. Gray 1856   EGF.1
   smithii (Hooker) Piper 1906   EGF.1-PGP

DODECATHEON Linnaeus 1753   *[Primulaceae]*
   alpinum (A. Gray) Greene 1895   CA-**DGP**
   campestrum Howell 1901
   clevelandii Greene 1888
     ssp. **insularis** H. J. Thompson 1953
   cusickii Greene 1890 = **D. pulchellum**
   dentatum Hooker 1838
     ssp. **ellisiae** (Standley) H. J. Thompson 1953
   ellisiae Standley 1913 = **D. dentatum** ssp. **ellisiae**
   hendersonii A. Gray 1886   CA
     Sooke Form
   jeffreyi Van Houtte 1865 (*D. tetrandum*)   PGP-RD
     var. *redolens* Hall 1901 = **D. redolens**
   meadia Linnaeus 1753   PGP-DGP-**RD**
     f. **album** Macbride 1930   **DGP**
   pauciflorum (Durand) Greene 1890 = **D. pulchellum**
   pulchellum (Rafinesque) Merrill 1948 (*D. cusickii, D. pauciflorum, D. radicatum*)
                           RD
     'Red Wings'
     'Queen Victoria'
   radicatum Greene 1895 = **D. pulchellum**
   redolens (Hall) H. J. Thompson 1953
   salinum A. Nelson 1899
   tetrandum Suksdorf 1895 = **D. jeffreyi**

DOODIA R. Brown 1810   *[Blechnaceae]*
   media R. Brown 1810   EGF.1

DORONICUM Linnaeus 1753   *[Asteraceae (Compositae)]*
   austriacum Jacquin 1774   PGP-**RD**
   caucasicum Marshall von Bieberstein 1808 = **D. orientale**
   clusii (Allioni) Tausch 1828
N   **columnae** Tenore 1811 (*D. cordatum*)   CA-**DGP-RD**

   cordatum (Wulfen) Schultz-Bip 1854 = **D. columnae**
   grandiflorum Lamarck 1786
   orientale Hoffmann 1808 (*D. caucasicum*)   DGP
N **pardalianches** Linnaeus 1753   PGP-RD
      'Goldstrauss'   [Beye 1935]
N **plantagineum** Linnaeus 1753   PGP-DGP-**RD**
L   **'Excelsum'** ('Harpur Crewe')   [Crewe 1876]   PGP-DGP-**RD**
      'Harpur Crewe' = **D. plantagineum 'Excelsum'**
      'Strahlengold'   [K. Partsch 1976]

   HYBRID CULTIVARS

      'Finesse'   [E. Benary 1976]
      'Frülingspracht' ('Spring Beauty')   [H. Hagemann 1962]   PGP-**DGP**-RD
      'Gerhard'   [H. Götz]
      'Goldzwerg'   [H. Klose 1962]
      'Magnificum'
      'Miss Mason'
      'Riedel's Goldkranz'   [Riedel 1956]
      'Riedel's Lichtspiegal'   [Riedel 1956]
      'Spring Beauty' = **D. 'Frülingspracht'**

DORONICUM Linnaeus 1753   [*Asteraceae (Compositae)*]
   austriacum Jacquin 1774   PGP-**RD**
   caucasicum Marshall von Bieberstein 1808 = **D. orientale**
   clusii (Allioni) Tausch 1828
N **columnae** Tenore 1811 (*D. cordatum*)   CA-**DGP**-**RD**
   cordatum (Wulfen) Schultz-Bip 1854 = **D. columnae**
   grandiflorum Lamarck 1786
   orientale Hoffmann 1808 (*D. caucasicum*)   DGP
N **pardalianches** Linnaeus 1753   PGP-RD
      'Goldstrauss'   [Beye 1935]
N **plantagineum** Linnaeus 1753   PGP-DGP-**RD**
L   **'Excelsum'** ('Harpur Crewe')   [Crewe 1876]   PGP-DGP-**RD**
      'Harpur Crewe' = **D. plantagineum 'Excelsum'**
      'Strahlengold'   [K. Partsch 1976]

   HYBRID CULTIVARS

      'Finesse'   [E. Benary 1976]
      'Frülingspracht' ('Spring Beauty')   [H. Hagemann 1962]   PGP-**DGP**-RD
      'Gerhard'   [H. Götz]
      'Goldzwerg'   [H. Klose 1962]
      'Magnificum'
      'Miss Mason'
      'Riedel's Goldkranz'   [Riedel 1956]
      'Riedel's Lichtspiegal'   [Riedel 1956]
      'Spring Beauty' = **D. 'Frülingspracht'**

DORYCNIUM Villars 1789   [*Fabaceae (Leguminosae)*]
S   **hirsutum** (Linnaeus) Sevastianov 1826
SN **pentaphyllum** Scopoli 1722 (*D. suffruticosum*)
    suffruticosum Villars 1789 = **D. pentaphyllum**

DOUGLASIA Lindley 1827 nom. cons.   [*Primulaceae*]
   laevigata A. Gray 1881 (*Androsace laevigata*)   CA
      var. **ciliolata** (Constantin) !
   montana A. Gray 1868 (*Androsace montana*)   CA
   nivalis Lindley 1827 (*Androsace nivalis*)
   vitaliana (Linnaeus) Bentham & Hooker f. 1865 = **Vitaliana primuliflora**

DRABA Linnaeus 1753   [*Brassicaceae (Cruciferae)*]
N‡   **aizoides** Linnaeus 1767   RD
    aizoon Wahlenberg 1814 = **D. lasiocarpa**
    arabisans Michaux 1803
    aspera Bertoloni 1819 (*D. bertolonii*)
    athoa (Grisebach) Boissier 1853
    bertolonii Nyman 1872 = **D. aspera**
    bruniifolia Steven 1812
        ssp. **olympica** (Sibthorp ex de Candolle) Coode & Cullen 1965 (*D. olympica*)
    bryoides de Candolle 1821 = **D. rigida** var. **bryoides**
    cantabrica Willkomm 1851   CA
    cappadocica Boissier 1859
    compacta Schott, Nyman & Kotschy 1854
    cossonii O. E. Schulz 1927
B   **crassifolia** Graham 1829
    cuspidata Marshall von Bieberstein 1819
    dedeana Boissier & Reuter 1845   CA
    densifolia Nuttall 1838
    dovrensis Fries 1846
    gigas Stur ex Boissier 1867 = **Arabis carduchorum**
    haynaldii Stur 1861
    hispanica Boissier 1838
BN‡   **incana** Linnaeus 1753
    incerta Payson 1917
    kitadakensis Koidzumi 1925
    lasiocarpa Rochel 1810 (*D. aizoon, D. athoa, D. scardica*)
    longisiliqua Schmalhausen ex Akinfiew 1892
    mollissima Steven 1812   CA-DGP
N‡   **norvegica** Gunn (*D. rupestris*)
    oligosperma Hooker 1830
    olympica sensu Boissier 1867 = **D. bruniifolia** ssp. **olympica**
    parnassica Boissier & Heldreich 1853
    paysonii MacBride 1918
    polytricha Ledebour 1842   CA-**RD**
    pyrenaica Linnaeus 1753 = **Petrocallis pyrenaica**
    repens Marshall von Bieberstein 1808 = **D. sibirica**
    rigida Willdenow 1802   CA-RD
        var. **bryoides** (de Candolle) Boissier 1867   CA-**RD**
        var. **imbricata** (C.A. Meyer) !   CA-**DGP**-RD
    rosularis Boissier 1842
    rupestris R. Brown in Aiton 1812 = **D. norvegica**
    x salomonii Sündermann (*D. bruniifolia* x *D. dedeana*)   [Sündermann c1900]
    sauteri Hoppe 1823
    scardica (Grisebach) Halacsy 1894 = **D. lasiocarpa**
    sibirica (Pallas) Thellung 1906 (*D. repens*)
    stellata Jacquin 1762
    stylaris Gay ex Koch 1843 (*D. stylosa* hort.)
    x suendermanii Sündermann (*D. dedeana* x ?)   [Sündermann]
    tomentosa Clairville 1811
    ussuriensis Pohle 1914

DRACOCEPHALUM Linnaeus 1753   [*Lamiaceae (Labiatae)*]
    argunense Fischer ex Link 1822
    bullatum Forrest ex Diels 1912
    calophyllum Handel-Mazzetti 1924
    forrestii W. W. Smith 1916   PGP
    govanianum Bentham 1831 = **Nepeta govaniana**
    nutans Linnaeus 1753
    prattii (Leveille) Handel-Mazzetti 1934

renatii Emberger 1935
ruyschianum Linnaeus 1753   PGP
sibiricum Linnaeus 1758 = **Nepeta sibirica**
speciosum Sweet 1825 = **Physotegia virginiana**
virginianum Linnaeus 1753 = **Physostegia virginiana**

DRACUNCULUS Miller 1754   [*Araceae*]
    muscivorus (Linneaus) Parlatore 1852 (*Helicodiceros muscivorus*)   EGF.2-**BB**
    vulgaris Schott 1832   EGF.2-PGP-**BB-DGP**

DROSANTHEMUM Schwantes 1927   [*Aizoaceae*]
    floribundum (Haworth) Schwantes 1927 (*Mesembryanthemum floribundum*)
    hispidum (Linnaeus) Schwantes 1927 (*Mesembryanthemum hispidum*)

DRYAS Linnaeus 1753   [*Rosaceae*]
    drummondii Richardson 1830
        '**Grandiflora**'
    integrifolia Vahl 1798 (*D. tenella*)
SN‡ **octopetala** Linnaeus 1753   **DGP-RD**
        var. *integrifolia* (Vahl) Hooker f. 1860 = **D. integrifolia**
        '**Lanata**' nom. dub.
        '**Minor**'   **CA**-DGP
        '**Silberteppich**'
    x suendermanii Kellerer 1925 (*D. drummondii* x *D. octopetala*)
                                                              [Sündermann 1910]
    tenella Pursh 1814 = **D. integrifolia**

DRYOPTERIS Adanson 1763 nom. cons.   [*Dryopteridaceae*]
    abbreviata (de Candolle) Newman 1854 = **D. affinis**
    abbreviata hort. non (de Candolle) Newman 1854 = **D. oreades**
N   **affinis** (Lowe) Fraser-Jenkins 1979 (*D. abbreviata, D. borreri, D. pseudo-mas*)
    affinis agg.   **PGP-RD**
        '**Angustata cristata**'
        '**Crispa**'
        '**Crispa congesta**'
        '**Cristata**' ('The King')
        '**Cristata nana**'
        'Cristata The King' = **D. affinis** agg. '**Cristata**'
        '**Grandiceps**'
        '**Grandiceps Askew**'
        '**Grandiceps Harvey**'
        '**Ramosissima Wright**'
        '**Pinderi**'
        '**Stableri**'
    atrata (Wallich ex Kunze) Ching 1933 = **D. cycadina**
    austriaca Woynar ex Schintz & Thellung 1915 = **D. dilatata**
    assimilis S. Walker 1961 = **D. expansa**
    borreri (Newman) Newman ex Oberholzer & Tavel 1937 = **D. affinis** subspecies
N   **carthusiana** (Villars) H. P. Fuchs 1958 (*D. spinulosa*)   EGF.1-PGP
        '**Cristata**'
    clintoniana (D. C. Eaton) Dowell 1906
N   **x complexa** Fraser-Jenkins 1987 (*D. affinis* x *D. filix-mas*) (*D. x tavellii*)
N   **cristata** (Linnaeus) A. Gray 1848   EGF.1-PGP-**RD**
    cycadina (Franchet & Savatier) C. Christensen (*D. atrata, D. hirtipes* hort.)   PGP
N   **dilatata** (Hoffmann) A. Gray 1848 (*D. austriaca*)   EGF.1-PGP-RD
        '**Crispa**'
        '**Crispa Whiteside**'
        '**Cristata**'
        '**Grandiceps**'
        '**Lepidota cristata**'

	erythrosora (D.C. Eaton) O. Kuntze 1891	EGF.1-**PGP**-RD
N	**expansa** (C. Presl) Fraser-Jenkins & Jermy 1977 (*D. assimilis*)	EGF.1
HNL	**filix-mas** (Linnaeus) Schott 1834	EGF.1-PGP-RD

      'Barnsii'
      'Congesta'
      'Crispa'
      'Crispa cristata'
      'Crispatissima'
      'Cristata'
      'Cristata Jackson'
      'Cristata Martindale'
      'Decomposita cristata'
      'Depauperata' = **D. filix-mas** 'Depauperata Padley'
      'Depauperata Padley'
      'Fluctuosa'
      'Fluctuosa cristata'
      'Foliosa'
      'Grandiceps'
      'Grandiceps Wills' ('Polydactyla Wills')
      'Linearis'
      'Linearis congesta'
      'Linearis crenata' nom. dub.
      'Linearis cristata'
      'Linearis polydactyla'
      'Oligodonta' = **D. oligodonta**
      'Polydactyla'
      'Polydactyla Dadds'
      'Polydactyla Wills' = **D. filix-mas** 'Grandiceps Wills'
      'Ramo-cristata'

	goldiana (Hooker) A. Gray 1848	PGP
	hirtipes hort. = **D. cycadina**	
	lacera (Thunberg) O. Kuntze 1891	
	marginalis (Linnaeus) A. Gray 1848	
	montana (Vogler) O. Kuntze 1891 comb. invalid. = **Oreopteris limbosperma**	
	odontoloma (Moore) C. Christensen 1924 = **D. pallida** ssp. **nigropaleacea**	
	oligodonta (Desvaux) Pichi-Sermolli	
N	**oreades** Fomin 1910 (*D. abbreviata* hort.p.p)	EGF.1
	pallida (Bory) C. Christensen ex Maire & Petitmengin 1908	
	ssp. **nigropaleacea** Fraser-Jenkins (*D. odontoloma*)	
	phegopteris (Linnaeus) C. Christensen 1905 = **Phegopteris connectilis**	
	pseudo-mas (Wollaston) Holub & Pouzar 1967 = **D. affinis**	
N	**remota** (A. Braun ex Doll) Druce 1908	
	spinulosa (O. F. Mueller) O. Kuntze 1891 = **D. carthusiana**	
N	**submontana** (Fraser-Jenkins & Jermy) Fraser-Jenkins 1977 (*D. villarii* ssp.	
	submontana)	EGF.1-RD
	x tavellii Rothmaler 1945 = **D. x complexa**	
	villarii (Bellardi) Woynar ex Schinz & Thellung 1915	
	ssp. *submontana* Fraser-Jenkins & Jermy 1977 = **D. submontana**	
	villarii UK hort. = **D. submontana**	
	wallichiana (Sprengel) Hylander 1953	EGF.1-**PGP**

	DUCHESNEA Smith 1811	[*Rosaceae*]
	chrysantha (Zollinger & Moritz) Miquel 1855 (*Fragaria chrysantha*)	
N	**indica** (Andrews) Focke 1888 (*Fragaria indica*)	
	'Variegata'	

	ECHINACEA Moench 1794	[*Asteraceae (Compositae)*]
	angustifolia de Candolle 1836	PGP
HL	**purpurea** (Linnaeus) Moench 1794 (*Rudbeckia purpurea*)	PGP-RD

'Abendsonne'		PGP
Bressingham Hybrids [A. Bloom]		
'Magnus'		
'Robert Bloom' [A. Bloom]		PGP-**DGP**-RD
'Rubinstern' [Weinreich]		
'The King'		PGP-**DGP-RD**
'White Lustre'		PGP-RD
'White Swan'		

ECHINOPS Linnaeus 1753   *[Asteraceae (Compositae)]*

N   **bannaticus** Rochel ex Schrader 1827   **RD**
    'Blue Ball' = **E. bannaticus 'Blue Globe'**
    'Blue Globe' ('Blue Ball')   RD
L   'Taplow Blue'   RD
    gmelinii Turczaninow 1832
    humilis Marshall von Bieberstein 1819   PGP-RD
    'Nivalis'   PGP
    nivea Wallach ex Royle 1835
    ritro Linnaeus 1753   PGP-DGP-RD
    'Tenuifolius' = **E. ritro** ssp. **ruthenicus**
L   ssp. **ruthenicus** (Marshall von Bieberstein) Nyman 1879 (*E. ruthenicus*) PGP
    'Veitch's Blue'   **DGP**
    ruthenicus Marshall von Bieberstein 1819 = **E. ritro** ssp. **ruthenicus**
N   **spaerocephalus** Linnaeus 1753   PGP

ECHIOIDES Ortega 1772   *[Boraginaceae]*
    longiflorum (K. Koch) I. M. Johnston 1954 = **Arnebia pulchra**

ECHIUM Linnaeus 1753   *[Boraginaceae]*
    fastuosum de Candolle 1846
    pininana Webb & Berthelot 1844   RD
    rubrum Jacquin 1788 non Forsskal 1744 = **E. russicum**
    russicum J. F. Gmelin 1791 (*E. rubrum* Jacquin)   RD
HN‡   **vulgare** Linnaeus 1753   RD
    wildpretii H. H. W. Pearson ex Hooker f. 1902   RD

EDRAIANTHUS (A. de Candolle) A. de Candolle 1839   *[Campanulaceae]*
    dalmaticus (A. de Candolle) A. de Candolle 1839   CA
    'Albus'
    dinaricus (A. Kerner) Wettstein 1887   CA
    graminifolius (Linnaeus) A. de Candolle 1839   **RD**
    'Albus'
    pumilio (Portenschlag) A. de Candolle 1839   **CA-DGP-RD**
    serbicus Petrovic 1882
    serpyllifolius (Visiani) A. de Candolle 1839   CA-DGP-**RD**
    'Major'   CA-**DGP**
    tenuifolius (Waldstein & Kitaibel) A. de Candolle 1839
    'Albus'

EGERIA Planchon 1849   *[Hydrocharitaceae]*
N   **densa** Planchon 1849 (*Elodea densa*)   EGF.1

EICHHORNIA Kunth 1843 nom. cons.   *[Pontederiaceae]*
    crassipes (C. Martius) Solms-Laubach 1883 (*E. speciosa*)   EGF.1-**RD**
    'Major'
    speciosa Kunth 1843 = **E. crassipes**

ELEOCHARIS R. Brown 1810   *[Cyperaceae]*
N‡   **acicularis** (Linnaeus) Roemer & Schultes 1817 non R. Brown 1810   EGF.2
N‡L   **palustris** (Linnaeus) Roemer & Schultes 1817
    pusilla R. Brown 1810

ELISENA Herbert 1837 = **HYMENOCALLIS**

ELMERA Rydberg 1905   [*Saxifragaceae*]
  racemosa (S. Watson) Rydberg 1905 (*Heuchera racemosa*)

ELODEA Michaux 1803   [*Hydrocharitaceae*]
N‡ **canadensis** Michaux 1803   EGF.1
  crispa hort. = **Lagarosiphon major**
  densa (Planchon) Caspary 1857 = **Egeria densa**

ELSHOLTZIA Willdenow 1790   [*Lamiaceae (Labiatae)*]
S **fruticosa** (D. Don) Rehder 1916
  stauntonii Bentham 1833

ELYMUS Linnaeus 1753   [*Poaceae (Gramineae)*]
  arenarius Linnaeus 1753 = **Leymus arenarius**
  giganteus Vahl 1794 = **Leymus racemosus**
  magellanicus (Desvaux) A. Löve 1984 (*Agropyron magellanicum*)
  virginicus Linnaeus 1753   EGF.2

EMINIUM (Blume) Schott 1856   [*Araceae*]
  albertii (Regel) Engler 1920   BB-SB
  intortum (Banks & Solander) O. Kuntze 1891   BB-SB
  lehmannii (Bunge) O. Kuntze 1891
  rauwolffii (Blume) Schott 1850   BB
  spiculatum (Blume) Schott 1856   BB

ENDYMION Dumortier 1827   [*Hyacinthaceae (Liliaceae)*]
  hispanicus (Miller) Chouard 1934 = **Hyacinthoides hispanica**
  non-scriptus (Linnaeus) Garcke 1849 = **Hyacinthoides non-scripta**

EOMECON Hance 1884   [*Papaveraceae*]
  chionantha Hance 1884   PGP

EPILOBIUM Linnaeus 1753   [*Onagraceae*]
  angustifolium Linnaeus 1753 = **Chamaenerion angustifolium**
  chloraefolium Haussknecht 1879
    var. **kaikourense** Cockayne 1918
S **crassum** Hooker f. 1855
  dodonaei Villars 1779 (*E. rosmarinifolium*)   PGP-RD
  fleischeri Hochstetter 1826   PGP
S **glabellum** Forster f. 1786   RD
    'Sulphureum'
N‡ **hirsutum** Linnaeus 1753
  luteum Pursh 1814
  obcordatum A. Gray 1865
  rosmarinifolium Haenke 1788 = **E. dodonaei**

EPIMEDIUM Linnaeus 1753   [*Berberidaceae*]

M-STEARN, W.T.: '*Epimedium and Vancouveria*' Journ. Linn. Soc. (Botany) v 51, no 340 (1938)

N‡ **alpinum** Linnaeus 1753   M
  x cantabrigiense Stearn 1979 (*E. alpinum* x *E. pubigerum*)
  davidii Franchet 1885   M
  diphyllum Loddiges 1832   M
  grandiflorum Morren 1834 (*E. macranthum*)   M-PGP-RD
    'Album' nom. dub.
    'Elfinkönigin'   [E. Pagels]
    f. **flavescens** Stearn 1938   M

var. **higoense** Shimizu
var. *hypoglaucum* Makino 1931 = **E. sempervirens**
ssp. **koreanum** (Nakai) Kitamura 1962
'Lilofee'   [E. Pagels]
'Nanum' nom. dub.
L **'Rose Queen'**   [Ruys]   M-PGP
'Rose Purple' nom. dub.
'Roseum' nom. dub.
f. **violaceum** (Morren) Stearn 1934   M-PGP
'White Queen'   PGP
koreanum Nakai 1936 = **E. grandiflorum** ssp. **koreanum**
macranthum Morren & Decaisne 1834 = **E. grandiflorum**
x perralchicum Stearn 1938 (*E. perralderianum* x *E. pinnatum* ssp. *colchicum*)
                                                                M-PGP

'Fröhnleiten'
'Wisley'
L **perralderianum** Cosson 1862   M-PGP-RD
pinnatum Fischer 1821   M-RD
L   ssp. **colchicum** (Boissier) Busch 1903 (*E. pinnatum 'Elegans'*)   M-PGP-RD
'Elegans' = **E. pinnatum** ssp. **colchicum**
pubigerum (de Candolle) Morren & Decaisne 1834   M-PGP
L **x rubrum** Morren 1854 (*E. alpinum* x *E. grandiflorum*)   M-PGP-**RD**
sempervirens Nakai ex Maekawa 1932 (*E. grandiflorum* var. *hypoglaucum*)   M
x versicolor Morren 1849 (*E. grandiflorum* x *E. pinnatum* ssp. *colchicum*)   M-PGP
'Cupreum' Morren 1849   M
'Neo-sulphureum' Stearn 1938   M
L **'Sulphureum'** (Morren) Stearn 1934   M-PGP-RD
'Versicolor' (Morren) Stearn 1934   M-PGP
L **x warleyense** Stearn 1938 (*E. alpinum* x *E. pinnatum* ssp. *colchicum*)   M-PGP-RD
x youngianum Fischer & C. A. Meyer 1846 (*E. diphyllum* x *E. grandiflorum*)
                                                                M-PGP-RD

'Album' = **E. x youngianum 'Niveum'**
'Lilacinum' = **E. x youngianum 'Roseum'**
'Merlin'   [A. Doncaster via E. Strangman]
'Niveum' (Vilmorin-Andrieux) Stearn 1934   M-RD
'Roseum' (Vilmorin-Andrieux) Stearn 1934   M

EPIPACTIS Zinn 1757 nom. cons.   [*Orchidaceae*]
N‡ **atrorubens** (Hoffman) Besser 1809   EGF.2-PGP
gigantea Douglas ex Hooker 1839   EGF.2-PGP
N‡ **palustris** (Linnaeus) Crantz 1769   EGF.2-PGP

EQUISETUM Linnaeus 1753   [*Equisetaceae*]
N **hyemale** Linnaeus 1753   EGF.1
var. **robustum** (A. Braun ex Englemann) A. A. Eaton 1903
N **palustre** Linnaeus 1753
robustum A. Braun ex Englemann 1843 = **E. hyemale** var. **robustum**
scirpoides Michaux 1803   EGF.1
N **variegatum** Schleicher ex Weber & Mohr 1807   EGF.1

ERAGROSTIS Wolf 1776   [*Poaceae (Gramineae)*]
curvula (Schrader) Nees 1841   EGF.2

ERANTHIS Salisbury 1804 nom. cons.   [*Ranunculaceae*]
N **cilicica** Schott & Kotschy 1854   BB-SB-**DGP**-RD
N‡ **hyemalis** (Linnaeus) Salisbury 1804   BB-SB-**DGP**-RD
longistipitata Regel 1870   **BB-SB**
pinnatifida Maximowicz 1877   SB
x tubergenii Bowles (*E. cilicica* x *E. hyemalis*)   **BB-DGP**-RD
'Guinea Gold'   [van Tubergen]   **BB**-SB-DGP-RD

EREMURUS Marshall von Bieberstein 1818   *[Asphodelaceae (Liliaceae)]*
  aitchisonii Baker 1881 (*E. elwesii*)   EGF.1-PGP-RD
    '**Albus**'   PGP-**RD**
  brachystemon Vvedensky 1946
  bungei Baker 1879 = **E. stenophyllus**
  comosus O. Fedtschenko 1904   EGF.1
  elwesii Micheli = **E. aitchisonii**
  fuscus (O. Fedtschenko) Vvedensky 1952
  himalaicus Baker 1876   EGF.1-PGP-RD
  x isabellinus P. L. Vilmorin 1905 (*E. olgae* x *E. stenophyllus*)   EGF.1-PGP
    '**Cleopatra**' ®   [N.C. Ruiter 1956]
    '**Feuerfackel**'
    '**Isobel**'
    '**Moonlight**'
    '**Rosalind**'
    Ruiter Hybrids
    '**Schneelanze**'
L   **Shelford Hybrids**   EGF.1-RD
    '**White Beauty**'
  olgae Regel 1873   EGF.1-PGP-**BB**-RD
L   **robustus** (Regel) Regel 1873   EGF.1-PGP-**DGP**-RD
  sogdianus (Regel) Franchet 1884   EGF.1
  spectabilis Marshall von Bieberstein 1819   EGF.1-PGP
  stenophyllus (Boissier & Buhse) Baker 1877 (*E. bungei*)   EGF.1-PGP-**BB**-**DGP**-RD
  suworowii Regel 1873

ERIANTHUS Michaux 1803   *[Poaceae (Gramineae)]*
  ravennae (Linnaeus) Palisot de Beavois 1812 = **Saccharum ravennae**

ERIGERON Linnaeus 1753   *[Asteraceae (Compositae)]*
  alpinus Linnaeus 1753 (*E. nanus* Schur)
  alpinus hort. non Linnaeus = **E. borealis**
  asper Nuttall 1818 = **E. glabellus**
  aurantiacus Regel 1879   PGP-RD
  aureus Greene 1891 = **Haplopappus brandegei**
N‡ **borealis** (Vierhapper) Simmons 1913
  compositus Pursh 1814   CA
    '**Albus**'
    var. **discoideus** A. Gray 1962 (*E. trifidus*)   CA
  delicatus Cronquist 1947
  elegantulus Greene 1895
  glabellus Nuttall 1818 (*E. asper*)
N **glaucus** Ker-Gawler 1815   PGP
    '**Albus**'
    '**Roseus**'
N **karvinskianus** de Candolle 1836 (*E. mucronatus*)   **DGP**
  leiomerus A. Gray 1884   CA
  linearis (Hooker) Piper 1906
  macranthus Nuttall 1840 = **E. speciosus** var. **macranthus**
  melanocephalus (A. Nelson) A. Nelson 1899
  mucronatus de Candolle 1836 = **E. karvinskianus**
  multiradiatus (Lindley ex de Candolle) C. D. Clarke 1876
  nanus Nuttall 1841 = **E. radicatus**
  nanus Schur 1866 = **E. alpinus**
  peregrinus (Pursh) Greene 1897
  pinnatisectus (A. Nelson) A. Nelson 1899
  radicatus Hooker 1834 (*E. nanus* Nuttall)
  roylei de Candolle 1836
  simplex Greene 1897
  speciosus (Lindley) de Candolle 1836   PGP-RD

var. **macranthus** (Nuttall) Cronquist 1943 (*S. macranthus*) PGP-**RD**
trifidus Hooker 1834 = **E. compositus** var. **discoideus**
N **uniflorus** Linnaeus 1753 CA

HYBRID CULTIVARS

    'Adria'   [H. Götz 1954]
    'Amity'   [A. Bloom]
    'Azure Blue'
    'Azure Fairy'
    'Birch Hybrid'   [Ingwersen]
    'Blaue Grotte'   [H. Götz]
    Bressingham Hybrids   [A. Bloom]
L   **'Charity'**   [A. Bloom] PGP-**DGP**
    'Darkest of All' = **E. 'Dunkelste Aller'**
    'Dignity'   [A. Bloom] **DGP**
    'Dimity'   [A. Bloom] PGP
    'Dominator'
L   **'Dunkelste Aller'** ('Darkest of All')   [Benary 1951] PGP-**RD**
L   **'Elstead Pink'**   [E. Ladhams] PGP
    'E. M. Beale'
    'Felicity'   [A. Bloom] **DGP-RD**
    'Festivity'   [A. Bloom] **DGP**
    'Foerster's Liebling'   [Benary/Walther 1951] PGP-RD
    'Four Winds'   [Four Winds Nursery]
    'Frivolity'   [A. Bloom]
    'Gaiety'   [A. Bloom] RD
    'Gratulant'
    'Hundstern'
    'Lilofee'   [H. Götz 1950] **DGP**
    'Märchenland'   [Bruske c1971]
    'Merstham Glory'
    'Mrs F. H. Beale'
    'Nachthimmel'   [H. Klose 1981]
    'Pink Jewel' = **E. 'Rosa Juwel'**
    'Pink Triumph' = **E. 'Rosa Triumph'**
    'Prosperity'   [A. Bloom] PGP-RD
    'Quakeress' RD
    'Quakeress Alba' = **E. 'White Quakeress'**
    'Rosa Juwel' ('Pink Jewel')
    'Rosa Triumph' ('Pink Triumph')   [Pötsche/Walther 1953]
    'Rosenballett'   [H. Klose 1981]
    'Rote Schönheit'
    'Rotes Meer'   [H. Götz 1970]
    'Schloss Hellenstein'
    'Schwarzes Meer'   [H. Götz 1970]
    'Sennen'
    'Serenity'   [A. Bloom]
    'Sincerity'   [A. Bloom] **DGP**
    'Sommerabend'
    'Sommerneuschnee'   [K. Foerster 1935]
    'Strahlenmeer'   [H. Götz 1949]
    'Unity'   [A. Bloom]
    'Veilchenballett'   [H. Klose 1982]
    'Viridis'
    'White Quakeress' (E. 'Quakeress Alba') PGP
    'Wuppertal'   [G. Arends 1932]

ERINACEA Adanson 1763   [*Fabaceae (Leguminosae)*]
s   **anthyllis** Link 1831 (*E. pungens*)   CA-DGP
    pungens Boissier 1839 = **E. anthyllis**

ERINUS Linnaeus 1753   [*Scrophulariaceae*]
NL   **alpinus** Linnaeus 1753   CA-**RD**
        'Albus'   CA-**RD**
        'Dr. Hähnle'   CA-**RD**
        'Mrs. Charles Boyle'   **RD**

ERIOGONUM Michaux 1803   [*Polygonaceae*]
    allenii S. Watson 1890
    douglasii Bentham 1856
    glaberrimum Gandy 1906 = **E. umbellatum** var. **subalpinum**
    jamesii Bentham 1856
    torreyanum A. Gray 1873 = **P. umbellatum** ssp. **polyanthum**
s   **umbellatum** Torrey 1828
        var. **polyanthum** (Bentham) M. E. Jones 1903 (*E. torreyanum*)
        var. **subalpinum** (Greene) M. E. Jones 1903 (*E. glaberrimum*)

ERIOPHORUM Linnaeus 1753   [*Cyperaceae*]
    angustifolium Honckeny 1782 = **Scirpus angustifolius**
    latifolium Hoppe 1800 = **Scirpus angustifolius** ssp. **latifolius**
    polystachion Linnaeus p.p. 1753 = **Scirpus angustifolius**
    vaginatum Linnaeus 1753 = **Scirpus fauriei** ssp. **vaginatus**

ERIOPHYLLUM Lagasca 1816   [*Asteraceae (Compositae)*]
    caespitosum Douglas ex Lindley 1828 = **E. lanatum**
    lanatum (Pursh) Forbes 1833 (*E. caespitosum*)   PGP

ERITRICHIUM Schrader ex Gaudin 1828   [*Boraginaceae*]
    nanum (Linnaeus) Schrader ex Gaudin 1828   **CA-DGP**
    rupestre Bunge 1836 (*E. strictum*)
        var. **pectinatum** (de Candolle 1846) !   CA-DGP
    strictum Decaisne 1844 = **E. rupestre**

ERODIUM L'Heritier 1789   [*Geraniaceae*]
    absinthoides Willdenow 1800
    balearicum hort. = **E. reichardii**
    carvifolium Boissier & Reuter 1842   PGP
    chamaedryoides L'Heritier 1792 = **E. reichardii**
    cheilanthifolium Boissier 1838 = **E. petraeum** ssp. **crispum**
    chrysanthum L'Heritier ex de Candolle 1824   CA-**RD**
N‡   **cicutarium** (Linnaeus) L'Heritier 1789
    corsicum Leman 1805   CA-DGP-**RD**
        'Album'   CA
    daucoides Boissier 1838
    gruinum (Linnaeus) L'Heritier 1789
    guttatum (Desfontaines) Willdenow 1800   **DGP**
    hymenodes L'Heritier 1792
    macradenum L'Heritier 1792 = **E. petraeum** ssp. **glandulosum**
    manescavi Cosson 1847   PGP
    pelargoniiflorum Boissier & Haussknecht ex Boissier 1849
    petraeum (Gouan) Willdenow 1800
        ssp. **crispum** (Lapeyrouse) Rouy 1897 (*E. cheilanthifolium*)
        ssp. **glandulosum** (Cavanilles) Bonnier 1913 (*E. macradenum*)   PGP-CA-**RD**
        'Pallidum'
        'Roseum'
    reichardii (Murray) de Candolle 1824 (*E. balearicum, E. chamaedryoides*)   CA-**RD**

rupestre (Pourret ex Cavanilles) Guittonneau 1963 (*E. supracanum*)   CA
supracanum L'Heritier 1789 = **E. rupestre**
x variabile Leslie 1980 (*E. corsicum* x *E. reichardii*)
    'Album'
    'Bishop's Form' nom. illegit.
    'Flore Pleno'
    'Roseum'   CA-**RD**
    'Roseum Plenum'

ERYNGIUM Linnaeus 1753   [*Apiaceae (Umbelliferae)*]
    agavifolium Grisebach 1874   **PGP**
    alpinum Linnaeus 1753   PGP-**DGP-RD**
        'Amethyst'
        'Blue Star'
        'Holden Blue'
        'Robustum'
        'Superbum'
    amethystinum Linnaeus 1753   PGP
L   **bourgatii** Gouan 1773   PGP-RD
        'Oxford Blue'
    bromelliifolium Delaroche 1808 = **E. monocephalum**
    bromelliifolium hort. non Delaroche 1808 = **E. eburneum**
    caeruleum Marshall von Bieberstein 1800
    decaisneana Urban 1879 (*E. pandanifolium*)   PGP
    eburneum Decaisne 1873 (*E. bromeliifolium* hort., *E. paniculatum* hort.)   PGP
B   **giganteum** Marshall von Bieberstein 1808   PGP-**DGP-RD**
    glaciale Boissier 1838
HN‡L **maritimum** Linnaeus 1753   **PGP-RD**
    monocephalum Cavanilles 1800 (*E. bromeliifolium*)
L   **x oliverianum** Delaroche 1808 (*E. alpinum* x])   PGP-**RD**
    pandanifolium Chamisso & Schlecht 1826 = **E. decaisneana**
    paniculatum Cavanilles & Dombey ex Delaroche 1808 = **E. eburneum**
    planum Linnaeus 1753   PGP-RD
        'Blauer Zwerg' ('Blue Dwarf')   PGP
    proteiflorum Delaroche 1808
    serra Chamisso & Schlecht 1826   PGP
    spinalba Villars 1779   PGP
    tricuspidatum Linnaeus
L   **x tripartitum** hort. non Linnaeus   PGP-**DGP-RD**
L   **variifolium** Cosson 1875   PGP-**DGP-RD**
    yuccifolium Michaux   PGP
    x zabelii Hort. ex Hegi 1926 (*E. alpinum* x *E. bourgatii*)   PGP
        'James Ivory'   PGP
        'Jewel'   PGP
        'Spring Hills'
        'Violetta'   PGP

ERYSIMUM Linnaeus 1753   [Brassicaceae (Cruciferae)]
    alpinum Persoon 1806   RD
    arkansanum Nuttall 1888
    asperum de Candolle 1821 = **E. capitatum**
    capitatum (Douglas) Greene 1891 (*E. asperum*)   RD
    concinnum Eastwood 1901
    helveticum (Jacquin) de Candolle 1805 (*E. pumilum*)
    kotschyanum Gay 1842
N   **linifolium** (Persoon) Gay 1842 (*Cheiranthus linifolius*)
        'Variegatum'
    murale Desfontaines 1804 = **E. suffruticosum**

mutabile Boissier & Heldreich 1849 (*Cheiranthus mutabilis*)
   'Variegatum' = **Cheiranthus x kewensis 'Variegatus'**
pulchellum (Willdenow) Gay 1842 (*E. rupestre*)   RD
pumilum hort. = **E. helveticum**
rupestre de Candolle 1821 = **E. pulchellum**
suffrutescens (Abrams) G. Rossbach 1958
S **suffruticosum** Sprengel 1819 (*E. murale*)

HYBRID CULTIVARS (including **CHEIRANTHUS** CULTIVARS)

     'Aunt May'
     'Bloody Warrior' = **Cheiranthus cheiri 'Bloody Warrior'**
     'E. A. Bowles' = **E. 'Bowles' Mauve'**
     'Bowles' Mauve'
     'Bredon'
     'Butterscotch'
     'Chequers'
     'Chevithorne'
     'Constant Cheer'
     'Ems'
     'Golden Flame'
     'Golden Gem'
     'Golden Jubilee'
     'Harpur-Crewe' = **Cheiranthus cheiri 'Harpur-Crewe'**
     'Ingwersen'
     'Jacob's Jacket'
     'Jubilee Gold'
     'Mrs L. K. Elmhirst'   RD
     'Moonlight'   **DGP**-RD
     'Primrose'
     'Orange Flame'
     'Rufus'
     'Semperflorens'   DGP
     'Sprite'   [via J. Elliott]
     'Sunbright'
     'Variegatum' = **Cheiranthus x kewensis 'Variegatus'**
     'Wenlock Beauty'   **DGP**-RD

ERYTHRAEA Renealme ex Borkhausen 1796   [*Gentianaceae*]
  chloodes (Brotero) Grenier & Godron 1852 = **Centaurium chloodes**
  diffusa J. Woods 1836 = **Centaurium scilloides**

ERYTHRONIUM Linnaeus 1753   [*Liliaceae*]
  *abchasicum
  albidum Nuttall 1818   EGF.1-CA-**BB**-SB
    var. **mesochoreum** (Knerr) Rickett 1937 (*E. mesochoreum*)   EGF.1-**BB**-SB
  americanum Ker-Gawler 1808   EGF.1-CA-**BB**-SB
  californicum Purdy 1904   EGF.1-CA-**BB**-SB
  caucasicum Woronow 1933   SB
  dens-canis Linnaeus 1753   EGF.1-CA-**BB**-SB-DGP-**RD**
    'Charmer' ®   [van Tubergen pe-1966]
    'Lilac Wonder' ® [N. Roozen]
    'Pink Perfection' ®   RD
    'Purple King' ®   [G. C. van Meeowen 1937]   RD
    'Rose Queen' ®   **DGP**
    'White Splendour' ® [van Tubergen pre-1961]   RD
  hendersonii S. Watson 1887   EGF.1-CA-**BB**-SB
  japonicum Decaisne 1854   EGF.1-**BB**-SB
  'Jeannine'
  johnsonii (Purdy) hort. = **E. revolutum** var. **johnsonii**

'Kondo' ®   [L. Slikker pre-1960] (*E. revolutum* x *E. tuolumnense*)
                                                                    EGF.1-SB-DGP-RD
mesochoreum Knerr 1891 = **E. albidum** var. **mesochoreum**
multiscapoideum (Kellogg) Nelson & Kellogg 1908 (*E. purdyi*)   EGF.1-SB
oregonum Applegate 1935   EGF.1-**BB**-SB
'Pagoda' ®   [L. Slikker via W. Blom & Sons pre-1959] (*E. revolutum*
                           'Album' x *E. tuolumnense*)   EGF.1-**BB**-SB-DGP-RD
purdyi hort. = **E. multiscapoideum**
revolutum Smith 1809   EGF.1-CA-**BB**-SB-RD
    'Album'
    var. **johnsonii** Purdy 1900   EGF.1-**BB**-SB
    'Knightshayes Pink'
    'Pink Beauty' ®   EGF.1-SB
    'Rose Beauty' ®   [C. Purdy 1935]
    'White Beauty' ®   [US pre-1938]   CA-**BB**-SB-**DGP**-RD
tuolumnense Applegate 1930   EGF.1-CA-**BB**-SB-DGP-**RD**
umbilicatum Parks & Hardin 1963   SB

EUCHARIS Planchon 1853   [*Amaryllidaceae*]
    amazonica Planchon 1881 (*E. grandiflora* hort.)   EGF.1-**DGP**
    grandiflora hort. non Planchon & Linden 1853 = **E. amazonica**

EUCOMIS L'Heritier 1788 nom. cons.   [*Hyacinthaceae (Liliaceae)*]
    autumnalis (Miller) Chittenden 1951 (*E. undulata*)   EGF.1-SB-RD
    bicolor Baker 1878   EGF.1-**PGP**-**BB**-SB-**DGP**-RD
        'Alba' ®   [van Tubergen]   EGF.1-PGP
    comosa (Houttuyn) hort. ex Wehrhahn 1929 (*E. punctata*)   EGF.1-**PGP**-SB-DGP-RD
        var. **striata** (Houttuyn) Wehrhahn 1929   EGF.1-PGP
    pallidiflora Baker 1887 (*E. pole-evansii* hort.)   EGF.1-PGP-SB
    pole-evansii hort., non Brown = **E. pallidiflora**
    punctata L'Heritier 1788 = **E. comosa**
    undulata Aiton 1810 = **E. autumnalis**
    zambesiaca Baker 1886   **SB**

EUNOMIA de Candolle 1821 = **AETHIONEMA**

EUPATORIUM Linnaeus 1753   [*Asteraceae (Compositae)*]
    aromaticum Linnaeus 1753
HN‡ **cannabinum** Linnaeus 1753   PGP-RD
        'Album'
        'Flore Pleno'   PGP-RD
    coelestinum Linnaeus 1753
    incarnatum Walter 1788
    maculatum Linnaeus 1755
        'Atropurpureum'   RD
    perfoliatum Linnaeus 1753
HL **purpureum** Linnaeus 1753   PGP-**DGP**-**RD**
        'Atropurpureum' = **E. maculatum 'Atropurpureum'**
    rugosum Houttuyn 1779 non Humboldt, Bonpland & Kunth 1820   RD
        'Album'
        'Braunlaub'
    sessilifolium Linnaeus 1753

EUPHORBIA Linnaeus 1753   [*Euphorbiaceae*]

M - TURNER, R.: *A Review of Spurges for the Garden* The Plantsman 5:3,157-162(1983)

N‡ **amygdaloides** Linnaeus 1753   M-PGP
L   var. **robbiae** (Turrill) Radcliffe-Smith 1976   M-PGP-**DGP**-**RD**
        'Purpurea' = **E. amygdaloides 'Rubra'**

	'Rubra' (`Purpurea`)	**M**-PGP
	'Variegata'	**M**-PGP
	biglandulosa Desfontaines 1808 = **E. rigida**	
	brittingeri Opiz ex Sampaio 1914 (*E. verrucosa* p.p.)	M
	capitulata Reichenbach 1832	M
	characias Linnaeus 1753	M-PGP-**DGP**-**RD**
	'Blue Hills'	
L	ssp. **wulfenii** (Hoppe) Radcliffe-Smith 1968	M-PGP-DGP-**RD**
	ssp. **wulfenii** **'Lambrook Gold'**	**M**-PGP
	ssp. **wulfenii** var. **sibthorpii** (Boissier) !	M-PGP
N	**corallioides** Linnaeus 1753	**M**
N‡	**cyparissias** Linnaeus 1753	M-PGP-RD
	'Tall Boy'	M
	'Bush Boy'	M
	'Baby'	M
	'Orange Man'	M
	decipiens Boissier & Buhse 1860	M
S	**dendroides** Linnaeus 1753	M
N	**dulcis** Linnaeus 1753	M-PGP
	epithymoides Linnaeus 1762 = **E. polychroma**	
N	**esula** Linnaeus 1753	M
	ssp. *tommasiniana* (Bertoloni) Nyman 1881 = **E. waldsteinii**	
	griffithii Hooker f. 1887	M-DGP-RD
	'Dixter' [H. Davenport-Jones via C. Lloyd]	**M**-PGP
L	**'Fireglow'** [A. Bloom]	M-**PGP**-**DGP**-**RD**
N‡	**hyberna** Linnaeus 1753	M-PGP
BHN‡	**lathyris** Linnaeus 1753	**M**-PGP
	longifolia D. Don 1825	M
	x **martinii** Rouy 1900 (*E. amygdaloides* x *E. charracias*)	M
	Green Form	
	mellifera Aiton 1789	M
L	**myrsinites** Linnaeus 1753	M-PGP-**DGP**-RD
	'Washfield' [H. Davenport-Jones]	M
	nicaeensis Allioni 1785	M-PGP
	ssp. **glareosa** (Pallas ex Bieberstein) Radcliffe-Smith 1968	M
	niciciana Borbas 1803 = **E. seguieriana** ssp. **niciciana**	
L	**palustris** Linnaeus 1753	M-PGP-**DGP**-**RD**
L	**polychroma** A. Kerner 1875 (*E. epithymoides*)	M-PGP-**DGP**-**RD**
	'Pilosa Major'	M
	'Purpurea'	
	'Sonnengold'	M
N‡	**portlandica** Linnaeus 1753	M
	x **pseudovirgata** (Schur) Soo 1930 (*E. uralensis*)	M
B	**pubescens** Vahl 1791 (*E. verrucosa* p.p.)	M
	rigida Marshall von Bieberstein 1808 (*E. biglandulosa*)	**M**-PGP-RD
	robbiae Turrill 1953 = **E. amygdaloides** var. **robbiae**	
	seguieriana Necker 1770	M
	ssp. **niciciana** (Borbas) Reichenbach f. 1948 (*E. niciciana*)	M-PGP
	serrulata Thuillier 1800 = **E. stricta**	
	sibthorpii Boissier 1860 = **E. characias** ssp. **wulfenii** var. **sibthorpii**	
	sikkimensis Boissier 1862	M-PGP-RD
	spinosa Linnaeus 1753	M
N	**stricta** Linnaeus 1759 (*E. serrulata*)	**M**
	uralensis hort. non Fischer ex Link 1822 = **E. x pseudovirgata**	
	veneta Willdenow 1809 = **E. characias** ssp. **wulfenii**	
	verrucosa Linnaeus 1758 nom. ambig. = **E. brittingeri** p.p., **E. pubescens** p.p.	
	virgata Waldstein & Kitaibel 1804 = **E. waldsteinii**	
	waldsteinii (Sojak) A. Radcliffe-Smith 1981 (*E. esula* ssp. *tommasiniana, E. virgata*)	M
	wallichii Hooker f. 1887	M-**PGP**
	wulfenii Hoppe 1829 = **E. characias** ssp. **wulfenii**	

EUSTEPHIA Cavanilles 1794   [*Amaryllidaceae*]
  *****jujuyensis**

FAGOPYRUM Miller 1754 nom. cons.   [*Polygonaceae*]
  cymosum (Treviranus) Meissner 1832 = **F. dibotrys**
  dibotrys (D. Don) Hara 1966 (*F. cymosum*)

FALLOPIA Adanson 1763   [*Polygonaceae*]
N   **japonica** (Houttuyn) Ronse Decraene 1988 (*Polygonum cuspidatum, P.*
                                        japonicum, P. reynoutria)   PGP
      var. **compacta** (Hooker f.)! (*Polygonum reynoutria* hort., non Makino)   **PGP**
      'Spectabilis'
    sachalinensis (F. Schmidt) Ronse Decraene 1988 (*Polygonum sachalinense*)

FASCICULARIA Mez 1891   [*Bromeliaceae*]
    bicolor (Ruiz & Pavon) Mez 1896   EGF.2-PGP
    pitcairniifolia (Verlot) Mez 1896   EGF.2-PGP

FELICIA Cassini 1818 nom. cons.   [*Asteraceae (Compositae)*]
    amelloides (Linnaeus) Voss 1894 (*Aster capensis, A. rotundifolius*)   **RD**
      'Santa Anita'
      'Santa Anita Variegated'   [B. Halliwell]
      'Variegata'
    amoena (Schulz-Bip) Levyns 1948 (*Aster pappei*)   CA-RD
      'Variegata'
    bergeriana (Sprengel) O. Hoffmann ex Zahlbruckner 1905   DGP-RD
    natalensis Schultz-Bip ex Walpers 1843 (*Aster natalensis*)
    pappei (Harvey) Hutchinson 1917 = **F. amoena**
    petiolata (Harvey) N. E. Brown 1906 (*Aster petiolatus*)
    uliginosa (Wood & Evans) Grau 1973

FERRARIA Burman ex Miller 1759   [*Iridaceae*]
    coelestina hort. = **Cypella plumbea**
    crispa Burman 1761 (*F. undulata*)   EGF.1
    undulata Linnaeus 1762 = **F. crispa**

FERULA Linnaeus 1753   [*Apiaceae (Umbelliferae)*]
    communis Linnaeus 1753   PGP
      'Gigantea'
    tingitana Linnaeus 1753   PGP

FESTUCA Linnaeus 1753   [*Poaceae (Gramineae)*]
    alpestris Roemer & Schultes 1817
    alpina Suter 1802   **RD**
    amethystina Linnaeus 1753   PGP-RD
    cinerea Villars 1785
      ssp. **pallens** (Host) Stohr 1960 (*F. pallens*)
    crassifolia (Gaudin) hort. = **F. curvula** ssp. **crassifolia**
    curvula Gaudin 1811
L   ssp. **crassifolia** (Gaudin) Markgraf-Dannenberg 1978
    eskia de Candolle 1805   EGF.2-PGP
    gautieri (Hackel) K. Richter 1890 (*F. scoparia*)
      'Pic Carlit'
N‡   **gigantea** (Linnaeus) Villars 1787
    glacialis Miegeville 1874   EGF.2-RD
      'Czakor'
    glauca Villars 1787 non Lamarck 1788 (*F. ovina* var. *glauca*)

L   F. GLAUCA GROUP CULTIVARS

PGP-DGP-RD

'Aprilgrün'   [H. Hagemann c1961]
'Azurit'   [H. Klose 1982]
'Bergsilber'
'Blaufink'   [H. Klose 1974]
'Blaufuchs'   [H. Klose 1974](F. 'Blue Fox')
'Blauglut'   [H. Klose 1972]
'Blausilber'
'Blue Fox' = F. 'Blaufuchs'
'Blue Sea' = F. 'Meerblau'
'Bronzeglanz'
'Frülingsblau'   [K. Foerster 1969]
'Harz'   [G. Arends 1963]
'Meerblau'   [H. Klose 1972](F. 'Blue Sea')
'Minima'
'Palatinat'   [T. Germann 1972]
'Seeigel'   [zur Linden]
'Severn Seas'
'Silberreiher'
'Silver Sea' = F. valesiaca 'Silbersee'
'Solling'   [H. Hagemann]
'Söhrewald'   [H. Klose 1982]
'Superba'

mairei Saint-Yves 1922 non Hackel ex Handel-Mazzetti 1936
novae-zealandiae (Hackel) Cockayne 1916 (F. ovina var. novae-zealandiae)
N‡   ovina Linnaeus 1753
    var. amethystina (Host) Koch 1837
    var. capillata (Lejeune) Mathieu 1853 = F. tenuifolia
    var. glauca (Villars) Hackel, non (Lamarck) Koch 1837, Fries 1828, Blytt
                         1861 = F. glauca
    var. novae-zealandiae Hackel 1903 = F. novae-zealandiae
pallens Host 1852 = F. cinerea ssp. pallens
pseudodalmatica Krajinaex Domin 1929
puccinellii Parlatore 1848
    'Laggin'
pumila Villars ex Chaix 1786 non Host 1802 = F. quadriflora
punctoria Smith 1806
quadriflora Honcheny 1782 (F. pumila)
*ramondii
N‡   rubra Linnaeus 1753
    var. viridis Petermann 1838
rupicola Heuffel 1858 (F. sulcata)
scoparia A. Kerner ex Nyman 1882 non Hooker f. 1844 = F. gautieri
sulcata (Hackel) Nyman 1882 = F. rupicola
N   tenuiflora Schrader 1806
tenuifolia Sibthorp 1794
    'Karl Foerster'
valesiaca Gaudin 1811
    var. glaucantha (Hackel) Ascherson & Graebner 1900   EGF.2
    'Silbersee' ('Silver Sea')   [K. Marx]
varia Haenke 1789
N   vivipara Smith 1800 non Hornemann 1832

FILIPENDULA Miller 1754
    hexapetala Gilibert 1781 nom. illegit. = F. vulgaris   [Rosaceae]
    kamtschatica (Pallas) Maximowicz 1879   RD
L   palmata (Pallas) Maximowicz 1879 (Spiraea digitata)   PGP-RD
    'Alba'

	'Digitata Nana' ('Nana')	
	'Elegantissima'	PGP
	'Nana' = **F. palmata 'Digitata Nana'**	
	'Rosea'	PGP
	'Rubra'	
L	**purpurea** Maximowicz 1879 (*Spiraea palmata* hort.)	PGP-**DGP**
	'Alba'	
	rubra (Hill) Robinson 1906	PGP-DGP-**RD**
	'Magnifica' = **F. rubra 'Venusta'**	
	'Venusta' ('Magnifica')	PGP-DGP-RD
HN‡L	**ulmaria** (Linnaeus) Maximowicz 1879	RD
	'Aurea'	PGP-RD
	'Flore Pleno'	PGP
	'Rosea'	
	'Variegata'	PGP
	vestita (Wallich ex G. Don) Maximowicz 1879	
HN‡	**vulgaris** Moench 1794 (*F. hexapetala*)	PGP-DGP-**RD**
L	'Flore Pleno'	**DGP**-RD
	'Grandiflora'	
	'Rosea'	

FOENICULUM Miller 1768		[*Apiaceae (Umbelliferae)*]
HN‡L	**vulgare** Miller 1768	PGP-**DGP**-RD
	var. **azoricum** (Miller) Thellung	
H	var. **dulce** Battandier & Trabut	RD
HL	'Purpurascens'	PGP

FONTINALIS Linnaeus 1753	[*Fontinalaceae*]
antipyretica Linnaeus 1753	

FRAGARIA Linnaeus 1753   [*Rosaceae*]
    alpina hort. = **F. vesca 'Semperflorens'**
N‡   **x ananassa** Duchesne 1766 (*F. chiloensis* x *F. virginiana*)
        'Variegata'
    'Baron Solemacher'
    chiloensis (Linnaeus) Duchesne 1766
    chrysantha Zollinger & Moritz 1846 = **Duchesnea chrysantha**
    daltoniana J. Gay 1877
    'Fraises des Bois'
    'Illa Martin'
    indica Andrews 1807 = **Duchesnea indica**
HN‡   **vesca** Linnaeus 1753
        'Flore Pleno'
        'Fructo-alba'
        var. **monophylla** Duchesne
        'Rügen'
H   'Semperflorens' (*F. alpina* hort.)
        'Variegata'

FRANCOA Cavanilles 1801		[*Saxifragaceae*]
	appendiculata Cavanilles 1824	PGP
	ramosa D. Don 1828	PGP
	sonchifolia Cavanilles 1801	**PGP**

FRANKENIA Linnaeus 1753		[*Frankeniaceae*]
SN‡	**laevis** Linnaeus 1753	CA
S	**thymifolia** Desfontaines 1789	CA

FREESIA Ecklon ex Klatt 1865	[*Iridaceae*]
alba (G. L. Meyer) Gumbleton (*F. refracta, F. xanthospila*)	

elimensis L. Bolus 1933
leichtlinii Klatt 1874 (*F. muirii*)
muirii N. E. Brown 1932 p.p. = **F. leichtlinii**
refracta (Jacquin) Ecklon ex Klatt 1865   EGF.1
refracta L. Bolus 1933 = **F. alba**
    var. *alba* G. L.Meyer = **F. alba**
sparrmannii (Thunberg) N. E. Brown 1921   EGF.1
xanthospila (de Candolle) Klatt 1865   EGF.1

HYBRID CULTIVARS   **DGP-RD**

    'Aurora' ®   [J. A. M. Goemans 1962]
    'Ballerina' ®   [J. A. M. Goemans 1957]   RD
    'Diana' ®   [J. A. M. Goemans pre-1961]   RD
    'Fantasy' ®   [J. A. M. Goemans via van Staaveren pre-1960]   DGP-**RD**
    Rainbow Hybrids
    'Red Lion' ®   [1972]
    'Romany' ®   [J. A. M. Goemans 1960]   **RD**
    'Rose Marie' ®   [J. A. M. Goemans pre-1961]   **RD**
    'Royal Blue' ®   [J. A. M. Goemans via van Staaveren]
    'Silvia' ®   [M. Penning & Sons 1972]

FREYLINIA Colla 1823   [*Scrophulariaceae*]
S   **lanceolata** Saccardo 1909

FRITILLARIA Linnaeus 1753   [*Liliaceae*]
   acmopetala Boissier 1846   EGF.1-CA-**BB**-SB-**DGP**-RD
   affinis (Schultes) J. R. Sealy 1980 (*F. lanceolata*)   EGF.1-CA-**SB**
     var. **gracile** (*F. phaeanthera* Purdy)   SB
   agrestis Greene 1895
   alburyana Rix 1971   EGF.1-**BB**-SB
   alfredae Post 1900   EGF.1-**BB**-SB
     ssp. **glaucoviridis** (Turrill) Rix 1979 (*F. glaucoviridis*)   **BB**-SB
   ariana (Losina-Losinskaya) Rix 1977   **BB**-SB
   armena Boissier 1846   EGF.1-CA-**BB**-SB
   assyriaca Baker 1874   EGF.1-**BB**-SB
     ssp. **melananthera** Rix 1983   SB
   assyriaca hort. non Baker 1874 = **F. uva-vulpis**
   atropurpurea Nuttall 1834   EGF.1-**BB**-SB
   aurea Schott 1854   EGF.1-CA-**BB**-SB
   aurea Schott x **F. pinardii** Boissier   **BB**
   biflora Lindley 1835   EGF.1-CA-**BB**-SB
   bithynica Baker 1874 (*F. citrina*)   EGF.1-CA-**BB**-SB
   bucharica Regel 1884   EGF.1-**BB**-SB
   camschatcensis (Linnaeus) Ker-Gawler 1809   EGF.1-CA-**BB**-SB-RD
   carduchorum Rix 1971 = **F. minuta**
   carica Rix 1975   EGF.1-**BB**-SB
   caucasica Adams 1805   EGF.1-CA-**BB**-SB
   cirrhosa D. Don 1825   EGF.1-CA-**BB**-**SB**
   citrina Baker 1893 = **F. bithynica**
   collina Adam 1806 (*F. lutea*)   EGF.1-**BB**-SB
   crassifolia Boissier & Reuter 1859   EGF.1-**BB**-SB
     ssp. **crassifolia**   BB
     ssp. **hakkarensis** Rix 1974   BB-SB
     ssp. **kurdica** (Boissier & Noe) Rix 1974 (*F. kurdica*)   EGF.1-**BB**-SB
     ssp. **poluninii** Rix 1974   **BB**-SB
   davisii Turrill 1940   EGF.1-**BB**-SB
   delphinensis Grenier & Godron 1855 = **F. tubiformis**
   drenovskyi Degen & Stojanoff 1931   EGF.1-CA-**BB**-SB
   eduardii Regel 1884   EGF.1-**BB**-SB

ehrhartii Boissier & Orphanides 1859   EGF.1-**BB**-SB
elwesii Boissier 1884   EGF.1-CA-**BB**-SB
epirotica Turrill ex Rix 1975   SB
forbesii Baker 1874   EGF.1-**BB**-SB
gibbosa Boissier 1846   **BB**-SB
glaucoviridis Turrill 1933 = **F. alfredae** ssp. **glaucoviridis**
gracilis (Ebel) Ascherson & Graebner = **F. messanensis** ssp. **gracilis**
graeca Boissier & Spruner 1841   EGF.1-CA-**BB**-SB
    ssp. **graeca**   **BB**
    ssp. **thessala** (Boissier) Rix 1978 (*F. ionica, F. thessalica*)   EGF.1-**BB**-SB
grayana Reichenbach f. & Baker 1878   EGF.1-**BB**-SB
gussichiae (Degen & Dörfler) Rix 1978   EGF.1-**BB**-SB
hermonis Fenzl 1855   EGF.1-SB
    ssp. **amana** Rix 1974   EGF.1-SB
    ssp. **amana EKB 1034**
    ssp. **amana Yellow Form**
imperialis Linnaeus 1753   EGF.1-PGP-**BB**-SB-DGP-**RD**
    'Aureo-marginata' ®   [Pre-1665]
    'Aurora' ®   PGP-**DGP-RD**
    'Blom's Orange Perfection'
    'Flava' ®('Lutea')   RD
    'Lutea' = **F. imperialis 'Flava'**
    'Maxima' ®('Maxima Rubra')   [Pre-1665]
    'Maxima Lutea' ®   [c1809]   **DGP**
    'Maxima Rubra' = **F. imperialis 'Maxima'**
    'Rubra'   RD
    'Sulphurino'
    'The Premier' ®
involucrata Allioni 1789   EGF.1-**BB**-SB
ionica Halacsy 1904 = **F. graeca** ssp. **thessala**
japonica Miquel 1867   EGF.1-SB
    var. **koidzumiana** (Ohwi) Rix   EGF.1-SB
karelinii (Fischer) Baker 1867   CA-SB
kurdica Boissier & Noe 1859 = **F. crassifolia** ssp. **kurdica**
lanceolata Pursh nom. illegit. = **F. affinis**
latakiensis Rix 1975   EGF.1-**BB**-SB
latifolia Willdenow 1799   EGF.1-CA-**BB**-SB-**RD**
    var. **nobilis** (Baker) ! (*F. nobilis*)   EGF.1-CA-**BB**-SB-RD
liliacea Lindley 1835   EGF.1-CA-**BB**-SB
lusitanica Wilkström 1821   EGF.1-**BB**-SB
lutea Marshall von Bieberstein 1808 non Miller 1768 = **F. collina**
N‡   **meleagris** Linnaeus 1753   EGF.1-CA-**BB**-SB-**DGP-RD**
    'Alba' ®   CA-**RD**
    'Aphrodite' ®   [J. Eckhart]   DGP-RD
    'Jupiter' ®   [J. Eckhart pre-1956]
    'Lutea'   SB
    'Orion' ®   [J. Eckhart]
    'Poseidon' ®   [J. Eckhart pre-1947]   RD
    'Purple King'   **DGP**
    'Saturnus' ®   [J. Eckhart]   DGP-RD
messanensis Rafinesque 1814   EGF.1-CA-**BB**-SB
    ssp. **messanensis**   **BB**
    ssp. **gracilis** (Ebel) Rix 1978 (*F. gracilis*)   EGF.1-**BB**-SB
michailovskyi Fomin 1905   EGF.1-**CA-BB-SB**
micrantha A. A. Heller 1910   SB
minima Rix 1971   **BB-SB**
minuta Boissier & Noe 1859 (*F. carduchorum*)   EGF.1-**BB**-SB
montana Hoppe 1832 (*F. nigra* hort.)   EGF.1-**BB**-SB
nigra hort. non Miller 1768 = **F. montana**
obliqua Ker-Gawler 1805 (*F. tristis*)   EGF.1-SB

olgae Vvedensky 1932   SB
olivieri Baker 1875   EGF.1-CA-**BB**-SB
orientalis Adams 1805 (*F. tenella*)   EGF.1-SB
pallidiflora Schrenk 1844   EGF.1-PGP-**BB**-SB-**DGP**-RD
persica Linnaeus 1753   EGF.1-PGP-**BB**-SB-DGP-RD
   'Adiyaman'   EGF.1-PGP-**BB**-RD
phaeanthera Purdy 1932 non Eastwood = **F. affinis** var. **gracilis**
pinardii Boissier 1846   EGF.1-**BB**-SB
pluriflora Torrey ex Bentham 1857   EGF.1-CA-**BB**-SB
pontica Wahlenberg 1828   EGF.1-**BB**-SB-RD
pudica (Pursh) Sprengel 1825   EGF.1-CA-**BB**-SB
pyrenaica Linnaeus 1753   EGF.1-PGP-**CA**-**BB**-SB-DGP-RD
raddeana Regel 1887   EGF.1-PGP-**BB**-SB
recurva Bentham 1857   **BB**-SB-RD
reuteri Boissier 1844   EGF.1-**BB**-SB
roylei Hooker 1852   EGF.1-PGP-CA-**BB**-SB
ruthenica Wilkström 1821   EGF.1-SB
sewerzowii Regel 1868 (*Korolkowia sewerzowii*)   EGF.1-**BB**-**SB**
sibthorpiana (Smith) Baker 1874   EGF.1-CA-**BB**-SB
stenanthera (Regel) Regel   EGF.1-**BB**-**SB**
straussii Bornmüller 1904   **BB**-SB
tenella Marshall von Bieberstein 1808 = **F. orientalis**
thessalica Spruner ex Nyman 1882 = **F. graeca** ssp. **thessala**
thunbergii Miquel 1867   EGF.1-**BB**-SB
rostristis Heldreich & Sartori 1859 = **F. obliqua**

tubiformis Grenier & Godron 1855 (*F. delphinensis*)   CA-**BB**-SB
tuntasia Heldreich & Halacsy 1904   EGF.1-**BB**-SB
uva-vulpis Rix 1974 (*F. assyriaca* hort.)   EGF.1-**BB**-SB-RD
verticillata Willdenow 1799   EGF.1-PGP-**BB**-SB
walujewii Regel 1893   EGF.1-**BB**-SB
whittallii Baker 1893   **BB**-SB
zagrica Stapf 1888   **BB**-SB

FURCRAEA Ventenat 1793   [*Agavaceae*]
  longaeva Karwinski & Zuccarini 1833

GAGEA Salisbury 1806   [*Liliaceae*]
N   **bohemica** (Zauschner) Schultes & Schultes f. 1829   EGF.1-**BB**

GAHNIA Forster & Forster f. 1776   [*Cyperaceae*]
  grandis (Labillardiere) S. T. Blake 1969

GAILLARDIA Fougeroux 1788   [*Asteraceae (Compositae)*]
N   **aristata** Pursh 1814   PGP-DGP
  x grandiflorum Hort ex Van Houtte (*G. aristata* x *G. pulchella*)   PGP-RD
    'Bremen'   [Benary/Walther 1929]
    'Büble'   [H. Klose 1974]
    'Burgunder'   [Benary/Walther 1931]   DGP-RD
    'Chloe'
    'Croftway Yellow'   PGP-RD
L   **'Dazzler'**   RD
    'Fackelschein' ('Torchlight')
    'Goblin' = **G. 'Kobald'**
    'Goldkobald'   [Benary/Walther 1949]
    'Ipswich Beauty'   PGP-RD
    Kelway's Hybrids   [Kelway]
    'Kobald' ('Goblin')   **DGP**-DR
    'Lorenziana'   **DGP**-RD
    'Mandarin'   [A. Bloom]   PGP-**RD**
    'Monarch'

'Nana Nieske'
'Regalis'
'Sommerfreude'
'Sonnengold'
'Tokajer'   [Benary/Walther ·1945]
'Torchlight' = **G. 'Fackelschein'**
'Wirral Flame'   PGP-**DGP**

N **pulchella** Fougeroux 1788   PGP-DGP

GALACTITES Moench 1794 nom. cons.   [*Asteraceae (Compositae)*
B **tomentosa** Moench 1794

GALANTHUS Linnaeus 1753   [*Amaryllidaceae*
allenii Baker 1891   EGF.1-**BB**-SB
byzantinus Baker 1893 = **G. plicatus** ssp. **byzantinus**
caucasicus (Baker) Grossheim 1926   EGF.1-CA-**BB**-SB
'Comet'
var. **hiemalis** Stern 1956   EGF.1-SB
corcyrensis Stern 1956 = **G. reginae-olgae**
elwesii Hooker f. 1875   EGF.1-CA-**BB**-SB-**DGP**
'Cassaba'
'Kingstone Double'
var. **whittallii** Moon 1900   CA
fosteri Baker 1889   EGF.1-CA-**BB**-SB
gracilis Celakovsky 1891 (*G. graecus* hort., non Boissier) EGF.1-CA-SB
graecus hort., non Boissier 1882 = **G. gracilis**
ikariae Baker 1893 (*G. woronowii*)   EGF.1-**BB**-SB-**DGP**-RD
ssp. **latifolius** (Ruprecht) Stern 1956 (*G. latifolius, G. platyphyllus*) EGF.1-**BB**-SB
imperati Bertoloni 1839 = **G. nivalis** ssp. **imperati**
kemulariae Kuthatheladze 1963 = **G. lagodechianus**
lagodechianus Kemularia-Natadze 1947 (*G. kemulariae*) EGF.1-SB
latifolius Ruprecht 1868, non Salisbury 1866 = **G. ikariae** ssp. **latifolius**
N‡ **nivalis** Linnaeus 1753   EGF.1-**BB**-SB-**DGP**-RD
'Bitton'
corcyrensis Stern ex hort. = **G. reginae-olgae**
'Flore Pleno'   SB-**RD**
'Gracilis' = **G. gracilis**
ssp. **imperati** (Bertoloni) Baker (*G. imperati*)   EGF.1-SB
'Lady Elphinstone'
var. **lutescens** Harpur-Crewe (*G. sandersii*)   **BB**-SB
'Orwell Green Tip'
'Poculiformis'
'Pusey Green Tip'
ssp. *reginae-olgae* (Orphanides) Gottlieb-Tannenhain 1904 = **G. reginae-olga**
'Sandhill Gate'
'Scharlockii'   EGF.1-**BB**-SB
'St. Annes'
'Tiny'
'Virescens'
'Viridi Apice'   SB
'Walrus'
platyphyllus Traub & Moldenke 1947 = **G. ikariae** ssp. **latifolius**
plicatus Marshall von Bieberstein 1819   EGF.1-CA-**BB**-SB-RD
ssp. **byzantinus** (Baker) D. A. Webb 1978   EGF.1-CA-**BB**-SB
'Warham'   **DGP**-RD
reginae-olgae Orphanides 1876 (*G. corcyrensis, G. nivalis* ssp. *reginae-olgae*)
                                                  EGF.1-**BB**-SB-**RD**
Sicilian Form
ssp. **vernalis** Kamari   EGF.1-SB
rizehensis Stern 1956   EGF.1-**BB-SB**

sandersii hort. = **G. nivalis** var. **lutescens**
woronowii Losina-Losinskaya 1935 = **G. ikariae**

HYBRID CULTIVARS

'Abington Gem'
'Atkinsii'
'Augustus'   **BB**-SB-DGP
'Backhouse No 12'
'Barbican'
'Benthall Beauty'
'Brenda Troyle'
'Clare Blakeway-Phillips'
'Desdemona'
'Dionysus'
'Eleanor Blakeway-Phillips'
'Galatea'
'Hill Poe'
'Hippolyta'
'Jacquenetta'
'John Gray'
'Ketton'
'Lady Beatrix Stanley'
'Lavinia'
'Magnet'
'Maidwell C'   **BB**-SB
'Maidwell L'
'Melvillei'
'Merlin'
'Mighty Atom'   **BB**
'Mrs Backhouse's Spectacles'
'Oliver Wyatt'
'Ophelia'
'Peg Sharples'
'Robin Hood'
'S. Arnott' ('Sam Arnott')
'Straffan'   **BB**-SB-**DGP**-RD
'Titania'
'Winifred Matthias'

GALAX Linnaeus 1753 nom. cons.   [*Diapensiaceae*]
    aphylla hort. non Linnaeus 1753 = **G. urceolata**
    urceolata (Poiret) Brummitt 1972 (*G. aphylla* hort.)   PGP

GALEGA Linnaeus 1753   [*Fabaceae (Leguminosae)*]
    bicolor Haussknecht 1865
    x hartlandii Hartland ex Clarke (*G. bicolor* x *G. officinalis*)   PGP
        'Alba'   DGP-**RD**
        'Candida'   PGP
        'His Majesty'   PGP-**DGP**-RD
        'Lady Wilson'   PGP-DGP-**RD**
HN‡ **officinalis** Linnaeus 1753
    officinalis hort. non Linnaeus = **G. x hartlandii**
    orientalis Lamarck 1788   **PGP**-RD

GALEOBDOLON Adanson 1763   [*Lamiaceae (Labiatae)*]
N‡ **luteum** Hudson 1778 (*Lamium galeobdolon, Lamiastrum galeobdolon*)   DGP-RD
        'Florentinum'
        'Silberteppich'   [E. Pagels]   RD
        'Silver Carpet' = **G. luteum** 'Silberteppich'

L   'Variegatum'   DGP-RD

GALIUM Linnaeus 1753   [*Rubiaceae*]
HN‡L **odoratum** (Linnaeus) Scopoli 1771 (*Asperula odorata*)
     perpusillum (Hooker f.) Allan 1961
     sylvaticum Linnaeus 1762
HN‡L **verum** Linnaeus 1753

GALTONIA Decaisne 1880   [*Hyacinthaceae (Liliaceae)*]
     candicans (Baker) Decaisne 1880 (*Hyacinthus candicans*)   PGP-**BB**-**DGP**-RD
     princeps (Baker) Decaisne 1880   PGP-**BB**
        'Praecox'
     viridiflora Verdoorn 1955

GAURA Linnaeus 1753   [*Onagraceae*]
     lindheimeri Englemann & A. Gray 1845   PGP

GAZANIA Gaertner 1791 nom. cons.   [*Asteraceae (Compositae)*]
     x hybrida hort. (*G. longiscapa* x *G. nivea* etc.)   DGP-RD
        'Cookie'
        'Cream Beauty'
        'Flash'
        'Magenta Green'
        'Michael'
        'Orange Beauty'
        'Silver Beauty'
        'Sir Francis'
        'Sunbeam'
     pectinata (Thunberg) Hartweg (*G. pinnata* Lessing)
     pinnata Lessing 1832 non de Candolle 1838 = **G. pectinata**
     rigens (Linnaeus) Gaertner 1791 (*G. splendens*)   RD
        'Aureo-variegata'
        'Torquay Silver'
        'Variegata'
     splendens E. G. & A. Henderson = **G. rigens**
     uniflora Sims 1821
        'Splendens' = **G. rigens**

GELASINE Herbert 1840   [*Iridaceae*]
     coerulea (Velloso) P. Ravenna 1977 (*Sisyrinchium coeruleum*)

GENTIANA Linnaeus 1753   [*Gentianaceae*]
     'Aberchalder' = **G. x hexa-farreri 'Aberchalder'**
     acaulis Linnaeus 1753   CA-**DGP**-RD
        'Alba'   CA
        'Alpina' = **G. alpina**
        'Belvedere'
        'Coelestina'
        'Dinarica' = **G. dinarica**
        'Gedanensis'
        'Helzmannii'
        'Krumrey'
        'Leith Vale'
        'Nora Bradshaw'
        'Rannach'
        'Trotter's Form'
        'Undulatifolia'
     affinis Grisebach ex Hooker 1838
     'Alpha' = **G. x hexa-farreri 'Alpha'**

L

alpina Villars 1779   CA
altaica Laxmann 1774 (*G. grandiflora*)
andrewsii Grisebach 1838
    'Alba'
'Angel's Wings' = **G. sino-ornata 'Angel's Wings'**
angulosa Marshall von Bieberstein 1808 = **G. verna** ssp. **pontica**
angustifolia Villars 1779
    'Auslese'
asclepiadea Linnaeus 1753   PGP-**DGP**-**RD**
    'Alba'   PGP
    'Knightshayes'   PGP
    'Phyllis'   PGP
bavarica Linnaeus 1753   CA-DGP
'Behnken'
bellidifolia Hooker f. 1844
'Belvedere' = **G. acaulis 'Belvedere'**
x bernardii hort. = **G. x stevenagensis 'Bernardii'**
bigelovii A. Gray 1883
bisetaea J. Howell 1897
'Blue Bonnets' = **G. x macaulayi 'Blue Bonnets'**
'Blue Dusk'
'Blue Flame'
'Blue Heaven'
brachyphylla Villars 1779   CA
    ssp. **favratii** (Rittener) Tutin 1971 (*G. favratii*)
'Brin Form' = **G. sino-ornata 'Brin Form'**
'Bucksburn Azure'
cachemirica Decaisne 1841   CA
'Carolii' (*G. farreri* x *G. lawrencei*)
'Christine Jean'
clusii Perrault & Songeon 1855   RD
    'Rochellii'
crinita Froelich 1796 = **Gentianopsis crinita**
cruciata Linnaeus 1753
dahurica Fischer 1812 (*G. kurroo* 'Brevidens')
decumbens Linnaeus f. 1781
dendrologii Marquand 1931
depressa D. Don 1825
'Devonhall' (*G. farreri* x *G. ornata*)
dinarica G. Beck 1887 (*G. acaulis* 'Dinarica')   DGP
doeringiana hort. = **G. septemfida** var. **lagodechiana 'Doeringiana'**
Drake's Hybrids (*G. farreri* x *G. ornata*)
'Drumcairn White'
'Dusk'
'Edinburgh' = **G. x macaulayi 'Edinburgh'**
'Edith Sarah' = **G. sino-ornata 'Edith Sarah'**
'Elizabeth'
'Elizabeth Brand'
'Emmen'
farreri I. B. Balfour 1918   CA-DGP-**RD**
'Fasta' (*G. farreri* x *G. x stevenagensis*)
'Fasta Highlands'
Fasta Hybrids
favratii (Rittener) Farrat 1887 = **G. brachyphylla** ssp. **favratii**
freyniana Bornmueller ex Freyn 1892
frigida Haenke 1788
gelida Marshall von Bieberstein 1808
'Glendevon' (*G. ornata* x *G. sino-ornata*)
gracilipes Turrill 1905 (*G. purdomi* hort.)   RD

'Yuatensis' = **G. wutaiensis**
grandiflora Laxmann 1774 non Lamarck 1779 = **G. altaica**
grossheimii Doluchanov 1948
x hascombensis hort. = **G. septemfida** var. lagodechiana 'Hascombensis'
'Helzmannii' = **G. acaulis 'Helzmannii'**
x hexa-farreri Hort. (*G. farreri x G. hexaphylla*)   CA
   'Aberchalder'
   'Alpha'   [J. Drake]
   'Omega'   [J. Drake]
hexapetala Maximowicz ex Kusnezow 1893   CA
'Ida K'
Inshriach Hybrids
'Inverleith' (*G. farreri x G. veitchiorum*)   CA-**DGP**
jesoana Nakai 1909 = **Crawfurdia japonica**
'Kidbrooke Seedling' = **G. x macaulayi 'Kidbrooke Seedling'**
'Kidora' (*G. x macaulayi* 'Kidbrooke Seedling' x *G. ornata*)
'Kingfisher' = **G. x macaulayi 'Kingfisher'**
kochiana Perrault & Songeon 1853 = **G. acaulis**
'Krumrey' = **G. acaulis 'Krumrey'**
kurroo Royle 1836   CA
   'Brevidens' = **G. dahurica**
kurroo hort. non Royle = **G. tibetica**
lagodechiana (Kusnezov) Grossheim ex Möllers 1931 = **G. septemfida**
                                                  var. **lagodechiana**
linearis Froelich 1796
H   **lutea** Linnaeus 1753   PGP-**RD**
x macaulayi Hort. (*G. farreri* x *G. sino-ornata*)   CA-DGP-RD
   'Blue Bonnets'
   'Edinburgh'
   'Elata'
   'Kidbrooke Seedling'   RD
   'Kingfisher'   RD
   'Praecox'
   'Wells' Variety' (*G. wellsii* hort.)
makinoi Kusnezov 1893   PGP
   'Royal Blue'
'Mary Lyle' = **G. sino-ornata 'Mary Lyle'**
'Midnight'   RD
'Mount Everest'
occidentalis Jakowatz 1899
olivieri Grisebach 1839
'Omega' = **G. x hexa-farreri 'Omega'**
oregana Engelmann ex A. Gray 1876 = **G. affinis**
oreodoxa H. Smith 1926
ornata (G. Don) Grisebach 1838   **CA**
pannonica Scopoli 1771
paradoxa Albov 1894
N‡   **pneumonanthe** Linnaeus 1753   PGP-RD
prolata Balfour f. 1918   CA
pumila Jacquin 1762
punctata Linnaeus 1753   PGP
purdomi hort. = **G. gracilipes**
purpurea Linnaeus 1753   PGP
pyrenaica Linnaeus 1767   CA
'Queen of the Blue'
'Rannach' = **G. acaulis 'Rannach'**
rochellii hort. = **G. clusii 'Rochellii'**
saxosa Forster f. 1777   CA-**DGP**-**RD**
'Sensation'

septemfida Pallas 1788   PGP-DGP-RD
   var. **cordifolia** (Koch) Boissier
   var. **lagodechiana** Kusnezov 1893 (*G. lagodechiana*)   **DGP**
   var. **lagodechiana** 'Doeringiana'
   var. **lagodechiana** 'Latifolia'
   var. **lagodechiana** 'Hascombensis'
sino-ornata I. B. Balfour 1918   **DGP-RD**
   'Alba'
   'Angels Wings'
   'Blauer Dom'
   'Brin Form'
   'Edith Sarah'
   'Mary Lyle'
   'Trogg's Form'
   'Woolgreaves'
x stevenagensis Hort. ex Barker 1934 (*G. sino-ornata* x *G. veitchiorum*)   RD
   'Bernardii'
   'Frank Barker'
straminea Maximowicz 1881
'Susan Jane' (*G. farreri* x *G. veitchiorum*)
tergestina G. Beck 1893 = **G. verna** ssp. **tergestina**
tenuifolia Petrie 1913
'The Souter'
tibetica King ex Hooker f. 1883 (*G. kurroo* hort.)
triflora Pallas 1789   PGP
'Trogg's Form' = **G. sino-ornata 'Trogg's Form'**
'Trotter's Form' = **G. alpina 'Trotter's Form'**
Tweeddale Hybrids
'Utterby Seedling'
veitchiorum Hemsley 1909   CA-DGP
N‡ **verna** Linnaeus 1753   **CA-DGP**-RD
   'Angulosa' = **G. verna** ssp. **pontica**
   ssp. **pontica** (Soltokovic) Hayek 1930 (*G. angulosa*)   CA-DGP-RD
   ssp. **tergestina** (G. Beck) Hayek 1930 (*G. tergestina*)
   *waltonii
'Wealdensis' (*G. x hexa-farreri* x *G. veitchiorum*)
wellsii hort. = **G. x macauleyi 'Wells' Variety'**
wilsonii Marquand 1928
'Woolgreaves' = **G. sino-ornata 'Woolgreaves'**
wutaiensis Marquand 1931

GENTIANELLA Moench 1794 nom. cons.   [*Gentianaceae*]
N‡ **amarella** (Linnaeus) Boerner 1912

GENTIANOPSIS Ma 1951   [*Gentianaceae*]
   crinita (Froelich) Ma 1951 (*Gentiana crinita*)

GERANIUM Linnaeus 1753   [*Geraniaceae*]

M - YEO, PETER,: *'Hardy Geraniums'* Croom Helm 1985

albiflorum Ledebour 1829   M
albiflorum hort. = **G. pratense** f. **albiflorum**
'Ann Folkard'   [O. G. Folkard c 1974] (*G. procurrens* x *G. psilostemon*)   **M-PGP**
anemonifolium L'Heritier = **G. palmatum**
argenteum Linnaeus 1756   M-CA
armenum Boissier 1867 = **G. psilostemon**
asphodeloides Burman 1759   **M**
atlanticum Boissier 1843   **M**
x cantabrigiense Yeo 1985 (*G. dalmaticum* x *G. macrorrhizum*)   **M**

'Biokovo' [H. Simon]	M
'Cambridge'	
'Ingwersen'	
'Ridsko'	
canariense Reuter 1858	M
candicans hort. = **G. lambertii**	
chinense hort. = **G. eriostemon**	
cinereum Cavanilles 1787	**M-CA-DGP-RD**
'Ballerina' [A. Bloom]	**M-DGP**-RD
'Laurence Flatman' [A. Bloom]	M-RD
var. **subcaulescens** (L'Heritier ex de Candolle) Knuth 1912	**M**-CA-**DGP**
var. **subcaulescens 'Giuseppii'**	M
var. **subcaulescens 'Splendens'** [J. Stormonth c1936]	**M**
clarkei Yeo 1985	M
'Kashmir Purple'	M-PGP
'Kashmir White'	**M**-PGP-RD
collinum Willdenow 1800	**M**
dalmaticum (Beck) Reichenbach	**M-CA-RD**
'Album' [via Bloom 1956]	M
'Roseum' = **G. dalmaticum**	
delavayi Franchet 1886	M-PGP
donianum Sweet 1827	M
endressii Gay 1832	M-PGP-RD
'Wargrave Pink' [Waterer 1930]	M-PGP-RD
erianthum de Candolle 1824	**M**
eriostemon Fischer ex de Candolle 1824 (*G. chinense* hort.)	M
farreri Stapf 1926 (*G. napuligerum* hort. non Franchet)	M-CA-RD
'Pink Panther'	
grandiflorum Edgeworth 1846 = **G. himalayense**	
var. *alpinum* hort. = **G. himalayense 'Gravetye'**	
himalayense Klotzsch 1862 (*G. grandiflorum*)	M-PGP-RD
'Album'	
'Birch Double' = **G. himalayense 'Plenum'**	
'Gravetye' (*G. grandiflorum* var. *alpinum* hort.)	**M-PGP**
'Irish Blue' [via G. Thomas c1947]	M
'Plenum' [pre-1928] ('Birch Double')	M-RD
ibericum Cavanilles 1787	**M-PGP-DGP-RD**
ssp. **jubatum** (Handel-Mazzetti) P. H. Davis 1955	M
incanum Burman 1759	M
'Johnson's Blue' (*G. pratense* x *G. himalayense*) [B. Ruys c1950]	M-PGP-**DGP**-RD
kishtvariense Knuth 1923	**M**
lambertii Sweet 1823	M-**PGP**-RD
libani P. H. Davis 1955	M
x lindavicum Sundermann ex Knuth 1912 (*G. argenteum* x *G. cinereum*)	M
'Alanah' [Gore-Booth pre-1946] ('Purpureum')	M
'Apple Blossom' [A. Bloom] ('Jenny Bloom')	M-RD
'Jenny Bloom' = **G. x lindavicum 'Apple Blossom'**	
'Lissadell' [Gore-Booth]	M
'Purpureum' = **G. x lindavicum 'Alanah'**	
lucidum Linnaeus 1753	M
macrorrhizum Linnaeus 1753	**M-PGP-DGP-RD**
'Album' [Ingwersen]	M-PGP-**DGP**
'Bevan's Variety' [Bevan via E. Strangman]	M-PGP
'Czakor'	
'Ingwersen's Variety' [Ingwersen 1929]	M-PGP-DGP-RD
'Roseum' = **G. macrorrhizum**	
'Spessart' [H. Simon]	M
'Variegatum'	M
'Velebit'	
macrostylum Boissier 1843	M-**BB**

The left-margin letter codes:

L   (next to 'Kashmir White')
N   (next to endressii)
L   (next to 'Johnson's Blue')
N‡ (next to lucidum)
N   (next to macrorrhizum)
L   (next to 'Album')
L   (next to 'Ingwersen's Variety')

maculatum Linnaeus 1753   M-**PGP**
    'Album'
maderense Yeo 1969   **M**
x magnificum Hylander 1961 (*G. ibericum* x *G. platypetalum*)   **M-PGP-RD**
malviflorum Boissier & Reuter 1852   **M-PGP**
microphyllum Hooker f. 1844
  x monacense Harz 1921 (*G. phaeum* x *G. reflexum*)   **M-PGP**
    var. **anglicum** Yeo 1985   M
    'Muldoon' ('Variegatum')   M
  napuligerum hort. non Franchet 1889 = **G. farreri**
nervosum Rydberg 1901   M
N **nodosum** Linnaeus 1753   M-PGP
  orientalitibeticum Knuth 1923 (*G. stapfianum roseum* hort.)   **M**
  x oxonianum Yeo 1985 (*G. endressii* x *G. versicolor*)   M
L   **'A. T. Johnson'**   [Johnston via Ingwersen pre-1937   M-PGP-RD
L   **'Claridge Druce'**   M-PGP-**RD**
    'Rose Clair'   [Johnston via Ingwersen pre-1946]   M-PGP-**RD**
    'Thurstonianum'   [pre-1914]   M
    'Wageningen'
    'Winscombe'   [M. Fish]   **M**
palmatum Cavanilles 1787 (*G. anemonifolium*)   M-PGP
palustre Linnaeus 1756   M
N‡ **phaeum** Linnaeus 1753   **M-PGP-RD**
    'Album'   [Ingwersen 1946]   M-PGP
    'Lily Lovell'   [T. Bath]   M
    var. **lividum** (L'Heritier) Persoon 1806   **M-PGP**
    var. **lividum 'Majus'**   M
    'Variegatum'   M
platypetalum Fischer & Meyer 1835   **M-PGP**
polyanthes Edgeworth & Hooker f. 1874   M
N‡L **pratense** Linnaeus 1753   **M-PGP-DGP-RD**
    f. **albiflorum** Opiz 1852 ('Album')   M
    'Bicolor' = **G. pratense 'Striatum'**
    'Birch Blue'
    'Galactic'   [via J. Forty pre-1971]   M
    'Kashmir White' = **G. clarkei 'Kashmir White'**
    'Mrs. Kendall Clark'   M-PGP-DGP-RD
    'Plenum Album'   M-PGP-DGP
    'Plenum Caeruleum'   **M-PGP-DGP**
    'Plenum Violaceum'   M-**PGP**
    'Silver Queen'   [Johnson pre-1946]   M
    'Striatum' ('Bicolor')   M-PGP
    'Wisley Blue'
procurrens Yeo 1973   M-RD
L **psilostemon** Ledebour 1842 (*G. armenum*)   M-PGP-DGP-**RD**
    'Bressingham Flair'   [A. Bloom 1973]   **M-PGP**
  punctatum hort. = **G. x monacense**
    'Variegatum' = **G. x monacense 'Muldoon'**
pylzowianum Maximowicz 1880   M-RD
N‡ **pyrenaicum** Burman f. 1759   M
  rectum album hort. = **G. x clarkei 'Kashmir White'**
reflexum Linnaeus 1771   **M-PGP**
L **renardii** Trautvetter 1882   **M-PGP-RD**
  x riversleaianum Yeo 1985 (*G. endressii* x *G. traversii*)   M
L   **'Russell Prichard'**   [Prichard]   **M-PGP-RD**
rivulare Villars 1779   **M**
HN‡L **robertianum** Linnaeus 1753   M
    'Album'   M
    'Celtic White'   M

B   **rubescens** Yeo 1969   M
N‡   **sanguineum** Linnaeus 1753   M-PGP-**DGP**
      'Album'   M-DGP-RD
      'Aviemore'
      'Cedric Morris'
      'Coccineum'
      'Compactum' nom. dub.
      Drake's Hybrids
      'Glenluce'   M-PGP
      'Elspeth'
      'Holden'   [R. Milne-Redhead pre-1975]   M
      'Jubilee Pink'   [J. Drake]   M
      lancastriense Nicholson 1885 = **G. sanguineum** var. **striatum**
      'Minutum'   [via Archer nom. illegit.]   M
      'Nanum'   [via Ingwersen nom. illegit]   M
      'Nyewoods'
      'Plenum'   M
      var. *prostratum* (Cavanilles) Persoon 1806 = **G. sanguineum** var. **striatum**
      'Shepherd's Warning'   [J. Drake]   M
L   var. **striatum** Weston 1771   **M-PGP**
      var. **striatum** 'Splendens'   M
   sessiliflorum Cavanilles 1787   M-CA
      ssp. **novaezelandiae** Carolin 1964   M
      ssp. **novaezelandiae** 'Nigricans'   M
   sinense Knuth 1912   M-PGP
   stapfianum roseum hort. = **G. orientalitibeticum**
   striatum Linnaeus 1759 = **G. versicolor**
   subcaulescens L'Heritier ex de Candolle 1824 = **G. cinereum** var. **subcaulescens**
N‡   **sylvaticum** Linnaeus 1753   M-PGP-DGP-RD
      'Album'   **M-PGP-DGP-RD**
      'Birch Lilac'
      'Mayflower'   [A. Bloom c1972]   M-PGP-**DGP**-RD
      'Meran'   [H. Klose 1972]
      f. **roseum** Murray   M
      'Silva'   [E. Pagels]
      var. **wanneri** Briquet 1889   M-PGP-RD
   thunbergii Siebold ex Lindley & Paxton 1851   M
   traversii Hooker f. 1867   M-PGP
      var. **elegans** Cockayne 1902   M-PGP
   tuberosum Linnaeus 1753   M-**BB**
      'Charlesii'
N‡   **versicolor** Linnaeus 1755 (*G. striatum*)   **M-PGP**
   viscosissimum Fischer & Meyer 1846   M
   wallichianum D. Don 1821   **M-PGP-DGP-RD**
L   **'Buxton's Variety'**   [E. C. Buxton c1920] ('Buxton's Blue')   **M-PGP-DGP**-RD
   wilfordii hort. non Maximowicz 1880 = **G. thunbergii**
   wlassovianum Fischer ex Link 1822   M-PGP-RD
   yesoense Franchet & Savatier 1878   M
   yunnanense Franchet 1889   M-PGP

GEUM Linnaeus 1753   [*Rosaceae*]
   aleppicum Jacquin 1784
      ssp. **strictum** (Aiton) Clausen 1949
L   **x borisii** Kellerer ex Sündermann 1906 (*G. bulgaricum* x *G. reptans*)   PGP-**DGP**-RD
      'Feuermeer'   [H. Klose 1964]
      'Werner Arends'   [G. Arends]
   borisii hort. p.p., non Kellerer ex Sündermann = **G. coccineum**
   bulgaricum Pancic 1886   RD
   chiloense Balbis 1825   PGP-DGP-RD

	'Bernstein' [H. Klose 1965]	
	'Carlskaer'	
	'Dolly North'	
	'Feuerball'	PGP
L	'Fire Opal' [1928]	PGP
	'Goldball' = **G. chiloense 'Lady Stratheden'**	
L	'Lady Stratheden' ('Goldball')	PGP-DGP-**RD**
L	'Mrs Bradshaw'	PGP-**DGP**-**RD**
	'Nordek'	
	'Princess Juliana' [1923]	PGP
	'Quellyon'	
	'Rubin' [G. Arends 1938]	

coccineum Smith 1806 (*G. borisii* hort. p.p.)

	'Coppertone'	
	'Prince of Orange'	RD
	'Red Wings'	DGP-**RD**

elatum Wallich ex G. Don 1832
x heldreichii hort. ex Bergmans 1924 (*G. coccineum* x *G. montanum*)

	'Georgenberg'	
	'Magnificum' ('Splendens')	PGP
	'Splendens' = **G. x heldreichii 'Magnificum'**	

N‡ **x intermedium** Ehrhardt (*G. urbanum* x *G. rivale*)
montanum Linnaeus 1753

	'Diana'	RD

peruvianum Focke 1906
reptans Linnaeus 1753   **CA-RD**
x rhaeticum Bruegger 1882 (*G. montanum* x *G. reptans*)
rhodopeum Stoyanoff & Stefanoff 1923
N‡ **rivale** Linnaeus 1753   PGP-DGP

	'Album'	
	'Leonard's Variety'	DGP-RD
	'Lionel Cox'	PGP

rossii (R. Brown) Sevastianov 1825   RD
strictum Aiton 1811 = **G. aleppicum** ssp. **strictum**
x tirolense Kerner 1867 (*G. montanum* x *G. rivale*)
triflorum Pursh 1814
   var. **campanulatum** (Greene) C. L. Hitchcock 1961
HN‡ **urbanum** Linnaeus 1753

GILLENIA Moench 1802   [*Rosaceae*]
H   **trifoliata** Moench 1802   **PGP**

GLADIOLUS Linnaeus 1753   [*Iridaceae*]
   atroviolaceus Boissier 1853   EGF.1-**BB**
   byzantinus Miller 1768 non Marshall von Bieberstein 1819 = **G. communis**
      ssp. **byzantinus**
   callianthus Marais 1973 (*Acidanthera bicolor, A. murieliae*)   EGF.1-PGP-**DGP-RD**
      'Zwanenburg'   [van Tubergen]
   carmineus C. H. Wright 1906   EGF.1
   carneus Delaroche 1766   EGF.1
   citrinus Klatt 1822
   x colvillei Sweet 1826 (*G. cardinalis* x *G. tristis*)   EGF.1-PGP-**BB**-RD
      'Albus'
N   **communis** Linnaeus 1753   EGF.1-PGP-**BB**
      ssp. **byzantinus** (Miller) A. P. Hamilton 1978 (*G. byzantinus*)   EGF.1-PGP-**RD**
      ssp. **byzantinus** 'Albus'
   cuspidatus Jacquin 1795 = **G. undulatus**
      var. *ventricosus* (Lamarck) Baker 1892 = **G. carneus**
   garnieri Klatt 1822
   gracilis Jacquin 1792

N‡   *grandis* (Thunberg) Thunberg 1784 = **G. liliaceus**
gueinzii Kunze 1847
halophilus Boissier & Heldreich 1854

N‡   **illyricus** K. Koch 1844   EGF.1-PGP-**BB**
imbricatus Linnaeus 1753   EGF.1-**BB**
    ssp. **kotschyanus** (Boissier) ! (*G. kotschyanus*)   **BB**

N   **italicus** Miller 1768 (*G. segetum*)   EGF.1-PGP-**BB**-DGP
kotschyanus Boissier 1854 = **G. illyricus** ssp. **kotschyanus**
liliaceus Houttuyn 1780 (*G. grandis*)   EGF.1
    'Christabel'
    'Gillian'
x nanceianus Hort. ex Baker 1892 (*G. x nanus*)
x nanus hort. non Andrews 1801 = **G. x nanceianus**
natalensis (Ecklon) Reinwardt ex Hooker 1831   EGF.1
    var. **primulinus** (Baker) ! (*G. primulinus*)   PGP
ochroleucus Baker 1876
    var. **macowanii** (Baker) Obermeyer 1972
palustris Gaudin 1828   EGF.1
papilio Hooker f. 1866 (*G. purpureo-auratus*)   EGF.1-PGP-**BB**
primulinus Baker 1890 = **G. natalensis** var. **primulinus**
purpureo-auratus Hooker f. 1872 = **G. papilio**
segetum Ker-Gawler 1804 = **G. italicus**
tristis Linnaeus 1762   EGF.1-PGP-**RD**
    var. **aestivalis** (Ingram) Lewis 1972   EGF.1
    var. **concolor** (Salisbury) Baker 1877
undulatus Linnaeus 1767   EGF.1

'MINIATURE' HYBRID CULTIVARS
Derived from:

1   **G. x colvillei**
2   **G. x nanceianus** (*G. x nanus*)
3   **G. recurvus** (*G. ramosus*)
4   **G. x tubergenii**
5   **G. tristis**

    'Agadir'
2   **'Amanda Mahy'** ®   [E. Mahy pre-1940]   PGP
    'Amusing'
    'Bellinda'
    'Blushing Bride'   DGP
4   **'Charm'** ®   [van Tubergen 1920]   **DGP**
4   **'Charming Beauty'** ®   [J. P. van der Hulst pre-1961]('Warmunda')
    'Charming May'
5   **'Corfe Castle'** ®   [T. T. Barnard 1959]
2   **'Elvira'** ®   [J. van Winsen 1956]
4   **'Fair Lady'**
2   **'Floriade'**
    'Fortuna'
2   **'Good Luck'**
    'Greenland'
2   **'Guernsey Glory'** ®   [E. Mahy via Wülfinghoff]
2   **'Herald Comet'**
2   **'Impressive'** ®   [E. Mahy via S. de Goede pre-1958]
    'Jackpot'
    'Lady Godiva'
    'Leonora'
    'Little Jade Green'
2   **'Nymph'** ®   [van Tubergen 1914]   DGP
    'Orith'

2	'Peach Blossom' ® [c1914]	PGP-DGP
2	'Prince Claus' ® [H. & J. van der Voet 1961]	
3	'Robinetta' ® [C. A. van der Wereld pre-1958]	**DGP**
	'Rosalind'	
	'Rosy Charm'	
	'Serafin'	
2	'Spitfire' ® [van Tubergen c1914]	DGP
1	'The Bride' ® [c1891]	PGP
	'Warmunda' = **G. 'Charming Beauty'**	
	'White Elegance'	

'PRIMULINUS' HYBRID CULTIVARS
Derived from **G. natalensis** (*G. primulinus*)

    'Atom'
    'Candy'
    'Carioca'
    'Columbine'   **RD**
    'Comet'
    'Dantino'
    'Essex'
    'Fantasy'
    'Helele'
    'Leonore'
    'Obelisk'
    'Pretoria'
    'Robin'
    'White City'
    'Treasure'
    'Yellow Special'

'LARGE FLOWERED' HYBRID CULTIVARS

434 LM	'Acapulco'	
414 LM	'Ace'	
454 M	'Action'	
4	'Albanberg'	
4	'Aldebarran'	
2	'Alice'	
500 LM	'Amsterdam'	
275 E	'Amy Beth'	
2	'Anchor'	
	'Andorra'	RD
	'Anglia'	RD
356 M	'Antares'	
475 M	'Applause'	
422 M	'Apricot Dream'	
378 L	'Aristocrat'	
201 M	'Arrows'	
447 LM	'Attraction'	
442 M	'Aubade'	
	'Avalanche'	
463 M	'Award'	
268 EM	'Back Lash'	
432 M	'Bel Ami'	
455	'Ben Trovata'	
256 M	'Blitzcrieg'	
4	'Bloemfontein'	

NORTH AMERICAN GLADIOLUS COUNCIL CLASSIFICATION

E   = Early flowering
EM   = Early mid-season
M   = Mid-season
LM   = Late mid-season
L   = Late flowering

1st digit indicates the **floret size**
2nd digit indicates the **colour**
3rd digit indicates the **shade**

FLORET SIZE DIGIT

1 = Miniature flowered (under 2.5')
2 = Small flowered (under 3.5')
3 = Medium flowered (under 4.5')
4 = Large flowered (under 5.5')
5 = Giant flowered (over 5.5')

COLOUR DIGITS

	PALE	LIGHT	MEDIUM	DEEP	OTHER
White	00				
Green		02	04		
Yellow	10	12	14	16	
Orange	20	22	24	26	
Salmon	30	32	34	36	*(includes Scarlet)*
Pink	40	42	44	46	
Red	50	52	54	56	58 *(Black)*
Rose	60	62	64	66	68 *(Black Rose)*
Lavender	70	72	74	76	78 *(Purple)*
Violet	80	82	84	86	
Tan	90				98 *(Brown)*
Smoky		92	94	96	

Violet includes Blue
Yellow includes Cream
Orange includes Buff

An odd number as the 3rd digit indicates a conspicuous mark or colour contrast.

285 E	'Bluebird'	
486	'Blue Conqueror'	RD
485 M	'Blue Heaven'	
486 M	'Blue Isle'	
	'Brevet'	RD
2	'Bristol'	
	Butterfly Hybrids	
2	'Camborne'	
	'Campanella'	**RD**
510 L	'Carmel Cream'	
594 M	'Carmen'	
4	'Carousel'	
536 M	'Carqueiranne'	
400 EM	'Carrara'	
445 M	'Cavalcade'	
534 LM	'Cecil T'	
512 M	'Celebrity'	
	'Chanson'	
	'City Lights'	
264 EM	'Claret'	
412 M	'Concorde'	
	'Confetti'	
454 M	'Cordula'	RD
460 LM	'Day Dream'	
456 LM	'D-Day'	
440	'Deciso'	
302 M	'Deios'	RD
532 LM	'Deja Vu'	
400 M	'Diana'	
500 M	'Divinity'	
454 M	'Dr Sjivago'	
237 E	'Doll Baby'	
2	'Donald Duck'	
496 M	'Dusty Miller'	
478 M	'Dynasty'	
513 E	'Early Yellow'	
444 M	'Easy Street'	
212 M	'Eden'	
235 EM	'Essex'	
522 M	'Esta Bonita'	
442 M	'European Song'	
454 M	'Eurovision'	
472 M	'Evening Dress'	RD
411 M	'Evening Glow'	
427 LM	'Fall Classic'	
440 M	'Fiance'	
478	'Fidelio'	
103 EM	'Fimbriata'	
	'Fine Fleur'	
445 M	'Flos Florium'	
416	'Flowersong'	
444 E	'Friendship'	**RD**
2	'Georgette'	RD
246 E	'Gigi'	
414 M	'Golden Monarch'	
412 LM	'Golden Morn'	
516 LM	'Golden Years'	
445 M	'Grand Finale'	
314 M	'Great Day'	
402 M	'Green Spire'	

402 EM	'Greenwich'	
305 M	'Greenwoodpecker'	DGP-RD
4	'Grock'	RD
425 M	'Hallmark'	
420 LM	'Happy Birthday'	
382 E	'High Seas'	
2	'Hoax'	
524 LM	'Holcombe'	
401 M	'Homecoming'	
4	'Hunting Song'	
	'Hypnose'	RD
400 M	'Ice Cap'	
2	'Ice Follies'	
413 EM	'Ice Gold'	
204 M	'Iceland'	
427 M	'Inca Chief'	
545 LM	'Incomparable'	
	'Introspection'	
	'Invitation'	
2	'Ivanhoe'	
400 M	'Jack Frost'	
214 EM	'Jayvee'	
424 E	'Jessica'	
	'Joyeuse Entree'	
595 M	'Krakatoa'	
256 M	'Krystal'	
105 EM	'Lady Bird'	
475 M	'Lavender Jewel'	
456	'Life Flame'	RD
253 E	'Lili'	
374 M	'Lochinvar'	
536 M	'Lovely Day'	
401 M	'Lowland Queen'	
400 M	'Madonna'	
442 M	'Maestro'	
468 M	'Marie Verne'	
4	'Mascagni'	
301 EM	'Melodie'	
4	'Memorial Day'	
	'Merry'	
500 L	'Miss Minnesota'	
	'Misty Eye'	
400 M	'Mont Blanc'	
512 LM	'Moon Mirage'	
500	'Morning Kiss'	
562	'My Love'	RD
4	'New Europe'	
	'Nova Lux'	
2	'Orange Diamond'	
460 M	'Orleans'	
556 LM	'Oscar'	RD
435 M	'Palm Springs'	
4	'Pandion'	
534 M	'Parade'	
476 M	'Par Excellence'	
445 L	'Patty Gay'	
454 M	'Peerless'	
425 M	'Peter Pears'	DGP-RD
478 EM	'Picasso'	
	'Piccolo'	RD

460 M	'Pink Attraction'	
345 M	'Pink Dawn'	
343 EM	'Pink Elf'	
445 M	'Pink Lady'	
442 LM	'Pink Miracle'	
260 EM	'Pink Pearl'	
464 M	'Pink Perfection'	
	'Plum Tart'	
277 E	'Poco'	
475 M	'Poets Dream'	
2	'Polar Beauty'	
400 M	'Polar Ice'	
444 EM	'Powder Puff'	
444 M	'Praha'	
	'Prince Carnaval'	
352 M	'Promise'	
	'Prosperity'	
400 M	'Pure Perfection'	
	'Queen of Night'	
571 M	'Rachelle'	
2	'Red Spot'	
4	'Reine de Holland'	
456 M	'Renegade'	
537 M	'Rivalry'	
443 M	'Riviera'	
478 M	'Roncalli'	
563 EM	'Rose Supreme'	
456 M	'Royal Beauty'	
474 M	'Royal Dutch'	
	'Royal Violet'	
300 EM	'Royal Wedding'	
305 M	'Sabrina'	
253 EM	'St Nick'	
	'Sancerre'	
452 LM	'Sans Souci'	RD
	'Saxony'	
	'Scout'	
	'Shamrock'	RD
	'Shell Pink'	
315 EM	'Shiloh'	
	'Shocking Pink'	
542 M	'Silver Jubilee'	
456 E	'Snoek's Favourite'	
200 M	'Snow Castle'	
400	'Snow Princess'	RD
237 EM	'South Seas'	
475 M	'Spartan'	
466	'Spic and Span'	RD
	'Spring Gem'	
470 E	'Springtime'	
262 M	'Stardust'	
564 M	'Stepping Out'	
	'Storiette'	**RD**
500 M	'Super White'	
	'Tangerine'	
344 M	'Tendresse'	
314 M	'Tesoro'	
323 LM	'Thanksgiving'	
310 M	'The Fairy'	
442 M	'The Queen'	
424 M	'Tijuana'	

425 M	'Topaz'
	'Tout a Toit'
557	'Trader Horn'
424 M	'Veerle'
400 M	'Vega'
354 M	'Vesuvius'
476 M	'Video'
386 EM	'Violetta'
327	'Vivaldi'
2	'West End'
400	'White Friendship'
4	'White Goddess'
400 LM	'White Prosperity'
465 E	'Wine & Roses'
211 M	'Winsome'
	'Yellow Supreme'

GLANDULARIA J. Gmelin 1791   [*Verbenaceae*]
    pulchella (Sweet) Trochain 1964 = **Verbena tenora**

GLAUCIDIUM Siebold & Zuccarini 1845   [*Paeoniaceae*]
    palmatum Siebold & Zuccarini 1845   PG-CA-**DGP**

GLAUCIUM Miller 1754   [*Papaveraceae*]
BN   **corniculatum** (Linnaeus) Rudolph 1781 (*G. rubrum*)   RD
N‡   **flavum** Crantz 1763   PGP-**DGP**
    rubrum Smith 1806 = **G. corniculatum**

GLECHOMA Linnaeus 1753   [*Lamiaceae (Labiateae)*]
HN‡ **hederacea** Linnaeus 1753 (*Nepeta hederacea*)   RD
      'Variegata'   RD

GLOBULARIA Linnaeus 1753   [*Globulariaceae*]
    aphyllanthes Crantz 1766
    aphyllanthes hort. non Crantz = **G. punctata**
    bellidifolia Tenore 1824 = **G. meridionalis**
S   **cordifolia** Linnaeus 1753   CA
      'Alba'   CA
      'Rosea'   [J. Elliott]
    elongata Hegetschweiler 1832 = **G. punctata**
    x fuxeensis Giraudias 1889 (*G. nudicaulis* x *G. repens*)
    incanescens Viviani 1808   CA
    meridionalis (Podpera) O. Schwarz 1938 (*G. bellidifolia, G. pygmaea* hort.)   CA
      'Hort's Variety'
    nana Lamarck 1788 = **G. repens**
    nudicaulis Linnaeus 1753
      'Alba'
    orientalis Linnaeus 1753
    punctata Lapeyrouse 1813 (*G. aphyllanthes* hort., *G. willkommii*)   CA
    pygmaea hort. = **G. meridionalis**
    repens Lamarck 1778 (*G. nana*)   CA
    trichosantha Fischer & Meyer 1839   CA
    vulgaris Linnaeus 1753
    willkommii Nyman 1854 = **G. punctata**

GLORIOSA Linnaeus 1753   [*Colchicaceae (Liliaceae)*]
    superba Linnaeus 1753   EGF.1-DGP-RD
      'Africana'   ®
      'Carsonii'   ®   [c1895]
      'Lutea'   ®   [Pre-1901]
      'Rothschildiana'   ®   [H. B. Rattray 1902]   DGP-**RD**

GLYCERIA R. Brown 1810 nom. cons.   [*Poaceae (Gramineae)*]
    aquatica (Linnaeus) Wahlenberg 1920 non (Linnaeus) J. & C. Presl 1819 =
                                                    G. maxima
N‡L   **maxima** (Hartmann) Holmberg 1919 (*G. aquatica*)   EGF.2-PGP
L   **'Variegata'**   [Boon & Ruys 1895]
                                                        PGP

GNAPHALIUM Linnaeus 1753   [*Asteraceae* Compositae)]
    filicaule (Hooker f.) Hooker f. 1864 = **Helichrysum filicaule**

GONIOLIMON Boissier 1848   [*Plumbaginaceae*]
    speciosum (Linnaeus) Boissier 1848
    tataricum (Linnaeus) Boissier 1848 = **Limonium tataricum**

GOODENIA Smith 1794   [*Goodeniaceae*]
    lunata J. M. Black 1927
    repens Labilliardiere 1804 (*Selliera radicans*)

GOODYERA R. Brown 1813   [*Orchidaceae*]
    oblongifolia Rafinesque 1833   EGF.2
    pubescens R. Brown 1813

GRATIOLA Linnaeus 1753   [*Scrophulariaceae*]
    nana Bentham 1846
H   **officinalis** Linnaeus 1753

GRINDELIA Willdenow 1807   [*Asteraceae (Compositae)*]
    chiloensis (Cornelisson) Cabrera 1932   PGP
    robusta Nuttall 1841 = **G. rubricaulis** var. **robusta**
    rubricaulis de Candolle
N   var. **robusta** (Nuttall) Steyermark (*G. robusta*)

GROELANDIA J. Gay 1854
N‡   **densa** (Linnaeus) Fourreau 1869 (*Potamogeton densus*)

GUNNERA Linnaeus 1767   [*Gunneraceae*]
    brasiliensis Schindler 1905 = **G. manicata**
    chilensis Lamarck 1789 = **G. tinctoria**
    flavida Colenso 1886
    hamiltonii Kirk 1895
    macrophylla hort. = **G. manicata**
    magellanica Lamarck 1789   CA
NL   **manicata** Lindley ex Andre 1873   PGP-**RD**
    prorepens Hooker f. 1852
N   **tinctoria** (Molina) Mirbel 1805 (*G. chilensis*)   PGP-RD

GYMNADENIA R. Brown 1813   [*Orchidaceae*]
N‡   **conopsea** (Linnaeus) R. Brown 1813   EGF.2

GYMNOCARPIUM Newman 1851   [*Woodsiaceae*]
N   **dryopteris** (Linnaeus) Newman 1851 (*Thelypteris dryopteris*)   EGF.1
    'Plumosum'
N   **robertianum** (Hoffmann) Newman 1851 (*Thelypteris robertianum*)   EGF.1

GYMNOSPERMIUM Spach 1839   [*Berberidaceae*]
    albertii (Regel) Takhtadjan 1970 (*Leontice albertii*)   **BB-SB**

GYNANDRIRIS Palatore 1854   [*Iridaceae*]
    sisyrinchium (Linnaeus) Parlatore 1854 (*I. sisyrinchium*)   **BB-SB**-DGP

GYNERIUM Palisot de Beauvois 1812   [*Poaceae (Gramineae)*]
    argenteum Nees 1829 = **Cortaderia selloana**

GYPSOPHILA Linnaeus 1753   [*Caryophyllaceae*]
    aretioides Boissier 1843   **CA**-RD
        'Caucasica' ('Compacta')   CA
        'Compacta' = **G. aretioides 'Caucasica'**
    briquetiana Schischkin 1928
    cerastioides D. Don 1825
        'Cooper's Variety'
    dubia hort. = **G. repens 'Dubia'**
    x monstrosa Gerbeaux (*G. repens* x *G. stevenii*)
    pacifica Komarov 1916
N   **paniculata** Linnaeus 1753   PGP-DGP-**RD**
L   **'Bristol Fairy'**   [Cuming 1928]   PGP-**DGP**-RD
        'Compacta Plena'   PGP-RD
        'Fairy Perfect'   [Maas & Van Stein 1950]
        'Flamingo'   [Kayser & Siebert 1938]   PGP
        'Hanikra'
        'Perfecta'
        'Pink Star'   PGP-DGP-RD
        'Plena'   [Ridel 1903]
        'Romano'
        'Rosy Veil' = **G. 'Rosenschleier'**
        'Schneeflocke' ('Snowflake')
        'Snowflake' = **G. paniculata 'Schneeflocke'**
        'Snow White'
        'Virgo'
    petraea (Baumgarten) Reichenbach 1832 (*G. transsylvanica*)
    repens Linnaeus 1753   **DGP**
        'Alba'
        'Dorothy Teacher'
        'Dubia'
        'Fratensis'   **RD**
        'Letchworth'
        'Monstrosa' = **G. x monstrosa**
        'Pink Beauty' = **G. repens 'Rosa Schönheit'**
        'Rosa Schönheit' ('Pink Beauty')
        'Rosea'
        'Rose Fountain'
    'Rosenschleier' (*G. paniculata* x *G. repens* 'Rosea')   [K. Foerster 1933]
        PGP-**DGP**-RD
    tenuifolia Marshall von Bieberstein 1808
        'Rosea'
    transsylvanica Sprengel 1827 = **G. petraea**

HAASTIA Hooker f. 1864   [*Asteraceae (Compositae)*]
S   **sinclairii** Hooker f. 1864

HABENARIA Willdenow 1805   [*Orchidaceae*]
    radiata (Thunberg) Sprengel 1826 (*Pecteilis radiata*)   EGF.2
        'Ginga'

HABERLEA Frivaldsky 1835   [*Gesneriaceae*]
    ferdinandi-coburgi Urumov 1902   CA-DGP-RD
    rhodopensis Frivaldsky 1835   **CA-DGP-RD**
        'Virginalis'   CA-DGP

HABRANTHUS Herbert 1824   [*Amaryllidaceae*]
    andersonii Herbert 1830 = **H. tubispathus**
    brachyandrus (Baker) Sealy 1894   EGF.1-**BB**-SB

phycelloides Herbert 1831 (*Hippeastrum phycelloides*)
  'Cherry Blossom'
robustus Herbert ex Sweet 1831   EGF.1-**BB**
texanus (Herbert) Herbert ex Steudel 1840   EGF.1-**BB**
tubispathus (L'Heritier) Traub 1951   EGF.1-**BB**-SB

HACQUETIA Necker 1790   [*Apiaceae (Umbelliferae)*]
  epipactis (Scopoli) de Candolle 1830   DGP-RD

HAEMANTHUS Linnaeus 1753   [*Amaryllidaceae*]
  albiflos Jacquin 1797   EGF.1-RD
  coccineus Forsskal 1775 non Linnaeus = **Scadoxus multiflorus**
  kalbreyeri Baker 1878 = **Scadoxus multiflorus**
  multiflorus Martyn 1795 = **Scadoxus multiflorus**

HAKONECHLOA Makino ex Honda 1930   [*Poaceae (Gramineae)*]
  macra Makino ex Honda 1930   EGF.2-PGP
L   **'Albo-aurea'** Makino 1940   PGP
      'Albo-variegata' Makino 1940   PGP
      'Aureola' Makino ex Honda 1930   PGP

HAPLOCARPHA Lessing 1831   [*Asteraceae (Compositae)*]
  nervosa (Thunberg) Beauverd 1915
  rueppellii (Schultes-Bip) Beauverd 1915

HAPLOPAPPUS Cassini 1818 nom. cons.   [*Asteraceae (Compositae)*]
  brandegei A. Gray 1884 (*Erigeron aureus*)   CA-DGP-RD
  coronopifolius de Candolle 1836 = **H. glutinosus**
  croceus A. Gray 1864
  glutinosus Cassini ex de Candolle 1830 (*H. coronopifolius*)
  lyallii A. Gray 1864
  reideri hort. = ?

HEDYCHIUM J. Koenig 1783   [*Zingiberaceae*]
  densiflorum Wallich 1853   EGF.2-**PGP**
  gardnerianum Sheppard ex Ker-Gawler 1824   PGP-**RD**

HEDYSARUM Linnaeus 1753   [*Fabaceae (Leguminosae)*]
B **coronarium** Linnaeus 1753   PGP-**RD**

HELENIUM Linnaeus 1753   [*Asteraceae (Compositae)*]
NL **autumnale** Linnaeus 1753 (*H. grandiflorum*)   PGP-DGP-RD
  bigelovii A. Gray 1857   PGP
      'The Bishop' ('Superba')   [Lubbe & Zoon 1937]   PGP
      'Superba' = **H. bigelovii 'The Bishop'**
  grandiflorum Nuttall 1841 = **H. autumnale**
  hoopesii A. Gray 1864   PGP
  pumilum Schlechtendal 1814
      'Magnificum'   RD

HYBRID CULTIVARS

      'Baudirektor Linne'   [G. Deutschmann/Hahn]   RD
      'Blütentisch'   [K. Foerster]
      'Bressingham Gold'   [A. Bloom]   PGP-RD
      'Bruno'   [A. Bloom]   PGP-RD
L   **'Butterpat'**   [A. Bloom]   PGP-**DGP**-RD
      'Chanctonbury'
      'Chipperfield Orange'
      'Coppelia'   [A. Bloom]   PGP-**DGP**-RD

	'Copper Spray'	
L	'Crimson Beauty'	PGP
	'Gartensonne'	
	'Feuersiegal' [K. Foerster]	
	'Flammenrad' [K. Foerster 1951]	
	'Goldene Jugend' ('Golden Youth') [Junge 1924]	RD
	'Golden Youth' = **H. 'Goldene Jugend'**	
	'Gold Fox'	
	'Goldlackzwerg' [K. Foerster]	
	'Goldrausch' [K. Foerster 1942]	
	'Indianerbraut'	
	'Julisamt' [K. Foerster]	
	'Kanaria' [K. Foerster 1949]	
	'Karneol'	
	'Königstiger' [K. Foerster 1964]	
	'Kupfersprudel' [K. Foerster 1940]	
	'Kupferzwerg' [Hage u. Schmidt]	
	'Madame Canivet'	
	'Mahogony'	RD
	'Margot' [K. Marx 1976]	
L	'Moerheim Beauty' [Ruys 1930]	PGP-**DGP**-RD
	'Riverton Beauty' [Prichard]	PGP
	'Riverton Gem' [Prichard]	PGP
	'Septemberfuchs'	
	'Septembergold' [Bornimer Staudenculturen 1975]	
	'Sonnenwunder' [K. Foerster]	
	'Spätrot'	PGP
	'Sunshine'	
	'Tawny Dwarf'	
	'Waldhorn'	
	'Waldtraut' [G. Deutschmann 1947]	
	'Wonadonga' [K. Foerster]	
L	'Wyndley'	PGP-**DGP**-RD
	'Zimbelstern' [K. Foerster 1956]	

HELIANTHELLA Torrey & A. Gray 1841   [*Asteraceae (Compositae)*]
quinquenervis (Hooker) A. Gray 1883 (*Helianthus quinquenervis*)

HELIANTHEMUM Miller 1754   [*Cistaceae*]
alpestre (Jacquin) de Candolle 1815 = **H. oelandicum** ssp. **alpestre**
  'Serpyllifolium' = **H. nummularium** ssp. **glabrum**
SN‡ apenninum (Linnaeus) Miller 1768 (*H. polifolium*)
  'Roseum'
SN‡ canum (Linnaeus) Baumgarten 1816
chamaecistus Miller 1768 = **H. nummularium**
globularifolium Persoon 1806 = **Tuberaria globularifolia**
italicum (Linnaeus) Persson 1806 = **H. oelandicum** ssp. **italicum**
A ledifolium (Linnaeus) Miller 1768 (*H. pilosum*)
S lunulatum (Allioni) de Candolle 1805   RD
S morisianum Bertoloni 1844
SN‡ nummularium (Linnaeus) Miller 1768 (*G. chamaecistus*)   DGP-**RD**
  'Amy Baring'
  ssp. **glabrum** (Koch) Wilczek 1922 (*H. alpestre* 'Serpyllifolium')   RD
  ssp. **grandiflorum** (Scopoli) Schinz & Thellung 1914
  ssp. **grandiflorum** 'Variegatum'
  ssp. **tomentosum** (Scopoli) Schinz & Thellung 1914
S oelandicum (Linnaeus) de Candolle 1805
  ssp. **alpestre** (Jacquin) Breistroffer 1947 (*H. alpestre*)   RD
  ssp. **italicum** (Linnaeus) Font Quer & Rothmayer 1934
S piliferum Boissier 1838

pilosum (Linnaeus) Persoon 1806 = **H. ledifolium**
polifolium Miller 1768 = **H. apenninum**
*scardicum
tuberaria (Linnaeus) Miller 1768 = **Tuberaria lignosa**

S   HYBRIDS

'Album Simplex'
'Alice Howorth'   [via J. Elliott]
'Amy Baring' = **H. nummularium 'Amy Baring'**
'Amabile Plenum' ('Rubin')
'Annabel'
'Apricot'
'Beech Park Red'
'Beech Park Scarlet'
'Ben Adler
'Ben Afflick'

'Ben Attow'   DGP
'Ben Avon'
'Ben Dearg'
'Ben Fhada'
'Ben Heckla'
'Ben Hope'   RD
'Ben Lawers'   **DGP**
'Ben Ledi'
'Ben Lomond'
'Ben Lui'
'Ben Macdhui'
'Ben More'
'Ben Nevis'   DGP-RD
'Ben Vane'
'Ben Vorlick'
'Bengal Rose'
'Blutströpfchen'
'Boughton Double Primrose'
'Braungold'
'Brilliant'
'Bronzeteppich'
'Broughty Beacon'
'Broughty Sunrise'
'Broughty Sunset'
'Brown Gold'
'Butter and Eggs'
'Butterball'
'Captivation'
'Cerise Queen'
'Cherry Red'
'Cherry Pink'
'Cheviot'
'Chocolate Blotch'
'Coppernob'
'Cupreum'
'Die Braut' = **H. 'The Bride'**
'Double Apricot'
'Double Cream'
'Double Orange'
'Double Pink'
'Double Primrose'
'Dr Phillips'
'Eisbär'

'Etna'
'Everton Flame'
'Everton Ruby'
'Fairy'
'Fire Ball' = **H. 'Mrs C. W. Earle'**
'Fire Brand'
'Fire Dragon' = **H. 'Mrs Clay'**
'Fire King'
'Fire Flame'
'Firefly'
'Fire Patt'
'Flame'
'Frau M Bachthaler'
'Frei'
'Gaiety'   [J. Elliott]
'Gaiety Variegated' = **'Gaiety'**
'Gelbe Perle' = **H. 'Sulphureum Plenum'**
'Gelber Findling'
'Georgeham'
'Glen Turret'
'Gloriosa'
'Golden Queen'
'Goldkitzel'
'Goldkugel'
'Goldtaler'
'Grandiflorum' = **H. nummularium** ssp. **grandiflorum**
'Harlequin'
'Henfield Brilliant'
'Highdown Apricot'
'Highdown Pink'
'Highdown Red'
'Honeymoon'
'Jack Scott'
L   'Jubilee'   RD
'Jubilee Variegated'
'Kathleen Druce'
'Lady Elizabeth'
'Lawrenson's Pink'
'Lemon Queen'
'L. Mette'
'Loxbeare Gold'
'Lucy Elizabeth'
'Luise Reuss'
'Magnificum'
'Mrs Clay' (H. 'Fire Dragon')   **DGP**
'Mrs Croft'
L   'Mrs C. W. Earle' (H. 'Fire Ball')   DGP-RD
'Mrs C. W. Earle Variegated'
'Mrs Jenkinson'
'Mrs Moules'
'Mrs Lake'
'Old Gold'
'Orange Queen'
'Orange Suprise'
'Peggy'
'Pilot'
'Pink Beauty'
'Pink Double'
'Pirol'
'Praecox'

'Prima Donna'
'Professor Mattern'
'Prostratum'
'Raspberry Ripple'
'Red Dragon'
'Red Orient' = **H. 'Supreme'**
'Rhodanthe Carneum' = **H. 'Wisley Pink'**
'Rosa Königin' ('Rose Queen')
'Rose of Leewood'
'Rose Perfection'
'Rose Queen' = **H. 'Rosa Königin'**
'Rostauge'
'Rosie'
'Rotkappchen'
'Rotring'
'Roxburgh Gold'
'Rubin' = **H. 'Amabile Plenum'**
'Rubro Plenum'
'Ruth'
'Salmon'
'Salmon Bee'
'Salmon Queen'
'Schatzalp'
'Shot Silk'
'Single Apricot'
'Snowball'
'Snow Queen' = **H. 'The Bride'**
'Southmead'
'Sterntaler'
'St. John's College Yellow'
'Sudbury Gem'
'Sulphureum'
'Sulphureum Plenum' ('Gelbe Perle', 'Yellow Queen')
'Sunbeam'
'Sunny Boy'
'Supreme' ('Red Orient')
'Tigrinum Plenum'

'The Bride' ('Snow Queen')		DGP-RD
'Venustum Plenum'		
'Voltaire'		
'Watergate Orange'		
'Watergate Rose'		
'Westfield Wonder'		
'Wine Red'		
L 'Wisley Pink' ('Rhodanthe Carneum')		DGP-**RD**
'Wisley Primrose'		RD
'Wisley White'		
'Wisley Yellow'		

'Yellow Queen' = **H. 'Sulphureum Plenum'**

HELIANTHUS Linnaeus 1753		*[Asteraceae (Compositae)]*
atrorubens Linnaeus 1753 (*H. sparsifolius* hort.)		PGP-RD
'Gullick's Variety'		PGP
'Monarch'		PGP-RD
NL decapetalus Linnaeus 1753 (*H. multiflorus* hort.)		PGP-RD
'Capenoch Star' [1938]		PGP-RD
L 'Loddon Gold' [Thos. Carlisle Ltd.]		PGP-RD
'Maximus'		
'Maximus Flore Pleno'		
'Meteor'		

'**Morning Sun**'
'Multiflorus Maximus' = **H. decapetalus 'Maximus Flore Pleno**'
'**Soleil d'Or**'   [Hartland 1889]   PGP-**RD**
'**Summer Sun**'
'**Triomphe de Gand**'   **RD**
'**Triomphe von Gent**'

N   **laetiflorus** Persoon 1807 (*H. rigidus* (Cassini) Desfontaines, *H. scaberrimus*
                                                    Elliot)   PGP
'**Latest of All**'
'**Miss Mellish**'   [1895]   PGP
'**Okterberstern**'
microcephalus Torrey & A. Gray 1842
multiflorus hort. = **H. decapetalus**
orgyalis de Candolle 1836 = **H. salicifolius**
quinquenervis Hooker 1847 = **Helianthella quinquenervis**
rigidus (Cassini) Desfontaines 1829 non Rydberg = **H. laetiflorus**
salicifolius A. Dietrich 1834 (*H. orgyalis*)   PGP-RD
'**Lemon Queen**'
scaberrimus Elliott 1824 non Britton & A. Brown = **H. laetiflorus**
sparsifolius hort. = **H. atrorubens**
HN   **tuberosus** Linnaeus 1753   **RD**

HELICHRYSUM Miller 1754 nom. cons.   [*Asteraceae (Compositae)*]
acuminatum Sweet
album N. E. Brown 1895
alveolatum de Candolle 1837 = **H. splendidum**
angustifolium (Lamarck) de Candolle 1829 = **H. italicum**
arenarium (Linnaeus) Moench 1794
'Nanum' = **H. stoechas 'Nanum**'
argyrophyllum de Candolle 1837
'Mo's Gold' = **H. argyrophyllum**
arwae J. R. I. Wood 1984
S   **bellidioides** (Forster f.) Willdenow 1800   CA-DGP-**RD**
var. **gracile** Allan 1961
'**Major**' nom. dub.
chionophilum Boissier & Balansa 1859
S   **coralloides** (Hooker f.) Bentham & Hooker f. 1873   **CA-RD**
depressum (Hooker f.) Bentham & Hooker f. 1873
filicaule Hooker f. 1853 (*Gnaphalium filicaule*)
B   **foetidum** (Linnaeus) Cassini 1822
S   **fontanesei** Cambessedes 1827
S   **frigidum** (Labillardiere) Willdenow 1803   **CA-DGP**
*gargan
hookerianum Wight & Arnold ex de Candolle 1837
SH   **italicum** (Roth) G. Don f. 1839 (*H. angustifolium*)   CA-**DGP**-RD
Cretan Form = **H. italicum** ssp. **microphyllum**
ssp. **microphyllum** (Willdenow) Nyman 1879 (*H. microphyllum*)
'Nanum' = **H. stoechas 'Nanum**'
ssp. **serotinum** (Boissier) P. Fournier 1940 (*H. serotinum*)
marginatum hort., nonde Candolle = **H. milfordiae**
microphyllum Willdenow non Bentham & Hooker f. = **H. italicum** ssp. **microphyllum**
microphyllum (Hooker f.) Bentham & Hooker f. 1873 non Willdenow
milfordiae Killick 1960 (*H. marginatum* hort.)   CA-DGP-RD
S   **orientale** (Linnaeus) Gaertner 1790   CA-RD
petiolare Hilliard & B. L. Burtt 1973 (*H. petiolatum* hort.)
'**Aureum**' ('Limelight')
'**Dragon Hill Monarch**'
'Limelight' = **H. petiolare 'Aureum**'
'**Skynet**'
'**Variegatum**'

petiolatum hort. = **H. petiolare**
plicatum de Candolle 1838   RD
plicatum hort., non de Candolle 1838 = **H. stoechas** ssp. **barrelieri**
plumeum Allan 1947
praecurrens Hilliard 1973
S   **retortum** (Linnaeus) Willdenow 1807
S   **scutellifolium** Bentham 1867
    'Schwefellicht' (*H.* 'Sulphur Light')   [H. Klose]   CA
    selaginoides F. Mueller ex Bentham 1867   PGP
S   **selago** (Hooker f.) Bentham & Hooker f. 1873   CA-RD
    'Major'
        var. **tumidum** Cheeseman 1925(*H. tumidum* hort.)
    serotinum Boissier 1829 = **H. italicum** ssp. **serotinum**
    sessile de Candolle 1837
    sibthorpii Rouy 1900 (*H. virgineum*)   CA-RD
    siculum (Sprengel) Boissier 1875 = **S. stoechas** ssp. **barrelieri**
S   **splendidum** (Thunberg) Lessing 1832 (*H. aveolatum*)   RD
S   **stoechas** (Linnaeus) Moench 1794
        ssp. **barrelieri** (Tenore) Nyman 1879 (*H. siculum*)
    'Nanum' nom. dub.
    'White Barn' ('Elmstead')   [B. Chatto]
    'Sulphur Light' = **H. 'Schwefellicht'**
    thianschanicum Regel 1879
    'Goldkind'
    tumidum hort. = **H. selago** var. **tumidum**
    virgineum (Smith) Grisebach 1843 non de Candolle 1837 = **H. sibthorpii**
    woodii hort. = **H. arwae**

HELICODICEROS Schott ex K. Koch 1853 nom. cons.   [*Araceae*]
    muscivorus (Linnaeus f.) Engler 1879 = **Dracunculus muscivorus**

HELICTOTRICHON Schultes 1827   [*Poaceae (Gramineae)*]
    montanum (Villars) Henrard 1940 = **H. sedenense**
    sedenense (de Candolle) J. Holub 1970 (*H. montanum*)
L   **sempervirens** (Villars) Besser ex Pilger 1938 (*Avena candida* hort.)   PGP-**DGP**-RD
    'Pendula'
    'Saphirsprudel'   [H. Klose 1982]

HELIOPSIS Persoon 1807 nom. cons.   [*Asteraceae (Compositae)*]
    helianthoides (Linnaeus) Sweet 1827   PGP
    'Ballerina'
    'Benzinggold'
    'Gigantea'   RD
    'Golden Plume' = **H. helianthoides 'Goldgefieder'**
    'Gold Greenheart' = **H. helianthoides 'Goldgrünherz'**
    'Goldranunkel'
L   **'Goldgefieder'** ('Golden Plume')   [K. Foerster]   PGP-**DGP**-RD
    'Goldspitze'   [VEB Bornim]
    'Goldgrünherz' ('Gold Greenheart')   RD
    'Hohlspiegel'   [K. Foerster 1954]
    'Incomparabilis'   [1932]   PGP-RD
    'Jupiter'   [H. Götz]
    'Karat'   [H. Götz]
    'Light of Loddon'   [Thos. Carlisle Ltd.]   PGP-**DGP**
    'Lohfelden'   [H. Klose 1971]
    'Mars'   [H. Götz]
    'Morning Sun'
    'Orion'   [H. Götz]
    'Patula'   PGP
        var. **scabra** (Dunal) Fernald 1942 (*H. scabra*)   PGP-DGP-RD

'**Sommesonne**' ('Summer Sun')   DGP
'**Sonnenglut**'   [H. Klose 1977]
'**Sonnenschild**'   [K. Foerster 1954]
'**Sonnenstrahl**'   [H. Klose 1977]
'**Spitzentänzerin**'   [K. Foerster 1949]
'Summer Sun' = **H. helianthoides 'Sommesonne'**
'**Sunburst**'
'**Venus**'
'**Wüstenkönig**'
scabra Dunal 1819 = **H. helianthoides** var. **scabra**

HELIOSPERMA (Reichenbach) Reichenbach 1841   [*Caryophyllaceae*]
alpestre (Jacquin) Reichenbach 1841 = **Silene alpestris**
pusillum (Waldstein & Kitaibel) Visiani 1852 = **Silene pusilla**

HELIPTERUM de Candolle 1837   [*Asteraceae (Compositae)*]
albicans de Candolle 1837
ssp. **alpinum** (F. Mueller) P. G. Wilson
'**Incanum**'
Yellow Form
anthemoides de Candolle 1837

HELLEBORUS Linnaeus 1753   [*Ranunculaceae*]

M - MATHEW, Brian: *'Hellebores'* Alpine Garden Society Guide 1989 *(in press)*

abschasicus A. Braun 1853 = **H. orientalis** ssp. **abchasicus**
antiquorum A. Braun 1853 = **H. orientalis**
NL   **argutifolius** Viviani 1825 (*H. corsicus, H. lividus* ssp. *corsicus*)   M-PGP-DGP-RD
atrorubens Waldstein & Kitaibel (*H. dumetorum* ssp. *atrorubens*)   M-PGP-RD
atrorubens hort., non Waldstein & Kitaibel = **H orientalis** ssp. **abschasicus**
bocconei Tenore 1822   M
Apennine Form
Calabrian Form
Sicilian Form
caucasicus A. Braun 1853 = **H. orientalis**
corsicus Schlechtendal in Willdenow 1814 = **H. argutifolius**
cyclophyllus Boissier 1867   M-PGP
dumetorum Waldstein & Kitaibel 1809   M-PGP
ssp. *atrorubens* (Waldstein & Kitaibel) Merxmueller & Podlech 1961 =
                              H. atrorubens
HN‡L   **foetidus** Linnaeus 1753   M-PGP-RD
Italian Form
Miss Jekyll's Scented Form
'**Wester Flisk**'   M
guttatus A. Braun & Sauer 1853 = **H. orientalis** ssp. **guttatus**
kochii Schiffner 1889 = **H. orientalis**
N   **lividus** Aiton 1789   M-PGP
ssp. *corsicus* (Willdenow) Tutin 1964 = **H. argutifolius**
multifidus Visiani 1829   M-PGP
ssp. *serbicus* (Adamovic) Merxmueller & Podlech 1961 = **H. torquatus**
HL   **niger** Linnaeus 1753   M-PGP-DGP-RD
'**Allerseelen**'
'**Altifolius**'   M-DGP
'**Grandiflorus**'   M
'**Ladhams' Variety**'   [E. Ladham]   M-PGP
'**Louis Cobbett**'   [L. Cobbett pre-1962]   M-PGP
ssp. **macranthus** (Freyn) Schiffner 1889   M-PGP
'**Madame Fourcade**'

Madame Fourcade Hybrids
Potter's Wheel Hybrids   [H. Davenport-Jones]   M-PGP-**DGP**-RD
'Praecox'   M
'St Brigid'   [Lawrenson via Burbidge and T. Smith c1850]   M-PGP
'Trotter's Form'   [R. Trotter c1970]
'Van Keesen'   M

x nigercors J. T. Wall 1934 (*H. niger* x *H. argutifolius*)
'Alabaster'   [Washfield Nursery 1971]   M-PGP
'Beatrix'   [E. B. Anderson 1967]   M-PGP
olympicus Lindley 1841 = **H. orientalis**   PGP

L   **orientalis** Lamarck 1789 (*H. antiquorum, H. caucasicus, H. kochii, H. olympicus*)
     M-PGP-**DGP**-RD
L   ssp. **abchasicus** (A. Braun) Mathew in press (*H. abchasicus*)   M-PGP-RD
        ssp. **guttatus** (A. Braun & Sauer) Mathew in press (*H. guttatus*)   M-PGP

H. ORIENTALIS GROUP HYBRIDS

'Agnes Brook'   [E. Raithby via Court Farm Nurseries 1985]   M
'Aldebaran'   [E. Smith c1970]   M
'Amethyst'   [H. Ballard 1986]   M
Anderson's Red Hybrids   [E. B. Anderson c1950]   M
'Apotheker Bogren'   [H. Heinemann c1880]   M
'Aquarius'   [E. Smith c1970]   M
'Ariel'   [E. Smith c1967]   M
'Aries'   [E. Smith c1970]   M
'Black Knight'   [Pre-1927]   M
'Blowsy'   [H. Ballard 1988]   M
'Blue Spray'   [H. Ballard 1988]   M
'Blue Wisp'   [H. Ballard 1983]   M
'Brünnhilde'   M
'Button'   [H. Ballard 1983]   M
'Capricornus'   [J. C. Archibald 1976]   M
'Carlton Hall'   [E. Raithby via Court Farm Nurseries 1985]   M
'Castor'   [E. Smith c1967]   M
'Cheerful'   [H. Ballard 1988]   M
'Citron'   [H. Ballard 1983]   M
'Cosmos'   [E. Smith c1973]   M
'Darley Mill'   [E. Raithby via Court Farm Nurseries 1985]   M
'Dawn'   [H. Ballard 1988]   M
'Dick Crandon'   [H. Ballard 1985]   M
'Dotty'   [H. Ballard 1986]   M
'Dusk'   [H. Ballard 1985]   M
'Elizabeth Coburn'   [E. Raithby via Court Farm Nurseries 1985]   M
'Ernest Raithby'   [E. Raithby via Court Farm Nurseries 1985]   M
'Fred Whitsey'   [E. Raithby via Court Farm Nurseries 1985]   M
'Frülingfreude'   [H. Klose 1978]   M
'Garnet'   [H. Ballard 1988]   M
'Gemini'   [J.C. Archibald 1976]   M
'Gertrude Raithby'   [E. Raithby via Court Farm Nurseries 1985]   M
'Greencups'   [H. Ballard 1985]   M
'Hades'   [H. Ballard 1988]   M
'Hazy Dawn'   M
Heartsease Hybrids   [A. Bloom]   M
'Hecate'   [H. Ballard 1985]   M
'Helen Ballard'   [H. Ballard 1987]   M
'Hercules'   [E. Smith c1970]   M
Highbury Hybrids   [S. Cherry]   M
'Hyades'   [E. Smith c1970]   M
'Ian Raithby'   [E. Raithby via Court Farm Nurseries 1985]   M

      '**Indigo**'   [H. Ballard 1983]   M
      '**Ingot**'   [H. Ballard 1983]   M
      '**John Cross**'   [E. Raithby via Court Farm Nurseries 1985]   M
      '**John Raithby**'   [E. Raithby via Court Farm Nurseries 1985]   M
      '**Lady Bonham Carter**'   [E. Raithby via Court Farm Nurseries 1985]   M
      '**Leo**'   [E. Smith c1974]   M
      '**Libra**'   [J. C. Archibald c1976]   M
      '**Longstock**'   [Longstock Park Gardens]   M
      '**Lynne**'   [H. Ballard 1988]   M
      '**Mary Petit**'   [E. Raithby via Court Farm Nurseries 1985]   M
      '**Mercury**'   [E. Smith pre-1964]   M
      '**Miranda**'   [E. Smith c1960]   M
      '**Nancy Ballard**'   [H. Ballard 1987]   M
      '**Nocturne**'   [H. Ballard 1988]   M
      '**Oberon**'   [E. Smith c1975]   M
      '**Orion**'   [J. C. Archibald 1978]   **M**
      '**Parrot**'   [H. Ballard 1987]   M
      '**Patchwork**'   [H. Ballard 1988]   M
      '**Pebworth White**'   [E. Raithby via Court Farm Nurseries 1985]   M
      '**Peggy Ballard**'   [H. Ballard 1987]   M
      '**Petsamo**'   M
      '**Philip Ballard**'   [H. Ballard 1987]   M
      '**Philip Wilson**'   [H. Ballard 1987]   M
      '**Pluto**'   [E. Smith c1960]   M-PGP
      '**Polaris**'   [E. Smith c1970]   M
      '**Pollux**'   [E. Smith c1967]   M
      '**Prince Rupert**'
      '**Rembrandt**'   [H. Ballard 1988]   M
      '**Rosa**'   [H. Ballard 1988]   M
      '**Rossini**'   [H. Ballard 1988]   M
      '**Rubens**'   [H. Ballard 1987]   M
      '**Sarah Ballard**'   [H. Ballard 1987]   M
      '**Scorpio**'   [E. Smith 1970]   M
      '**Sirius**'   [E. Smith pre-1964]   M
      '**Sunny**'   [H. Ballard 1988]   M
      '**Sylvia**'   [H. Ballard 1987]   M
      '**Taurus**'   [E. Smith c1972]   M
      '**Titania**'   [J. C. Archibald c1980]   M
      '**Trotter's Spotted**'   [R. Trotter c1960]   M
      '**Upstart**'   [H. Ballard 1987]   M
      '**Ushba**'   [H. Ballard 1987]   M
      '**Victoria Raithby**'   [E. Raithby via Court Farm Nurseries 1985]   M
      Winter Cheer Hybrids   [A. Bloom c1970]   M
      '**Yellow Button**'   [H. Ballard 1987]   M
  purpurascens Waldstein & Kitaibel 1802   **M-PGP-RD**
  serbicus Adamovic 1906 = **H. torquatus**
  x sternii Turrill 1937 (*H. argutifolius* x *H. lividus*)   M-PGP
      Blackthorn Hybrids   [A. R. White 1987]   M
      '**Boughton Beauty**'   [V. Finnis]   **M**
      Boughton Hybrids   [V. Finnis]
      Valerie Finnis Hybrids = **H. x sternii Boughton Hybrids**
  torquatus Archer-Hind 1884 (*H. serbicus, H. multifidus* ssp. *serbicus*)   **M**
N‡ **viridis** Linnaeus 1753   **M-PGP-RD**
    ssp. **occidentalis** (Reuter) Schiffner 1896   **M-PGP**

HELONIOPSIS A. Gray 1858   [*Melanthiaceae (Liliaceae)*]
  orientalis (Thunberg) T. Taneka 1925   EGF.1
    var. **breviscapa** (Maximowicz) Ohwi   EGF.1

HELXINE Requien 1825   [*Urticaceae*]
   soleirolii Requien 1825 = **Soleirolia solierolii**

HEMEROCALLIS Linnaeus 1753   [*Hemerocallidaceae (Liliaceae)*]

M - STOUT, A. B.: *'Daylilies'* 1934 Reprint: Sagapress Inc., 1986

aurantiaca Baker 1890		EGF.1-M-PGP
citrina Baroni 1897		EGF.1-M-PGP-DGP-RD
'Baroni' = **H. 'Baroni'**		
dumortieri Morren 1834		EGF.1-M-PGP
exaltata Stout 1934		M-PGP
exilis Satake 1936		
flava Linnaeus 1762 = **H. lilio-asphodelus**		
forrestii Diels 1912		EGF.1-M-PGP
'Perry's Variety' = **H. 'Perry's Variety'**		

N   **fulva** (Linnaeus) Linnaeus 1762   EGF.1-MPGP-RD
   fulva hort. non Linnaeus 1762 = **H. fulva 'Europa'**

L   **'Europa'**(*H. fulva* hort.)   M-PGP
      'Fisher Variegated' ® [Fisher 1948] = **H. fulva 'Kwanso Variegata'**
      'Green Kwanso' ® [Stout 1917]   M
      'Kwanso' = **H. fulva 'Kwanso Variegata'**
      'Kwanso Flore Pleno' = **H. fulva 'Flore Pleno'**
      'Kwanso Variegata'   EGF.1-M-PGP
      'Flore Pleno'   M-PGP
      var. **littorea** (Makino) ! (*H. littorea*)   PGP
      var. **longituba** Maximowicz 1835   EGF.1-M
      f. **maculata**   M-PGP
      'Rosea'   EGF.1-M-PGP

NL   **lilio-asphodelus** Linnaeus 1753 (*H. flava*)   EGF.1-M-**PGP**
   littorea Makino 1929 = **H. fulva** var. **littorea**
   middendorfii Trautvetter & Meyer 1856
   minor Miller 1768   EGF.1-M-PGP
   multiflora Stout 1929   EGF.1-M-PGP
      'Isis' = **H. 'Isis'**   EGF.1-M-PGP
   nana W. W. Smith & Forrest 1917   EGF.1-M-PGP
   serotina Focke 1889 = **H. thunbergii**
   thunbergii Baker 1890 (*H. serotina, H. vespertina*)   EGF.1-M-RD
   vespertina Hara 1941 = **H. thunbergii**

L   HYBRID CULTIVARS

      'Adah' ® [Harris-Petree 1977]
      'Admiral' ® [Hall 1955]
      'Adoration' ® [Claar-Parry 1959]
      'A La Mode' ® [Mederer 1960]
      'Alan' ® [Claar 1953]
      'Alison' ® [Peck 1968]   PGP-RD
      'Amazon Amethyst' ® [Wild 1966]
      'Ambassador' ® [Smith 1951]
      'Amber Star'
      'Angel Face' ® [Terry 1956]
      'Angels Flight' ® [Hall 1969]
      'Anosia'   [Perry]
      'Anzac' ® [Parry 1968]
      'Apollo' ® [Emigholz 1946]
      'Appasionata' ® [Lambert 1970]
      'Apricot' ® [Yeld 1913]   M

'Apricot Dawn'   ®   [Rudolph 1973]
'Ariadne'   ®   [Emigholz 1949]
'Aten'   ®   [Kraus 1951]
'Atlas'   ®   [Kraus 1951]
'Atomic Age'   ®   [Claar 1960]
'August Pink'   ®   [Kraus 1954]
'Autumn Princess'
'Ava Michelle'   ®   [Flory 1960]
'Azor'   ®   [Claar 1963]
'Baby Girl'   ®   [Christian-Stateler 1976]
'Bajamar'   ®   [Peck 1977]
'Ballerina'   ®   [Saxton 1948]
'Ballet Dancer'   ®   [Nesmith 1946]
'Bambi Doll'   ®   [Wild 1965]
'Banbury Canary'   ®   [Brummitt 1962]   **DGP**
'Banbury Cinnamon'   ®   [Brummitt 1965]
'Banbury Contrast'   ®   [Brummitt 1964]
'Baroni'   ®   [Sprenger 1903]   EGF.1-M-**DGP**
'Bed of Roses'   ®   [Wynne 1963]
'Bess Vestal'   ®   [House-Schreiner 1949]
'Bejewelled'   ®   [Childs 1970]
'Bel'   ®   [Wynne 1964]
'Belconto'   ®   [Fischer 1965]
'Belinda'   ®   [Hardy 1956]
'Bella Manelis'   ®   [Winniford 1974]
'Bellringer'   ®   [Lester 1960]
'Beloved Returns'   ®   [Wild 1969]
'Bertie Ferris'   ®   [Winniford 1969]
'Bess Vestal'   ®   [House 1949]
'Beth Standard'   ®   [Standard 1968]
'Bibury'   ®   [Randall 1969]
'Big World'   ®   [Hall 1960]
'Bitsy'   ®   [Warner 1963]
'Black Falcon'   ®   [Nesmith 1941]
'Black Magic'   ®   [Douglas 1949]
'Black Prince'   ®   [Russell 1942]
'Blaze of Fire'   ®   [Wild 1966]
'Blue Nile'   ®   [Hite 1981]
'Blütenfülle'
'Blithe Spirit'   ®   [Fischer 1955]
'Bold Courtier'   ®   [Nesmith 1939]
'Bold Ruler'   ®   [Hall 1958]
'Bonanza'   ®   [Ferrick 1954]   RD
'Bonheur'   ®   [Lambert 1966]
'Bourbon Kings'   ®   [Wild 1968]
'Bourbon Prince'   ®   [Buttrich 1969]
'Brass Buckles'   ®   [Kennedy 1972] (H. 'Puddin')
'Bright Banner'   ®   [Hall 1957]
'Bright Charm'   ®   [Douglas 1954]
'Bright Spangles'   ®   [Baker 1956]
'Brilliant Red'   ®   [Claar 1963]
'Broad Ripples'   ®   [Lake 1960]
'Brunette'   ®   [Stout 1941]
'Bruno Muller'   ®   [Coe 1974]
'Buccaneer'   ®   [Russell 1943]
'Buffy's Doll'   ®   [Williamson 1969]
'Buried Treasure'   ®   [Moldovan 1961]
'Burlesque'   ®   [Lambert 1963]
'Burning Daylight'   ®   [Fischer 1957]
'Button Box'   ®   [Irish 1975]

'Buzz Bomb' ®   [Hall 1961]
'By Jove' ®   [Wild 1968]
'By Myself' ®   [Peck 1971]
'Cadence' ®   [Fay-Hardy 1960]
'Caerphilly' ®   [Lambert 1973]
'Canary Bird' ®   [Lord 1938]
'Canary Glow' ®   [Benzinger 1968]
'Candle Glow' ®   [Nesmith 1952]
'Candy Fluff' ®   [Hall 1965]
'Capri' ®   [Milliken 1952]
'Carey Quinn' ®   [Hall 1960]
'Carriage Trade' ®   [Lambert 1965]
'Carrot Curls' ®   [Mannoni 1961]
'Carrot Top' ®   [Lambert 1969]
'Cartwheels' ®   [Fay 1956]   PGP-**RD**
'Catherine Woodberry' ®   [Childs 1967]
'Chantilly Lace' ®   [Childs 1963]
'Charlemagne' ®   [Moldovan 1966]
'Charlotte Holman' ®   [Childs 1964]
'Chartreuse Cream' ®   [Gersclorff 1949]
'Chartreuse Magic' ®   [Wild 1963]
'Chartreuse Queen' ®   [Wild 1965]
'Cherry Cheeks' ®   [Peck 1968]
'Cherry Point' ®   [Lambert 1973]
'Chetco' ®   [Kraus 1977]
'Chicago Royal Robe' ®   [Marsh 1977]
'Chic Bonnet'
'Chief Sarcoxie' ®   [Wild 1964]
'Childscraft' ®   [Childs 1965]
'Chinese Coral' ®   [Smith 1957]
'Chivalry' ®   [Hall 1948]
'Chloe's Child' ®   [Nesmith 1951]
'Chosen Love' ®   [Maxwell 1970]
'Christmas Candles' ®   [Hall 1966]
'Clarence Simon' ®   [McMillan 1966]
'Claret Cup' ®   [Buttrick 1960]
'Classic Simplicity' ®   [Wild 1965]
'Cologne Cake'   [Stobberg]
'Cologne Cathedral'   [Stobberg]
'Cologne Fascination'   [Stobberg]
'Cologne Mystery'   [Stobberg]
'Colonel Joe' ®   [Lester 1951]
'Colonial Dame' ®   [Milliken 1948]
'Comet' ®   [Russell 1943]
'Conspicua' ®   [Perry 1946]
'Constitutional Island' ®   [Wild 1970]
'Contessa' ®   [Fischer 1955]
'Coquinna' ®   [Claar-Parry 1965]
'Corky' ®   [Fischer 1959]   PGP
'Creamade' ®   [Coe 1968]
'Crestwood Lucy' ®   [Fay-Griesbach 1963]
'Crimson Glory' ®   [Carpenter 1950]
'Crimson Pirate' ®   [Sass 1951]
'Croesus' ®   [Grull 1951]
'Cuddlesome' ®   [Fass 1957]
'Curls' ®   [Kraus 1958]
'Dainty' ®   [Betscher 1937]
'Dainty'   [Sutton 1956]
'Daily Bread' ®   [Hager 1973]
'Danish Duchess' ®   [Hall 1958]

'Dauntless' ®   [Stout 1935]
'Dawn Play' ®   [Nesmith 1938]
'Dawn Supreme' ®   [Rudolph 1961]
'Dearly Beloved' ®   [Lambert 1969]
'Delft Rose' ®   [Fischer 1963]
'Delicate Splendor' ®   [Hall 1958]
'Demure' ®   [Lester 1963]
'Deva'
'Devon Cream' ®   [Nesmith 1945]
'Diamond Dust' ®   [Fischer 1957]
'Dido' ®   [Grull 1950]
'Display' ®   [Hall 1948]
'Dorothy Bullard'
'Dorothy Lambert' ®   [Lambert 1966]
'Dorothy McDade' ®   [Sass 1941]   PGP
'Double Encore' ®   [McEwen 1974]
'Double Pleasure' ®   [Krauss 1957]
'Doubloon' ®   [Nesmith 1945] (H. 'Golden Orchid')   PGP-DGP-RD
'Down Town' ®   [Wild 1966]
'Dresden Gleam' ®   [Lester 1959]
'Earlianna' ®   [Betscher 1938]
'Eden' ®   [Claar-Parry 1964]
'Eden Phillips'
'Edna Spalding' ®   [Spalding 1962]
'Ella Gee' ®   [Holman 1975]
'Ella Thomas Riggins' ®   [Cunningham 1972]
'Elsie Kearny' ®   [Lambert 1967]
'Erin Prairie' ®   [Fay 1971]
'Esther Murray' ®   [Buttrick 1959]
'Esther Walker'   [Kelway]
'Europa' = **H. fulva 'Europa'**
'Eva Sandford' ®   [Perry 1949]
'Evelyn Claar' ®   [Kraus 1949]
'Evening Bell' ®   [Peck 1971]
'Exalted Ruler' ®   [Hall 1962]
'Fairy Jewels' ®   [Nesmith 1947]
'Fairy Wings' ®   [Lester 1953]
'Fandango' ®   [Smith 1951]
'Fantasia' ®   [Stout 1946]
'Far Afield' ®   [Butterick 1959]
'Far East' ®   [Fay 1961]
'Fashion Model' ®   [Lester 1960]
'Felicity' ®   [Nesmith 1947]
'Festivity' ®   [Wheeler 1956]
'Finlandia' ®   [Claar-Parry 1959]
'Fire Dance' ®   [Smith 1951]
'First Formal' ®   [Moldovan 1960]
'First Romance' ®   [Lester 1960]
'Fisher Variegated' = **H. fulva 'Kwanso Variegata'**
'Flair' ®   [Fischer 1960]
'Flaming Sunset' ®   [Claar-Parry 1965]
'Floye Cope' ®   [Lacy 1973]
'Folklore' ®   [Wild 1966]
'Fond Caress' ®   [Milliken 1952]
'Fortyniner' ®   [Ferrick 1951]
'Frances Bland' ®   [Lambert 1968]
'Frances Fay' ®   [Fay 1957]
'Frans Hals' ®   [Flory 1955]
'Fraulein' ®   [Schlumph 1967]
'Frau Lina'   [Köhlein]

'Friar Tuck'   ®   [Lester 1951]
'Full Reward'   ®   [McVicker-Murphy 1957]
'Garden Portrait'
'Gay Garland'
'Gay Music'   ®   [Childs 1965]   PGP
'Gay Nineties'   ®   [Nesmith 1957]
'Gay Rapture'   ®   [Claar-Parry 1965]
'Gay Troubadour'   ®   [Nesmith 1941]
'George Cunningham'   ®   [Hall 1957]
'Georgia Peach'   ®   [Childs 1960]   RD
'Giant Moon'   ®   [Kraus 1956]
'Gideon'   ®   [Moldovan 1974]
'Giraffe'
'Glowing Dewdrop'
'Glowing Gold'   ®   [Nesmith 1940]
'Glowing Lights'   ®   [Hall 1963]   DGP
'Glow Worm'   ®   [Davis 1958]
'Gold Ball'   ®   [Mueller 1907]
'Gold Dust'   ®   [Yeld pre-1906]   M
'Gold Imperial'   ®   [Perry 1925]   M
'Golden Ball' = H. 'Gold Ball'   M
'Golden Bell'   ®   [Wallace & Co 1915]
'Golden Casket'   M
'Golden Chance'   ®   [Wild 1970]
'Golden Chimes'   ®   [Fischer 1954]
'Golden Dewdrop'   ®   [Taylor 1955]   PGP
'Golden Galeon'   ®   [Milliken 1954]
'Golden Gate'   ®   [Christenson 1949]
'Golden Geisha'   ®   [Munson 1967]
'Golden Glory'   ®   [Perry 1946]
'Golden Hind'   ®   [Perry 1942]
'Golden Imperial' = H. 'Gold Imperial'
'Golden Orchid' = H. 'Doubloon'
'Golden Prize'   ®   [Peck 1968]
'Golden Showpiece'   ®   [Pittard 1958]
'Goldensong'   ®   [Krauss 1951]
'Golden West'   ®   [Sass 1932]
'Grape Velvet'   ®   [Wild 1960]
'Grecian Gift'   ®   [Spalding 1959]
'Green Kwanso' = H. fulva 'Green Kwanso'
'Green Magic'   ®   [Hall 1955]
'Gusto'   ®   [Hall 1955]
'Gypsy Dazzler'   ®   [Cruse 1976]
'Hallmark'   ®   [Kennell 1954]
'Halolight'   ®   [Nesmith 1954]
'Happy Apple'   ®   [Wild 1976]
'Hassie Garren'   ®   [Lambert 1968]
'Heathcliff'   ®   [Lambert 1968]
'Heirloom Lace'   ®   [Wild 1963]
'Helicon'   ®   [Dennett 1948]
'Helios' = H. 'Helicon'
'Her Majesty'   ®   [Nesmith 1951]
'Hesperus'   ®   [Sass 1940]
'Hidden Dream'   ®   [Moldovan 1973]
'High Glory'   ®   [Claar 1961]
'High Time'   ®   [Claar-Parry 1965]
'High Tor'
'Hippity Hop'   ®   [Fischer 1960]
'Holiday Harvest'   ®   [Hall 1965]
'Holiday Mood'   ®   [Hall 1955]
'Holiday Wreath'   ®   [Wild 1966]

'Honey Redhead'   ®   [Nesmith 1942]
'Hornby Castle'   [Randall]   RD
'Hortensia'   ®   [Branch 1964]
'Hyperion'   ®   [Mead 1924]   M
'Illinois'   ®   [Hall 1955]
'Imperator'   ®   [Perry 1931]   M
'Indian Seranade'   ®   [Claar-Parry 1965]
'Inlaid Gold'   ®   [Fass 1960]
'Invictus'   ®   [Hall 1955]
'Irene Felix'   ®   [Claar-Parry 1965]
'Iron Gate Glacier'   ®   [Sellers 1971]
'Isaac'   ®   [Harris 1973]
'Isis'   ®   [Munson 1972]
'Isis'   ®   [Perry 1936] (H. multiflora 'Isis')   PGP
'Jack Frost'   ®   [Lester 1953]
'Jake Russell'   ®   [Russell 1956]
'Jay'   ®   [Warner 1972]
'Jekyll Lass'   ®   [Yancey 1978]
'Joan Green'
'John Paul Morton'
'Jo-Jo'   ®   [Fischer 1960]
'J S Gayner'   ®   [Yeld 1928]
'July Gold'   ®   [Weld 1971]
'June Royalty'   ®   [Childs 1963]
'Karl Foerster'
'Kelway's Gold'   [Kelway]
'King of Hearts'   ®   [King 1965]
'Kwanso' = H. fulva 'Kwanso Variegata'
'Lady Fair'   ®   [Nesmith 1946]
'Lady Fermoy Hesketh'   ®   [Perry 1924]   M
'Lady Inara Cubiles'   ®   [Hall 1956]
'Lady Laurel'   ®   [Atkins 1978]
'Lady Liz'   ®   [Lachman 1983]
'Lark Song'   ®   [Fay 1952]   PGP
'Late Date'   ®   [Lake 1961]
'Laura Lambert'   ®   [Lambert 1975]
'Laurel Anne'   ®   [Fischer 1960]
'Lavender Bonanza'   ®   [MacMillan 1965]
'Lavender Flight'   ®   [Spalding 1963]
'Lemon Bells'   ®   [Coe 1969]
'Lemon King'   ®   [Betscher 1952]
'Lester Pastel'
'Lexington'   ®   [Claar 1959]
'Lilac Chiffon'   ®   [Lester 1959]
'Lilly Dache'   ®   [Hall 1957]
'Limonero'   ®   [Kraus 1955]
'Limonetta'   [Feldmaier]
'Linda'   ®   [Stout 1936]
'Little Butterfly'   ®   [Hall 1960]
'Little Cherub'   ®   [Claar 1945]
'Little Fellow'   ®   [Tanner 1968]
'Little Grapette'   ®   [Williamson 1970]
'Little Greenie'   [Winniford 1973]
'Little Joy'   ®   [Lewis 1977]
'Little Love'   ®   [Wild 1966]
'Little Tyke'   ®   [Wild 1962]
'Little Wart'   ®   [Spalding 1964]
'Little Wine Cup'   ®   [Carter 1969]
'Lively Set'   ®   [Wild 1965]
'Lochinvar'   ®   [Taylor 1947]

'Lotus Land'   ®   [Nesmith 1955]
'Louise Talley'   ®   [Lambert 1968]
'Lucretius'   ®   [Traub 1959]
'Lula Mae Purnell'   ®   [Kraus-Schilling 1961]
'Lunar Frills'   ®   [Himottu 1971]
'Luxury Lace'   ®   [Spalding 1959]
'Lynn Hall'   ®   [Hall 1957]
'Mabel Fuller'   ®   [Kraus 1949]
'Magic Dawn'   ®   [Hall 1955]
'Mai Königen' = H. 'Queen of May'
'Mantra'
'Marcus' = H. 'Marcus Perry'
'Marcus Perry'   ®   [Perry 1932]   M
'Margaret Perry'   ®   [Perry 1925]   M
'Marion Vaughn'   ®   [Smith 1951]   PGP-DGP
'Mary Anne'   ®   [Hall 1957]
'Mary Guenther'   ®   [Russell 1942]
'Mary Randall'   ®   [Perry 1958]
'Mary Rippengale'
'Mary Todd'   ®   [Fay 1967]
'Mascot'   ®   [Childs 1962]
'Maurine'   ®   [Murphy 1963]
'Mavoureen Nesmith'   ®   [Nesmith 1953]
'McPick'   ®   [Lexington 1957]
'Meadow Gold'   ®   [Hall 1948]
'Melody Lane'   ®   [Hall 1955]
'Melon Balls'   ®   [Wild 1960]
'Melotone'   ®   [Sass 1954]
'Mighty Mogul'   ®   [Moldovan 1973]
'Mildred Hobbs'   ®   [Coe 1974]
'Mildred Kelley'   ®   [Lambert 1968]
'Mikado'   ®   [Stout 1929]   M
'Missouri Beauty'   ®   [Wild 1965]
'Miss Violetta'
'Misty'   ®   [Hall 1962]
'Modesty'   ®   [Betscher 1929]   M
'Momento'   ®   [Way 1943]
'Moment of Truth'   ®   [McMillan 1969]
'Morocco Red'   ®   [Nesmith 1940]
'Mount Joy'   ®   [Nesmith 1952]
'Mrs B F Bonner'   ®   [Russell 1942]
'Mrs David Hall'   ®   [Kraus 1948]
'Mrs Hugh Johnson'   ®   [Russell 1942]
'Mrs John J Tigert'   ®   [Watkins 1939]
'Mrs Lester'
'Multiflora Isis' = H. 'Isis'
'Multnomah'   ®   [Kraus 1954]
'Music Man'   ®   [Wild 1971]
'My Belle'   ®   [Durio 1973]
'Nashville'   ®   [Claar 1952]
'Nehoiden'   ®   [Merry 1950]
'Neyron Rose'   ®   [Kraus 1950]
'Netsuke'   ®   [Moldovan 1973]
'Night Hawk'   ®   [Fay 1954]
'Nigrette'   ®   [Grullemans 1950]
'Nob Hill'   ®   [Hall 1962]
'Northbrook Star'   ®   [Fay 1968]
'Northfield Orange'
'Norton Orange'   ®   [Coe 1971]
'North Star'   ®   [Hall 1948]

'Nouvelle'
'Old Vintage' ® [Russell 1942]
'Ophir' ® [Farr 1924]   M
'Orange Beauty' ® [Sass 1945]
'Orange Bowl' ® [McEwen 1973]
'Orangeman' ® [Yeld pre-1906]   M
'Orangette'
'Ozark Lass' ® [Stahl 1959]
'Painted Lady' ® [Russell 1942]
'Pale Rider' ® [Peck 1979]
'Pamela' ® [Kraus 1948]
'Paprika Velvet' ® [Hardy 1969]
'Paradise Beach' ® [Buttrich 1959]
'Paradise Prince' ® [Lewis 1975]
'Pardon Me' ® [Apps 1982]
'Parsifal' [Köhlein]
'Party Partner' ® [Wild 1967]
'Patricia Fay' ® [Fay 1960]
'Paul Boussier'
'Peach Amber'
'Peach Flush'
'Peach Supreme' ® [Corley 1961]
'Perry's Variety' ® [Perry 1946]
'Persian Princess' ® [Nesmith 1938]
'Pewter Chalice' ® [Lambert 1970]
'Pink Charm' ® [Nesmith 1940]
'Pink Charmer' ® [Monette 1976]
'Pink Damask' ® [Stevens 1951]   DGP-RD
'Pink Embers' ® [Wild 1976]
'Pink Lady' ® [Perry 1945]
'Pink Lighting' ® [Hall 1962]
'Pink Maid' [Coe]
'Pink Mist' ® [Russell 1951]
'Pink Perfection' ® [Russell 1951]
'Pink Prelude' ® [Nesmith 1949]   DGP-RD
'Pink Reflection' ® [Childs 1959]
'Pioneer Lady' ® [Lacey 1968]
'Pixie Parasol' ® [Hudson 1975]
'Pizza' ® [Warner 1969]
'Playboy' ® [Wheeler 1954]
'Polar Bear' ® [Fass 1961]
'Polly's Gold' ® [Mayo 1975]
'Pony' ® [Durio 1972]
'Port' ® [Stout 1941]
'Powder Puff' ® [Lester 1951]
'Prairie Blue Eyes' ® [Marsh 1970]
'Prairie Charmer' ® [Marsh 1962]
'Prairie Sunset' ® [Wild 1963]
'Precious' ® [Nesmith 1951]
'Precious Treasure' ® [Nesmith 1951]
'Premier' ® [Hall 1951]
'President Rice' ® [Claar 1953]
'Pretty P' [Coe]
'Preview Party' ® [Pride 1983]
'Prima Donna' ® [Taylor 1946]
'Primrose Mascotte' ® [Grullemans 1950]
'Prophet' ® [Claar 1963]
'Puddin' = H. 'Brass Buckles'
'Purity' ® [Traub 1949]
'Purple Splendor' ® [Pittard]

'Queen of May' ®   [Van Veen 1906]   M
'Radiant' ®   [Yeld 1931]   M
'Rajah' ®   [Stout 1935]
'Rapport' ®   [Wynne 1968]
'Rare China' ®   [Hall 1968]
'Red Cup' ®   [Douglas 1954]
'Red Knight' ®   [Stout 1949]
'Red Marvel' ®   [Douglas 1950]
'Red Mittens' ®   [Heinemann 1966]
'Red Ochre'
'Red Precious' ®   [Coe 1968]
'Red Perfect' ®   [Coe 1974]
'Red Riches' ®   [Richards-Skeidel 1970]
'Red Torch' ®   [Smith 1951]
'Red Waves' ®   [Schreiner 1968]
'Renee' ®   [Dill 1962]
'Resplendent' ®   [Nesmith 1951]
'Rev Traub' ®   [Traub 1959]
'Revolute' ®   [Sass 1944]
'Rhodora' ®   [Kraus 1951]
'Robert' ®   [Emigholz 1956]
'Romany' ®   [Lord 1938]
'Rose Motif' ®   [Lester 1963]
'Rosetta' ®   [Hall 1960]
'Roseway' ®   [Fischer 1962]
'Royal Command' ®   [Hall 1955]
'Royalty' ®   [Nesmith 1940]
'Royski' ®   [Peck 1977]
'Rozavel' ®   [Lambert 1965]
'Ruffled Apricot' ®   [Baker 1972]
'Ruffled Pinafore' ®   [Milliken 1948]
'Rundblick' ®   [Tamberg 1979]
'Russell Prichard'
'Russia Leather' ®   [Lambert 1970]
'Saladin' ®   [Stevens 1947]
'Salmon Sheen' ®   [Taylor 1950]   PGP
'Sammy Russell' ®   [Russell 1951]
'Sanders Walker' ®   [Wood 1954]
'Satans Torch' ®   [Lambert 1977]
'Satin Glass' ®   [Fay 1960]
'Scotland' ®   [Wild 1966]
'Sea Gold' ®   [Hall 1963]
'Sea Gypsy' ®   [Claar 1965]
'Secret Ways' ®   [Wild 1968]
'Serene Madonna' ®   [Childs 1972]
'Sewanna Belle'
'Shadyside' ®   [Lambert 1969]
'Shell Cameo' ®   [Fischer 1968]
'Sherwood' ®   [Fischer 1957]
'Shooting Star' ®   [Hall 1951]
'Silent Love' ®   [Claar 1964]
'Silent World' ®   [Hall 1964]
'Silver King' ®   [Lake 1959]
'Singalong' ®   [Peck 1968]
'Sirius' ®   [Yeld 1931]
'Sleeping Beauty' ®   [Munson 1959]   M
'Sleigh Ride' ®   [Wild 1966]
'Snappy Rhythm' ®   [Claar 1960]
'Snow Elf' ®   [Bryant 1974]
'Soledad' ®   [Kraus 1951]

'Songster' ®   [Wynne 1956]
'Sophie's Choice' ®   [Lachman 1983]
'Sovereign' ®   [Yeld 1906]   M
'Spanish Gold' ®   [Smith 1951]   PGP
'Spectacular' ®   [Pattison 1956]
'Stafford' ®   [Randall 1959]   PGP-DGP
'Staten Island' ®   [Smith 1952]
'Stella de Oro' ®   [Jablonski 1975]
'Stolen Hours' ®   [Hall 1964]
'Sugar Plum Fairy' ®   [Hall 1961]
'Summer Interlude' ®   [Hall 1955]
'Summer Wine' ®   [Wild 1973]
'Sunday Afternoon' ®   [Fischer 1963]
'Sunny Face' ®   [Trank 1968]
'Suzie Wong' ®   [Kennedy 1962]
'Sweet Georgia Brown' ®   [McMillan 1967]
'Sweet Surprise' ®   [Allgood 1973]
'Sweetheart Supreme' ®   [Sutton 1954]
'Taj Mahal' ®   [Russel 1945]
'Tang' ®   [Lambert-Wynne 1965]
'Tasmania' ®   [Grullemans 1950]
'Tejas' ®   [Russell 1945]
'Telemark' ®   [Wild 1970]
'Telstar' ®   [Richardson 1962]
'Temple Bells' ®   [Hall 1954]
'Theresa Hall' ®   [Hall 1957]
'Three Cheers' ®   [Hall 1951]
'Three Tiers' ®   [Grooms 1971]
'Thumbelina'   [Fischer 1960]
'Tigress' ®   [Maugham 1954]
'Tinker Bell' ®   [Stevens 1954]
'Tiny Pumpkin' ®   [Hudson 1975]
'Tiny Tex' ®   [Hara 1960]
'Tis Midnight' ®   [Russell 1961]
'Todd Monroe' ®   [Sholar 1974]
'Tonkin' ®   [Claar-Hall 1965]
'Torpoint' ®   [Fischer 1963]
'Towhead' ®   [Hall 1955]
'Tralee' ®   [Hoar-Parry 1965]
'Trendy' ®   [Coe 1970]
'Varsity' ®   [Hall 1960]
'Vespers' ®   [Nesmith 1941]
'Vintage Wine' ®   [Munson 1976]
'Virgin's Blush' ®   [Childs 1958]
'Viscountess Byng' ®   [Perry 1931]   M
'Walt Disney' ®   [Wild 1967]
'Wanetta' ®   [Spalding 1963]
'War Clouds' ®   [Russell 1958]
'Waxwing' ®   [Nesmith 1951]
'Whichford'
'Whir of Lace' ®   [Wild 1964]
'White Jade' ®   [Fay 1954]
'Wideyed' ®   [Craig 1954]
'Wild Welcome' ®   [Wild 1965]
'Windsor Castle' ®   [Hall 1966]
'Windsor Tan' ®   [Nesmith 1948]
'Winne The Pooh' ®   [Wild 1964]
'Winning Ways' ®   [Wild 1963]
'Yardley' ®   [Lambert 1969]
'Yellow Beacon' ®   [Childs 1959]

'**Yellow Rain**' ®   [Schlumpf 1950]
'**Zampa**' ®   [Claar 1963]
'**Zara**' ®   [Perry 1936]
'**Zola**' ®   [Norton 1954]
'**Zorba**' ®   [Munson 1969]
'**Zorro**' ®   [Durio 1975]

HEMIPHRAGMA Wallich 1822   *[Scrophulariaceae]*
    heterophyllum Wallich 1822

HEPATICA Miller 1754   *[Ranunculaceae]*
    acutiloba de Candolle 1824
    '**Ada Scott**'
    americana Ker-Gawler 1819
    angulosa de Candolle 1817 = **H. transsilvanica**
    x media (*H. nobilis* x *H. transsilvanica*)
        '**Ballardii**'   [E. Ballard 1938]   **DGP**-RD
N   **nobilis** Garsault 1764 (*Anemone nobilis, H. triloba*)   **DGP**-RD
        '**Alba**'
        '**Caerulea**'
        Marbled Leaf Form
        '**Marmorata**'
        '**Rosea**'
        '**Rosea Plena**'
        '**Rubra**'
        '**Rubra Plena**'
    transsilvanica Fuss 1850 (*Anemone transsylvanica*)   RD
        '**Alba**'
        '**Buis**'
        '**Lilacina**'
        '**Loddon Blue**'
        '**Rosea**'
    triloba Chaix 1786 = **H. nobilis**

HERACLEUM Linnaeus 1753   *[Apiaceae (Umbelliferae)]*
N   **mantegazzianum** Sommier & Levier 1895   PGP-**RD**
    minimum Lamarck 1778
    '**Roseum**'

HERMODACTYLUS Miller 1752   *[Iridaceae]*
N‡   **tuberosus** (Linnaeus) Miller 1752 (*Iris tuberosa*)   EGF.1-**BB-SB-DGP**

HERNIARIA Linnaeus 1753   *[Caryophyllaceae]*
    caucasica Ruprecht 1869
HN‡   **glabra** Linnaeus 1753
N   **hirsuta** Linnaeus 1753
    latifolia Lapeyrouse 1813 (*H. pyrenaica*)
    pyrenaica Gay 1832 = **H. latifolia**

HERPOLIRION Hooker f. 1853   *[Anthericaceae (Liliaceae)]*
    novae-zealandiae Hooker f. 1853   EGF.1

HERTIA Lessing 1831   *[Asteraceae (Compositae)]*
    cheirifolia (Bentham & Hooker f.) Kuntze 1891 = **Othonnopsis cheirifolia**

HESPERALOE Englemann 1871   *[Agavaceae]*
    parviflora (Torrey) Coulter 1894 (*Yucca parviflora*)   EGF.1

HESPERANTHA Ker-Gawler 1805   [*Iridaceae*]
    buhrii L. Bolus 1931   EGF.1
    stanfordiae L. Bolus 1931 = **H. vaginata**
    vaginata (Sweet) Goldblatt 1970 (*H. stanfordiae*)   EGF.1

HESPERIS Linnaeus 1753   [*Brassicaceae (Cruciferae)*]
HN‡L **matronalis** Linnaeus 1753   PGP-**RD**
      'Alba'
      'Alba Plena'

HESPEROCHIRON S. Watson 1871 nom. cons.   [*Hydrophyllaceae*]
    californicus (Bentham) S. Watson 1871
    pumilus (Grisebach) Porter 1872 (*Villarsia pumila*)

HEUCHERA Linnaeus 1753   [*Saxifragaceae*]
    americana Linnaeus 1753 (*H. glauca*)   PGP
L   **'Purpurea'** (*H. rubescens* hort.)   PGP
    x brizoides Hort. ex Lemoine (*H. x sanguinea* hort.)   PGP-DGP-**RD**
      'Apple Blossom'
      'Bressingham Blaze'   [A. Bloom]   PGP-**RD**
      Bressingham Hybrids   [A. Bloom]   **DGP**
      'Carmen'
      'Coral'
      'Coral Bells' = **H. sanguinea**
L   **'Coral Cloud'**   PGP
      'Damask'
      'Feuerregen' = **H. 'Pluie de Feu'**
      'Firebird'
      'Firefly'
      'Freedom'
      'Gloriana'
      'Gracillima'   PGP
      'Greenfinch' = **H. cylindrica 'Greenfinch'**
      'Green Ivory'
      'Huntsman'
      'Hyperion' = **H. cylindrica 'Hyperion'**
      'Ibis'
      'Lady Romney'
      'Leuchtkäfer'
      'Mary Rose'
L   **'Oakington Jewel'**   PGP
L   **'Pearl Drops'**   PGP
      'Pluie de Feu' ('Feuerregen')
      'Pretty Polly'   RD
      'Pruhoniciana'
      'Pruhoniciana Rikard'
      'Rakete'
      'Red Pimpernel'
      'Red Spangles'   PGP-**RD**
      'Rosenrot'
      'Ruberrima'
      'Scintillation'   **DGP**-RD
      'Schneeweissen'
      'Schneewittchen'
      'Shere Variety'   PGP
      'Silberregen'
      'Sparkler'   PGP
      'Sunset'   RD
      'Titania'
      'Taff's Joy'

'Weserlachs'
'Widar'
'William How'
cylindrica Douglas ex Hooker 1833
   'Greenfinch'   [A. Bloom]
   'Hyperion'   PGP
glauca Rafinesque 1828 = **H. americana**   PGP
grossulariifolia Rydberg 1900
micrantha Douglas ex Lindley 1830   PGP
   var. **diversifolia** (Rydberg) Rosendahl, Butters & Lakela 1936
   var. **diversifolia** 'Palace Purple'
pubescens Pursh 1814
   'Alba'
rubescens hort. non Torrey 1852 = **H. americana** 'Purpurea'
sanguinea Engelmann 1848
   'Alba'
   'Atrosanguinea'
   'Grandiflora'
   'Robusta'
   'Rosea'
   'Splendens'
   'Variegata'
sanguinea hort. non Engelmann 1848 = **H. x brizoides**
villosa Michaux 1803   PGP

X HEUCHERELLA Wehrhahn 1930   [*Saxifragaceae*]
L   **alba** (Lemoine) Stearn 1948 (*Heuchera x brizoides* x *Tiarella cordifolia*)
     'Bridget Bloom'   [A. Bloom]
     'Rosalie'   RD
   tiarelloides (Lemoine) Wehrhahn ex Stearn 1948 (*Heuchera x brizoides* x
                              Tiarella cordifolia)
    'Alba' = **H. alba**   RD

HIERACIUM Linnaeus 1753   [*Asteraceae (Compositae)*]
N   **aurantiacum** Linnaeus 1753
     ssp. **carpathicola** Naegeli & Peter 1885 (*H. brunneo-croceum*)   PGP
   bombycinum Boissier & Reuter ex Fries
   brunneo-croceum Pugsley 1921 = **H. aurantiacum** ssp. **carpathicola**
   lanatum (Linnaeus) Villars 1779 (*Andryala lanata*)   PGP
N‡   **maculatum** Smith 1810
   mixtum Froelich 1838
N‡   **pilosella** Linnaeus 1753
     'Kupferteppich' = **H. x rubrum**
     'Niveum' = **H. tardans**
     'Rubrum' = **H. x rubrum**
   praecox Schultz-Bip 1851
   x rubrum Peter 1884 (*H. aurantiacum* x *H. flagellare*)
   tardans Peter 1884 (*H. pilosella* 'Niveum')
   tomentosum Allioni 1785
   villosum Jacquin 1762
   waldsteinii Tausch 1828   PGP-**DGP**
   wilczekii Zahn 1935

HIMANTOGLOSSUM Koch 1837 nom. cons.   [*Orchidaceae*]
N‡   **hircinum** (Linnaeus) Koch 1837
   longibracteatum (Bernardi) Schlechter 1914 nom. illegit. = **Barlia robertiana**

HIPPEASTRUM Herbert 1821 nom. cons.   [*Amaryllidaceae*]
   bifidum (Herbert) Baker 1878 (*Rhodophiala bifida*)   EGF.1
   gracilifolium Baker 1878

'Donau'
'Pamela'
phycelloides (Herbert) Baker 1878 = **Habranthus phycelloides**

HYBRID CULTIVARS

'Acramanii'	PGP
'Apple Blossom'	RD
'Belinda'	
'Beautiful Lady'	
'Best Seller'	
'Blossfeldii'	
'Bouquet'	RD
'Candy Cane'	RD
'Christmas Joy' ('Xmas Joy')	
'Cinderella'	
'Day Dream'	
'Dutch Belle'	
'Excelsior'	
'Fantasia'	
'Fantastica'	
'Firedance'	
'Firey Diamond'	
'Hecuba'	
'Intokasi'	
'King of the Striped'	
'Lilac Favourite'	
'Lucky Strike'	
'Ludwig's Dazzler'	
'Ludwig's Goliath'	
'Maria Goretti'	
'Minerva'	
'Mont Blanc'	
'Orange Sovereign'	
'Picotee'	
'Purple Sensation'	
'Queen of Sheba'	
'Red Lion'	
'Rilone'	
'Rotterdam'	
'Scarlet Elegance'	
'Scarlet Globe'	
'Telstar'	
'United Nations'	
'White Dazzler'	
'White Lady'	

'Xmas Joy' = **H. 'Christmas Joy'**

HIPPOCREPIS Linnaeus 1753   [*Fabaceae (Leguminosae)*]
N‡   **comosa** Linnaeus 1753
    'E. R. Jaines'

HIPPURIS Linnaeus 1753   [*Hippuridaceae*]
N‡   **vulgaris** Linnaeus 1753

HOLCUS Linnaeus 1753 nom. cons.   [*Poaceae (Gramineae)*]
N‡   **lanatus** Linnaeus 1753
    'Variegatus' = **H. mollis 'Albo-variegatus'**
N‡   **mollis** Linnaeus 1759   EGF.2
L   **'Albo-variegatus'** Bull 1869   PGP

HOMERIA Ventenat 1808   *[Iridaceae]*
    breyniana (Linnaeus) G. Lewis 1941 (*H.collina*)   EGF.1
        var. **aurantiaca** (Zuccagni) G. Lewis 1941   EGF.1
        var. **ochroleuca** (Salisbury) G. Lewis 1941   EGF.1
    collina (Thunberg) Ventenat 1808 = **H. breyniana**
    comptonii L. Bolus 1929

HOMOGLOSSUM Salisbury 1812
    huttonii N.E. Brown 1932   *[Iridaceae]*

HOMOGYNE Cassini 1821
N   **alpina** (Linnaeus) Cassini 1821   *[Asteraceae (Compositae)]*

HORMINIUM Linnaeus 1753
    pyrenaicum Linnaeus 1753   *[Lamiaceae (Labiatae)]*

HOSTA Trattinnick 1812 nom. cons.   *[Hostaceae (Liliaceae)]*
    aequinoctiiantha Koidzumi ex Araki 1942 (*H. longipes* var. *aequinoctiiantha*)
    albomarginata (Hooker) Ohwi 1942 = **H. sieboldii**
    amanuma Maekawa 1940 = **H. capitata 'Amanuma'**
    capitata (Koidzumi) Nakai 1930   EGF.1
        'Amanuma'
        'Nakaimo' ®   [Imperial Gardens, Japan]
    caput-avis (Maekawa) Nakai 1952 = **H. kikutii** var. **caput-avis**
    clausa Nakai 1930   PGP
        var. **normalis** Maekawa 1937
    crispula Maekawa 1930 (H. 'Thomas Hogg' hort., p.p.)   EGF.1-PGP-**DGP-RD**
        f. **viridis** Brickell 1981
L   **decorata** Bailey 1930 (H. 'Thomas Hogg' hort., p.p.)   EGF.1-PGP-RD
        var. *marginata* Stearn 1931 = **H. decorata** var. **decorata**
        var. **normalis** Stearn 1931   EGF.1-PGP
    elata Hylander 1954, non Bailey 1915 = **H. montana**
    fluctuans Maekawa 1940
        'Parviflora'
        'Variegated' (*H. montana* 'Sagae')
L   **fortunei** (Baker) Bailey 1930   EGF.1-PGP-DGP-RD
        'Albo-marginata'
L   var. **albopicta** (Miquel) Hylander 1954   EGF.1-PGP-**DGP-RD**
        var. **albopicta 'Maya'**   [Summers]
        'Aoki'
        'Aoki Variegated'   PGP
        'Aurea'
        'Aurea' Dwarf Form   EGF.1-PGP-RD
        'Aureo-alba' = **H. fortunei 'Spinners'**
L   **'Aureo-maculata'** nom. illegit.   [N. Lindsay via The Plantsmen]   EGF.1
        'Aureo-marginata' (*H. fortunei* var. *obscura* 'Marginata')   EGF.1-PGP-**RD**
        'Aureo-minor' nom. illegit. = **H. fortunei** 'Aurea' Dwarf Form
        'Aureo-picta' = *H. fortunei* var. *albopicta*
        'Aureo-variegata'
        'Bensheim'
        'Charon' = **H. fortunei 'Sharmon'**
        'Elizabeth Campbell' ®   [via George](H. 'Panache Jaune')
        'Francee'   [Klopping]
        'Freising'   [Munich Botanic Garden]
        'Gloriosa' ®   [Krossa-Summers]
        'Goldbrook'   [S. Bond]
        'Gold Haze' ®   [Smith c.1973]
        'Gold Leaf' ®   [Smith]   EGF.1

'**Gold Standard**' ®   [Banyai]   EGF.1
'**Green Gold**' ®   [Mack-Savory]
'**Hadspen White**'   [Smith post-1975]
var. **hyacinthina** Hylander 1954   EGF.1-PGP
var. **hyacinthina** '**Helen Field Fischer**' ®   [Minks]
var. **hyacinthina** '**Variegated**'
var. **hyacinthina** '**Viette's Yellow Edge**' ®   [Viette]
'**Iona**' ®   [Lavender-Chappell]
'**Japonica**' nom. dub.
var. *marginato-alba* Bailey 1930 = **H. crispula**
'**Moerheim**'   [Ruys]
'**Nancy Lindsay**' ®   [N. Lindsay via D. Grenfell 1986]
'**North Hills**' ®   [Summers]   EGF.1
var. **obscura** Hylander 1954   EGF.1-PGP
var. *obscura* 'Marginata' = **H. fortunei** '**Aureo-marginata**'
'**Pagoda**' ®   [Smith post-1975]
'**Phyllis Campbell**' ®   [Smith]
'Picta' = **H. fortunei** var. **albopicta**
'**Robusta**'   EGF.1
var. **rugosa** Hylander 1954   EGF.1-PGP
'**Sharmon**' ®   [Donahue]
'**Spinners**' ®   [Smith-Chappell]
var. **stenantha** Hylander 1954   EGF.1-PGP
'**Thea**'   [Barcock via S. Bond]
'Viridis' = **H. crispula** f. **viridis**
'**Yellow Edge**'   [ex Japan via J. Sirkett]
glauca (Siebold) Stearn 1931 = **H. sieboldiana**
glauca hort., non (Siebold) Stearn = **H. sieboldiana** '**Elegans**'
gracillima Maekawa 1936   EGF.1
'**Vera-Verde**' ('Variegated')
helonioides Maekawa 1937   EGF.1
f. **albopicta** Maekawa 1937   EGF.1-PGP
hypoleuca Murata 1962   EGF.1-PGP
kikutii Maekawa 1937   PGP
var. **caput-avis** Maekawa 1950 (*H. caput-avis*)   PGP
'**Gala**'   [Aden]
'**Green Fountain**' ®   [via Aden]
var. **polyneuron**
var. **yakusimensis** (Masamune) Maekawa 1940
kiyosumiensis Maekawa 1935
L   **lancifolia** (Thunberg) Engler 1888   EGF.1-PGP-RD
var. *albo-marginata* (Hooker) Stearn 1930 = **H. sieboldii**
'**Argentea**' nom. dub.
'**Chinese Sunrise**' ('Variegated')
'Subcrocea' = **H. sieboldii** '**Subcrocea**'
'Variegated' = **H. lancifolia** '**Chinese Sunrise**'
longipes (Franchet & Savatier) Matsumura 1894   EGF.1-PGP
var. *aequinoctiiantha* (Koidzumi ex Araki) Kitamura 1966 = **H. aequinoctiiantha**
longissima (Honda) Honda 1935   EGF.1-PGP
var. *angustifolia* Koidzumi 1936 = **H. longissima**
var. *brevifolia* Maekawa 1937 = **H. longissima**
'**Yakushima**' nom. dub.
minor Nakai 1911   EGF.1
'Alba' = **H. sieboldii** '**Alba**'
montana Maekawa 1940 (*H. elata*)   PGP
'**Aureo-marginata**' Maekawa 1940   **PGP**
'**Praeflorens**' Maekawa 1940
'Sagae' = **H. fluctuans** '**Variegated**'
mukayama hort. = **H. nakaiana**

nakaiana Maekawa 1937   EGF.1-PGP
    'Candy Hearts' ®   [Fisher]
    'Golden' [Smith c.1973](H. 'Birchwood Parky's Gold)   EGF.1
    'Pastures New' [Smith c.1973]   EGF.1
nigrescens (Makino) Maekawa 1937   EGF.1
    f. **elatior** Maekawa 1940   EGF.1
nokogyriana nom. nudum et illegit.

L **plantaginea** (Lamarck) Ascherson 1863   EGF.1-PGP-DGP-RD
    var. **grandiflora** (Siebold & Zuccarini) Ascherson & Graebner 1905

                                       EGF.1-PGP-**DGP**

L   **'Honeybells'** ® [Cumming]   EGF.1-PGP
    'Royal Standard' ® [Wayside Gardens]   EGF.1-PGP-RD
    'Sugar and Cream' ® [TC sport from 'Honeybells']
    'Summer Fragrance' ® [Vaughn]
    'Sweet Susan' ® [Williams]
    'Wayside Perfection' = **H. plantaginea 'Honeybells'**
rectifolia Nakai 1930
    var. **chionea** Maekawa 1938   EGF.1-PGP-RD
    'Foliis Luteus' nom. illegit.
    var. **sachalinensis** (Koizumi) Maekawa 1938
    'Tallboy' ® [Savill]
rohdeifolia Maekawa 1937   EGF.1-PGP
    'Variegated' = **H. rohdeifolia**   PGP
rupifraga Nakai 1930
    Tetraploid Form [Hirao]   EGF.1-PGP
sieboldiana (Hooker) Engler & Prantl 1888 (*H. glauca* (Siebold) Stearn)
                                      EGF.1-PGP-**DGP-RD**
    'Aureo-marginata' = **H. sieboldiana 'Frances Williams'**
    'Coerulea' = **H. sieboldiana 'Elegans'**
    var. **cucullata** (Siebold) ?
    var. *elegans* Hylander 1954 = **H. sieboldiana 'Elegans'**
    'Elegans' [G. Arends 1905] (*H. glauca* hort., non (Siebold) Stearn,
                       H. sieboldiana 'Coerulea')   EGF.1-**PGP**-RD
    'Elegans Alba' nom. illegit. [N. Lindsay via The Plantsmen]
    var. *fortunei* (Regel) Ascherson & Graebner 1905 = **H. tokudama**
    'Frances Williams' ® [Williams] (*H. sieboldiana* 'Aureo-marginata',
                   H. sieboldiana 'Yellow Edge')   EGF.1-**PGP**-RD
    var. **glauca** Makino & Matsumura
                                          PGP
    'Golden' = **H. sieboldiana 'Golden Sunburst'**
    'Golden Sunburst' ® [TC sport from 'Frances Williams']
    var. *longipes* (Franchet & Savatier) Matsumura 1905 = **H. longipes**
    var. **mira** Maekawa 1940
    'Semperaurea' [Foerster pre-1946]
    'Yellow Edge' = **H. sieboldiana 'Frances Williams'**
L **sieboldii** (Paxton) Ingram 1967 (*H. albomarginata. H. lancifolia* var.
                           albo-marginata)   EGF.1-PGP-RD
    'Alba' (*H. minor* var. *alba*)   EGF.1-PGP-RD
    'Emerald Isle' [Smith c1970]   EGF.1
    'Frühlingsgold' [Klose]
    'Golden Isle' [Smith]
    'Haku-chu-han' ® [ex Japan]
    'Hakujima'
    'Inaho' (*H. tardiva* hort. non Nakai)
    f. **kabitan** Maekawa 1940
    'Lavender Lady' [Williams]   EGF.1-PGP
    'Louisa' ® [Williams]
    'Medio-picta' = **H. sieboldii 'Shirokabitan'**   EGF.1.
    'Nishiki' nom. dub. [Hirao]
    'Sentinels' [Williams 1966]
    'Shirokabitan' (*H. sieboldii* 'Medio-picta')

'Slim Polly' ® [Williams]
f. **spathulata** (Siebold) Miquel
'Subcrocea' (*H. lancifolia* 'Subcrocea')
'Viride-marginata' = *H. sieboldii* var. *kabitan*
'Wogon' ('Wogon Gold' hort.)   PGP
'Yakushima Mizu'
x **tardiana** hort., nom. non rite publ. (*H. sieboldiana* x *H. tardiflora*)   EGF.1-PGP
    'Blaue Venus' [Smith-Klose]
    'Blaumeise' [Smith-Klose]
    'Blauspecht' [Smith-Klose]
    'Blue Belle' ® [Smith-Morss]
    'Blue Blush' ® [Smith-Morss]
    'Blue Danube' ® [Smith 1970-5]
    'Blue Dimples' ® [Smith 1970-5]
    'Blue Diamond' ® [Smith 1970-5]
    'Blue Moon' ® [Smith 1970-5]
    'Blue Skies' ® [Smith 1970-5]
    'Blue Wave' [Smith 1970-5]
    'Blue Wedgwood' ® [Smith-Summers]
    'Bright Glow' [Smith-Aden]
    'Deven Blue' [Smith-Bowden]
    'Dorset Blue' ® [Smith post 1975]
    'Dorset Charm' [Smith post 1975]
    'Dorset Flair' [Smith post 1975]
    'Fumiko' [Smith-Klose]
    'Glockenspiel' [Smith-Klose]
    'Hadspen Hawk' ® [Smith post 1975]
    'Hadspen Heron' ® [Smith post 1975]
    'Halcyon' ® [Smith c1970]   EGF.1
    'Happiness' ® [Smith post 1975]
    'Harmony' ® [Smith post 1975]   EGF.1
    'Irische See' [Smith-Klose]
    'Naomi' [Smith-Klose]
    'Nicola' ® [Smith-Eason]
    Multiscaped Form
    'North Atlantic' [Smith-Archibald 1976]
    'Silberpfeil' [Smith-Klose]
    'Tomoko' [Smith-Klose]
tardiflora (Irving) Stearn 1938   EGF.1-PGP
tardiva Nakai 1930
tardiva hort. non Nakai = **H. sieboldii 'Inaho'**
tokudama Maekawa 1940 (*H. sieboldiana* var. *fortunei*)   EGF.1-PGP
    var. **aureo-nebulosa** Maekawa 1940 ('Variegated')   EGF.1-**PGP**
    'Big Daddy' ® [Aden]
    'Buckshaw Blue' ® [Smith c1967]   EGF.1-PGP
    var. **flavo-circinalis** Maekawa 1940
    var. **flavo-planata** Maekawa 1940
    'Golden Medallion' ® [TC sport from H. tokudama var. aureo-nebulosa]
    'Hadspen Blue' [Smith post 1975]
    'Little Aurora' ® [Aden]
    'Love Pat' ® [Aden]
    'Moscow Blue' ® [Arett]
    Tetraploid Form [Hirao]
    'Variegated' = *H. tokudama* var. *aureo-nebulosa*
tortifrons Maekawa 1940   EGF.1
tsushimensis Fujita 1960
undulata (Otto & Dietrich) Bailey 1923 (*H. undulata* 'Medio-variegata')
                                                      EGF.1-PGP-**DGP-RD**
    var. **albo-marginata** Maekawa 1936 (H. 'Thomas Hogg' hort., p.p.)   EGF.1
    'Cream Delight'

    var. **erromena** (Stearn) Maekawa 1936   EGF.1-PGP-RD
    'Medio-variegata' = **H. undulata** var. **undulata**
    var. **univittata** (Miquel) Hylander 1954
    'Variegated' = **H. undulata** var. **undulata**   EGF.1-PGP

L **ventricosa** Stearn 1930   EGF.1-PGP-RD
    var. **aureo-maculata** Henson 1963   EGF.1-PGP

L   '**Aureo-marginata**' (*H. ventricosa* 'Variegated')   EGF.1-RD
    'Maculata' = **H. ventricosa** var. **aureo-maculata**
    'Nana' = **H. minor**
    'Variegated' = **H. ventricosa** '**Aureo-marginata**'
venusta Maekawa 1935   EGF.1
    'Variegated'
yakusimensis Masamune = **H. kikutii** var. **yakusimensis**

HYBRID CULTIVARS

    '**Allan P. McConnell**' ®   [McConnell]
    '**Alpine Aire**' ®   [Minks]
    '**Anne Arett**' ®   [Arett]
    '**Animachi**'
    '**Antioch**' ®   [Tompkins]
    '**Aspen Gold**' ®   [Grapes]
    '**August Moon**'   [Summers]   PGP
    '**Beatrice**'   [Williams]
    '**Bengee**'   [Palmer]
    '**Betsy King**' ®   [Williams]
    '**Big Mama**' ®   [Aden]
    '**Birchwood Gold**' ®   [Shaw]
    '**Blauglut**'   [Klose]
    '**Blaue Wolke**'   [Klose]
    '**Blue Angel**' ®   [Aden]
    '**Blue Boy**' ®   [Stone]
    '**Blue Cadet**' ®   [Aden]
    '**Blue Mammoth**'   [Aden]
    '**Blue Piecrust**' ®   [Summers]
    '**Blue Present**'
    '**Blue Seer**'   [Aden]
    '**Blue Umbrellas**' ®   [Aden]
    '**Blue Vision**' ®   [Aden]
    '**Blütenspiel**'   [Klose]
    '**Bonanza**'   [Nesmith]
    '**Bressingham Blue**'   [Bloom]
    '**Butter Rim**' ®   [Summers]
    '**Celebration**'   [Aden]
    '**Chartreuse Wiggles**' ®   [Aden]
    'Clausa' = **H. clausa**
    '**County Park**' ®   [Hutchins]
    '**Cream Puff**'
    '**Crinkle Cup**' ®   [Fisher]
    '**Crown Jewel**' ®   [Wayside Gardens Inc.]
    '**Dorothy**' ®   [Williams]
    '**Ellerbroek**'   [Ellerbroek]
    '**Excitation**'   [Aden]
    '**Fascination**'   [Aden]
    '**Flamboyant**' ®   [Aden]   PGP
    '**Fringe Benefit**'   [Aden]
    '**Gaiety**' ®   [Aden]
    '**Ginko Craig**' ®   [Craig-Summers]
    '**Gold Cadet**' ®   [Aden]
    '**Gold Drop**' ®   [Anderson]

'Gold Edger' ®   [Aden]
'Golden Anniversary'
'Golden Circles'   [Williams]   PGP
'Golden Prayers' ®   [Aden]   RD
'Golden Scepter' ®   [TC sport from H. 'Golden Tiara']
'Golden Tiara' ®   [Savory]
'Golden Waffles' ®   [Aden]
'Gold Pan' ®   [Aden]
'Goldpfeil' = **H. fortunei 'Gold Leaf'**
'Gold Regal' ®   [Aden 1974]
'Gold Seer'   [Aden]
'Goldsmith'   [Smith c1973]
'Goliath'   [Harrison]
'Good as Gold'   [Aden]
'Granary Gold' ®   [Smith post 1975]
'Green Acres' ®   [Geissler]
'Green Gold'   [Savory-Mackwood]
'Green Piecrust' ®   [Williams]
'Green Wedge' ®   [Aden]
'Green Wiggles' ®   [Carpenter]
'Grey Piecrust' ®   [Donahue]
'Ground Master' ®   [Smith]
'Grünspecht'   [Klose]
'Hadspen Samphire'   [Smith post 1975]
'Helen Doriot' ®   [Reath]
'Herifu'   [ex Japan via Stone]
'Hokkaido' nom. dub.
'Hoopla'   [Aden]
'Hydon Gleam'   [George]
'Hydon Sunset' ®   [George]
'Janet' ®   [Shugart]
'Japan Boy'   [Köhlein]
'Japan Girl'   [Köhlein]
'Jingle Bells' ®   [Grapes]
'Jolly Green Giant' ®   [Armstrong]
'Julie Morss' ®   [Morss]
'June Beauty' ®   [Zager]
'Iron Gate Bouquet' ®   [Sellers]
'Kasseler Gold'   [Klose]
'Kilowatt' ®   [Armstrong]
'Krossa Regal' ®   [Krossa]   EGF.1-PGP
'Krossa's Cream Edge'
'Lady Helen'   [Holly 1963]
'Lemon Lime' ®   [Savory]
'Liliput'   [Klose]
'Little Blue'   [Englerth]
'Maple Leaf' ®   [Minks]
'Midas Touch' ®   [Aden]
'Midwest Gold' ®   [Cooley]
'Minnie Klopping' ®   [Klopping]
'Mount Kirishama' ('Kirishima')
'Neat Splash'   [Aden]
'Pearl Lake' ®   [Paine 1974]
'Piedmont Gold' ®   [Piedmont Gardens]   RD
'Pixie Power'   [Aden]
'Purple Profusion'   [Williams via Nesmith]
'Reginald Kaye'   [Kaye via Klose]
'Resonance'   [Aden]
'Reversed' ®   [Aden]
'Rheingold'   [Köhlein]

'Rough Waters' ® [Armstrong]
'Ruffles' ® [Lehman]
'Saishu Jima' [ex Japan via Davidson]
'Samurai' [Aden]
'Satin Flare' ® [Fisher]
'Schneewittchen' [Klose]
'Schwarzer Ritter'
'Sea Drift' ® [Seaver]
'Sea Sprite' ® [Seaver]
'See Saw' ® [Summers]
'Shade Fanfare' [TC sport from H. 'Flamboyant']
'Shade Master' ® [Aden]
'Shiro Sasa' [Hirao]
'Shogun' [Aden]
'Silver Crown' = **H. fortunei 'Albo-marginata'**
'Silverdale' [Kaye]
'Silver Streak' [Eisel-Krossa]
'Snowdon' ® [Smith c1970]   EGF.1
'Snow Mound' [Summers]
'Squiggles' ® [Aden]
'Stone's Fantasy' [D. Stone 1974]
'Sturtevant'
'Sum and Substance' ® [Aden]
'Summer Gold' [Hamblin c1962]
'Sun Glow' ® [Aden]
'Sun Power' ® [Aden]
'Sunlight Sister' ® [Nesmith]
'Tess Hoop'
'Thomas Hogg' USA hort. = **H. decorata**
'Thomas Hogg' UK hort. = **H. crispula**, p.p., **H undulata** var.
                          albo-marginata, p.p., etc. **PGP**
'True Blue' ® [Aden]
'Valentine Lace' ® [Armstrong]
'Vanilla Cream' ® [Aden]
'Vilmoriniana' [Vilmorin via New York Botanic Gardens]
'Wagon Wheels' ® [Minks]
'Weihenstephan' [Munich Botanic Gardens]
'Weisse Glocke' [Klose]
'White Colossus' ® [Aden]
'White Christmas' ® [Krossa]
'White Gold'
'White Magic' ® [Aden]
'Wide Brim' ® [Aden]
'Windsor Gold'
'Woad Courts'
'Wogon Gold' ® [Krossa]   EGF.1
'Yellow Splash' ® [Aden]
'Zitronenfalter' [Klose]
'Zounds' ® [Aden]

L

HOTTONIA Linnaeus 1753   [*Primulaceae*]
N‡   **palustris** LInnaeus 1753

HOUSTONIA Linnaeus 1753   [*Rubiaceae*]
   coerulea Linnaeus 1753   CA-**RD**
      'Alba'   CA
      'Millard's Variety' [F. W. Millard pre-1948]   CA-RD

longifolia Gaertner 1788
serpyllifolia Michaux 1803   CA
tenuifolia Nuttall 1808

HOUTTUYNIA Thunberg 1784 nom. cons.   [*Saururaceae*]
   cordata Thunberg 1784   PGP-RD
     'Chameleon' ('Tricolor','Variegata')
     'Plena'   PGP-RD
     'Tricolor' = **H. cordata 'Chameleon'**
     'Variegata' = **H. cordata 'Chameleon'**

HUGUENINIA Reichenbach 1832   [*Brassicaceae (Cruciferae)*]
   tanacetifolia (Linnaeus) Reichenbach 1832

HUMULUS Linnaeus 1753   [*Cannabidaceae*]
CHN‡ **lupulus** Linnaeus 1753   PGP
     'Aureus'   PGP

HUTCHINSIA R. Brown 1812   [*Brassicaceae (Cruciferae)*]
   alpina (Linnaeus) R. Brown 1812
     ssp. **auerswaldii** (Willkomin) Lainz 1957
     ssp. **brevicaulis** (Hoppe) Arcangeli 1882

HYACINTHELLA Schur 1857   [*Hyacinthaceae (Liliaceae)*]
   azurea (Fenzl) Chouard 1931 = **Pseudomuscari azureum**
   dalmatica (Baker) Chouard 1931 = **H. pallens**
   glabrescens (Boissier) Persson & Wendelbo 1981   EGF.1-SB
   heldreichii (Boissier) Chouard 1931   SB
   lineata (Steudel) Chouard 1931 (*Hyacinthus lineatus*)   EGF.1-CA-**BB**-SB
   millingenii (Post) Feinbrun 1961
   pallens Schur 1857 (*H. dalmatica, Hyacinthus dalmaticus*)   EGF.1-**BB**-**SB**
     'Alba'
   siirtensis Mathew 1973   **BB**

HYACINTHOIDES Heister ex Fabricius 1759   [*Hyacinthaceae (Liliaceae)*]
N‡ **hispanica** (Miller) Rothmaler 1944 (*Endymion hispanicus, Scilla campanulata,*
                 S. hispanica)   EGF.1-PGP-**BB**-DGP-**RD**
     'Alba'   ®   [1849]
     'Azalea'
     'Danube'   ®   [J. Valkering] ('Donau')
     'Donau' = **H. hispanica 'Danube'**
     'Excelsior'   ®   [G. C. van Meeuwen 1906]   DGP-RD
     'La Grandesse'   ®
     'Mount Everest'   ®   [J. Valkering pre-1939]   DGP

     'Myosotis'   ®   [J. Valkering pre-1939]   DGP-RD
     'Queen of the Pinks'   ®   [J. Valkering pre-1939]   DGP-RD
     'Rosabella'   ®   [J. Valkering pre-1944]
     'Rose'   ®   [J. Valkering pre-1939]
     'White City'   ®   [J. Valkering]
N‡L **non-scripta** (Linnaeus) Chouard ex Rothmaler 1944 (*Endymion non-scriptus,*
              Scilla non-scripta, S. nutans)   EGF.1-PGP-**BB**-**DGP**-RD
     'Alba'   ®   [1596]
     'Rosea'

HYACINTHUS Linnaeus 1753   [*Hyacinthaceae (Liliaceae)*]
   amethystinus Linnaeus 1753 = **Brimeura amethystina**
   azureus (Fenzl) Baker 1871 = **Pseudomuscari azureum**

dalmaticus Baker 1871 = **Hyacinthella pallens**
lineatus Steudel 1830 = **Hyacinthella lineata**
orientalis Linnaeus 1753

		EGF.1-**BB**-SB-RD
'Amethyst' ®	[Langelaan-Hulsebosch pre-1950]	
'Amsterdam' ®	[C. J. Briejer 1933]	RD
'Anna Marie' ®	[N. C. Berbee pre-1949]	RD
'Apollo' ®	[P. van Dijk & Sons 1970]	
'Apple Blossom'		
'Ben Nevis' ®	[M. van Waveren pre-1942]	
'Bismark' ®	[D. J. Ziegler 1875]	
'Blue Giant' ®	[E. H. Krelage]	**BB**-RD
'Blue Jacket' ®	[C. J. Zonneveld pre-1953]	
'Blue Magic' ®	[G. van der Mey 1946]	
'Blushing Dolly' ®	[G. van der Mey 1971]	
'Borah' ®	[G. van der Veld pre-1946]	
'Carnegie' ®	[A. Lefeber]	
'Cherry Blossom'		**BB**-RD

ssp. **chionophilus** Wendelbo 1980

		EGF.1-SB
'City of Haarlem' ®	[J. H. Kersten 1893]	DGP-**RD**
'Colosseum' ®	[G. van der Veld 1935]	
'Concorde' ®	[Walter Blom & Son 1971]	
'Cote d'Azure' ®	[G. van der Mey 1927]	
'Debutante'		
'Delft Blue' ®	[J. W. A. Lefeber 1944]	**RD**
'Distinction' ®	[C. W. F. Hoogeveen 1880]	
'Fireball'		
'Gainsborough' ®	[M. van Waveren]	
'Gipsy Queen' ®	[G. van der Mey 1927]	
'Grace Darling'		
'Hollyhock' ®	[A. C. van der Schoot 1936]	
'Indian Prince'		
'Jan Bos' ®	[J. Bos 1910]	DGP-RD
'King of the Blues' ®	[F. van Velsen Jr. 1863]	DGP
'Lady Derby' ®	[J. H. Veen 1875]	DGP-RD
'La Victoire' ®	[D. Bakker 1875]	RD
'L'Innocence' ®	[V. van der Vinne 1863]	**BB**-DGP-RD
'Lord Balfour' ®	[J. W. van der Veldt 1883]	
'Marconi' ®	[A. van der Vlugt 1900]	RD
'Marie' ®	[J. Prinsen 1860]	
'Maryon'		
'Mont Blanc' ®	[Segers Bros 1944]	
'Morning Star'		
'Mulberry Rose' ®	[G. van der Mey 1946]	
'Myosotis' ®	[C. Rijnsburger 1896]	DGP-RD
'Orange Queen'		
'Oranje Boven' ®	[A. van Schie 1870] ('Salmonetta')	RD
'Ostara' ®	[G. van Waveren-Kruyff via Segers Bros 1942]	DGP-**RD**
'Paul Herman'		
'Pearle Brilliante' ®	[Pre-1895]	**DGP**
'Pink Pearl' ®	[J.W.A. Lefeber 1922]	**BB**-DGP-RD
'Pink Princess'		
'Princess Victoria'		
'Queen of the Pinks' ®	[c1903]	RD
'Rosalie' ®	[G. van Waveren-Kruyff via Eggink Bros pre-1948]	
'Rose Dream'		**BB**-DGP

'Salmonetta' = **H. 'Oranje Boven'**
'Sneeuwitje' ®   [P. van Reisen 1950]('Snow White')
'Snow Princess'

    'Snow Queen'   ®   [Verdegaal Bros 1945]
    'Snow White' = **H. 'Sneeuwwitje'**
    'Sunflower'
    'Tubergen's Scarlet'   ®   [van Tubergen 1920]   DGP-RD
    'Violet Pearl'   ®   [G. H. Went & Sons 1970]
    'White Pearl'   ®   [A. C. Paardekoper 1954]
    'Yellow Hammer'   ®   [J. H. Veen 1883]   RD

HYDRASTIS Ellis ex Linnaeus 1759   *[Ranunculaceae]*
H   **canadensis** Linnaeus 1759

HYDRILLA Richard 1811   *[Hydrocharitaceae]*
N   **verticillata** (Linnaeus f.) Royle 1839   EGF.1

HYDROCHARIS Linnaeus 1753   *[Hydrocharitaceae]*
N‡L   **morsus-ranae** Linnaeus 1753   EGF.1

HYDROCOTYLE Linnaeus 1753   *[Apiaceae (Umbelliferae)]*
N   **moschata** Forster f. 1786
N‡   **vulgaris** Linnaeus 1753

HYLOMECON Maximowicz 1853   *[Papaveraceae]*
    japonicum (Thunberg) Prantl & Kuendig 1889   PGP-**DGP**

HYMENOCALLIS Salisbury 1812   *[Amaryllidaceae]*
    amancaes (Ruiz & Pavon) Nicholson 1886   EGF.1-**RD**
    calathina (Ker-Gawler) Nicholson 1886 = **H. narcissiflora**
    x festalis (Worsley) Schmarse 1933 (*H. longipetala* x *H. narcissiflora*) EGF.1-PGP-**RD**
        'Sulphur Queen'   [van Tubergen pre-1889]   PGP
        'Zwanenburg'   [van Tubergen 1912]   PGP
    harrisiana Herbert 1840   EGF.1
    longipetala (Lindley) MacBride 1931 (*Elisena longipetala*)   EGF.1
    narcissiflora (Jacquin) MacBride 1931 (*H. calathina, Ismene calanthina*)
                EGF.1-PGP-DGP-RD
        'Advance'   [van Tubergen pre-1932]   DGP

HYMENOXYS Cassini 1828   *[Asteraceae (Compositae)]*
    acaulis (Pursh) Parker 1950
    grandiflora (Torrey & A. Gray ex A. Gray) Parker 1950

HYOSCYAMUS Linnaeus 1753   *[Solanaceae]*
B   **albus** Linnaeus 1753
BHN‡   **niger** Linnaeus 1753

HYPERICUM Linnaeus 1753   *[Clusiaceae (Guttiferae)]*
    adenotrichum Spach 1836
    annulatum Moris 1827 (*H. degenii*)
S   **balearicum** Linnaeus 1753
SN‡   **calycinum** Linnaeus 1767   **DGP-RD**
    capitatum Choisy 1821
S   **cerastoides** (Spach) N. Robson 1967 (*H. rhodoppeum*)   CA-**DGP**
    coris Linnaeus 1753   CA
    cuneatum Poiret 1813 = **H. pallens**
    degenii Bornmueller 1910 = **H. annulatum**
    elodeoides Choisy 1824 (*H. napaulense*)
N‡   **elodes** Linnaeus 1759
    napaulense Choisy 1824 = **H. elodeoides**
    nummularium Linnaeus 1753

SL **olympicum** Linnaeus 1753
    f. **minus** Haussknecht 1893 (*H. repens* hort., non Linnaeus)   CA-RD
    f. **minus** 'Edith'   CA-**DGP**-RD
    f. **minus** 'Schwefelperle'   [H. Klose 1971]
    f. **minus** 'Sulphureum'
    f. **minus** 'Variegatum'
    f. **minus** 'Zitronenfalter'
    f. **uniflorum** D. Jordan & Kozevnikov 1970
L   f. **uniflorum** 'Citrinum'
    f. **uniflorum** 'Sunburst'   DGP-RD
  orientale Linnaeus 1753
S   **pallens** Banks & Solander 1794 (*H. cuneatum*)
  polyphyllum hort., non Boissier & Balansa 1856 = **H. olympicum** f. **minus**   CA
  pseudopetiolatum A. Keller 1897
  repens hort., non Linnaeus 1753 = **H. olympicum** f. **minus**
  rhodoppeum Frivaldsky 1836 = **H. cerastoides**
S   **trichocaulon** Boissier & Heldreich 1849
  yakusimense Koidzumi 1928

HYPOLEPIS Bernhardi 1806   [*Dennstaedtiaceae*]
  millefolium Hooker 1852
  punctata (Thunberg) Mettenius 1868   EGF.1-PGP

HYPSELA C. Presl 1836   [*Campanulaceae*]
  longiflora (Hooker) Bentham & Hooker f. 1865 = **H. reniformis**
  reniformis (Kunth) C. Presl 1836 (*H. longiflora*)
    'Greencourt White'
  rivalis F. Wimmer 1943

HYSSOPUS Linnaeus 1753
SHNL   **officinalis** Linnaeus 1753   [*Lamiaceae (Labiatae)*]
    'Albus'   PGP-**RD**
H   ssp. **aristatus** (Godron) Briquet 1893   RD
    'Purpurascens' ('Ruber')   DGP
    'Roseus'
    'Ruber' = **H. officinalis** 'Purpurascens'   RD

HYSTRIX Moench 1794
  patula Moench 1794   [*Poaceae (Gramineae)*]
    EGF.2

IBERIS Linnaeus 1753
A   **attica** Jordan 1847 (*I. jordanii*)   [*Brassicaceae (Cruciferae)*]
  candolleana Jordan 1847 = **I. pruitii**
  commutata Schott & Kotschy ex Boissier 1867 = **I. sempervirens**
S   'Correifolia' (*I. sempervirens* x *I. tenoreana*)
S   **gibraltarica** Linnaeus 1753   CA
  jordanii Boissier 1853 = **I. attica**   CA-RD
  jucunda Schott & Kotschy ex Boissier 1867 = **I. pruitii**
  pruitii Tineo 1817 (*I. candolleana, I. jucunda*)
  pygmaea hort. = **I. sempervirens** 'Nana'
S   **saxatilis** Linnaeus 1756
SNL   **sempervirens** Linnaeus 1753   CA-**DGP**-RD
    'Compacta'   PGP-**DGP**-RD
    'Correifolia' = **I. 'Correifolia'**
    'Elfenreigen'
    'Findel'   [Helfert c1950]
    'Garrexiana'
    'Gracilis'

'Little Gem' = **I. sempervirens 'Weisser Zwerg'**
'Nana' (*I. pygmaea* hort.)
'Schneeflocke' = **I. sempervirens 'Snowflake'**
'Snowdrift' = **I. sempervirens 'Zwergschneeflocke'**
'Snowflake'   [T. Smith c1925]('Schneeflocke')
'Weisser Zwerg'   [G. Arends 1894]('Little Gem')   CA-**RD**
'Winterzauber'
'Zwergschneeflocke'   [Lindner]('Snowdrift')
tenoreana de Candolle 1825   CA

IMPATIENS Linnaeus 1753   [*Balsaminaceae*]
hookeriana Arnott 1835 = **I. grandis**
grandis Heyne 1832 (*I. hookeriana*)

IMPERATA Cyrillo 1792   [*Poaceae (Gramineae)*]
sacchariflora Maximowicz 1859 = **Miscanthus sacchariflorus**

INCARVILLEA Jussieu 1789   [*Bignoniaceae*]
arguta (Royle) Royle 1836 = **Amphicome arguta**
brevipes hort. = **I. mairei**
delavayi Bureau & Franchet 1891   **PGP-DGP-RD**
'Bees' Pink'   [Bees' Nurseries]   PGP-DPG
emodi (Wallich ex Royle) Chaterjee 1961 = **Amphicome emodi**
grandiflora Bureau & Franchet 1891 = **I. mairei** var. **grandiflora**
'Brevipes' = **I. mairei**
mairei (Leveille) Grierson 1961 (*I. brevipes*, *I. grandiflora* 'Brevipes')   **PGP**
var. **grandiflora** (Wehrhahn) Grierson 1961 (*I. grandiflora*)   CA-**DGP-RD**
'Frank Ludlow'   PGP
'Nyoto Sama'   PGP
S   **olgae** Regel 1880   PGP
sinensis Lamarck 1789
variabilis Batalin 1892

INULA Linnaeus 1753   [*Asteraceae (Compositae)*]
acaulis Schott & Kotschy ex Boissier 1875   CA-RD
afghanica hort. = **I. magnifica**
barbata Wallich 1831
N   **britannica** Linnaeus 1753
L   **ensifolia** Linnaeus 1753   PGP
'Compacta'
'Goldammer'
glandulosa Willdenow 1803 non Lamarck = **I. orientalis**
'Golden Beauty' = **Buphthalmum salicifolium**
HN‡   **helenium** Linnaeus 1753
hirta Linnaeus 1753
hookeri C. B. Clarke 1876   **DGP-RD**
macrocephala hort., non Kotschy & Boissier = **I. royleana**
L   **magnifica** Lipsky 1898 (*I. afghanica* hort.)   PGP
oculus-christi Linnaeus 1751   PGP
orientalis Lamarck 1789 (*I. glandulosa*)   PGP
rhizocephala Schrenk 1844
royleana de Candolle 1830 (*I. macrocephala* hort.)   PGP-RD

IONOPSIDIUM Reichenbach 1829   [*Brassicaceae (Cruciferae)*]
A   **acaule** (Desfontaines) Reichenbach 1829

IPHEION Rafinesque 1836   [*Alliaceae (Liliaceae)*]
ixiodes (Aiton) hort. = **Triteleia ixiodes**
laxa (Bentham) hort. = **Triteleia laxa**
sellowianum (Kunth) Traub 1949 (*Triteleia sellowiana*)   SB

tubergenii hort. = **Triteleia x tubergenii**

N **uniflorum** (Graham) Rafinesque 1837 (*Triteleia uniflora*)   EGF.1-**BB**-SM-**DGP**
    'Album'
    'Froyle Mill'
    'Lilacinum'   EGF.1-**BB**
    'Rolf Fiedler'
    'Violaceum'   ®   [c1884]
    'Wisley Blue'   ®   [via van Tubergen 1961]   **BB**

IRIS

M - BRIAN MATTHEW, *'The Iris'* Batsford 1981   [*Iridaceae*]

Classification as in above, viz:

1	**Iris** *subgenus*	**Iris**
A	*Section*	**Iris** (The bearded or pogon irises)
B	*Section*	**Psammiris**
C	*Section*	**Oncocyclus**
D	*Section*	**Regelia**
E	*Section*	**Hexapogon**
F	*Section*	**Pseudoregelia**
2	**Iris** *subgenus*	**Limniris** (The beardless irises)
A	*Section*	**Lophiris** (The evansia irises)
B	*Section*	**Limniris**
(a)	*Series*	**Chinenses**
(b)	*Series*	**Vernae**
(c)	*Series*	**Ruthenicae**
(d)	*Series*	**Tripetalae**
(e)	*Series*	**Sibiricae**
(f)	*Series*	**Californicae**
(g)	*Series*	**Longipetalae**
(h)	*Series*	**Laevigatae**
(i)	*Series*	**Hexagonae**
(j)	*Series*	**Prismaticae**
(k)	*Series*	**Spuriae**
(l)	*Series*	**Foetidissimae**
(m)	*Series*	**Tenuifoliae**
(n)	*Series*	**Ensatae**
(o)	*Series*	**Syriacae**
(p)	*Series*	**Unguiculares**
3	**Iris** *subgenus*	**Nepalensis**
4	**Iris** *subgenus*	**Xiphium**
5	**Iris** *subgenus*	**Scorpiris** (The juno irises)
6	**Iris** *subgenus*	**Hermodactyloides** (The reticulata irises)

1C   **acutiloba** C. A. Meyer 1831   EGF.1-M-**DGP**
       ssp. **lineolata** (Trautvetter) Mathew & Wendelbo 1975   EGF.1-M
1D   **afghanica** Wendelbo 1972   EGF.1-**M**
       aintabensis (Baker) hort. = **I. histrio** var. **aintabensis**
5   **aitchisonii** (Baker) Boissier 1882   EGF.1-M-SB
       alata Poiret 1789 = **I. planifolia**
1A   **albicans** Lange 1860   EGF.1-M
5   **albo-marginata** R. C. Foster 1936 (*I. caerulea*)   EGF.1-**M-SB**
       anglica Steudel = **I. latifolia**
1A   **aphylla** Linnaeus 1753
                                          EGF.1-M

arenaria Waldstein & Kitaibel 1802 = **I. humilis**

1C	**atropurpurea** Baker 1889	EGF.1-**M**-PGP
1A	**attica** Boissier & Heldreich 1859 (*I. pumila* ssp. *attica* hort.)	EGF.1-**M**
5	**aucheri** (Baker) Sealy 1950 (*I. sindjarensis*)	EGF.1-**M**-CA-**BB**-SB-**DGP**-RD
6	**bakeriana** Foster 1889 (*I. reticulata* var. *bakeriana*)	EGF.1-M-CA-**BB**-SB-**DGP**
5	**baldschuanica** B. Fedtschenko 1909	EGF.1-M-SB
1C	**barnumae** Baker & Foster 1888	EGF.1-**M**

    f. **protonyma** (Stapf) Mathew & Wendelbo 1975   M

    f. **urmiensis** (Hoog) Mathew & Wendelbo   EGF.1-M

2A	**'Bourne Elegant'** (*I. confusa* x *I. japonica*) [J. Ellis]	
2B(f)	**bracteata** S. Watson 1885	EGF.1-M-PGP
5	**bucharica** Foster 1902	EGF.1-**M**-PGP-**DGP-RD**
2B(e)	**bulleyana** Dykes 1910	EGF.1-M

caerulea B. Fedtschenko 1904 non Spach 1846 = **I. albo-marginata**

5	**caucasica** Hoffmann 1808	EGF.1-**M**-**BB**-SB

    var. **kharput** Foster 1892 (*I. kharput*)   M

    'Major' = **I. magnifica**

cengialtii Ambrosi 1854 = **I. pallida** ssp. **cengialtii**

chamaeiris Bertoloni 1837 = **I. lutescens**

2B(e)	**chrysographes** Dykes 1911	EGF.1-M-PGP-DG
	Black Form	
	'Black Knight'	PGP
	'Black Velvet'	
	'Inshriach'	
	'Mandarin Purple' ® [J. Drake 1950]	
	Red Form	
	'Rubella' ® [J. B. Stevenson c1927]	EGF.1-M
	'Stjerneskud'	
2B(f)	**chrysophylla** Howell 1902	EGF.1-M
2B(e)	**clarkei** Baker 1892	EGF.1-M-PGP
2A	**confusa** Sealy 1937	EGF.1-M-**PGP**

cretensis Baker 1877 = **I. unguicularis 'Cretensis'**

cretica Herbert 1892 = **I. cretensis**

2A	**cristata** Solander 1789	EGF.1-**M**-CA-RD
	'Alba' ®	

    var. *lacustris* (Nuttall) hort. = **I. lacustris**

5	**cycloglossa** Wendelbo 1958	EGF.1-M-**BB**-SB

dalmatica hort. = **I. pallida**

6	**danfordiae** (Baker) Boissier 1884	EGF.1-**M**-CA-**BB**-SB-**DGP-RD**
3	**decora** Wallich 1832 (*I. nepalensis*)	EGF.1-**M**
2B(e)	**delavayi** Micheli 1895	EGF.1-M-PGP-**DGP**
	'Didcot'	
2B(i)	**'Dorothea K Williamson'** (*I. fulva* x *I. brevicaulis*) ® [Williamson 1918]	
2B(f)	**douglasiana** Herbert 1841	EGF.1-M-PGP-**DGP-RD**
	'Southcombe Velvet' [T. Woods]	

elegantissima Sosnowsky 1915 = **I. iberica** ssp. **elegantissima**

2B(h)	**ensata** Thunberg 1794 non Dykes 1913 (*I. kaempferi*)	EGF.1-M-PGP-**RD**
	'Alba'	
	'Apollo' ® [V. H. Hallock c1885]	
	'Blue Peter'	
	'Embossed' ® [L. Marx 1956]	
	'Galatea' ® [Kelway 1890]	
	'Gei-sho-ui' ® [Barr 1938]	PGP
	'Hercule' ® [Vilmorin 1910]	
	Higo Hybrids	
	'Hokkaido'	
	'Kuma-funjin' ® [Kelway 1910]	
	'Laced'	
	'Landscape at Dawn' ® [Perry 1940	
	'Mandarin' ® [Wallace 1910]	

	'Moonlight Waves'	®	[Wallace 1910]
	'Oku-banri' ®	[Chivers c1911]	
	Pale Mauve		
	'Pink Frost' ®	[L. Marx 1955]	
	Purple		
	'Purple East' ®	[Barr 1938]	
	Tokyo Hybrids		
	'White Swan' ®	[J. K. Alexander 1930]	
	'Variegata'		

	4	**filifolia** Boissier 1839	EGF.1-M
		florentina Linnaeus 1762 = **I. germanica 'Florentina'**	
HN‡	2B(l)	**foetidissima** Linnaeus 1753	EGF.1-M-PGP-**DGP**-**RD**
		'Chinese Yellow' = **I. foetidissima** var. **citrina**	
		var. **citrina** Syme	
		var. **lutescens** Maire	M-PGP
		'Variegata'	M
	2B(e)	**forrestii** Dykes 1910	PGP-RD
	5	**fosteriana** Aitchison & Baker 1888	EGF.1-M-PGP
	2B(i)	**fulva** Ker-Gawler 1812	EGF.1-**M**-SB
	2B(i)	**x fulvala** Dykes 1913 (*I. fulva x I. lamancei*)	EGF.1-M-PGP-RD
	5	**galatica** Siehe 1905	EGF.1-M-PGP-RD
	1C	**gatesii** Foster 1890	EGF.1-M-SB
N‡	1A	**germanica** Linnaeus 1753	EGF.1-**M**-RD
			EGF.1-M-PGP-RD
		'Amas' ® [Forster 1885]	
H		**'Florentina'** (*I. florentina*) ®	M
		'Kharput'	EGF.1-M
			M
		gormanii Piper 1924 = **I. tenax**	
	2A	**gracilipes** A. Gray 1859	EGF.1-M-CA-RD
	5	**graeberiana** van Tubergen ex Sealy	EGF.1-M-PGP-SB
	2B(k)	**graminea** Linnaeus 1753	EGF.1-M-PGP-RD
		halophila Pallas 1773 = **I. spuria** ssp. **halophila**	
	2B(f)	**hartwegii** Baker 1876	EGF.1-M-PGP
		ssp. **australis** (Parish) Lenz 1958	M
		ssp. **columbiana** Lenz 1958	M
		ssp. **pinetorum** (Eastwood) Lenz 1958	M
	1C	**haynei** Baker 1876	EGF.1-M
	6	**histrio** Reichenbach f. 1872	EGF.1-**M**-CA-**BB**-**SB**
		var. **aintabensis** Baker	M-CA-**BB**-SB
	6	**histrioides** (G. F.Wilson) S. Arnott	EGF.1-**M**-CA-**BB**-SB
		var. **major** Grey	
		'Major' [van Tubergen ex Armenia]	EGF.1-**BB**-**DGP**-RD
		var. **sophenensis** (Foster) Dykes	EGF.1-M
	2B	**'Holden Clough'** ® [D. Patton 1971] (*I. foetidissima* x *I. pseudacorus* ?)	
	1D	**hoogiana** Dykes 1916	PGP
			EGF.1-**M**-PGP-RD
		'Alba'	
		'Bronze Beauty' ® [van Tubergen]	RD
		'Noblesse' ® [van Tubergen pre-1968]	
		'Purpurea'	RD
		hookeri Penny 1840 = **I. setosa** ssp. **canadensis**	
	1B	**humilis** Georgi (*I. arenaria*)	EGF.1-M
		humilis Marshall von Bieberstein 1808 non Georgi = **I. pontica**	
	6	**hyrcana** Woronow ex Grossheim 1928	M-**BB**-SB
	1C	**iberica** Hoffmann 1808	EGF.1-M
		ssp. **elegantissima** (Sosnowsky) Fedorov & Takhtadjan 1972	
		(*I. elegantissima*)	EGF.1-**M**
		ssp. **lycotis** (Woronow) Takhtadjan 1972 (*I. lycotis*)	EGF.1-**M**
		iliensis Poljakav 1950 = **I. lactea**	
	2B(f)	**innominata** Henderson 1930	EGF.1-**M**-PGP-CA-**DGP**-**RD**
		'Alba' nom. dub.	

'**Aurea**' nom. dub.

2A   **japonica** Thunberg 1794   EGF.1-M-PGP-**RD**
　　　'**Aphrodite**' ('Variegata')　 ®　　[Sprenger c1907]   EGF.1-**M**-PGP
　　　'**Ledger's Variety**'　 ®　　[Lugard 1925]   PGP-**DGP**-RD
　　　'Variegata' = **I. japonica 'Aphrodite**'
1C   **jordana** Dinsmore 1933   M
　　　kaempferi Siebold 1858 = **I. ensata**
1F   **kamaonensis** Wallich ex D. Don   EGF.1-**M**
1A   **kashmiriana** Baker 1877   EGF.1-M
　　　'Alba' = **I. kashmiriana 'Kashmir White**'
　　　'**Kashmir White**'　 ®　　[Foster 1912]
　　　kasruwana Dinsmore 1933 = **I. sofarana** ssp. **kasruwana**
2B(k) **kerneriana** Ascherson & Sintensis 1884   EGF.1-M-**PGP**
　　　kharput (Foster) hort. = **I. caucasica** var. **kharput** or **germanica 'Kharput**'
　　　klattii Kemularia-Natadze 1949 = **I. spuria** ssp. **musulmanica**
6   **kolpakowskiana** Regel 1877   EGF.1-M
5   **kopetdagensis**(Vvedensky) Mathew & Wendelbo 1975   M
1E   **korolkowii** Regel 1873   EGF.1-**M**-PGP
　　　'**Concolor**'　 ®　　[Baker 1888]   M-PGP
　　　'**Violacea**'　 ®　　[Kreleage 1905]   M-PGP
　　　kumaonensis hort. = **I. kamaonensis**
2B(n) **lactea** Pallas (*I. iliensis*)   EGF.1-M
2A   **lacustris** Nuttall 1818   EGF.1-M-CA-**DGP**
2B(h) **laevigata** Fischer 1837   EGF.1-**M**-PGP-DGP-RD
　　　'**Alba**'　 ®　　[R. Wallace 1915]   PGP-**DGP**-RD
　　　'**Albo-purpurea**'　 ®　　[R Wallace 1916]   PGP
　　　'**Blue Beauty**'　 ®
　　　'**Colchesterensis**'　 ®　　[Wallace 1910]
　　　'**Monstrosa**'   **DGP**-RD
　　　'**Mottled Beauty**'　 ®　　[Perry 1946]
　　　'**Variegata**'　 ®　　[van Tubergen 1916]   EGF.1-PGP-**RD**

I. LAEVIGATA HYBRIDS ('Japanese' cultivars)

　　　'**Adonis**'   [S. J. Grubb 1986]
　　　'**Arctic Sea**'   [S. J. Grubb 1986]
　　　'**Blue Spangles**'   [S. J. Grubb 1986]
　　　'**Blue Surf**'   [S. J. Grubb 1986]
　　　'**Elegante**'　 ®　　[Prichard 1939]
　　　'**Evening Star**'   [S. J. Grubb 1986]
　　　'**Gainsborough**'   [S. J. Grubb 1986]
　　　'**Lilac Time**'   [S. J. Grubb 1986]
　　　'**Midnight**'　 ®　　[Mitchell 1924]
　　　'**Moorland Mist**'   [S. J. Grubb 1986]
　　　'**Murakumo**'　 ®　　[Chugai 1928]
　　　Newlake Hybrids
　　　'**Rose Queen**'　 ®　　[Ruys 1921]   PGP
　　　'**Silver Cloud**'   [S. J. Grubb 1986]
　　　'**Sorrento**'   [S. J. Grubb 1986]
　　　'**Snowdrift**'　 ®　　[Elliot]
　　　'**Weymouth**'

4   **latifolia** Miller (*I. anglica* hort, *I. xiphioides*)   EGF.1-**M**-**BB**-**RD**

'DUTCH' IRISES (*I. latifolia x I. tingitana* etc.)

　　　'**Apollo**'　 ®　　[G. D. Hommes 1971]
　　　'**Blue Champion**'　 ®　　[J. Heere pre-1941]   **DGP**
　　　'**Blue Diamond**'　 ®　　[Koomen Bros 1975]
　　　'**Blue Magic**'　 ®　　[P. Aker 1959]

'Bronze Queen' ®   [J. de Goede pre-1944]
'Golden Emperor' ®   [D. van Buggenum pre-1937]
'Golden Harvest' ®   [D. van Buggenum pre-1937]
'H C van Vliet' ®   [De Graaff Bros pre-1931]
'Hildegarde' ®   [H. S. van Waveren 1939]
'Ideal' ®   [C. N. Koomen via G. Hommes 1956]
'Imperator' ®   [Tubergen via Arn. Bijvoet pre-1915]
'Juliette' ®   [P. Nijssen 1975]
'Lemon Queen' ®   [J. de Goede Sz. pre-1940]   **DGP**
'Professor Blaauw' ®   [H. S. van Waveren pre-1949]
'Purple Sensation' ®   [H. S. van Waveren pre-1959]
'Royal Yellow' ®   [D. van Buggenum pre-1949]
'Sapphire Beauty' ®   [De Graaff Bros 1953]
'Sunrise' ®   [P. Nijssen 1971]
'Symphony' ®   [P. Nijssen pre-1968]
'Telstar' ®   [G. D. Hommes 1971]
'Wedgwood' ®   [Lowe-Shawyer via De Graaff Bros. pre-1925]
                                                                  DGP-RD
'White Exelsior' ®   [De Graaff Bros pre-1920]
'White van Vliet' ®   [De Graaff Bros pre-1934]
'White Wedgwood' ®   [G. Hommes 1961]
'Yellow Queen' ®   [De Graaf Bros. pre-1921]

2B(p)	**lazica** Albov 1895 (*I. unguicularis* var. *lazica*)	EGF.1-M
	lilacina Borbas 1882 = **I. spuria** ssp. **sogdiana**	
1D	**lineata** Foster ex Regel 1887	M
2B(g)	**longipetala** Herbert 1841	EGF.1-**M**-PGP
1C	**lortetii** Barbey in Boissier 1881	EGF.1-**M**-PGP-CA
1A	**lutescens** Lamarck 1789 (*I. chamaeiris*)	EGF.1-**M**-PGP-**RD**
	'Campbellii' ®	
	'Nancy Lindsey' ® [N. Lindsey via S. Linnegar 1986]	
	lycotis Woronow 1915 = **I. iberica** ssp. **lycotis**	
5	**magnifica** Vvedensky 1935 (*I. caucasica* 'Major')	EGF.1-**M**-PGP-**BB**-SB-DGP
	'Alba'	
2B	'Margot Holmes' ® [Perry 1927] (*I. crysographes x I. douglasiana*)	
		PGP-RD
	mellita Janka 1874 = **I. suaveolens**	
2A	**milesii** Foster 1883	EGF.1-M-PGP
2B(g)	**missouriensis** Nuttall 1834 (*I. tolmeiana*)	EGF.1-M-PGP
2B(k)	**monnieri** De Candolle in Redoute 1808	EGF.1-M-PGP
2B(f)	**munzii** R. C. Foster 1938	EGF.1-M
5	**narbutii** O. Fedtschenko 1869	M-**SB**
	nepalensis D. Don 1825 non Wallich = **I. decora**	
5	**nicolai** Vvedensky 1935	EGF.1-**M**-SB
1C	**nigricans** Dinsmore 1933	EGF.1-M
5	**nusairiensis** Mouterde 1966	M-SB
	ochroleuca Linnaeus 1771 = **I. orientalis**	
5	**orchioides** Carriere 1880	M-**BB**
	orchioides hort. non Carriere 1880 = **I. bucharica** (form)	
2B(k)	**orientalis** Miller 1768 (*I. ochroleuca*)	EGF.1-**M**-PGP-**DGP**-RD
	orientalis Thunberg 1794 non Miller 1768 = **I. sanguinea**	
1A	**pallida** Lamark 1789 (*I. dalmatica* hort.)	EGF.1-M-PGP-DGP-RD
	'Albo-variegata' = **I. pallida** 'Argentea Variegata'	
	'Argentea Variegata' ® [Goos & Koennemann 1906]	DGP-RD
	'Aureo-variegata' = **I. pallida** 'Variegata'	
	ssp. **cengialtii** (Ambrosi) Foster (*I. cengialtii*)	EGF.1-**M**
	'Dalmatica' = **I. pallida**	
	'Variegata' ® [Barr 1901]	EGF.1-PGP-**DGP**-RD
6	**pamphylica** Hedge 1961	EGF.1-**M**-**BB**-SB
1C	**paradoxa** Steven 1817	EGF.1-**M**

		f. **choschab** (Hoog) Mathew & Wendelbo	EGF.1-M
	5	**parvula** Vvedensky 1935	M-SB
	5	**persica** Linnaeus 1753	EGF.1-**M**-CA-**BB**-SB-DGP
		var. *stenophylla* (Haussknecht & Siehe ex Baker) hort. = **I. stenophylla**
		var. *tauri* (Siehe ex Mallet) hort. = **I. stenophylla**
	5	**planifolia** (Miller) Fiori & Paoletti 1896 (*I. alata*)	EGF.1-M-CA-**BB**-SB-**DGP**
	2B(k)	**pontica** Zapalowicz 1906 (*I. humilis*)	EGF.1-M
HN‡	2B(h)	**pseudacorus** Linnaeus 1753	EGF.1-M-PGP-**DGP**-RD
		var. **bastardii** (Bureau) Lynch	EGF.1-M-PGP-DGP-RD
		Cream Form	
		'Empress of India' ® [Barr 1921]	
		'Flore Pleno'	
		'Golden Fleece'	PGP
		'Golden Queen' ® [Gibson 1938]	RD
		'Mandshurica' ® [Berry 1938]	
		'Marginatus' nom. dub.	
		'Primrose Beauty' = **I. pseudacorus** var. **bastardii**	
		'Sulphur Queen'	
		'Turnispeed'	
		'Variegata' ® [Perry 1906]	EGF.1-PGP-**RD**
	5	**pseudocaucasica** Grossheim 1916	EGF.1-**M**-**BB**-SB
	1A	**pumila** Linnaeus 1753	EGF.1-M-CA-**RD**
		ssp. *attica* (Boissier & Heldreich) Hayek = **I. attica**	
	2B(f)	**purdyi** Eastwood 1897	EGF.1-M-PGP
	1A	**reichenbachii** Heuffel 1858 (*I. serbica*)	EGF.1-**M**-CA-**BB**-**SB**-**DGP**-**RD**
	6	**reticulata** Marshall von Bieberstein 1808	EGF.1-**M**
		ex **Armenia**	
		var. *bakeriana* (Foster) Mathew & Wendelbo 1975 = **I. bakeriana**	

'RETICULATA' IRISES (*I.histrioides x I.reticulata x I. winogradowii etc.*)

'Angel's Tears' ® [W. Blom & Son 1974]	M
'Cantab' ® [E. A. Bowles 1914]	CA-**BB**-**DGP**-RD
'Clairette' ® [van Tubergen pre-1919]	**BB**-**DGP**-RD
'Edward'	
'Frank Elder'	EGF.1-M-SB
'George' ® [P. B. van Eeden 1973]	
'Gordon' ® [P. B. van Eeden 1971]	
'G P Baker' ® [G. P. Baker c1909]	M
'Harmony' ® [van Tubergen pre-1953]	**DGP**-RD
'Hercules' ® [A. van den Berg Gzn. pre-1933]	
'Ida' ® [P. B. van Eeden 1973]	
'Jeannine' ® [van Tubergen 1958]	
'Joyce' ® [van Tubergen pre-1943]	**BB**-DGP-RD
'J S Dijt' ® [J. S. Dijt pre-1938]	
'Katharine Hodgkin' ® [E. B. Anderson 1960]	EGF.1-M-**BB**-SB
'Natascha' ® [P. B. van Eeden 1973]	
'Pauline' ® [van Tubergen pre-1953]	**RD**
'Purple Gem' ® [van Tubergen]	
'Royal Blue' ® [A. L. Hutley pre-1936]	DGP
'Spring Time' ® [van Tubergen 1950]	
'Violet Beauty' ® [De Graaff Bros 1954]	DGP

	2B(h)	**x robusta** E. B. Anderson (*I. versicolor x I. virginica*)	
		'Gerald Darby' ® [G. Darby via Coe 1968]	
	5	**rosenbachiana** Regel 1884	EGF.1-M-**BB**-SB
		rudskyi Horvat 1947 = **I. variegata**	
	2B(c)	**ruthenica** Ker-Gawler 1808	EGF.1-M-CA-RD
	1C	**samariae** Dinsmore 1933	EGF.1-M
	1A	**x sambuciana** Linnaeus 1750 (*I. pallida x I. variegata*)	EGF.1-M

2B(e)   **sanguinea** (Don) Hornemann 1813 (*I. orientalis* Thunberg, *I. thunbergii*)

        'Alba'   EGF.1-M

        'Gigantea'   EGF.1-M

1C   **sari** Schott ex Baker 1876   EGF.1-**M**

1A   **schachtii** Markgraf   EGF.1-M

     serbica Pancic 1883 = **I. reichenbachii**

2B(d) **setosa** Pallas ex Link 1875   EGF.1-**M**-PGP-RD

         var. **arctica** (Eastwood) Dykes   EGF.1-M

         ssp. **canadensis** (M. Forster) Hulten (*I. hookeri*) EGF.1-M

         Dwarf Form = **I. setosa** var. **arctica**

2B(e) **sibirica** Linnaeus 1753   EGF.1-M-PGP-**RD**

        'Alba' ®   [Van Houtte 1879]

'SIBERIAN' HYBRIDS

        'Ann Dasch' ®   [S. Varner 1977]

        'Anniversary' ®   [M. Brummitt 1965]   PGP

        'Avon' ®   [S. Varner 1978]

        'Bee' ®   [C. McEwen 1976]

        'Blue Brilliant' ®   [Cassebeer 1959]

        'Blue Burgee' ®   [C. McEwen 1971]

        'Blue Celeste' ®   [Roy 1919]

        'Blue King' ®   [Barr 1902]   RD

        'Blue Mere' ®   [P. Hutchinson 1959]   **DGP**

        'Blue Pennant' ®   [C. McEwen 1971]

        'Bracknell' ®   [Waterer 1934]

        'Butter and Sugar' ®   [C. McEwen 1976]

        'Caesar' ®   [Morgan 1930]   PGP

        'Caesar's Brother' ®   [Morgan 1932]]   PGP-**DGP**

        'Cambridge' ®   [M. Brummitt 1964]   PGP

        'Chartreuse Bounty' ®   [C. McEwen 1983]

        'Chine Blue' ®   [Preston pre-1938]

        'Clee Hills' ®   [J. Hewitt 1979]

        'Cleve Dodge' ®   [C. McEwen 1968]

        'Clouded Moon' ®   [E. Hunt 1972]

        'Cool Spring' ®   [Kellogg 1939]   **DGP**

        'Dark Desire' ®   [S. Varner 1974]

        'Dragonfly' ®   [Dykes 1923]

        'Dreaming Green' ®   [C. McEwen 1981]

        'Dreaming Spires' ®   [M. Brummitt 1964]

        'Dreaming Yellow' ®   [C. McEwen 1969]

        'Ego' ®   [McGarvey 1965]

        'Elmeney' ®   [E. Berlin 1980]

        'Ellesmere' ®   [P. Hutchinson 1956]

        'Emperor' ®   [Barr 1916]   PGP

        'Eric The Red' ®   [Whitney 1947]   PGP

        'Ewen' ®   [C. McEwen 1970]

        'Flight of Butterflies' ®   [J. Witt 1972]

        'Fourfold Lavender' ®   [C. McEwen 1982]

        'Fourfold White' ®   [C. McEwen 1969]

        'Gatineau' ®   [Preston 1932]   RD

        'Grand Junction' ®   [F. McCord 1968]

        'Harpswell Haze' ®   [C. McEwen 1977]

        'Heavenly Blue' ®   [Waterer 1928]   PGP-RD

        'Helen Astor' ®   [Whitney via Kellogg 1938]   PGP-RD

        'Hubbard' ®   [C. McEwen 1982]

        'Illini Encore' ®   [Varner 1966]

        'Kismet' ®   [S. Varner 1979]

        'Kobaltblau' ®   [T. Tamberg 1978]

'**Langthorn's Pink**'
'**Laurenbuhl**' ®   [E. Berlin 1979]
'**Lavender Bounty**' ®   [C. McEwen 1981]
'**Lavender Light**' ®   [C. McEwen 1973]
'**Lavender Royal**' ®   [M. Brummitt 1982]
'**Letitia**' ®   [S. Varner 1974]
'**Limeheart**' ®   [M. Brummitt 1968]   RD
'**Limelight**'
'**Little Blue**' ®   [C. McEwen 1976]
'**Little White**' ®   [C. McEwen 1968]
'**Maranatha**' ®   [S. Varner 1973]
'**Marilyn Holmes**' ®   [C. McEwen 1968]
'**Mike's Find**'
'**Miss Underwood**'
'**Mountain Lake**' ®   [Gersdorff 1938]
'**My Love**' ®   [Scheffy 1949]
'**Nottingham Lace**' ®   [P. Hutchinson 1959]
'**On and On**' ®   [C. McEwen 1977]
'**Orville Fay**' ®   [C. McEwen 1969]
'**Ottawa**' ®   [Preston 1928]   RD
'**Outset**' ®   [C. McEwen 1976]
'**Papillon**' ®   [Dykes 1923]   RD
'**Pearl Queen**'
'**Peg Edwards**' ®   [C. McEwen 1975]
'**Perry's Blue**'   [Perry]
'**Perry's Favourite**'   [Perry]
'**Perry's Pygmy**'   [Perry]
'**Persimmon**' ®   [Wallace 1939]
'**Phosphorflamme**'
'**Pickanock**' ®   [Preston 1937]
'**Pirate Prince**' ®   [S. Varner 1977]
'**Placid Waters**' ®   [Cassebeer 1962]
'**Polly Dodge**' ®   [C. McEwen 1968]
'**Purple Cloak**' ®   [P. Hutchison 1963]
'**Purple Mere**' ®   [P. Hutchinson 1959]   DGP
'**Red Flag**'
'**Red Flare**'
'**Red Flash**'
'**Reddy Maid**' ®   [C. McEwen 1978]
'**Rejoice Always**' ®   [S. Varner 1975]
'**Rimouski**' ®   [Preston 1937]
'**Roanoke's Choice**' ®   [W. McGarvey 1975]
'**Royal Blue**' ®   [Taylor 1932]
'**Royal Ensign**' ®   [Hall via Nesmith 1950]
'**Ruffled Velvet**' ®   [C. McEwen 1973]
'**Sally Kerlin**' ®   [C. McEwen 1968]
'**Savoir Faire**' ®   [S. DuBose 1974]
'**Sea Shadows**' ®   [Brummitt 1964]   PGP
'**Shirley Pope**' ®   [C. McEwen 1979]
'**Silver Edge**' ®   [C. McEwen 1973]
'**Sky Wings**' ®   [W. Peck 1971]
'**Snow Bounty**' ®   [C. McEwen 1973]
'**Snow Crest**' ®   [Gage 1932]
'**Snow Princess**'
'**Snow Queen**' ®   [Barr 1900]   RD
'**Soft Blue**' ®   [C. McEwen 1979]
'**Sparkling Rose**' ®   [B. Hager 1967]
'**Steve**' ®   [S. Varner 1974]
'**Steve Varner**' ®   [H. Briscoe 1976]
'**Strandperle**' ®   [Goos & Koennemann 1927]

'**Summer Sky**' ®   [Cleveland 1935]
'**Superba**' ®   [Bergmanns 1924]
'**Swank**' ®   [B. Hager 1968]
'**Teal Velvet**' ®   [C. McEwen 1981]
'**Towanda Redflare**' ®   [Scheffy 1949]
'**Tropic Night**' ®   [Morgan 1937]
'**Tunkhannock**' ®   [Scheffy 1944]
'**Turquoise Cup**' ®   [Cleveland 1927]
'**Tycoon**' ®   [Cleveland 1938]
'**Valda**' ®   [A. Back 1976]
'**Vee One**' ®   [A. Back via A. Blanco-White 1982]
'**Vi Luihn**' ®   [S. DuBose 1973]
'**Violetmere**' ®   [P. Hutchinson 1963]
'**Weihenstephan**
'**Weisser Orient**' ®   [Steiger 1958]
'**White Horses**' ®   [Kitton 1964]
'**White Queen**'
'**White Swirl**' ®   [Cassebeer 1957]   PGP-**DGP**
'**Wine Wings**' ®   [S. Varner 1976]
'**Wisley White**' ®   [Wisley Gardens 1940]   PGP

sindjarensis Boissier & Haussknecht 1882 = **I. aucheri**
5   '**Sindpers**' (*I. aucheri* x *I. persica*) ®   [van Tubergen 1889]
                                                          EGF.1-M-**BB**-SB
2B(k)   **sintenisii** Janka 1874   EGF.1-**M**
        sisyrinchium Linnaeus 1753 = **Gynandriris sisyrinchium**
IC   **sofarana** Foster 1899 (*I. susiana* hort.)   EGF.1-M
        ssp. **kasruwana** (Dinsmore) Chaudhary (*I. kasruwana*)   M
        sogdiana Bunge 1847 = **I. spuria** ssp. **sogdiana**
2B(m)   **songarica** Schrenk 1841   EGF.1-**M**
1C   **sprengeri** Siehe 1904   EGF.1-**M**
N‡   2B(k)   **spuria** Linnaeus 1753   EGF.1-M-PGP-DGP-RD
        ssp. **halophila** (Pallas) Mathew & Wendelbo 1975 (*I. halophila*)
                                                          EGF.1-M-PGP
        ssp. **maritima** (Lamarck) Fournier   M
        ssp. **musulmanica** (Fomin) Takhtadjan 1972 (*I. klattii*)   EGF.1-**M**
        '**Ochroleuca**' = **I. orientalis**
        ssp. **sogdiana** (Bunge) Mathew 1981 (*I. lilacina, I. sogdiana*)   M

IRIS SPURIA GROUP CULTIVARS

'**Adobe Sunset**' ®   [E. McCown 1976]
'**Airy Fancy**' ®   [B. Hager 1977]
'**Archie Owen**' ®   [B. Hager 1970]
'**Barbara's Kiss**' ®   [E. McCown 1981]
'**Belief**'
'**Betty Cooper**' ®   [E. McCown 1981]
'**Blue Pinafore**' ®   [T. Craig 1950]
'**Blue Zephyr**' ®   [Washington 1943]
'**Buttered Chocolate**' ®   [O. D. Niswonger 1973]
'**Burnished Brass**' ®   [B. Roe 1971]
'**Cambridge Blue**' ®   [Barr 1924]
'**Cameltone**' ®   [O. D. Niswonger 1976]
'**Charmglow**' ®   [B. Roe 1971]
'**Char-True**' ®   [Muhlestein 1965]
'**Cherokee Chief**' ®   [Nies 1949]
'**Cinnamon Roll**' ®   [O. D. Niswonger 1979]
'**Cinnamon Stick**' ®   [D. Niswonger 1982]
'**Clarke Cosgrove**' ®   [B. Hager 1974]
'**Connoisseur**' ®   [B. Hager 1965]

'Counterpoint' ®   [Ferguson 1961]
'Dawn Candle' ®   [Ferguson 1965]
'Dorothy Foster' ®   [Foster 1889]
'Elixir' ®   [B. Hager 1963]
'Essay' ®   [B. Hager 1963]
'Farolito' ®   [B. Hager 1965]
'Fort Ridge' ®   [W. Ferguson 1970]
'Golden Chocolate' ®   [D. Niswonger 1973]
'Golden Lady' ®   [Combs 1957]
'Good Nature' ®   [Ferguson 1958]
'Grand Illusion' ®   [B. Williamson 1971]
'Happy Choice' ®   [O. D. Niswonger 1976]
'Highline Lavender' ®   [E. McCown 1968]
'Imperial Bronze' ®   [E. McCown 1970]
'Janice Chesnik' ®   [E. McCown 1983]
'Just Reward' ®   [J. Ghio 1977]
'La Senda' ®   [W. Ferguson 1972]
'Lord Wolsely' ®   [Barr 1899]
'Lydia Jane' ®   [M. Walker 1964]
'Mariposa Tarde' ®   [E. McCown 1975]
'Media Luz' ®   [B. Hager 1967]
'Missouri Gal' ®   [D. Niswonger 1976]
'Neophyte'
'Orange Maid' ®   [W. Ferguson 1965]
'Oroville' ®   [M. Walker 1967]
'Penny Bunker' ®   [E. McCown 1981]
'Port of Call' ®   [B. Hager 1965]
'Protege' ®   [B. Hager 1966]
'Proverb' ®   [W. Ferguson 1971]
'Red Clover' ®   [W. Ferguson 1970]
'Red Oak' ®   [W. Ferguson 1965]
'Redwood Supreme' ®   [D. Niswonger 1976]
'Ripe Wheat' ®   [W. Ferguson 1972]
'Sahara Sands' ®   [D. Niswonger 1976]
'Sarong' ®   [B. Hager 1974]
'Sierra Nevada' ®   [M. Walker 1973]
'Spring Reverie' ®   [B. Hager 1976]
'Stability' ®   [M. Walker 1964]
'Sunlit Sea' ®   [M. Walker 1956]
'Sunny Day' ®   [Sass 1931]
'Sunny Side' ®   [T. Craig 1951]
'Suspense' ®   [B. Hager 1966]
'Thrush Song' ®   [Ferguson 1958]
'Vintage Year' ®   [D. Niswonger 1979]
'Wakerobin' ®   [W. Ferguson 1958]

1A	**x squalens** Linnaeus 1759 (*I. germanica x I. variegata*)	PGP
5	**stenophylla** Haussknecht & Siehe ex Baker 1900 (*I. persica* var. *stenophylla*,	
		I. tauri) EGF.1-M-**BB**
1D	**stolonifera** Maximowicz 1880	EGF.1-M-PGP-RD
	'George Barr'	
	stylosa Dammann 1901 = **I. unguicularis**	
1A	**suaveolens** Boissier & Reuter 1853 (*I. mellita*)	EGF.1-**M**-CA
1A	**subbiflora** Brotero 1804	EGF.1-M
1C	**susiana** Linnaeus 1753	EGF.1-**M**
	susiana hort. non Linnaeus 1753 = **I. sofarana**	
5	**svetlanae** Vvedensky	M-SB
2B(k)	**swertii** Hort. ex Lamarck	
	tauri Siehe 1905 = **I. stenophylla**	
2A	**tectorum** Maximowicz 1871	EGF.1-M-PGP-**DGP-RD**
	'Alba' ® [Sprenger 1901]	EGF.1-**M**-PGP

2B(f)	**tenax** Douglas ex Lindley 1829 (*I. gormanii*)	EGF.1-M-PGP-CA-RD
	'Alba'	
	ssp. **klamathensis** Lenz 1958	
2A	**tenuis** S. Watson 1882	EGF.1-M
	thunbergii Lundström 1914 = **I. sanguinea**	
	tolmeiana Herbert = **I. missouriensis**	
1A	**trojana** Kerner ex Stapf 1887	EGF.1-M-PGP
	'Miss Rowe' ® [Perry 1911]	
	tuberosa Linnaeus 1753 = **Hermodactylus tuberosus**	
2B(p)	**unguicularis** Poiret 1785 (*I. stylosa*)	EGF.1-M-**DGP-RD**
	'Abingdon Purple'	
	'Alba' ® [Arkwright pre-1988]	M-**DGP**
	'Angustifolia' ®	M
	'Cretensis'= **I. cretensis**	**M**
	var. *lazica* (Albov) Dykes = **I. lazica**	
	'Marginata' ® [Dammann 1901]	M
	'Mary Barnard' ® [Barnard via E. B. Anderson 1962]	M-PGP-DGP
	'Oxford' nom. dub.	
	'Oxford Dwarf'	
	'Walter Butt' ® [E. B. Anderson 1962]	M
	'Winter Treasure' ® [E. Cleaves 1966]	M-PGP
1A	**variegata** Linnaeus 1753 (*I. rudskyi*)	EGF.1-M
2B(b)	**verna** Linnaeus 1753	EGF.1-M-CA-**DGP**
2B(h)	**versicolor** Linnaeus 1753	EGF.1-**M**-PGP-RD
	'Kermesina' ® [Barr 1901]	EGF.1-**PGP**-RD
	Lavender	
	Violet Form	
5	**vicaria** Vvedensky 1935	M-**BB-SB**
5	**warleyensis** Foster 1902	EGF.1-M-PGP-**BB-SB**
5	**'Warlsind'** ® [van Tubergen 1936] (*I. aucheri x I. warleyensis*)	
		EGF.1-M-BB-SB
5	**willmottiana** Foster 1901	EGF.1-M-**BB-SB**
	'Alba' [van Tubergen 1936]	EGF.1-M
2B(e)	**wilsonii** C. H. Wright 1907	EGF.1-M
6	**winogradowii** Fomin 1924	EGF.1-**M-CA-BB**-SB-DGP-RD
	xiphioides Ehrhart 1792 = **I. latifolia**	
4	**xiphium** Linnaeus 1753	EGF.1-M-**BB**-RD
	var. *filifolia* (Boissier) hort. = **I. filifolia**	
	'Taitii'	EGF.1-M

'PACIFIC COAST' or 'CALIFORNIAN' IRISES
(*I. douglasiana x I. innominata etc.*)

'Arnold Sunrise' ® [V. Humphrey 1975]
'Banbury Fair' ® [M. Brummitt 1969]
'Banbury Melody' ® [M. Brummitt 1973]
'Banbury Yellow'
'Blue Ballerina' ® [Bootle/Wilbraham 1973]
'Broadleigh Ann'
'Broadleigh Dorothy'
'Broadleigh Emily'
'Broadleigh Florence'
'Broadleigh Joan'
'Broadleigh Lavinia'
'Broadleigh Mitre'
'Broadleigh Rose'
'Broadleigh Sybil'
'Dr Riddle'
Edith Piaf Hybrids

'Hirao'
'Lavender Lilt' ®   [F. Knowles 1973]
'Lavender Royal' ®   [M. Brummitt 1982]
'Reuthe's Bronze'
'Silf'
'Western American'

'ARIL' IRISES (*REGELIOCYLYS HYBRIDS*)
(Hybrids from section Onocyclus x section Regelia)

'Ancilla' ®   [van Tubergen pre-1957]
'Chione' ®   [van Tubergen pre-1919]   DGP-RD
'Clotho' ®   [van Tubergen pre-1922]
'Dardanus'   ®   [van Tubergen]
'Hipermestra'
'Theseus'   ®   [P. W. Voet pre-1914]
'Thor' ®   [van Tubergen]   RD
'Vera' ®   [van Tubergen 1956]   RD

'ARIL-MEDIAN' IRISES
(Aril x Miniature Tall Bearded (MTB) irises)

'Canasta'   ®   [L. Rich 1975]
'Little Orchid Annie'   ®   [D. Foster 1973]

'ARILBRED' IRISES
(Aril x Tall Bearded (TB) irises)

'Big Black Bumblebee'   ®   [Danielson 1965]
'Calypso Clown'   ®   [L. Rich 1977]
'Desert Dream'   ®   [L. Flanagan 1974]
'Lady Mohr' ®   [Salback 1943]   DGP
'Little Sheba'   ®   [Abell 1962]
'Loudmouth'   ®   [L. Rich 1970]
'Jessaboo' ®   [F. Gadd 1977]
'Nineveh'   ®   [Keppel 1965]
'Nightlight' ®   [L. Rich 1975]
'Pogo Doll' ®   [L. Christlieb 1967]
'Prophetic Message' ®   [H. Nichols 1978]
'Real Gold' ®   [Austin 1956]
'Saffron Charm' ®   [Benbow 1953]
'Speckled Bird' ®   [Crandall 1957]
'Wee Scot' ®   [Street 1958]

'BEARDED' (POGON) IRISES

classification:

BB	Border Bearded
IB	Intermediate Bearded
MDB	Miniature Dwarf Bearded
MTB	Miniature Tall Bearded
SDB	Standard Dwarf Bearded
TB	Tall Bearded

SDB	'Abracadabra' ®	[B. Hager 1976]
DB	'Ablaze' ®	[Welch 1955]
TB	'Action Front' ®	[N. Cook 1942]
TB	'Actress' ®	[K. Keppel 1975]
TB	'Alastor' ®	[Spender 1940]

TB	'Albatross' ®	[Barr 1907]	
TB	'Allaglow' ®	[Tompkins 1958]	
TB	'Allegiance' ®	[P. Cook 1957]	
TB	'Alenette' ®	[DeForest 1969]	
MDB	'Already' ®	[Warburton 1961]	
SDB	'Amaranth Gem' ®	[Muhlestein 1962]	
	'Amas' = **I. germanica 'Amas'**		
SDB	'Amazon Princess' ®	[H. Nichols 1973]	
TB	'Ambassadeur' ®	[Vilmorin 1920]	
DB	'Amber Queen' ®	[Ouden c1940]	
TB	'Amethyst Flame' ®	[R. Schreiner 1957]	RD
MTB	'Amethyst Sunset' ®	[W. Welch 1973]	
TB	'Amigo' ®	[Williamson 1934]	
SDB	'Amphora' ®	[J. D. Taylor 1972]	
MDB	'Angel Eyes' ®	[B. Jones 1958]	
SDB	'Angelic' ®	[C. Palmer 1974]	
TB	'Annabel Jane' ®	[B. Dodsworth 1973]	
SDB	'Anne Elizabeth' ®	[J. D. Taylor 1973]	
TB	'Antarctic' ®	[Kelway 1957]	
IB	'Apache Warrior' ®	[A. Brown 1971]	
IB	'Appleblossom Pink' ®	[J. Boushay 1973]	
SDB	'Appledore' ®	[J. D. Taylor 1973]	
MDB	'April Accent' ®	[A. Brown 1965]	
MDB	'April Ballet' ®	[C. Palmer 1973]	
TB	'Arab Chief' ®	[Whiting 1942]	
TB	'Arabi Pasha' ®	[Anley 1951]	
IB	'Arabi Treasure' ®	[Burnett 1962]	
IB	'Arabic Night'		
IB	'Arctic Fancy' ®	[A. Brown 1964]	PGP
TB	'Arctic Star' ®	[Kelway 1959]	
TB	'Arctic Tern' ®	[B. Dodsworth 1983]	
TB	'Argus Pheasant' ®	[DeForest 1947]	
SDB	'Arnold Velvet' ®	[V. Humphrey 1971]	
BB	'Aunt Martha' ®	[J. Allen 1970]	
SDB	'Austrian Sky' ®	[Darby 1959]	
TB	'Autumn Leaves' ®	[K. Keppel 1972]	
IB	'Avanelle' ®	[W. Jones 1976]	
SDB	'Aztec Star' ®	[D. Niswonger 1981]	
SDB	'Baby Blessed' ®	[L. Zurbrigg 1979]	
TB	'Baby Face' ®	[K. Mohr 1976]	
MDB	'Baby Kid' ®	[D. Rawdon 1971]	
TB	'Baccarat' ®	[Gaulter 1966]	
DDB	'Banbury Ruffles' ®	[D. Reath 1970]	
TB	'Bang' ®	[T. Craig 1955]	
IB	'Baria' ®	[P. Cook 1951]	
SDB	'Barnstormer' ®	[A. Brown 1973]	
SDB	'Batsford' ®	[J. D. Taylor 1975]	
IB	'Battle Shout' ®	[J. Boushay 1975]	
TB	'Bavarian Cream' ®	[G. Plough 1977]	
TB	'Beach Girl' ®	[B. Blyth 1983]	
SDB	'Be Dazzled' ®	[J. Boushay 1975]	
MTB	'Bellboy' ®	[M. Dunderman 1973]	
TB	'Belle Embellie' ®	[P. Anfosso 1981]	
TB	'Benton Nigel' ®	[C. Morris 1955]	
TB	'Benton Yellow' nom. dub.		
TB	'Berkeley Gold' ®	[Salback 1942]	RD
TB	'Betty Chatten' ®	[Mrs C. McClanahan 1975]	
SDB	'Betty Wood' ®	[S. Varner 1978]	
TB	'Beverly Sills' ®	[B. Hager 1978]	
TB	'Bewick Swan' ®	[B. Dodsworth 1980]	

TB	'Beyond' ®	[J. Gibson 1978]	
BB	'Bibelot' ®	[Willbanks 1962]	
SDB	'Bibury' ®	[J. D. Taylor 1975]	
TB	'Big Peach' ®	[T. Muhlestein 1975]	
TB	'Black Forest' ®	[Schreiner 1944]	
TB	'Black Hills' ®	[Fay 1950]	
TB	'Black Ink' ®	[Kelway 1958]	
TB	'Black Swan' ®	[Fay 1960]	
TB	'Black Taffeta' ®	[Songer 1953]	RD
MDB	'Blauer Zweiklang' ®	[van Nes 1966]]	
MDB	'Blauer Pfeil' ®	[van Nes 1959]	
SDB	'Blockley' ®	[J. D. Taylor 1979]	
SDB	'Blonde Carmen' ®	[Denkewitz 1985]	
TB	'Blue Admiral' ®	[Kelway 1959]	
IB	'Blue Asterisk' ®	[Greenlee 1955]	
MDB	'Blue Beret' ®	[E. Roberts 1966]	
TB	'Bluebird Wine' ®	[B. Blyth 1981]	
SDB	'Blue Delph' ®	[N. Scopes 1984]	
SDB	'Blue Denim' ®	[Warburton 1958]	
MDB	'Blue Doll' ®	[Marburton 1958]	
TB	'Blue Duchess' ®	[Kelway 1966]	
DB	'Blue Frost' ®	[Doriot 1956]	
SDB	'Blue Pigmy' ®	[Ouden 1933]	RD
SDB	'Blue Pools'	[B. Jones 1972]	
TB	'Blue Rhythm' ®	[Whiting 1945]	**RD**
TB	'Blue Sapphire' ®	[B. Schreiner 1953]	
TB	'Blue Shimmer' ®	[Sass 1941]	
TB	'Blue Smoke' ®	[Kelway 1963]	
SDB	'Blue Sparks' ®	[Welch 1963]	
TB	'Blue Staccato' ®	[J. Gison 1976]	
TB	'Blue Valley' ®	[Smith 1945]	
TB	'Bobby Dazzler' ®	[N. Scopes 1986]	
IB	'Bold Print' ®	[J. Gatty 1981]	
TB	'Bolivia' ®	[Kelway 1960]	RD
SDB	'Boo' ®	[L. Markham 1971]	
IB	'Boy Wonder' ®	[J. Ghio 1976]	
TB	'Braithwaite' ®	[Randall 1952]	RD
SDB	'Brannigan' ®	[J. D. Taylor 1966]	
SDB	'Brassie' ®	[Warburton 1957]	
SDB	'Brass Tacks' ®	[K. Keppel 1977]	
SDB	'Bravita' ®	[L. Blyth 1980]	
TB	'Bridal Crown' ®	[Schreiner's 1981]	
DB	'Bride' ®	[W. J. Caparne 1901]	
IB	'Brighteyes' ®	[Darby 1957]	RD
SDB	'Bright Moment' ®	[B. Hager 1982]	
MDB	'Bright White' ®	[Welch 1957]	
SDB	'Broadwell' ®	[J. D. Taylor 1979]	
SDB	'Bromyard' ®	[J. D. Taylor 1979]	
TB	'Bronze Bird' ®	[Kelway 1963]	
TB	'Bronze Cloud' ®	[Kelway 1962]	
BB	'Brown Lasso' ®	[E. Buckles via D. Niswonger 1972]	
TB	'Brown Trout' ®	[Kelway 1959]	RD
DB	'Buster Brown' ®	[Zickler 1953]	
IB	'Butter Cookie' ®	[J. Gatty 1979]	
TB	'Buttercup Bower' ®	[Tompkins 1960]	
MDB	'Buttercup Charm' ®	[A. Brown 1969]	
TB	'Butterscotch Kiss' ®	[Plough 1955]	
SDB	'Byword' ®	[J. Boushay 1975]	
TB	'Caliente' ®	[Luihn 1967]	
TB	'California Gold' ®	[Mohr-Mitchell 1933]	
TB	'Camelot Rose' ®	[Tompkins 1965]	

TB	'Canary Bird' ®	[Kelway 1957]	
SDB	'Candy Apple' ®	[M. Hamblen 1972]	
BB	'Candy Cane' ®	[Z. G. Benson 1969]	
TB	'Captain Gallant' ®	[Schmelzer 1957]	
TB	'Carnaby' ®	[Schreiner's 1973]	
BB	'Carnival Glass' ®	[B. Jones 1964]	
TB	'Carnton' ®	[Wills 1950]	RD
TB	'Carolina Gold' ®	[L. Powell 1970]	
MTB	'Carolyn Rose' ®	[M. Dunderman 1970]	
SDB	'Carrot Curls' ®	[D. Sindt 1981]	
SDB	'Cascade Sprite' ®	[Fothergill 1963]	
TB	'Celestial Glory' ®	[Reckamp 1961]	
SDB	'Chalk Mark' ®	[G. Plough 1974]	
TB	'Chantilly' ®	[Hall 1943]	
TB	'Chapeau' ®	[S. Babson 1969]	
SDB	'Chapel Hill' ®	[A. & D. Willott 1976]	
IB	'Charm Song' ®	[A. Brown 1968]	
IB	'Cheers' ®	[B. Hager 1974]	
SDB	'Cherry Garden' ®	[B. Jones 1966]	
TB	'Cherry Orchard' ®	[B. Long 1956]	
SDB	'Cherub Tears' ®	[J. Boushay 1975]	
TB	'Chesterton' ®	[J. D. Taylor 1977]	
TB	'Chief Moses' ®	[Plough 1967]	
TB	'Chieftain's' ®	[L. MacKay 1972]	RD
TB	'Chinese Coral' ®	[Fay 1960]	
TB	'Chinese Treasure' ®	[B. Blyth 1981]	
TB	'Christabel' ®	[E. G. Lapham 1936]	
TB	'Christmas Angel' ®	[DeForest 1959]	
MDB	'Chromeling' ®	[H. Fothergill 1973]	
SDB	'Church Stoke' ®	[J. D. Taylor 1979]	
SDB	'Cindy Mitchell' ®	[C. Palmer 1978]	
SDB	'Circlette' ®	[Goett 1962]	
TB	'City of David' ®	[J. Boushay 1976]	
TB	'City of Lincoln' ®	[Sass 1936]	
SDB	'Clap Hands' ®	[B. Hager 1974]	
SDB	'Clay's Caper' ®	[B. Hager via M. Hamblen 1975]	
TB	'Cliffs of Dover' ®	[Fay 1952]	DGP
IB	'Cloud Fluff' ®	[Greenlee 1955]	
TB	'Columbia' ®	[Tompkins 1951]	
SDB	'Combo' ®	[B. Hager 1976]	
SDB	'Concord Touch' ®	[A. & D. Willott 1974]	
IB	'Confederate Soldier' ®	[H. Nichols 1974]	
TB	'Confetti' ®	[R. Schreiner 1948]	
TB	'Constance Meyer' ®	[Meyer pre-1938]	
MTB	'Consummation' ®	[W. Welch 1977]	
TB	'Copper Rose' ®	[Cook 1941]	
TB	'Corrida' ®	[Millet & fils 1914]	
SDB	'Cotton Blossom' ®	[B. Jones 1969]	
TB	'Craithie'		
TB	'Credo' ®	[Babson 1964]	
TB	'Crispette' ®	[R. Schreiner 1954]	
MDB	'Crispy' ®	[Welch 1958]	
TB	'Crushed Velvet' ®	[J. Ghio 1976]	
SDB	'Cuban Cutie' ®	[P. Dyer 1977]	
TB	'Cup Race' ®	[Buttrick 1962]	
MDB	'Curio' ®	[B. Hager 1971]	
DB	'Cyanea' ®	[Goos & Koenemann 1899]	
MDB	'Dainty Belle' ®	[M. Hamblen 1976]	
SDB	'Dainty Toddler' ®	[M. Wright 1976]	
TB	'Daisy Powell' ®	[Hinkle 1963]	

DB	'Dale Dennis' ®	[D. Dennis 1955]	
TB	'Dame Judy' ®	[Kelway 1958]	
TB	'Dancer's Veil' ®	[Hutchison 1959]	**DGP-RD**
SDB	'Dancing Eyes' ®	[D. Sindt 1968]	
TB	'Dante' ®	[Kelway 1958]	
SDB	'Dark Fairy' ®	[A. Brown 1960]	
TB	'Dark Rosaleen' ®	[N. Scopes 1976]	
SDB	'Dark Spark' ®	[D. Sindt 1967]	
SDB	'Darkover' ®	[N. Scopes 1983]	
BB	'Dashing Deb' ®	[A. Brown 1966]	
SDB	'Dawn Favour' ®	[Soper 1960]	
IB	'Dawn Chorus' ®	[N. Scopes 1977]	
TB	'Deep Black' ®	[P. Cook 1953]	
TB	'Deep Pacific' ®	[E. Burger 1975]	
TB	'Deep Space' ®	[Tompkins 1961]	
SDB	'Deering-Do' ®	[Warburton 1957]	
TB	'Deft Touch' ®	[C. Tompkins 1977]	
SDB	'Delicate Air' ®	[Warburton 1961]	
TB	'Demelza' ®	[R. Nichol 1984]	
SDB	'Demon' ®	[B. Hager 1971]	
TB	'Depute Nomblot' ®	[Cayeaux 1929]	
SDB	'Derry Down' ®	[N. Scopes 1979]	
TB	'Derwentwater' ®	[Randall 1953]	
TB	'Desert Echo' ®	[D. Meek 1980]	
MTB	'Desert Quail' ®	[E. Roberts 1958]	
TB	'Desert Song' ®	[Fay 1946]	**RD**
IB	'Dew Point' ®	[G. Plough 1970]	
DB	'Die Braut'	[Junge 1906] = **I. 'Bride'**	
SDB	'Diligence' ®	[A. Brown via J. Boushay 1975]	
SDB	'Dixie Pixie' ®	[B. Jones 1977]	
MDB	'Doll House' ®	[A. Brown 1968]	
MTB	'Doll Ribbons' ®	[M. Dunderman 1977]	
IB	'Doll Type' ®	[Hager 1963]	
TB	'Dotted Swiss' ®	[Sass 1956]	
SDB	'Double Lament' ®	[J. D. Taylor 1969]	
TB	'Double Scoop' ®	[J. Ghio 1980]	
IB	'Downland' ®	[R. Usher 1969]	
TB	'Dovedale' ®	[B. Dodsworth 1980]	
IB	'Doxa' ®	[H. P. Sass 1929]	
MDB	'Dragons in Amber' ®	[B. Hager 1976]	
TB	'Dreamcastle' ®	[N. Cook 1943]	
TB	'Dresden Green' ®	[E. Sellman 1977]	
MDB	'Dunlin' ®	[J. D. Taylor 1977]	
TB	'Dusky Dancer' ®	[W. Luihn 1966]	
IB	'Early Edition' ®	[K. Keppel 1968]	
IB	'Early Frost' ®	[J. Gatty 1976]	
TB	'East Indies' ®	[K. Smith 1953]	
SDB	'Easy Strolling' ®	[J. Boushay 1979]	
TB	'Edward Windsor' ®	[Morris 1945]	
TB	'Eleanor's Pride' ®	[E. Watkins 1952]	**RD**
TB	'Elizabeth Arden' ®	[Kelway 1957]	
TB	'Elizabeth Nobel' ®	[K. Smith 1953]	
TMB	'Elmohr' ®	[Loomis-Long 1942]	RD
IB	'Elusive Quest' ®	[C. Palmer 1970]	
TB	'Elysian Fields' ®	[L. Gaulter 1976]	
TB	'Embassadora' ®	[B. Blyth 1978]	
SDB	'Encanto' ®	[A. Brown 1973]	
SDB	'Enchanted Blue' ®	[C. Palmer 1973]	
TB	'Esther Fay' ®	[Fay 1960]	**DGP**
TB	'Etched Apricot' ®	[J. Gibson 1967]	

TB	'Evening Écho'	®	[M. Hamblen 1976]
DB	'Excelsior'	®	[Goos & Koenemann 1899]
TB	'Exotic Gem'	®	[M. Olson 1970]
TB	'Exotic Star'	®	[G. Plough 1974]
SDB	'Eyebright'	®	[J. D. Taylor 1977]
SDB	'Eye Shadow'	®	[E. Roberts 1962]
IB	'Fancy Caper'	®	[Warburton 1963]
SDB	'Fantasy Isle'	®	[J. Boushay 1978]
IB	'Fantasy World'	®	[A. Brown 1975]
SDB	'Faraway'	®	[N. Scopes 1982]
TB	'Feminine Charm'	®	[E. Kegerise 1973]
TB	'Festive Skirt'	®	[F. Hutchins 1973]
TB	'Festive Spirit'	®	[Plough 1968]
TB	'Fiery Song'	®	[Kelway 1962]
TB	'Fine Precedent'	®	[P. Blyth 1976]
MDB	'Fiorellino'	®	[J. D. Taylor 1970]
SDB	'Fire One'	®	[G. Plough 1978]
TB	'Fire and Rain'	®	[G. Plough 1974]
TB	'Firecracker'	®	[D. N. Hall 1942]
IB	'First Lilac'	®	[Greenlee 1957]
TB	'Flair'	®	[J. Gatty 1975]
TB	'Flamenco'	®	[K. Keppel 1975]
TB	'Flamingo'	®	[Williamson 1929]
TB	'Flareup'	®	[J. Ghio 1977]
SDB	'Flirty Mary'	®	[D. Rawdon 1977]
	'Florentina' = **I. germanica 'Florentina'**		
TB	'Focus'	®	[K. Keppel 1975]
TB	'Foggy Dew'	®	[K. Keppel 1968]
MDB	'Footlights'	®	[B. Hager 1979]
SDB	'Forest Light'	®	[J. D. Taylor 1962]
IB	'Foxcote'	®	[J. D. Taylor 1977]
TB	'Foxfire'	®	[E. Fox 1951]
TB	'French Gown'	®	[B. Blyth 1983]
BB	'Frenchi'	®	[B. Jones 1958]
TB	'Fresno Frolic'	®	[J. Weiler 1980]
TB	'Frost and Flame'	®	[D. Hall 1956]
SDB	'Frosted Angel'	®	[T. Blyth 1984]
IB	'Frosted Crystal'	®	[J. Gatty 1977]
SDB	'Funtime'	®	[A. Peterson 1964]
SDB	'Furnaceman'	®	[J. D. Taylor 1971]
SDB	'Galleon Gold'	®	[Schreiner's 1977]
BB	'Garda'	®	[J. D. Taylor 1971]
MDB	'Garnet Elf'	®	[M. Hamblen 1976]
BB	'Gemini'	®	[Knopf 1965]
SDB	'Gentle Grace'	®	[J. Boushay 1979]
SDB	'Gentle Sky'	®	[B. Warburton 1977]
SDB	'Gentle Smile'	®	[A. Brown 1972]
TB	'Gigi'	®	[Schreiner's 1971]
TB	'Gilded Minaret'	®	[H. Fothergill 1969]
TB	'Gilston Gwyneth'	®	[H. Fletcher 1963]
SDB	'Gingerbread Man'	®	[B. Jones 1968]
MDB	'Gizmo'	®	[B. Hager 1976]
SDB	'Gleaming Gold'	®	[Roberts 1965]
TB	'Glory of June'	®	[Kelway 1962]
IB	'Gold Intensity'	®	[Austin 1954]
TB	'Gold Flake'	®	[Murrell 1933]
TB	'Golden Alps'	®	[L. Brummitt 1952]
SDB	'Golden Dewdrops'	®	[C. Palmer 1975]
SDB	'Golden Fair'	®	[Warburton 1960]
TB	'Golden Glow'	®	[Glutzbeck 1939]

TB	'Golden Harvest' ®	[Sass 1929]	
TB	'Golden Planet' ®	[Kelway 1956]	
TB	'Golden Veil' ®	[Kelway 1958]	
TB	'Goldfackel' ®	[Steffen 1955]	
TB	'Goldilocks' ®	[Wayman 1930]	
TB	'Gold Trimmings' ®	[Schreiner's 1973]	
TB	'Grace Abounding' ®	[H. Fothergill via P. McCormick 1976]	
TB	'Grace Sturtevant' ®	[Bliss 1926]	
DB	'Grandma's Hat' ®	[Mahood 1955]	
MTB	'Grandpa's Girl' ®	[K. Fisher 1983]	
DB	'Green Halo' ®	[Greenlee 1955]	
TB	'Green Ice' ®	[Kelway 1960]	
IB	'Green Spot' ®	[P. Cook 1951]	RD
SDB	'Greenstuff' ®	[A. Farrington 1986]	
MDB	'Grey Pearls' ®	[B. Hager 1978]	
TB	'Gringo' ®	[Keppel 1963]	
TB	'Gudrun' ®	[Dykes 1930]	
SDB	'Gypsy Boy' ®	[R. Blodgett 1977]	
TB	'Gypsy Caravan' ®	[S. Moldovan 1978]	
SDB	'Gypsy Eyes' ®	[J. Wadekamper via G. Hanson 1980]	
IB	'Gypsy Smoke' ®	[A. Brown 1968]	
TB	'Happy Birthday' ®	[D. Hall 1952]	
BB	'Happy Song' ®	[M. Hamblen 1977]	
IB	'Happy Thought' ®	[G. Douglas 1953]	RD
TB	'Harbor Blue' ®	[E. Christiansen 1966]	
TB	'Harriet Thoreau' ®	[Cook 1944]	
TB	'Harvest Gold' ®	[Kelway 1957]	
MTB	'Hazy Skies' ®	[F. Williams 1978]	
TB	'Headlines' ®	[L. Brummitt 1953]	
TB	'Heather Blush' ®	[B. Hamner 1976]	
TB	'Helen McGregor' ®	[N. Graves 1943]	DGP
TB	'Helen Traubel' ®	[C. Benson 1959]	
TB	'High Barbaree' ®	[Tompkins 1958]	
TB	'High Command' ®	[B. R. Long 1945]	
SDB	'Hilmteich' ®	[van Nes 1960]	
SDB	'Hocus Pocus' ®	[B. Hager 1974]	
TB	'Honey Girl' ®	[Kelway 1962]	
IB	'Honey Glazed' ®	[D. Niswonger 1982]	
BB	'Honey Spice' ®	[M. Hamblen 1970]	
SDB	'Honington' ®	[J. D. Taylor 1980]	
IB	'Honorabile' ®	[Lemon 1840]	
SDB	'Hooligan' ®	[J. Boushay 1978]	
TB	'Hugh Miller' ®	[Forbes 1910]	
MDB	'Hula Doll' ®	[A. Brown 1963]	
TB	'Hurley Burley' ®	[J. Boushay 1978]	
SDB	'Imagette' ®	[B. Blythe 1983]	
BB	'Impelling' ®	[J. Boushay 1979]	
BB	'Impetuous' ®	[J. Boushay 1980]	
IB	'Indeed' ®	[Hager 1963]	
TB	'Indian Chief' ®	[Ayres 1929]	
SDB	'Indian Jewel' ®	[A. Brown 1973]	
IB	'Innocent Heart' ®	[A. Howe via M. Howe 1974]	
SDB	'Inscription' ®	[J. Boushay 1978]	
TB	'Intuition' ®	[J. Ghio 1975]	
MDB	'Irish Doll' ®	[A. Brown 1962]	
MDB	'Irish Baby' ®	[D. Rawdon 1977]	
IB	'Irish King' ®	[Goos & Koenemann 1907]	
SDB	'Ishmael' ®	[J. Boushay 1976]	
TB	'Ivory Gown' ®	[E. Smith 1962]	
IB	'Jack O' Hearts' ®	[G. Douglas 1953]	

MDB	'Jackanape' ®	[W. Marx 1961]	
SDB	'Jade Mist' ®	[P. Dyer 1977]	
SDB	'Jan Reagan' ®	[K. Shaver 1976]	
TB	'Jane Phillips' ®	[Graves 1946]	**DGP**-RD
SDB	'Jane Taylor' ®	[J. D. Taylor 1968]	
MDB	'Jasper Gem' ®	[Welch 1963]	
SDB	'Jennie Grace' ®	[B. Warburton 1977]	
SDB	'Jeremy Brian' ®	[B. Price 1975]	
SDB	'Jerry Rubin' ®	[van Nes 1964]	
SDB	'Jersey Lilli' ®	[D. Dennis 1958]	
SDB	'Jewel Bright' ®	[N. Scopes 1983]	
TB	'Jill Rosalind' ®	[B. Dodsworth 1976]	
TB	'Joan Lay' ®	[Chadburn 1939]	
TB	'Joanna' ®	[Stern 1936]	
MDB	'Joanna Taylor' ®	[J. D. Taylor 1971]	
MTB	'Joette' ®	[F. Williams 1977]	
BB	'John's Joy' ®	[A. Ensminger 1971]	
SDB	'Jolly Fellow' ®	[A. Brown 1972]	
TB	'Jovian Magic' ®	[B. Blyth 1976]	
SDB	'Joyful' ®	[J. Gatty 1977]	
TB	'Jubilee Gem' ®	[Kelway 1960]	
TB	'Juliet' ®	[Klein 1946]	RD
TB	'June Sunset' ®	[D. Niswonger 1980]	
TB	'Jungle Fires' ®	[Schreiner's 1960]	
BB	'Jungle Shadows' ®	[Sass via Graham 1959]	
BB	'Just Jennifer' ®	[J. D. Taylor 1983]	
SDB	'Just So' ®	[Z. Benson 1962]	
SDB	'Katherine Helen' ®	[B. Price 1984]	
SDB	'Katy Petts' ®	[J. D. Taylor 1978]	
SDB	'Kayo' ®	[D. Niswonger 1979]	
TB	'Kent Pride' ®	[Hutchison 1958]	RD
SDB	'Kentucky Bluegrass' ®	[B. Jones 1970]	
	'Kharput' = **I. germanica** 'Kharput'		
TB	'Kildonan' ®	[B. Dodsworth 1976]	
TB	'Kirkstone' ®	[Randall 1957]	
SDB	'Kista' ®	[B. Blythe 1973]	
MDB	'Knick Knack' ®	[Greenlee 1959]	
SDB	'Knotty Pine' ®	[Goett 1959]	
BB	'La Nina Rosa' ®	[Sundt 1959]	
SDB	'Laced Lemonade' ®	[B. Warburton 1969]	
TB	'Lady Boscawen' ®	[Graves 1942]	
TB	'Lady River' ®	[Kelway 1966]	
TB	'Langley' ®	[J. D. Taylor 1977]	
IB	'Langport Carnival'	[Kelways]	
IB	'Langport Chapter'	[Kelways]	
IB	'Langport Chief'	[Kelways]	RD
IB	'Langport Chimes'	[Kelways]	
IB	'Langport Duchess'	[Kelways]	
IB	'Langport Fairy'	[Kelways]	
IB	'Langport Finch'	[Kelways]	RD
IB	'Langport Flame'	[Kelways]	RD
IB	'Langport Flash'	[Kelways]	
IB	'Langport Flush'	[Kelways]	
IB	'Langport Girl'	[Kelways]	
IB	'Langport Honey'	[Kelways]	RD
IB	'Langport Jane'	[Kelways]	
IB	'Langport Judy'	[Kelways]	
IB	'Langport Kestral'	[Kelways]	
IB	'Langport Lady'	[Kelways]	
IB	'Langport Magic'	[Kelways]	

IB	**'Langport Minstral'**	[Kelways]	
IB	**'Langport Pagan'**	[Kelways]	
IB	**'Langport Pansy'**	[Kelways]	RD
IB	**'Langport Pearl'**	[Kelways]	
IB	**'Langport Pinnacle'**	[Kelways]	
IB	**'Langport Prince'**	[Kelways]	
IB	**'Langport Robin'**	[Kelways]	
IB	**'Langport Romance'**	[Kelways]	
IB	**'Langport Secret'**	[Kelways]	
IB	**'Langport Smoke'**	[Kelways]	
IB	**'Langport Snow'**	[Kelways]	
IB	**'Langport Song'**	[Kelways]	
IB	**'Langport Star'**	[Kelways]	
IB	**'Langport Storm'**	[Kelways]	
IB	**'Langport Sultan'**	[Kelways]	
IB	**'Langport Sun'**	[Kelways]	
IB	**'Langport Tartan'**	[Kelways]	
IB	**'Langport Vale'**	[Kelways]	
IB	**'Langport Violet'**	[Kelways]	
IB	**'Langport Vista'**	[Kelways]	
IB	**'Langport Warrior'**	[Kelways]	
IB	**'Langport Wren'**	[Kelways]	
SDB	**'Lanka'** ®	[J. Taylor 1972]	
TB	**'Lavanesque'** ®	[R. Schreiner 1953]	
SDB	**'Lemon Flare'** ®	[Muhlestein 1958]	RD
IB	**'Lemon Flurry'** ®	[Muhlestein 1965]	
TB	**'Lemon Ice'** ®	[N. Tharp 1939]	
MDB	**'Lemon Puff'** ®	[Dunbar 1965]	
TB	**'Lemon Tree'** ®	[B. Jones 1965]	
TB	**'Lent A Williamson'** ®	[Williamson 1918]	
MDB	**'Libation'** ®	[B. Hager 1974]	
IB	**'Light Laughter'** ®	[N. Scopes 1984]	
TB	**'Lilac Mist'** ®	[W. Luihn 1968]	
TB	**'Lilac Queen'** ®	[G. Saxton 1971]	
SDB	**'Lilli-White'** ®	[Welch 1957]	
SDB	**'Lime Grove'** ®	[Fothergill 1958]	
IB	**'Lime Ripples'** ®	[A. Brown 1959]	
MDB	**'Linda Jean'** ®	[A. Farrington 1974]	
IB	**'Listowel'** ®	[Zurbrigg 1957]	
SDB	**'Little Bill'** ®	[W. Jones 1977]	
SDB	**'Little Black Belt'** ®	[D. Niswonger 1978]	
SDB	**'Little Blackfoot'** ®	[M. Reinhardt 1966]	
SDB	**'Little Bucaneer'** ®	[Schriener's 1973]	
SDB	**'Little Black Belt'** ®	[D. Niswonger 1978]	
SDB	**'Little Chestnut'** ®	[M. Brizedine 1970]	
SDB	**'Little Cottage'** ®	[Muhlestein 1958]	
SDB	**'Little Dandy'** ®	[J. Riley 1975]	
SDB	**'Little Dogie'** ®	[E. Roberts 1958]	
IB	**'Little Idol'** ®	[G. Plough 1977]	
MDB	**'Little May Dancer'** ®	[H. Hite 1974]	
MTB	**'Little Paul'** ®	[K. Fisher 1983]	
SDB	**'Little Rosy Wings'** ®	[G. Douglas 1957]	
IB	**'Little Shadow'** ®	[G. Douglas 1953]	RD
BB	**'Little Sir Echo'** ®	[Tompkins 1962]	
SDB	**'Little Suki'** ®	[N. Scopes 1970]	
BB	**'Little Swinger'** ®	[M. Hamblen 1975]	
IB	**'Little Wonder'** ®	[T. Craig 1967]	
MTB	**'Lively Rose'** ®	[K. Fisher 1985]	
TB	**'L'lita'** ®	[Tams 1960]	
TB	**'Lodestar'** ®	[Hall 1925]	

TB	'Lodore' ®	[Randall 1958]
TB	'Lord Warden' ®	[J. D. Taylor 1966]
TB	'Lorilee' ®	[Schreiner's 1981]
TB	'Lothario' ®	[Schreiner 1942]
TB	'Loudon Lassie' ®	[G. Crossman 1971]
TB	'Louvois' ®	[Cayeux 1936]
TB	'Love Chant' ®	[B. Blyth 1979]
SDB	'Love Lisa' ®	[L. Boushay 1979]
TB	'Lovely Again' ®	[R. G. Smith 1963]
TB	'Lovely Kay' ®	[M. Hamblen 1979]
TB	'Lovely Letty' ®	[D. Hall 1960]
TB	'Lucky Dip' ®	[N. Scopes 1983]
TB	'Lugano' ®	[Cayeux 1959]
DB	'Lutea' ®	[Kreleage 1875]
TB	'Lynn Hall' ®	[D. Hall 1956]
TB	'Magic Carpet' ®	[Schreiner 1942]
TB	'Magic Hills' ®	[Kelway 1959]
MDB	'Magic Flute' ®	[Beattie 1962]
SDB	'Mairi' ®	[N. Scopes 1977]
MDB	'Marhaba' ®	[J. D. Taylor 1969]
TB	'Marie Pinel'	
TB	'Mariner's Cove' ®	[W. Luihn 1981]
BB	'Marmalade Skies' ®	[D. Niswonger 1978]
MDB	'Marmot' ®	[Simonson 1964]
IB	'Maroon Caper' ®	[Warburton 1963]
TB	'Marshlander' ®	[J. Taylor 1966]
IB	'Marty' ®	[W. Jones 1977]
TB	'Mary Frances' ®	[L. Gaulter 1971]
SDB	'Mary McIlroy' ®	[J. D. Taylor 1984]
TB	'Mary Randall' ®	[Fay 1950]
TB	'Mary Todd' ®	[H. Randall 1960]
TB	'May Magic' ®	[R. Schreiner 1955]
TB	'May Melody' ®	[Hamblen 1964]
SDB	'May Thirty-First' ®	[A. Farrington 1986]
SDB	'Meadow Court' ®	[Neel 1965]
SDB	'Meadow Moss' ®	[B. Jones 1968]
TB	'Melbreak' ®	[Randall 1957]
TB	'Melody Lane' ®	[D. Hall 1947]
SDB	'Melon Honey' ®	[E. Roberts 1972]
IB	'Melrose' ®	[H. P. Simpson 1926]
TB	'Memphis Delight' ®	[E. Kegerise 1977]
IB	'Merry Day' ®	[H. L. Danenhauer 1934]
SDB	'Merseyside' ®	[A. Farrington 1982]
TB	'Millrace' ®	[L. Gaulter 1973]
TB	'Minisa' ®	[H. Wall 1973]
TB	'Minnie Colquitte' ®	[H. P. Sass 1941]
TB	'Mission Sunset' ®	[Reckamp 1962]
TB	'Misty Watercolors' ®	[D. Niswonger 1975]
MTB	'Mockingbird' ®	[E. Roberts 1962]
TB	'Monaco' ®	[R. Brown 1976]
TB	'Moonlight' ®	[Dykes 1923]
SDB	'Moon Shadows' ®	[D. Sindt 1968]
TB	'Morwenna' ®	[R. Nichol 1984]
IB	'Mrs Reuthe' ®	[Ware 1899]
SDB	'Mrs Nate Rudolph' ®	[H. Briscoe 1972]
TB	'Mulberry Rose' ®	[Schreiner 1941]
TB	'Muriel Neville' ®	[Fothergill 1963]
TB	'Murmuring Morn' ®	[C. Corlew 1969]
TB	'My Mary' ®	[Kelway 1960]
TB	'My Smoky' ®	[Kelway 1956]

RD

DGP

RD

TB	'Mystic Eye'	®	[D. Denney 1977]	
SDB	'Myra's Child'	®	[W. Greenlee 1971]	
TB	'Mysterious'	®	[Schreiner's 1972]	
IB	'Nambe'	®	[Williamson 1946]	
TB	'Nampara'	®	[R. Nichol 1984]	
MDB	'Nancy Hardy'	®	[J. D. Taylor 1971]	
TB	'Nancy's Khaki'			
TB	'Nashborough'	®	[Wills 1954]	
TB	'Neon Rainbow'	®	[Schreiner's 1971]	
MTB	'New Idea'	®	[B. Hager 1970]	
TB	'New Snow'	®	[Fay 1946]	RD
TB	'Night Owl'	®	[Schreiner's1970]	
TB	'Normandie'	®	[Gaulter 1968]	
SDB	'Nylon Ruffles'	®	[Doriot 1961]	
IB	'Of Course'	®	[B. Hager 1978]	
TB	'Ola Kala'	®	[J. Sass 1942]	DGP-RD
SDB	'Oliver'	®	[H. Nichols 1971]	
TB	'Olympic Torch'	®	[R. Schreiner 1956]	DGP
BB	'Oracle'	®	[J. Ghio 1971]	
TB	'Orchardist'	®	[Kelway 1965]	
MDB	'Orchid Flare'	®	[Mahood 1960]	
TB	'Orelio'	®	[De Forest 1947]	
TB	'Oriental Glory'	®	[Salbach 1952]	
TB	'Oritam'	®	[J. & P. Hoffmeister 1975]	
SDB	'Ornament'	®	[B. Hager 1971]	
BB	'Ouija'	®	[N. Scopes 1974]	
SDB	'Owlet'	®	[J. D. Taylor 1976]	
TB	'Pacemaker'	®	[Lapham 1949]	
TB	'Pagan Princess'	®	[G. Douglas 1948]	
MTB	'Painted Rose'	®	[E. Roberts 1964]	
TB	'Palace Gossip'	®	[R. Blyth 1981]	
TB	'Pale Primrose'	®	[Whiting 1946]	
TB	'Paradise Pink'	®	[Lapham 1949]	
MTB	'Parakeet'	®	[E. Roberts 1957]	
SDB	'Paricutin'	®	[J. D. Taylor 1969]	
TB	'Paris Kiss'	®	[R. Blyth 1983]	
TB	'Party Dress'	®	[Muhlestein 1950]	RD
BB	'Passport'	®	[J. Ghio 1970]	
DB	'Path of Gold'	®	[Hodson 1941]	RD
TB	'Patina'	®	[K. Keppel 1976]	
TB	'Patterdale'	®	[Randall 1955]	
BB	'Peaches a la Mode'	®	[W. Vallette 1973]	
TB	'Peach Float'	®	[O. Brown 1973]	
SDB	'Peach Top'	®	[L. Delany 1977]	
IB	'Peachy Face'	®	[Bennett Jones 1975]	
TB	'Pearly Dawn'	®	[Anley 1952]	
IB	'Peggy Chambers'	®	[J. D. Taylor 1976]	
MDB	'Penny Candy'	®	[M. Hamblen 1976]	
SDB	'Pepper Mill'	®	[B. Hager 1976]	
MDB	'Perky'	®	[Welch 1958]	
TB	'Persian Fancy'	®	[Schortman 1963]	
TB	'Persian Romance'	®	[Kelway 1962]	
IB	'Pharoah's Daughter'	®	[J. Boushay 1973]	
BB	'Picayune'	®	[K. Keppel 1976]	
IB	'Pigmy Gold'	®	[Douglas 1953]	
TB	'Pink Charm'	®	[Stevens 1946]	
TB	'Pink Chimes'	®	[Hall 1956]	
TB	'Pink Clover'	®	[D. Hall 1956]	
TB	'Pink Confetti'	®	[J. Gibson 1975]	
IB	'Pink Kitten'	®	[V. Wood 1976]	

IB	'Pink Ruffles' ®	[K. Smith 1939]	
TB	'Pinnacle' ®	[W. R. Stevens 1945]	RD
TB	'Pipes of Pan' ®	[O. Brown 1963]	
TB	'Piute Pass' ®	[M. Daling 1974]	
DB	'Pixie' ®	[Sass 1932]	RD
SDB	'Pixie Plum' ®	[M. Hamblen 1970]	
SDB	'Pixie Princess' ®	[Schreiner's 1972]	
TM	'Pluie d'Or' ®	[Cayeux 1928]	
BB	'Pocket Size' ®	[G. Plough 1974]	
IB	'Pogo' ®	[Douglas 1953]	
IB	'Pony' ®	[B. Hager 1977]	
IB	'Poppet' ®	[N. Scopes 1969]	
TB	'Portrait of Larrie' ®	[L. Gaulter 1977]	
IB	'Pot Luck' ®	[B. Hager 1976]	
TB	'Powder Pink' ®	[Kelway 1959]	
TB	'Prairie Sunset' ®	[Sass 1939]	
TB	'Pretender' ®	[P. Cook 1951]	
TB	'Pretty Lady' ®	[J. Gatty 1981]	
TB	'Primrose Drift' ®	[L. Brummitt 1960]	
SDB	'Prince' ®	[A. Brown via J. Boushay 1975]	
TB	'Princely' ®	[B. Long 1953]	
SDB	'Puppet' ®	[B. Hager 1968]	
SDB	'Purple Landscape' ®	[L. Brummitt 1973]	
TB	'Queechee' ®	[Knowlton 1947]	
TB	'Queen's Taste' ®	[G. Douglas 1950]	
TB	'Quicksilver' ®	[R. Schreiner 1950]	
SDB	'Quiet Lagoon' ®	[J. Boushay 1980]	
MTB	'Quirk' ®	[A. Brown 1971]	
TB	'Radiant Apogee' ®	[J. Gibson 1964]	
TB	'Rainbow Trout' ®	[B. Dodsworth 1978]	
SDB	'Rain Dance' ®	[Bennett Jones 1978]	
TB	'Rajah' ®	[K. Smith 1942]	
TB	'Ramadan' ®	[A. Harrison 1951]	
TB	'Ranger' ®	[Klein 1943]	
IB	'Rare Edition' ®	[J. Gatty 1980]	
IB	'Raspberry Acres' ®	[W. Greenlee 1968]	
IB	'Raspberry Blush' ®	[M. Hamblen 1975]	
SDB	'Raspberry Jam' ®	[D. Niswonger 1980]	
TB	'Raspberry Ripples' ®	[Niswonger 1967]	
BB	'Raspberry Sundae' ®D.	[Niswonger 1970]	
IB	'Rathe Primrose' ®	[Fothergill 1963]	
TB	'Raven Hill' ®	[F. Carr 1973]	
SDB	'Real Coquette' ®	[B. Blyth 1976]	
MDB	'Red Atlast' ®	[L. Mahood 1969]	
TB	'Red Flash' ®	[Maples 1940]	
SDB	'Red Heart' ®	[A. Brown 1966]	
IB	'Red Orchid' ®	[Sass 1934]	
TB	'Red Rufus' ®	[J. D. Taylor 1979]	
TB	'Redwing' ®	[Sass 1926]	
TB	'Redwyne' ®	[McKee 1944]	
SDB	'Regards' ®	[B. Hager 1966]	
TB	'Repartee' ®	[C. & K. Smith 1966]	
TB	'Ribbon Round' ®	[Tompkins 1962]	
SDB	'Rickshaw' ®	[Hager 1961]	
MTB	'Riff-Raff' ®	[A. Farrington 1986]	
TB	'Right Royal' ®	[Wills 1950]	
SDB	'Ripe Raspberry' ®	[Dunbar-Sindt 1970]	
TB	'Rippling Waters' ®	[Fay 1961]	DGP
TB	'River Hawk' ®	[G. Plough 1978]	
TB	'River Patrol' ®	[H. Stahly 1978]	

TB	'Rococo' ®	[R. Schreiner 1959]	
TB	'Rocket' ®	[Whiting 1945]	
TB	'Rockette' ®	[O. Brown 1971]	
TB	'Romance' ®	[Murrell 1928]	
TB	'Roman Emperor' ®	[B. Dodsworth 1980]	
TB	'Rose Violet' ®	[Kirk 1939]	
TB	'Rosy Wings' ®	[Gage 1935]	
MDB	'Rotkäppchen' ®	[van Nes 1966]	
SDB	'Roustabout' ®	[A. Brown 1975]	
TB	'Rowella' ®	[R. Nichol 1985]	
TB	'Royal Ascot' ®	[N. Scopes 1975]	
SDB	'Royal Blush' ®	[H. Nichols 1978]	
SDB	'Royal Elf' ®	[A. Brown via J. Boushay 1978]	
TB	'Royal Knight' ®	[A. Brown1960]	
TB	'Royal Moon' ®	[Kelway 1966]	
TB	'Royal Ruffles' ®	[Purviance 1962]	
TB	'Royal Touch' ®	[Schreiner's 1966]	
SDB	'Royal Wine' ®	[H. Fletcher 1972]	
IB	'Ruby Chimes' ®	[A. Brown 1971]	
SDB	'Ruby Contrast' ®	[A. Brown 1970]	
TB	'Ruby Gleam' ®	[E. Fankhauser 1985]	
IB	'Runaway' ®	[A. Brown 1970]	
TB	'Rustam' ®	[Kelway 1956]	
TB	'Ruth Couffer' ®	[T. Craig 1956]	
TB	'Sable' ®	[Cook 1938]	RD
TB	'Sable Night' ®	[P. Cook 1950]	
SD	'Saintbury' ®	[J. D. Taylor 1977]	
SDB	'Saltwood' ®	[J. D. Taylor 1971]	
MTB	'Sand Princess' ®	[K. Fisher 1983]	
TB	'San Leandro' ®	[Gaulter 1968]	
TB	'Sanderling' ®	[B. Dodsworth 1979]	
IB	'Sandy Caper' ®	[Warburton 1965]	
IB	'Sangreal' ®	[Sass 1935]	
SDB	'Sapphire Gem' ®	[H. Schmelzer 1975]	
TB	'Sapphire Hills' ®	[Schreiner's 1971]	
SDB	'Sapphire Jewel' ®	[M. Hamblen 1977]	
SDB	'Sassenach' ®	[J. D. Taylor 1979]	
TB	'Satin Gown' ®	[J. Gatty 1977]	
BB	'Saucy Peach' ®	[Muhlestein 1959]	
DB	'Schneekuppe' ®	[Goos & Koenemann 1910]	
SDB	'Scintilla' ®	[Fothergill 1959]	DGP
MDB	'Scribe' ®	[J. D. Taylor 1975]	
SDB	'Sea Holly' ®	[H. Catton 1982]	
TB	'Shah's Court' ®	[B. Blyth 1976]	
IB	'Shampoo' ®	[V. Messick 1975]	
TB	'Shawsii'nom. dub.		
TB	'Shekinah' ®	[Sturtevant 1918]	
TB	'Shepherd's Delight' ®	[H. Fothergill 1969]	
SDB	'Sherborne' ®	[J. D. Taylor 1975]	
IB	'Short Distance' ®	[J. Gatty 1979]	
MTB	'Shrinking Violet' ®	[Hager 1965]	
IB	'Silent Strings' ®	[P. Dyer 1978]	
SDB	'Silkie' ®	[Hager 1968]	
TB	'Silver Shower' ®	[Schreiner's 1973]	
IB	'Sing Again' ®	[Plough 1965]	
TB	'Siva Siva' ®	[J. Gibson 1961]	
TB	'Sketch Me' ®	[G. Plough 1975]	
SDB	'Skip Stitch' ®	[D. Rawdon 1977]	
SDB	'Sky Bolt' ®	[A. Brown 1968]	
MTB	'Slim Jim' ®	[F. Williams 1978]	

SDB	'Small Sky' ®	[Muhlestein 1963]	
SDB	'Small Wonder' ®	[G. Douglas 1953]	**DGP**
BB	'Smarty Pants' ®	[A. White 1949]	
TB	'Smokey Dream' ®	[Kelway 1965]	
BB	'Smoky Valley' ®	[A. Brown 1970]	
TB	'Smooth Orange'		
SDB	'Snow Elf' ®	[A. Brown 1958]	
SDB	'Snow Troll' ®	[Goett 1963]	
IB	'Snow Festival' ®	[C. Palmer 1974]	
TB	'Snowy Owl' ®	[R. Blodgett 1977]	
IB	'Solent Breeze' ®	[J. D. Taylor 1962]	
TB	'Solid Gold' ®	[Kleinsorge 1951]	
TB	'Solid Mahogany' ®	[J. Sass 1943]	
BB	'Something Special' ®	[B. Hager 1976]	
TB	'Soul Kiss' ®	[B. Blyth 1984]	
SDB	'Southern Clipper' ®	[S. Street 1971]	
MTB	'Spanish Coins' ®	[J. Witt 1976]	
SDB	'Sparkling Cloud' ®	[D. Sindt 1967]	
BB	'Sparkling Lemonade' ®	[N. Scopes 1977]	
TB	'Sparkling Waters' ®	[R. Schreiner 1959]	
SDB	'Spring Bells' ®	[Bennett Jones 1971]	
SDB	'Spring Fern' ®	[E. Roberts 1963]	
TB	'Spring Festival' ®	[D. Hall 1957]	
IB	'Spring Signal' ®	[Zurbrigg 1959]	
TB	'St Crispin' ®	[Meyer 1937]	RD
SDB	'Stanway' ®	[J. D. Taylor 1975]	
TB	'Stardom' ®	[D. Hall 1941]	
TB	'Starlit River' ®	[G. Plough 1980]	
SDB	'Starry Eyed' ®	[J. Gatty 1974]	
TB	'Star Shine' ®	[Wills 1947]	**DGP**
TB	'Staten Island' ®	[K. Smith 1945]	RD
TB	'Stepping Out' ®	[Shreiner's 1964]	
TB	'Sterling Silver' ®	[Moldovan 1961]	
TB	'Stitch in Time' ®	[Schreiner's 1975]	
SDB	'Stockholm' ®	[B. Warburton 1971]	
TB	'Strawberry Sensation' ®	[L. Powell 1980]	
TB	'Strawberry Sundae' ®	[H. Schmelzer 1977]	
DB	'Stylish' ®	[Welch 1951]	RD
SDB	'Sudeley' ®	[J. D. Taylor 1979]	
IB	'Sugar' ®	[Warburton 1961]	
BB	'Sugar Pie' ®	[Cassebeer 1965]	
SDB	'Summer Nights' ®	[L. Boushay 1979]	
TB	'Summer Pearl' ®	[Kelway 1963]	
IB	'Sundown Red' ®	[P. Blyth 1982]	
TB	'Sunday Chimes' ®	[M. Hamblen 1977]	
SDB	'Sun Glint' ®	[N. Scopes 1974]	
SDB	'Sunlit Trail' ®	[A. Brown 1968]	
SDB	'Sunny Smile' ®	[N. Scopes 1977]	
IB	'Sunrising' ®	[J. D. Taylor 1976]	
SDB	'Sun Symbol' ®	[B. Jones 1964]	
TB	'Superlation' ®	[P. Cook 1957]	
TB	'Superstition' ®	[Schreiner's 1977]	
TB	'Susan Bliss' ®	[Bliss 1922]	
IB	'Svelte' ®	[B. Hager 1970]	
SDB	'Sweet Bess' ®	[N. Scopes 1974]	
SDB	'Sweet Kate' ®	[N. Scopes 1985]	
TB	'Sylvia Murray' ®	[Norton 1943]	
TB	'Tall Chief' ®	[DeForest 1955]	
TB	'Tangerine Sunrise' ®	[B. Dodsworth 1979]	
IB	'Tan Tingo' ®	[B. Blyth 1981]	

TB	**'Tarn Hows'** ®	[Randall 1951]
BB	**'Tarot'** ®	[N. Scopes 1973]
SDB	**'Taupkin'** ®	[E. Wood 1969]
SDB	**'Tease'** ®	[B. Hager 1974]
TB	**'Techny Chimes'** ®	[Charles 1955]
TB	**'Theatre'** ®	[K. Keppel 1981]
IB	**'The Bride'** ®	[K. Smith 1945]
TB	**'The Citadel'** ®	[R. Graves via E. Watkins 1951]
TB	'The Rocket = **I. 'Rocket'**	
TB	**'Thick and Creamy'** ®	[J. Weiler 1977]
MDE	**;'Three Cherries'** ®	[B. Hager 1971]
TB	**'Three Oaks'** ®	[Whiting 1940]
TB	**'Thundercloud'** ®	[K. Keppel 1972]
DB	**'Tid-Bit'** ®	[Sturtevant 1925]
BB	**'Tidle-De-Winks'** ®	[Stern 1957]
BB	**'Timmie Too'** ®	[Wolff 1961]
SDB	**'Tinker Bell'** ®	[G. Douglas 1954]
MDE	**;'Tiny Freckles'** ®	[A. Farrington 1986]
SDB	**'Tirralirra'** ®	[N. Scopes 1985]
TB	**'Tombola'** ®	[N. Scopes 1976]
SDB	**'Tomingo'** ®	[E. Roberts 1966]
MDE	**;'Toni Lynn'** ®	[E. Smith 1962]
SDB	**'Toots'** ®	[F. Williams 1977]
TB	**'Top Flight'** ®	[D. Hall 1953]
MTB	**'Topsy Turvy'** ®	[Welch 1963]
TB	**'Torchlight'** ®	[Kelway 1957]
BB	**'Toskaner Prinz'** ®	[E. Berlin 1980]
TB	**'Touch of Sky'** ®	[Schreiner's 1980]
TB	**'Tracey'** ®	[J. D. Taylor 1976]
TB	**'Tranquil Star'** ®	[B. Blyth 1978]
TB	**'Treasure'** ®	[Sturtevant 1929]
TB	**'Trenwith'** ®	[R. Nichol 1985]
SDB	**'Tropic Babe'** ®	[A. Brown 1972]
SDB	**'Truly'** ®	[B. Warburton 1977]
MDB	**'Tuscany'** ®	[J. D. Taylor 1973]
MTB	**'Two Bits'** ®	[Albright 1957]
TB	**'Tyrian Robe'** ®	[C. Hall 1968]
TB	**'Ultrapoise'** ®	[Noyd 1961]
TB	**'Velvet Robe'** ®	[Schreiner's 1960]
MDB	**'Velvet Toy'** ®	[B. Dunbar via D. Sindt 1971]
TB	**'Viking Admiral'** ®	[E. Burger 1973]
MTB	**'Violet Bouquet'**	
TB	**'Violet Classic'** ®	[L. Zurbrigg 1976]
DB	**'Violetta'** ®	[Benbow 1956]
IB	**'Virtue'** ®	[J. Gatty 1975]
IB	**'Voila'** ®	[J. Gatty 1972]
TB	**'Wabash'** ®	[Williamson 1936]
TB	**'War and Peace'** ®	[B. Long 1943]
SDB	**'Webelos'** ®	[J. Seeden 1977]
IB	**'Wenlock'** ®	[J. D. Taylor 1979]
TB	**'Wensleydale'** ®	[B. Dodsworth 1985]
TB	**'Western Hostess'** ®	[S. Babson 1977]
SDB	**'Westwell'** ®	[J. D. Taylor 1978]
SDB	**'Wheels'** ®	[B. Blyth 1977]
TB	**'Whernside'** ®	[B. Dodsworth 1976]
MDB	**'Whisky'** ®	[A. Farrington 1986]
MTB	**'White Canary'** ®	[E. Roberts 1972]
TB	**'White City'** ®	[Murrell 1939]
TB	**'White Knight'** ®	[Saunders 1916]
IB	**'Whiteladies'** ®	[J. D. Taylor 1975]

DGP

RD

BB	**'Whoop 'Em Up'** ®	[D. Brady 1973]
IB	**'Why Not'** ®	[B. Hager 1979]
SDB	**'Widicombe Fair'** ®	[J. D. Taylor 1965]
IB	**'Wigit'** ®	[Williamson 1943]
TB	**'Wild Ginger'** ®	[J. Gibson 1960]
TB	**'Winged Melody'** ®	[C. Tompkins 1977]
IB	**'Winkieland'** ®	[D. Boen 1979]
TB	**'Winter Olympics'** ®	[O. Brown 1961]
TB	**'Wisteria'** ®	[Loth 1934]
IB	**'Wisteria Sachet'** ®	[C. Palmer 1972]
SDB	**'Wizard of Id'** ®	[P. Dyer 1980]
SDB	**'Wow'** ®	[A. Brown 1969]
SDB	**'Wyckhill'** ®	[J. D. Taylor 1975]
TB	**'Zambezi'** ®	[P. Blyth 1984]
TB	**'Zantha'** ®	[Fay 1947]
BB	**'Zeeland'** ®	[N. Scopes 1984]
MDB	**'Zipper'** ®	[D. Sindt 1978]
IB	**'Zua'** ®	[Crawford 1914]
SDB	**'Zuyder Zee'** ®	[N. Scopes 1972]

RD

ISATIS Linnaeus 1753   *[Brassicaceae (Cruciferae)]*
BHN‡ **tinctoria** Linnaeus 1753
PGP

ISMENE Salisbury 1812   *[Amaryllidaceae]*
   calathina (Ker-Gawler) Herbert 1826 = **Hymenocallis narcissiflora**

ISNARDIA Linnaeus 1753   *[Onagraceae]*
   palustris Linnaeus 1753 = **Ludwigia palustris**

ISOPYRUM Linnaeus 1753   *[Ranunculaceae]*
   nipponicum Franchet 1879
      var. **sarmentosum** Ohwi
   ohwianum (Ohwi) Koidzumi 1940 = **I. nipponicum** var. **sarmentosum**
   stoloniferum Maximowicz 1883
   thalictroides Linnaeus 1753
CA

ISOTOMA (R. Brown) Lindley 1826   *[Campanulaceae]*
   axillaris Lindley 1826
   fluviatilis F. Mueller ex Bentham 1868 = **Pratia pedunculata**

IXIA Linnaeus 1753 nom. cons.   *[Iridaceae]*
   paniculata D. Delaroche 1766
EGF.1-DGP

   HYBRID CULTIVARS

   'Blauwe Vogel' = **I. 'Blue Bird'**
   'Blue Bird' ®   [N. S. Boogaard pre-1944]
   'Castor' ®   [N. S. Boogaard pre-1949]
   'Cupido'
   'Giant' ®   [N. S. Boogaard pre-1953]
   'Hogarth' ®
   'Hubert' ®   [P. Rumphorst]
   'Marquette' ®   [N. S. Boogaard]
   'Panorama' ®   [J. Zweeris 1954]
   'Rose Emperor' ®   [J. Zweeris]
   'Spotlight' ®   [J. Zweeris 1954]
   'Titia' ®   [W. Blokker Jzn. 1954]
   'Uranus' ®   [N. S. Boogaard pre-1937]
   'Venus' ®   [N. S. Boogaard pre-1937]

IXIOLIRION Herbert 1821   [*Ixioliriaceae (Liliaceae)*]
  ledebourii Fischer & Meyer 1853 = **I. tataricum** ssp. **ledebourii**
  montanum (Labillardiere) Herbert 1821 = **I. tataricum** ssp. **montanum**
  pallasii hort., non Fischer & Meyer ex Labillardiere 1853 = **I. tataricum**
                                                              ssp. **montanum**
    tataricum (Pallas) Herbert 1821   EGF.1-**SB**-DGP
      ssp. **ledebourii** (Fischer & Meyer) R. Miller 1984 (*I. ledebourii*)
      ssp. **montanum** (Labillardiere) Takhtadjan 1972 (*I. montanum, I. pallasii* hort.)

JABOROSA Jussieu 1789   [*Solanaceae*]
  integrifolia Lamarck 1789   PGP

JANKAEA Boissier 1879   [*Gesneriaceae*]
  heldreichii (Boissier) Boissier 1879   CA-**DGP**

JASIONE Linnaeus 1753   [*Campanulaceae*]
  crispa (Pourret) G. Sampaio 1921 (*J. humilis*)
B **heldreichii** Boissier & Orphanides 1859 (*J. jankae*)
  humilis (Persoon) Loiseleur 1810 = **J. crispa**
  jankae Neilreich 1870 = **J. heldreichii**
  laevis Lamarck 1795 (*J. perennis*)
    'Blaulicht' ('Blue Light')
  perennis Villars ex Lamarck 1789 = **J. laevis**

JASONIA Cassini 1815   [*Asteraceae (Compositae)*]
  tuberosa de Candolle 1836

JEFFERSONIA Barton 1793   [*Berberidaceae*]
  diphylla (Linnaeus) Persoon 1805 (*Podophyllum diphyllum*)   CA
  dubia (Maximowicz) Bentham & Hooker ex Baker & Moore 1879
                              (*Plagiorhegma dubium*)   CA-**DGP**-**RD**
    'Alba'

JOVELLANA Ruiz & Pavon   [*Scrophulariaceae*]
S **sinclairii** (Hooker) Kranzlin 1907

JOVIBARBA Opiz 1852   [*Crassulaceae*]
  allionii (Jourdan & Fourreau) D. A. Webb 1963 (Sempervivum allionii)   C
  allionii x **J. hirta**
  allionii ex Estang x **J. hirta** ex Biele
  allionii x **J. hirta** ssp. **glabrescens** ex Smeryouka
  allionii x **J. sobolifera**
  arenaria (Koch) Opiz 1852
      ex Murtal
  arenaria x **J. heuffelii**
  heuffelii (Schott) A.& D. Löve 1961 (*Sempervivum heuffelii*)   CA-**RD**
      var. **glabra** Beck & Szyszylowicz
      var. **glabra** ex Anabakanak
      var. **glabra** ex Anthoborio
      var. **glabra** ex Anthomorica
      var. **glabra** ex Backovo
      var. **glabra** ex Haila
      var. **glabra** ex Jakupica
      var. **glabra** ex Koipo
      var. **glabra** ex Kopronovik
      var. **glabra** ex Kosovo

var. **glabra** ex Kratovo
var. **glabra** ex Krusevo
var. **glabra** ex Ljubotin
var. **glabra** ex Mega Chorion
var. **glabra** ex Osljak
var. **glabra** ex Ostrovica
var. **glabra** ex Parentkoff
var. **glabra** ex Pasina Glava
var. **glabra** ex Rhodope
var. **glabra** ex Rujen
var. **glabra** ex Rila
var. **glabra** ex Sapka
var. **glabra** ex Stogovo
var. **glabra** ex Treska Gorge
var. **glabra** ex Trigrad
var. **glabra** ex Uranae
var. **glabra** ex Vitse
var. **glabra** ex Vlasic
var. **kopaonikense** (Pancic) P. J. Mitchell 1983
var. **patens** (Grisebach & Schrenk) P. J. Mitchell 1983
var. *randolphii* hort. = **J. 'Randolph'**
heuffelii x **J. hirta** ssp. **glabrescens**
heuffelii var. **glabra** x **J. allionii**
heuffelii var. **glabra** x **J. hirta** ssp. **glabrescens**

CULTIVARS OF **J. HEUFFELII**

'Apache' ®   [Payne]
'Aquarius' ®   [Fearnley]
'Beacon Hill' ®   [Fearnley 1973]
'Belcore' ®   [Payne]
'Bermuda' ®   [Ford 1975]
'Brocade' ®   [Ford]
'Bronze Ingot' ®   [Ford]
'Bronze King'
'Cameo' ®   [Ford 1975]
'Chocoleto' ®   [Ford]
'Cloverdale' ®   [Ford]
Dark Green Form = **J. 'Millers Violet'**
'Emerald Spring' ®   [Vaughn]
'Fandango' ®   [Nixon 1972]
'Gento' ®   [Ford 1980]
'Giuseppi Spiny' ®
'Greenstone' ®   [Ford]
'Grignense'
'Henry Correvon' ®
'Hystyle' ®   [Ford]
'Inferno' ®   [Nixon 1976]
'Kapo' ®   [van der Steen]
'Mary Ann' ®   [Fearnley]
'Miller's Violet' ®
'Minuta' ®
'Nannette' ®   [Nixon 1976]
'Orion' ®   [1981]
'Pallasii' ®
'Pink Skies' ®   [Smith 1979]
'Prisma' ®   [Ford 1980]
'Purple Haze' ®   [Ford]
Red Form
'Randolph' ®   [Nixon]

        'Sundancer'   ®   [Nixon 1972]
        'Suntan'   ®   [Smith 1980]
        'Tan'   ®   [Fearnley]
        'Tancredi'   ®   [Ford]
        'Torrid Zone'   ®   [Nixon 1976]
        'Tuxedo'   ®   [Ford]
        'Tyke'
        'Violet'   ®   [Fearnley]
        'Vulcan'   ®   [Ford]
        'Wotan'   ®
        'Xanthoheuff'   ®   [Skrocki]

    hirta (Linnaeus) Opiz 1852
        ssp. **borealis** (Huber) R. Soo 1978
        'Bulgarien'
        ssp. **glabrescens** (Sabransky) R. Soo & Javorka 1951
        ssp. **glabrescens** ex Belansky Tatra
        ssp. **glabrescens** ex High Tatra
        ssp. **glabrescens** ex Smeryouka
        ssp. **glabrescens** ex Wintergraben
        ssp. **glabrescens** var. **neilreichii** (Schott, Nyman & Kotschy) R. Konop
                                              & O. Bendak 1981
        f. **hildebrandtii** (Schott) R. Konop & O. Bendak 1981
    x **kwediana** P. J. Mitchell 1982 (*J. allionii* x *J. heuffelii*)
        'Pickwick'   ®   [Smith 1970]
        'Linn'
        'Luteum'
    x **nixonii** B. J. M. Zonneveld 1981 (*J. heuffelii* x *J. sobolifera*)
        'Jowan'   ®   [Zonneveld]
        'Stefan'   ®   [Zonneveld]
    preissiana (Domin) Omel'chuk-Myakushko & Chopik 1975
    sobolifera (Sims) Opiz 1852 (*Sempervivum soboliferum*)   RD
        'Green Globe'   ®
        'Nitra'

JUNCUS Linnaeus 1753   *[Juncaceae]*
N‡   **effusus** Linnaeus 1753
        * var. **spiralis**   RD
    ensifolius Wilström 1823
    glaucus Sibthorp 1794 non Ehrhart 1791 = **J. inflexus**
N‡   **inflexus** Linnaeus 1753 (*J. glaucus*)   RD
    pusillus Buchanan 1879
    spiralis hort. = **J. effusus** var. **spiralis**
    tenageia Ehrhart ex Linnaeus f. 1781

JURINEA Cassini 1821   *[Asteraceae (Compositae)]*
    ceratocarpa Bentham & Hooker 1873

KELSEYA (S. Watson) Rydberg 1900   *[Rosaceae]*
S   **uniflora** (S. Watson) Rydberg 1900   CA

KENTRANTHUS Necker 1790 = **CENTRANTHUS**

KIRENGESHOMA Yatabe 1890   *[Hydrangeaceae]*
    koreana Nakai 1935   PGP
L   **palmata** Yatabe 1890   PGP

KITAIBELA Willdenow 1799   *[Malvaceae]*
    vitifolia Willdenow 1799

KNAUTIA Linnaeus 1753   [*Dipsacaceae*]
HN‡L **arvensis** (Linnaeus) Coulter 1823
    macedonica Grisebach 1846 (*Scabiosa rumelica*)   PGP

KNIPHOFIA Moench 1794 nom. cons.   [*Asphodelaceae (Liliaceae)*]

M - TAYLOR, J.: '*Kniphofia - A Survey*' The Plantsman, 7:3 129-160 (1985)

    aloöides Moench 1794 = **K. uvaria**
    caulescens Baker 1872   M- EFG.1-PGP
    ensifolia Baker 1885   M-EGF.1-PGP
    galpinii hort. non Baker 1896 = **K. triangularis**
    gracilis Harvey ex Baker 1874   M-EFG.1-PGP
    macowanii Baker 1874 = **K. triangularis**
    natalensis Baker 1885   M
    nelsonii Masters 1892 = **K. triangularis**
    northiae Baker 1889   M-EFG.1-PGP
    praecox Baker 1870   M-PGP
    rooperi (Moore) Lemoine 1854 (*K.* 'C. M. Prichard' hort.)   M-EGF.1
    rufa Baker 1900   M-EFG.1-PGP
    snowdenii C. H. Wright 1919 = **K. thomsonii** var. **snowdenii**
    thomsonii Baker 1885   M-EFG.1
        var. **snowdenii** (C. H.Wright) Marais 1973 (*K. snowdenii*)   M-EFG.1-**PGP**
L   **triangularis** Kunth 1843 (*K. galpinii* hort., *K. macowanii, K. nelsonii*)   M-EFG.1-**PGP**
    uvaria (Linnaeus) Hooker 1854 (*K. aloöides*)   **M**-EGF.1-PGP-**RD**
        '**Grandiflora**'   PGP
        '**Nobilis**'   M-PGP

    HYBRID CULTIVARS & GROUPS

      '**Abendsonne**'
      '**Ada**'   [Slieve Donard]   M-PGP-RD
      '**Alcazar**'   [Lubbe]   M
      '**Amberlight**'   [Slieve Donard]   M-PGP
      '**Apricot**'   [Prichard]   M
      '**Atlanta**'   [N. Treseder]   M-PGP
      '**Bees' Lemon**'   [Bees]   M-PGP-**RD**
      '**Bees' Sunset**'   [Bees]   M
      '**Bernock's Triumph**'
      '**Border Ballet**'
L   '**Bressingham Flame**'   [A. Bloom]   M-PGP
      '**Bressingham Glow**'   [A. Bloom]   M-PGP
      Bressingham Hybrids   [A. Bloom]
      '**Bressingham Torch**'   [A. Bloom]   M-PGP.RD
      '**Brimstone**'   M-PGP
      '**Bronceleuchter**'   [Kayser & Siebert]
      '**Burnt Orange**'   [B. Chatto]   M-RD
      '**Buttercup**'   M-PGP
      '**Canary Bird**'   [Slieve Donard]   M-PGP
      '**Cardinal**' (K. 'Kardinal')   M
      '**Candlelight**'   [A. Bloom]   M-RD
      'C. M. Prichard' hort. non Prichard = **K. rooperi**
      '**Comet**'   [Coe 1968]   M
      '**Cool Lemon**'   [B. Chatto]   M-RD
      '**Corallina**'   M-PGP
      '**David**'   [Thos. Carlile Ltd.]   M
      '**Earliest of All**'   M
      '**Early Buttercup**'   M
      '**E. M. Mills**'   M

'Enchantress'   [Slieve Donard]   M-PGP
'Erecta'   M-PGP
'Evered'   [Coe 1970]   M
Express Hybrids   M
'Fiery Fred'   [A. Bloom]   M-RD
'Firefly'   [The Plantsmen 1977]   M-RD
'Fyrwerkeri'
'Gold Else'   [Wallace 1906]   M-PGP-**RD**
'Goldkackel'
'Goldfinch'   [Slieve Donard]   M-PGP
'Green Jade'   [B. Chatto]   M-PGP
'Ice Queen'   [A. Bloom]
'Indian'   [Lubbe]   M
L   'Jenny Bloom'   [A. Bloom]   M-PGP
'John Benary'   [Pre-1889]   M
'Kardinal' = **K. 'Cardinal'**
'La Citronaire'
'Lemon Ice'   [Coe 1969]   M
'Little Elf'   M
'Little Maid'   [B. Chatto]   **M**-PGP-RD
'Lye End'   [Pole]   M
'Maid of Orleans'   [Grullemans via Perry c1953]   M-PGP-RD
'Modesta'   M-PGP
'Percy's Pride'   [A. Bloom]   RD
'Pfitzeri'   [Pfitzer pre-1893]   M
'Prince Igor'   [Prichard 1953]   M
'Red Prince'
'Redstart'   [Slieve Donard]   M-PGP
L   'Royal Standard'   [Prichard 1921]   M-PGP
'Safranvogel'
'Samuel's Sensation'   [Samuel]   M-PGP-RD
'Saturn'   [J. Metcalf 1986]
'Scarlet Cap'   [Coe 1969]   M
'Schneewittchen'
'Shining Sceptre'   [A. Bloom]   M
'Slim Coral Red'   [B. Chatto]   M
L   'Snow Maiden'   M-PGP
'Springtime'   M-**RD**
Stark's Hybrids   M
'Star of Baden-Baden'   [M. Leichtlin pre-1889]   M-PGP
'Strawberries and Cream'   [B. Chatto]   M
'Sunningdale Yellow'   [Bryce Wilson]   M
'Sunset'   [J. Metcalf 1986]   M
'The Rocket'   M
'Timothy'   [Thos. Carlile Ltd.]   M-PGP
'Toffee Nosed'   [J. Metcalf 1986]   M
'Torchbearer'   M
'Tubergeniana'   [van Tubergen]   M-PGP
'Tuckii'   [pre-1906]   M
'Underway'   [N. Hadden pre-1947]   M-PGP
'Vuurflame'
'Wrexham Buttercup'   [W. Samuel]   M-PGP
'Yellow Hammer'   [Slieve Donard]   M-PGP
'Zeal Primrose'   [T. Jones]   M

KOELERIA Persoon 1805   [*Poaceae (Gramineae)*]
N   **glauca** (Schkuhr) de Candolle 1813

KOROLKOWIA Regel 1873   [*Liliaceae*]
    sewerzowii (Regel) Regel 1873 = **Fritillaria sewerzowii**

LACHENALIA Jacquin f. 1787   *[Hyacinthaceae (Liliaceae)]*

M - TREVOR S. CROSBY, `The Genus Lachenalia` The Plantsman 8-129-166 (1987)

aloides (Linnaeus f.) hort. ex Ascherson & Graebner 1905 (*L. tricolor*)

	M-EGF.1-DGP-**RD**
var. **aurea** (Lindley) hort. ex Ascherson & Graebner 1905	M-EGF.1-RD
'Nelsonii' [Nelson 1878]	M-EGF.1-RD
'Pearsonii' [ex New Zealand pre-1955]	**M**-EGF.1-**DGP**-RD
var. **quadricolor** (Jacquin) Chittenden 1951	M
var. **vanzyliae** Barker 1984	M
arbuthnotiae Barker 1984	M
bachmannii Baker 1893	M
bulbifera (Cyrillo) hort. ex Ascherson & Graebner 1905 (*L. pendula*)	M
	M-EGF.1-**RD**
contaminata Solander in Aiton 1789	**M**-EGF.1
glaucina Jacquin 1794	M-EGF.1-RD
mutabilis Sweet 1832	M-EGF.1-RD
pallida Solander in Aiton 1789	M-EGF.1
pendula Solander in Aiton 1789 = **L. bulbifera**	
tricolor Jacquin f. 1795 = **L. aloides**	
unifolia Jacquin f. 1798	M-EGF.1
'Violet Queen' (*L. bulbifera* x *L. glaucina*)	
zeyheri Baker 1871	M

LACTUCA Linnaeus 1753   *[Asteraceae (Compositae)]*
    perennis Linnaeus 1753
    tenerrima Pourret 1788

LAGAROSIPHON Harvey 1842   *[Hydrocharitaceae]*
L   **major** (Ridley) Moss ex Wager 1928 (*Elodea crispa*)   EGF.1

LAGENOPHORA Cassini 1818   *[Asteraceae (Compositae)]*
    pinnatifida Hooker f. 1853
    pumila (Forster f.) Cheeseman 1909
    stipitata (Labillardiere) Druce 1917

LAGOTIS Gaertner 1770   *[Scrophulariaceae]*
    stolonifera Maximowicz 1881

LAMIASTRUM Heister ex Fabricius 1759   *[Lamiaceae (Labiatae)]*
    galeobdolon (Linnaeus) Ehrendorfer & Polatschek 1906 comb. illegit.
        = **Galeobdolon luteum**

LAMIUM Linnaeus 1753   *[Lamiaceae (Labiatae)]*
    galeobdolon (Linnaeus) Linnaeus 1756 = **Galeobdolon luteum**
    garganicum Linnaeus 1763   RD
        ssp. **pictum** (Boissier) Mennema
N   **maculatum** (Linnaeus) Linnaeus 1763   DGP-RD
L   **'Album'**   RD
        'Argenteum'
        'Aureum'   DGP
        `Beacon Silver` = **L. maculatum 'Silbergroschen'**
        'Beedham's White'
L   **'Chequers'**
        'Hatfield'
        'Pink Pewter'
        'Roseum'
        'Salmoneum'   DGP
        'Shell Pink'
L   **'Silbergroschen'** (`Beacon Silver`)   [H. Klose 1978]   RD
        'Silberlicht' (`Silver Light`)

'White Nancy'   RD
orvala Linnaeus 1759   PGP-RD
    'Album'   PGP

LAMPRANTHUS N. E. Brown 1930   [*Aizoaceae*
S   **aurantiacus** (de Candolle) Schwantes 1938 (*Mesembryanthemum aurantiacum*)
S   **aureus** (Linnaeus) N. E. Brown 1930 (*Mesembryanthemum aureum*)
S   **blandus** (Haworth) Schwantes 1938 (*Mesembryanthemum blandum*)
S   **brownii** (Hooker f.) N. E. Brown 1930 (*Mesembryanthemum brownii*)
S   **falciformis** (Haworth) N. E. Brown 1930 (*Mesembryanthemum falciforme*)
S   **glaucus** (Linnaeus) N. E. Brown 1930 (*Mesembryanthemum glaucum*)
S   **multiradiatus** (Jacquin) N. E. Brown 1930 (*Mesembryanthemum multiradiatum,*
                                                                 L. roseus
    roseus (Willdenow) Schwantes 1938 = **L. multiradiatus**
S   **spectabilis** (Haworth) N. E. Brown 1930 (*Mesembryanthemum spectabile*)
        'Tresco Apricot'
        'Tresco Brilliant'
        'Tresco Red'
    zeyheri (Salm-Dyck) N. E. Brown 1930 (*Mesembryanthemum zeyheri*)

LAPEIROUSIA Pourret 1788   [*Iridaceae*
    laxa (Thunberg) N. E. Brown 1928 = **Anomatheca laxa**
    viridis (Aiton) L. Bolus 1932 = **Anomatheca viridis**

LASIAGROSTIS Link 1827   [*Poaceae (Gramineae)*
    calamagrostis (Linnaeus) Link 1827 = **Stipa calamagrostis**
    splendens (Trinius) Kunth 1829 = **Stipa splendens**

LASTREA Bory 1826   [*Thelypteridaceae*
    montana (Vogler) T. Moore 1853 comb. invalid. = **Oreopteris limbosperma**
    nipponica (Frivalti & Savatier) Copeland 1947 = **Thelypteris nipponica**

LATHYRUS Linnaeus 1753   [*Fabaceae (Leguminosae)*
    aurantius C. Koch 1841 (*Vicia crocea*)
    aureus hort. non (Steven) Brandza = **L. luteus 'Aureus'**
N   **latifolius** Linnaeus 1753   PGP-**RD**
        'Albus'   PGP
        'Blushing Bride'
        'Pink Pearl' = **L. latifolius 'Rosa Perle'**
        'Red Beauty'
L   'Rosa Perle' ('Pink Pearl')
        'Roseus'
        'Snow Queen'
        'Splendens'
L   'Weisse Perle' ('White Pearl')   PGP-**RD**
        'White Pearl' = **L. latifolius 'Weisse Perle'**
    luteus (Linnaeus) Peterman   PGP
        'Aureus'   PGP
    magellanicus D. Don 1837 = **L. nervosus**
    nervosus Lamarck 1786 (*L. magellanicus*)   PGP
N   **niger** (Linnaeus) Bernhardi 1800
    rotundifolius Willdenow 1802   PGP-RD
A   **sativus** Linnaeus 1753
A   **tingitanus** Linnaeus 1753
N‡   **tuberosus** Linnaeus 1753   PGP
L   **vernus** (Linnaeus) Bernhardi 1800   PGP-**DGP**-RD
        'Albo-roseus'   RD
        'Caeruleus'
        'Flaccidus'
        f. **roseus** Beck   PGP
        'Spring Delight'
        'Spring Melody'

LAVATERA Linnaeus 1753   *[Malvaceae]*
BSN‡   **arborea** Linnaeus 1753   **DGP**-RD
    arborea hort. non Linnaeus 1753 = **L. thuringiaca**
    cachemiriana Cambessedes 1844
B‡   **cretica** Linnaeus 1753   **PGP**
    maritima Gouan
S   **olbia** Linnaeus 1753   PGP
    olbia hort. non Linnaeus = **L. thuringiaca**   PGP-DGP
S   **thuringiaca** Linnaeus 1753 (*L. arborea* hort., *L. olbia* hort.)   PGP
    'Barnsley'   [Mrs R Verey via Hopleys Nursery 1986]
    'Kew Rose' M Cheek 1989
L   **'Rosea'**   [E Ladhams pre-1920]   PGP-**DGP**
    'Rosea' hort. p.p. non Ladhams = **L. thuringiaca 'Kew Rose'**
    'Wembdon Variegated' M Cheek 1989
    'Variegata' hort. = **L. thuringiaca 'Wembdon Variegated'**

LEDEBOURIA Roth 1821   *[Hyacinthaceae (Liliaceae)]*
    cooperi (Hooker f.) J. P. Jessop 1970 (*Scilla adlamii*)   EGF.1

LEMNA Linnaeus 1753   *[Lemnaceae]*
N‡   **gibba** Linnaeus 1753
N‡   **minor** Linnaeus 1753
    'Major' nom. dub.
    polyrhiza Linnaeus 1753 = **Spirodela polyrhiza**
N‡   **trisulca** Linnaeus 1753

LEONTICE Linnaeus 1753   *[Berberidaceae]*
    albertii Regel 1881 = **Gymnospermium albertii**

LEONTOPODIUM R. Brown ex Cassini 1822   *[Asteraceae (Compositae)]*
    aloysiodorum hort. = **L. haplophylloides**
    alpinum Cassini 1822   CA-**DGP**-RD
        'Alpengarten'
        'Alpenstern'
        ssp. **nivale** (Tenore) Tutin 1973 (*L. nivale*)
        'Silberstern'
    calocephalum (Franchet) Beauverd 1909
    discolor Beauverd 1909
    haplophylloides Handel-Mazzetti 1927 (*L. aloysiodorum* hort.)   PGP
    jacotianum Beauverd 1909
    kurilense Takeda 1911
    nivale (Tenore) Huet & Handel-Mazzetti 1927 = **L. alpinum** ssp. **nivale**
    sibiricum Cassini 1822   DGP
    souliei Beauverd 1909
        'Mignon'
    stracheyi (Hooker f.) C. B. Clarke ex Hemsley 1894

LEONURUS Linnaeus 1753   *[Lamiaceae (Labiatae)]*
HN   **cardiaca** Linnaeus 1753

LEOPOLDIA Parlatore 1845 nom. cons.   *[Hyacinthaceae (Liliaceae)]*
    caucasica (Grisebach ex Baker) Losina-Losinskaja 1934 (*Muscari caucasicum*)
                                                     BB-SB
N   **comosa** (Linnaeus) Parlatore 1847 (*Muscari comosum, M. pinardii*)
                                          EGF.1-**BB**-SB-RD
        'Plumosum'   ®   [c1612]   EGF.1-**DGP**-RD

LEPIDIUM Linnaeus 1753   *[Brassicaceae (Cruciferae)]*
    nanum S. Watson 1871

LEPTINELLA Cassini 1822   [*Asteraceae (Compositae)*]
    atrata (Hooker f.) D. Lloyd & C. Webb 1987 (*Cotula atrata*)
        ssp. **luteola** (D. Lloyd) D. Lloyd & C. Webb 1987
    dendyi (Cockayne) D. Lloyd & C. Webb 1987 (*Cotula dendyi*)
    dioica Hooker f. 1852 (*Cotula dioica*)
    goyenii (Petrie) D. Lloyd & C. Webb 1987 (*Cotula goyenii*)
    pectinata (Hooker f.) D. Lloyd & C. Webb 1987 (*Cotula pectinata*)
        var. **sericea** (Kirk) D. Lloyd & C. Webb 1987
    potentillina F. Mueller 1864 (*Cotula potentillina*)
    pyrethrifolia (Hooker f.) D. Lloyd & C. Webb 1987 (*Cotula pyrethrifolia*)
        var. **linearifolia** (Cheeseman) D. Lloyd & C. Webb 1987 (*Cotula linearifolia*)
    rotundata (Cheeseman) D. Lloyd & C. Webb 1987 (*Cotula rotundata*)
    scariosa Cassini 1822 (*Cotula scariosa*)
L   **squalida** Hooker f. 1852 (*Cotula squalida*)
    traillii (Kirk) D. Lloyd & C. Webb 1987 (*Cotula traillii*)

LESQUERELLA S. Watson 1888   [*Brassicaceae (Cruciferae)*]
    fendleri (A. Gray) S. Watson 1888

LEUCANTHEMELLA Tzvelev 1961   [*Asteraceae (Compositae)*]
L   **serotina** (Linnaeus) Tzvelev 1961 (*Chrysanthemum serotinum, C. uliginosum*)
                                              PGP-RD

        'Herbststern'   [H. Klose 1978]

LEUCANTHEMOPSIS (Giroux) Heywood 1975   [*Asteraceae (Compositae)*]
    alpina (Linnaeus) Heywood 1975 (*Chrysanthemum alpinum*)   **CA-RD**
        ssp. **tomentosa** (Loiseleur) Heywood 1975
    pallida (Miller) Heywood 1975
        ssp. **spathulifolia** (Gay) Heywood 1975

LEUCANTHEMUM Miller 1754   [*Asteraceae (Compositae)*]
    atlanticum (Ball) Maire 1923 = **Chrysanthemopsis atlanticum**
    atratum (Jacquin) de Candolle 1838 (*Chrysanthemum atratum*)
        ssp. **ceratophylloides** (Allioni) Horvatic 1935
    catananche (Ball) Maire 1923 = **Chrysanthemopsis catananche**
    gayanum (Cosson & Durieu) Maire 1923 = **Chrysanthemopsis gayanum**
    hosmariense (Ball) Font-Quer 1930 = **Chrysanthemopsis hosmariense**
    maresii (Cosson) Maire 1923 = **Chrysanthemopsis maresii**
    mawii (Hooker f.) hort. = **Chrysanthemopsis gayanum**
N   **maximum** (Ramond) de Candolle 1838 (*Chrysanthemum maximum*)
    maximum hort. non (Ramond) de Candolle = **L. x superbum**
    nipponicum Franchet ex Maximowicz 1872 = **Nipponicanthemum nipponicum**
    x superbum Bergmans ex J. Ingram (*L. lacustre* x *L. maximum*)   DGP-RD
        'Aglaia'   PGP-RD
        'Alaska'
        'Anna Camilla'
        'Andernach'
        'Beaute Nivelloise'
        'Beethoven'
        'Bishopstone'   PGP
        'Christine Hagemann'
        'Cobham Gold'   PGP
        'Dieneren Riesen'
        'Droitwich Beauty'
        'Eisrevue'
        'Eisstern'
        'Elizabeth'
        'Esther Read'   PGP-**DGP**-RD
        'Fiona Coghill'   PGP
        'Everest'

    'Firnglanz'
    'Grünherz'
    'H. Seibert'
    'Horace Read'   RD
    'Inka'   RD
    'Jennifer Read'
    'Julischnee'
    'Juno'
    'Little Princess'
    'May Beauty'
    'Moonlight'
    'Perlenkranz'
    'Phyllis Smith'   PGP-**RD**
    'Polaris'
    'Powis Castle'   PGP
    'Rhine View'
    'Saturn'
    'Schwabengruss'
    'September Snow'   PGP
    'Silberprinzesschen' ('Silver Princess')
    'Silver Dollar'
    'Silver Princess' = **L. maximum 'Silberprinzesschen'**
    'Snowcap'
    'Starburst'
    'Stern von Antwerpen'
    'T. Killin'   PGP
    'Universal'
    'Wirral Pride'   **DGP**-RD
L   'Wirral Supreme'   PGP-RD
    'Worthing'
    'Yvonne'
    'Zuzanna'
NL‡ **vulgare** Lamarck 1778 (*Chrysanthemum leucanthemum*)   PGP
    'Edelstein'
    'Hofenkrone'
    'Maikönigin' ('May Queen')
    'Maistern'   [Bergel 1953]   PGP
    'May Queen' = **L. vulgare 'Maikönigin'**
    'Rheinblick'
    'Wunderkind'

LEUCOCORYNE Lindley 1830   *[Alliaceae (Liliaceae)]*
    ixioides (Hooker) Lindley 1830   EGF.1

LEUCOGENES Beauverd 1910   *[Asteraceae (Compositae)]*
S **grandiceps** (Hooker f.) Beauverd 1910   CA-DGP
S **leontopodium** (Hooker f.) Beauverd 1910   CA-**DGP**

LEUCOJUM Linnaeus 1753   *[Amaryllidaceae]*
N‡ **aestivum** Linnaeus 1759   EGF.1-PGP-**BB**-SB-DGP-**RD**
    'Gravetye' ('Gravetye Giant')   [W. Robinson]   EGF.1-PGP-**BB**-**DGP**-RD
    'Gravetye Giant' = **L. aestivum 'Gravetye'**
    autumnale Linnaeus 1753   EGF.1-PGP-CA-**BB**-SB-**RD**
      *var. **oporanthum**   SB
    hiemale de Candolle 1815 = **L. nicaeence**
    longifolium (Gay ex Roemer) Grenier 1855   EGF.1-**BB**-SB
    nicaeense Ardoino 1867 (*L. hiemale*)   EGF.1-**BB**-SB
    roseum F. Martin 1804   EGF.1-NN-SB
    trichophyllum Schousboe 1800   EGF.1-CA-**BB**-**SB**
    valentinum Pau 1914   SB

N‡   **vernum** Linnaeus 1753   EGF.1-PGP-**BB**-SB-DGP
        ssp. **carpathicum** (Loudon) E. Murray 1983   **BB**-SB-**DGP-RD**
        var. **vagneri** Stapf   EGF.1-**BB**-SB

X LEUCORAOULIA Allan 1939 nom. nud.   *[Asteraceae (Compositae)]*
    loganii (Buchanan) Cockayne & Allan 1934 nom. nud. (*Leucogenes grandiceps*
                                                              x *Raoulia goyenii*)

LEUZEA de Candolle 1805   *[Asteraceae (Compositae)]*
    conifera (Linnaeus) de Candolle 1805
    rhapontica (Linnaeus) Holub 1973

LEVISTICUM Hill 1756 nom. cons.   *[Apiaceae (Umbelliferae)]*
HN   **officinale** Koch 1824

LEWISIA Pursh 1814   *[Portulacaceae]*
    brachycalyx Englemann 1868   CA-RD
        'Alba' nom. dub
    cantelovii J Howell 1842
    columbiana (J. Howell) Robinson 1897   CA-RD
        'Alba'
        'Rosea' nom. dub.   CA-RD
        var. **rupicola** (English) C. L. Hitchcock 1964
        var. **wallowensis** C. L. Hitchcock 1964
    congdonii (Rydberg) Clay 1937
    cotyledon (S. Watson) Robinson 1897   CA-**DGP-RD**
        'Alba'
        'Ashwood White'
        'Ashwood Yellow'
        Birch Hybrids
        'Feuerrad'
        'Harold Judd'
        var. **heckneri** (Morton) Munz 1958 (*L. heckneri*)   CA-**RD**
        var. **howellii** (S. Watson) Jepson 1915 (*L. howellii*)   CA-**DGP-RD**
        'Jean Turner'
        'Kathy Kline'
        Kathy Kline Hybrids
        'Luminosa'
        Magenta Hybrids
        'Mars'
        'Matthew'
        'Orange Giant'
        'Orange Zwerg'
        Peach and Pink Hybrids
        Pink Hybrids
        'Pink Queen'
        'Rose Splendour'
        'Sun Dance'
        Sunset Hybrids
        Yellow Hybrids
    'George Henley' (*L. columbiana* x *L. cotyledon*)   RD
    heckneri (Morton) R. B. Smith 1931 = **L. cotyledon** var. **heckneri**
    howellii (S. Watson) Robinson 1897 = **L. cotyledon** var. **howellii**
    leana (Porter) Robinson 1897   CA
    longipetala (Piper) Clay 1937
    'Margaret Williams' (*L. cotyledon* x *L. leana*)
    nevadensis (A. Gray) Robinson 1897   CA-RD
    oppositifolia (S. Watson) Robinson 1897   CA
    'Paula'
    'Pinkie' (*L. cotyledon* x *L. longipetala*)

pygmaea (A. Gray) Robinson 1897   **CA**
   ssp. *longipetala* (Piper) Ferris 1944 = **L. longipetala**
rediviva Pursh 1814   CA-RD
   'Alba'
sierrae Ferris 1944
'Susan'
'Trevosia' (*L. columbiana* x *L. cotyledon* var. *howellii*)   CA
triphylla (S. Watson) Robinson 1897
tweedyi (A. Gray) Robinson 1897   CA-**DGP**-RD
   'Alba'
     'Rosea'   [J. Elliott]   DGP-RD

LEYMUS Hochstetter 1848   *[Poaceae (Gramineae)]*
N‡L   **arenarius** (Linnaeus) Hochstetter 1848 (*Elymus arenarius*)   PGP
    racemosus (Lamarck) Tzvelev 1960 (*Elymus giganteus*)

LIATRIS Gaertner ex Schreber 1791 nom. cons.   *[Asteraceae (Compositae)]*
   callilepis hort. = **L. spicata**
   pycnostachya Michaux 1803
   scariosa (Linnaeus) Willdenow 1804   PGP
     'Alba'   PGP
     'Magnifica'
H   **spicata** (Linnaeus) Willdenow 1804 (*L. callilepis* hort.)   PGP-**DGP**-RD
     'Alba'   PGP-DGP
     'Blue Bird'
     'Floristan Violett'
     'Floristan Weiss'
     'Kobald'
     'Picador'   PGP-RD
     'Snow Queen'

LIBERTIA Sprengel 1825 nom. cons.
   caerulescens Kunth 1847   *[Iridaceae]*
                EGF.1
   chilensis Klotzsch ex Baker 1877 = **Solenomelus chilensis**
   formosa R. Graham 1833   EGF.1-PGP
     'Glauca'
   grandiflora (R. Brown) Sweet 1830   EGF.1-PGP
   ixioides (Forster f.) Sprengel 1825   EGF.1-PGP
   paniculata (R. Brown) Sprengel 1825
   peregrinans Cockayne & Allan 1927
   pulchella Sprengel 1825 = **Sisyrinchium pulchellum**

LIGULARIA Cassini 1816 nom. cons.   *[Asteraceae (Compositae)]*
   clivorum (Maximowicz) Maximowicz 1871 = **L. dentata**
N   **dentata** (Gray) Hara 1939 (*L. clivorum, Senecio clivorum, S. dentata*)   PGP-**DGP**
L   **'Desdemona'**   [Hesse 1940]   PG-DGP
     'Golden Queen'
     'Moorblut'
     'Orange Princess'   PGP
     'Orange Queen'
     'Othello'   [1915]   PGP
     'Sommergold'   [Bornimer Staudenkulturen 1973]   PGP
L   **'Gregynog Gold'**   [Hesse 1950] (*L. dentata* x *L. veitchiana*)   PGP-**DGP**
   x hessei Hesse ex Bergmans (*L. dentata* x *L. veitchiana* x *L. wilsoniana*)   PGP-**DGP**
   hodgsonii Hooker f. 1863   PGP-**DGP**
   japonica (Thunberg) Lessing 1832   PGP-**DGP**
   macrophylla (Ledebour) de Candolle 1838 (*Senecio ledebourii*)   **PGP**
   x palmatiloba Hesse (*L. dentata* x *L. japonica*)   PGP
   przewalskii (Maximowicz) Diels (*Senecio przewalskii*)   PGP
   smithii (de Candolle) hort. = **Senecio smithii**

L   **stenocephala** (Maximowicz) Matsumura ex Chen 1934 (*Senecio stenocephalus*)
PGP

        'Globosa'
        'The Rocket'   PGP
        'Weihenstephan'
        tangutica (Maximowicz) Chen 1934 = **Senecio tanguticus**
        veitchiana (Hemsley) Greenman 1917   PGP
        wilsoniana (Hemsley) Greenman 1917   PGP
        'Zepter'   [K. Partsch 1975] (*L. przewalskii x L. veitchiana*)

LIGUSTICUM Linnaeus 1753   [*Apiaceae (Umbelliferae)*]
    mutellina (Linnaeus) Crantz 1767
HN‡   **scoticum** Linnaeus 1753

LILIUM Linnaeus 1753   [*Liliaceae*]

M - SYNGE, P.M., **'Lilies'** B. T. Batsford Ltd, London, 1980

CLASSIFICATION: in accord with the *'International Lily Register'* (Third Edition) 198
and supplements to 1988 inclusive, published by The Royal Horticultural Society
London.

    Division

    I   'Hybrids derived from such species or hybrid groups as *L. tigrinum*
              L. cernuum, L. davidii, L. leichtlinii, L. x maculatum, L. x hollandicum
              L. amabile, L. pumilum, L. concolor and *L. bulbiferum*.

    I (a)   'Early-flowering lilies with upright flowers, single or in an umbel.
    I (b)   'Those with outward-facing flowers.
    I (c)   'Those with pendent flowers.

    II   'Hybrids of Martagon type of which one parent has been a form
             L. martagon or *L. hansonii*.

    III   'Hybrids derived from *L. candidum, L. chalcedonicum* and other relat
             European species (but excluding *L. martagon*).

    IV   'Hybrids of American species.

    V   'Hybrids derived from *L. longiflorum* and *L. formosanum*.

    VI   'Hybrid Trumpet Lilies and Aurelian Hybrids derived from Asia
             species including *L. henryi*, but excluding those derived from *L. auratu*
             L. speciosum, L. japonicum and *L. rubellum*.

    VI (a) 'Those with trumpet-shaped flowers.
    VI (b) 'Those with bowl-shaped and outward-facing flowers.
    VI (c) 'Those with pendent flowers.
    VI (d) 'Those with flat, star-shaped flowers.

    VII   'Hybrids of Far Eastern species such as *L. auratum, L. speciost*
            L. japonicum and *L. rubellum*, including any of their hybrids w
            L. henryi.

VII (a) 'Those with trumpet-shaped flowers.
VII (b) 'Those with bowl-shaped flowers.
VII (c) 'Those with flat flowers.
VII (d) 'Those with recurved flowers.

VIII 'To contain all hybrids not provided for in any other division.

IX 'To contain all species and their varieties and forms.

IX **alexandrae** (Wallace) Coutts 1934   **M**-EGF.1
IX **amabile** Palibin 1901   M-EGF.1-**RD**
    'Luteum'   M-EGF.1
    'Unicolor'
IX **auratum** Lindley 1862   M-EGF.1-**BB**=**DGP**-**RD**
    'Citronella' ®
    'Crimson Beauty' ®   [J de Graaff c1960]
    Red Band (grex) ®   [J de Graaff c 1958]
    var. **platyphyllum** Baker 1880   M-EGF.1-PGP-RD
  bukosanense Honda = **L. x maculatum** var. **bukosanense**
IX **bulbiferum** Linnaeus 1753   M-EGF.1-**BB**-RD
    var. **croceum** (Chaix) Persoon 1805   M-EGF.1-PGP-**BB**-RD
IX **canadense** Linnaeus 1753   **M**-EGF.1-**DGP**-RD
    'Chocolate Chips' ®   [R M Adams 1981]
    var. **coccineum** Pursh 1814   M-EGF.1
    var. **editorum** Fernald 1943   M-EGF.1
    'Fire Engine' ®   [R M Adams 1981]
    'Melted Spots' ®   [R M Adams 1981]
    'Peaches and Pepper' ®   [R M Adams 1981]
IX **candidum** Linnaeus 1753   **M**-PGP-**BB**-DGP-RD
IX **carniolicum** Bernhardi ex Kock 1837   M-EGF.1-**BB**
    ssp. **albanicum** (Grisebach) Hayek 1932   M-EGF.1
IX **catesbaei** Walter 1788   M-EGF.1
  centifolium Stapf & Elwes 1921 = **L. leucanthum** var. **centifolium**
IX **cernuum** Komarov 1901   **M**-EGF.1-**RD**
IX **chalcedonicum** Linnaeus 1753   **M**-EGF.1-**BB**
IX **columbianum** Hanson ex Baker 1874   **M**-EGF-1-**BB**
IX **concolor** Salisbury 1806   M-EGF
    'Partheneion' (Siebold & De Vriese) Baker 1876
    var. **pulchellum** (Fischer) Regel 1876   M-EGF.1
  croceum Chaix 1786 = **L. bulbiferum** var. **croceum**
II **x dalhansonii** Powell 1893 (*L. hansonii* x *L. martagon* var. *cattaniae*)
                            M-EGF.1-**RD**
IX **dauricum** Ker-Gawler 1809   M-EGF.1-RD
    var. **alpinum** Kuseneva
IX **davidii** Duchartre 1877   **M**-EGF.1-PGP
    'Unicolor' (Hoog) Cotton 1938
    var. **willmottiae** (Wilson) Raffill 1938   **M**-EGF.1
IX **duchartrei** Franchet 1887   M-EGF.1-PGP-**BB**
IX **formosanum** Wallace 1891   **M**-EGF.1-**RD**
    var. **pricei** Stoker 1935   M-EGF.1
    'Snow Queen' ®
  fortunei (Standish) hort. = **L. lancifolium** var. **fortunei**
  giganteum Wallich 1824 = **Cardiocrinum giganteum**
IX **grayi** S. Watson 1879   **M**-EGF.1
    'Gulliver's Thimble' ®   [R M Adams 1981]
IX **hansonii** Leichtlin ex D. T. Moore 1871   M-EGF.1-PGP-DGP-**RD**
IX **henryi** Baker 1888   **M**-EFG.1-PGP-**BB**-**DGP**-RD

	'Citrinum'	EGF.1
I (a)	**x hollandicum** Bergmans ex Stearn 1950 (*L. umbellatum* hort.)	
	(*L. bulbiferum* x *L. maculatum*)	M-EGF.1-PGP-DGP-**RD**
IX	**humboldtii** Roezl & Leichtlin ex Ducharte 1870	M-EGF.1
VI (a)	**x imperiale** Wilson 1920 (*L. regale* x *L. sargentiae*)	M-EFG.1-RD
	Creelman Hybrids	RD
IX	**iridollae** M. G. Henry 1947	M-EGF.1
IX	**japonicum** Thunberg ex Houttuyn 1780	**M**-EFG.1-**DGP**-**RD**
IX	**kelloggii** Purdy 1901	**M**-EFG.1-**BB**
IX	**lancifolium** Thunberg 1794 (*L. tigrinum*)	M-EFG.1-**BB**-DGP-**RD**
	'Album'	
	var. **flaviflorum** Makino 1933	**M**-EGF.1
	'Flore Pleno' Regel 1870	EGF.1
	var. **fortunei** (Standish) Matthews 1985	**M**-EFG.1-PGP-RD
	var. **splendens** (Van Houtte) Matthews 1985	M-EFG.1-DGP
	'Yellow Tiger' ® [C A Best c1953]	
IX	**lankongense** Franchet 1892	**M**-EGF.1-PGP-**BB**
IX	**leichtlinii** Hooker f. 1867	M-EFG.1-**BB**-**RD**
	var. **maximowiczii** (Regel) Baker 1871 (*L. maximowiczii*)	M-EFG.1-RD
IX	**leucanthum** (Baker) Baker 1901	M
	var. **centifolium** (Stapf) Stearn 1935	**M**-EGF.1-PGP
IX	**longiflorum** Thunberg 1794	M-EGF.1-**RD**
	'Albomarginatum' T. Moore 1874	
	'Arai No 5' = **L. longiflorum 'Georgia'**	
	'Georgia' ('Arai No 5') ® [c1940]	
	Holland's Glory (grex) ® [Van Zonneveld Bros & Philippo 1948]	
	'Mount Everest' [De Long Lelies Ltd]	
	'White Europe' ® [G A van Veen 1979]	
IX	**mackliniae** Sealy 1949	**M**-EFG.1-**BB**-**RD**
I (a)	**x maculatum** Thunberg 1794 (*L. concolor* x *L. dauricum*)	M-EFG.1-PGP-**BB**
	var. **bukosanense** (Honda) !	M
IX	**maritimum** Kellogg 1875	**M**-EFG.1
N IX	**martagon** Linnaeus 1753	M-EFG.1-PGP-**BB**-**DGP**-**RD**
	var. **album** Weston 1772	M-EFG.1-DGP-RD
	ssp. **caucasicum** Mischckenko 1928	M-EFG.1
	maximowiczii Regel 1868 = **L. leichtlinii** var. **maximowiczii**	
IX	**michauxii** Poiret 1813	M-EFG.1
IX	**michiganense** Farwell 1915	M-EFG.1
IX	**monadelphum** Marshall von Bieberstein 1808	M-EFG.1-PGP-**BB**-RD
	var. **szovitsianum** (Fischer & Ave-Lallemant) Baker 1871	
	(*L. szovitsianum*)	**M**-PGP-**BB**-**DGP**-**RD**
IX	*myriophyllum* Franchet 1892 non Wilson = **L. sulphureum**	
	myriophyllum Wilson 1905 non Franchet = **L. regale**	
IX	**nanum** Klotzsch & Garcke 1862 (*Nomocharis nana*)	M-EFG.1-CA
	var. **flavidum** (Rendle) Sealy 1952	M-EFG.1-CA
IX	**nepalense** D. Don 1821	**M**-EFG.1-**BB**
IX	**nobilissimum** (Makino) Makino 1914	M-EFG.1
IX	**oxypetalum** (Royle) Baker 1874 (*Nomocharis oxypetala*)	**M**-EFG.1-CA
	var. **insigne** Sealy 1952	M-EFG.1
IX	**pardalinum** Kellogg 1859	M-EFG.1-PGP-**BB**-**DGP**-**RD**
	'Giganteum' Woodcock & Coutts 1935	**M**-EFG.1
VII (b)	**x parkmannii** T. Moore 1875 (*L. auratum* x *L. speciosum*)	M-EFG.1-**DGP**
IX	**philadelphicum** Linnaeus 1762	M-EFG.1
IX	**philippinense** Baker 1876	M-EFG.1
IX	**pitkinense** Beane & Vollmer 1955	M-EFG.1
IX	**polyphyllum** D. Don 1840	M-EFG.1-**BB**
IX	**pomponium** Linnaeus 1753	M-EFG.1-**BB**
IX	**ponticum** K. Koch 1849	M-EFG.1
	pricei (Stoker) hort. = **L. formosanum** var. **pricei**	
IX	**pumilum** Delile 1812 (*L. tenuifolium*)	M-EFG.1-**RD**

NÉ   IX   **'Golden Gleam'** ⊛   [E Huptelen 1911]   M
    pyrenaicum Gouan 1773   **M**-EFG.1-PGP-**BB**-DGP-**RD**
    'Aureum'   EGF.1
    'Rubrum'   EGF.1-PGP-**BB**-DGP
IX   **regale** Wilson 1912(*L. myriophyllum* Wilson)   **M**-EFG.1-**DGP**-**RD**
    Album (grex) ⊛   [J Tensen c1935]
    Royal Gold (grex) ⊛   [J de Graaff c1955]
IX   **rhodopaeum** Delipavlov 1952   **DGP**
IX   **rubellum** Baker 1898   M-EGF.1
IX   **speciosum** Thunberg 1794   **M**-EGF.1-**DGP**-**RD**
    M-EGF.1-PGP-**BB**-DGP-RD
    var. **album** Masters ex Baker 1873
    'Benikoshiki'   [H Nagahama c1962]
    'Ellabee' ⊛   [F M Wilson c1953]
    'Grand Commander' ⊛   [F M Wilson]
    var. **gloriosoides** Baker 1880   EGF.1
    'Ida Uchida'
    'Lucie Wilson' ⊛   [F M Wilson c1940]
    var. **magnificum** Wallace 1904   M
    'Melpomene' ⊛   [C M Hovey 1884]   M-**DGP**
    'Namazu Beauty' ⊛   [Hakoneya Nurseries 1955]
    'Rosemede'
    var. **roseum** Masters ex Baker 1873
    var. **rubrum** Masters ex Baker 1873   DGP
    'Uchida' ⊛   [M Uchida 1960]   M
    'Uchida Kanoka'
    sulphureum Baker 1892 (*L. myriophyllum* Franchet)   M-EGF.1
IX   **superbum** Linnaeus 1762   **M**-EFG.1-**RD**
    szovitsianum Fischer & Ave-Lallemant 1839 = **L. monadelphum**
    var. **szovitsianum**
III   *tenuifolium* Fischer 1812 nom. nudum = **L. pumilum**
    x **testaceum** Lindley 1842 (*L. candidum* x *L. chalcedonicum*)
    M-EFG.1-**PGP**-**BB**-**DGP**-**RD**
    tigrinum Ker-Gawler 1810 = **L. lancifolium**
IX   **tsingtauense** Gilg 1904   **M**-PGP-**BB**-**RD**
IX   **umbellatum** Pursh 1814
    umbellatum hort. non Pursh = **L. x hollandicum**
IX   **wallichianum** Kellogg 1859   **M**-EFG.1
IX   **washingtonianum** Schultes f. 1830   M-EFG.1-**BB**
    var. **purpurascens** Stearn 1948   M-EFG.1-**BB**
    willmottiae Wilson 1913 = **L. davidii** var. **willmottiae**
IX   **wilsonii** Leichlin ex Woodcock & Stearn 1950 nom. nudum.   M-EFG.1

HYBRID CULTIVARS & GROUPS
(The epithet '(grex)' indicates a group name)

I (a)   **'Achilles'** ⊛   [C North c1977]
I (a)   **'Admiral'** ⊛   [Bischoff Tulleken Leliecultuur 1979]
VI (a)   **'African Queen'** ⊛   [J de Graaff c1958]
VI (a)   **African Queen** (grex) ⊛   [J de Graaff c1958]   RD
V   **Albino** (grex) ⊛   [Z K Tvrtkovic-Sahin c1964]
    'Aleida' = **L. 'Edith'**
VII (d)   **'Allegra'**   [S L Emsweller c1955]   DGP
    'Amigos'
I (c)   **'Angela North'** ⊛   [C North 1973]
I (a)   **'Anne Boleyn'** ⊛   [D B Fox 1970]
I (c)   **'Apeldoorn'** ⊛   [N & B Laan Bros c1965]
I (a)   **'Apricot'** ⊛   [K Zaadnoordijk c1928]
I (b)   **'Apricot Beauty'** ⊛   [N & B Laan Bros c1964]
I (c)   **'Ariadne'** ⊛   [C North 1976]
    'Aristo' = **L. 'Orange Aristo'**

I (a)	**'Astarix'** ® [P Hoff & Sons c1978]	
I (b)	**'Attila'** ® [N & B Laan Bros c1966]	
VII (a)	**Aurelian Hybrids** ® [C Yerex c1938]	
I (a)	**'Avignon'** ® [Gebr Vletter & J A den Haan 1984]	
I (c)	**'Barbara North'** ® [C North 1973]	
I (c)	**'Beckwith Tiger'** ® [R A Beckwith 1982]	
IV	**Bellingham Hybrids** ® [D Griffiths c1933]	EGF.1-PGP-**DGP**-RD
IV	**Bellmaid Hybrids** ® [D B Fox 1967]	
I (a)	**'Bellona'** ® [N & B Laan Bros c1975]	
I (b)	**'Bingo'** ® [L D Marshall 1975]	
VII (d)	**'Black Beauty'** ® [L Woodriff c1957]	**BB**
VI (a)	**'Black Dragon'** ® [J de Graaff c1950]	**DGP**-RD
VI (a)	**'Black Magic'** ® [J de Graaff c1959]	
VII (b)	**'Bonfire'** ® [J de Graaff c1962]	
I (a)	**'Bora'** ® [N & B Laan Bros 1984]	
I (b)	**'Brandywine'** ® [S L Emsweller c1953]	
I (a)	**'Bravissimo'** ® [Bischoff Tulleken Leliecultuur 1983]	
I (a)	**'Bright Beauty'** ® [N & B Laan Bros 1975]	
VI (d)	**'Bright Star'** ® [J de Graaff c1959]	**RD**
	'Bronze' = **L. 'Marksuv Bronz'**	
IV	**Bullwood Hybrids** ® [D B Fox 1967]	
I (c)	**Burgundy** (grex) ® [J de Graaff c1959]	
I (a)	**'Butterfly'** ® [G M Chandler 1953]	
I (b)	**'Camborne'** ® [Rosewarne E H S c1969]	
I (c)	**'Cambridge'** ® [H J Eaton c1984]	
I (a)	**'Capri'** ® [Gebr Vletter & J A den Haan 1984]	
	'Caprice'	
VII (b)	**'Casa Blanca'** ® [Gebr Vletter & J A den Haan 1975]	
I (b)	**'Charm'** ® [J Boon pre-1982]	
IV	**'Cherrywood'** ® [D B Fox 1982]	
I (a)	**'Chinook'** ® [Oregon Bulb Farms 1972]	
I (c)	**Citronella** (grex) ® [J de Graaff c1958]	**RD**
	'Citronella' = **L. auratum 'Citronella'**	
I (a)	**'Claudia'** ® [S en S Ltd 1985]	
I (a)	**'Colleen'** ® [E A McRae 1982]	
I (a)	**'Concorde'** ® [Vletter Bros & J A den Haan c1976]	
I (a)	**'Connecticut King'** ® [D M Stone & F H Payne c1967]	
I (b)	**'Connecticut Lemonglow'** ® [D M Stone & F H Payne c1965]	
I (c)	**'Connecticut Yankee'** ® [D M Stone c1959]	
I (a)	**'Corina'** ® [De Jong Lelies Ltd 1978]	
I (a,b)	**Cornish Hybrids** ® [Rosewarne E H S 1974]	
	'Coronne d'Or'	
I (b)	**'Corsage'** ® [J de Graaff c1961]	
	'Crimson Beauty' = **L. auratum 'Crimson Beauty'**	
VI (a)	**'Damson'** ® [J de Graaff c1954]	
I (a)	**'Destiny'** ® [J de Graaff c1949]	**DGP**-RD
I (c)	**'Discovery'** ® [J de Graaff c1962]	
VII	**'Dominique'** ® [Sun Valley Bulb Farms 1973]	
I (a)	**'Duet'** ® [Bischoff Tulleken Leliecultuur 1975]	
I (c)	**'Dukat'** ® [V Jost 1977]	
I (a)	**'Edith'** ® [D B Fox 1981]	
I (a)	**'Enchantment'** ® [J de Graaff c1947]	**DGP**-RD
I (c)	**'Eros'** ® [C North c1976]	
I (a)	**'Esther'** ® [J Boon c1980]	
I (a)	**'Eurovision'** ® [Gebr Vletter & J A den Haan 1979]	
I (b)	**'Exception'** ® [N & B Laan Bros c1978]	
	Faberge Hybrids	
I (c)	**'Falmouth'** ® [Rosewarne E H S 1974]	
I (a)	**'Festival'** ® [P Hoff & Sons c1980]	
I (b)	**'Feuerzauber'** ® [N & B Laan Bros c1970]	

I (c)	**Fiesta Hybrids** ®	[J de Graaff 1946]	RD
I (a)	**'Firecracker'** ®	[Oregon Bulb Farms 1975]	
I (b)	**'Fire King'** ®	[J E H Stooke c1933]	
I (a)	**'Flamin Star'** ®	[Gebr Vletter & J A den Haan 1984]	
VII (c)	**'Furore'** ®	[Sun Valley Bulb Farms 1984]	
I (a)	**Golden Chalice Hybrids** ®	[J de Graaff c1947]	
VI (a)	**Golden Clarion** (grex) ®	[J de Graaff 1948]	**DGP-RD**
	'Golden Gleam' = **L. pumilum 'Golden Gleam'**		
I (c)	**'Golden Melody'** ®	[Vletter Bros & J A den Haan c1976]	
I (b)	**'Golden Souvenir'** ®	[N & B Laan Bros c1968]	
VI (a)	**Golden Splendour** (grex) ®	[J de Graaff 1957]	**RD**
VI (d)	**Golden Sunburst** (grex) ®	[J de Graaff c1956]	RD
I (a)	**'Gold Medal'** ®	[E A McRae 1971]	
I (b)	**'Gold Rush'** ®	[J de Graaff 1951]	
	'Grand Commander' = **L. speciosum 'Grand Commander'**		
I (a)	**'Gran Paradiso'** ®	[Vletter Bros & J A den Haan 1983]	
VI (a)	**'Green Dragon'** ®	[J de Graaff c1949]	
VI (a)	**'Greenlight'**	[N & B Laan Bros]	
VI (a)	**Green Magic** (grex) ®	[J de Graaff c1956]	
I (a)	**'Greenpeace'** ®	[Bischoff Tulleken Leliecultuur 1982]	
I (c)	**Harlequin Hybrids** ®	[J de Graaff c1950]	RD
I (a)	**'Harmony'** ®	[J de Graaff c1950]	
I (a)	**'Harvest'** ®	[Oregon Bulb Farms c1978]	
	'Highland Flame'		
	'Highland Primrose'		
I (a)	**'Hilde'** ®	[J Boon pre-1982]	
VI (a)	**'Honeydew'** ®	[J de Graaff c1954]	
I (c)	**'Hornback's Gold'** ®	[Oregon Bulb Farms 1972]	
VII (c)	**Imperial Crimson** (grex) ®	[J de Graaff c1960]	DGP-RD
VII (c)	**Imperial Gold** (grex) ®	[J de Graaff c1960]	**RD**
	'Imperial Red Band'		
VII (c)	**Imperial Silver** (grex) ®	[J de Graaff]	DGP-RD
I (a)	**'Inferno'** ®	[E A McRae 1979]	
I (c)	**'Iona'** ®	[C North pre-1982]	
II	**'Jacques S Dijt'** ®	[H C Dijt c1950]	
VII (d)	**Jamboree** (grex) ®	[J de Graaff c1960]	RD
	'Jeanne d'Arc' = **L. 'Colleen'**		
I (a)	**'Joanna'** ®	[Oregon Bulb Farms 1973]	
	'Jolanda'		
VII (d)	**'Journey's End'** ®	[J S Yeates c1957]	RD
VII (b)	**'Joy'** ®	[T Kirsch 1981]	
I (a)	**'Juliana'** ®	[Oregon Bulb Farms c1976]	
I (a)	**'Juno'** ®	[V Jost c1980]	
I (b)	**'King Pete'** ®	[H Peters pre-1975]	
I (c)	**'La Boheme'** ®	[J Koeman c1965]	
VI (b)	**'Lady Ann'** ®	[N & B Laan Bros 1982]	
I (c)	**'Lady Bowes Lyon'** ®	[G W Darby c1956]	PGP
I (a)	**'Ladykiller'** ®	[N & B Laan Bros c1974]	
I (c)	**'Langtry'** ®	[D B Fox 1975]	
VII	**'Laura'** ®	[Sun Valley Bulb Farms 1980]	
	'Lauralee' = **L. 'Laura'**		
	'Le Reve' = **L. 'Joy'**		
I (c)	**'Levant'** ®	[N & B Laan Bros c1975]	
	'Liberation'		
VI (a)	**'Limelight'** ®	[J de Graaff c1958]	**DGP-RD**
	'Little Snow White'		
VI (a)	**Mabel Violet** (grex) ®	[N & B Laan Bros 1970]	
I (a)	**'Manuella'** ®	[N & B Laan Bros c1975]	
	'Marhan' = **L. x dalhansonii**		
I (c)	**'Marie North'** ®	[C North 1973]	

I (a)	**'Marilyn Monroe'** ®	[I D Parsons 1973]	
I (c)	**'Marksuv Bronz'** ®	[J Marks pre-1969]	
I (a)	**'Matchless'** ®	[Oregon Bulb Farms 1979]	
I (c)	**'Maxwill'** ®	[F L Skinner c1932]	PGP
I (a)	**'Medaillon'** ®	[Vletter Bros & J A den Haan c1970]	
VII	**'Merci'** ®	[Sun Valley Bulb Farms 1974]	
I (a)	**Mid-Century Hybrids** ®	[J de Graaff c1949]	RD
I (c)	**'Minos'** ®	[C North 1976]	
I (a)	**'Mirage'** ®	[W Windus 1975]	
I (a)	**'Mont Blanc'** ®	[Vletter Bros & J A den Haan c1978]	
I (c)	**'Montreaux'** ®	[Gebr Vletter & J A den Haan 1984]	
VI (a)	**Moonlight** (grex) ®	[J de Graaff]	
I (b)	**'Moulin Rouge'** ®	[Vletter Bros & J A den Haan c1978]	
II	**'Mrs R O Backhouse'** ®	[Mrs R O Backhouse pre-1921]	
I (a)	**'Musical'** ®	[Bischoff Tulleken Leliecultuur 1983]	
	'Nell Gwynn'		
I (b)	**'Odysseus'** ®	[C North pre-1976]	
I (a)	**'Olivia'** ®	[L Woodriff pre-1983]	
VI (a)	**Olympic Hybrids** ®	[J de Graaff 1946]	RD
I (a)	**'Orange Aristo'** ®	[Bischoff-Tulleken Ltd 1980]	
	'Orange Sensation'		
I (a)	**'Orange Triumph'** ®	[F Rijnveld & Sons 1939]	
	'Orchid Beauty'		
I (b)	**'Orestes'** ®	[C North pre-1976]	
VII (b)	**Oriental Hybrids** ®	[L B Tuffery c1954]	
	'Oriental Sunrise' = **L. 'Roter Cardinal'**		
I (c)	**'Pan'** ®	[C North c1976]	
I (a)	**'Pandora'** ®	[C North c1976]	
I (a)	**'Papillon'** ®	[N & B Laan Bros pre-1979]	
I (b)	**'Paprika'** ®	[J de Graaff 1958]	DGP
	'Peach Blossom'		
I (a)	**'Peachblush'** ®	[Oregon Bulb Farms c1976]	
IV	**'Peachwood'** ®	[D B Fox 1960]	
I (c)	**'Peggy North'** ®	[C North 1973]	
I (a)	**'Phoebus'** ®	[C North c1976]	
VII (c)	**'Pink Beauty'** ®	[Y S Yeates c1952]	
I (c)	**'Pink Giant'** ®	[N & B Laan Bros 1976]	
	'Pink Panther'		
VI (a)	**Pink Pearl Trumpets** (grex) ®	[C Yerex c1958]	
VI (a)	**Pink Perfection** (grex) ®	[J de Graaff c1950]	
I (b)	**'Pink Tiger'** ®	[N & B Laan Bros c1976]	
I (a)	**'Pirate'** ®	[J de Graaff 1971]	
VI (d)	**'Prince Charming'** ®	[G E Holland]	
	'Prince Constantine' = **L. 'Prins Constantijn'**		
I (b)	**'Prins Constantijn'** ®	[N & B Laan Bros c1970]	
	'Prominence'		
I (b)	**'Prosperity'** ®	[J de Graaff]	
I (a)	**'Prune'** ®	[Gebr N & B Laan 1984]	
	'Prunus' = **L. 'Prune'**		
VII (d)	**Rangitoto Hybrids** ®	[N Copsey]	
	Red Band = **L. auratum Red Band**		
I (c)	**'Red Fox'** ®	[N & B Laan Bros c1963]	
I (c)	**Red Jewels** (grex) ®	[J F McRae 1979]	
	'Red Marvel'		
	'Red Night' = **L. 'Roter Cardinal'**		
I (b)	**'Redruth'** ®	[Rosewarne E H S c1975]	
I (b)	**'Redstart'** ®	[J C Taylor 1960]	
I (a)	**'Rosefire'** ®	[E A McRae 1973]	
I (a)	**'Rosita'** ®	[De Jong Lelies Ltd 1979]	
I (a)	**'Roter Cardinal'** ®	[N & B Laan Bros c1974]	

Royal Gold = **L. regale Royal Gold**
I (a)	**'Safari'** ®	[L Woodriff 1981]
I (a)	**'Sahara'** ®	[Bischoff-Tulleken Ltd 1980]
I (b)	**'Saint Blazey'** ®	[Rosewarne E H S 1974]
I (b)	**'Saint Day'** ®	[Rosewarne E H S 1974]
I (a)	**'Saint Ives'** ®	[Rosewarne E H S 1974]
I (a)	**'Saint Just'** ®	[Rosewarne E H S 1974]
I (a)	**'Salut'** ®	[Bischoff-Tulleken Ltd 1980]
I (a)	**'Samba'** ®	[Bischoff-Tulleken Ltd 1979]
VII (d)	**'Sans Souci'** ®	[L Woodriff 1971]
I (a)	**'Santana'** ®	[P Hoff & Sons c1974]
VI (a)	**Sentinel** (grex) ®	[J de Graaff c1958]
IV	**'Shuksan'** ®	[D Griffiths c1924]
I (a)	**'Silvia'**	[De Jong Lelies Ltd 1978]
I (a)	**'Sinai'** ®	[Bischoff-Tulleken Ltd 1980]
I (a)	**'Simoen'** ®	[N & B Laan Bros 1984]
I (a)	**'Sirocco'** ®	[N & B Laan Bros 1984]
	'Snow Princess'	
I (a)	**'Sorrento'** ®	[Gebr Vletter & J A Haan 1984]
VII (d)	**'Stardrift'** ®	[A C Imanse 1975]
VII (c)	**'Star Gazer'** ®	[Sun Valley Bulb Farms 1975]
I (a)	**'Sterling Star'** ®	[Oregon Bulb Farms 1973]
I (a)	**'Striped Beauty'** ®	[N & B Laan Bros 1975]
I (a)	**'Sundrop'** ®	[Oregon Bulb Farms 1972]
I (a)	**'Sun Ray'** ®	[D M Stone & F H Payne c1965]
I (c)	**Sutter's Gold** (grex) ®	[J de Graaff c1964]
I (a)	**'Sylvester'** ®	[Bischoff-Tulleken Ltd 1979]
I (a)	**'Tabasco'** ®	[J de Graaff c1958]
I (b)	**'Tamara'** ®	[De Jong Lelies Ltd c1978]
II	**Terrace City Hybrids** ®	[N E Pfeiffer]
I (c)	**'Theseus'** ®	[C North c1976]
I (c)	**'Tiger White'** ®	[N & B Laan 1981]
I (a)	**'Tip-Top'** ®	[Bischoff-Tulleken Ltd 1980]
VI (b)	**'Trance'** ®	[Bischoff Tulleken Leliecultuur 1983]
VII (c)	**'Troubadour'** ®	[Bischoff Tulleken Leliecultuur 1984]
I (c)	**'Truro'** ®	[Rosewarne E H S 1974]
II	**'Tsingense'** ®	[E Robinson c1964]
	'Uchida' = **L. speciosum 'Uchida'**	
I (a)	**'Utopia'** ®	[Oregon Bulb Farms 1981]
I (a)	**'Venture'** ®	[Oregon Bulb Farms 1979
I (a)	**'Vermillion Brilliant'** ®	[K Zaadnoordijk c1927]
I (c)	**'Viking'** ®	[E F Palmer c1942]
	'White Europe' = **L. longiflorum 'White Europe'**	
I (a)	**'White Happiness'** ®	[N & B Laan Bros 1979]
VI (a)	**'White Lady'** ®	[V P Orekhov c1960]
VII (c)	**'White Mountain'** ®	[J C Smit 1979]
V	**'White Superior'** ®	[A J van der Zwet & Sons 1946]
	'White Tiger' = **L. 'Tiger White'**	
I (a)	**Yellow Blaze** (grex) ®	[D M Stone & F H Payne c1965]
	'Yellow Enchantment' nom. dub.	
	'Yellow Giant' = **L. 'Joanna'**	
	'Yellowhammer'	
	'Yellow Present'	
VII (c)	**'Yellow Ribbons'** ®	[H J Strahm]
I (b)	**'Yellow Star'** ®	[De Jong Lelies Ltd 1964]
	'Yellow Tiger' = **L. lancifolium 'Yellow Tiger'**	
I (a)	**'Yoma'** ®	[D B Fox c1969]

PGP-RD

LIMNANTHEMUM S. Gmelin 1770   [*Menyanthaceae*]
   indicum (Linnaeus) Thwaites 1860 = **Nymphoides indica**
   peltatum S. Gmelin 1770 = **Nymphoides peltata**

LIMNANTHES R. Brown 1833 nom. cons.   [*Limnanthaceae*]
A   **douglasii** R. Brown 1833   **DGP-RD**

LIMONIUM Miller 1754 nom. cons.   [*Plumbaginaceae*]
N‡   **bellidifolium** (Gouan) Dumortier 1827 (*L. caspium*)   CA-RD
         'Filigran'
     bellidifolium hort. non (Gouan) Dumortier = **L. companyonis**
     caspium (Willdenow) Gam 1880 = **L. bellidifolium**
N   **companyonis** (Grenier & Billot) O. Kuntze (*L. bellidifolium* hort.)
     cosyrense (Gussone) O. Kuntze 1891   CA
     dumosum hort. = **L. tataricum** var. **angustifolium**
     globulariifolium O. Kuntze 1891 = **L. ramosissimum**
     latifolium (Smith) O. Kuntze 1891 non Moench 1794 = **L. platyphyllum**
     minutum (Linnaeus) Fourreau 1869 (*Statice minuta*)   CA
     platyphyllum Linczevski 1964 (*L. latifolium* (Smith) O. Kuntze, *Statice latifolium*)
                                                                    PGP-**RD**

         'Blauschleier'
         'Blue Gown'
         'Grandiflorum'
         'Violetta'   PGP
     ramosissimum (Poiret) Maire 1936 (*L. globulariifolium*)
     tataricum Miller 1754 (*Goniolimon tataricum*)
         var. **angustifolium** (*L. dumosum* hort.)

LINARIA Miller 1754   [*Scrophulariaceae*]
     aequitriloba (Viviani) Sprengel 1825 = **Cymbalaria aequitriloba**
     alpina (Linnaeus) Miller 1768   CA-**RD**
         'Rosea'   CA
     anticaria Boissier & Reuter 1852
     cymbalaria (Linnaeus) Miller 1768 = **Cymbalaria muralis**
         var. *globosa* Hort. ex Gerbault 1917 = **Cymbalaria muralis 'Globosa'**
N   **dalmatica** (Linnaeus) Miller 1768 (*L. genistifolia* ssp. *dalmatica*)   PGP-**RD**
     genistifolia (Linnaeus) Miller 1768   PGP
         ssp. *dalmatica* (Linnaeus) Maire & Petitmengin 1908 = **L. dalmatica**
     hepaticifolia (Poiret) Steudel 1821 = **Cymbalaria hepaticifolia**
     lilacina Lange 1855
     origanifolia (Linnaeus) Chazelles de Prizy 1790 = **Chaenorhinum origanifolium**
     pallida (Tenore) Gussone 1826 = **Cymbalaria pallida**
     pilosa (Jacquin) Chazelles de Prizy 1790 = **Cymbalaria pilosa**
N‡   **purpurea** (Linnaeus) Miller 1768   PGP-DGP-RD
         'Canon J. Went'   PGP-**DGP**-RD
N‡   **repens** (Linnaeus) Miller 1768
N   **supina** (Linnaeus) Chazelles de Prizy 1790   CA
     triornithophora (Linnaeus) Willdenow 1809   PGP-RD
         'Rosea'
HN‡L **vulgaris** Miller 1768
         'Flore Pleno'

LINDELOFIA Lehmann 1850   [*Boraginaceae*]
     longiflora (Bentham) Baillon 1890   PGP

LINNAEA Linnaeus 1753   [*Caprifoliaceae*]
SN‡ **borealis** Linnaeus 1753   **RD**
         ssp. **americana** (Forbes) Hulton   RD

LINUM Linnaeus 1753   [*Linaceae*]
  alpinum Jacquin 1762 = **L. perenne** ssp. **alpinum**
S   **arboreum** Linnaeus 1753
S   **campanulatum** Linnaeus 1753   CA-DGP-RD
    capitatum Kitaibel ex Schultes 1814   RD
    dolomiticum Borbas 1897
    flavum Linnaeus 1753   CA-**RD**
        'Compactum'
    'Gemmell's Hybrid' (*L. campanulatum* x *L. elegans*)   [Gemmells Nursery c1940]
    julicum Hayek 1907 = **L. perenne** ssp. **alpinum**
S   **monogynum** Forster f. 1786
        'Nelson'
SL **narbonense** Linnaeus 1753   PGP-**DGP**-RD
        'Heavenly Blue'
        'Six Hills'
    paniculatum Moench 1802 = **L. narbonense**   PGP
SHN‡ **perenne** Linnaeus 1753
        'Album'
        ssp. **alpinum** (Jacquin) Ockenden 1967 (*L. alpinum, L. julicum*)   CA
        'Blau Saphir'
        'Saphir'
        'Tetra Blue Mist'
    rhodopeum Velenovsky 1896
    salsoloides Lamarck 1792 = **L. suffruticosum** ssp. **salsoloides**
    suffruticosum Linnaeus 1753
        ssp. **salsoloides** (Lamarck) Rouy 1897 (*L. salsoloides*)   CA
AN **usitatissimum** Linnaeus 1753   PGP-RD
    viscosum Linnaeus 1762   PGP

LIPPIA Linnaeus 1753   [*Verbenaceae*]
  canescens Kunth 1817 = **Phyla canescens**
  nodiflora (Linnaeus) Richard 1803 = **Phyla nodiflora**
  repens hort. = **Phyla canescens**

LIRIOPE Loureiro 1790   [*Convallariaceae (Liliaceae)*]
    exiliflora (Bailey) Bailey 1961
        'Silvery Sunproof'   PGP
    graminifolia (Linnaeus) Baker 1879 = **L. spicata**
    minor (Maximowicz) Makino 1893
L   **muscari** (Decaisne) Bailey 1929   EGF.1-PGP-**RD**
        'China'
        'Christmas Tree'   [W. L. Monroe c1957]
        'Curly Twist'   [Riegel Plant Co.]
        'Gold-banded'   [Riegel Plant Co.]
        'Ingwersen'
        'John Burch'
        'Lilac Beauty'   [Riegel Plant Co.]
        'Majestic'   [Russell Gardens]
        'Monroe White'   [W. L. Monroe c1957]   PGP
        'Variegata'
    platyphylla F. T. Wang & Tang 1951   PGP
    spicata (Thunberg) Loureiro 1790 (*L. graminifolia*)   PGP
        'Alba'   EGF.1-RD

LISTERA R. Brown 1813 nom. cons.   [*Orchidaceae*]
N‡ **ovata** (Linnaeus) R. Brown 1813   EGF.2

LITHODORA Grisebach 1844   [*Boraginaceae*]
S   **diffusa** (Lagasca) I. M. Johnson 1924 (*Lithospermum diffusum*)   CA-DGP-**RD**

	'Alba'	CA
	'Cambridge Blue'	
	'Grace Ward'	CA-**DGP**-RD
	'Heavenly Blue' [W. H. Lowe via A. Perry]	CA-DGP-RD
S	**fruticosa** (Linnaeus) Grisebach 1844	
S	**hispidula** (Smith) Grisebach 1844	
S	**oleifolia** (Lapeyrouse) Grisebach 1844 (*Lithospermum oleifolium*)	CA-**DGP**-RD
	'Barker's Form'	
S	**rosmarinifolia** (Tenore) I. M. Johnson 1924	CA
S	**zahnii** (Heldreich ex Halascy) I. M. Johnson 1924	

LITHOPHRAGMA (Nuttall) Torrey & A. Gray 1840 nom. cons.   [*Saxifragaceae*]
    parviflora (Hooker) Nuttall ex Torrey & A. Gray 1840 (*Tellima parviflora*)

LITHOSPERMUM Linnaeus 1753   [*Boraginaceae*]
    diffusum Lagasca 1805 = **Lithodora diffusa**
    oleifolium Lapeyrouse 1813 = **Lithodora oleifolia**
SN‡ **purpureocaerulea** Linnaeus 1753 (*Buglossoides purpureocaerulea*)

LITTORELLA P. Bergius 1768   [*Plantaginaceae*]
    lacustris (Linnaeus) Linnaeus 1771 = **L. uniflora**
N‡ **uniflora** (Linnaeus) Ascherson 1864 (*L. lacustris*)

LLOYDIA Salisbury ex Reichenbach 1830 nom. cons.   [*Liliaceae*]
    flavonutans Hara 1974   **SB**
N‡ **serotina** (Linnaeus) Sweet 1830   EGF.1-CA-**BB**-SB

LOBELIA Linnaeus 1753   [*Campanulaceae*]

	anceps Linnaeus f. 1781	
	angulata Forster f. 1786 = **Pratia angulata**	
	cardinalis Linnaeus 1753	
	'Alba'	
	fulgens Willdenow 1809	PGP-**DGP**-RD
	'Blinkfeuer'	
	'Illumination'	
	gattingeri Gray 1881	
	x gerardii Chabanne ex Nicholas (*L. cardinalis* x *L. siphilitica*)	PGP
	'Blauzauber'	
	'Rosenkavalier' [Müller]	
	'Tania'	PGP
L	'Vedrariensis' (*L. x vedrariensis*)	PGP-RD
	laxiflora Humboldt, Bonpland & Kunth 1820	
	var. **angustifolia** de Candolle	**PGP**
	lindblomii Mildbraed 1922	
	linnaeoides (Hooker f.) Petrie 1891 (Pratia linnaeoides)	CA
	'Dobson' [G. Hutchins]	
	'Sutton' [G. Hutchins]	
	roughii Hooker f. 1864	
	sequinii A. Leveille & Vaniot 1913	
	sessilifolia Lambert 1811	
H	**siphilitica** Linnaeus 1753	PGP-**RD**
	'Alba'	RD
	'Arctic Blue'	
	'Nana'	CA
	'Nana Alba'	
	x speciosa Sweet 1833 (L. cardinalis x L. fulgens x L. siphilitica)	
	'Bees' Flame'	PGP-DGP-RD
	'Brightness' [A. Chan via Wisley Gardens]	

      'Cherry Ripe'   PGP
      'Dark Crusader'   [A. Chan via Wisley Gardens]   PGP
      'Huntsman'
      'Jack McMaster'

L   **'Queen Victoria'**
      'Russian Princess'   PGP-RD
      'Will Scarlet'   [A. Chan via Wisley Gardens]   PGP
  'Tim Rees'
      tupa Linnaeus 1762   **PGP**
      x vedrariensis hort. = **L. x gerardii 'Vedrariensis'**

LOBULARIA Desvaux 1814 nom. cons.   *[Brassicaceae (Cruciferae)]*
N‡   **maritima** (Linnaeus) Desvaux 1814

LOMARIA Willdenow 1809   *[Blechnaceae]*
      alpina Sprengel 1827 = **Blechnum penna-marina** ssp. **alpinum**

LOPHOSPERMUM D. Don 1827   *[Scrophulariaceae]*
C   **erubescens** D. Don 1830 (*Maurandya erubescens*)   **RD**
C   **purpusii** (T. S. Brandegee) Rothmaler 1943 (*Maurandya purpusii*)
C   **scandens** D. Don 1827 (*Maurandya scandens* (D. Don) A. Gray)

LOTUS Linnaeus 1753   *[Fabaceae (Leguminosae)]*
      berthelotii Masferrer 1881
N‡L   **corniculatus** Linnaeus 1753   **DGP**
      'Flore Pleno'   DGP

LUDWIGIA Linnaeus 1753   *[Onagraceae]*
      minor hort. = **L. parviflora**
N‡   **palustris** (Linnaeus) Elliott 1821 (*Isnardia palustris*)
      parviflora Roxburgh 1820 (*L. minor* hort.)

LUETKEA Bongard 1833   *[Rosaceae]*
S   **pectinata** (Pursh) Kuntze 1891

LUNARIA Linnaeus 1753   *[Brassicaceae (Cruciferae)]*
AN   **annua** Linnaeus 1753   PGP-**DGP**-**RD**
      'Variegata'
N   **rediviva** Linnaeus 1753   **PGP-DGP**-RD

LUPINUS Linnaeus 1753   *[Fabaceae (Leguminosae)]*
S   **albifrons** Bentham 1835   PGP
SHN   **arboreus** Sims 1803   PGP-**RD**
      'Golden Spire'
      'Snow Queen'   [E. Ladhams pre-1899]
      argenteus Pursh 1814
S   **chamissonis** Eschscholtz 1826
      confertus Kellogg 1863   CA
      latifolius Lindley ex J. G. Agardh 1835
      lepidus Douglas ex Lindley 1828
         var. **lobbii** (A. Gray ex S. Watson) C. L. Hitchcock 1961
      littoralis Douglas ex Lindley 1828
N   **nootkatensis** Don ex Sims 1810
      perennis Linnaeus 1753
      rivularis Douglas ex Lindley 1833
NL   **polyphyllus** Lindley 1827
S   **saxatilis** Ulbrich 1906   PGP-RD
      tomentosus de Candolle 1825

L   HYBRID CULTIVARS & GROUPS

'Barnsdale'
'Betty Astell'
'Blushing Bride'   RD
'Blue Jacket'   RD
'Boningale Lass'
'Catherine of York'
'Celandine'
'Chandelier'   RD
'Cherry Pie'   RD
'City of York'
'Clifford Star'   [Woodfield Bros.]
'Commando'
'Corn Dolly'
'Daydream'
'Deborah Woodfield'   [Woodfield Bros.]
'Dwarf Lulu' = L. 'Lulu'
'Edelknaben'
'Fireglow'
'Fraülein'
'Fred Yule'
'Freedom'   DGP-RD
'George Russell'
'Gold Dust'
'Halina'
'Harvester'
'Household Brigade'   [Woodfield Bros.]
'Josephine'   DGP
'Joy'
'Judy Harper'   [Woodfield Bros.]
'Julie'   [Woodfield Bros.]
'Kastellan'
'King's Royal'   [Woodfield Bros.]
'Kronleuchter'
'La Chatelaine'   RD
'Lady Beatrix Stanley'
'Lady Diana Abdy'
'Lady Fayre'
'Lady Gay'
'Lilac Time'   RD
'Limelight'
'Loveliness'
'Lulu'   RD
'Masterpiece'
'Mein Schloss' = L. 'My Castle'
'Minarette'
'Misty'   [Woodfield Bros.]
'Monkgate'
'Moonraker'
'Mrs Noel Terry'
'Mrs Micklethwaite'
'My Castle'   RD
'Nellie B Allen'
'Noble Maiden'   RD
'Orangeade'   [Woodfield Bros.]
'Pope John Paul'   [Woodfield Bros.]
'Prosperity'
'Red Rover'
Roggli Hybrids

'Rougham Beauty'   [K. Harbutt]
'Rote Flamme'
'Royal Parade'
Russell Hybrids
'Sailor Boy'   [Woodfield Bros.]
'Saxby'
'Schlössfrau' = **L.** 'La Chatelaine'
'Shy Princess'   [Woodfield Bros.]
'The Governor'
'The Page'   RD
'Thundercloud'   RD
'Venus'   RD
'Viscountess Cowdray'
'Vogue'
'Walton Lad'
'Washington Yellow'
'Wheatsheaf'

LURONIUM Rafinesque 1840   [*Alismataceae*]
N‡   **natans** (Linnaeus) Rafinesque 1840 (*Alisma natans*)   EGF.1

LUZULA de Candolle 1805 nom. cons.
   alopecuros Desveaux 1808   [*Juncaceae*]
   banksiana E. Meyer 1849
   celata Edgar 1966
   maxima (Reichard) de Candolle 1805 = **L. sylvatica**
N   **nivea** (Linnaeus) de Candolle 1805
       'Arctic Hair' hort.! = **L. nivea** 'Schneehäschen'
       'Schneehäschen' ('Snow Leveret')
   parviflora (Ehrhart) Desvaux 1808
N‡   **pilosa** (Linnaeus) Willdenow 1809
       'Grünfink'   [zur Linden]
   pumila Hooker f. 1864
   purpureosplendens Seubert 1844
   rufa Edgar 1966
N‡   **sylvatica** (Hudson) Gaudin 1811 (*L. maxima*)   EGF.2
       'Aurea Marginata' = **L. sylvatica** 'Marginata'
       'Farnfreund'
       'Hohe Tatra'
       'Marginata' ('Aureo Marginata', 'Variegata')
       'Nivea' = **L. nivea**
       'Silberhaar'
       'Tauernpass'   [H. Klose 1968]
       'Variegata' = **L. sylvatica** 'Marginata'
       'Wäldler'

LUZURIAGA Ruiz & Pavon 1802 nom. cons.   [*Philesiaceae (Liliaceae)*]
S   **radicans** Ruiz & Pavon 1802   EGF.1

LYCHNIS Linnaeus 1753   [*Caryophyllaceae*]
N‡   **alpina** Linnaeus 1753 (*Viscaria alpina*)   RD
       'Alba'   RD
       'Rosea'   RD
   x **arkwrightii** hort. ex Heydt 1932 (*L. chalcedonica* x *L. haageana*)   PGP-RD
       'Vesuvius'   PGP
NL   **chalcedonica** Linnaeus 1753   PGP-**DGP**-**RD**
       'Alba'   PGP-DGP
       'Alba Plena'
       'Carnea'
       'Rosea'

'Rosea Plena'
'Rubra Plena'

N   **coronaria** (Linnaeus) Desvaux 1792 (*Agrostemma coronaria, A. tomentosa*)
PGP-**DGP**-**RD**
    'Alba'   PGP-DGP
    'Atrosanguinea'
    'Flore Pleno'
    'Oculata'   PGP
    coronata Thunberg 1784 (*L. grandiflora*)
        var. **sieboldii** (Van Houtte) Bailey (*L. sieboldii*)
        var. **sieboldii** '**Alba**'
    dioica Linnaeus 1753 = **Silene dioica**
    grandiflora Jacquin 1787 = **L. coronata**

N‡L   **flos-cuculi** Linnaeus 1753
    'Alba'
    'Alba Plena'
    'Nana'
    'Rosea Plena'

N   **flos-jovis** (Linnaeus) Desvaux 1792   PGP-**DGP**-**RD**
    'Alba'   DGP
    'Hort's Variety'   [A. Hort c1920]   PGP-DGP
    'Minor' = **L. flos-jovis** '**Nana**'
    'Nana' ('Minor')
    x haageana Lemoine 1859 (*L. coronata* var. *sieboldii* x *L. fulgens*)   PGP-**DGP**-**RD**
    kiusiana Makino 1903
    lagascae Hooker f. 1868 = **Petrocoptis glaucifolia**
    oculata Backhouse 1844 = **Silene coeli-rosa**
    sieboldii Van Houtte 1854 = **L. coronata** var. **sieboldii**
    sibirica Linnaeus 1753 = **Silene sibirica**
    viscaria Linnaeus 1753 (*Viscaria viscosa*)   DGP-**RD**
    'Alba'
    ssp. **atropurpurea** (Grisebach) Chater 1964
    'Enzettfeuer'
    'Flore Pleno' = **L. viscaria** '**Splendens Plena**'
    'Fontaine'
    'Kugelblitz'   [Pötschke/Walther 1971]
    'Nana' nom. dub.
    'Splendens Plena' ('Flore Pleno')   DGP-**RD**
    'Thurnau'   [Karlheinz Marx]
    'Viscashnee'
    x walkeri (Dickson ex Düsberg 1890) ! (*L. coronaria* x *L. flos-jovis*)
    'Abbotswood Rose'   DGP
    wilfordii Regel ex Maximowicz 1872
    yunnanensis Baker f. 1903

LYCOPUS Linnaeus 1753   [*Lamiaceae (Labiatae)*]
HN‡   **europaeus** Linnaeus 1753

LYCORIS Herbert 1821   [*Amaryllidaceae*]
    albiflora Koidzumi 1924 = **L. radiata** var. **albiflora**
    aurea (L'Heritier) Herbert 1821   EGF.1
    incarnata Comes ex Sprenger 1906 = **L. squamigera**
    radiata (L'Heritier) Herbert 1821   EGF.1
        var. **albiflora** (Koidzumi) !
    squamigera Maximowicz 1885 (*L. incarnata*)   EGF.1

LYSICHITON Schott 1857   [*Araceae*]
N‡L   **americanus** Hulten & H. St. John 1931   EGF.2-PGP-**DGP**-**RD**
L   **camtschatcensis** (Linnaeus) Schott 1857 (*L. japonicus* hort.)   EGF.2-**PGP**-**DGP**-**RD**
    japonicus hort. = **L. camtschatcensis**

LYSIMACHIA Linnaeus 1753   [*Primulaceae*]
   barystachys Bunge 1833

N‡   **ciliata** Linnaeus 1753

   clethroides Duby 1844   PGP

L   **ephemerum** Linnaeus 1753   PGP-**RD**

   henryi Hemsley 1889   **PGP-DGP-RD**

   japonica Thunberg 1784
      'Minutissima'

   lichiangensis Forrest 1908

N‡   **nemorum** Linnaeus 1753

HN‡L   **nummularia** Linnaeus 1753
      'Aurea'   **DGP-RD**

   pseudo-henryi Pampanini 1910

NL   **punctata** Linnaeus 1753   **PGP-DGP-RD**
      'Adelheid'   [H. Klose 1985]

N‡   **thyrsiflora** Linnaeus 1753
N   **vulgaris** Linnaeus 1753

LYTHRUM Linnaeus 1753   [*Lythraceae*]
HN‡L   **salicaria** Linnaeus 1753   PGP-DGP-RD
      'Brightness'
      'Feuerkerze' ('Firecandle')   PGP-DGP
      'Firecandle' = **L. salicaria 'Feuerkerze'**   PGP
      'Happy'
      'Lady Sackville'
      'Morden's Pink'   **RD**
      'Rakete'   PGP
L   **'Robert'**   [Copijn]
      'Rose'   PGP-DGP-RD
      'Roseum Superbum'
      'Stichflamme'
      'The Beacon'
      'Zigeunerblut'   [H. Klose 1981]   **DGP-RD**
      'Zigeurnerliebe'
   virgatum Linnaeus 1753
      'Dropmore Purple'   PGP-DGP-RD
      'Rose Queen'   DGP-RD
L   **'Rosy Gem'**   PGP-**DGP-RD**
      'The Rocket'   PGP-RD

MACLEAYA R. Brown 1826   [*Papaveraceae*]
L   **cordata** (Willdenow) R. Brown 1826   PGP-**DGP-RD**
      'Alba' = **M. cordata**
      var. **yedoensis** (Andre) Fedde
   microcarpa (Maximowicz) Fedde   PGP-**DGP-RD**
L   **'Kelway's Coral Plume'** ('Korallenfeder')   [Kelway c1930]   PGP-RD
      'Korallenfeder' = **M. microcarpa 'Kelway's Coral Plume'**

MAIANTHEMUM Weber 1780 nom. cons.   [*Convallariaceae (Liliaceae)*]
N‡   **bifolium** (Linnaeus) F. W. Schmidt 1794   EGF.1-CA
      var. *kamtschaticum* (Gmelin) Jepson 1911 = **M. dilatatum**
   canadense Desfontaines 1807
   dilatatum (Wood) Nelson & MacBride 1916 (*M. kamtschaticum*)   EGF.1
   kamtschaticum (Gmelin) Nakai 1917 = **M. dilatatum**
   nipponicum Nakai 1924 (*Smilacina japonica*)   EGF.1
L   **racemosum** (Linnaeus) Link 1831 (*Smilacina racemosa*)   EGF.1-PGP-**DGP-RD**
   stellatum (Linnaeus) Link 1821 (*Smilacina stellata*)   EGF.1-PGP-RD

MALEPHORA N. E. Brown 1927   [*Aizoaceae*]
S   **lutea** (Haworth) Schwantes 1928

MALVA Linnaeus 1753   [*Malvaceae*]
N   **alcea** Linnaeus 1753   PGP-DGP-**RD**
        var. **fastigiata** Cavanilles   PGP-**DGP**-RD
BHN‡ **moschata** Linnaeus 1753   PGP-**RD**
        '**Alba**'   PGP-RD
        '**Romney Marsh**'
N‡   **sylvestris** Linnaeus 1753

MALVASTRUM A. Gray 1849 nom. cons.   [*Malvaceae*]
    lateritium Nicholson 1886

MANDRAGORA Linnaeus 1753   [*Solanaceae*]
H   **officinarum** Linnaeus 1753

MARRUBIUM Linnaeus 1753   [*Lamiaceae (Labiatae)*]
    cyllenum Boissier & Heldreich 1859
        '**Velvetissimum**'
    incanum Desvaux 1792   PGP
        '**Les Merriennes**'
    sericeum Boissier 1838 = **M. supinum**
    supinum Linnaeus 1753 (*M. sericeum*)
    velutinum Smith 1809
HN‡ **vulgare** 1753

MARSILEA Linnaeus 1753   [*Marsileaceae*]
    quadrifolia Linnaeus 1753   EGF.1

MATRICARIA Linnaeus 1753   [*Asteraceae (Compositae)*]
    aurea (Loefling) Schultz-Bip 1844 (*Chamomilla aurea*)
    caucasica (Willdenow) Poiret 1814 = **Tripleurospermum caucasicum**
    chamomilla Linnaeus 1753 p.p. = **M. recutita**
HAN‡ **recutita** Linnaeus 1753(*Chamomilla recutita*)

MATTEUCCIA Todaro 1866 nom. cons.   [*Woodsiaceae*]
    orientalis (Hooker) Trevisan 1869   PGP
    pensylvanica (Willdenow) Raymond 1950 = **M. struthiopteris North American form**
NL   **struthiopteris** (Linnaeus) Todaro 1866   EFG.1-PGP-**RD**
        North American form (*M. pensylvanica*)

MATTHIOLA Linnaeus 1753 nom. cons.   [*Brassicaceae (Cruciferae)*]
    fruticulosa (Linnaeus) Maire 1932
        ssp. **valesiaca** (Gay ex Gaudin) P. W. Ball 1962

MAURANDYA Ortega 1797   [*Scrophulariaceae*]
    antirrhiniflora Humboldt & Bonpland ex Willdenow 1806
C   **barclaiana** Lindley 1827   RD
    erubescens (D. Don) A. Gray 1868 = **Lophospermum erubescens**
    maurandioides (A. Gray) hort. = **Antirrhinum maurandioides**
    purpusii T. S. Brandegee 1908 = **Lophospermum purpusii**
C   **scandens** (Cavanilles) Persoon 1806 non (D. Don) A. Gray 1868
    scandens (D. Don) A. Gray 1868 = **Lophospermum scandens**

MAZUS Loureiro 1790   [*Scrophulariaceae*]
    pumilio R. Brown 1810   CA
        '**Albus**'
    radicans (Hooker f.) Cheeseman 1906 (*Mimulus radicans*)   CA-RD
    reptans N. E. Brown 1914   CA-**RD**
        '**Albus**'

MECONOPSIS Viguier 1814   [*Papaveraceae*]

M - **TAYLOR, G.**, '*An Account of the Genus Meconopsis* 'New Flora & Silva Ltd., London 1934

	aculeata Royle 1834	M
	baileyi Prain 1915 = **M. betonicifolia**	
	bella Prain 1894	M-CA
NL	**betonicifolia** Franchet 1889 (*M. baileyi*)	**M-PGP-DGP-RD**
	'Alba'	
N‡	**cambrica** (Linnaeus) Viguier 1814	**M-PGP-DGP-RD**
	var. **aurantiaca** Hort. ex Wehrhahn 1930	M
	'Flore Pleno' Nicholson 1901	
	chelidonifolia Bureau & Franchet 1891	**M-PGP**
	dhwojii G. Taylor ex Hay 1932	**M**
	grandis Prain 1895	**M-PGP-DGP-RD**
	'Alba'	
	'Early Sikkim'	
	horridula Hooker f. & Thomson 1885	**M**
	integrifolia (Maximowicz) Franchet 1886	**M-DGP-RD**
	latifolia (Prain) Prain 1915	**M**
	nepaulensis de Candolle 1824 (*M. wallichii*)	**M-PGP-RD**
	'Alba'	
	'Coerulea'	
	'Rosea'	
	paniculata (D. Don) Prain 1896	**M-PGP**
	punicea Maximowicz 1889	**M-PGP**
	quintuplinervia Regel 1876	**M-PGP-CA-DGP-RD**
	regia G. Taylor 1929	**M-PGP-DGP-RD**
	x sarsonsii Sarsons 1930 (*M. betonicifolia* x *M. integrifolia*)	**M-PGP**
	x sheldonii G. Taylor 1936 (*M. betonicifolia* x *M. grandis*)	**PGP**
	'Branklyn'	**PGP-DGP**
	Crewdson Hybrids	PGP
	'Slieve Donard' [T. Smith]	**PGP**
	simplicifolia (D. Don) Walpers 1842	**M-PGP**
	superba King ex Prain 1896	**M-PGP**
L	**villosa** (Hooker f.) G. Taylor 1934	**M-PGP**
	wallichii Hooker 1852 = **M. nepaulensis**	

MEEHANIA Britton 1893   [*Lamiaceae (Labiatae)*]
    cordata (Bentham) Britton 1894
    urticifolia (Miquel) Makino 1899

MEGACARPAEA de Candolle 1821   [*Brassicaceae (Cruciferae)*]
    polyandra Bentham 1855   PGP

MELANDRIUM Roehling 1812   [*Caryophyllaceae*]
    elisabethae (Jan ex Reichenbach) Rohrbach 1868 = **Silene elisabethae**
    keiskei (Miquel) Ohwi 1936 = **Silene keiskei**
    rubrum (Weigel) Garcke 1858 = **Silene dioica**
    zawadzkii (Herbich) A. Braun 1843 = **Silene zawadzkii**

MELICA Linnaeus 1753   [*Poaceae (Gramineae)*]
	altissima Linnaeus 1753	EGF.2-PGP
	'Atropurpurea' Platz 1888	PGP
	ciliata Linnaeus 1753	EGF.2-PGP
	var. *transsilvanica* (Schur) Hackel ex Halacsy & Braun 1882 = **M. transsilvanica**	
N‡	**nutans** Linnaeus 1753	EGF.2-PGP
	transsilvanica Schur 1866 (*M. ciliata* var. *transsilvanica*)	
N‡	**uniflora** Retzius 1779	EGF.2-PGP
	'Variegata'	

MELILOTUS Miller 1754   [*Fabaceae (Leguminosae)*]
BHN‡ **officinalis** (Linnaeus) Pallas 1776

MELISSA Linnaeus 1753   [*Lamiaceae (Labiatae)*]
HN‡ **officinalis** Linnaeus 1753
     'All Gold' = **M. officinalis 'Aurea'**
L   **'Aurea'** ('All Gold')   PGP
      'Variegata'

MELITTIS Linnaeus 1753   [*Lamiaceae (Labiatae)*]
N‡   **melissophyllum** Linnaeus 1753   PGP
     ssp. **albida** (Gussone) P. W. Ball 1971   PGP

MENTHA Linnaeus 1753   [*Lamiaceae (Labiatae)*]
HN‡L **aquatica** Linnaeus 1753
AHN‡ **arvensis** Linnaeus 1753
     cervina Linnaeus 1753 (*Preslia cervina*)
     citrata Ehrhart 1792
H   **gattesfossei** Maire 1954
     'Variegata'
HN‡ **x gentilis** Linnaeus 1753 (*M. arvensis* x *M. spicata*)   RD
     'Aurea'
     'Crispa'
     'Variegata'   PGP-**RD**
H‡   **longifolia** (Linnaeus) Hudson 1762   PGP
     'Crispa'
H   **niliaca** Jussieu ex Jacquin 1776
N‡   **x piperita** Linnaeus 1753 (*M. aquatica* x *M. spicata*)
H   nm. **citrata** (Ehrhart) Briquet
     'Crispa'
     'Cristata'
H   nm. **officinalis**
H   nm. **piperita**
HN‡L **pulegium** Linnaeus 1753
     raripila hort. = **M. x smithiana**
HN   **requienii** Bentham 1833   RD
     x rotundifolia (Linnaeus) Hudson 1762 (*M. longifolia* x *M. suaveolens*)   PGP-**RD**
     'Crispa'
     Flecked Form
     'Variegata' = **M. suaveolens 'Variegata'**
     sativa Roxburgh 1814 nom.nud. = **M. spicata**
HN   **x smithiana** R. M. Graham 1949 (*M. aquatica* x *M. arvensis* x *M. spicata*)
     'Rubra'
HN‡ **spicata** Linnaeus 1753 (*M. sativa, M. viridis*)
HN‡ **suaveolens** Ehrhart 1753
     'Bowles' Variety' = **M. villosa** nm. *alopecuroides*
H   **'Variegata'**
     sylvestris Linnaeus 1763 = **M. longifolia**
N   **x villosa** Hudson 1778 (*M. spicata* x *M. suaveolens*)
H   nm. **alopecuroides**
H   **x villosonervata** Opitz (*M. longifolia* x *M. spicata*)
     viridis (Linnaeus) Linnaeus 1763 = **M. spicata**

MENYANTHES Linnaeus 1753   [*Menyanthaceae*]
     crista-galli Menzies ex Hooker 1830 (*Villarsia crista-galli*)
HN‡L **trifoliata** Linnaeus 1753

MERENDERA Ramond 1798   [*Colchicaceae (Liliaceae)*]
     attica (Tommasini) Boissier & Spruner 1884   EGF.1-SB
     bulbocodium Ramond 1798 non Balbis = **M. montana**

caucasica Marshall von Bieberstein 1808 = **M. trigyna**
eichleri Boissier 1882 = **M. trigyna**
kurdica Bormueller 1899
montana Lange 1862 (*M. bulbocodium, M. pyrenaica*)   EGF.1-**BB**-SB
pyrenaica (Pourret) Fournet 1935 = **M. montana**   EGF.1-CA-**BB**-SB
raddeana Regel 1880   EGF.1-SB
robusta Bunge 1852   EGF.1-CA-SB
sobolifera Fischer & Meyer 1835   EGF.1-CA-SB
trigyna (Steven ex Adam) Stapf 1885 (*M. caucasica, M. eichleri*)   EGF.1-CA-**BB**-SB

MERTENSIA Roth 1797 nom. cons.   [*Boraginaceae*]
   asiatica (Takeda) Macbride 1916 = **M. simplicissima**
   ciliata (James) G. Don 1838   PGP-DGP-RD
   echioides Bentham ex C. B. Clarke 1883   CA-RD
   franciscana A. A. Heller 1899
N‡   **maritima** (Linnaeus) S. F. Gray 1821   PGP-CA
     ssp. *asiatica* Takeda = **M. simplicissima**
   primuloides C. B. Clarke 1883   RD
   pterocarpa (Turczaninow) Tatewaki & Ohwi 1933
L   **pulmonariodes** Roth 1797 (*P. virginica*)   PGP-CA-**DGP-RD**
   sibirica (Linnaeus) G. Don 1838
     'Alba'
   simplicissima G. Don 1838 (*M. asiatica, M. maritima* ssp. *asiatica*)   PGP
   virginica Link 1829 = **M. pulmonariodes**

MESEMBRYANTHEMUM Linnaeus 1753 nom. cons.   [*Aizoaceae*]
   aurantiacum de Candolle ex Haworth 1803 = **Lampranthus aurantiacus**
   aureum Linnaeus 1759 = **Lampranthus aureus**
   'Basutoland' = **Delosperma 'Basutoland'**
   blandum Haworth 1819 = **Lampranthus blandus**
   brownii Hooker f. 1888 = **Lampranthus brownii**
   cooperi Hooker f. 1877 = **Delosperma cooperi**
   falciforme Haworth 1818 = **Lampranthus falciforme**
   floribundum Haworth 1819 = **Drosanthemum floribundum**
   glaucum Linnaeus 1753 = **Lampranthus glaucus**
   hispidum Linnaeus 1753 = **Drosanthemum hispidum**
   luteum Haworth 1826 = **Malephora lutea**
   othona hort. = **Delosperma linearis**
   puterillii L. Bolus 1925
   roseum Willdenow 1809 = **Lampranthus multiradiatus**
   zeyheri Salm-Dyck = **Lampranthus zeyheri**

MEUM Miller 1754   [*Apiaceae (Umbelliferae)*]
N‡   **athamanticum** Jacquin 1776   PGP

MIBORA Adanson 1763   [*Poaceae (Gramineae)*]
AN‡   **minima** (Linnaeus) Desvaux 1818   EGF.2

MICROMERIA Bentham 1829 nom. cons.   [*Lamiaceae (Labiatae)*]
   corsica (Bentham) Leveille 1916 = **Acinos corsicus**
   croatica (Persoon) Schott 1857
   dalmatica Bentham 1848
S   **graeca** (Linnaeus) Bentham ex Reichenbach 1831   CA
S   **varia** Bentham 1834 (*Thymus ericifolius*)
     'Aurea'

MILIUM Linnaeus 1753   [*Poaceae (Gramineae)*]
N‡   **effusum** Linnaeus 1753   EGF.2
L   **'Aureum'**   PGP

MIMULUS Linnaeus 1753   [*Scrophulariaceae*]
    'Andean Nymph'   [Watson]
S   **aurantiacus** Curtis 1796 (*M. glutinosus, Diplacus glutinosus*)   PGP-DGP-RD
    x bartonianus hort. = **M. lewisii**
    'Boydii'
N   **x burnetii** S. Arnott (*M. cupreus x M. guttatus*)   **DGP**-RD
    cardinalis Douglas ex Bentham 1835   PGP-**RD**
    cupreus Regel 1864   CA-DGP-RD
    glutinosus J. C. Wendland 1798 = **M. aurantiacus**
N‡   **guttatus** Fischer ex de Candolle 1838 (*M. langsdorfii*)   PGP-RD
    x hybridus Hort. ex Wettstein 1891 (*M. guttatus* x *M. luteus* etc.)
        'Andean Nymph' = **M. 'Andean Nymph'**
        'Andean Pink'
        'Andean Princess'
        'A. T. Johnson'   PGP-**DGP**-**RD**
        'Bees' Dazzler'
        'Bees' Major'
        'Bees' Scarlet'   **RD**
        'Brilliant'
        Calypso Hybrids
        'Firedragon'
        'Fireflame'
        'Fire King'
        'Highland Pink'
        'Highland Red'
        Highland Hybrids
        'Highland Yellow'
        Hose-in-Hose
        'Inshriach Crimson'
        'Kibble's Scarlet'
        'Leopard'
        'Malibu'
        'Mandarin'
        'Manifique'
        'Orchid'
        'Orange Glow'
        'Plymtree'
        'Queen's Prize' = **M. x hybridus 'Tigrinus Queen's Prize'**
        'Red Emperor' = **M. x hybridus 'Roter Kaiser'**
        'Roter Kaiser' ('Red Emperor')   CA-DGP
        'Royal Velvet'
        'Scarlet Bee' = **C. x hybridus 'Bees' Scarlet'**
        'Shep'
        'Tigrinus Grandiflorus'
        'Tigrinus Queen's Prize'   DGP-**RD**
        'Whitecroft Scarlet'   CA-**DGP**-**RD**
        'Wildwoods'
        'Wisley Red'
    langsdorfii Don 1812 = **M. guttatus**
S   **lewisii** Pursh 1814 (*M. bartonianus*)   PGP-RD
S   **longiflorus** (Nuttall) Grant 1924
N   **luteus** Linnaeus 1763 non Greene 1895   DGP-**RD**
N   **moschatus** Douglas ex Lindley 1828   **RD**
    primuloides Bentham 1835   CA-**DGP**
S   **puniceus** (Nuttall) Steudel 1841 (*Diplacus puniceus*)
    radicans Hooker f. 1854 = **Mazus radicans**
    ringens Linnaeus 1753   PGP-RD
        'Lilacina'
    tilingii Regel 1869
        var. **caespitosus** (Greene) Grant 1924

MINUARTIA Linnaeus 1753   [*Caryophyllaceae*]
    biflora (Host) Schinz & Thellung 1907 (*Arenaria sajanensis*)
    circassica (Albov) Woronow ex Grossheim 1930 (*Arenaria pinifolia*)
    gerardii (Willdenow) Hayek 1908 = *M. verna* ssp. *gerardii*
S   **graminifolia** (Schrader) Javorka 1914
    imbricata (C. A. Meyer) Nakai 1929 (*Arenaria imbricata*)
    juniperina (Linnaeus) Maire & Petitmengin 1908
    kashmirica (Edgeworth) Mattfeld 1921
    laricifolia (Linnaeus) Schinz & Thellung 1907
    parnassica hort. = **M. stellata**
    stellata (E. D. Clarke) Maire & Petitmengin 1908 (*M. parnassica*)
N‡ **verna** (Linnaeus) Hiern 1899
        ssp. **caespitosa** (Ehrhart) ! (*Arenaria caespitosa*)
        ssp. **caespitosa 'Aurea'**
        ssp. **gerardii** (Willdenow) Graebner (*M. gerardii*)

MIRABILIS Linnaeus 1753   [*Nyctaginaceae*]
    jalapa Linnaeus 1753   PGP-**DGP**-**RD**

MISCANTHUS Andersson 1856   [*Poaceae (Gramineae)*]
    floridulus (Labillardiere) Warburg ex Schumacher & Lauterbach 1901
                            (*M. japonicus*)   RD
    japonicus Andersson 1856 = **M. floridulus**
    oligostachyus Stapf 1898
L   **sacchariflorus** (Maximowicz) Hackel 1887 (*Imperata sacchariflora*)   EGF.2-**PGP**
       'Robustus'
    sinensis Andersson 1855   EGF.2-**PGP**-**DGP**-RD
        var. **condensatus** (Hackel) Makino 1913
        'Giganteus' = **M. floridulus**
        'Goldfeder'
L   **'Gracillimus'**   [1878]   PGP-RD
        'Graziella'   [E. Pagels]
        'Hercules'   [H. Simon]
        'Malepartus'   [E. Pagels]
        var. **purpurascens** (Andersson) Rendle 1904
        'Rotsilber'   [E. Pagels]
        'Silberfeder'   [H. Simon c1971] ('Silver Feather')   **PGP**
        'Silberpfeil'   [H. Klose 1978] ('Silver Arrow')
        'Silver Arrow' = **M. sinensis 'Silberpfeil'**
        'Silver Feather' = **M. sinensis 'Silberfeder'**
        'Sirene'   [E. Pagels]
        'Strictus'
L   **'Variegatus'** Beal 1896   PGP-**RD**
        'Yakushima Dwarf' nom. dub.
        'Zebrinus' Beal 1896   PGP-RD

MITCHELLA Linnaeus 1753   [*Rubiaceae*]
    repens Linnaeus 1753   CA

MITELLA Linnaeus 1753   [*Saxifragaceae*]
    breweri A. Gray 1864
    caulescens Nuttall ex Torrey & A. Gray 1840
    diphylla Linnaeus 1753
    nuda Linnaeus 1753
    ovalis Greene 1887
    pentandra Hooker 1829
    stauropetala Piper 1899

MOEHRINGIA Linnaeus 1753   [*Caryophyllaceae*]
    muscosa Linnaeus 1753

MOLINIA Schrank 1789   [*Poaceae (Gramineae)*]
    altissima Link 1827 = **M. litoralis**
N‡ **caerulea** (Linnaeus) Moench 1794   EGF.2-PGP
    ssp. *arundinacea* (Shrank) H. Paulex Grabherr 1940 = **M. litoralis**
      'Dauerstrahl'   [H. Klose 1982]
      'Heidebraut'   [Zillmer 1967]
      'Moorhexe'   [H. Hagemann 1963]
      'Strahlenquelle'
      'Variegata'   PGP
    litoralis Host 1827 (*M. altissima, M. caerulea* ssp. *arundinacea*)   PGP
      'Bergfreund'   [K. Partsch]
      'Karl Foerster'   [K. Foerster]
      'Fontäne'   [Kayser & Siebert 1975]
      'Transparent'   [K. Partsch]
      'Windspiel'   [K. Partsch]

MOLTKIA Lehmann 1817   [*Boraginaceae*]
    graminifolia (Viviani) Nyman 1881 = **M. suffruticosa**
S **x intermedia** (Froebel) J. Ingram 1958 (*M. petraea* x *M. suffruticosa*)   CA-**DGP**
S **petraea** (Trattinnick) Grisebach 1845   CA
S **suffruticosa** (Linnaeus) Brand 1902 (*M. graminifolia*)   CA

MONARDA Linnaeus 1753   [*Lamiaceae (Labiatae)*]
H **didyma** Linnaeus 1753   PGP-DGP-RD
H **fistulosa** Linnaeus 1753   PGP
  russeliana Nuttall 1837

    HYBRID CULTIVARS

      'Adam'   PGP-RD
      'Aquarius'
      'Beauty of Cobham'
      'Blaustrumpf' ('Blue Stocking')   [Kayser & Siebert 1955]   RD
      'Blue Stocking' = **M. 'Blaustrumpf'**
      'Bowman'
L   **'Cambridge Scarlet'**   [Prichard pre-1913]   PGP-**DGP-RD**
      'Capricornus'
L   **'Croftway Pink'**   [c1932]   PGP-DGP-**RD**
      'Dark Ponticum'
      'Donnerwolke'   [Marx 1973]
      'Fishes'
      'Kardinal'   [E. Pagels]
      'Loddon Crown'
      'Magnifica'   PGP
      'Mahogany'
      'Melissa'   RD
      'Morgenröte'   [Marx 1975]
      'Mrs. Perry'   [M. Perry]
      'Pale Ponticum'   RD
      'Panorama'
      'Präriebrand'   [Kayser & Siebert 1955]
      'Prärieglut' ('Prairie Glow')   [Kayser & Siebert 1955]   PGP-DGP
L   **'Prärienacht'** ('Prairie Night')   [Kayser & Siebert 1955]   PGP-RD
      'Prairie Glow' = **M. 'Prärieglut'**
      'Prairie Night' = **M. 'Prärienacht'**
      'Purple Night' = **M. 'Prärienacht'**
      'Red Explosion'
      'Schneewittchen' ('Snow Maiden')   [K. Foerster 1956]   PGP-DGP-RD
      'Scorpion'

'Snow Maiden' = **M. 'Schneewittchen'**
'Twins'
'Vintage Wine'

MONTBRETIA de Candolle 1803 = **CROCOSMIA**

MONTIA Linnaeus 1753   *[Portulacaceae]*
   australasica (Hooker f.) Paxton & Hoffmann 1934 = **Neopaxia australasica**
A   **chamissoi** (Ledebour) Robinson & Fernald 1908
   chamissonis Greene 1891
A   **parvifolia** (Mocino) Greene 1891
AN‡ **perfoliata** (Don ex Willdenow) J. Howell 1893
AN‡ **sibirica** (Linnaeus) J. Howell 1893 (*Claytonia sibirica*)
   'Alba'

MORAEA Miller 1762 nom. cons.   *[Iridaceae]*

M - GOLDBLATT, P.: *'The Moraeas of Southern Africa'* Ann. Kirstenbosch Bot. Gar.
Vol 14 (1986)

   aristata (Delaroche) Ascherson & Graebner 1906 (*M. glaucopis*) **M**-EGF.1
   bellendenii (Sweet) N. E. Brown 1929 (*M. pavonia* var. *lutea*) **M**-EGF.1
   gigandra L. Bolus 1927 **M**-EGF.1
   glaucopis (de Candolle) Drapiez 1841 = **M. aristata**
   iridoides Linnaeus 1767 = **Dietes iridoides**
   moggii N. E. Brown 1929 M-EGF.1-PGP
   neopavonia R. Forster 1947 (*M. pavonia*) **M**-EGF.1
   papilionacea (Linnaeus f.) Ker-Gawler 1804 **M**-EGF.1
   pavonia (Linnaeus f.) Ker-Gawler 1805 nom. illegit. = **M. neopavonia**
     var. *lutea* (Ker-Gawler) Baker 1896 = **M. bellendenii**
   ramosissima (Linnaeus f.) Druce 1914 **M**-EGF.1
   spathacea (Thunberg) Ker-Gawler 1808 = **M. spathulata**
   spathulata (Linnaeus f.) Klatt 1895 (*M. spathacea*) **M**-EGF.1-PGP-**BB**
   stricta Baker 1904 M-EGF.1-**SB**
   villosa (Ker-Gawler) Ker-Gawler 1805 **M**-EGF.1

MORINA Linnaeus 1753   *[Morinaceae]*
   coulteriana Royle 1839
   longifolia Wallich ex de Candolle 1830 PGP-**DGP-RD**

MORISIA J. Gay 1829   *[Brassicaceae (Cruciferae)]*
   hypogaea Schreber 1789 = **M. monanthos**
   monanthos (Viviani) Ascherson 1884 (*M. hypogaea*) CA-**DGP**

MUHLENBERGIA Schreber 1789   *[Poaceae (Gramineae)]*
   capillaris (Lamarck) Trinius 1824 (*Stipa capillaris*)
   mexicana (Linnaeus) Trinius 1824 EGF.2

MUSCARI Miller 1754   *[Hyacinthaceae (Liliaceae)]*
   ambrosiacum Moench 1794 = **Muscarimia muscari**
   'Argaei Album' ® [van Tubergen]
   armeniacum Leichtlin ex Baker 1878 (*M. pallens*) EGF.1-CA-**BB**-SB-**DGP-RD**
     'Album'
     'Blue Spike' ® [J. A. van Zanten pre-1963] EGF.1
     'Cantab' ® [H. Rollo Meyer via van Tubergen]
     'Dark Eyes'
     'Early Giant' = **M. armenaicum**
     'Saphir'
     'Sky Blue'
     'White Beauty'

aucheri (Boissier) Baker 1871   EGF.1-**BB**-SB
    '**Tubergenianum**' ®   [van Tubergen 1940]   EGF.1-**BB**-SB-**DGP**-RD
azureum Fenzl 1859 = **Pseudomuscari azurea**
botryoides (Linnaeus) Miller 1769   EGF.1-CA-**BB**-SB-**DGP-RD**
    '**Album**' ®   [Pre-1596]   CA
bucharicum Regel nom. nud. = **M. neglectum**
caucasicum Grisebach ex Baker 1871 = **Leopoldia caucasica**
commutatum Gussone 1827   EGF.1-**BB**-SB
comosum (Linnaeus) Miller 1768 = **Leopoldia comosa**
latifolium Armitage & Playne ex Kirk 1868   EGF.1-CA-**BB**-SB-**DGP-RD**
macrocarpum Sweet 1827 = **Muscarimia macrocarpa**
moschatum Willdenow 1809 = **Muscarimia muscari**
N‡   **neglectum** Gussone 1842 (*M. bucharicum, M. racemosum*)   EGF.1-CA-**BB**-SB-RD
pallens (Marshall von Bieberstein) Fischer 1812 = **Pseudomuscari pallens**
paradoxum hort., non (Fischer & C. A. Meyer) Baker = **Bellevalia pycnantha**
parviflorum Desfontaines 1798 = **Pseudomuscari parviflora**
pinardii (Boissier) Boissier 1846 = **Leopoldia comosa**
racemosum Lamarck & de Candolle 1806 = **M. neglectum**
racemosum Miller 1758 = **Muscarimia muscari**
tubergenianum Hoog ex Turrill 1952 = **M. aucheri 'Tubergenianum'**

MUSCARIMIA Kosteletzky ex Losina-Losinskaja 1935   [*Hyacinthaceae (Liliaceae)*]
ambrosiaca (Moench) hort. = **M. muscari**
  macrocarpa (Sweet) Garberi 1968 (*Muscari macrocarpum*)   SB-RD
  muscari Losina-Losinskaja 1935 (*Muscari ambrosiacum, Muscari moschatum,*
                Muscari racemosum Miller)   EGF.1-CA-**BB**-SB-DGP-**RD**
    '**Major**'

MYOSOTIDIUM Hooker 1859   [*Boraginaceae*]
  hortensia (Decaisne) Baillon 1891   PGP-**RD**

MYOSOTIS Linnaeus 1753   [*Boraginaceae*]
N‡   **alpestris** F. W. Schmidt 1794   CA-DGP-RD
    '**Nana**' nom. dub.
BN‡L   **arvensis** (Linnaeus) Hill 1764
  australis R. Brown 1810
  azorica H. C. Watson 1844   CA
caespitosa C. F. Schultz 1819 = **M. laxa** ssp. **caespitosa**
    ssp. *rehsteineri* (Wartmann) Nyman = **M. rehsteineri**
  colensoi (Kirk) Macbride 1916 (*M. decora*)
decora Kirk ex Cheeseman 1906 = **M. colensoi**
  explanata Cheeseman 1906   CA
BN‡   **laxa** Lehmann 1818
    ssp. **caespitosa** (C. F. Schultz) Hylander & Nordhagen 1940 (*M. caespitosa*)
                       CA
palustris (Linnaeus) Linnaeus 1756 = **M. scorpioides**
  pulvinaris Hooker f. 1864
  rakiura L. B. Moore 1961
  rehsteineri Wartmann 1884 (*M. caespitosa* ssp. *rehsteineri*)   CA
  rupicola Smith 1813   **CA**
N‡   **scorpioides** Linnaeus 1753 (*M. palustris*)   RD
    '**Mermaid**'   CA
    '**Semperflorens**'   RD
    '**Thuringen**'
    *****symphytifolia**
  traversii Hooker f. 1864

MYRIOPHYLLUM Linnaeus 1753   [*Haloragidaceae*]
N   **aquaticum** (Vellozo Conceicao) Verdcourt (*M. brasiliense, M. prosperinacoides*)

brasiliense Cambessedes 1829 = **M. aquaticum**
proserpinacoides Gillies ex Hooker & Arnott 1833 = **M. aquaticum**
N‡L   **spicatum** Linnaeus 1753
N‡   **verticillatum** Linnaeus 1753

MYRRHIS Scopoli 1772   [*Apiaceae (Umbelliferae)*]
HN‡L   **odorata** Scopoli 1772
                                                                        PGP

NARCISSUS Linnaeus 1753   [*Amaryllidaceae*]
   abscissus(Haworth) Schultes f. 1830 (*N. pseudonarcissus* ssp. *abscissus*) EGF.1-SB
   albus plenus odoratus hort. = **N. poeticus 'Plenus'**
   assoanus Dufour 1830 nom. confus. = **N. requienii**
   asturiensis (Jordan) Pugsley 1933 (*N. minimus* hort.)   EGF.1-CA-**BB**-**SB**-DGP-RD
   bicolor Linnaeus 1762 (*N. pseudonarcissus* ssp. *bicolor*)   EGF.1-**BB**-SB
   bulbocodium Linnaeus 1753 (*Corbularia bulbocodium*)   EGF.1-CA-**BB**-SB-DGP-RD
      ssp. *albidus* (Emberger & Maire) Maire 1959 = **N. romieuxii** ssp. **albidus**
      ssp. *albidus* var. *zaianicus* Maire, Weiller & Wilczek 1959 = **N. romieuxii**
                                                           ssp. **albidus** var. **zaianicus**
      ssp. **bulbocodium** var. **citrinus** Baker 1888   EGF.1-CA-SB
      ssp. **bulbocodium** var. **conspicuus** (Haworth) Baker 1875   EGF.1-CA-SB-**DGP**
      ssp. **obesus** (Salisbury) Maire 1931 (*N. obesus*)   EGF.1-SB-RD
      ssp. *romieuxii* (Braun-Blanquet & Maire) Maire 1959 = **N. romieuxii**
      ssp. *romieuxii* var. *mesatlanticus* Maire 1959 = **N. romieuxii** var. **mesatlanticus**
      'Tenuifolius' (*N. tenuifolius* Salisbury 1796)   CA
   calcicola Mendonça 1930   EGF.1-CA-SB-RD
   canaliculatus Gussone 1854 = **N. 'Canaliculatus'**
   cantabricus de Candolle 1816   EGF.1-**BB**-SB-RD
      ssp. **cantabricus** var. **foliosus** (Maire) A. Fernandes 1968 (*N. foliosus* hort.)
                                                                           SB
      ssp. **cantabricus** var. **petunioides** A. Fernandes 1968   SB
      ssp. **monophyllus** (Durieu) A. Fernandes 1968 (*Corbularia monophyllus*)
                                                              EGF.1-CA-**BB**-SB
   concolor (Haworth) Link 1839 (*N. triandrus* var. *concolor, N. triandrus*
                                              'Pallidulus')   EGF.1-**BB**-SB-RD
   cyclamineus de Candolle 1815   EGF.1-CA-**BB**-SB-DGP-**RD**
   eystettensis hort. = **N. 'Eystettensis'**
   fernandesii G. Pedro 1947   EGF.1-SB
   foliosus (Maire) A. Fernandes ex hort. = **N. cantabricus** ssp. **cantabricus** var. **foliosus**
   gaditanus Boissier & Reuter 1859   EGF.1-**BB**-SB
   gayi (Henon) Pugsley 1933 (*N.* 'Princeps', *N. pseudonarcissus* ssp. *gayi*)
                                                              EGF.1-**BB**-SB
   x gracilis Sabine 1824 = **N. x tenuior**
   hellenicus Pugsley 1915 = **N. poeticus** var. **hellenicus**
   heminalis Schultes f. 1830 = **N. x infundibulum**
   henriquesii (Sampaio) hort. = **N. jonquilla** var. **henriquesii**
   hispanicus Gouan 1773 (*N. major, N. maximus* hort., *N. pseudonarcissus* ssp.
                                              major)   EGF.1-**BB**-SB
   humilis (Cavanilles) Traub (*Tapeinanthus humilis*)   EGF.1-**SB**
N   **x infundibulum** Poiret 1796 (*N. abscissus* x *N. jonquilla*) (*N. heminalis,*
                                              N. x odorus 'Heminalis')
   x intermedius Loiseleur 1828 (*N. jonquilla* x *N. tazetta*)   EGF.1-SB
   italicus Ker-Gawler 1808 (*N. tazetta* ssp. *italicus*)   EGF.1-**BB**-SB
   jonquilla Linnaeus 1753   EGF.1-**BB**-DGP-**RD**
      var. **henriquesii** Sampaio 1947 (*N. henriquesii*)   SB
      'Flore Pleno'   DGP
   juncifolius Lagasca 1816, non Salisbury 1796 = **N. requienii**
   lobularis hort., non Haworth = **N. nanus** Spach p.p. & **N. pseudonarcissus**
                                                          Dwarf Form p.p.
   major Curtis 1788 & hort p.p. = **N. hispanicus**
   maximus hort. = **N. hispanicus**

minimus hort., non Haworth = **N. asturiensis**
minor Brotero 1804 & hort. p.p., non Linnaeus 1762 = **N. pumilus**
minor Linnaeus 1762, non Brotero (*N. nanus* hort. p.p., non Spach)
  EGF.1-CA-**BB**-RD
  var. *conspicuus* (Haworth 1819) Anon = **N. nanus** Spach
    'Major' = **N. nanus** Spach
  var. *pumilus* (Salisbury) A. Fernandes 1951 = **N. pumilus**
moschatus Linnaeus 1762 (*N. pseudonarcissus* ssp. *moschatus*) EGF.1CA-**BB**-SB-RD
nanus Spach 1846 (*N. lobularis* hort. p.p., non Haworth, *N. minor* var. *conspicuus*,
        N. pseudonarcissus 'Minor', *N. minor* 'Major') EGF.1-SB
nanus hort. p.p., non Spach = **N. minor**
obesus Salisbury 1796 = **N. bulbocodium** ssp. **obesus**
N‡ **obvallaris** Salisbury 1796 (*N. pseudonarcissus* ssp. *obvallaris*) EGF.1-SB-RD
ochroleucus Loiseleur (*N. tazetta* ssp. *ochroleucus*) EGF.1-SB
N **x odorus** Linnaeus 1756 (*N. hispanica* x *N. jonquilla*) EGF.1-SB-RD
  'Giganteus'
  'Heminalis' = **N. x infundibulum**
  'Minor'
  'Plenus'
  'Rugulosus'
  'Rugulosus Maximus'
pallidiflorus Pugsley 1933 (*N. pallidus praecox* hort., *N. pseudonarcissus*
          ssp. *pallidiflorus*) EGF.1-**BB**-SB
pallidus praecox hort. = **N. pallidiflorus**
papyraceus Ker-Gawler 1806 (*N. tazetta* ssp. *papyraceus*) EGF.1-SB-RD
N **poeticus** Linnaeus 1753 EGF.1-**RD**
  var. **hellenicus** (Pugsley) A. Fernandes 1968 (*N. hellenicus*) EGF.1-SB
  'Plenus' (*N. albus plenus odoratus* hort.)
  'Physaloides'
  var. **recurvus** (Haworth) A. Fernandes 1968 EGF.1-**BB**
N‡L **pseudonarcissus** Linnaeus 1753 EGF.1-**BB**-SB-**DGP**
  ssp. *abscissus* (Schultes f.) A. Fernandes 1951 = **N. abscissus**
  ssp. *bicolor* (Linnaeus) Baker 1888 = **N. bicolor**
  ssp. *gayi* (Henon) A. Fernandes 1951 = **N. gayi**
  ssp. *major* (Curtis) Baker 1888 = **N. hispanicus**
    'Minor' = **N. nanus** Spach
  ssp. *moschatus* (Linnaeus) Baker 1888 = **N. moschatus**
  ssp. *obvallaris* (Salisbury) A. Fernandes 1951 = **N. obvallaris**
  ssp. *pallidiflorus* (Pugsley) A. Fernandes 1951 = **N. pallidiflorus**
    'Princeps' = **N. gayi**
x pulchellus Salisbury 1796 (*N. concolor* x *N. triandrus* var. *cernuus*) (*N. triandrus*
          var. *pulchellus*) EGF.1-SB
pumilus Salisbury 1796 (*N. minor* var. *pumilus*, *N. minor* Brotero & hort. p.p.,
          non Linnaeus) SB
  'Plenus' = **N. 'Rip van Winkle'**
requienii Roemer 1847 (*N. assoanus, N. juncifolius* Lagasca, non Salisbury)
  EGF.1-CA-**BB**-SB-**DGP**-RD
romieuxii Braun-Blanquet & Maire 1922 (*N. bulbocodium* ssp. *romieuxii*)
  EGF.1-**CA**-**BB**-**SB**-**DGP**-RD
  ssp. **albidus** (Emberger & Maire) A. Fernandes 1968 EGF.1
  ssp. **albidus** var. **zaianicus** (Maire, Weiller & Wilczek) A. Fernandes 1968
        (*N. bulbocodium* ssp. *albidus* var. *zaianicus*) EGF.1-SB
  var. **mesatlanticus** (Maire) ! (*N. bulbocodium* ssp. *romieuxii* var. *mesatlanticus*)
  SB
rupicola Dufour 1830 EGF.1-CA-**BB**-SB-RD
  ssp. **marvieri** (Jahand & Maire) Maire & Weiller 1925 EGF.1-CA-SB
scaberulus Henriques 1888 EGF.1-CA-**BB**-SB-RD
serotinus Linnaeus 1753 EGF.1-CA-**SB**
tazetta Linnaeus 1753 EGF.1-CA-**BB**-SB-**RD**
  ssp. *italicus* (Ker-Gawler) Baker 1888 = **N. italicus**

ssp. **lacticolor** Baker 1888   SB
ssp. *ochroleucus* (Loiseleur) Baker 1888 = **N. ochroleucus**
ssp. *papyraceus* (Ker-Gawler) Baker 1888 = **N. papyraceus**
telamonius plenus hort. = **N. 'Van Sion'**
x tenuior Curtis 1797 (*N. jonquilla* x *N. poeticus*) (*N. x gracilis*)   EGF.1-SB-RD
triandrus Linnaeus 1762   EGF.1-CA-**BB**-SB-DGP
    var. *albus* (Haworth) Baker 1888 = **N. triandrus** var. **triandrus**
    var. *concolor* (Haworth) Baker 1875 = **N. concolor**
    var. **triandrus** (*N. triandrus* var. *albus*)
    'Pallidulus' = **N. concolor**   EGF.1-**CA-RD**
    var. *pulchellus* (Salisbury) Baker 1875 = **N. x pulchellus**
watieri Maire 1921
                                                                              EGF.1-CA-**BB**-SB-**DGP**

CULTIVARS OF GARDEN ORIGIN

Classification in accord with the system published by the Royal Horticultural Society viz:

The classification consists of a Division number followed by a colour code.

DIVISION

1 **TRUMPET DAFFODILS OF GARDEN ORIGIN**
    One flower to a stem; corona ('trumpet') as long as, or longer than the perianth segments ('petals').

2 **LARGE-CUPPED DAFFODILS OF GARDEN ORIGIN**
    One flower to a stem; corona ('cup') more than one-third, but less than equal to the length of the perianth segments ('petals').

3 **SMALL-CUPPED DAFFODILS OF GARDEN ORIGIN**
    One flower to a stem; corona ('cup') not more than one-third the length of the perianth segments ('petals').

4 **DOUBLE DAFFODILS OF GARDEN ORIGIN**
    One or more flowers to a stem, with doubling of the perianth segments or the corona or both.

5 **TRIANDRUS DAFFODILS OF GARDEN ORIGIN**
    Characteristics of *N. triandrus* predominant.Usually two or more pendent flowers to a stem; perianth segments reflexed.

6 **CYCLAMINEUS DAFFODILS OF GARDEN ORIGIN**
    Characteristics of *N. cyclamineus* predominant. Usually one flower to a stem; perianth segments reflexed; flower at an acute angle to the stem, with a very short pedicle ('neck').

7 **JONQUILLA DAFFODILS OF GARDEN ORIGIN**
    Characteristics of the *N. jonquilla* group predominant. Usually one to three flowers to a rounded stem; leaves narrow, dark green; perianth segments spreading, not reflexed; flowers fragrant.

8 **TAZETTA DAFFODILS OF GARDEN ORIGIN**
    Characteristics of *N. tazetta* group predominant. Usually three to twenty flowers to a stout stem; leaves broad; perianth segments spreading, not reflexed; flowers fragrant.

9 **POETICUS DAFFODILS OF GARDEN ORIGIN**
    Characteristics of the *N. poeticus* group predominant.Usually one flower to a stem; perianth segments pure white; corolla usually disc-shaped, with a green or yellow centre and a red trim; flowers fragrant.

10 **SPECIES, WILD VARIANTS AND WILD HYBRIDS**
    All species and wild or reputedly wild variants and hybrids, including those with double flowers.

11 **SPLIT-CORONA DAFFODILS OF GARDEN ORIGIN**
    Corona split rather than lobed and usually for more than half its length.

12 **MISCELLANEOUS DAFFODILS**
    All daffodils not falling into any one of the foregoing Divisions.

COLOUR CODES

W	White or Whitish
G	Green
Y	Yellow
P	Pink
O	Orange
R	Red

The group of letters before the hyphen describe the perianth ('petal') colour.

The group of letters after the hyphen describe the corona (the 'trumpet' or 'cup')

M - Barnes, Don; *'Daffodils for Home, Gardens and Show'* David & Charles 1987

2W-YYR	**'Abadan'**	[W. Blom 1954]	
2W-YYP	**'Abalone'**	[G. E. Mitsch 1962]	
2W-P	**'Accent'**	[G. E. Mitsch 1960]	
4W-R	**'Acclamation'**	[J. L. Richardson 1968]	
3W-R	**'Accolade'**	[J. L. Richardson 1956]	
9W-GOR	**'Ace of Diamonds'**	[Rev. G. H. Engleheart 1923]	
3Y-R	**'Achduart'**	[J. S. B. Lea 1972]	M
4W-R	**'Achentoul'**	[J. S. B. Lea 1970]	
3W-W	**'Achnasheen'**	[J. S. B. Lea 1964]	
4W-R	**'Acropolis'**	[J. L. Richardson 1955]	**M**-RD
9W-GYR	**'Actaea'**	[G. Lubbe 1927]	M-**BB**-**DGP**-RD
3Y-GYY	**'Advocat'**	[B. S. Duncan 1977]	
3W-ORR	**'Aflame'**	[Warnaar & Co Ltd 1938]	
3W-YYR	**'After All'**	[J. Gerritsen 1961]	
2Y-Y	**'Agathon'**	[A. M. Wilson 1949]	
3W-O	**'Agena'**	[C. R. Wooton 1968]	
3W-O	**'Agora'**	[G. H. Johnstone 1959]	
2Y-O	**'Air Marshal'**	[J. L. Richardson 1953]	
3W-Y	**'Aircastle'**	[G. E. Mitsch 1958]	**BB**
1Y-Y	**'Akala'**	[W. Jackson Jnr. 1970]	
3W-YOW	**'Albacrest'**	[T. Bloomer 1985]	
8W-YOO	**'Albany'**	[Frylink 1932]	
	'Albus Plenus Odoratus' = **N. poeticus 'Plenus'**		
2W-Y	**'Aldergrove'**	[W. J. Dunlop 1953]	
2W-W	**'Aldringham'**	[Ballydorn Bulb Farm 1978]	
2W-GPP	**'Algarve'**	[T. Bloomer 1984]	
2W-P	**'Alice's Pink'**	[Carncairn Daffodils 1978]	
1Y-Y	**'Alliance'**	[van der Wereld 1983]	
1Y-Y	**'Alray'**	[J. O'More 1968]	
2Y-O	**'Altruist'**	[F. E. Board 1965]	M
2Y-WPP	**'Amber Castle'**	[Mrs J. L. Richardson 1976]	
2W-P	**'Amber Light'**	[J. L. Richardson 1967]	
2O-R	**'Ambergate'**	[Milne 1950]	
2Y-Y	**'Amberglow'**	[G. E. Mitsch 1969]	
3W-YYO	**'Amor'**	[Leewen 1971]	
6Y-YYR	**'Andalusia'**	[C. F. Coleman 1961]	
9W-GYR	**'Andrew Marvell'**	[J. M. de Navarro 1950]	
1Y-Y	**'Angola'**	[J. L. Richardson 1973]	
3W-GWO	**'Annalong'**	[Ballydorn Bulb Farm 1982]	
2W-YPP	**'Ann Abbott'**	[G. H. Johnstone 1947]	
2W-P	**'Ann Cameron'**	[Fairbain 1968]	
	'Anniversary'		
2W-YOR	**'Anthea'**	[J. L. Richardson 1975]	

1W-P	'Apia' [J. O'More 1980]	
4Y-O	'Apotheose' [Oregon Bulb Farms 1975]	
1W-P	'Apricot' [de Graff 1898]	
4W-P	'Apricot Sundae' [Carncairn Daffodils 1984]	
2W-WWY	'April Charm' [G. E. Mitsch 1966]	
1W-W	'April Love' [Mrs J. Abel Smith 1974]	M
1W-W	'April Message' [T. Bloomer 1964]	
1W-W	'April Parade' [T. Bloomer 1964]	
5Y-Y	'April Tears' [A. Gray 1939]	M-DGP-RD
2Y-YYO	'Aranjuez' [Warnaar & Co Ltd 1933]	
2W-O	'Arbar' [J. L. Richardson 1948]	M-DGP-RD
2W-YWP	'Arcady' [M. J. Jefferson-Brown 1985]	
2W-YOO	'Arctic Flame' [J. M. de Navarro 1968]	
1Y-Y	'Arctic Gold' [J. L. Richardson 1951]	M-BB-RD
2W-GWW	'Ardbane' [G. L. Wilson 1938]	
3W-GRY	'Ardglass' [Ballydorn Bulb Farm 1983]	
2WR	'Ardour' [G. E. Mitsch 1952]	
2W-GYY	'Ardress' [B. S. Duncan 1982]	
1Y-Y	'Argosy' [J. L. Richardson 1959]	
5W-W	'Arish Mell' [D. Blanchard 1961]	M
1Y-Y	'Arkle' [J. L. Richardson 1968]	M
2Y-O	'Armada' [G. L. Wilson 1938]	DGP
1Y-Y	'Armagh' [W. J. Dunlop 1961]	
2Y-YOR	'Armley Wood' [W. A. Noton 1976]	
2W-R	'Arndilly' [J. S. B. Lea 1972]	
2W-W	'Arpege' [F. E. Board 1965]	
2W-P	'Arpeggio' [G. E. Mitsch 1972]	
2Y-R	'Arragon' [J. M. de Navarro 1958]	
3W-R	'Artillery' [J. L. Richardson 1961]	
4Y-O	'Ascot' [J. L. Richardson 1962]	
2W-GWW	'Ashmore' [J. W. Blanchard 1974]	M
8W-Y	'Aspasia' [van der Schoot 1910]	
2O-R	'Attrus' [M. E. Jefferson-Brown 1985]	
5Y-Y	'Auburn' [D. Blanchard via A. Gray 1951]	
3W-YYP	'Audubon' [G. E. Mitsch 1965]	M
8W-Y	'Avalanche' [Pre-1906]	M
2Y-W	'Avalon' [Mrs J. L. Richardson 1977]	
2W-W	'Ave' [G. L. Wilson 1935]	M
2W-R	'Avenger' [J. L. Richardson 1957]	
6Y-Y	'Baby Doll' [M. P. Williams 1957]	
7Y-Y	'Baby Moon' [J. Gerritsen 1958]	M
11Y-Y	'Baccarat' [J. Gerritsen 1960]	RD
6Y-Y	'Backchat' [P. Phillips 1971]	
3W-YYO	'Badanloch' [J. S. B. Lea 1981]	
3Y-YYR	'Badbury Rings' [J. W. Blanchard 1985]	
2Y-YYR	'Balalaika' [J. L. Richardson 1956]	
1Y-Y	'Ballindalloch' [J. S. B. Lea 1981]	
2Y-R	'Ballintoy' [W. J. Dunlop 1950]	
1Y-Y	'Ballyarnett' [Carncairn Daffodils 1976]	
3W-WWO	'Ballycastle' [W. J. Dunlop 1947]	
1W-W	'Ballyfrema' [Carncairn Daffodils 1986]	
1W-Y	'Ballygarvey' [W. J. Dunlop 1947]	
1W-W	'Ballylough' [Carncairn Daffodils 1978]	
2Y-WWY	'Ballymore' [B. S. Duncan 1979]	
2W-P	'Ballyroan' [Mrs J. L. Richardson 1979]	
1Y-Y	'Ballyrobert' [W. J. Dunlop 1968]	
2Y-Y	'Ballytrim' [Mrs J. L. Richardson 1979]	M
2W-GPP	'Balvenie' [J. S. B. Lea 1976]	
1W-Y	'Bambi' [Dutch origin 1948]	
1Y-Y	'Banbridge' [J. L. Richardson 1955]	M

2W-OOY	**'Bandolier'** [T. Bloomer 1977]	
2Y-O	**'Bandleader'** [M. E. Jefferson-Brown 1968]	
2Y-YRR	**'Bantam'** [Barr 1950]	
2W-R	**'Barbados'** [J. L. Richardson 1963]	
2W-Y	**'Barley Cove'** [Carncairn Daffodils 1981]	
1W-Y	**'Bar None'** [P. Phillips 1966]	M
3W-YYO	**'Barley Sugar'** [Carncairn Daffodils 1978]	
6Y-Y	**'Barlow'** [G. E. Mitsch 1969]	
3W-Y	**'Barnby Moor'** [Mrs J. Abel Smith 1979]	
2W-GWW	**'Barnwell Alice'** [Carncairn Daffodils 1986]	
1Y-Y	**'Baronscourt'** [Carncairn Daffodils 1973]	
3W-WRR	**'Barrett Browning'** [J. W. A. Lefeber 1945]	RD
3Y-YYR	**'Barrii Conspicuus'** [W. Backhouse 1884]	
6Y-Y	**'Bartley'** [J. C. Williams 1934]	DGP
1Y-Y	**'Bastion'** [G. L. Wilson 1944]	
2Y-R	**'Battle Cry'** [T. Bloomer 1977]	
1Y-Y	**'Bayard'** [J. L. Richardson 1956]	
	'Beauvallet' = **N. 'Castle Dobbs'**	
4Y-R	**'Beauvallon'** [D. A. Lloyd 1969]	M
2Y-O	**'Beefeater'** [Barr 1959]	
1W-W	**'Beersheba'** [Rev. G. H. Engleheart 1923]	M-**BB**-RD
3Y-Y	**'Beige Beauty'** [G. E. Mitsch 1966]	
11W-Y	**'Belcanto'** [J. Gerritsen 1977]	
2W-YYO	**'Belisana'** [van Tubergen 1946]	
7W-P	**'Bell Song'** [G. E. Mitsch 1966]	M
2W-GPP	**'Beltrim'** [Carncairn Daffodils 1976]	
1W-W	**'Ben Avon'** [J. S. B. Lea 1978]	
2W-W	**'Ben Hee'** [J. S. B. Lea 1964]	**M**
2W-YYO	**'Ben Ledi'** [J. S. B. Lea 1985]	
2W-R	**'Ben Loyal'** [J. S. B. Lea 1964	
3W-R	**'Ben Rinnes'** [J. S. B. Lea 1972]	
2W-YOO	**'Ben Vorlich'** [J. S. B. Lea 1970]	
3W-W	**'Benvarden'** [Carncairn Daffodils 1969]	
3W-GWW	**'Benvoy'** [Mrs J. L. Richardson 1977]	
4W-O	**'Bere Ferrers'** [Mrs J. L. Richardson 1979]	
2Y-O	**'Bermuda'** [Warnaar & Co Ltd 1939]	
6Y-O	**'Beryl'** [P. D. Williams 1907]	
3W-YOR	**'Best of Luck'** [Ballydorn Bulb Farm 1984]	
2Y-W	**'Bethany'** [G. E. Mitsch 1958]	M
1W-W	**'Betoateione'** [F. E. Board pre-1986]	
2Y-YOO	**'Better Times'** [Warnaar & Co Ltd 1944]	
1Y-W	**'Big John'** [M. W. Evans 1975]	
6W-GPP	**'Bilbo'** [B. S. Duncan]	
2Y-YRR	**'Bilboa'** [S. C. Gaspar 1955]	
2Y-W	**'Binkie'** [Wolfhagen 1938]	M-**BB**
3W-O	**'Birchill'** [Mrs J. Abel Smith 1974]	**BB**
2W-GWW	**'Birdalone'** [J. M. de Navarro 1969]	
3W-YYR	**'Birdsong'** [Carncairn Daffodils 1978]	
2W-W	**'Birkdale'** [B. S. Duncan 1981]	
3Y-O	**'Birma'** [J. W. A. Lefeber 1960]	RD
2W-GWW	**'Birthday Girl'** [B. S. Duncan 1983]	
1W-W	**'Birthright'** [G. L. Wilson 1956]	
1Y-Y	**'Biscayne'** [de Jager 1966]	
3W-YOO	**'Bittleford'** [B. S. Duncan via du Plessis Bros 1987]	
2W-WWY	**'Bit O' Gold'** [G. E. Mitsch 1965]	
3W-WWO	**'Bithynia'** [G. E. Mitsch 1954]	
2W-Y	**'Bizerta'** [J. L. Richardson 1943]	
2W-GYP	**'Blair Atholl'** [Mrs J. Abel Smith 1988]	
2W-P	**'Blaris'** [G. L. Wilson 1960]	**BB**
3W-OOY	**'Blarney'** [J. L. Richardson 1935]	DGP

2W-OOY	'Blarney's Daughter' [J. L. Richardson 1948]	
1Y-Y	'Bleasby Gorse' [Mrs J. Abel Smith 1973]	
2Y-YWY	'Blessing' [Origin unknown c1978]	
3W-WYO	'Blithe Spirit' [F. E. Board 1965]	
2W-W	'Blue Bird' [M. E. Jefferson-Brown 1969]	
1Y-Y	'Bob Minor' [Rosewarne E. H. S. 1980]	
7Y-YYO	'Bobbysoxer' [A. Gray 1949]	M
2W-GYO	'Bobolink' [G. E. Mitsch 1965]	
1W-Y	'Bobster' [B. S. Duncan 1980]	
2W-Y	'Bodilly' [P. D. Williams 1925]	
2Y-O	'Bold Lad' [Mrs J. L. Richardson 1974]	
7Y-Y	'Bolton' [P.D. Williams 1935]	
2Y-YYR	'Bombay' [J. L. Richardson 1945]	
2W-YYO	'Bonamargy' [Carncairn Daffodils 1975]	
1W-P	'Bon Rose' [J. Erp 1956]	
6Y-Y	'Bonus' [G. E. Mitsch 1972]	
2Y-O	'Border Chief' [J. L. Richardson 1953]	
2Y-R	'Border Flame' [J. L. Richardson 1972]	
2Y-O	'Border Legend' [G. L. Wilson 1963]	
2W-R	'Borrobol' [J. S. B. Lea 1963]	
3O-R	'Bossa Nova' [B. S. Duncan 1983]	
1W-P	'Boudoir' [Carncairn Daffodils 1967]	
2W-YYO	'Bovagh' [Carncairn Daffodils 1975]	
1Y-Y	'Brabazon' [G. H. Johnstone 1950]	M
2Y-GWY	'Bracken Hill' [Carncairn Daffodils 1985]	
2Y-O	'Brackenhurst' [Mrs J. Abel Smith 1977]	
3W-GYR	'Braddock' [Ballydorn Bulb Farm 1980]	
2W-ORR	'Brahms' [J. M. de Navarro 1957]	
2W-P	'Bramley' [Mrs J. Abel Smith 1977]	
11Y-OYY	'Brandaris' [J. Gerritsen 1976]	
2W-O	'Brave Adventure' [Ballydorn Bulb Farm 1979]	
2W-YYO	'Brave Journey' [Carncairn Daffodils 1986]	
1W-Y	'Bravoure' [van der Wereld 1974]	M
3W-R	'Bravura' [G. L. Wilson 1937]	
2Y-R	'Break of Day' [T. Bloomer 1962]	
2Y-GYY	'Breakthrough' [M. E. Jefferson-Brown 1965]	
1Y-O	'Brer Fox' [W. O. Backhouse 1959]	
4W-Y	'Bridal Crown' [Schoorl 1953]	
2W-WPP	'Bridesmaid' [Ballydorn Bulb Farm 1970]	
2W-GWW	'Brierglass' [J. S. B. Lea 1985]	
2W-P	'Bright Flame' [Mrs J. Abel Smith 1970]	
3W-R	'Bright Spark' [J. M. de Navarro 1977]	
2W-P	'Bright Star' [Mrs J. Abel Smith 1983]	
11Y-YYR	'Brilliant Star' [J. W. A. Lefeber 1960]	
2YW-P	'Brindisi' [B. S. Duncan 1977]	
2W-W	'Broadland' [Dye 1984]	
2W-GPP	'Broadway Rose' [J. M. de Navarro 1977]	
11W-WOO	'Broadway Star' [J. W. A. Lefeber 1975]	
2Y-YRR	'Broadway Village' [C. Postles 1985]	
2W-W	'Brookfield' [W. J. Dunlop 1947]	
2Y-Y	'Broomgrove' [F. E. Board 1965]	
2W-W	'Broomhill' [F. E. Board 1965]	M
1W-W	'Broughshane' [G. L. Wilson 1938]	
2W-Y	'Brunswick' [P. D. Williams 1931]	BB
2Y-Y	'Bryanston' [J. W. Blanchard 1977]	
3W-GWW	'Bryher' [R. V. Favell 1939]	
1Y-O	'Buckskin' [M. W. Evans 1973]	
7Y-Y	'Buffawn' [Morrill 1977]	
2Y-Y	'Bulbarrow' [J. W. Blanchard 1985]	
3W-YOO	'Bullseye' [F. E. Board 1975]	

2Y-R	**'Bunclody'** [J. S. B. Lea 1963]	
2W-O	**'Buncrana'** [J. L. Richardson 1938]	
7Y-O	**'Bunting'** [G. E. Mitsch 1965]	
2W-P	**'Burgage Hill'** [Mrs J. Abel Smith 1978]	
2Y-GYO	**'Burma Star'** [Carncairn Daffodils 1984]	
11Y-OYO	**'Burning Heart'** [J. W. A. Lefeber 1958]	
2Y-R	**'Burning Torch'** [J. L. Richardson 1967]	
1W-W	**'Burntollet'** [J. S. B. Lea 1974]	M
3W-YYO	**'Bushmills'** [W. J. Dunlop 1961]	
2Y	**'Buster'** [Barr 1954]	
7Y-Y	**'Buttercup'** [Rev. G. H. Engleheart 1890]	
2Y-Y	**'Butterscotch'** [G. E. Mitsch 1962]	
1Y-Y	**'By Jove'** [M. J. Jefferson-Brown 1968]	
1Y-Y	**'Cabra'** [Carncairn Daffodils 1979	
3W-GYO	**'Cadence'** [G. E. Mitsch 1958]	
9W-GYR	**'Caedmon'** [Rev. G. H. Engleheart 1913]	
3W-ORR	**'Cairn Toul'** [J. S. B. Lea 1978]	M
2W-GPP	**'Cairndhu'** [Carncairn Daffodils 1975]	
2Y-W	**'Cairngorm'** [Mrs J. L. Richardson 1976]	
2Y-Y	**'Calabar'** [A. Wilson via Wallace & Barr 1957]	
2Y-YOO	**'California'** [P. D. Williams 1945]	
2YW-YPP	**'Camelford'** [T. Bloomer 1986]	
4Y-Y	**'Camellia'** [van der Zalm 1930]	DGP
2Y-Y	**'Camelot'** [J. L. Richardson 1962]	M
1Y-Y	**'Camowen'** [B. S. Duncan 1974]	
9W-GYR	**'Campion'** [B. S. Duncan 1980]	
8	**'Canaliculatus'**	**BB**-SB
8Y-GOO	**'Canarybird'** [Berghuis 1959]	
10W-Y	**'Canasta'** [J. Gerritsen 1957]	RD
2W-P	**'Canby'** [G. E. Mitsch 1970]	
4W-Y	**'Candida'** [J. L. Richardson 1956]	
1W-YPP	**'Candyfloss'** [M. E. Jefferson-Brown 1985]	
3W-WYO	**'Canford'** [J. W. Blanchard 1983]	
2W-W	**'Canisp'** [J. S. B. Lea 1960]	M
9W-GGR	**'Cantabile'** [G. L. Wilson 1932]	RD
1W-W	**'Cantatrice'** [G. L. Wilson 1936]	M-DGP-**RD**
9W-GYR	**'Canticle'** [Ballydorn Bulb Farm 1984]	
2W-W	**'Cape Cool'** [Carncairn Daffodils 1981]	
3W-GYO	**'Capisco'** [Ballydorn Bulb Farm 1969]	M
2Y-YYO	**'Capitol Hill'** [J. S. B. Lea 1979]	
3W-GYR	**'Caprice'** [D. S. Bell 1962]	
2W-YRR	**'Capstan'** [R. H. Bath 1929]	
2Y-R	**'Caracas'** [J. L. Richardson 1963]	
2Y-O	**'Carbineer'** [A. M. Wilson 1927]	DGP
3W-O	**'Cardinham'** [T. Bloomer 1986]	
2W-Y	**'Careysville'** [J. L. Richardson 1958]	
2Y-Y	**'Carlton'** [P. D. Williams 1927]	**BB**-DGP
1W-Y	**'Caroline Fox'** [G. H. Johnstone 1952]	
2W-WPP	**'Caro Nome'** [G. E. Mitsch 1954]	
3W-GWW	**'Carrara'** [Mrs J. L. Richardson 1979]	
1Y-Y	**'Carrickbeg'** [J. L. Richardson 1963]	
2W-P	**'Carrickmannon'** [J. L. Richardson 1968]	
2W-W	**'Carrigeen'** [Carncairn Daffodils 1967]	
3W-GWW	**'Cascade'** [J. L. Richardson 1961]	
11W-W	**'Cassata'** [J. Gerritsen 1963]	M-**RD**
2Y-O	**'Casterbridge'** [J. W. Blanchard 1986]	
4Y-R	**'Castle Dobbs'** [Carncairn Daffodils 1979]	
3W-YYR	**'Castlehill'** [Ballydorn Bulb Farm 1981]	
2W-GWW	**'Castle of Mey'** [G. L. Wilson 1953]	
2Y-R	**'Castle Upton'** [Carncairn Daffodils 1970]	

Code	Name	Breeder	
1Y-Y	'Castlewellan'	[W. J. Dunlop 1959]	
2Y-R	'Cathay'	[J. L. Richardson 1962]	
2Y-R	'Cattistock'	[J. W. Blanchard 1974]	
2W-YPP	'Cavatina'	[J. L. Richardson 1967]	
2W-GPP	'Cavoda'	[J. Radcliffe 1977]	
2Y-O	'Cawdron'	[du Plessis Bros 1976]	
2W-Y	'Cawsand'	[Mrs J. L. Richardson 1978]	
1W-W	'Celilo'	[M. W. Evans 1968]	
2Y-Y	'Celtic Gold'	[Mrs J. L. Richardson 1974]	
2W-WWP	'Celtic Song'	[J. L. Richardson 1967]	
2Y-O	'Ceylon'	[J. L. Richardson 1943]	M-DGP
11W-PPY	'Chablis'	[J. Gerritsen 1971]	
6W-GPP	'Cha Cha'	[B. S. Duncan 1986]	
2Y-GOO	'Chagall'	[Carncairn Daffodils 1985]	
1W-W	'Chania'	[Carncairn Daffodils 1984]	
2Y-YRR	'Chancellorsville'	[J. M. de Navarro 1960]	
11Y-Y	'Chanterelle'	[J. Gerritsen 1962]	RD
2W-Y	'Chapeau'	[M. W. Evans 1972]	
2Y-Y	'Charade'	[M. W. Evans 1976]	
1Y-Y	'Charioteer'	[G. H. Johnstone 1954]	
6Y-Y	'Charity Fair'	[Ballydorn Bulb Farm 1983]	
6Y-Y	'Charity May'	[C. F. Coleman 1948]	M-DGP-RD
2O-R	'Charleston'	[B. S. Duncan 1983]	
2Y-W	'Charter'	[G. E. Mitsch 1964]	
7Y-W	'Chat'	[G. E. Mitsch 1968]	M
2Y-R	'Checkmate'	[D. S. Bell 1957]	
4W-Y	'Cheerfulness'	[van der Schoot 1923]	M-BB-RD
2W-GPP	'Chelsea China'	[G. H. Johnstone 1954]	
2W-P	'Chelsea Derby'	[G. H. Johnstone 1968]	
2Y-OOY	'Chemawa'	[G. E. Mitsch 1963]	
2W-WWP	'Chenoweth'	[B. S. Duncan 1980]	
2W-GPP	'Cherrygardens'	[N. A. Burr 1978]	M
9W-GYR	'Chesterton'	[B. S. Duncan 1980]	
2Y-R	'Chianti'	[W. G. Pannill 1970]	
6Y-O	'Chicadee'	[G. E. Mitsch 1959]	
3Y-YYR	'Chickerell'	[J. W. Blanchard 1984]	
1W-Y	'Chief Inspector'	[T. Bloomer 1982]	
2W-P	'Chiffon'	[S. J. Bisdee 1950]	
2W-GWW	'Chig'	[M. E. Jefferson-Brown 1985]	
1Y-W	'Chiloquin'	[G. E. Mitsch 1968]	M
1W-W	'Chinchilla'	[B. S. Duncan 1983]	
2W-WWP	'China Doll'	[C. Postles 1985]	M
3W-GWW	'Chinese White'	[G. L. Wilson 1937]	M-DGP
8Y-YRR	'Chinita'	[H. Chapman 1922]	
2W-Y	'Chinook'	[G. E. Mitsch 1952]	
1W-W	'Chivalry'	[J. L. Richardson 1955]	
2W-P	'Chloe'	[M. Evams 1973]	
3Y-R	'Chungking'	[G. L. Wilson 1942]	DGP
2W-GWP	'Church Bay'	[Carncairn Daffodils 1987]	
2W-W	'Churchfield'	[Carncairn Daffodils 1969]	
2W-GWW	'Churchman'	[Ballydorn Bulb Farm 1968]	
4W-O	'Churston Ferrers'	[B. S. Duncan via du Plessis Bros 1987]	
2Y-Y	'Cibola'	[G. E. Mitsch 1952]	
1Y-W	'Cindywood'	[Mrs J. Abel Smith 1980]	
3Y-Y	'Citronita'	[W. A. Noton 1976]	M
2W-YYR	'City Lights'	[D. S. Bell 1957]	M
2W-Y	'Clady Cottage'	[Carncairn Daffodils 1987]	
7Y-Y	'Clare'	[A. Gray 1968]	M
2W-P	'Clare Park'	[Carncairn Daffodils 1976]	
2W-P	'Clochmerle'	[G. L. Wilson 1962]	

3W-YYR	'Clockface'	[G. L. Wilson 1947]
2W-WWP	'Cloudcap'	[G. E. Mitsch 1967]
2Y-W	'Cloud Nine'	[G. E. Mitsch 1972]
2Y-Y	'Cloyfin'	[W. J. Dunlop pre-1970]
3W-Y	'Clumber'	[Mrs J. Abel Smith 1975]
2W-GWW	'Cold Overton'	[W. A. Noton 1976]
3W-GOR	'Collector's Choice'	[Carncairn Daffodils 1983]
3W-YOR	'Colley Gate'	[J. S. B. Lea 1985]
2W-W	'Colliford'	[B. S. Duncan 1986]
2W-Y	'Colloggett'	[B. S. Duncan via du Plessis Bros 1987]
11Y-O	'Colorange'	[J. Gerritsen 1962]
3W-WWO	'Coloratura'	[G. E. Mitsch 1956]
2W-W	'Columbus'	[Carncairn Daffodils 1976]
1Y-Y	'Comal'	[W. Jackson jnr. 1968]
1Y-Y	'Commissar'	[W. A. Noton 1976]
9W-YOR	'Como'	[D. W. Gourlay 1973]
2W-P	'Confusion'	[C. O. Fairbairn pre-1964]
4W-W	'Conglass'	[J. S. B. Lea 1983]
11Y-YYO	'Congress'	[J. Gerritsen 1976]
2W-GWW	'Connor'	[Carncairn Daffodils 1986]
2Y-W	'Cool Autumn'	[W. A. Noton 1976]
3W-GWW	'Cool Crystal'	[G. E. Mitsch 1966] M
2W-P	'Cool Flame'	[G. E. Mitsch 1969]
2W-GRR	'Cool Waters'	[T. Bloomer 1964]
2W-P	'Coolah'	[J. Radcliff 1966]
2W-Y	'Coolattin'	[Carncairn Daffodils 1969]
3W-GYY	'Coolgreany'	[Carncairn Daffodils 1967]
1Y-Y	'Cophetua'	[Carncairn Daffodils 1973]
4W-Y	'Coppins'	[Mrs J. L. Richardson 1977]
7W-Y	'Cora Ann'	[Mitchell 1939]
2W-R	'Coral Fair'	[Mrs J. Abel Smith 1984]
2W-WWP	'Coral Light'	[Kanouse 1972]
6W-P	'Coralline'	[B. S. Duncan 1981]
2W-P	'Coral Luster'	[G. E. Mitsch 1967]
2W-WWP	'Coral Ribbon'	[G. E. Mitsch 1964]
2W-Y	'Corbridge'	[G. Harrison 1968]
2W-W	'Corby'	[G. L. Wilson 1948]
2W-P	'Cordial'	[M. W. Evans 1970]
2W-PPO	'Coreen'	[Carncairn Daffodils 1973]
2Y-O	'Cornerstone'	[M. E. Jefferson-Brown 1984]
6Y-Y	'Cornet'	[A. Gray 1953]
3W-YYR	'Corofin'	[J. L. Richardson 1943]
1W-W	'Cotehele'	[T. Bloomer 1981]
3W-GOO	'Country Morning'	[Mrs J. L. Richardson 1985]
1Y-Y	'Courier'	[B. S. Duncan 1979]
2Y-R	'Court Martial'	[J. L. Richardson 1956] M
2W-YYO	'Coverack Perfection'	[The Brodie of Brodie 1930]
3W-GWW	'Coylum'	[J. M. de Navarro 1956]
4Y-O	'Crackington'	[D. A. Lloyd 1986]
8W-R	'Cragford'	[P. D. Williams 1930] DGP-RD
2W-OOY	'Craigdun'	[Carncairn Daffodils 1979]
2Y-O	'Craigtara'	[Carncairn Daffodils 1975]
2Y-R	'Craigywarren'	[W. J. Dunlop 1949] DGP
2Y-R	'Cranborne'	[J. W. Blanchard]
2Y-GRR	'Crater'	[J. M. de Navarro 1956]
2O-R	'Creag Dubh'	[J. S. B. Lea 1978] M
2W-GWW	'Creme de Menthe'	[Carncairn Daffodils 1976]
2W-W	'Crenelet'	[B. S. Duncan 1977]
2W-R	'Crimpelene'	[P. Phillips 1968]
2W-W	'Crinoline'	[G. L. Wilson

2W-P	'Crinoline' [J. N. Hancock 1956]	
1W-Y	'Cristobal' [J. L. Richardson 1968]	
1Y-Y	'Crock of Gold' [G. L. Wilson 1948]	
2Y-Y	'Crocus' [P. D. Williams 1927]	**BB**-DGP
2W-GWW	'Croila' [J. S. B. Lea 1978]	
2W-YYO	'Crown Royalist' [Ballydorn Bulb Farm 1976]	
1Y-Y	'Crumlin' [W. J. Dunlop 1958]	
3W-W	'Crystal River' [G. E. Mitsch 1967]	
3W-R	'Cul Beag' [J. S. B. Lea 1971]	
1W-P	'Curley' [Mrs C. O. Fairbairn]	
3W-GWW	'Cushendall' [G. L. Wilson 1931]	
3W-Y	'Cushendun' [Ballydorn Bulb Farm 1980]	
4W-Y	'Cypri Plena' [Pre-1629]	
2W-Y	'Cyros' [W. Jackson jnr. 1966]	
2W-P	'Dailmanach' [J. S. B. Lea 1972]	M
2Y-O	'Dalboyne' [G. L. Wilson 1947]	M
3W-R	'Dalhuaine' [J. S. B. Lea 1961]	
1Y-O	'Dalinda' [Backhouse]	
3W-GWW	'Dallas' [The Brodie of Brodie 1948]	
2YW-GWY	'Dalliance' [Carncairn Daffodils 1985]	
2W-GYO	'Dancer' [M. E. Jefferson-Brown 1984]	
2Y-OOR	'Dancing Flame' [J. L. Richardson 1968]	
2W-P	'Dancing Partner' [M. E. Jefferson-Brown 1969]	
2W-W	'Danes Balk' [F. E. Board 1965]	
3W-O	'Darite' [T. Bloomer 1986]	
3Y-O	'Dateline' [B. S. Duncan 1986]	
2W-OOY	'Daviot' [The Brodie of Brodie 1950]	
2W-YPP	'Davlyn' [M. J. Jefferson-Brown 1985]	
5W-Y	'Dawn' [Rev. G. H. Engleheart 1907]	
2W-PPW	'Dawncrest' [G. E. Mitsch 1978]	
2Y-W	'Daydream' [G. E. Mitsch 1960]	
2W-P	'Dear Me' [T. H. Piper 1977]	
2W-P	'Debbie Rose' [B. S. Duncan 1976]	
4W-P	'Debenture' [D. Jackson 1983]	
2W-P	'Debutante' [J. L. Richardson 1956]	DGP-RD
2Y-YYR	'Delabole' [Mrs J. L. Richardson 1986]	
2W-P	'Delamont' [Carncairn Daffodils 1971]	
2W-WWP	'Delectable' [G. E. Mitsch 1972]	
6W-YWP	'Delia' [B. S. Duncan 1984]	
2Y-O	'Delibes' [Rijnveld 1950]	
3W-GYY	'Delightful' [G. E. Mitsch 1969]	
3W-WWO	'Dell Chapel' [J. S. B. Lea 1970]	
4W-P	'Delnashaugh' [J. S. B. Lea 1978]	
3W-GWW	'Delos' [J. M. de Navarro 1968]	
6W-P	'Delta Wings' [B. S. Duncan 1977]	
2Y-Y	'Demand' [P. & G.Phillips 1970]	
1Y-Y	'Derg Valley' [B. S. Duncan 1978]	
1W-Y	'Descanso' [M. W. Evans 1965]	M
2W-W	'Desdemona' [G. L. Wilson 1964]	**RD**
1Y-Y	'Deseado' [W. O. Backhouse 1956]	
2W-P	'Desert Rose' [Mrs J. L. Richardson 1979]	
6W-GPP	'Diane' [B. S. Duncan 1983]	
7Y-W	'Dickcissel' [G. E. Mitsch 1963]	M
4Y-Y	'Dick Wilden' [P. T. Zwetsloot 1962]	
3Y-YYO	'Dilemma' [B. S. Duncan 1983]	
3Y-YYR	'Dinkie' [H. Chapman 1927]	
3W-GYR	'Diversion' [Carncairn Daffodils 1983]	
7W-P	'Divertimento' [G. E. Mitsch 1967]	
2W-P	'Divine' [P. Phillips 1968]	
3W-GOO	'Doctor Hugh' [B. S. Duncan 1975]	M

11W-OWO	'Dolly Mollinger' [J. W. A. Lefeber 1958]	
2W-R	'Don Carlos' [J. L. Richardson 1962]	M
1Y-Y	'Donore' [G. L. Wilson 1956]	
2W-PPW	'Dorada Dawn' [T. Bloomer 1985]	
4W-YYP	'Double Blush' [Carncairn Daffodils 1987]	
4Y-Y	'Double Diamond' [Valkering 1972]	
4W-O	'Double Eagle' [J. L. Richardson 1960]	
4W-Y	'Double Event' [J. L. Richardson 1952]	DGP
4Y-Y	'Double Fortune' [M. Zandbergen-Terwegen 1954]	
4W-W	'Double Ming' [A. M. Wilson pre-1950]	
	'Double White Polyanthus' = N. 'Romanus'	
3Y-O	'Doubtful' [J. L. Richardson 1953]	
6W-O	'Dove of Peace' [Ballydorn Bulb Farm 1980]	M
6W-Y	'Dove Wings' [C. F. Coleman 1940]	M-DGP-RD
2W-W	'Dover Cliffs' [F. E. Board 1956]	M
3W-W	'Downhill' [W. J. Dunlop 1960]	
1W-Y	'Downpatrick' [W. J. Dunlop 1959]	M
2W-R	'Doctor Alex Fleming' [J.W. A. Lefeber 1948]	
3W-R	'Dragoman' [J. L. Richardson 1956]	
3W-W	'Dream Castle' [G. E. Mitsch 1963]	
2W-P	'Drenagh' [Carncairn Daffodils 1969]	
3W-YYR	'Dress Circle' [T. Bloomer 1976]	
2W-Y	'Dromona' [Carncairn Daffodils 1973]	
1Y-Y	'Drumadarragh' [Carncairn Daffodils 1971]	
2W-O	'Drumadoon' [Carncairn Daffodils 1981]	
2Y-W	'Drumawillan' [Carncairn Daffodils 1970]	
2W-P	'Drumboe' [G. L. Wilson 1960]	M
2W-PPR	'Drumcairne' [Carncairn Daffodils 1970]	
2Y-WWY	'Drumnabreeze' [Carncairn Daffodils 1978]	
3W-Y	'Drumnasole' [Carncairn Daffodils 1970]	
1Y-Y	'Drumragh' [B. S. Duncan 1979]	
2Y-O	'Drumrunie' [J. S. B. Lea 1971]	
2W-WWP	'Drumtullagh' [Carncairn Daffodils 1971]	
3W-GWW	'Duchess of Abercorn' [T. Bloomer 1973]	
4W-O	'Duet' [W. P. van Eeden 1980]	
2W-Y	'Duke of Windsor' [Uit den Boogaard 1937]	RD
2W-WWP	'Dulcie Joan' [Mrs J. Abel Smith 1972]	
9W-YYR	'Dulcimer' [Rev. G. H. Engleheart 1913]	
3W-GWW	'Dulnan' [J. M. de Navarro 1968]	
1Y-Y	'Dumbleton' [J. M. de Navarro 1959]	
2Y-R	'Dundarave' [Carncairn Daffodils 1969]	
2W-Y	'Dundrod' [Ballydorn Bulb Farm 1975]	
2Y-O	'Dunkeld' [The Brodie of Brodie 1935]	
2W-Y	'Dunlambert' [Ballydorn Bulb Farm 1975]	
2W-Y	'Dunmurry' [W. J. Dunlop 1958]	BB
2Y-WYY	'Duntroon' [Mrs J. Abel Smith 1984]	
3W-W	'Dunskey' [B. S. Duncan 1977]	
1Y-Y	'Dutch Master' [Unknown Origin via G. Zandbergen-Terwegen 1948]	RD
2W-O	'Dynamite' [M. E. Jefferson-Brown 1964]	
4W-Y	'Earlicheer' [M. Gardiner pre-1934]	M
1W-P	'Early Blossom' [Mrs J. Abel Smith 1980]	
2W-WO	'Early Bride' [Reeuwijk 1961]	
1Y-Y	'Early Glory' [van der Meer 1942]	
2Y-O	'Early Light' [Warnaar & Co pre-1953]	
2W-W	'Early Mist' [J. L. Richardson 1953]	
8W-O	'Early Splendour' [van der Schoot 1938]	
3Y-WYY	'Earthlight' [Dr T. D. Throckmorton 1976]	
2W-WWP	'Easter Bonnet' [Rev R. Meyer 1956]	
1W-W	'Easter Bride' [G. L. Wilson 1957]	

2W-GWW	'Easter Moon' [G. L. Wilson 1954]	M
2W-W	'Easter Morn' [Rev. G. H. Engleheart 1931]	
4Y-Y	'Eastertide' [M. Zandbergen-Terwegen 1959]	M
3W-R	'Eaton Park' [T. Bloomer 1984]	
2W-YPP	'Eclat' [G. E. Mitsch 1970]	
2W-YYO	'Eddy Conzony' [J. W. A. Lefeber 1953]	
3Y-OOR	'Edward Buxton' [Sandys-Winsch 1932]	
11W-Y	'Egard' [J. Gerritsen 1973]	RD
4W-Y	'Egg Nogg' [Mrs J. L. Richardson 1975]	
6Y-Y	'El Camino' [G. E. Mitsch 1978]	
7W-W	'Eland' [G. E. Mitsch 1968]	
6W-GWP	'Elizabeth Ann' [B. S. Duncan 1983]	
2W-W	'Ellanne' [Miss M. Verry 1974]	M
3W-ORR	'Ellbridge' [Mrs J. L. Richardson 1977]	
1Y-Y	'Elmley Castle' [J. M. de Navarro 1949]	
2Y-R	'Elmwood' [W. J. Dunlop 1958]	
4W-P	'Elphin' [J. S. B. Lea 1965]	
6W-W	'Elrond' [B. S. Duncan 1981]	
2W-Y	'Elsie Gunter' [R. Ward 1973]	
2W-Y	'Elton Legget' [J. W. A. Lefeber 1958]	
8W-Y	'Elvira [der Schoot 1904]	
6W-W	'Elwing' [B. S. Duncan 1981]	BB
	'Elysian' = N. 'Elysian Fields'	
2W-P	'Elysian Fields' [M. E. Jefferson-Brown 1977]	
2Y-Y	'Emily' [Mrs J. Abel Smith 1974]	
3W-GYY	'Eminent' [G. E. Mitsch 1963]	BB
1Y-Y	'Emperor' [W. Backhouse 1865]	
1W-W	'Empress of Ireland' [G. L. Wilson 1952]	BB
2Y-R	'Enfield' [Mrs H. K. Richardson via du Plessis Bros 1987]	M-DGP-RD
4Y-O	'Enterprise' [Oregon Bulb Farm 1958]	
1Y-W	'Entrancement' [G. E. Mitsch 1958]	
1W-W	'Envoy' [G. L. Wilson]	
2W-R	'Eribol' [J. S. B. Lea 1964]	
2W-W	'Erinvale' [W. J. Dunlop 1962]	
4W-Y	'Eriskay' [J. S. B. Lea 1979]	
3W-GWY	'Ernevale' [B. S. Duncan 1983]	
2Y-Y	'Eskylane' [Carncairn Daffodils 1975]	
3W-GYY	'Esmeralda' [J. L. Richardson 1971]	
2Y-O	'Estio Pinza' [J. W. A. Lefeber pre-1977]	
3W-YYO	'Estrella' [Bulman 1956]	
2Y-O	'Estremadura' [J. M. de Navarro 1967]	
3W-Y	'Ethel' [G. H. Johnstone 1959]	
2Y-Y	'Euphony' [G. E. Mitsch 1968]	
2W-GWW	'Evendine' [M. J. Jefferson-Brown 1985]	
2W-WWY	'Evenlode' [J. M. de Navarro 1949]	
1Y-Y	'Exception' [D. van Buggenum 1971]	
4Y-R	'Extol' [J. L. Richardson 1959]	
3W-GYR	'Eyecatcher' [Carncairn Daffodils 1982]	
4Y-Y	'Eystettensis' [pre-1601]	
	'Eystettensis Plenus' = N. 'Eystettensis'	
3W-GYO	'Fairgreen' [Ballydorn Bulb Farm 1965]	
9W-GYP	'Fair Head' [Ballydorn Bulb Farm 1982]	
2W-P	'Fair Prospect' [J. L. Richardson 1962]	M
3W-GYY	'Fairmaid' [Ballydorn Bulb Farm 1980]	
3W-GYO	'Fairmile' [Ballydorn Bulb Farm 1980]	
3W-GYO	'Fairsel' [Ballydorn Bulb Farm 1978]	
2W-P	'Fair William' [Mrs J. Abel-Smith 1987]	
3W-GWW	'Fairy Footsteps' [Ballydorn Bulb Farm 1982]	
4W-O	'Falaise' [J. L. Richardson 1945]	
2Y-R	'Falstaff' [J. L. Richardson 1960]	M

2W-P	**'Famille Rose'** [G. H. Johnstone 1942]	
3W-GRR	**'Faraway'** [Ballydorn Bulb Farm 1976]	
2W-GYP	**'Far Country'** [Carncairn Daffodils 1976]	
1W-P	**'Farnsfield'** [Mrs J. Abel Smith 1979]	**BB**
1W-W	**'Faro'** [Ballydorn Bulb Farm 1965]	
2W-W	**'Fastidious'** [G. E. Mitsch 1971]	
3W-GYR	**'Favor Royal'** [Ballydorn Bulb Farm 1976]	
2W-Y	**'Favourite'** [F. E. Board 1965]	
3W-Y	**'Fearless'** [Rev. G. H. Engleheart pre-1904]	
6Y-Y	**'February Gold'** [de Graaf Bros. 1923]	M-**BB**-DGP-RD
6W-W	**'February Silver'** [de Graaf Bros. 1949]	**BB**-RD
2Y-R	**'Feeling Lucky'** [J. L. Richardson 1969]	
9W-GYR	**'Felindre'** [A. M. Wilson 1930]	
2W-YYP	**'Fellowship'** [B. S. Duncan 1978]	
2Y-ORR	**'Fergie'** [M. E. Jefferson-Brown 1985]	
2W-YOO	**'Fermoy'** [J. L. Richardson 1938]	DGP-RD
3Y-Y	**'Ferndown'** [J. W. Blanchard pre-1979]	M
2W-Y	**'Festivity'** [G. E. Mitsch 1954]	
1Y-Y	**'Fettle'** [M. W. Evans 1977]	
2O-R	**'Fiery Flame'** [J. L. Richardson 1962]	
4Y-Y	**'Fiji'** [J. L. Richardson 1956]	M
2W-W	**'Filly'** [J. van de Wereld via Tom Parker Farms Ltd 1984]	
2Y-R	**'Film Star'** [G. Lewis 1935]	
1W-W	**'Fincool'** [Ballydorn Bulb Farm 1965]	
2W-Y	**'Finland'** [R. V. Favell pre-1940]	
2W-WWP	**'Finnebrogue'** [Carncairn Daffodils 1971]	
2W-P	**'Fintona'** [G. L. Wilson 1956]	
2W-P	**'Fionn'** [J. S. B. Lea 1962]	
2Y-O	**'Fire Flash'** [Mrs J. L. Richardson 1976]	
2O-O	**'Fire Raiser'** [Carncairn Daffodils 1981]	
2W-O	**'Fire Rocket'** [J. L. Richardson 1967]	
2O-O	**'Fireman'** [Carncairn Daffodils 1982]	
2Y-R	**'Firemaster'** [J. L. Richardson 1948]	
2Y-R	**'Firestorm'** [Ballydorn Bulb Farm 1979]	
3W-YYR	**'Firgrove'** [Carncairn Daffodils 1971]	
3W-Y	**'First Date'** [Carncairn Daffodils 1982]	
1Y-Y	**'Firvale'** [F. E. Board 1965]	
2Y-O	**'Flamboyant'** [J. L. Richardson 1963]	
2Y-R	**'Flaming Meteor'** [G. E. Mitsch 1962]	
2Y-YYR	**'Fleurimont'** [P. D. Williams 1948]	
6Y-Y	**'Flirt'** [Mrs J. L. Richardson 1985]	
3W-GYO	**'Florida Manor'** [Ballydorn Bulb Farm 1979]	
4W-O	**'Flower Drift'** [van Paridon 1966]	
2W-OOR	**'Flower Record'** [J. W. A. Lefeber 1943]	RD
2Y-R	**'Fly Half'** [T. Bloomer 1984]	
7Y-Y	**'Flycatcher'** [G. E. Mitsch 1970]	
2W-Y	**'Flying Saucer'** [G. E. Mitsch 1954]	
2Y-W	**'Focal Point'** [G. E. Mitsch 1972]	
3W-GWW	**'Foggy Dew'** [G. L. Wilson 1941]	
4W-Y	**'Fool's Gold'** [Carncairn Daffodils 1984]	
2W-YYP	**'Foray'** [G. E. Mitsch 1964]	
1Y-Y	**'Forerunner'** [Rev. G. H. Engleheart 1927]	
1W-Y	**'Foresight'** [G. L. Wilson 1944]	RD
2Y-GOO	**'Forge Mill'** [Carncairn Daffodils 1976]	
1W-Y	**'Form Master'** [B. S. Duncan 1977]	
1Y-Y	**'Fort Knox'** [M. E. Jefferson-Brown 1975]	
2Y-Y	**'Forthright'** [The Brodie of Brodie 1949]	
2Y-GYY	**'Fortitude'** [B. S. Duncan 1977]	
2Y-O	**'Fortune'** [W. Ware 1923]	M-**DGP**-RD
2W-R	**'Fortune's Queen'** [Mrs R. O. Backhouse 1929]	

1Y-Y	'Fortwilliam' [W. J. Dunlop 1960]	
6W-P	'Foundling' [Carncairn Daffodils 1969]	M
2W-P	'Fount [M. W. Evans 1976]	
3W-GYR	'Fourways' [Ballydorn Bulb Farm 1979]	
2W-GWO	'Foxfire' [M. W. Evans 1968]	
2Y-R	'Foxhunter' [G. L. Wilson 1953]	
2W-GPP	'Fragrant Rose' [B. S. Duncan 1978]	M
9W-GGR	'Frank's Fancy' [Ballydorn Bulb Farm 1979]	
2W-GPP	'Freshman' [B. S. Duncan 1977]	
3W-GGW	'Frigid' [G. L. Wilson 1953]	DGP
1W-Y	'Frolic' [G. E. Mitsch 1958]	
2Y-YYO	'Front Royal' [J. M. de Navarro 1958]	
9W-GGY	'Frost In May' [Ballydorn Bulb Farm 1981]	
6W-W	'Frostkist' [G. E. Mitsch 1968]	
4W-W	'Frou-Frou' [Carncairn Daffodils 1984]	
2Y-R	'Fuego' [Mrs J. L. Richardson 1976]	
4Y-O	'Furbelow' [J. L. Richardson pre-1961]	
2W-P	'Gainsborough' [Carncairn Daffodils 1975]	
2Y-O	'Gala King' [Mrs J. L. Richardson 1974]	
1Y-Y	'Galahad' [T. Bloomer 1978]	
2Y-Y	'Galway' [J. L. Richardson 1943]	M-RD
2Y-O	'Gambler's Gift' [J. L. Richardson 1968]	
3W-YOO	'Ganaway' [Ballydorn Bulb Farm 1984]	
6Y-Y	'Garden Princess' [de Graff 1974]	
2W-OOY	'Gardenvale' [Carncairn Daffodils 1969]	
3W-R	'Gaucho' [Brogden 1964]	
4Y-O	'Gay Cavalier' [J. L. Richardson 1967]	
4W-R	'Gay Challenger' [J. L. Richardson 1962]	M
2W-GOR	'Gay Colours' [T. Bloomer 1962]	
4W-O	'Gay Kybo' [Mrs J. L. Richardson 1980]	M
2W-P	'Gay Mood' [G. E. Mitsch 1962]	
4W-O	'Gay Record' [J. L. Richardson 1964]	
4W-W	'Gay Song' [J. L. Richardson 1968]	
4W-Y	'Gay Symphony' [J. L. Richardson 1973]	
4W-R	'Gay Time' [J. L. Richardson 1952]	
2W-YYO	'Gaybrook' [Carncairn Daffodils 1973]	
2W-O	'George Leak' [J. L. Richardson 1960]	
2Y-Y	'Georgia Moon' [Warnaar & Co Ltd 1962]	
8W-O	'Geranium' [van der Schoot 1930]	M-DGP-RD
2W-Y	'Gerbrandt Kieft' [Onderwater 1967]	
2Y-GYR	'Gettysburg' [J. M. de Navarro 1979]	
2Y-Y	'Gigantic Star' [G. Helmus 1960]	
3W-GRR	'Gilford' [W. J. Dunlop 1958]	
6W-P	'Gimli' [B. S. Duncan 1981]	
1Y-GWW	'Gin and Lime' [Carncairn Daffodils 1973]	M
2W-W	'Gipsy Moth' [Carncairn Daffodils 1967]	
1Y-WWY	'Gipsy Queen' [A. Gray 1969]	
1W-W	'Glacier' [J. L. Richardson 1956]	DGP-RD
2Y-O	'Glad Day' [G. E. Mitsch 1974]	
2W-W	'Glandore' [Ballydorn Bulb Farm 1972]	
2W-ORR	'Glaston' [P. Phillips 1966]	
3W-W	'Glen Cassley' [J. S. B. Lea 1983]	
2Y-ORR	'Glen Clova' [J. S. B. Lea 1978]	
1W-GMW	'Glen Isla' [J. S. B. Lea 1981]	
2W-P	'Glen Lorne' [Mrs J. Abel Smith 1975]	
2W-P	'Glen Rothes' [J. S. B. Lea 1976]	
1W-Y	'Glenamoy' [Carncairn Daffodils 1979]	
2W-Y	'Glencraig' [Ballydorn Bulb Farm 1977]	
2W-GWW	'Glendermott' [G. L. Wilson 1957]	
1Y-O	'Glenfarclas' [J. S. B. Lea 1976]	

2W-GWW	'Glenside' [F. E. Board 1976]	
3W-R	'Glenwherry' [W. J. Dunlop 1947]	
2W-YOO	'Glorification' [G. Lubbe 1944]	
8W-R	'Glorious' [J. C. Williams 1923]	
8W-Y	'Gloriosus' [Pre-1850]	
2W-R	'Glowing Ember' [Mrs J. L. Richardson 1973]	
1Y-Y	'Gold Bullion' [Carncairn Daffodils 1982]	
1Y-Y	'Gold Convention' [J. S. B. Lea 1978]	M
1Y-Y	'Gold Medal' [G. Lubbe & Son 1938]	
2Y-Y	'Gold Mine' [Ballydorn Bulb Farm 1983]	
1Y-Y	'Gold Phantom' [J. L. Richardson 1968]	
1Y-Y	'Gold Strike' [Carncairn Daffodils 1984]	
2Y-ORR	'Golden Amber' [Ballydorn Bulb Farm 1975]	M
2Y-Y	'Golden Aura' [J. L. Richardson 1964]	M-BB
8Y-O	'Golden Dawn' [Oregon Bulb Farms 1958]	
4Y-Y	'Golden Ducat' [Speelman 1947]	BB-DGP-RD
2Y-WWO	'Golden Halo' [Ballydorn Bulb Farm 1983]	
1Y-Y	'Golden Harvest' [Warnaar 1927]	M-DGP-RD
2Y-GYY	'Golden Jewel' [T. Bloomer 1973]	M
2Y-Y	'Golden Joy' [T. Bloomer 1973]	M
1Y-Y	'Golden Marvel' [Warnaar 1938]	
7Y-Y	'Golden Perfection' [de Graaf 1927]	
1Y-Y	'Golden Radiance' [Ballydorn Bulb Farm 1974]	
2Y-Y	'Golden Ranger' [Mrs J. L. Richardson 1976]	
1Y-Y	'Golden Rapture' [J. L. Richardson 1952]	RD
1Y-Y	'Golden Riot' [G. L. Wilson 1948]	
1Y-Y	'Golden Rupee' [W. A. Noton]	
1Y-Y	'Golden Sand' [The Brodie of Brodie pre-1910]	
1Y-Y	'Golden Showers' [Mrs J. Abel Smith 1982]	
1Y-Y	'Golden Sovereign' [Ballydorn Bulb Farm 1975]	
2Y-O	'Golden Treasure' [G. Lewis pre-1940]	
1Y-Y	'Golden Vale' [F. E. Board 1976]	M
6Y-Y	'Golden Wings' [Ballydorn Bulb Farm 1977]	
2Y-Y	'Goldsithney' [A. Gray 1949]	
4W-Y	'Golly' [J. L. Richardson 1968]	
2W-W	'Good Measure' [M. E. Jefferson-Brown 1975]	
9W-GYR	'Goose Green' [Ballydorn Bulb Farm 1983]	
3W-YYP	'Gossamer' [G. E. Mitsch 1962]	
3W-GGY	'Grace Note' [G. E. Mitsch 1966]	
2W-GWY	'Graceland' [T. Bloomer 1982]	
2W-P	'Gracious Lady' [Mrs J. L. Richardson 1974]	M
2W-GPP	'Graduate' [B. S. Duncan 1980]	
8W-Y	'Grand Monarque' [Dutch origin]	M
8W-Y	'Grand Primo Citroniere' [Dutch origin]	
2Y-W	'Grand Prospect' [Mrs J. L. Richardson 1974]	M-BB
8Y-O	'Grand Soleil d'Or' [French origin]	M-BB-DGP-RD
3W-GOR	'Gransha' [Ballydorn Bulb Farm 1977]	
11W-Y	'Grapillon' [J. Gerritsen 1968]	
2Y-Y	'Great Expectations' [Mrs J. L. Richardson 1977]	
4Y-Y	'Great Leap' [E. & J. C. Martin pre-1923]	
2W-GYY	'Green Glens' [Carncairn Daffodils 1981]	
2Y-GYY	'Green Gold' [G. E. Mitsch 1975]	
2W-GWW	'Greenholm' [B. S. Duncan 1981]	
3W-GYY	'Green Howard' [G. H. Johnstone 1944]	
2W-GWW	'Green Ice' [B. S. Duncan 1981]	
2W-GWY	'Green Island' [J. L. Richardson 1938]	M
2W-GGY	'Green Peace' [Ballydorn Bulb Farm 1984]	
2Y-W	'Green Rival' [Konyneburg & Mark 1962]	
2W-GYR	'Green Woodpecker' [J. M. de Navarrro 1954]	
3W-GGR	'Greenfinch' [J. L. Richardson 1962]	

4G-G	'Greenstar'	[Pre-1956]
2W-GWW	'Greenvale'	[B. S. Duncan 1981]
2W-Y	'Greeting'	[P. D. Williams 1934]
3W-WWR	'Grey Lady'	[G. L. Wilson 1935]
2Y-ORR	'Gunsynd'	[W. Jackson jnr. 1966]
3W-YYR	'Halgarry'	[J. S. B. Lea 1985]
2W-YYR	'Halley's Comet'	[Mrs J. Abel Smith 1986]
2Y-W	'Halolight'	[G. E. Mitsch 1960]
2Y-W	'Halstock'	[J. W. Blanchard 1986]
2Y-WWO	'Hambledon'	[J. W. Blanchard 1983]
3W-Y	'Hammoon'	[D. Blanchard 1968]
2Y-W	'Handcross'	[Sir F. Stern 1957]
2W-O	'Happy Face'	[Carncairn Daffodils 1979]
5Y-Y	'Harmony Bells'	[Fowlds 1962]
2W-P	'Hartington'	[F. E. Board 1965]
4Y-R	'Hawaii'	[J. L. Richardson 1956] M
5Y-Y	'Hawera'	[Dr Thomson 1938] **M-BB-DGP**
2Y-O	'Haye'	[Mrs J. L. Richardson 1977]
2W-P	'Hazel Winslow'	[B. S. Duncan 1983]
4W-Y	'Hearts Desire'	[J. L. Richardson 1969]
2Y-R	'Heat Haze'	[Carncairn Daffodils 1978]
2Y-O	'Heath Fire'	[J. L. Richardson 1964]
1Y-O	'Hero'	[M. E. Jefferson-Brown 1984] M
7Y-GYY	'Hesla'	[P. D. Williams 1908]
3W-YYR	'Heslington'	[C. Postles 1985] M
2Y-R	'Hessenford'	[Mrs J. L. Richardson 1981]
9W-YYR	'Hexameter'	[The Brodie of Brodie 1927]
3W-WYY	'Hexworthy'	[Ballydorn Bulb Farm 1985]
2W-GWW	'High Church'	[Ballydorn Bulb Farm 1986]
2W-YYO	'High Life'	[Uit den Boogaard 1951]
7Y-W	'High Note'	[G. E. Mitsch 1974]
2W-GYP	'High Society'	[B. S. Duncan 1979]
3W-GWY	'High Tower'	[Ballydorn Bulb Farm 1982]
8Y-GYO	'Highfield Beauty'	[H. R. Mott 1964] M
2W-GWP	'Highland Wedding'	[J. L. Richardson 1956]
3W-GYO	'Highway Song'	[Carncairn Daffodils 1987]
2W-O	'Hilford'	[Ballydorn Bulb Farm 1979]
2W-WPP	'Holiday Fashion'	[G. E. Mitsch 1967]
11W-Y	'Holiday Inn International'	[J. Gerritsen 1968]
2Y-R	'Holly Berry'	[W. J. Dunlop 1950]
2Y-O	'Hollywood'	[Warnaar 1939]
2W-GWW	'Homage'	[G. L. Wilson 1955]
2Y-R	'Home Fires'	[G. L. Wilson 1950] RD
1Y-W	'Honeybird'	[G. E. Mitsch 1965] M
1Y-Y	'Honeymoon'	[M. W. Evans 1969]
4W-R	'Honolulu'	[J. L. Richardson 1956]
4W-Y	'Hope'	[J. L. Richardson 1971]
9W-YOR	'Horace'	[Rev G. H. Engleheart 1907]
2Y-R	'Hot Stuff'	[J. T. Gray 1964]
3W-GRY	'Hot Sun'	[W. A. Noton 1985]
4Y-O	'Hot Toddy'	[Carncairn Daffodils 1983]
2W-R	'Hotspur'	[J. L. Richardson 1959] M
3W-GYR	'Howard's Way'	[Mrs J. Abel-Smith 1987]
1Y-Y	'Hunter's Moon'	[The Brodie of Brodie 1941] DGP
3W-YYO	'Ibberton'	[J. W. Blanchard 1974]
11W-WWY	'Ice Crystal'	[J. Gerritsen 1965]
2W-W	'Ice Follies'	[Konynenburg & Mark 1953] M-RD
11W-Y	'Ice King'	[A. P. van den Berg-Hytuna]
5W-W	'Ice Wings'	[C. F. Coleman 1958]
2W-YRW	'Ida May'	[R. H. Glover 1968]

8W-O	'Ideal'	[van der Schoot 1907]	
2W-P	'Imogen'	[J. L. Richardson 1958]	
3W-GYY	'Impala'	[G. E. Mitsch 1966]	
2Y-Y	'Imperial'	[G. E. Mitsch 1972]	
7O-R	'Indian Maid'	[W. G. Pannill 1972]	
2Y-R	'Indian Summer'	[G. L. Wilson 1940]	
2W-GYP	'Infatuation'	[J. L. Richardson 1954]	
4Y-Y	'Inglescombe'	[J. Walker 1914]	
2W-GWW	'Innis Beg'	[Carncairn Daffodils 1976]	
3W-WWY	'Innisfree'	[Carncairn Daffodils]	
1W-W	'Inniswood'	[Carncairn Daffodils 1978]	M
2W-YYP	'Interim'	[G. L. Wilson 1948]	
2W-GYP	'Interval'	[Ballydorn Bulb Farm 1975]	
2W-W	'Inverpolly'	[J. S. B. Lea 1980]	
9W-GYR	'Ireland's Eye'	[Ballydorn Bulb Farm 1979]	
4W-Y	'Irene Copeland'	[W. F. M. Copeland 1923]	RD
2W-OOY	'Irish Charm'	[W. J. Dunlop 1952]	
3Y-YYO	'Irish Coffee'	[G. E. Mitsch 1967]	
2Y-R	'Irish Light'	[J. L. Richardson 1972]	
3W-GWW	'Irish Linen'	[Carncairn Daffodils 1979]	
1Y-Y	'Irish Luck'	[G. L. Wilson 1948]	
2W-Y	'Irish Minstrel'	[J. L. Richardson 1958]	BB
2W-Y	'Irish Mist'	[J. L. Richardson 1972]	
3W-GYO	'Irish Nymph'	[Carncairn Daffodils 1981]	
3W-R	'Irish Ranger'	[Carncairn Daffodils 1975]	
2W-P	'Irish Rose'	[G. L. Wilson 1953]	
2W-OOY	'Irish Rover'	[J. L. Richardson 1967]	
3W-R	'Irish Splendour'	[W. J. Dunlop 1962]	
3W-YYO	'Islandhill'	[Ballydorn Bulb Farm 1984]	
1W-W	'It's True'	[M. E. Jefferson-Brown 1968]	M
6Y-R	'Itzim'	[G. E. Mitsch 1982]	
2W-YOY	'Ivory Crown'	[F. E. Board]	
1W-Y	'Ivy League'	[M. W. Evans 1972]	
6W-Y	'Jack Snipe'	[M. P. Williams 1951]	RD
2Y-O	'Jaguar'	[J. L. Richardson 1951]	
3W-GYY	'Jamestown'	[Ballydorn Bulb Farm 1978]	
6Y-Y	'Jana'	[A. Gray 1949]	
2W-WWP	'Janis Babson'	[M. W. Evans 1968]	
6W-W	'Jenny'	[C. F. Coleman 1943]	M
3W-YYO	'Jessiman'	[Mrs J. Abel Smith 1971]	
6Y-R	'Jetfire'	[G. E. Mitsch 1966]	M
2W-P	'Jewel Song'	[J. L. Richardson 1967]	BB
3Y-R	'Jezebel'	[A. M. Wilson 1948]	
6Y-Y	'Jingle'	[P. & G. Phillips 1975]	
5Y-Y	'Johanna'	[A. Gray 1950]	
2W-Y	'John of Salisbury'	[M. E. Jefferson-Brown 1975]	
2W-Y	'Jolity'	[M. E. Jefferson-Brown 1985]	
2W-Y	'Jolly Roger'	[M. W. Evans 1969]	
7Y-YYO	'Joppa'	[du Plessis Bros 1987]	
1Y-Y	'Joseph Macleod'	[Warnaar & Co Ltd 1946]	
2W-Y	'Joy' = N. 'Jolity'		
6W-Y	'Joybell'	[J. L. Richardson 1969]	
10Y-Y	'Joy Bishop'	[J. C. Archibald 1968]	
2Y-GYY	'Joyland'	[B. S. Duncan 1977]	
2W-Y	'Jubilation'	[G. E. Mitsch 1959]	
	'Julia Jane'		
6Y-O	'Jumblie'	[A. Gray 1952]	
1Y-Y	'Jumbo Gold'	[B. S. Duncan 1979]	
2W-YOY	'Juno'	[Carncairn Daffodils 1978]	
1Y-Y	'Kapuni'	[G. C. Yeats 1968]	

2Y-YYR	**'Karachi'** [J. L. Richardson 1949]	
1W-Y	**'Karamudli'** [D. Blanchard 1949]	M
3W-R	**'Kazuko'** [J. O'More 1975]	
9W-GGY	**'Keats'** [A. Gray 1968]	
2Y-WP	**'Kelanne'** [T. Bloomer 1982]	
6W-P	**'Kelpie'** [J. L. Richardson 1968]	
2W-P	**'Ken's Favourite'** [M. W. Evans 1978]	
2W-R	**'Kentucky Cardinal'** [J. M. de Navarro 1966]	
2W-W	**'Kibo'** [G. L. Wilson 1948]	
2W-P	**'Kildavin'** [J. S. B. Lea 1963]	
3W-R	**'Kildrum'** [W. J. Dunlop 1950]	
1Y-Y	**'Kilkenny'** [J. L. Richardson 1938]	
6Y-Y	**'Killdeer'** [G. E. Mitsch 1970]	
9W-GYR	**'Killearnan'** [J. S. B. Lea 1985]	
2Y-O	**'Killeen'** [Ballydorn Bulb Farm 1980]	
2W-W	**'Killymoon'** [S. J. Bisdee 1951]	
2Y-O	**'Kilmorack'** [The Brodie of Brodie 1950]	
3W-O	**'Kilmurry'** [J. L. Richardson 1938]	
2W-W	**'Kilrea'** [W. J. Dunlop 1952]	
2W-GRR	**'Kilworth'** [J. L. Richardson 1938]	M-DGP-**RD**
3W-YYO	**'Kimmeridge'** [D. Blanchard 1966]	**M**
3W-W	**'Kincorth'** [The Brodie Gardens 1957]	
2Y-R	**'Kindled'** [G. L. Wilson 1950]	
1Y-Y	**'King Alfred'** [J. Kendall 1899]	**M-BB**-DGP
2Y	**'Kingcup'** [C. L. Adams pre-1908]	
11Y-Y	**'King Size'** [J. Gerritsen 1969]	M-RD
1Y-Y	**'King's Bridge'** [B. S. Duncan 1980]	
1Y-Y	**'King's Ransom'** [J. L. Richardson 1950]	
1Y-Y	**'King's Stag'** [J. W. Blanchard 1974]	
8Y-GOO	**'Kingcraft'** [P. D. Williams 1915]	
3W-GYR	**'Kingfisher'** [J. L. Richardson 1958]	
7Y-O	**'Kinglet'** [G. E. Mitsch 1959]	
1Y-Y	**'Kingscourt'** [J. L. Richardson 1963]	**M**
1Y-Y	**'Kingsmill'** [du Plessis Bros 1976]	
3W-GYR	**'Kipling'** [B. S. Duncan 1978]	
3W-GYO	**'Kirkinriola'** [Carncairn Daffodils 1986]	
2W-P	**'Kirklington'** [Mrs J. Abel Smith 1979]	
2Y-O	**'Kissproof'** [Warnaar & Co 1964]	
6Y-O	**'Kitten'** [C. F. Coleman 1962]	
2W-Y	**'Klamath'** [G. E. Mitsch 1960]	
2W-P	**'Knightwick'** [J. L. Richardson 1963]	**BB**
1Y-Y	**'Knockstacken'** [W. J. Dunlop 1965]	
2W-W	**'Knowehead'** [G. L. Wilson 1954]	**BB**
3Y-R	**'Kopi'** [W. Jackson jnr. 1968]	
2Y-R	**'Krakatoa'** [J. L. Richardson 1937]	
8W-GOO	**'La Fiancee'** [Warnaar & Co Ltd 1937]	
3W-GYO	**'La Riante'** [van Deursen 1933]	
9W-GYR	**'Lady Serena'** [P. D. Williams 1976]	
1W-W	**'Ladybank'** [B. S. Duncan 1981]	M
2Y-R	**'Lamerton'** [Mrs J. L. Richardson 1985]	
	'L'Amour' = **N. 'Madelaine'**	
3Y-GYY	**'Lalique'** [Dr T. D. Throckmorton 1975]	
7Y-Y	**'Lanarth'** [P. D. Williams 1907]	DGP
3W-GYO	**'Lancaster'** [Ballydorn Bulb Farm 1977]	
1Y-Y	**'Lancelot'** [T. Bloomer 1979]	
2W-O	**'Landmark'** [Brogden 1963]	
3W-YYR	**'Langford Grove'** [Mrs J. Abel Smith 1977]	**BB**
2W-Y	**'Langwith'** [Mrs J. Abel Smith 1969]	**BB**
2Y-YRR	**'Lansallos'** [T. Bloomer 1986]	
2Y-WWY	**'Lark'** [G. E. Mitsch 1976]	

6Y-O	'Larkelly'	[P. D. Williams 1930]
2W-O	'Larkfield'	[W. J. Dunlop 1969]
3W-GYO	'Larry'	[F. E. Board 1976]
3W-GYY	'Last Word'	[M. E. Jefferson-Brown 1985]
3W-GYR	'Late Call'	[Ballydorn Bulb Farm 1984]
6W-GPP	'Lavender Lass'	[B. S. Duncan 1976]
2Y-O	'Leader'	[M. J. Jefferson-Brown 1975]
2Y-Y	'Lemnos'	[A. H. Ahrens pre-1949]
11W-WWY	'Lemon Beauty'	[J. W. A. Lefeber 1962]
2Y-WWY	'Lemon Candy'	[Mrs J. L. Richardson 1977]
1Y-Y	'Lemon Cloud'	[M. E. Jefferson-Brown 1969]
5W-Y	'Lemon Heart'	[Barr 1952]
1y-Y	'Lemon Meringue'	[G. E. Mitsch 1954]
2W-GYY	'Lemon Sherbet'	[Carncairn Daffodils 1979]
3Y-Y	'Lemonade'	[J. L. Richardson 1963]
1W-Y	'Lenz'	[Chambers 1972]
2W-P	'Leonaine'	[G. E. Mitsch 1959] **BB**
3W-RRY	'Leonora'	[J. L. Richardson 1963]
1W-GWW	'Leslie Hill'	[Carncairn Daffodils 1985]
2W-WWY	'Lewannick'	[Mrs H. K. Richardson via du Plessis Bros 1987]
5Y-Y	'Liberty Bells'	[Rijnveld 1950] M-DGP-**RD**
2W-WWO	'Liberty Light'	[J. L. Richardson 1952]
2W-R	'Libya'	[J. L. Richardson 1959]
3W-GYR	'Lichfield'	[C. R. Wooton 1956]
3W-R	'Lighthouse'	[B. S. Duncan 1981]
6W-GPP	'Lilac Charm'	[B. S. Duncan 1973] M
2W-P	'Lilac Delight'	[G. E. Mitsch 1968]
2O-R	'Limbo'	[B. S. Duncan 1984]
2Y-W	'Limeade'	[G. E. Mitsch 1962]
3Y-GYY	'Limegrove'	[C. R. Wooton 1985]
2YW-W	'Limehurst'	[T. Bloomer 1982]
1Y-Y	'Limelight'	[B. S. Duncan 1958]
3W-R	'Limerick'	[J. L. Richardson 1938]
8W-Y	'L'Innocence'	[C. P. Alkemede 1930]
7Y-O	'Lintie'	[Barr 1937]
4W-Y	'Lionheart'	[Mrs J. L. Richardson 1975]
3W-GYR	'Lisbane'	[Ballydorn Bulb Farm 1975]
3W-GRR	'Lisbarnett'	[Ballydorn Bulb Farm 1984]
1W-Y	'Lisrenny'	[Carncairn Daffodils 1973]
1W-Y	'Little Beauty'	[J. Gerritsen 1953]
1W-Y	'Little Dancer'	[A. Gray 1977]
1Y-Y	'Little Gem'	[J. Gerritsen 1959] M
6W-P	'Little Princess'	[Mrs J. L. Richardson 1978]
7Y-Y	'Little Sentry'	[A. Gray 1984] M
6Y-Y	'Little Witch'	[Mrs R. O. Backhouse 1929]
2Y-O	'Liverpool Festival'	[J. S. B. Lea 1985] M
2Y-O	'Lizard Light'	[M. P. Williams pre-1947]
3W-GWO	'Loch Assynt'	[J. S. B. Lea 1963] **M**
3W-ORR	'Loch Broom'	[J. S. B. Lea 1979]
2W-O	'Loch Brora'	[J. S. B. Lea 1979] M
2Y-R	'Loch Carron'	[J. S. B. Lea 1980]
3W-R	'Loch Coire'	[J. S. B. Lea 1983] M
2Y-R	'Loch Fada'	[J. S. B. Lea 1972]
2Y-O	'Loch Garvie'	[J. S. B. Lea 1971]
2Y-R	'Loch Hope'	[J. S. B. Lea 1970] M
2Y-R	'Lock Loyal'	[J. S. B. Lea 1980]
2Y-R	'Loch Lundie'	[J. S. B. Lea 1978]
2Y-R	'Loch Maberry'	[J. S. B. Lea 1983]
2Y-O	'Loch Meadie'	[J. S. B. Lea 1979]
2Y-ORR	'Loch Naver'	[J. S. B. Lea 1963]

2Y-O	'Loch Owskeich'	[J. S. B. Lea 1971]	
2Y-YRR	'Loch Rimsdale'	[J. S. B. Lea 1985]	M
3W-R	'Loch Roag'	[J. S. B. Lea 1983]	M
2Y-R	'Loch Stac'	[J. S. B. Lea 1961]	M
2W-YRR	'Loch Trool'	[J. S. B. Lea 1983]	
2W-R	'Loch Turnaig'	[J. S. B. Lea 1979]	
7	'Logan Rock'	[R. V. Favell pre-1953]	
2W-O	'Lorenzo'	[J. L. Richardson 1959]	
3W-GYY	'Loth Lorien'	[B. S. Duncan 1981]	
2W-Y	'Lothario'	[van Deursen 1938]	
2Y-R	'Lough Bawn'	[Carncairn Daffodils 1975]	
1Y-Y	'Lough Cuan'	[Ballydorn Bulb Farm 1984]	
1Y-Y	'Loughanisland'	[Ballydorn Bulb Farm 1986]	
1Y-Y	'Loughanmore'	[Carncairn Daffodils 1969]	
2W-P	'Louise De Coligny'	[van Leeuwen 1948]	
3W-W	'Lovable'	[G. E. Mitsch 1967]	
2W-O	'Love Song'	[Grullemans 1957]	
2Y-Y	'Lucinius'	[de Graaf 1915]	
3W-R	'Lucky Star'	[T. Bloomer 1973]	
1Y-W	'Lunar Sea'	[G. E. Mitsch 1954]	M-DGP
1Y-Y	'Lurgain'	[J. S. B. Lea 1957]	
3W-GYO	'Lusky Mills'	[Ballydorn Bulb Farm 1978]	
2W-Y	'Luxulyan'	[T. Bloomer 1986]	
2Y-Y	'Lyles'	[McNairny 1974]	
1W-W	'Lynwood'	[Carncairn Daffodils 1975]	
9W-GYR	'Lyric'	[B. S. Duncan 1977]	
2W-YYO	'Lysander'	[J. L. Richardson 1959]	
2Y-O	'Madelaine'	[Mrs J. L. Richardson 1975]	
2W-WWY	'Madrigal'	[G. E. Mitsch 1956]	
2Y-R	'Magherally'	[G. L. Wilson 1944]	
4W-Y	'Magic'	[J. L. Richardson 1962]	
2W-YYR	'Magic Circle'	[J. L. Richardson 1938]	
2WGWP	'Magic Flute'	[Carncairn Daffodils 1984]	
2W-R	'Magic Maiden'	[T. Bloomer 1982]	
1W-Y	'Magnet'	[van Leeuwen 1931]	RD
1Y-Y	'Magnificence'	[Rev. G. H. Engleheart 1914]	DGP-RD
2W-R	'Mahmoud'	[J. L. Richardson 1937]	DGP
2W-YYR	'Maid of Ulster'	[T. Bloomer 1982]	
2W-P	'Maiden's Blush'	[Rev R. Meyer 1945]	
1W-W	'Majestic Star'	[T. Bloomer 1982]	M
1Y-Y	'Malvern City'	[C. W. Pierson pre-1951]	
2W-Y	'Manchu'	[Barr 1947]	
1Y-Y	'Mando'	[G. L. Wilson 1959]	
2W-P	'Mandolin'	[G. L. Wilson 1959]	
4Y-O	'Manly'	[J. L. Richardson 1972]	M
2W-GPP	'Mantle'	[B. S. Duncan via Rathowen Daffodils 1987]	
2W-WWP	'Maplebeck'	[Mrs J. Abel Smith 1979]	
1Y-Y	'Maraval'	[G. L. Wilson 1945]	
2Y-R	'March Madness'	[Carncairn Daffodils 1976]	
6Y-Y	'March Sunshine'	[de Graaf 1923]	BB-RD
2W-P	'Marcola'	[G. E. Mitsch 1969]	
2W-WWP	'Margaret Clare'	[Mrs J. Abel Smith 1973]	
3W-YYR	'Margaret Mitchell'	[G. Lubbe 1943]	
2W-YOR	'Marshfire'	[M. W. Evans 1970]	
8W-O	'Martha Washington'	[Frylink 1948]	
1W-W	'Martigny'	[J. L. Richardson 1968]	
7Y-O	'Martinette'	[Tuggle 1985]	
2Y-O	'Mary Bohannon'	[M. P. Williams 1957]	
4W-O	'Mary Copeland'	[W. F. M. Copeland 1914]	RD
3W-WWY	'Mary Isabel'	[Mrs J. Abel Smith 1982]	
6W-GWP	'Mary Kate'	[B. S. Duncan 1983]	

1W-Y	**'Mary Sumner'**	[Carncairn Daffodils 1975]
2W-P	**'Mary's Pink'**	[Carncairn Daffodils 1975]
2Y-O	**'Masked Light'**	[J. L. Richardson 1951]
2W-R	**'Masquerade'**	[D. S. Bell 1955]
8Y-GWO	**'Matador'**	[Oregon Bulb Farms 1958]
3W-R	**'Matapan'**	[J. L. Richardson 1941]
2W-GYY	**'May Queen'**	[J. L. Richardson 1973]
1W-W	**'Meavy'**	[Mrs J. L. Richardson 1978]
2W-YPP	**'Medalist'**	[G. E. Mitsch 1967]
8W-GRR	**'Medusa'**	[P. D. Williams 1907]
2W-Y	**'Megalith'**	[T. Bloomer 1984]
2W-P	**'Melbury'**	[J. W. Blanchard 1977]
1Y-Y	**'Meldrum'**	[J. S. B. Lea 1976]
3W-O	**'Mellon Park'**	[T. Bloomer 1984]
2W-P	**'Melody Lane'**	[G. E. Mitsch 1962]
2W-GPP	**'Mentor'**	[T. Bloomer via Rathowen Daffodils 1982]
2W-GWW	**'Menucha'**	[Carncairn Daffodils 1984]
2W-YDR	**'Mercato'**	[Berbee 1945]
3W-YYR	**'Merlin'**	[J. L. Richardson 1956] **M**
2W-GWY	**'Mermaid's Spell'**	[Carncairn Daffodils 1975]
5W-Y	**'Merry Bells'**	[Oregon Bulb Farms 1958]
4Y-R	**'Merrymaker'**	[M. E. Jefferson-Brown 1978]
2Y-O	**'Mexico City'**	[W. J. Toal via Ballydorn Bulb Farm 1967]
1Y-Y	**'Midas Touch'**	[T. Bloomer 1977]
9W-GYR	**'Milan'**	[A. H. Wilson 1932]
2Y-P	**'Milestone'**	[G. E. Mitsch 1968]
2W-O	**'Milford'**	[Mrs J. Abel Smith 1978]
2Y-R	**'Mill Grove'**	[W. A. Noton 1976]
1Y-Y	**'Mill Reef'**	[J. L. Richardson 1973]
4W-R	**'Minard'**	[M. Zandbergen 1978]
3W-GYR	**'Minikin'**	[M. W. Evans 1969]
8W-Y	**'Minnow'**	[A. Gray 1962] **M-RD**
3Y-Y	**'Minster Lodge'**	[Mrs J. Abel Smith 1977]
3W-GWY	**'Mint Cup'**	[Carncairn Daffodils 1983]
3Y-GYY	**'Mint Julep'**	[B. S. Duncan 1981]
3W-GYR	**'Minx'**	[M. W. Evans 1969]
2Y-O	**'Missouri'**	[M. Zandbergen 1945]
11W-Y	**'Mistral'**	[J. Gerritsen 1965]
2W-GWW	**'Misty Glen'**	[F. E. Board 1976] **M**
3W-WWO	**'Misty Moon'**	[G. L. Wilson 1936]
7Y-W	**'Mockingbird'**	[G. E. Mitsch 1971]
2W-P	**'Modest Maiden'**	[B. S. Duncan 1976]
11Y-Y	**'Modesta'**	[J. Gerritsen 1961]
2W-Y	**'Modulux'**	[P. & G. Phillips 1978]
3W-WWO	**'Moina'**	[C. E. Radcliffe 1938]
11Y-Y	**'Mol's Hobby'**	[J. W. A. Lefeber 1960]
2W-P	**'Mondaine'**	[G. L. Wilson 1956]
2Y-R	**'Moneymore'**	[W. J. Dunlop 1960]
3W-GWW	**'Monk Silver'**	[F. E. Board 1976]
2Y-R	**'Montalto'**	[Carncairn Daffodils 1971]
2W-YYP	**'Montclair'**	[Mrs J. Abel-Smith 1967]
3Y-YYO	**'Montego'**	[J. L. Richardson 1968]
4W-O	**'Monterrico'**	[J. L. Richardson 1962]
2Y-Y	**'Monument'**	[M. W. Evans 1969]
4Y-YR	**'Monza'**	[B. S. Duncan 1986]
	'Moon Empress'	
1Y-Y	**'Moon Goddess'**	[G. L. Wilson 1953]
3W-GWY	**'Moon Jade'**	[Ballydorn Bulb Farm 1982]
2Y-Y	**'Moon Orbit'**	[Warnaar & Co Ltd 1969]
3Y-O	**'Moon Rhythm'**	[Ballydorn Bulb Farm 1980]

3Y-YOO	'Moon Tide'	[Ballydorn Bulb Farm 1984]
2W-GWW	'Moon Valley'	[B. S. Duncan via Rathowen Daffodils 1983]
1Y-W	'Moonlight Sonata'	[G. E. Mitsch 1960]
1Y-Y	'Moonrise'	[G. Lubbe 1947]
1Y-Y	'Moonshot'	[G. E. Mitsch 1963]
2Y-W	'Moonspell'	[Ballydorn Bulb Farm 1972]
3W-Y	'Morning Cloud'	[Mrs J. Abel Smith 1973]
3W-YYR	'Mount Angel'	[B. S. Duncan 1978]
1W-W	'Mount Hood'	[van Deursen 1938] M-DGP-RD
2W-W	'Mount Fuji'	[B. S. Duncan via Rathowen Daffodils 1987]
2W-GWO	'Mount Ida'	[Ballydorn Bulb Farm 1976]
2W-P	'Mount Vernon'	[G. E. Mitsch 1968]
7Y-Y	'Mountjoy'	[Barr 1950]
2W-Y	'Mountpleasant'	[Ballydorn Bulb Farm 1968]
9W-GYO	'Moyle'	[Ballydorn Bulb Farm 1982]
2W-P	'Moyola'	[Carncairn Daffodils 1976]
1W-W	'Mrs Ernst H Krelage'	[E. H. Krelage & Son 1912]
2W-P	'Mrs Oscar Ronalds'	[O. Ronalds 1956]
2W-P	'Mrs R O Backhouse'	[Mrs R. O. Backhouse 1923]
4W-W	'Mrs William Copeland'	[W. F. M. Copeland 1930]
1W-GWW	'Muirfield'	[B. S. Duncan 1981]
1Y-Y	'Mulatto'	[van Tubergen 1931]
3W-GYO	'Murrayfield'	[T. Bloomer 1984]
2W-Y	'Muscadet'	[J. Gerritsen 1960]
1W-Y	'Music Hall'	[J. L. Richardson 1923]
2W-P	'My Lady'	[M. E. Jefferson-Brown 1978]
2W-Y	'My Love'	[J. L. Richardson 1948]
2W-P	'My My'	[J. L. Richardson 1967]
2W-P	'My Word'	[Mrs E. Murray 1979]
3W-YYR	'Myriantha'	[G. H. Johnstone 1959]
1Y-W	'Nampa'	[G. E. Mitsch 1958]
2Y-GYR	'Namraj'	[T. Bloomer via Rathowen Daffodils 1988]
7W-W	'Nancegollan'	[M. P. Williams 1937]
2Y-R	'Narvik'	[J. L. Richardson 1940]
3Y-R	'Narya'	[B. S. Duncan 1978]
1W-W	'Navarone'	[T. Bloomer 1985]
2Y-W	'Nazareth'	[G. E. Mitsch 1958]
3W-R	'Nendrum'	[Ballydorn Bulb Farm 1975]
2Y-R	'Nevta'	[J. M. de Navarro via Rathowen Daffodils 1988]
7Y-W	'New Day'	[G. E. Mitsch 1972]
3Y-Y	'New Penny'	[W. G. Pannill 1972]
2W-GYY	'New Song'	[G. E. Mitsch 1963]
2W-P	'New Star'	[Mrs J. L. Richardson 1978]
2Y-YYP	'New World'	[M. E. Jefferson-Brown 1984]
1W-Y	'Newcastle'	[W. J. Dunlop 1957] M-DGP
4Y-O	'Newton Ferres'	[Mrs J. L. Richardson 1986]
5W-W	'Niveth'	[H. Backhouse 1931]
2W-GPP	'Normanton'	[Mrs J. L. Richardson 1978]
2W-ORR	'Northern Light'	[J. L. Richardson 1958]
2W-YYR	'Northern Sceptre'	[Ballydorn Bulb Farm 1975]
2W-R	'Norval'	[J. L. Richardson 1959]
3W-R	'Norwood'	[Mrs J. L. Richardson 1977]
6W-Y	'Noss Mayo'	[Rosewarne E. H. S. 1986]
3W-GYO	'Notable'	[Ballydorn Bulb Farm 1979]
3W-YPO	'Nouvelle'	[Ballydorn Bulb Farm 1969]
3W-WWY	'Noweta'	[G. E. Mitsch 1963]
2W-W	'Nuage'	[G. H. Johnstone 1949]
12W-W	'Nylon'	[D. Blanchard 1949] M
6W-P	'Nymphette'	[B. S. Duncan 1978]
1Y-Y	'Oadby'	[W. A. Noton 1985]

3Y-Y	'Oakwood' [S. J. Bisdee 1966]	
4Y-O	'Ocarino' [J. L. Richardson 1964]	
1W-W	'Ocean Mist' [P. Phillips 1966]	
7W-W	'Ocean Spray' [G. E. Mitsch 1966]	
11Y-GYY	'Oecumene' [J. Gerritsen 1970]	
2W-P	'Oharabrook' [Mrs J. L. Richardson 1978]	
2W-ORR	'Ohio' [J. M. de Navarro 1966]	
2W-Y	'Old Satin' [G. E. Mitsch 1967]	
1Y-Y	'Olympic Gold' [J. L. Richardson 1963]	
3W-GOO	'Omagh' [T. Bloomer 1968]	
3W-YYR	'Omaha' [Ballydorn Bulb Farm 1974]	
2Y-Y	'Oneonta' [M. W. Evans 1968]	
2W-P	'Opal Pearl' [Mrs J. Abel Smith 1976]	
2W-PPY	'Opalescent' [G. E. Mitsch 1972]	
2W-P	'Ophelia' [J. L. Richardson 1967]	
2W-O	'Orange Beacon' [Carncairn Daffodils 1978]	
2W-O	'Orange Lodge' [B. S. Duncan 1978]	
7O-O	'Orange Queen' [The Brodie of Brodie pre-1908]	
2Y-YOY	'Orange Sherbet' [Carncairn Daffodils 1979]	
11W-POY	'Orangery' [J. Gerritsen 1957]	RD
1Y-Y	'Oratia' [Mrs M. Verry 1965]	
2W-Y	'Oratorio' [G. E. Mitsch 1959]	
2W-O	'Orion' [J. L. Richardson 1959]	M
2Y-Y	'Ormeau' [W. J. Dunlop 1949]	BB
7Y-W	'Oryx' [G. E. Mitsch 1969]	
3W-R	'Osmington' [J. W. Blanchard 1974]	
2W-GYR	'Ottoman Gold' [Ballydorn Bulb Farm 1986]	
1Y-Y	'Owen Roe' [Ballydorn Bulb Farm 1983]	
1W-Y	'Owston Wood' [W. A. Noton 1976]	
3W-Y	'Oykel' [J. S. B. Lea 1978]	
3Y-GYO	'Painted Desert' [T. D. Throckmorton 1974]	
3W-YYR	'Pakatoa' [G. Lewis 1968]	
2Y-Y	'Pale Sunlight' [Carncairn Daffodils 1983]	
1W-W	'Pallidus Praecox' = N. pallidiflorus	
3W-YRR	'Palmyra' [G. E. Mitsch 1970]	
1W-W	'Panache' [G. L. Wilson 1962]	M
2W-GWY	'Pankot' [Carncairn Daffodils 1984]	
8W-W	'Paper White' [Pre-1576]	RD
8W-W	'Paper White Grandiflora' [Pre-1887]	DGP
11W-W	'Papillon Blanc' [J. W. A. Lefeber 1960]	M-RD
4Y-Y	'Papua' [J. L. Richardson 1961]	
7Y-O	'Parcpat' [M. P. Williams 1937]	
4W-P	'Parfait' [M. W. Evans 1975]	
2Y-R	'Paricutin' [G. E. Mitsch 1952]	
11W-O	'Parisienne' [J. Gerritsen 1961]	RD
2Y-YYR	'Park Royal' [A. Gibson 1951]	
3W-WWY	'Park Springs' [Mrs J. Abel Smith 1972]	M
2W-O	'Parkdene' [T. Bloomer 1984]	
2W-W	'Parkmore' [G. L. Wilson 1969]	
2W-R	'Parkridge' [T. Bloomer via Rathowen Daffodils 1984]	
2W-Y	'Parterre' [T. Bloomer 1983]	
4W-Y	'Parthenon' [J. L. Richardson via Carncairn Daffodils 1988]	
2W-P	'Passionale' [G. L. Wilson 1956]	M-BB-RD
2Y-WWY	'Pastorale' [G. E. Mitsch 1965]	
2Y-R	'Patabundy' [Rathowen Daffodils 1987]	
3W-WWY	'Paula Cottell' [A. Gray 1961]	
11W-P	'Pearlax' [J. Gerritsen 1971]	
11W-Y	'Pearl-shell' [J. Gerritsen 1969]	
1W-W	'Pearly King' [W. A. Noton]	M
6Y-Y	'Peeping Tom' [P. D. Williams 1927]	DGP-RD

4Y-Y	'Pencrebar'	[H. G. Hawker pre-1929] **M**
1W-Y	'Pennine Way'	[F. E. Board 1965]
2W-GPP	'Pennybridge'	[Carncairn Daffodils 1975]
7Y-Y	'Penpol'	[P. D. Williams 1935]
1Y-Y	'Pentille'	[Mrs J. L. Richardson 1979]
2W-Y	'Penvose'	[P. D. Williams 1927]
1W-Y	'Penyoke'	[du Plessis Bros] **BB**
2Y-R	'Pepper'	[J. C. Williams 1933]
9W-GYR	'Perdita'	[D. W. Gourlay 1963]
3Y-YYR	'Perimeter'	[J. L. Richardson 1956]
6W-Y	'Perky'	[G. E. Mitsch 1970]
1W-W	'Perseus'	[J. L. Richardson 1963]
7Y-O	'Pet Finch'	[M. E. Jefferson-Brown 1975]
4Y-P	'Petit Four'	[Rijnveld 1961]
5W-W	'Petrel'	[G. E. Mitsch 1970]
1W-W	'Petsamo'	[J. L. Richardson 1944]
3W-YYO	'Picasso'	[Carncairn Daffodils 1984]
11W-O	'Pick Up'	[J. Gerritsen 1968] **RD**
2Y-R	'Pimm'	[T. Bloomer 1985]
2W-W	'Pinafore'	[G. E. Mitsch 1966]
2W-P	'Pink Beauty'	[G. L. Wilson 1957]
4W-P	'Pink Champagne'	[Mrs J. L. Richardson 1972]
4W-P	'Pink Chiffon'	[Kanouse 1963]
1W-P	'Pink Delight'	[Mrs C. O. Fairbairn]
2W-YYP	'Pink Fancy'	[van Leeuwen 1943]
4W-P	'Pink Gin'	[Mrs J. L. Richardson 1976]
2Y-P	'Pink Mink'	[B. S. Duncan 1978]
2W-P	'Pink Monarch'	[C. E. Radcliffe 1950]
4W-P	'Pink Pageant'	[B. S. Duncan 1976]
2W-P	'Pink Panther'	[Mrs J. Abel Smith 1974] **M**
4W-P	'Pink Paradise'	[B. S. Duncan 1976]
2W-YYP	'Pink Rim'	[van Leeuwen 1939]
2W-P	'Pink Smiles'	[W. J. Dunlop 1953]
2W-P	'Pink Whispers'	[Mrs J. Abel Smith 1976]
2Y-YOR	'Pinza'	[J. L. Richardson 1962]
2Y-R	'Pipe Major'	[F. E. Board 1965] **BB**
7Y-Y	'Piper's Barn'	[A. Gray 1947]
3W-GWW	'Piper's End'	[Mrs J. Abel Smith 1984]
7Y-W	'Pipit'	[G. E. Mitsch 1963]
2W-O	'Pirate King'	[J. L. Richardson 1956]
2W-WWP	'Pismo Beach'	[B. S. Duncan 1978]
2W-GWW	'Pitchroy'	[J. S. B. Lea 1973]
3W-Y	'Pixie's Parlour'	[Carncairn Daffodils 1970]
3W-GGY	'Pixie's Pool'	[Carncairn Daffodils 1979]
3Y-YYO	'Planet'	[G. E. Mitsch 1982]
2Y-O	'Playboy'	[G. L. Wilson 1944]
3W-YYO	'Playschool'	[Carncairn Daffodils 1969]
9W-GYR	'Poet's Way'	[T. Bloomer 1975]
9W-GYR	'Poet's Wings'	[T. Bloomer 1976]
2W-P	'Pol Dornie'	[J. S. B. Lea 1978]
2W-P	'Pol Voulin'	[J. S. B. Lea 1983]
2W-W	'Polar Circle'	[Carncairn Daffodils 1982]
3W-W	'Polar Ice'	[G. Lubbe 1937]
3W-W	'Polar Imp'	[Rev. Philpott 1973]
2Y-R	'Polbathic'	[B. S. Duncan 1986]
3W-GWW	'Polglass'	[J. S. B. Lea 1980]
8W-R	'Polglase'	[P. D. Williams 1927]
2W-Y	'Polindra'	[P. D. Williams 1927]
7Y-Y	'Polnesk'	[P. D. Williams 1927] **BB**-DGP
2W-P	'Polonaise'	[Mrs J. L. Richardson 1974]

2W-Y	'Pontresina'	[J. L. Richardson 1958]
3W-GGW	'Port Erin'	[Ballydorn Bulb Farm 1980]
2W-w	'Portavo'	[Carncairn Daffodils 1978]
7Y-Y	'Porthchapel'	[R. V. Favell pre-1953]
3W-GWW	'Portrush'	[G. L. Wilson 1947]
3W-W	'Portstewart'	[Ballydorn Bulb Farm 1971]
6Y-Y	'Post Horn'	[Rosewarne E. H. S.]
1W-Y	'Preamble'	[G. L. Wilson 1946] **DGP**-DGP
2W-YPP	'Precedent'	[G. L. Wilson 1947]
2W-GPP	'Premiere'	[B. S. Duncan 1973]
2Y-GYY	'President Carter'	[D. van Buggenum 1978]
1W-Y	'President Lebrun'	[P. D. Williams 1942]
2W-P	'Pretty Polly'	[J. L. Richardson 1958]
8W-YRR	'Pride of Cornwall'	[P. D. Williams 1933]
2W-P	'Primrose Path'	[Carncairn Daffodils 1983]
3W-YYR	'Prince'	[A. T. van Craven pre-1934]
1Y-Y	'Prince Igor'	[J. O. Sherrard pre-1943]
2W-Y	'Prince of Brunswick'	[Ballydorn Bulb Farm 1976]
	'Princeps' = **N. gayi**	
3W-GWW	'Princess Zaide'	[Mrs J. Abel Smith 1986]
1Y-Y	'Priority'	[G. L. Wilson 1945]
3W-O	'Privateer'	[J. L. Richardson 1958]
1Y-Y	'Prizewinner'	[D. van Buggenum 1971]
2W-R	'Professor Einstein'	[J. W. A. Lefeber 1946] **RD**
1W-Y	'Prologue'	[G. E. Mitsch 1962]
1Y-YYP	'Prophet'	[H. R. Barr 1975]
3W-O	'Prospero'	[J. L. Richardson 1958]
7W-W	'Pueblo'	[G. E. Mitsch 1966]
5Y-O	'Puppet'	[G. E. Mitsch 1970]
6Y-Y	'Puppy'	[M. E. Jefferson-Brown 1984]
3W-YYO	'Purbeck'	[J. W. Blanchard 1971] M
2W-W	'Purity'	[G. L. Wilson 1960]
7Y-Y	'Quail'	[G E. Mitsch 1974]
1W-Y	'Queen of Bicolors'	[E. H. Krelage 1940] RD
3W-Y	'Queen of the North'	[Barr 1908]
1W-W	'Queenscourt'	[G. L. Wilson 1956] M
2W-P	'Queensland'	[G. H. Barr 1954]
9W-GYR	'Quetzal'	[G. E. Mitsch 1965]
7W-P	'Quick Step'	[G. E. Mitsch 1965]
2W-GPP	'Quiet Day'	[Carncairn Daffodils 1983]
6Y-Y	'Quince'	[A. Gray 1953]
2Y-YRR	'Quirinus'	[G. Lubbe 1939]
2Y-R	'Rademon'	[Carncairn Daffodils 1973]
2W-P	'Radiation'	[G. E. Mitsch 1954]
6Y-Y	'Radical'	[Rosewarne E. H. S. 1985]
2W-WWP	'Rainbow'	[J. L. Richardson 1961] M
2W-GYO	'Ramada'	[B. S. Duncan 1978]
1Y-Y	'Rame Head'	[B. S. Duncan 1981]
2W-R	'Rameses'	[J. L. Richardson 1960]
2W-P	'Rarkmoyle'	[Carncairn Daffodils 1969]
1W-W	'Rashee'	[G. L. Wilson 1952]
2W-GWP	'Raspberry Ring'	[J. M. de Navarro 1977]
2W-Y	'Rathgar'	[W. J. Dunlop 1960]
2Y-R	'Rathowen Flame'	[T. Bloomer 1973]
1Y-Y	'Rathowen Gold'	[T. Bloomer 1973]
3W-GYO	'Ravenhill'	[T. Bloomer 1984]
3W-GYR	'Reckless'	[Carncairn Daffodils 1987]
1Y-O	'Red Arrow'	[W. O. Backhouse 1968]
2Y-R	'Red Bay'	[W. J. Dunlop 1978]
2W-YYR	'Red Cottage'	[Carncairn Daffodils 1973]
1Y-R	'Red Curtain'	[W. O. Backhouse 1956]

2W-R	'Red Devil'	[Carncairn Daffodils 1973]
2Y-O	'Red Devon'	[E. B. Champernowne 1943]	RD
2W-O	'Red Hackle'	[The Brodie of Brodie 1937]
3W-O	'Red Hall'	[Carncairn Daffodils 1983]
2O-R	'Red Hot'	[J. O'More 1975]
2Y-R	'Red Lory'	[G. E. Mitsch 1970]
2Y-YYR	'Red Mars'	[D. S. Bell 1963]
2W-O	'Red Marshal'	[Mrs J. L. Richardson 1976]
2Y-R	'Red Ranger'	[W. J. Dunlop 1953]
2Y-R	'Red Rascal'	[Warnaar & Co pre-1950]
3W-R	'Red Rooster'	[B. S. Duncan 1978]
2Y-R	'Red Rum'	[Mrs J. L. Richardson 1973]
3Y-R	'Red Snapper'	[Mrs J. Abel-Smith 1988]
2Y-R	'Red Spartan'	[B. S. Duncan 1983]
2Y-R	'Redman'	[Ballydorn Bulb Farm 1975]
3W-GWO	'Redstart'	[G. E. Mitsch 1959]
2W-GWW	'Regal Bliss'	[B. S. Duncan 1982]
3W-YOO	'Regality'	[Rijnveld 1957]
6W-GPP	'Reggae'	[B. S. Duncan 1981]
2W-Y	'Reliance'	[M. E. Jefferson-Brown 1975]
1Y-Y	'Rembrandt'	[G. Lubbe 1930]	DGP-RD
1W-Y	'Renvyle'	[J. L. Richardson 1963]
4W-P	'Replete'	[M. W. Evans 1975]	M
3W-GWY	'Reprieve'	[G. L. Wilson 1947]
2Y-R	'Resplendent'	[G. E. Mitsch 1977]
2Y-R	'Revelry'	[J. L. Richardson 1964]
1Y-Y	'Revenge'	[J. L. Richardson 1964]
2YW-W	'Reverie'	[B. S. Duncan 1979]
1Y-Y	'Reuter'	[G. Tarry via du Plessis Bros 1988]
4W-R	'Revival'	[M. J. Jefferson-Brown pre-1985]
1Y-Y	'Reward'	[G. W. E. Brogden 1963]
1W-Y	'Rhinestone'	[B. S. Duncan 1979]
1Y-W	'Rich Reward'	[G. E. Mitsch 1968]
2Y-YYR	'Richhill'	[W. J. Dunlop 1958]
3W-Y	'Riding Mill'	[G. Harrison 1968]
11W-WWY	'Riesling'	[J. Gerritsen 1974]
2Y-R	'Right Royal'	[Ballydorn Bulb Farm 1980]
1Y-Y	'Rijnvald's Early Sensation'	[F. H. Chapman 1943]
1W-P	'Rima'	[G. E. Mitsch 1954]	M
3W-GWY	'Rimmon'	[B. S. Duncan 1981]
2W-YWP	'Rimski'	[B. S. Duncan 1984]
2W-YWP	'Rimster'	[B. S. Duncan 1984]
2W-YYR	'Ringleader'	[Mrs J. L. Richardson 1972]
2Y-YYO	'Ringmaster'	[J. L. Richardson 1953]
3W-YYR	'Ringway'	[B. S. Duncan 1978]
2O-R	'Rio Bravo'	[Ballydorn Bulb Farm 1986]
2O-R	'Rio Gusto'	[Ballydorn Bulb Farm 1981]
2O-R	'Rio Rouge'	[Ballydorn Bulb Farm 1974]
5W-W	'Rippling Waters'	[Barr 1932]	M-RD
1Y-W	'Riptide'	[D. S. Bell 1971]
4	'Rip van Winkle' (N. pumilus 'Plenus')	[Irish Origin pre-1885]
1Y-Y	'Ristin'	[W. Jackson jnr. 1979]	M
3W-GYY	'Rivendell'	[B. S. Duncan 1981]
3W-GYY	'Rob Roy'	[J. L. Richardson 1975]
3W-R	'Rockall'	[J. L. Richardson 1955]	M-BB-DGP
2W-YYO	'Rococo'	[van Tubergen 1944]
6Y-O	'Roger'	[A. Gray 1952]
4W-O	'Romanus'	[Pre-1576]
2W-YYP	'Roman Tile'	[G. H. Johnstone 1959]
2W-P	'Romance'	[J. L. Richardson 1959]

3O-R	'Romany Red' [B. S. Duncan 1983]	
8Y-O	'Romeo' [van der Wereld 1962]	
9W-GYR	'Rondo' [A. H. Aherns 1945]	
3W-GPP	'Rosapenna' [Carncairn Daffodils 1978]	
2W-P	'Rose Caprice' [J. L. Richardson 1952]	
2W-P	'Rose City' [M. W. Evans 1969]	
2W-P	'Rose Noble' [G. L. Wilson 1957]	
4W-W	'Rose of May' [G. L. Wilson 1950]	
2W-P	'Rose Royale' [J. L. Richardson 1958]	
2W-P	'Roseate Tern' [J. M. de Navarro 1975]	
2W-P	'Rosedew' [J. L. Richardson 1962]	
2W-P	'Roseworthy' [D. Blanchard 1953]	RD
2W-GYR	'Rossferry' [Ballydorn Bulb Farm 1986]	
4W-P	'Rosy Cloud' [van Zanten 1968]	
2W-WWP	'Rosy Diamond' [G. L. Wilson 1960]	
2W-YYP	'Rosy Sunrise' [Rijnveld 1939]	
1W-P	'Rosy Trumpet' [R. O. Backhouse 1952]	
3Y-R	'Rotarian' [T. Bloomer 1982]	
2Y-YYR	'Round Robin' [Carncairn Daffodils 1985]	
1Y-Y	'Rowallane' [G. L. Wilson 1960]	
1Y-Y	'Royal Armour' [O. Ronalds 1967]	
2W-WPP	'Royal Ballet' [B. S. Duncan 1984]	
2W-GYO	'Royal Coachman' [M. W. Evans 1969]	
	'Royal Command' = N. 'Royal Decree'	
2W-YPP	'Royal Decree' [M. J. Jefferson-Brown 1985]	
1Y-Y	'Royal Oak' [J. L. Richardson 1961]	
2W-WPP	'Royal Occasion' [Mrs J. Abel Smith 1982]	
2W-O	'Royal Orange' [Uit den Boogaard 1953]	
2W-WWR	'Royal Princess' [Mrs J. Abel Smith 1985]	
2W-R	'Royal Regiment' [J. L. Richardson 1955]	
2Y-O	'Royal Revel' [J. L. Richardson 1967]	
2W-GWY	'Royal Wedding' [Carncairn Daffodils 1982]	
2W-ORR	'Rubh Mor' [J. S. B. Lea 1971]	M
2W-R	'Ruby Tail' [J. L. Richardson 1959]	
2W-P	'Rubythroat' [G. E. Mitsch 1969]	M
2W-P	'Rufford' [Mrs J. Abel Smith 1983]	BB
	'Rugulosus' = N. x odorus 'Rugulosus'	
3W-Y	'Rushcliffe' [Mrs J. Abel Smith 1983]	
2Y-W	'Rushlight' [A. Wilson 1957]	
5Y-Y	'Ruth Haller' [C. R. Phillips 1968]	
2W-W	'Rutland Water' [W. A. Noton 1985]	M
3Y-GYY	'Ryan Son' [Mrs J. Abel Smith 1986]	
2Y-O	'Rytha' [Mrs J. L. Richardson 1978]	
3O-R	'Sabine Hay' [D. B. Milne 1970]	M
2Y-O	'Sacajawea' [G. E. Mitsch 1954]	
3W-GWW	'Sacramento' [J. M. de Navarro 1949]	
2Y-O	'Safari' [J. L. Richardson 1972]	
2W-GWP	'Salmon Leap' [Carncairn Daffodils 1979]	
2W-P	'Salmon Spray' [J. L. Richardson 1967]	
2W-P	'Salmon Trout' [J. L. Richardson 1948]	DGP
2W-PPY	'Salome' [J. L. Richardson 1958]	BB-RD
1W-WYY	'Saltermill' [Mrs J. L. Richardson 1976]	
4W-P	'Samantha' [Mrs J. L. Richardson 1972]	
3W-W	'Samaria' [The Brodie of Brodie 1923]	
5Y-R	'Samba' [Barr 1952]	
1W-W	'Samite' [G. L. Wilson 1930]	
2W-O	'Sammy Boy' [Barr 1972]	
11W-Y	'Sancerre' [J. Gerritsen 1974]	M
4W-W	'Santa Claus' [G. L. Wilson 1950]	
2W-WWP	'Santa Rosa' [J. L. Richardson 1973]	

9W-GYR	'Sarchedon' [Rev. G. H. Engleheart 1913]	
	'Sarah'	
2W-YPP	'Sateen' [Barr 1968]	
6Y-O	'Satellite' [G. E. Mitsch 1962]	
2W-P	'Satin Pink' [J. L. Richardson 1958]	
3W-GYO	'Saturn' [Carncairn Daffodils 1978]	
3Y-R	'Scarlet Elegance' [P. D. Williams 1938]	
8Y-R	'Scarlet Gem' [P. D. Williams 1910]	
2Y-R	'Scarlet Royal' [G. Lubbe 1948]	
3W-GYR	'Scarlet Thread' [J. M. de Navarro 1977]	
2Y-R	'Scarlett O'Hara' [H. P. Zwetsloot & Sons 1950]	
2W-O	'Scolboa' [Carncairn Daffodils 1973]	
1Y-Y	'Scoreline' [B. S. Duncan 1977]	
1Y-Y	'Scotney Castle' [N. A. Burr 1985]	
3W-GWW	'Sea Dream' [J. O'More 1968]	
9W-GGR	'Sea Green' [Rev. G. H. Engleheart 1930]	M
3W-GYY	'Sea Princess' [Mrs J. Abel Smith 1984]	
3W-GRR	'Sealed Orders' [J. M. de Navarro 1977]	
2Y-R	'Sealing Wax' [Barr 1957]	M
3W-YYO	'Seaton' [Mrs J. L. Richardson 1981]	
2W-Y	'Sebastapol' [J. L. Richardson 1945]	
2W-P	'Sedate' [P. Phillips 1967]	
2W-Y	'Segovia' [F. M. Gray 1962]	M
2W-P	'Seltan' [G. L. Wilson 1960]	
2W-O	'Sempre Avanti' [de Graaf 1938]	M
6W-GWW	'Sextant' [B. S. Duncan 1981]	
7Y-Y	'Shah' [Barr 1949]	
2W-YOY	'Shandon' [B. S. Duncan 1979]	
1Y-Y	'Shanes Castle' [Carncairn Daffodils 1978]	
2W-P	'She' [M. E. Jefferson-Brown 1978]	
2W-YOY	'Sheik' [Carncairn Daffodils 1978]	
2W-P	'Shell Bay' [J. W. Blanchard 1974]	
1W-W	'Sherpa' [B. S. Duncan 1986]	
2Y-O	'Sheviock' [T. Bloomer via du Plessis Bros 1987]	
2Y-YYO	'Shieldaig' [J. S. B. Lea 1964]	
2Y-ORR	'Shining Light' [F. E. Board 1965]	M
5W-R	'Shot Silk' [de Graaf 1933]	
2W-YYO	'Showboat' [M. W. Evans 1970]	
2W-Y	'Shriner' [M. W. Evans 1972]	
6W-O	'Shuttlecock' [B. S. Duncan 1977]	
2W-GWP	'Shy Face' [Carncairn Daffodils 1982]	
3W-GYY	'Sidley' [T. Bloomer 1982]	
2W-O	'Signal Light' [J. L. Richardson 1948]	
3W-YYR	'Silent Beauty' [T. Bloomer 1964]	
3W-YYR	'Silent Cheer' [T. Bloomer 1964]	M
3W-YYR	'Silent Grace' [T. Bloomer 1964]	
3W-YYO	'Silent Morn' [T. Bloomer 1964]	
1W-W	'Silent Valley' [T. Bloomer 1964]	M
3W-YYO	'Silent Wonder' [T. Bloomer 1964]	
2W-GWW	'Silk Cut' [B. S. Duncan 1986]	
3W-WWY	'Silken Sails' [G. E. Mitsch 1964]	
5W-W	'Silver Bells' [G. E. Mitsch 1962]	
2W-GWW	'Silver Blaze' [B. S. Duncan 1978]	
8W-W	'Silver Chimes' [E. Martin 1916]	DGP
1W-W	'Silver Convention' [J. S. B. Lea 1978]	M
3Y-Y	'Silver Howard' [G. H. Johnstone 1971]	
3W-WWY	'Silver Leopard' [J. L. Richardson 1972]	M
3W-W	'Silver Moon' [Barr & Sons 1908]	
3W-GWY	'Silver Phantom' [Mrs J. Abel-Smith 1987]	
3W-GWW	'Silver Princess' [W. J. Dunlop 1953]	

2W-Y	'Silver Standard'	[van Tubergen 1944]
2W-W	'Silver Surf'	[B. S. Duncan via Rathowen Daffodils 1978]
2W-W	'Silvermere'	[B. S. Duncan 1981]
2W-W	'Silversmith'	[W. A. Noton 1985] M
2W-GPP	'Simile'	[J. L. Richardson 1973]
1Y-Y	'Sir Ivor'	[Mrs J. L. Richardson 1972]
2W-GRR	'Sir Knight'	[T. Bloomer 1962]
4W-O	'Sir Winston Churchill'	[H. A. Holmes 1966]
3Y-Y	'Skookum'	[M. W. Evans 1976]
3Y-Y	'Slaney'	[Carncairn Daffodils 1987]
1Y-Y	'Slieveboy'	[G. L. Wilson 1953]
3W-GYO	'Slowcoach'	[B. S. Duncan 1979]
2Y-R	'Smiling Maestro'	[G. E. Mitsch 1964]
4O-R	'Smokey Bear'	[B. S. Duncan 1978] M
9W-GOR	'Smyrna'	[The Brodie of Brodie 1927]
6W-GPP	'Snoopie'	[B. S. Duncan 1979]
7W-Y	'Snow Bunting'	[P. D. Williams 1935]
2W-W	'Snow Dream'	[W. J. Dunlop 1953]
3W-R	'Snow Gem'	[Culpepper 1957]
1W-GWW	'Snow Gleam'	[B. S. Duncan 1977]
3W-W	'Snow Magic'	[Carncairn Daffodils 1973]
3W-GWW	'Snowcrest'	[Mrs J. L. Richardson 1972] M
4W-R	'Snowfire'	[Mrs J. L. Richardson 1976]
2W-GWW	'Snowshill'	[J. M. de Navarro 1949]
2Y-R	'Soldier Brave'	[M. E. Jefferson-Brown 1978]
2W-W	'Soledad'	[Mrs J. L. Richardson 1978]
	'Soleil d'Or' = N. 'Grand Soleil d'Or'	
9W-GYR	'Sonata'	[Rev. G. H. Engleheart 1910]
2YW-Y	'Sophia'	[Mrs J. L. Richardson 1980]
2W-P	'Sophie Girl'	[Mrs J. Abel Smith 1984]
3W-YYR	'Sorcerer'	[Carncairn Daffodils 1982]
2W-P	'Southgrove'	[F. E. Board 1965]
1Y-Y	'Southgate'	[W. A. Noton pre-1985]
2Y-Y	'Space Age'	[M. W. Evans 1965]
1Y-Y	'Spanish Gold'	[J. L. Richardson 1948]
1W-GWW	'Spanish Moon'	[G. L. Wilson 1965]
8W-GOO	'Sparkling Eye'	[van der Schoot 1931]
3W-R	'Spectrum'	[D. S. Bell 1963]
2W-W	'Spelga'	[Ballydorn Bulb Farm 1975]
1Y-W	'Spellbinder'	[G. L. Wilson 1944] BB-DGP-RD
2W-O	'Spencer Tracy'	[J. W. A. Lefeber 1943]
2W-O	'Spey Bay'	[B. S. Duncan 1981]
11W-W	'Split'	[J. Gerritsen 1957]
2W-P	'Sportsman'	[B. S. Duncan 1979]
2W-P	'Spring Fashion'	[Mrs J. L. Richardson 1977]
2W-R	'Spring Magic'	[T. Bloomer 1970]
2Y-YPP	'Spring Morn'	[G. E. Mitsch 1984]
3W-GYY	'Spring Valley'	[Carncairn Daffodils 1984]
2W-W	'Springston Charm'	[L. J. Chambers 1980]
2W-W	'Springston Gem'	[L. J. Chambers 1980]
2W-GWW	'Springwood'	[B. S. Duncan 1986]
6W-YYP	'Sputnik'	[B. S. Duncan 1978]
1Y-Y	'Squire'	[Mrs J. Abel Smith 1969]
8W-O	'St Agnes'	[P. D. Williams pre-1926]
3W-R	'St Anns'	[Mrs J. L. Richardson 1978]
2Y-Y	'St Egwin'	[P. D. Williams 1927]
2W-W	'St Dilpe'	[B. S. Duncan via du Plessis Bros 1987]
2Y-Y	'St Keverne'	[P. D. Williams 1949] M-RD
8W-O	'St Keyne'	[P. D. Williams 1927]
2Y-O	'St Mawes'	[T. Bloomer 1985]

2W-OOY	'St Mellion' [Mrs J. L. Richardson 1978]	
2Y-Y	'St Patrick's Day' [Konyenburg & Mark 1964]	
2W-Y	'Stadium' [J. L. Richardson 1948]	
2W-W	'Stainless' [G. L. Wilson 1960]	
1Y-Y	'Standard Value' [Geerlings 1949]	
1Y-Y	'Standfast' [T. Bloomer 1982]	
2Y-R	'Star War' [T. Bloomer 1984]	
7Y-O	'Starfire' [Hyde 1959]	
3W-R	'Starlight Express' [Mrs J. Abel-Smith 1978]	
2Y-GOO	'State Express' [B. S. Duncan 1983]	
2W-Y	'Statue' [J. L. Richardson 1938]	
2W-WWP	'Staythorpe' [Mrs J. Abel Smith 1985]	
7Y-W	'Step Forward' [G. E. Mitsch 1970]	
1Y-Y	'Sterling' [G. L. Wilson 1956]	
6Y-Y	'Stint' [M. Fowlds 1970]	
3W	'Stocken' [A. M. Wilson pre-1950]	
2Y-YOO	'Stourbridge' [J. S. B. Lea 1974]	M
3W-GYR	'Strangford' [Ballydorn Bulb Farm 1970]	
1Y-Y	'Strathkanaird' [J. S. B. Lea 1959]	
7Y-O	'Stratosphere' [G. E. Mitsch 1968]	M
6W-WPP	'Stray' [Carncairn Daffodils 1983]	
1Y-Y	'Strephon' [Carncairn Daffodils 1982]	
2Y-Y	'Strines' [F. E. Board 1965]	M
2W-O	'Stromboli' [J. L. Richardson 1959]	
2W-P	'Student Prince' [B. S. Duncan 1977]	
3Y-Y	'Suave' [Dr T. D. Throckmorton 1976]	M
2Y-GOO	'Suda Bay' [Carncairn Daffodils 1984]	
7W-YYW	'Sugarbush' [A. Gray 1946]	RD
3W-W	'Suilven' [J. S. B. Lea 1956]	BB
4W-PPY	'Suisgill' [J. S. B. Lea 1983]	
1Y-W	'Sun 'n Snow' [G. E. Mitsch 1970]	
2Y-O	'Sun Chariot' [J. L. Richardson 1943]	DGP
1Y-Y	'Sun City' [Mrs J. Abel Smith 1983]	
7Y-Y	'Sun Disc' [A. Gray 1946]	M
3Y-R	'Sun Gleam' [T. Bloomer 1972]	
2Y-R	'Sun Salver' [Ballydorn Bulb Farm 1976]	
3Y-YYR	'Sunapee' [M. W. Evans 1969]	M
2Y-R	'Sunbather' [Carncairn Daffodils 1984]	
7Y-Y	'Sundial' [A. Gray 1955]	
7Y-R	'Susan Pearson' [R. V. Favell 1954]	
7Y-O	'Suzy' [R. V. Favell 1954]	M-RD
6Y-O	'Swallowcliffe' [J. W. Blanchard 1986]	
1Y-Y	'Swallownest' [F. E. Board 1965]	
4W-W	'Swansdown' [The Brodie of Brodie 1939]	
2W-WWY	'Sweet Harmony' [Rijnveld 1956]	
4W-W	'Sweet Music' [G. E. Mitsch 1965]	
7Y-O	'Sweet Pepper' [R. V. Favell 1939]	
7Y-Y	'Sweetness' [B. S. Duncan 1982]	BB
6W-GPP	'Swing Wing' [B. S. Duncan 1982]	
3W-ORR	'Sword Play' [F. E. Board 1965]	
5W-GWW	'Sydling' [J. W. Blanchard 1977]	
1W-W	'Sylvan Hill' [Ballydorn Bulb Farm 1984]	
2Y-Y	'Symphonette' [G. E. Mitsch 1975]	
3W-WWY	'Syracuse' [J. L. Richardson 1958]	
12W-W	'Taffeta' [D. Blanchard 1952]	
4Y-R	'Tahiti' [J. L. Richardson 1956]	M-RD
1W-W	'Tain' [The Brodie of Brodie 1933]	
4Y-R	'Tamar Fire' [Mrs J. L. Richardson 1976]	
2W-GWW	'Tamar Snow' [B. S. Duncan 1986]	
2Y-ORR	'Tanera' [J. S. B. Lea 1959]	

2W-P	'Tangent' [G. E. Mitsch 1969]	
1W-Y	'Tannaghmore' [T. Bloomer 1973]	
2W-P	'Tara Rose' [Mrs J. L. Richardson 1972]	
1W-GPP	'Tardree' [Carncairn Daffodils 1987]	
2Y-R	'Target' [G. H. Johnstone pre-1960]	
12W-W	'Tarlatan' [D. Blanchard 1952]	
2O-R	'Tawny Lad' [Mrs J. L. Richardson 1976]	
1W-W	'Tedstone' [M. E. Jefferson-Brown 1978]	
1Y-Y	'Tenterfield' [Mrs J. Abel Smith 1985]	
2W-YPP	'Testament' [M. E. Jefferson-Brown 1985]	
6Y-O	'Tete-a-Tete' [A. Gray 1949]	M-**BB**-RD
4Y-O	'Texas' [Mrs R. O. Backhouse 1928]	
9W-GYR	'Thackeray' [B. S. Duncan 1979]	
5W-W	'Thalia' [van Waveren 1916]	DGP-**RD**
2W-Y	'Theano' [G. L. Wilson 1959]	
	'The Prince' = **N. 'Prince'**	
	'The Star' = **N. 'The Sun'**	
3W-O	'The Sun' [C. van Zonneveld pre-1926]	
5Y-Y	'Thoughtful' [A. Gray 1951]	
1Y-Y	'Thrumpton' [Mrs J. Abel Smith 1984]	
1Y-O	'Thunderbolt' [M. E. Jefferson-Brown 1975]	
2W-W	'Tibet' [G. L. Wilson 1942]	
6W-P	'Tiger Moth' [B. S. Duncan 1981]	
3Y-R	'Timandaw' [W. Jackson jnr 1970]	
3Y-GYR	'Timolin' [Carncairn Daffodils 1985]	
3W-GWY	'Tingford' [Mrs J. Abel-Smith 1987]	
2Y-O	'Tinker' [G. L. Wilson 1937]	
1W-Y	'Tinnell' [Mrs J. L. Richardson 1978]	
11Y-O	'Tiritomba' [J. Gerritsen 1974]	
6W-W	'Titania' [J. L. Richardson 1958]	
7Y-Y	'Tittle Tattle' [C. R. Wooton 1953]	
3W-GWW	'Tobernaveen' [G. L. Wilson 1960]	
2Y-R	'Toby' [M. P. Williams 1957]	
2W-P	'Tollymore' [Ballydorn Bulb Farm 1984]	
3W-YYO	'Tommy Lawton' [Rijnveld 1957]	
2W-WWP	'Tomphubil' [J. M. de Navarro 1979]	
4Y-R	'Tonga' [J. L. Richardson 1958]	
2Y-Y	'Toorak Gold' [J. N. Hancock 1965]	
3W-Y	'Top Gallant' [Ballydorn Bulb Farm 1971]	
2Y-Y	'Top Notch' [G. E. Mitsch 1970]	
3W-GWY	'Top of The Hill' [Ballydorn Bulb Farm 1981]	
2W-OOY	'Topkapi' [Ballydorn Bulb Farm 1975]	
1Y-Y	'Topolino' [J. Gerritsen 1965]	
2Y-Y	'Torch Bearer' [Ballydorn Bulb Farm 1975]	
3W-R	'Toreador' [J. L. Richardson 1961]	**BB**
2W-W	'Tornamona' [G. L. Wilson 1945]	
2Y-R	'Torridon' [J. S. B. Lea 1964]	
3W-Y	'Torrish' [J. S. B. Lea 1964]	
2W-GWW	'Touch of Silver' [W. A. Noton 1985]	
1Y-Y	'Toujours' [F. E. Board 1965]	
1W-Y	'Tradition' [M. E. Jefferson-Brown 1965]	
3W-WYY	'Tranquil Morn' [G. E. Mitsch 1962]	
4Y-R	'Transmitter' [Mrs J. L. Richardson 1978]	
2W-P	'Tredinnick' [Unknown Origin via du Plessis Bros 1987]	
2Y-OOR	'Tregarrick' [J. S. B. Lea 1985]	
3Y-O	'Trelay' [P. Phillips 1972]	M
2Y-O	'Trematon' [T. Bloomer 1986]	
6W-Y	'Trena' [M. Verry 1971]	
5W-W	'Tresamble' [P. D. Williams 1930]	RD
2W-YPP	'Trevelmond' [T. Bloomer 1986]	

7Y-Y	'Trevithian'	[P. D. Williams 1927]	M-**DGP**-RD
2W-P	'Trewidland'	[B. S. Duncan via du Plessis Bros 1987]	
6Y-Y	'Trewirgie'	[P. D. Williams 1928]	
1Y-Y	'Trewithen'	[G. H. Johnstone 1971]	
2Y-O	'Trifine'	[G. H. Johnstone 1978]	
7Y-O	'Triller'	[G. E. Mitsch 1979]	
3W-GYR	'Trillick'	[B. S. Duncan 1978]	
11Y-Y	'Tripartite'	[R. L. Brook 1980]	
2Y-Y	'Tristram'	[Mrs J. L. Richardson 1976]	
1W-Y	'Trocadero'	[G. Lubbe 1938]	
2W-W	'Troon'	[B. S. Duncan 1978]	
1W-Y	'Trousseau'	[P. D. Williams 1934]	M-DGP-**RD**
3W-GWW	'Troutbeck'	[Mrs J. Abel Smith 1977]	
2W-Y	'Trouville'	[Mrs J. L. Richardson 1974]	
3W-O	'Trudy'	[G. H. Johnstone 1959]	
1W-Y	'Tudor Dance'	[Mrs J. L. Richardson 1977]	
2W-Y	'Tudor Grove'	[Mrs J. L. Richardson 1982]	
2W-Y	'Tudor Love'	[J. L. Richardson 1973]	
2W-Y	'Tudor Minstrel'	[J. L. Richardson 1948]	M-**DGP**-RD
2W-Y	'Tudor Rose'		
5W-Y	'Tuesday's Child'	[D. Blanchard 1964]	M
3W-GYR	'Tullybeg'	[Ballydorn Bulb Farm 1979]	
2W-P	'Tullycore'	[Ballydorn Bulb Farm 1976]	
2W-W	'Tullygirvan'	[Carncairn Daffodils 1976]	
2W-WWY	'Tullyglass'	[J. L. Richardson 1956]	
2W-P	'Tullyroyal'	[Ballydorn Bulb Farm 1975]	
6W-O	'Turncoat'	[B. S. Duncan 1984]	
2W-GWW	'Tutankhamun'	[Mrs J. Abel Smith 1972]	BB
9W-YYR	'Tweedsmouth'	[G. Harrison 1968]	
2W-P	'Tynan'	[Carncairn Daffodils 1973]	
3W-R	'Tyneham'	[J. W. Blanchard 1974]	
3YO-ORR	'Ulster Bank'	[B. S. Duncan 1978]	
2Y-Y	'Ulster Bullion'	[Ballydorn Bulb Farm 1984]	
1Y-Y	'Ulster Prince'	[G. L. Wilson 1950]	
1W-W	'Ulster Queen'	[G. L. Wilson 1962]	DGP
2W-R	'Ulster Star'	[T. Bloomer 1964]	
2Y-O	'Ultimus'	[van Tubergen 1947]	
2Y-O	'Uncle Ben'	[Mrs J. Abel Smith 1980]	
1Y-O	'Uncle Remus'	[W. O. Backhouse 1975]	
2Y-P	'Undertone'	[B. S. Duncan 1977]	
4W-Y	'Unique'	[J. L. Richardson 1961]	M
1Y-Y	'Unsurpassable'	[G. Lubbe 1929]	RD
2W-GWP	'Upper Broughton'	[Mrs J. Abel Smith 1980]	M
6W-P	'Urchin'	[B. S. Duncan 1981]	
2Y-R	'Vagabond'	[J. L. Richardson 1975]	
11W-Y	'Valdrome'	[J. Gerritsen 1965]	RD
3W-GWW	'Valediction'	[Mrs J. L. Richardson 1976]	
2W-P	'Valhalla'	[J. L. Richardson 1962]	
2W-P	'Valinore'	[B. S. Duncan 1978]	
1Y-Y	'Valley Gold'	[E. W. Cotter 1968]	
4Y-Y	'Van Sion'	[Very Old Cultivar] (*N. telamonius* 'Plenus') M-**BB**-RD
2W-WPP	'Vantage'	[M. W. Evans 1970]	
1Y-GYY	'Verdant'	[B. S. Duncan 1979]	
7Y-W	'Verdin'	[G. E. Mitsch 1965]	
3W-R	'Verger'	[van Deursen 1930]	
2W-GYY	'Vernal Prince'	[T. Bloomer 1982]	
3W-GWW	'Vernedale'	[B. S. Duncan 1981]	
3W-W	'Verona'	[J. L. Richardson 1958]	M-RD
9W-GYR	'Vers Libre'	[B. S. Duncan 1984]	

2W-YYO	'Verve' [M. W. Evans 1978]	
3Y-Y	'Verwood' [J. W. Blanchard 1980]	
2W-Y	'Victorious' [R. V. Favell 1954]	
2W-R	'Victory' [J. L. Richardson 1961]	
4W-P	'Viennese Rose' [Mrs J. L. Richardson 1976]	
1W-W	'Vigil' [G. L. Wilson 1947]	M-**BB**-**DGP**
1W-W	'Vigilante' [B. S. Duncan 1977]	M
1Y-Y	'Viking' [J. L. Richardson 1956]	M
2W-W	'Vilna' [A. M. Wilson pre-1944]	
2W-GPP	'Violetta' [B. S. Duncan 1975]	
2W-P	'Violin' [B. S. Duncan 1976]	
7Y-GYY	'Vireo' [G. E. Mitsch 1962]	
9W-GYO	'Virgil' [Rev G. H. Engleheart 1900]	
2Y-Y	'Virtue' [G. L. Wilson 1942]	
11Y-O	'Vivarino' [J. W. A. Lefeber 1968]	
2W-P	'Vocation' [B. S. Duncan 1976]	
2Y-O	'Vulcan' [J. L. Richardson 1956]	
2W-Y	'Wahkeena' [M. W. Evans 1965]	
6W-P	'Waif' [Carncairn Daffodils 1983]	
2W-P	'Walesby' [Mrs J. Abel Smith 1985]	
2Y-P	'Warleigh' [T. Bloomer via du Plessis Bros 1987]	
7W-P	'Waterperry' [R. V. Favell 1953]	
5W-W	'Waxwing' [M. Fowlds 1967]	
9W-GYR	'Webster' [B. S. Duncan 1981]	
2W-W	'Wedding Bell' [W. J. Dunlop 1950]	
1Y-Y	'Wee Bee' [Dutch origin 1948]	
1Y-Y	'Welbeck' [Mrs J, Abel Smith 1975]	
2W-P	'Wellow' [Mrs J. Abel Smith 1979]	
2W-GYY	'Westholme' [B. S. Duncan 1986]	
7Y-O	'Westhorpe' [Mrs J. Abel Smith 1971]	
4W-Y	'Westward' [J. L. Richardson 1962]	
3W-YYR	'Wetherby' [B. S. Duncan 1983]	
5Y-Y	'Whisper' [M. E. Jefferson-Brown 1960]	
3W-GYR	'Whitbourne' [M. E. Jefferson-Brown 1975]	
2W-W	'White Butterfly' [The Brodie of Brodie 1940]	
1W-W	'White Chief' [M. E. Jefferson-Brown 1975]	
2W-W	'White Crystal' [Mrs J. Abel Smith 1986]	
2W-GWW	'White Cross' [Ballydorn Bulb Farm 1983]	
1W-W	'White Diamond' [Mrs J. Abel Smith 1982]	
1W-GWW	'White Empress' [T. Bloomer 1970]	
2W-GWW	'White Ermine' [B. S. Duncan 1978]	
1W-W	'White Hills' [Hancock 1966]	
4W-Y	'White Lion' [de Graaf 1949]	**BB**-**RD**
1W-W	'White Majesty' [T. Bloomer 1970]	
4W-W	'White Marvel' [M. Zandbergen 1950]	
2W-W	'White Mist' [W. A. Noton 1976]	
1W-W	'White Phantom' [Carncairn Daffodils 1975]	
1W-W	'White Prince' [G. L. Wilson 1952]	
1W-W	'White Princess' [Mrs J. Abel Smith 1978]	
1W-W	'White Prospect' [J. L. Richardson 1948]	
2W-W	'White Spray' [J. O'More 1968]	
1W-W	'White Star' [T. Bloomer 1970]	M
2Y-PPY	'Widgeon' [G. E. Mitsch 1975]	
2W-P	'Wild Rose' [The Brodie of Brodie 1939]	
6Y-Y	'Willet' [G. E. Mitsch 1975]	
1W-Y	'Willow Green' [Mrs J. Abel Smith 1977]	M
2Y-YOO	'Winchester' [Barr 1954]	
1Y-Y	'Windjammer' [B. S. Duncan 1964]	
2W-W	'Winfrith' [D. Blanchard 1966]	
3W-YYR	'Winifred van Graven' [van Graven 1954]	

3W-YYO	**'Winkburn'** [Mrs J. Abel Smith 1977]	
3W-YYO	**'Witch Doctor'** [Ballydorn Bulb Farm 1983]	
6Y-Y	**'Woodcock'** [M. P. Williams 1949]	
2W-WYY	**'Woodgreen'** [B. S. Duncan 1956]	
6Y-Y	**'Woodcock'** [M. P. Williams 1949]	
3W-R	**'Woodland Beauty'** [T. Bloomer 1964]	
3W-Y	**'Woodland Prince'** [T. Bloomer 1964]	
3W-R	**'Woodland Splendour'** [T. Bloomer 1970]	
3W-R	**'Woodland Star'** [T. Bloomer 1962]	
2W-WWY	**'Woodvale'** [W. J. Dunlop 1947]	
2W-W	**'Worcester'** [M. E. Jefferson-Brown 1975]	
1W-W	**'W P Milner'** [W. Backhouse 1884]	M-**DGP**
4Y-Y	**'Wren'** [G. L. Wilson 1959]	
1Y-Y	**'Xanthin Gold'** [D. S. Duncan via Rathowen Daffodils 1987]	
4Y-Y	**'Yellow Cheerfulness'** [Aggink Bros 1938]	RD
2Y-Y	**'Yellow Standard'** [Barr & Sons pre-1918]	
2Y-Y	**'Yellow Sun'** [G. Lubbe 1940]	
2W-P	**'Yes Please'** [F. E. Board 1965]	
2W-Y	**'Yester'** [Pre-1985]	
7W-Y	**'Young Idea'** [M. J. Jefferson-Brown 1987]	
1W-W	**'Zelah'** [T. Bloomer 1979]	
2Y-R	**'Zeus'** [Carncairn Daffodils 1978]	

NARDUS Linnaeus 1753   *[Poaceae (Gramineae)]*
N‡   **stricta** Linnaeus 1753

NASSAUVIA Commerson ex Jussieu 1789   *[Asteraceae (Compositae)]*
    lagascae Benthan & Hooker 1873
    revoluta D. Don 1832

NECTAROSCORDUM Lindley 1836   *[Alliaceae (Liliaceae)]*
    bulgaricum Janka 1873 = **N. siculum** ssp. **bulgaricum**
    siculum (Ucria) Lindley 1836 (*Allium siculum*)   EGF.1-PGP-**BB-DGP-RD**
        ssp. **bulgaricum** (Janka) Stearn 1978 (*N. bulgaricum*)   EGF.1-PGP-**BB**

NELUMBO Adanson 1763   *[Nelumbonaceae]*
    lutea (Willdenow) Persoon 1807
    nucifera Gaertner 1788 (*Nymphaea nelumbo*)

NEOPAXIA O. Nilsson 1966   *[Portulacaceae]*
    australasica (Hooker f.) O. Nilsson 1966 (*Claytonia australasica, Montia australasica*)

NEOTINIA Reichenbach f. 1852   *[Orchidaceae]*
N   **maculata** (Desfontaines) Stearn 1974

NEPETA Linnaeus 1753   *[Lamiaceae (Labiatae)]*
    'Blue Beauty' = **N. 'Souvenir d'Andre Chaudron'**
HN‡   **cataria** Linnaeus 1753
H   **'Citriodora'**
    crinita Montbret & Aucher ex Bentham 1836
HL   **x faassenii** Bergmans ex Stearn 1950 (*N. mussinii* x *N. nepetella*)   PGP-DGP-**RD**
      'Blauknirps' ('Blue Dwarf')   PGP
      'Blue Dwarf' = **N. x faassenii 'Blauknirps'**
      'Little Titch'
      'Superba' nom. dub.
      'Variegata'
      'Walker's Low'   PGP
    glechoma Bentham 1832 = **Glechoma hederacea**
    glutinosa Bentham 1835
    govaniana Bentham 1834 (*Dracocephalum govanianum*)   **PGP**

hederacea Trevisan 1842 = **Glechoma hederacea**
mussinii Sprengel ex Henckel 1806
mussinii hort. non Henckel = **N. x faassenii**
nepetella Linnaeus 1758   PGP
nervosa Royle ex Bentham & Hooker 1883   RD
nuda Linnaeus 1753   PGP
   ssp. *albiflora* (Boissier) Gams 1927 = **N. sulphurea**
phyllochlamys P. H. Davis 1951
sibirica Linnaeus 1753 (*Dracocephalum sibiricum*)   PGP
L   **'Six Hills Giant'**   [C. Elliott]   PGP-**DGP-RD**
'Souvenir d'Andre Chaudron' (N. 'Blue Beauty')   PGP
sulphurea C. Koch 1848 (*N. nuda* ssp. *albiflora*)

NERINE Herbert 1820 nom. cons.   [*Amaryllidaceae*]
  alta W. F. Barker 1935
  angustifolia (Baker) W. Watson 1889   EGF.1
  appendiculata Baker 1894   EGF.1
  bowdenii W. Watson 1904   EGF.1-PGP-**BB-DGP**-RD
    'Fenwick's Variety'   PGP-**BB-DGP-RD**
    'Hera'   PGP
    'Manina'
    'Pink Triumph'   PGP
    'Wellsii'   **BB**
  corusca (Ker-Gawler) Herbert 1820 = **N. sarniensis** var. **corusca**
  crispa Hort. ex Vilmorin 1895 = **N. undulata**
  curvifolia (Jacquin) Herbert 1820 = **N. sarniensis** var. **curvifolia**
  filifolia Baker 1881   EGF.1
  flexuosa (Jacquin) Herbert 1820   EGF.1-PGP-**BB-RD**
    'Alba'
  *****forbesii**
  fothergillii (Andrews) M. Roemer = **N. sarniensis** var. **fothergillii**
  frithii L. Bolus 1921
  gibsonii K. H. Douglas 1968
  gracilis R. A. Dyer 1937
  *****hirsuta**
  humilis (Jacquin) Herbert 1820   EGF.1-PGP
  krigei W. F. Barker 1935
  laticoma Durieu ex Schinz 1893
  masonorum L. Bolus 1930   EGF.1
  peersii W. F. Barker 1935
  platypetala G. McNeil 1971
  pudica Hooker f. 1871   EGF.1
  sarniensis (Linnaeus) Herbert 1820   EGF.1-DGP-RD
    var. **corusca** (Ker-Gawler) Baker 1894 (*N. corusca*)   EGF.1-RD
    var. **corusca** 'Major'   **DGP**
    var. **curvifolia** (Jacquin) Traub (*N. curvifolia*)   EGF.1
    var. **fothergillii** (Andrews) Traub (*N. fothergillii*)   EGF.1
  undulata (Linnaeus) Herbert 1820 (*N. crispa*)   EGF.1-PGP-**BB-RD**

HYBRID CULTIVARS

    'Afterglow'   [Exbury Gardens]
    'Ancilla'   [van Tubergen]
    'Baghdad'   [Exbury Gardens]
    'Belladonna'
    'Bennett Poe'   [Poe]
    'Bettina'
    'Betty Hudson'
    'Blanchefleur'   [C. A. Norris]
    'Brocade'

'Canasta'   [Exbury Gardens]
'Carlos'   [C. A. Norris]
'Caroline'
'Carolside'   [Exbury Gardens pre-1960]
'Caryatid'   [Exbury Gardens pre-1942]
'Cassio'   [Exbury Gardens]
'Catkin'
'Christmas'
'Clent Charm'
'Coralina'
'Countess Maria Plater'
'Cranfield'   [F. Stern]
'Curiosity'   [C. A. Norris pre-1976]
'Cynthia Chance'
'Daphne'
'Eve'   [Exbury Gardens]
'Evelyn Emmett'
'Fairylight'   [Exbury Gardens]
'Gay Girl'
'Gipsy Queen'
'Gloaming'   [F. Stern]
'Guy Fawkes'   [Findlater]
'Hon. Miss Gibbs'
'Jenny Wren'
'Lady Clementine Mitford'
'Lady Keane'
'Lady Llewelyn'
'Lady Lucy Hicks Beech'
'Lady Montague'   [Exbury Gardens]
'Lady Redesdale'
'Mansellii'   [J. L. Mansell c1875]
'Margaret Rose'   [Exbury Gardens]
'Mertoun'   [Exbury Gardens]
'Miss Battye'
'Miss E. Cator'   [pre-1924]
'Miss Edith Godman'   DGP
'Miss Rosamund Elwes'
'Miss Willmott'   [pre-1899]
'Mrs Bromley'
'Mrs Mackworth Praed'
'Mrs Vivian Graham'
'Nina'
'Plymouth'   [Exbury Gardens pre-1960]
'Robert Berkeley'
'Rushmere Star'   [pre-1966]
'Sheelagh Mullholland'
'Stephanie'   [pre-1949]
'Theresa Buxton'
'Xanthia'
'Zella'

NERTERA Banks & Solander 1788 nom. cons.   [*Rubiaceae*]
    balfouriana Cockayne 1911
    depressa Banks & Solander ex Gaertner 1788 = **N. granadensis**
    granadensis (Mutis) Druce 1917 (*N. depressa*)

NIEREMBERGIA Ruiz & Pavon 1794   [*Solanaceae*]
S   **caerulea** Gillies ex Miers 1846   CA-DGP-RD
S   **frutescens** Durieu 1866   PGP-RD

'Dwarf Purple Robe'
repens Ruiz & Pavon 1794 (*N.rivularis*)   CA-**DGP**-RD
'Violet Queen'
rivularis Miers 1846 = **N. repens**

NIPPONANTHEMUM (Kitamura) Kitamura 1978   [*Asteraceae (Compositae)*]
nipponicum (Franchet & Maximowicz) Kitamura 1978 (*Chrysanthemum*
nipponicum, Leucanthemum nipponicum)   PGP

NOMOCHARIS Franchet 1889   [*Liliaceae*]

M - SYNGE, P.M., *'Lilies'* : B. T. Batsford Ltd, London, 1980

aperta (Franchet) Wilson 1925   M-EGF.1-PGP-CA-**BB**-RD
farreri (W. E. Evans) Harrow 1929   M-EGF.1-PGP-CA
x finlayorum Synge 1969 (*N. farreri* x *N. pardanthina*)   M-EGF.1-RD
mairei Leveille 1913   M-EGF.1-PGP-**CA**-DGP-RD
nana (Klotzch) Wilson 1925 = **Lilium nanum**
oxypetala (Royle) Wilson 1925 = **Lilium oxypetalum**
pardanthina Franchet 1889   M-EGF.1-**PGP**-CA-**DGP**-RD
saluenensis Balfour f. 1918   M-PGP-CA-**DGP**-RD

NOTHOLIRION Wallich ex Boissier 1882   [*Liliaceae*
bulbuliferum (Lingelsheim) Stearn 1950   EGF.1-PGP
macrophyllum (D. Don) Boissier 1882   EGF.1-PGP-**BB**
thomsonianum (Royle) Stapf 1934   EGF.1-PGP-**BB**

NOTHOSCORDUM Kunth 1843 nom. cons.   [*Alliaceae (Liliaceae)*]
fragrans (Ventenat) Kunth 1843 = **N. gracile**
N   **gracile** (Aiton) Stearn 1986 (*N. fragrans, N. inodorum* hort.)   EGF.1-**BB**-SB
inodorum hort. = **N. gracile**
neriniflorum (Herbert) Traub 1960 = **Caloscordum neriniflorum**

NUPHAR J.E. Smith 1808 nom. cons.   [*Nymphaecaceae*
N   **advena** R. Brown 1811 (*N. variegata*)
japonica de Candolle 1825
'Rubrotincta' (Caspary) Ohwi
N‡ **lutea** (Linnaeus) Smith 1809
minima Spenner 1811 = N. pumila
N‡ **pumila** (Timm) de Candolle 1821 (*N. minima*)
variegata Engelmann ex S. Watson 1878 = **N. advena**

NYMPHAEA Linnaeus 1753 nom. cons.   [*Nymphaeaca*

M - SWINDELLS, PHILLIP ; *'Waterlilies'* : Croom Helm 1983

N‡L **alba** Linnaeus 1753   **M-RD**
   * ssp. **occidentalis** ('Minor')   **M**
   'Albatross'   [Marliac 1910]   **M**
   'Amabilis'   [Marliac 1921]   **M**
   'American Star'
   'Andreana'   [Marliac 1895]   **M**
   'Arc-en-ciel'   [Marliac 1901]   **M**
   'Atropurpurea'   [Marliac 1901]   **M**
   'Attraction'   [Marliac 1910]   **M**
   'August Koch'   [Koch 1922]   **M**
   'Aurora'   [Marliac 1895]   **M**
   'Bateau'   [Marliac]   **M**
   'Brackleyi Rosea'   [Pre-1909]   **M**
   candida J. Presl 1921   **M**

	'Candidissima'	M
	capensis Thunberg 1800	M-DGP-RD
	* var. zanzibariensis	M
	var. zanzibariensis 'Rosea'	M-DGP
	'Charles de Meurville' [Marliac c1931]	M
	'Chrysantha' [Marliac 1905]	M
L	'Collosea' [Marliac 1901]	M
	'Colonel A. J. Welch' [Marliac]	M
	'Comanche' [Marliac 1908]	M
L	'Conqueror' [Marliac 1910]	M-RD
	'Darwin' [Marliac 1909]	M
	'Daubeniana' [Daubeny 1863]	M-DGP
	'Ellisiana' [Marliac 1896]	M
L	'Escarboucle' [Marliac 1906]	M-DGP-RD
	'Fabiola' [Marliac 1913]	M
	flava Leitner ex Audobon 1838 = N. mexicana	
	'Froebelii' [Froebel 1898]	M-RD
	'Galatee' [Marliac 1909]	M
	'Gladstoniana' [Richardson 1897]	M-DGP-RD
	'Gloire de Temple-sur-Lot' [Marliac 1913]	M
	'Gloriosa' [Marliac 1896]	M
	'Goliath' [Marliac 1912]	M
	'Gonnere' [Marliac]	M
	'Graziella' [Marliac 1902]	M-RD
	'Green Smoke' [Randig]	M
	'Hermine' [Marliac 1910]	M
	'Hollandia'	
	'Indiana' [Marliac 1912]	M
	'Irene'	M
	'James Brydon' [Dreer 1902]	M-DGP-RD
	'James Hudson' [Marliac 1912]	M
	'Lactea' [Marliac 1907]	M
	'Laydekeri' [Marliac]	M
	'Laydekeri Fulgens' [Marliac 1895]	M-RD
L	'Laydekeri Lilacea' [Marliac]	M-RD
	'Leydekeri Lucida' [Marliac 1894]	M
L	'Leydekeri Purpurata' [Marliac 1895]	M-RD
	'Leydekeri Rosea' [Marliac 1893]	M
	'Leydekeri Rubra' = N. 'Leydekeri Fulgens'	
	'Livingstone' [Marliac 1909]	M
	lotus Linnaeus 1753	M
	* var. dentata	M-DGP
	'Lusitania' [Marliac 1912]	M
	'Lustrous'	M
	'Madame de Bonseigneur' [Marliac 1937]	M
	'Madame Wilfron Gonnere' [Marliac]	M
	'Marguerite Laplace' [Marliac 1913]	M
L	'Marliacea Albida' [Marliac 1880]	M-RD
	'Marliacea Carnea' [Marliac 1887]	M-RD
L	'Marliacea Chromatella' [Marliac 1886]	M-DGP-RD
L	'Marliacea Rosea' [Marliac 1879]	M-RD
	'Masaniello' [Marliac 1908]	M-RD
	'Maurice Laydeker' [Marliac]	M
	mexicana Zuccarini 1832 (N. flava)	M
	'Moorei' [Adelaide Botanic Garden 1900]	M
	'Mrs George C. Hitchcock' [Pring 1926]	M-RD
	'Mrs Richmond' [Marliac 1910]	M
	'Murillo' [Marliac 1910]	M
	'Newton' [Marliac 1910]	M
	nouchali Burman f. 1769 (N. stellata)	M-RD

'Odalisque' [Marliac 1908]		M
odorata Dryander 1811		M-RD
'Alba' = **N. odorata**		
'Caroliniana Nivea' [Marliac 1893]		M
'Caroliniana Perfecta' [Marliac 1893]		M
'Eugene de Land' [Marliac]		M
'Firecrest'		**M-DGP**-RD
'Juliana'		
'Luciana' [Dreer]		M
var. **minor** Sims 1814		RD
'Sauvissima' [Marliac 1899]		M
'Sulphurea' [Marliac 1879]		**M-RD**
'Sulphurea Grandiflora' [Marliac 1888]		M-**DGP**-RD
'Turicensis'		M-RD
'William B. Shaw' [Dreer]		M
'Paul Hariot'		**DGP**
'Perfection'		
'Phoebus' [Marliac 1909]		M
'Picciola' [Marliac 1913]		M
'Pink Glory'		M
'Pinkie'		
'Pink Opal' [Fowler 1915]		M
'Pink Sensation' [Slocum 1948]		M
'Princess Elizabeth' [Perry 1935]		M
x pygmaea (Salisbury) Dryander 1811		M
L	'Alba'	M
L	**'Helvola'** [Marliac 1879]	**M-RD**
	'Rosea'	
	'Rubra'	M
'Queen Wilhelmina'		
'Rembrandt'		M
'Rene Gerard' [Marliac 1914]		**M**
'Robinsoniana' [Marliac 1895]		M
'Rose Arey' [Fowler 1913]		**M-RD**
'Rose Magnolia'		M
'Rosennymphe' [Junge]		M
'Rosy Morn' [Johnson 1932]		M
'Sanguinea' [Marliac 1894]		M
'Seignourettii' [Marliac 1893]		M
'Sioux' [Marliac 1908]		M
'Sirius' [Marliac 1913]		**M**
'Solfatare' [Marliac 1906]		M
'Somptuosa' [Marliac 1909]		M
'Splendida' [Marliac 1904]		M
stellata Willdenow 1799 = **N. nouchali**		
'Sunrise'		M-**DGP**-RD
tetragona Georgi 1775		M
'Thetis'		
'Trudy Slocum' [Slocum 1948]		M
tuberosa Paine 1865		**M-RD**
*var. **maxima**		M
'Paeslingberg' [Buggele]		M
'Richardsonii' [Richardson 1894]		M-RD
'Rosea'		M-RD
'Vesuve' [Marliac 1906] ('Vesuvius')		M
'William Doogue' [Dreer 1899]		M
'William Falconer' [Dreer c1899]		**M**

NYMPHOIDES Hill 1757   [*Menyanthacea*

indica (Linnaeus) O. Kuntze 1891 (*Limnanthemum indicum*)

NL   **peltata** (S. G. Gmelin) O. Kuntze 1891 (*Limnanthemum peltatum, Villarsia*
      'Bennettii' nom. dub.   *nymphaeoides*)

OAKESIELLA Small 1903   [*Convallariaceae (Liliaceae)*]
      sessilifolia (Linnaeus) S. Watson 1879 = **Uvularia sessilifolia**

OCHAGAVIA R. Philippi 1856
      lindleyana (Lemoine) Mez 1935   [*Bromeliaceae*]

OCIMUM Linnaeus 1753
AH   **basilicum** Linnaeus 1753   [*Lamiaceae (Labiatae)*]
AH   **minimum** Linnaeus 1753

ODONTOSTOMUM Torrey 1856   [*Amaryllidaceae*]
      hartwegii Torrey 1856   SB

OENOTHERA Linnaeus 1753
      acaulis Cavanilles 1798 (*O. taraxacifolia*)   [*Onagraceae*]
      'Aurea'   RD
      albicaulis Pursh 1814
BHN   **biennis** Linnaeus 1753 (*O. glabra*)
      caespitosa Nuttall 1813   RD
      cinaeus hort. = **O. tetragona** var. **fraseri**
      elata Humboldt, Bonpland & Kunth 1820 (*O. hookeri*)
      erythrosepala Borbas 1903 = **O. glazioviana**
      flava (A. Nelson) Garrett 1927
      fruticosa Linnaeus 1753   DGP-RD
N   *glazioviana* Micheli ex Martius (*O. erythrosepala*)
      glabra Miller 1768 = **O. biennis**
      hookeri Torrey & A. Gray 1840 = **O. elata**
      kunthiana (Spach) Munz 1932
      lamarckiana DeVries 1959 non Seringe 1828 = **O. glazioviana**
      lamarckiana Seringe 1828 non DeVries 1959 = **O. biennis**
L   **missouriensis** Sims 1814
      'Greencourt Lemon'   PGP-**DGP**-RD
      nuttallii Sweet 1830
      nuttallii Torrey & A. Gray 1840 = **O. tanacetifolia**
      odorata hort. non Jacquin 1786 = **O. stricta**
      pallida Lindley 1828
          ssp. *trichocalyx* (Nuttall ex Torrey & A. Gray) Munz & W. Klein 1965
                                                                  = **O. trichocalyx**
      perennis Linnaeus 1758 (*O. pumila*)   RD
      pumila Linnaeus 1762 = **O. perennis**
      speciosa Nuttall 1821
          var. **childsii** (Bailey) Munz 1937
N   **stricta** Ledebour ex Link (*O. odorata* hort.)
      'Sulphurea'
      tanacetifolia Torrey & A. Gray 1840
      taraxacifolia Hort. ex Sweet 1827 non Leveille & Guffroy 1902 = **O. acaulis**
      tetragona Roth 1806   PGP-DGP-RD
          var. **fraseri** (Pursh) Munz 1937   PGP-**DGP**-RD
      'Fireworks' = **O. tetragona 'Fyrverkeri'**
L   **'Fyrverkeri'** ('Fireworks')   PGP-**DGP**
      'Highlight' = **O. tetragona 'Hohes Licht'**
      'Hohes Licht'   [Baltin 1961] ('Highlight')   DGP-RD
          var. **riparia** (Nuttall) Munz 1937   **DGP**-RD
      'Sonnenwende'   [Marx 1983]
      'Sundrops'
L   **'Yellow River'**
                                                                        PGP-RD

trichocalyx Nuttall ex Torrey & A. Gray 1840 (*O. pallida* ssp. *trichocalyx*)   RD
    'Wedding Bells'
A   **triloba** Hooker 1847

OMPHALODES Miller 1754   [*Boraginaceae*]
L   **cappadocica** (Willdenow) de Candolle 1846   **DGP-RD**
    'Anthea Bloom'   [A. Bloom]
    'Cherry Ingram'
A   **linifolia** (Linnaeus) Moench 1794
    luciliae Boissier 1844   CA-**DGP-RD**
    lusitanica hort. non (Linnaeus) Lange = **O. nitida**
    nitida Hoffmanns & Link 1816 (*O. lusitanica* hort.)
N   **verna** Moench 1794   RD
    'Alba'
    'Grandiflora'

OMPHALOGRAMMA (Franchet) Franchet 1898   [*Primulaceae*]
    elegans Forrest 1923
    minus Handel-Mazzettii 1922
    vinciflorum (Franchet) Franchet 1898   CA-**DGP**

ONOBRYCHIS Miller 1754   [*Fabaceae (Leguminosae)*]
HN‡ **viciifolia** Scopoli 1772

ONOCLEA Linnaeus 1753   [*Woodsiaceae*]
NL   **sensibilis** Linnaeus 1753   EGF.1-PGP-RD
    'Rotstiel'

ONONIS Linnaeus 1753   [*Fabaceae (Leguminosae)*]
    cenisia Linnaeus 1771 = **O. cristata**
    cristata Miller 1768 (*O. cenisia*)
S   **natrix** Linnaeus 1753
    procurrens Wallroth 1822 = **O. repens** var. **procurrens**
SN‡L **repens** Linnaeus 1753
    var. **procurrens** (Wallroth) I. Grintescu 1957 (*O. procurrens*)
    rotundifolia Linnaeus 1753
N‡   **spinosa** Linnaeus 1753

ONOPORDUM Linnaeus 1753   [*Asteraceae (Compositae)*]
BHN‡ **acanthium** Linnaeus 1753   PGP-**RD**
    arabicum hort. = **O. nervosum**
    nervosum Boissier 1839   RD

ONOSMA Linnaeus 1762   [*Boraginaceae*
S   **albo-roseum** Fischer & C. A. Meyer 1839
S   **cinereum** Schrader 1767
S   **tauricum** Pallas ex Willdenow 1799   **RD**

OPHIOPOGON Ker-Gawler 1807   [*Convallariaceae (Liliaceae)*
    intermedius D. Don 1825
    jaburan (Kunth) Loddiges 1832   EGF.1-RD
    'Variegatus' = **L. jaburan 'Vittatus'**
    'Vittatus' ('Variegatus')   **RD**
    japonicus (Linnaeus f.) Ker-Gawler 1807   EGF.1-RD
    'Minor'
    planiscapus Nakai 1920   EGF.1-RD
L   **'Nigrescens'**   EGF.1-RD

OPHRYS Linnaeus 1753   [*Orchidaceae*
N‡   **apifera** Hudson 1762   EGF.2-CA

bombyliflora Link 1800
exaltata Tenore 1819 = **O. fuciflora** ssp. **exaltata**   CA
N   **fuciflora** (Schmidt) Moench 1802
   ssp. **exaltata** (Tenore) E. Nelson 1962 (*O. exaltata*)   EGF.2
   ssp. **oxyrrhynchos** (Todaro) Soo 1927
fusca Link 1800
holoserica (Burmann f.) Greuter 1968   EGF.2-CA
N‡ **insectifera** Linnaeus 1753   EGF.2
lunulata Parlatore 1838   EGF.2
lutea (Gouan) Cavanilles 1993
speculum Link 1800 (*O. vernixia*)   EGF.2-CA
N‡ **sphegodes** Miller 1768   CA
   ssp. **mammosa** (Desfontaines) Soo ex Nelson 1962   EGF.2
tenthredinifera Willdenow 1805   EGF.2
vernixia Brotero 1804 = **O. speculum**   EGF.2

OPUNTIA Miller 1754   [*Cactaceae*]
compressa (Salisbury) MacBride 1922 = **O. macrorhiza**
engelmannii Salm-Dyck 1844
   var. **discata** (Griffith) C.Z. Nelson 1919
erinacea Engelmann 1856
   var. **utahensis** (Engelmann) L. Benson (*O. rhodantha, O. utahensis*)
fragilis (Nuttall) Haworth 1819
humifusa (Rafinesque) Rafinesque 1820
juniperina Britton & Rose 1919 = **O. polyacantha**
macrocentra Engelmann 1857
   var. **martiniana** L. Benson 1950
macrorhiza Engelmann 1850 (*O. compressa*)
monacantha (Willdenow) Haworth 1819
phaeacantha Engelmann 1849
   'Albispina'   DGP
   var. **camanchica** (Engelmann & Bigelow) Bory
   'Longispina'
polyacantha Haworth 1819 (*O. juniperina*)
rhodantha K. Schumann 1896 = **O. erinacea** var. **utahensis**
utahensis J. H. Purpus 1909 = **O. erinacea** var. **utahensis**
vulgaris Miller 1768
   'Variegata Monstrosa'

ORCHIS Linnaeus 1753   [*Orchidaceae*]
anatolica Boissier 1844   EGF.2
fuchsii Druce 1915 = **Dactylorhiza fuchsii**
italica Poiret 1798
lactea Poiret 1798   EGF.2
longicornu Poiret 1798
maderensis Summerhayes 1948 = **Dactylorhiza foliosa**
N‡ **mascula** (Linnaeus) Linnaeus 1755   EGF.2-CA
N‡ **militaris** Linnaeus 1753   EGF.2-PGP-CA
N‡ **morio** Linnaeus 1753   EGF.2-CA
   ssp. **picta** (Loiseleur) Arcangeli 1894
papilionacea Linnaeus 1759   EGF.2-CA
provincialis Balbis ex de Candolle 1806   EGF.2
N‡ **purpurea** Hudson 1762   EGF.2-PGP-CA
pyramidalis Linnaeus 1753 = **Anacamptis pyramidalis**
N‡ **simia** Lamarck 1779
spectabilis Linnaeus 1753 non Pursh 1814   CA
tridentata Scopoli 1772   CA

OREOBOLUS R. Brown 1810
pectinatus Hooker f. 1844   [*Cyperaceae*]

OREOPTERIS Holub 1969   *[Thelypteridaceae]*
N   **limbosperma** (Bellardi ex Allioni) Holub 1969 (*Dryopteris montana, Lastrea*
                                        montana, Thelypteris limbosperma)   PGP

ORIGANUM Linnaeus 1753   *[Lamiaceae (Labiatae)]*
        amanum G. E. Post 1895   CA-**DGP**-**RD**
        'Barbara Tingey' (*O. calcaratum* x *O.rotundifolium*)
        'Birch Farm'   [Ingwersen]
        'Buckland' (*O.amanum* x *O. calcaratum*)
        calcaratum Jussieu 1789
        dictamnus Linnaeus 1753   CA-RD
        'Erntedank' (*O. laevigatum* x ?)
        heracleoticum Linnaeus 1753 = **O. vulgare** ssp. **hirtum**
        'Herrenhausen'
        x hybridum Miller 1768 (*O. dictamnus* x *O. sipyleum*)   **DGP**-RD
        'Kent Beauty' (*O. rotundifolium* x *O. scabrum*)   [E. Strangman]
        kopetdaghense Borissova-Bekrjashera 1954
        laevigatum Boissier 1854   PGP
            'Hopleys'   [D. Barker]
SH   **marjorana** Linnaeus 1753   PGP
S   **microphyllum** (Bentham) Boissier 1879
        'Nymphenburg'
SH   **onites** Linnaeus 1753
H   **'Aureo-crispum'**
H   **'Aureum'**
H   **'Variegatum'**
        prismaticum hort. = **O. vulgare 'Prismaticum'**
        rotundifolium Boissier 1859   RD
        scabrum Boissier & Heldreich 1846
            ssp. **pulchrum** (Boissier & Heldreich) P. H. Davis 1949
        tournefortii Aiton 1789 = **O. calcaratum**
        tytthanthum Gontsch 1939 = **O. vulgare** ssp. **gracile**
HN‡L **vulgare** Linnaeus 1753   DGP
            'Aureum'   PGP-**DGP**
H   **'Compactum'**
            'Curly Gold'
            'Gold Tip'
            ssp. **gracile** (C. Koch) Letswaart 1980 (*O. tytthanthum*)
H   ssp. **hirtum** (Link) Letswaart 1980 (*O. heracleoticum*)
            'Prismaticum'
            'Roseum'
            'Thumble's Variety'
            'Tracy's Yellow'
            'Variegatum'

ORNITHOGALUM Linnaeus 1753   *[Hyacinthaceae (Liliaceae)]*
        arabicum Linnaeus 1753   EGF.1-SB-DGP
        arcuatum Steven 1829, non Velenovsky   SB
        balsanae Boissier 1884   EGF.1-**BB**-SB-RD
        caudatum Jacquin 1788   EGF.1
        lanceolatum Labillardiere 1812   EGF.1-**SB**
        magnum Krascheninnikov & Schischkin 1935
        nanum Smith 1809, non Thunberg 1794 = **O. sigmoideum**
        narbonense Linnaeus 1756   EGF.1-**BB**-SB
N‡   **nutans** Linnaeus 1753   EGF.1-PGP-**BB**-SB-**DGP**-RD
        oligophyllum E. D. Clarke 1816   EGF.1-SB
N‡   **pyramidale** Linnaeus 1753   EGF.1-PGP
        pyrenaicum Linnaeus 1753   EGF.1-PGP-**BB**-SB
        sibthorpii Greuter 1967 = **O. sigmoideum**
        sigmoideum Freyn & Sintensis 1896 (*O. nanum* Smith, *O. sibthorpii*)   SB

    thrysoides Jacquin 1813   EGF.1-**DGP-RD**
HN‡ **umbellatum** Linnaeus 1753   EGF.1-SB-**DGP-RD**

ORONTIUM Linnaeus 1753   [*Araceae*]
    aquaticum Linnaeus 1753   EGF.2

OROSTACHYS (de Candolle) Fischer ex A. Berger 1930   [*Crassulaceae*]
    aggregata (Makino) Hara 1935 (*O. malacophyllus*)
       'Roseus' Sugaya 1956
    chanetii (Leveille) Berger 1930   CA
    erubescens (Maximowicz) Ohwi 1942
    furusei Ohwi 1954
    iwarenge (Makino) Hara 1935
    malacophyllus (Pallas) Fischer 1808 nom. nud. = **O. aggregata**
B   **spinosus** (Linnaeus) Berger 1930   CA

ORTHROSANTHUS Sweet 1827   [*Iridaceae*]
    chimboracensis (Humboldt, Bonpland & Kunth) Baker 1876   EGF.1
    multiflorus Sweet 1827   EGF.1
    polystachyus Bentham 1868

OSMUNDA Linnaeus 1753   [*Osmundaceae*]
    cinnamomea Linnaeus 1753   EGF.1-PGP
    claytoniana Linnaeus 1753   EGF.1-**PGP**
    gracilis hort. = **O. regalis 'Gracilis'**
    japonica Thunberg 1784   EGF.1
NL **regalis** Linnaeus 1753   EGF.1-**PGP-RD**
       'Cristata'   PGP-RD
       'Gracilis'   PGP
       'Purpurascens'   PGP-RD
       'Purpurascens Willstedt'
       'Undulata'

OSTEOSPERMUM Linnaeus 1753   [*Asteraceae* (*Compositae*)]
    barberiae (Harvy) Norlindh 1943
    barberiae hort. non (Harvy) Norlindh 1943 = **O. jucundum**
    ecklonis (A. de Candolle) Norlindh 1943 (*Dimorphotheca ecklonis*) PGP-DGP-RD
       'Prostratum'   RD
    jucundum (E. Phillips) Norlindh 1943 (*Dimorphotheca jucunda*) PGP-**DGP**-RD
       var. **compactum** (Higgins) !
       'Compactum' = **O. jucundum 'Nanum'**
       'Nanum' ('Compactum')   PGP-DGP

HYBRID CULTIVARS

       'African Queen'
       'Bloemhof Belle'
       'Blue Streak'
       'Buttercup'
       'Cannington Roy'
       'Falmouth'
       'Hopleys'
       'Lady Liatrum'
       'Langtrees'
       'Pale Face'
       'Peggyi' = **O. 'Tresco Purple'**
       'Pink Whirls'
       'Tresco Pink'
       'Tresco Purple' ('Peggyi')
       'Tresco Sally'

'Weetwood'
'Whirlygig'
'Wine Purple'
'Wisley' nom. dub.

OSTROWSKIA Regel 1884   [*Campanulaceae*]
    magnifica Regel 1884   PGP

OTHONNOPSIS Jaubert & Spach 1852   [*Asteraceae (Compositae)*]
S   **cheirifolia** Bentham & Hooker f. 1873 (*Hertia cherifolia*)   CA

OURISIA Commerson ex Jussieu 1789   [*Scrophulariaceae*]
    breviflora Bentham 1846
    caespitosa Hooker f. 1853
       var. **gracilis** Hooker f. 1867
    coccinea Persoon 1806   CA-DGP-**RD**
    'Loch Ewe' (*O. coccinea* x *O. macrophylla*)
    macrophylla Hooker 1843   PGP-**RD**
    'Snowflake' (*O. macrocarpa* x *O. caespitosa* var. *gracilis*)   [J. Drake]

OXALIS Linnaeus 1753   [*Oxalidaceae*]
N‡L   **acetosella** Linnaeus 1753   **RD**
      'Rubra'
    adenophylla Gillies 1833   CA-**BB**-SB-**DGP**-RD
      'Minima' nom. dub.
    articulata Savigny 1798 (*O. floribunda*)
    brasiliensis Loddiges 1833   CA
    cernua Thunberg 1781 = **O. pes-caprae**
    chrysantha Progel 1877   CA-RD
N‡   **corniculata** Linnaeus 1753
       var. **atropurpurea** Planchet
    deppei Loddiges ex Sweet 1831 = **O. tetraphylla**
    depressa Ecklon & Zeyher 1835 (*O. inops*)   **BB**-SB-**DGP**-RD
    enneaphylla Cavanilles 1799   **CA-BB**-SB-RD
      'Alba'
      'Minutifolia'   RD
      'Rosea'   CA-**RD**
      'Rubra'
      'Ruth Tweedie'
    floribunda Lehmann 1826 = **O. articulata**
    hirta Linnaeus 1753   CA
      'Gothenburg'
    inops Ecklon & Zeyher 1834 = **O. depressa**
    'Ione Hecker' (*O. enneaphylla* x *O. laciniata*) [E.B. Anderson via J. Elliott]   **SB**
    laciniata Cavanilles 1799   CA-**BB-SB-DGP**-RD
    lactea Hooker 1836 = **O. magellanica**
    lasiandra Zuccarini 1834
    lobata Sims 1823   CA-**BB**-SB
    magellanica Forster f. 1789 (*O. lactea*)   CA-RD
    melanosticta Sonder 1860
    obtusa Jacquin 1794   SB
    oregana Nuttall ex Torrey & A. Gray 1838   CA
    patagonica Spegazzini 1897
N   **pes-caprae** Linnaeus 1753 (*O. cernua*)   RD
    purpurea Linnaeus 1753 (*O. speciosa, O. variabilis*)   CA-SB
      'Bowles' White'
      'Ken Aslet'   **SB**
      'Rosea'
    racemosa Savignone 1798
      'Aureo-reticulata'

N
    speciosa Ecklon & Zeyher 1835 = **O. purpurea**
    tetraphylla Cavanilles 1795 (*O. deppei*)   CA-SB
      'Alba'
      'Iron Cross' ®   [W. Blokker Jzn 1969]
    variabilis Jacquin 1794 = **O. purpurea**
    versicolor Linnaeus 1753
    violacea Linnaeus 1753

OXYPETALUM R. Brown 1809 nom. cons.   [*Asclepiadaceae*]
    caeruleum Decaisne 1844 = **Tweedia caerulea**

OXYRIA Hill 1768
N‡   **digyna** (Linnaeus) Hill 1768   [*Polygonaceae*]

OXYTROPIS de Candolle 1802 nom. cons.   [*Fabaceae (Leguminosae)*]
N‡   **campestris** (Linnaeus) de Candolle 1802
N‡   **halleri** Bunge ex Koch 1843
    uralensis de Candolle 1802

PACHYPHRAGMA (de Candolle) Reichenbach 1841   [*Brassicaceae (Cruciferae)*]
    macrophyllum (Thlaspi m.) Busch 1908 (*Cardamine asarifolia* hort.)

PAEDEROTA Linnaeus 1762
    bonarota (Linnaeus) Linnaeus 1762 (*Veronica bonarota*)   [*Scrophulariaceae*]
                                                  CA

PAEONIA Linnaeus 1753   [*Paeoniaceae*]
    albiflora Pallas 1788 = **P. lactiflora**
    anemoniflora hort. = **P. officinalis 'Anemoniflora'**
    anomala Linnaeus 1771
        var. **intermedia** (C. A. Meyer) O. & B. Fedtschenko 1905   PGP
    arietina Anderson 1818 = **P. mascula** ssp. **arietina**   PGP
    bakeri Hort. ex Lynch 1890
    broteroi Boissier & Reuter 1842   PGP
    cambessedesii Willkomm 1880   PGP-CA-**DGP**
    clusii Stern & Stearn 1940 (*P. peregrina* var. *glabra*)   PGP
    corallina Retzius 1873 = **P mascula**
    daurica Andrews 1807 = **P. mascula** ssp. **tridentata**
    emodi Wallich ex Royle 1834   **PGP-RD**
    humilis Retzius 1783 = **P. officinalis** ssp. **humilis**
    kavachensis Aznavour 1917 = **P. mascula**
N   **lactiflora** Pallas 1776 (*P. albiflora*, P. 'La Fiancee', 'The Bride', 'Whitleyi Major')
                                                 PGP-DGP-**RD**
    lobata Desfontaines 1804 = **P. peregrina** Miller
N‡   **mascula** (Linnaeus) Miller 1768 (*P. corallina, P. kavachensis, P. romanica,*
                                   P. officinalis var. *mascula*)   PGP
    ssp. **arietina** (Anderson) Cullen & Heywood 1964 (*P. arietina, P. peregrina*
                                     Bornmüller)   PGP-RD
      ssp. **arietina 'Northern Glory'**   [Barr ? 1890]   PGP
      ssp. **arietina 'Purple Emperor'**
      ssp. **arietina 'Rose Gem'**
      ssp. **russii** (Bivona) Cullen & Heywood 1964 (*P. russii*)   PGP
      ssp. **russii** var. **reverchonii** (Le Grand) !   PGP
      ssp. **tridentata** (Boissier) Gürke (*P. dahurica, P. tridentata*)   PGP
L   **mlokosewitschii** Lomakin 1897   **PGP-DGP-RD**
      'Chameleon'
    mollis Anderson 1818   PGP
    obovata Maximowicz 1859
        var. **alba** Saunders 1934   **PGP-RD**
      'Grandiflora'

officinalis Linnaeus 1753   PGP-**DGP**-RD
L   'Alba Plena'   PGP-DGP-RD
         'Anemoniflora'
         'Anemoniflora Rosea'   PGP
         'China Rose'   PGP
         'Crimson Globe'   PGP
         ssp. **humilis** (Retzius) Cullen & Heywood 1964 (*P. humilis*)
         'James Crawford Weguelin'   PGP
         'Lize van Veen'
         var. *mascula* (Linnaeus) Fiori 1924 = **P. mascula**
         'Mutabilis Plena'   PGP
         'Rosea Superba'
         'Rosea Superba Plena'   PGP
         'Rosea Plena'   DGP-**RD**
L   'Rubra Plena'   PGP-DGP-**RD**
peregrina Miller 1768 (*P. lobata, P. romanica, P.* 'Fire King', *P.* 'Sunbeam') PGP-RD
         'Fire King'   [Prichard pre-1920] = **P. peregrina** Miller
         var. *glabra* Boissier 1867 = **P. clusii**
L   'Otto Froebel'   [Barr 1898] ('Sunshine')   PGP
         'Sunbeam'   [Barr 1895] = **P. peregrina** Miller
         'Sunshine' = **P. peregrina 'Otto Froebel'**
peregrina Bornmüller 1768 = **P. mascula** ssp. **arietina**
romanica Brandza 1879 = **P. peregrina** Miller
russii Bivona 1816 = **P. mascula** ssp. **russii**
         var. *reverchonii* Le Grand 1899 = **P. mascula** ssp. **russii** var. **reverchonii**
x smouthii Hort. ex Lemoine = **P. 'Smouthii'**
tenuifolia Linnaeus 1759   PGP
         'Flore Pleno'   PGP
         'Latifolia'
         'Rosea'   PGP
triternata Pallas 1795 = **P. mascula** ssp. **triternata**
veitchii Lynch 1905   PGP
         'Alba'
         var. **woodwardii** (Stapf & Cox) Stern 1943   PGP
wittmanniana Hartwiss ex Lindley 1846   PGP
         var. **macrophylla** (Albov) Busch 1930   PGP
woodwardii Stapf & Cox 1930 = **P. veitchii** var. **woodwardii**

CULTIVARS & HYBRID CULTIVARS

classification:

S   =   single
D   =   double
SD   =   semi-double
J   =   'japanese' (petaloid)

P. LACTIFLORA CULTIVARS ('CHINESE' VARIETIES)

D   'A. Delatour'
D   'Abel Carriere'
D   'Adolphe Rousseau'   [Dessert & Mechin 1890]
D   'Agida'   [Origin Unknown pre-1930]
J   'Airway'   [Wild 1967]
J   'Akalu'   [Dessert]
D   'Albert Crousse'   [Crousse 1893]   DGP-RD
D   'Alesia'   [Lemoine 1927]
D   'Alexander Fleming'   [Raiser Unknown]
D   'Alexandre Dumas'   [Guerin 1862]
D   'Alice Harding'   [Lemoine 1922]

J	**'Alstead'**	[Auten 1939]	
J	**'Ama-No-Sode'**	[ex Japan pre-1928]	
D	**'Amabilis'**		
J	**'Angelika Kauffmann'**	[Goos & Koenemann 1912]	
D	**'Angel Cheeks'**	[Klehm]	
D	**'Ann Cousins'**	[Cousins 1946]	
J	**'Antwerpen'**	[Origin Unknown]	
D	**'Arabian Prince'**	[Kelway]	
D	**'Argentine'**		
D	**'Armance Dessert'**	[Doriat 1929]	
D	**'Armistice'**	[Kelsey 1938]	
D	**'Asa Gray'**	[Crousse 1886]	
D	**'Assmannshausen'**	[Goos & Koenemann 1912]	
D	**'Attar of Roses'**	[Murawska 1951]	
D	**'Auguste Dessert'**	[Dessert 1920]	PGP
D	**'Augustin d'Hour'**	[Calot 1867] ('Marechal MacMahon')	
J	**'Aureolin'**	[Shaylor 1917]	
D	**'Avalanche'**	[Crousse 1886]	
D	**'Ballerina'**	[Kelway]	
S	**'Balliol'**	[Origin Unknown]	
J	**'Barrington Belle'**	[Klehm]	
J	**'Barrymore'**	[Kelway]	
D	**'Baroness Schroeder'**	[Kelway 1889]	PGP
S	**'Baron Hulot'**		
J	**'Beacon Flame'**	[Kelway]	
J	**'Beatrice Kelway'**	[Kelway]	
D	**'Beau Geste'**	[Kelway]	
S	**'Beauty Spot'**	[Kelway]	
S	**'Beersheba'**	[Kelway]	PGP
D	**'Best Man'**	[Klehm]	
D	**'Better Times'**	[Franklin 1941]	
D	**'Big Ben'**	[Auten 1943]	
D	**'Big Red Boomer Sooner'**	[Wild & Son 1962]	
D	**'Bingen'**	[Goos & Koenemann 1919]	
D	**'Blush Queen'**	[Hoogendoorn 1949]	
J	**'Bo-Peep'**	[Auten 1944]	
D	**'Bonanza'**	[Franklin 1947]	
D	**'Border Gem'**	[Hoogendoorn 1949]	
D	**'Bossuet'**		
D	**'Boule de Neige'**	[Calot 1867]	
J	**'Bowl of Beauty'**	[Hoogendoorn 1949]	PGP-**DGP**-RD
D	**'Bowl of Cream'**	[Klehm 1963]	
J	**'Break o' Day'**	[Murawska 1947]	
D	**'Bridal Gown'**	[Klehm 1981]	
D	**'Bridal Veil'**	[Kelway]	
J	**'Bride's Dream'**	[Krekler 1965]	
D	**'British Beauty'**	[Kelway 1926]	PGP
S	**'British Empire'**	[Kelway]	
D	**'Buchhügel'**	[Goos & Koenemann]	
D	**'Bunker Hill'**	[Hollis 1906]	
SD	**'Butch'**	[Kreckler 1959]	
J	**'Bu-Te'**	[Wassenberg 1954]	
J	**'Butter Ball'**		
J	**'Calypso'**	[Andrews 1925]	PGP
D	**'Campfire'**	[Auten 1956]	
D	**'Canari'**	[Guerin 1861]	
D	**'Candeur'**	[Dessert 1920]	
S	**'Captivation'**	[Kelway]	
D	**'Carmen'**	[Lemoine 1898]	PGP
D	**'Carnival'**	[Kelway]	PGP

D	'Carolina Moon'	[Auten 1940]
J	'Carrara'	[Bigger 1952]
D	'Caub'	[Goos & Koenemann 1919]
D	'Cecilia Kelway'	[Kelway 1912]
D	'Celebration'	[Nicholls - Wild & Son 1964]
D	'Charlemagne'	[Crousse 1880]
D	'Charles White'	[Klehm 1951]
J	'Charm'	[Franklin 1931]
D	'Cheddar Cheese'	[Klehm 1973]
SD	'Cheddar Gold'	[Klehm 1959]
D	'Cherry Hill'	[Thurlow 1915]
D	'Cherry Royal'	[Wild 1967]
D	'Chestine Gowdy'	[Brand 1913]
S	'Chocolate Soldier'	[Kelway]
D	'Chippewa'	[Murawska 1943]
D	'Claire Dubois'	[Crousse 1886]
D	'Clemenceau'	[Dessert 1920]
J	'Colonel Heneage'	[Kelway]

PGP

J	'Cora Stubbs'	[Krekler]
D	'Cornelia Shaylor'	[Shaylor 1977]
J	'Corronach'	[Kelway]
S	'Countess of Altamont'	[Kelway]
S	'Country Girl'	[Kelway]
D	'Couronne d'Or'	[Calot 1873]
D	'Crimson Banner'	[Kelway]
J	'Crimson Glory'	[Sass 1937]
J	'Curiosity'	[Dessert & Mechin]
S	'Daimio'	[Millet 1926]
D	'Dawn Crest'	[Kelway]
S	'Dawn Pink'	[Sass 1946]
S	'Dayspring'	[Kelway]

PGP

D	'Dinner Plate'	[Klehm 1968]
J	'Dominion'	[Kelway]
J	'Doreen'	[Sass 1949]
J	'Do Tell'	[Auten 1946]
J	'Dragon's Nest'	[Auten 1933]
	'Dr Alexander Fleming' = P. 'Alexander Fleming'	
D	'Dr H Barnsby'	[Dessert 1913]
D	'Doris Cooper'	[Cooper 1946]
S	'Dresden'	[Kelway]
D	'Duchesse de Nemours'	[Calot 1856]

PGP

D	'Duke of Devonshire'	[Kelway 1895]
S	'Dürer'	[Goos & Koenemann]
D	'Edith Cavell'	[Kelway 1916]
D	'Eduard Doriat'	[Doriat 1929]
D	'Edulis Superba'	[Lemon 1824]
D	'Ella Christiansen'	[Brand 1925]
D	'Elsa Sass'	[Sass 1930]
D	'Emma Klehm'	[Klehm 1951]
D	'Emmchen'	[Goos & Koenemann 1919]
D	'Emperor of India'	[Kelway 1912]
S	'English Princess'	[Kelway]
D	'Etienne Mechin'	[Mechin 1880]
	'Etincelante' = P. 'L'Etincelante'	
D	'Eugenie Verdier'	[Calot 1864]
J	'Eva'	[Origin Unknown pre-1952]
J	'Evening World'	[Kelway]

PGP

J	'Fairbanks'	[Auten 1945]
D	'Fairy's Petticoat'	[Klehm]
J	'Fancy Nancy'	[Auten 1944]

D	**'Fause'** [Miellez 1855]		
D	**'Feather Top'** [Wild 1967]		
D	**'Felix Crousse'** [Crousse 1881]	PGP	
D	**'Felix Supreme'** [Kriek 1955]		
D	**'Festiva Maxima'** [Miellez 1851]	PGP-DGP	
SD	**'Fireball'** [Brand 1938]		
D	**'First Lady'** [Klehm]		
D	**'F Koppius'** [Rijnstroom 1931]		
S	**'Flamingo'** [Andrews 1925]		
D	**'Florence Ellis'** [Nicholls 1948]		
D	**'Florence Nicholls'** [Nicholls 1938]		
D	**'Fokker'** [Ruys 1928]		
D	**'Francois Ortegat'** [Parmentier 1850]		
J	**'Fuigi-No-Mine'** [Origin Unknown]		
D	**'Garden Beauty'** [Kelway]		
J	**'Gartenbaudirektor Heide'** [Klose 1981]		
D	**'Gayborder June'** [Hoogendoorn 1949]		
S	**'Gay Ladye'** [Kelway]		
J	**'Gay Paree'** [Auten 1933]		
D	**'General Bertrand'** [Guerin 1846]		
S	**'General Wolfe'** [Kelway]		
D	**'Germaine Bigot'** [Dessert 1902]		
	'G F Hemerick' = **P. 'Mr G F Hemerick'**		
D	**'Gilbert Barthelot'** [Doriat 1931]		
J	**'Gleam of Light'** [Kelway]		
D	**'Globe of Light'** [Kelway 1928]	PGP-RD	
D	**'Gloire de Chenonceaux'** [Mechin 1880]		
D	**'Gloriana'** [Neeley 1918]		
D	**'Glory Hallelujah'** [Klehm]		
D	**'Glory of Somerset'** [Kelway 1887]		
J	**'Go-Daigo'** [Millet 1926]		
D	**'Gold Medal'** [ex Netherlands]		
D	**'Grace Loomis'** [Saunders 1920]		
S	**'Granat'** [Goos & Koenemann 1951]		
J	**'Great Sport'** [Kelway]		
D	**'Gretchen'** [Goos & Koenemann 1911]		
D	**'Guidon'** [Nicholls 1941]		
J	**'Hakodate'** [Millet]		
D	**'Hargrove Hudson'** [Wild 1949]		
J	**'Hari-Ai-Nin'** [Babcock 1929]		
J	**'Hawaiian Sunset'**		
D	**'Heimburg'** [Goos & Koenemann 1926]		
D	**'Heinrich Hagemann'** [Klose 1981]		
D	**'Heirloom'** [Kelway]		
S	**'Helen'** [Thurlow 1922]		
D	**'Helen Hayes'** [Murawska 1943]		
J	**'Henri Potin'** [Doriat 1924]		
S	**'Her Grace'** [Kelway]		
J	**'Her Majesty'** [Kelway]		
D	**'Hiawatha'** [Franklin 1931]		
D	**'Highlight'** [Auten-Wild 1952]		
S	**'Hit Parade'** [Nicholls 1965]		
S	**'Hogarth'** [Goos & Koenemann 1912]		
S	**'Holbein'** [Goos & Koenemann 1910]		
D	**'Honey Gold'** [Klehm]		
D	**'Hoosierland'** [Klehm 1968]		
D	**'Ingenieur Doriat'** [Doriat 1931]		
D	**'Inspecteur Lavergne'** [Doriat 1924]		
J	**'Instituteur Doriat'** [Doriat 1925]	PGP	
J	**'Isani-Gidui'** [Origin Unknown pre-1928]		

J	**'Jacques Doriat'**	[Doriat 1928]	
D	**'James Kelway'**	[Kelway 1900]	
D	**'James Pillow'**	[Pillow 1936]	
J	**'Jan van Leeuwen'**	[van Leeuwen 1928]	
D	**'Jay Cee'**	[Klehm 1959]	
D	**'Jean Claude Allard'**		
S/J	**'Jeanne Cayeux'**	[Cayeux pre-1937]	
D	**'Jeanne d'Arc'**	[Calot 1858]	
D	**'Jennie E Richardson'**	[Hollis 1909]	
S	**'Jeso'**		
D	**'Jessie Gist'**	[Nicholls-Wild & Son 1953]	
D	**'John Howard Wigell'**	[Wigell 1942]	
J	**'Johnny'**	[Origin Unknown 1955]	
J	**'Joseph Aletti'**	[Doriat 1934]	
D	**'Judy Ann'**	[Wild & Son 1964]	
D	**'June Morning'**	[Kelway]	
D	**'June Rose'**	[Jones 1935]	
J	**'Kameno Kegoromo'**	[Flamboyant]	
S	**'Kankakee'**	[Auten 1931]	
D	**'Kansas'**	[Bigger 1940]	
J	**'Karatzu'**	[Millet]	
D	**'Karl Rosenfield'**	[Rosenfield 1908]	RD
S	**'Kaskaskia'**	[Auten 1931]	
D	'Kaub' = **P. 'Caub'**		
J	**'Kelway's Brilliant'**	[Kelway]	PGP
D	**'Kelway's Glorious'**	[Kelway 1909]	PGP
S	**'Kelway's Gorgeous'**	[Kelway]	
D	**'Kelway's Lovely'**	[Kelway]	PGP
J	**'Kelway's Majestic'**	[Kelway]	PGP
D	**'Kelway's Rosemary'**	[Kelway 1916]	
D	**'Kelway's Supreme'**	[Kelway]	
S	**'Kestral'**	[Kelway]	
J	**'King Arthur'**	[Kelway 1902]	
D	**'King Midas'**	[Lins 1942]	
J	**'King George VI'**	[Kelway]	
J	**'King of England'**	[Kelway 1902]	
D	**'Koenigswinter'**	[Goos & Koenemann 1912]	
J	**'Kojiki'**	[Millet 1926]	
S	**'Krinkled White'**	[Brand 1928]	
J	**'Kuni-Mori'**	[Origin Unknown]	
J	**'Laciniata'**	[Origin Unknown]	
D	**'Lady Alexandra Duff'**	[Kelway 1902]	PGP-RD
D	**'Lady Anna'**	[Calot 1856]	
D	**'Lady Orchid'**	[Bigger 1942]	
D	**'Lady of the Snows'**	[Brethour 1938]	
S	**'Lady Wolseley'**	[Kelway]	
S	'La Fiancee' = **P. lactiflora**		
D	**'La France'**	[Lemoine 1901]	
D	**'Lake O' Silver'**	[Franklin 1920]	
D	**'La Lorraine'**	[Lemoine 1901]	
S	**'Langport Cross'**	[Kelway 1929]	
D	**'La Perle'**	[Crousse 1886]	
J	**'Largo'**	[Vories 1929]	
D	**'Laura Dessert'**	[Dessert 1913]	PGP
D	**'Lavender Bouquet'**	[Nicholls-Wild 1964]	
D	**'Le Cygne'**	[Lemoine 1907]	
J	**'Lemon Queen'**	[Origin Unknown]	
S	**'L'Etincelante'**	[Dessert 1905]	
S	**'Liebchen'**	[Murawska 1959]	
J	**'Lilac Time'**	[Lins 1958]	

D   'Lois Kelsey'   [Kelsey 1934]
D   'Longfellow'   [Brand 1907]
D   'Lora Dexheimer'   [Brand 1913]
D   'Lorch'   [Goos & Koenemann 1913]
D   'Lord Avebury'   [Kelway]
S   'Lord Kitchener'   [Kelway]   PGP
J   'Lotus Queen'   [Murawska 1947]
SD   'Louis Barthelot'   [Doriat 1927]
D   'Lowell Thomas'   [Rosenfield 1934]
S   'Lucky Day'   [Auten 1934]
D   'Madelon'   [Dessert 1922]
D   'Magic Melody'   [Kelway]
D   'Magic Orb'   [Kelway]
D   'Mainz'   [Goos & Koenemann 1926]
D   'Margarete Klose'   [Klose 1972]
D   'Marguerite Gerard'   [Crousse]
       'Marechal MacMahon' = P. 'Augustin d'Hour'
D   'Marie Crousse'   [Crousse 1892]   PGP
D   'Marie Lemoine'   [Calot 1869]
D   'Marietta Sisson'   [Sass 1933]
D   'Marksburg'   [Goos & Koenemann 1930]
D   'Marquis C Lagergren'   [Dessert 1911]
D   'Martha Bulloch'   [Brand 1907]
D   'Mary Brand'   [Brand 1907]
D   'Masterpiece'   [Kelway 1895]
D   'Matilda Lewis'   [Saunders 1921]
J   'Meadow Lark'   [Bigger 1977]
SD   'Minnie Shaylor'   [Shaylor 1919]
S   'Mischief'   [Auten 1925]
SD   'Miss America'   [Mann-van Steen 1936]
D   'Miss Eckhart'   [Roelof-van der Meer 1928]
D   'Mister Ed'   [Klehm]
S   'Mistral'   [Dessert 1905]
D   'Mlle Jeanne Riviere'   [Riviere 1908]
D   'Mlle Leonie Calot'   [Calot 1861] ('Mons Charles Leveque')
S   'Mme Antoine Riviere'   [Riviere]
S   'Mme Benoit Riviere'   [Riviere 1911]
J   'Mme Butterfly'   [Franklin 1933]
D   'Mme Calot'   [Miellez 1856]   RD
D   'Mme Claude Tain'   [Doriat 1927]
D   'Mme Crousse'   [Calot 1866]
D   'Mme de Verneville'   [Crousse 1885]
D   'Mme Ducel'   [Mechin 1880]
       'Mme Durufle' = P. 'Mons Durufle'
D   'Mme Edouard Doriat'   [Dessert-Doriat 1924]
D   'Mme Emile Debatene'   [Dessert-Doriat 1927]
D   'Mme Emile Galle'   [Crousse 1881]
D   'Mme Geissler'   [Crousse 1880]
S   'Mme Henry Fuchs'   [Riviere]
D   'Mme Julie Berthier'
D   'Mme Jules Dessert'   [Dessert 1909]
D   'Mme Lemoine'   [Calot 1864]
D   'Mme Lemoinier'   [Calot 1865]
       'Mme Leonie Calot' = P. 'Mlle Leonie Calot'
J   'Mobuchi'   [Millet]
D   'Modeste Guerin'   [Guerin 1845]
       'Mons Charles Leveque' = P. 'Mlle Leonie Calot'
D   'Mons Adam Modzelewski'   [Doriat 1935]
D   'Mons Durufle'   [Origin Unknown]
D   'Mons Jules Elie'   [Crousse 1888]   RD

D	**'Mons Martin Cahuzac'** [Dessert 1899]	PGP
D	**'Moonglow'** [Rosefield 1939]	
J	**'Moon of Nippon'** [Auten 1936]	
D	**'Moon River'** [Klehm]	
D	**'Moonstone'** [Murawska 1943]	
D	**'Mother's Choice'** [Glasscock 1950]	
J	**'Mr G F Hemerick'** [Van Leeuwen]]	
S	**'Mr Thim'** [Van Leeuwen 1926]	
D	**'Mrs Edward Harding'** [Shaylor 1918]	
D	**'Mrs Franklin D Roosevelt'** [Franklin 1932]	
S	**'Mrs F J Hemerick'**	
D	**'Mrs J V Edlund'** [Franklin 1929]	
D	**'Mrs Livingstone Farrand'** [Nicholls 1935]	
J	**'Mrs Wilder Bancroft'** [Nicholls 1935]	
S	**'Murillio'** [Goos & Koenemann 1910]	
D	**'Music Man'** [Wild 1967]	
D	**'My Pal Rudy'** [Klehm 1952]	
D	**'Nancy Nicholls'** [Nicholls 1941]	
D	**'Newfoundland'**	
SD	**'Nice Gal'** [Krekler 1965]	
D	**'Nick Shaylor'** [Allison 1931]	
J	**'Nippon Beauty'** [Auten 1927]	
J	**'Nippon Parade'** [Auten 1935]	
D	**'Noemie Demay'** [Calot 1867]	
J	**'Nymphe'** [Dessert 1913]	
J	**'Ohirama'** [Origin Unknown]	
J	**'Okinawa'** [Origin Unknown]	
J	**'Okushimo'**	
J	**'Opal Hamilton'** [Nicholls-Wild 1957]	
D	**'Ornament'** [Kelway]	
D	**'Osage'** [Bigger 1977]	
D	**'Painted Desert'** [Nicholls 1965]	
D	**'Paul M Wild'** [Wild 1964]	
D	**'Peace'** [Murawska 1955]	
D	**'Peach Fluff'** [Wild 1954]	
D	**'Peppermint'** [Nicholls-Wild 1958]	
S	**'Peregrine'** [Kelway]	
D	**'Peter Brand'** [ex Netherlands pre-1937]	
J	**'Petite Renee'** [Dessert 1899]	
D	**'Pfeiffer's Red Triumph'** [Pfeiffer 1947]	
D	**'Philippe Rivoire'** [Riviere 1911]	
D	**'Philomele'** [Calot 1861]	
S	**'Pico'** [Freeborn 1934]	
D	**'Pierre Dessert'** [Dessert-Mechin 1890]	
D	**'Pillow Talk'** [Klehm 1973]	
J	**'Pink Champagne'** [Nicholls 1964]	
S	**'Pink Dawn'** [Klehm]	
J	**'Pink Delight'** [Kelway]	PGP-**RD**
D	**'Pink Jazz'** [Klehm]	
D	**'Pink Lemonade'** [Klehm 1951]	
D	**'Pink Parfait'** [Klehm 1975]	
S	**'Pink Perfection'** [Kelway]	
D	**'Pink Radiance'** [Wild 1959]	
J	**'Plainsman'** [Bigger 1949]	
S	**'Poetic'** [Kelway]	PGP
J	**'Polar Star'** [Sass 1932]	
D	**'Pottsi Plena'** [Calot 1857]	
D	**'President Poincare'** [Kelway]	PGP
D	**'President Franklin D Roosevelt'** [Franklin 1933]	RD
	'President Taft' = **P. 'Reine Hortense'**	

D	'President Wilson'	[Thurlow 1918]	
S	'Pride of Somerset'	[Kelway 1928]	
D	'Primevere'	[Lemoine 1907]	
J	'Princess Duleepsingh'	[Kelway]	
D	'Princess Margaret'	[Murawska 1960]	
D	'Purpurea Suberba'	[Delache pre-1930]	
J	'Queen Alexandra'	[Kelway 1902]	
D	'Queen of Sheba'	[Sass 1937]	
S	'Queen of the Belgians'	[Kelway]	
J	'Raspberry Joe'	[Klehm 1981]	
D	'Raspberry Sundae'	[Klehm 1968]	
D	'Rauenthal'	[Goos & Koenemann 1913]	
D	'Red Carpet'	[Wild 1965]	
D	'Red Comet'	[Auten 1956]	
J	'Red Emperor'	[Auten 1931]	
S	'Red Flag'		
J	'Red Star'	[Nicholls 1941]	
S	'Red Velvet'	[Auten 1945]	
D	'Reine Hortense'	[Calot 1857] ('President Taft')	
S	'Rembrandt'	[Goos & Koenemann 1926]	
D	'Richard Carvel'	[Brand 1913]	
J	'Rigolote'	[Doriat 1931]	
J	'Roberta'	[Auten 1936]	
D	'Rosa Klose'	[Klose 1983]	
D	'Rose d'Amour'	[Calot 1857]	
S	'Rose of Delight'		
D	'Rose Shaylor'	[Shaylor 1920]	
D	'Rüdesheim'	[Goos & Koenemann]	
D	'Ruth Clay'	[Kelsey 1935]	
D	'Ruth Cobb'	[Wild 1963]	
J	'Sagamore'	[Jones 1943]	
S	'Sang Gaulois'	[Riviere]	
SD	'Santa Fe'	[Auten 1937]	
D	'Sarah Bernhardt'	[Lemoine 1906]	PGP-DGP-RD
J	'Schaffe'	[Krekler 1965]	
S	'Schwindt'	[Goos & Koenemann 1910]	
S	'Sea Shell'	[Sass 1937]	
J	'Seioba'	[Origin Unknown]	
J	'Shaylor's Sunburst'	[Allison 1931]	
D	'Shimmering Velvet'	[Kelway]	
D	'Shirly Temple'	[Origin Unknown]	RD
D	'Silberschmelze'	[Goos & Koenemann pre-1937]	
S	'Silver Flare'		
SD	'Sinbad'	[Auten 1941]	
S	'Sir Edward Elgar'	[Kelway]	PGP
J	'Sitka'	[Auten 1945]	
J	'Sky Pilot'	[Auten 1939]	
D	'Snow Cloud'	[Hoogendoorn 1949]	
D	'Snow Mountain'	[Bigger 1946]	
J	'Snow Wheel'	[Origin Unknown]	
D	'Solange'	[Lemoine 1907]	RD
D	'Solfartare'	[Calot 1861]	
J	'Some Ganoko'	[Origin Unknown]	
J	'Soshi'	[Millet]	
D	'Souvenir d'A Millet'	[Millet 1924]	
D	'Souvenir de Francois Ruitton'	[Riviere 1908]	
S	'Souvenir de Marguerite Lemoine'	[Riviere]	
D	'Souvenir de Mme Collette Veillet'	[Riviere 1825]	
S	'Souvenir d'Haraucourt'		
S	'Spellbinder'	[Bigger 1960]	

D	**'St Goar'**	[Goos & Koenemann 1919]
D	**'Strassburg'**	[Goos & Koenemann 1911]
S	**'Strephon'**	[Kelway]
J	**'Surugu'**	[Origin Unknown]
D	**'Susie Q'**	[Klehm]
D	**'Sweet Sixteen'**	[Klehm]
J	**'Sword Dance'**	[Auten 1933]
J	**'Tamate-Boku'**	[Origin Unknown]
D	**'The Mighty Mo'**	[Wild & Son 1950]
S	**'The Moor'**	[Barr]
D	**'Therese'**	[Dessert 1904]
S	**'Thoma'**	[Goos & Koenemann 1919]
D	**'Thura Hires'**	[Nicholls 1938]
SD	**'Tiny Tim'**	[Kelsey 1941]
D	**'To Kalon'**	[Kelsey 1936]
J	**'Tokio'**	[pre-1910]
J	**'Tom Eckhardt'**	[Krekler 1965]
D	**'Top Brass'**	[Klehm 1968]
J	**'Toro-No-Maki'**	[pre-1928]
J	**'Torpilleur'**	[Dessert 1913]
D	**'Triomphe de L'Exposition de Lille'**	[Calot 1865]
J	**'Tudor Rose'**	[Kelway]
S	**'Uhde'**	[Goos & Koenemann 1919]
J	**'Variety Girl'**	[Kelway]
J	**'Velma Atkinson'**	[Wild 1964]
D	**'Veronica Klose'**	[Klose 1983]
J	**'Vicomte de Noaillis'**	
D	**'Viola Klose'**	[Klose 1983]
D	**'Victoire de la Marne'**	[Dessert 1915]
D	**'Victoire Lemon'**	[Miellez 1858]
S	**'Victoria'**	[Origin Unknown]
D	**'Ville de Nancy'**	[Calot 1872]
D	**'Virgo Maria'**	[Calot 1859]
D	**'Vivid Rose'**	[Klehm 1952]
D	**'Vogue'**	[Hoogendoorn 1949]
D	**'Walter Faxon'**	[Richardson 1904]
S	**'Watteau'**	[Goos & Koenemann 1911]
J	**'Westerner'**	[Bigger 1942]
J	**'White Cap'**	[Winchell 1956]
D	**'White Charm'**	[Glasscock-Falk 1964]
J	**'White Sands'**	[Wild 1968]
S	**'White Wings'**	[Hoogendoorn 1949]
D	**'Wiesbaden'**	[Goos & Koenemann 1911]
S	**'Wilbur Wright'**	[Kelway 1909]
J	**'Yellow King'**	[via Harding]
SD	**'Zuzu'**	[Krekler 1955]

RD
DGP

HYBRID CULTIVARS

S	**'Alexander Steffen'**	[Steffen]
SD	**'Alexander Woollcott'**	[Saunders 1941]
D	**'Angelo Cobb Freeborn'**	[Freeborn 1943]
S	**'Archangel'**	[Saunders 1950]
S	**'Arrow Maker'**	[Auten 1968]
S	**'Athena'**	[Saunders c1955]
D	**'Auten's Red'**	[Auten 1951]
D	**'Ballerina'**	[Saunders 1941]
D	**'Belle Center'**	[Mains 1956]
SD	**'Black Gold'**	[Auten 1946]
D	**'Black Monarch'**	[Glasscock 1939]

SD   'Blaze'   [Fay 1973]
S   'Bravura'   [Saunders 1943]
S   'Bright Diadem'   [Saunders 1950]
D   'Bright Eyes'   [Auten 1950]
S   'Bright Knight'   [Glasscock 1939]
SD   'Buckeye Belle'   [Mains 1956]
S   'Burma Ruby'   [Glasscock 1951]
S   'Burst of Joy'   [Auten 1968]
   'Byzantine'
SD   'Camellia'   [Saunders 1942]
S   'Campagna'   [Saunders 1941]
S   'Cardinal's Robe'   [Saunders 1940]
SD   'Carina'   [Saunders 1944]
D   'Carol'   [Bockstoce 1955]
S   'Carolina'   [Saunders 1950]
S   'Chalice'   [Saunders 1929]
D   'Cherry Red'   [Glasscock 1939]   PGP
SD   'Chief Justice'   [Auten 1941]
SD/D   'Chief Logan'   [Mains 1961]
S   'China Boy'   [Auten 1942]
   'China Rose' = **P. officinalis** 'China Rose'
J   'Chocolate Soldier'   [Auten 1939]
S   'Claire de Lune'   [White-Wild 1954]
SD   'Claudia'   [Saunders 1944]
D   'Commando'   [Glasscock 1944]
SD   'Constance Spry'   [Saunders 1941]   PGP
J   'Coral 'n Gold'   [Cousins-Klehm 1981]
SD   'Coral Charm'   [Wissing 1964]
SD   'Coral Fay'   [Fay 1973]
SD   'Coral Sunset'   [Wissing 1965]
SD   'Coral Supreme'   [Wissing 1964]
S   'Coralie'   [Saunders 1940]
SD   'Crusader'   [Glasscock 1940]
SD   'Cytherea'   [Saunders 1953]   PGP
J   'Dainty Lass'   [Glasscock 1935]
S   'Dakota'   [Auten 1941]
D   'Dandy Dan'   [Auten 1946]
S   'Dauntless'   [Glasscock 1944]
S   'Daystar'   [Saunders 1949]   PGP
S   'Dazzler'   [Auten 1956]
S   'Defender'   [Saunders 1929]   **PGP-DGP**
D   'Diana Parks'   [Bockstoce 1942]
S   'Early Daybreak'   [Saunders 1949]
S   'Early Scout'   [Auten 1952]
S   'Early Windflower'   [Saunders 1939]   PGP
S   'Echo'   [Saunders 1951]
D   'Edgar Jessep'   [Bockstoce 1958]
J/D   'Eldorado'   [Auten 1956]
SD   'Ellen Cowley'   [Saunders 1940]
S   'Eventide'   [Glasscock 1945]
J   'Fancy Free'   [Auten 1951]
S   'Favorita'   [Auten 1956]
SD   'Fayette'   [Fay 1970]
S   'Fiesta'   [Auten 1956]
SD   'Firebell'   [Mains 1959]
D   'Fire Bird'   [Auten 1956]
SD   'Firelight'   [Saunders 1950]
S   'Flame'   [Glasscock 1939]
S   'Friendship'   [Glasscock-Falk 1955]
S   'Garden Peace'   [Saunders 1941]

S	**'Gay Cavalier'**	[Glasscock 1944]	
S	**'Golden Glow'**	[Glasscock 1935]	
S	**'Good News'**	[Auten 1946]	
S	**'Green Ivory'**	[Saunders 1938]	
S	**'Halcyon'**	[Saunders 1948]	
D	**'Heavenly Pink'**	[Smirnow]	
SD	**'Helen Matthews'**	[Saunders-Krekler 1953]	
D	**'Henry Bockstoce'**	[Bockstoce 1955]	
SD	**'Heritage'**	[Saunders 1950]	
D	**'Hi-Fi'**	[Auten-Wild 1971]	
SD	**'Hoffnung'**	[Steffen 1954]	
SD	**'Hope'**	[Saunders 1929]	
S	**'Horizon'**	[Saunders 1943]	
D	**'Howard R Watkins'**	[Bockstoce 1947]	
SD	**'Illini Belle'**	[Glasscock 1941]	
S	**'Illini Chief'**	[Glasscock 1940]	
S	**'Illini Warrior'**	[Glasscock 1954]	
S	**'Janice'**	[Saunders 1939]	
D	**'Jean E Bockstoce'**	[Bockstoce 1933]	
S/D	**'Jewel'**	[Glasscock 1939]	
S/D	**'John Harvard'**	[Auten 1939]	
S	**'Laddie'**	[Glasscock 1941]	
S	**'Late Windflower'**	[Saunders 1939]	PGP
SD	**'Laura Magnuson'**	[Saunders 1941]	
S/D	**Lavender Hybrids**	[Saunders 1939]	
S/SD	**'Legion of Honor'**	[Saunders 1941]	PGP
S	**'Little Dorrit'**	[Saunders 1949]	PGP
SD/D	**'Lois Arlene'**	[Moots 1962]	
SD	**'Lovely Rose'**	[Saunders 1942]	
SD	**'Ludovica'**	[Saunders 1941]	
S	**'Lustrous'**	[Saunders 1942]	
S	**'Mai Fleuri'**	[Lemoine 1905]	PGP
S	**'Massasoit'**	[White 1954]	
S	**'May Apple'**	[Wolf-Bigger 1977]	
S	**'Mid May'**	[Saunders 1950]	
S/SD	**'Montezuma'**	[Saunders 1943]	
S	**'Moonrise'**	[Saunders 1949]	PGP
SD	**'Nadia'**	[Saunders 1941]	
S	**'Nancy'**	[White 1954]	
D	**'Nathalie'**	[Saunders 1939]	
S	**'Nevada'**	[Auten 1950]	
D	**'Ole Faithful'**	[Glasscock-Falk 1964]	
D	**'Old Main'**	[Auten 1939]	
S	**'Orange Glory'**	[Auten 1956]	
SD	**'Pageant'**	[Saunders 1941]	
S	**'Paladin'**	[Saunders 1950]	
S	**'Patriot'**	[Saunders 1943]	
S	**'Paula Fay'**	[Fay 1968]	
D	**'Peachy Rose'**	[Smirnow]	
SD	**'Pink Hawaian Coral'**	[Klehm 1981]	
S	**Playmate Hybrids**	[Saunders 1950]	
	'Polindra'		
SD	**'Postilion'**	[Saunders 1941]	
SD	**'Prairie Moon'**	[Fay 1959]	
J	**'Raspberry Rose'**	[Auten 1956]	
J	**'Red Beauty'**	[Auten 1956]	
D	**'Red Charm'**	[Glasscock 1944]	
SD	**'Red Glory'**	[Auten 1937]	
D	**'Red Grace'**	[Glasscock-Klehm 1980]	
D	**'Red Monarch'**	[Auten-Glasscock 1937]	

SD	'Red Red Rose'	[Saunders 1942]	
S	'Red Romance'	[Auten 1968]	
S	'Red Signal'	[Freeborn 1941]	
S	'Requiem'	[Saunders 1941]	
SD	'Robert W Auten'	[Auten 1948]	
S	'Rosalba'	[Saunders 1941]	
S	'Rose Crystal'	[Saunders 1955]	
SD	'Rosedale'	[Auten 1936]	
S	'Rose Diamond'	[Saunders 1943]	
S	'Roselette'	[Saunders 1950]	
SD	'Rosy Cheek'	[Saunders 1943]	
SD	'Royal Rose'	[Reath 1974]	
S	'Rubinschale'	[von Stein-Zeppelin]	
S	'Rushlight'	[Saunders 1950]	
D	'Salmon Beauty'	[Glasscock-Auten 1935]	
S	'Salmon Glow'	[Glasscock 1947]	
S	'Sanctus'	[Saunders 1952-55]	
S	'Scarlet O'Hara'	[Glasscock-Falk 1956]	
D	'Simple Simon'	[Auten]	
S	'Sky Queen'	[Auten 1956]	
S	'Smouthii'	[ex France 1845]	PGP-RD
SD	'Sophie'	[Saunders 1940]	
S	'Sprite'	[Saunders 1950]	
S	'Starlight'	[Saunders 1949]	
	'Sunbeam' = **P. peregrina**		
S	'Sunlight'	[Saunders 1973]	
S	'Tango'	[Auten 1956]	
S	'Tecumseh'	[White 1954]	
	'The Bride' = **P. lactiflora**		
D	'Veritas'	[Auten 1939]	
D	'Victoria Lincoln'	[Saunders 1938]	PGP
J	'Walter Mains'	[Mains 1957]	
S	'White Innocence'	[Saunders 1947]	PGP
	'Whitleyi Major' = **P. lactiflora**		
S	'Wildfire'	[Schroeder-Glasscock 1947]	
S	'Winged Victory'	[Saunders 1950]	
S	'Your Majesty'	[Saunders 1947]	

PAESIA J. Saint-Hilaire 1833   [*Dennstaedtiaceae*]
    scaberula (A. Richard) Kuhn 1882   EGF.1-PGP

PANCRATIUM Linnaeus 1753   [*Amaryllidaceae*]
    illyricum Linnaeus 1753   EGF.1-PGP-**BB-RD**
    maritimum Linnaeus 1753   EGF.1-PGP-**BB**-RD

PANICUM Linnaeus 1753   [*Poaceae (Gramineae)*]
AN   **capillare** Linnaeus 1753   EGF.2
    clandestinum Linnaeus 1753   EGF.2
    maximum Jacquin 1786
AN   **miliaceum** Linnaeus 1753   EGF.2
    virgatum Linnaeus 1753   EGF.2-PGP
          'Hänse'   [H. Herms]
          'Rehbraun'
          'Rotbraun' = **P. virgatum 'Rehbraun'**
          'Rotstrahlbusch'   [K. Foerster]
          'Rubrum'
          'Strictum'   PGP

PAPAVER Linnaeus 1753   [*Papaveraceae*]
    alpinum Linnaeus 1753 = **P. nudicaule**

alpinum Markgraf non Linnaeus 1753 = **P. burseri**
    ssp. *kerneri* (Hayek) Fedde = **P. kerneri**
    ssp. *rhaeticum* (Leresche) Hayek = **P. rhaeticum**
    ssp. *sendtneri* (Kerner ex Hayek) Schinz & R. Keller = **P. sendtneri**

N	**atlanticum** (Ball) Cosson 1882	PGP
	bracteatum Lindley 1821	PGP
	burseri Crantz 1763 (*P. alpinum* Markgraf)	DGP-RD
AN	**commutatum** Fischer & C.A. Meyer 1837	
	corona-sancti-stephani Zapalowicz 1911	
	heldreichii Boissier 1867 = **P. spicatum**	
	kerneri Hayek 1903 (*P. alpinum* ssp. *kerneri*)	RD
	faurei Fedde 1909 = **P. miyabeanum**	
N	**lateritium** Koch 1855	**PGP**
	miyabeanum Tatewaki 1936 (*P. faurei*)	
N	**nudicaule** Linnaeus 1753	PGP-DGP-RD

    'Constance Finnis'
    'Garden Gnome' = **P. nudicaule 'Gartenzwerg'**
    'Gartenzwerg' ('Garden Gnome')   [E. Benary]
    'Illumination'
    'Kelmscott Giant'
    Meadhome Hybrids
    'Oregon Rainbow'

N	**orientale** Linnaeus 1753	**DGP**

    'Allegro'
    'Arwide'
    'Avebury Crimson'
    'Beauty of Livermere'
    'Beauty Queen'
    'Black and White'
    'Blue Moon'
    'Brilliant'
    'Catherina'   [Zeppelin 1970]
    'Cedric's Pink'
    'China Boy'
    'Colosseum'
    'Cowichan'
    'Curlilocks'
    'Degas'
    'Derwisch'   [Zeppelin 1976]
    'Ethel Swete'
    'Fatima'
    'Fireball' ('Nana Plena')   PGP
    'Fireglobe'
    'Frühot'   [Zeppelin]
    'Garden Glory'
    'Glowing Embers'
    'Goliath'   PGP-RD
    'Haremstraum'
    'Helen Elizabeth'
    'Harvest Moon'
    'Indian Chief'   [A. Perry]   PGP-DGP
    'John III'
    'Karine'   [Zeppelin 1976]
    'King George'   **RD**
    'Kleine Tanzerin'
    'Ladybird'
    'Lighthouse'
    'Lord Lambourne'
    'Maiden's Blush'

L   **'Marcus Perry'**   [A. Perry 1942]   PGP-DGP-RD

'Mahony'
'May Sadler'
'Midnight'
L 'Mrs Perry'   [A. Perry]   PGP-**DGP**-**RD**
   'Mrs Stobart'   [A. Perry]
   'Nana Allegro'
   'Nana Plena' = **P. orientale 'Fireball'**
   'Olympia'   PGP
   'Orange Glow'
   'Oriana'
   'Pale Face'
   'Pale White'
L 'Perry's White'   [A. Perry]   PGP-RD
   'Peter Pan'   [A. Perry]   PGP
   'Picotee'
   'Pink Chiffon'
   'Prinzessin Victoria Louise'
   'Rembrandt'
   'Salmon Glow'   PGP-RD
   'Salome'
   'Sindbad'   [Zeppelin 1975]
   'Snowflame'
   'Springtime'
   'Storm Torch' = **P. orientale 'Sturmfackel'**
   'Sturmfackel' ('Storm Torch')   [Goos & Koenemann]   PGP
   'Suleika'
   'Sultana'   **DGP**
   'Turkenlouis' ('Turkish Delight')
   'Turkish Delight' = **P. orientale 'Turkenlouis'**
   pilosum Smith 1806   PGP-RD
   pyrenaicum (Linnaeus) Willdenow 1809 = **P. rhaeticum** p.p., **P. sendtneri** p.p.
N **radicatum** Rottboell 1770
   rhaeticum Leresche 1881 (*P. alpinum* ssp. *rhaeticum, P. pyrenaicum* p.p.) DGP-**RD**
AN‡L **rhoeas** Linnaeus 1753   **DGP**-RD
   rupifragum Boissier & Reuter 1852   PGP
   sendtneri Kerner ex Hagek 1903 (*P. alpinum* ssp. *sendtneri, P. pyrenaicum* p.p.)
                                                                 RD
AN‡ **somniferum** Linnaeus 1753   RD
   'Paeoniiflorum'   RD
   'Proliferum'
   spicatum Boissier & Balansa 1856 (*P. heldreichii*)   PGP
B **triniifolium** Boissier 1867

PARADISEA Mazzucato 1814 nom. cons.   [*Asphodelaceae (Liliaceae)*]
   liliastrum (Linnaeus) Bertoloni 1840   EGF.1-PGP
   'Major'   EGF.1
   lusitanica (Coutinho) Sampaio 1913   PGP

PARAHEBE W. R. B. Oliver 194   [*Scrophulariaceae*]
   x bidwillii (Hooker) W. R. B. Oliver 1944 (*P. decora* x *P. lyallii*)
      'Kea'   [G. Hutchins]
      'Rosea'
   canescens W. R. B. Oliver 1944   CA
   catarractae (Forster f.) W. R. B. Oliver 1944 (*Veronica catarractae*) **RD**
      'Alba'
      'Delight' ('Greencourt Hybrid', 'Porlock')   RD
      ssp. **diffusa** (Hooker f.) P. J. Garnock-Jones 1980
      'Greencourt Hybrid' = **P. catarractae 'Delight'**
      ssp. **martinii** P. J. Garnock-Jones 1980
      'Porlock' = **P. catarractae 'Delight'**

decora M. B. Ashwin 1961   CA
derwentiana (Andrews) B. G. Briggs & Ehrendorfer 1968
x edinensis hort. (*P. hectori* x *P. pimeleoides*)
hookeriana (Walpole) W. R. B. Oliver 1944 (*Veronica compacta, V. nivea*)
    var. **olsenii** (Colenso) M. B. Ashwin 1961 (*P. olsenii*)
linifolia (Hooker f.) W. R. B. Oliver 1944
    'Blue Skies'
lyallii (Hooker f.) W. R. B. Oliver 1944   RD
    'Julie-Anne'
    'Rosea'
'Mervyn'   [M.T. Feesey]
olsenii (Colenso) W. R. B. Oliver 1944 = **P. hookeriana** var. **olsenii**
perfoliata (R. Brown) B. G. Briggs (*Veronica perfoliata*)   **PGP**
trifida (Petrie) W. R. B. Oliver 1944

PARAQUILEGIA J. R. Drummond & Hutchinson 1920   [*Ranunculaceae*]
    anemonoides (Willdenow) Ulbrich 1922 (*P. grandiflora*)   **CA**
    grandiflora (Fischer ex de Candolle) J. R. Drummond & Hutchinson 1920 =
                                        P. anemonoides

PARIETARIA Linnaeus 1753   [*Urticaceae*]
HN‡ **judaica** Linnaeus 1753
    officinalis hort., non Linnaeus 1753 = **P. judaica**

PARNASSIA Linnaeus 1753   [*Saxifragaceae*]
N‡ **palustris** Linnaeus 1753

PAROCHETUS Buchanan-Hamilton ex D.Don 1825   [*Fabaceae (Leguminosae)*]
    communis Buchanan-Hamilton ex D.Don 1925   **CA-RD**

PARONYCHIA Miller 1754   [*Caryophyllaceae*]
    argentea Lamarck 1778   CA
    capitata (Linnaeus) Lamarck 1778 (*P. nivea*)   CA
    kapela (Hacquet) Kerner 1869   CA
        ssp. **serpyllifolia** (Chaix) Graebner 1919
    nivea de Candolle 1797 = **P. capitata**

PATRINIA Jussieu 1807 nom. cons.   [*Valerianaceae*]
    gibbosa Maximowicz 1867   PGP
    palmata Maximowicz 1868 = **P. triloba** var. **palmata**
    triloba Miquel 1870
        var. **palmata** (Maximowicz) Hara (*P. palmata*)
    villosa (Thunberg) Jussieu 1807

PECTEILIS Rafinesque 1836   [*Orchidaceae*]
    radiata Rafinesque 1836 = **Habenaria radiata**

PELARGONIUM L'Heritier 1789   [*Geraniaceae*]
    endlicherianum Fenzl 1856

PELTANDRA Rafinesque 1819 nom. cons.   [*Araceae*]
    undulata (Linnaeus) Rafinesque 1819 (*P. virginica*)   EGF.2
        'Alba'
    virginica (Linnaeus) Schott & Endlicher 1856 = **P. undulata**

PELTIPHYLLUM (Engler) Engler 1890   [*Saxifragaceae*]
    peltatum (Torrey) Engler 1890 = **Darmera peltata**

PELTOBOYKINIA (Engler) Hara 1937   [*Saxifragaceae*]
    tellimoides (Maximowicz) Hara 1937 (*Boykinia tellimoides*)

PENNISETUM Richard 1805   *[Poaceae (Gramineae)]*
    alopecuroides (Linnaeus) Sprengel 1825 non Desvaux ex Hamilton 1825
                           (*P. compressum, P. japonicum*)   EGF.2-PGP-**DGP**-RD
       'Compressum' = **P. alopecuroides**
       'Hameln'   [H. Junge]
       f. **purpurascens** (Thunberg) Ohwi 1953
       'Weserbergland'   [H. Junge]
       'Woodside'   [M. Feesey]
    compressum R. Brown 1810 = **P. alopecuroides**
    flaccidum Grisebach 1868   PGP
    incomptum Nees ex Steudel 1854 = **Cenchrus ciliaris**
    japonicum Trinius 1821 = **P. alopecuroides**
    orientale (Willdenow) Richard 1805   EGF.2-PGP-**DGP**-RD
    ruppelii Steudel ex Steudel 1854 = **P. setaceum**
    setaceum (Forsskal) Chiovenda 1923   EGF.2-**RD**
    villosum R. Brown ex R. Brown 1837   EGF.2-PGP-**DGP**-RD

PENSTEMON Schmidel 1762
    alpinus Torrey 1824 = **P. glaber**   *[Scrophulariaceae]*
S   **ambiguus** Torrey 1828
    angustifolius Pursh 1814 (*P. coeruleus*)   CA
S   **antirrhinoides** Bentham 1846
      ssp. **microphyllus** (A. Gray) Keck 1951
    arizonicus A. Heller 1899 = **P. whippleanus**
L   **barbatus** (Cavanilles) Roth 1800 (*Chelone barbata*)   PGP-**DGP**-RD
      'Coccineus'
      'Nana Rondo'
      'Praecox'
      'Praecox Nanus'
S   **barrettae** A. Gray 1886
    caeruleus Hort. ex Vilmorin = **P. hartwegii**   CA
    caespitosus Nuttall ex A. Gray 1862
S   **campanulatus** Willdenow 1800 (*P. kunthii, P. pulchellus*)   PGP
S   **cardwellii** J. Howell 1901   CA
    coeruleus Nuttall 1818 = **P. angustifolius**
    cobaea Nuttall 1837
      ssp. **purpureus** (Pennell) Pennell 1935
    confertus Douglas 1829
S   **cordifolius** Bentham 1835
S   **corymbosus** Bentham 1846
    crandallii A. Nelson 1899   CA
      ssp. **procumbens** (Greene) Keck 1937
    cristatus Nuttall 1818 = **P. eriantherus**
S   **davidsonii** Greene 1892   CA-RD
      var. **menziesii** (Keck) Cronquist 1959 (*P. menziesii*)   CA-RD
    diffusus Douglas ex Lindley 1828 = **P. serrulatus**
    digitalis (Sweet) Nuttall 1833 (*P. laevigatus* var. *digitalis*)
S   **eriantherus** Pursh 1814 (*P. cristatus*)   CA
      'Nanus' nom. dub.
    fendleri Torrey & A. Gray 1857 = **P. nitidus**
S   **fruticosus** (Rafinesque) Pursh 1814   DGP
      var. *cardwellii* (J. Howell) Piper 1906 = **P. cardwellii**
      var. **scouleri** (Lindley) Cronquist 1959 (*P. scouleri*)   CA-**DGP**-RD
      var. **scouleri 'Albus'**
      var. **scouleri 'Hopleys'**   [D. Barker]
      var. **scouleri 'Purple Gem'**
      var. **scouleri Red Form**
    gentianoides Poiret
    gentianoides Lindley 1838 non Poiret = **P. hartwegii**
    glaber Pursh 1814 (*P. alpinus*)

'Roseus'
gormanii Greene 1902
hartwegii Bentham 1840 (*P. caeruleus* Vilmorin, *P. gentianoides* Lindley)
                                                            PGP-DGP-RD

S   **heterophyllus** Lindley 1836   RD
      'Blue Gem'
      'Blue Springs'
      'Heavenly Blue'
      'True Blue'
      'Züriblau'
hirsutus (Linnaeus) Willdenow 1801   PGP
      'Pygmaeus' nom. dub.
humilis Nuttall ex A. Gray 1862 (*P. virens*)
S   **isophyllus** Robson   PGP
jamesii Bentham 1864
kunthii G. Don 1830 = **P. campanulatus**
laetus A. Gray 1859
      ssp. **roezlii** (Regel) Keck 1932 (*P. roezlii*)   RD
laevigatus (Linnaeus) Solander 1789 (*Chelone penstemon*)
      var. **digitalis** A. Gray 1878 = **P. digitalis**
linarioides A. Gray 1854
menziesii Hooker 1837 = **P. davidsonii** var. **menziesii**
      ssp. *davidsonii* (Piper) Piper 1906 = **P. davidsonii**
mexicanus Hort. ex A. de Candolle 1846
microphyllus A. Gray 1857 = **P. antirrhinoides** ssp. **microphyllus**
S   **newberryi** A. Gray 1857   CA-**DGP-RD**
      f. **humilior** Sealy 1948
nitidus Douglas ex Bentham 1846 (*P. fendleri*)
ovatus Douglas 1829   PGP-RD
S   **pinifolius** Greene 1881
pulchellus Lindley 1828 = **P. campanulatus**
S   **richardsonii** Douglas 1827
roezlii Regel 1827 = **P. laetus** ssp. **roezelii**
roezlii hort., non Regel = **P. rupicola**
rubicundus hort. = **P. 'Rubicunda'**
S   **rupicola** (Piper) J. Howell 1901   CA-RD
      'Albus'
rydbergii A. Nelson 1898
scouleri Lindley 1829 = **P. fruticosus** var. **scouleri**
S   **serrulatus** Menzies ex Smith 1813 (*P. diffusus*)
strictus Bentham 1846   PGP
venustus Douglas 1830
virens Pennell 1917 = **P. humilis**
watsonii A. Gray 1878
whippleanus A. Gray 1862 (*P. arizonicus*)

HYBRID CULTIVARS

      'Alice Hindley'   PGP
L   'Andenken an Friedrich Hahn' ('Garnet')
      'Apple Blossom'
      'Blue Bedder'
      'Blue Eye'
      'Blue King'
      'Burford Seedling'
      'Burgundy'
      'Castle Forbes'
      'Catherine de la Mare'
      'Charles Rudd'

'Cherry Ripe'
'Chester Scarlet'
'Claret'
'Dazzler'
'Deep Purple'
'Drinkstone'
'Edithae'
'Eva'
'Evelyn' ('Phyllis')
'Firebird' = **P. 'Schönholzeri'**   PGP
'Flame'
'Garnet' = **P. 'Andenken an Friedrich Hahn'**
'Gentianoides'
'George Home'   PGP
'Greencourt Purple'
'Hewell's Pink'
'Hidcote Pink'
'Hyacinth'   PGP
'John Nash'
'Jupiter'
'King George'
'Lilac Time'   **RD**
'MacPenny's Pink'
'Margery Fish'
'Modesty'
'Mother of Pearl'
'Mrs Morse'
'Myddelton Gem'
'Papal Purple'
'Pennington Gem'   **RD**
'Pennington Pink' = **P. 'Pennington Gem'**
'Phyllis' = **P. 'Evelyn'**
'Pink Dragon'
'Pink Endurance'   PGP
'Port Wine'
'Prairie Fire'
'Purple Bedder'
'Red Emperor'
'Rich Ruby'
'Roseo-campanulus' nom. dub.
'Rubicunda'   [c1906]   PGP
'Ruby' = **P. 'Schönholzeri'**
'Scarlet Queen'
'Schönholzeri' ('Firebird', 'Ruby')   PGP-**DGP**-RD
'Sissinghurst Pink'
'Six Hills'   CA-**DGP**
'Snow Storm'
'Sour Grapes'
'Southgate Gem'   PGP
'Souvenir d'Adrian Reginier'   PGP
'Souvenir d'Andre Torres'
'Stapleford Gem'   PGP
'Sulphurasacens' nom. dub.
'Thorn'
'Threave Pink'
'Waterloo'
'White Bedder'
'Whitethroat'
'Windsor Red'

L

PENTAGLOTTIS Tausch 1829   [*Boraginaceae*]
N‡   **sempervirens** (Linnaeus) Tausch ex Bailey 1949 (*Anchusa sempervirens*)   PGP

PENTSTEMON Mitchell 1748 = **PENSTEMON**

PEREZIA Lagasca 1811   [*Asteraceae (Compositae)*]
      linearis Lessing 1830
      recurvata Lessing 1830

PEROVSKIA Karelin 1841   [*Lamiaceae (Labiatae)*]
S   **abrotanoides** Karelin 1841   PGP-**DGP**-RD
SH   **atriplicifolia** Bentham 1848   PGP
      'Blue Spire' (*P. abrotanoides* x *P. atriplicifolia*)   [Notcutt]   PGP-**RD**
      scrophulariaefolia Bunge 1851
      'Superba' (*P. abrotanoides* x *P. atriplicifolia*)

PERSICARIA Miller 1754   [*Polygonaceae*]
      affinis (D. Don) Ronse Decraene 1988 (*Bistorta affinis, Polygonum affine, Polygonum*
                                    brunonis)   PGP-DGP-RD
            'Darjeeling Red'   RD
            'Dimity' = **B. affinis 'Superba'**
L   **'Donald Lowdnes'**   **DGP**-RD
            'Superba'   PGP-**RD**
      alata (D. Don) H. Gross 1913 (*Polygonum alatum* D. Don)
      alpina (Allioni) ! (*Polygonum alpinum, Polygonum sericeum* hort, non Pallas)
N‡L   **amphibia** (Linnaeus) S.F. Gray 1821 (*Polygonum amphibium*)
N   **amplexicaulis** (D. Don) Ronse Decraene 1988 (*Bistorta amplexicaulis, Polygonum*
            amplexicaule, Polygonum oxypetalum, Polygonum speciosum)   PGP-**DGP**
            'Arun Gem' = **P. amplexicaulis** var. **pendula**
            'Atropurpurea' nom. dub.
L   **'Atrosanguinea'**   **PGP-RD**
            'Firetail'   PGP-DGP-RD
            'Inverleith'   PGP
            var. **pendula** (Hara 1975) !   PGP-**RD**
HN   **bistorta** (Linnaeus) Sampaio 1946 (*Bistorta major, Polygonum bistorta, Polygonum*
                                    regelianum)   DGP
            ssp. **carnea** (C. Koch) ! (*Polygonum carneum*)
            'Hohe Tatra' nom. dub.
L   **'Superba'**   PGP-**DGP-RD**
N‡L   **campanulata** (Hooker f.) Ronse Decraene 1988 (*Aconogonum campanulatum,*
                                    Polygonum campanulatum)   PGP-**DGP-RD**
            'Album'
            'Rosenrot'
            var. **lichiangense** (W. Smith) !
            'Southcombe White'   [Southcombe Garden Plant Nursery]
      capitata (Buchanan-Hamilton ex D. Don) H. Gross 1913 (*Polygonum capitatum*)
      emodi (Meissner) ! (*Bistorta emodi, Polygonum emodi*)
      filiformis (Thunberg) Nakai (*Polygonum filiforme, Tovara filiformis*)   PGP
            'Painter's Palette'   PGP
      macrophylla (D. Don) ! (*Bistorta macrophylla, Polygonum macrophyllum, Polygonum*
                                    sphaerostachyum)   PGP-RD
      milletii (Leveille) ! (*Bistorta milletii, Polygonum milletii*)   PGP-RD
      molle (D. Don) ! (*Aconogonum molle, Polygonum molle*)   PGP
            var. **rude** (Meissner) ! (*Polygonum rude*)   PGP
      polymorpha (Ledebour) ! (*Aconogonum polymorphum, Polygonum polymorphum*)
N‡   **polystachya** (Wallich ex Meissner) H. Gross 1913 (*Aconogonum polystachya,*
                                    Polygonum polystachyum)   PGP
      runcinata (Buchanan-Hamilton ex D.Don) H. Gross 1913 (*Polygonum runcinatum*)
      sericea (Pallas) H. Gross 1913 (*Aconogonum sericeum, Polygonum sericeum* Pallas)
      tenuicaulis (Bisset & Moore) ! (*Bistorta tenuicaulis, Polygonum tenuicaule*)

vacciniifolia (Wallich ex Meissner) Ronse Decraene 1988 (*Bistorta vacciniifolia,*
                              Polygonum vacciniifolium)   CA-**DGP-RD**
virginianum (Linnaeus) Gaertner (*Polygonum virginianum, Tovara virginiana*)
                                                                PGP
    'Variegatum'   PGP
N   **vivipara** (Linnaeus) Ronse Decraene 1988 (*Bistorta vivipara, Polygonum viviparum*)
    weyrichii (F. Schmidt) Ronse Decraene 1988 (*Aconogonum weyrichii, Polygonum*
                                                    weyrichii)   PGP

PETASITES Miller 1754   [*Asteraceae (Compositae)*]
HN‡ **fragrans** (Villars) C. Presl 1826   PGP
N   **japonicus** (Siebold & Zuccarini) F. Schmidt 1868   PGP
        var. **giganteus** (F. Schmidt) Nicholson

PETROCALLIS R. Brown 1812   [*Brassicaceae (Cruciferae)*]
    pyrenaica (Linnaeus) R. Brown 1812 (*Draba pyrenaica*)   CA
        'Alba'

PETROCOPTIS A. Braun ex Endlicher 1843   [*Caryophyllaceae*]
    crassifolia Rouy 1895
    glaucifolia (Lagasca) Boissier 1853 = **P. lagascae**
    lagascae (Willkomm) Willkomm 1851 (*Lychnis lagascae, P. glaucifolia*)   CA
    pyrenaica (J.P. Bergeret) A. Braun 1842   CA

PETROMARULA Ventenat ex Hedwig f. 1806   [*Campanulaceae*]
    pinnata (Linnaeus) A. de Candolle 1830

PETROPHYTON Rydberg 1900   [*Rosaceae*]
S   **caespitosum** (Nuttall) Rydberg 1900
S   **cinerascens** (Piper) Rydberg 1908
S   **hendersonii** (Canby & Greene) Rydberg 1908

PETRORHAGIA (Sevastianov ex de Candolle) Link 1831   [*Caryophyllaceae*]
N   **saxifraga** (Scopoli) Link 1831 (*Tunica saxifraga*)
        'Alba'
        'Alba Plena'
        'Rosette'   [Thos. Hilling]

PETROSELINUM Miller 1756   [*Apiaceae (Umbelliferae)*]
BHN **crispum** (Miller) A.W. Hill 1925   **RD**
H   **'Tuberosum'**   RD

PEUCEDANUM Linnaeus 1753   [*Apiaceae (Umbelliferae)*]
    cervaria (Linnaeus) Lapeyrouse
N   **ostruthium** (Linnaeus) Koch
    verticillare (Linnaeus) K. Koch ex de Candolle 1830

PHACELIA Jussieu 1789   [*Hydrophyllaceae*]
    sericea (Graham) A. Gray 1862   CA

PHAEDRANASSA Herbert 1845   [*Amaryllidaceae*]
    carmiolii Baker 1869   EGF.1

PHALARIS Linnaeus 1753   [*Poaceae (Gramineae)*]
N‡L **arundinacea** Linnaeus 1753   EGF.2-**DGP-RD**
        var. **picta** Linnaeus 1753
        var. **picta 'Feesey'**   [M.T. Feesey]
L   var. **picta 'Picta'**   PGP-**DGP-RD**
        var. *variegata* Parnell 1845 = **P. arundinacea** var. **picta**

PHARBITIS Choisy 1833 nom. cons.   [*Convolvulaceae*]
C   **learii** Lindley 1841

PHEGOPTERIS (C. Presl) Fee 1852   [*Thelypteridaceae*]
N   **connectilis** (Michaux) Watt 1867 (*Dryopteris phegopteris, Thelypteris phegopteris*)
                                                                    EGF.1
        decursive-pinnata (Van Hall) Fee 1852   EGF.1
        hexagonoptera (Michaux) Fee 1852

PHLOMIS Linnaeus 1753   [*Lamiaceae (Labiatae)*]
        bracteosa Royle ex Bentham 1833
SH   **fruticosa** Linnaeus 1753   **DGP-RD**
S   **italica** Linnaeus 1759
S   **purpurea** Linnaeus 1753
L   **russeliana** (Sims) Bentham 1834 (*P. samia* hort., *P. viscosa* hort.)   PGP-RD
        samia Linnaeus 1753   **RD**
        samia Boissier 1879 non Linnaeus 1753 = **P. russeliana**
        tuberosa Linnaeus 1753   PGP
S   **viscosa** Poiret 1804
        viscosa hort. non Poiret 1804 = **P. russeliana**

PHLOX Linnaeus 1753   [*Polemoniaceae*]

M - WHERRY, E. T.: *'The Genus Phlox'* 1955

        adsurgens Torrey ex A. Gray 1870   M-CA-**DGP**-RD
            'Black Buttes'
            'Blue Buttes'
            'Red Buttes'
            'Wagon Wheels'
            'White Buttes'
        amoena Sims 1810   M-**DGP**-RD
        amoena hort. non Sims = **P. x procumbens**
        x arendsii hort. (*P. divaricata* x *P. paniculata*)   M
            'Anja'   [G. Arends 1966]   PGP
            'Hilde'   [G. Arends]   PGP
            'Suzanne'   [G. Arends]   PGP
        bifida Beck 1826   M-**DGP**
            'Alba'
            Blue Form
            'Colvin's White'
            'Minima Colvin' nom. dub.
            'Starbright'
            ssp. **stellaria** A. Gray 1870 (*P. stellaria*)   M
        borealis Wherry 1955   M
            'Porea'
        brittonii Small 1900 = **P. subulata** ssp. **brittonii**
        caespitosa Nuttall 1834   M-CA
            'Alba'
            ssp. *condensata* (E. Nelson) Wherry 1941 = **P. condensata**
        camlaensis hort. = **P. nivalis 'Camla'**
        canadensis Sweet 1827 = **P. divaricata**
        carolina Linnaeus 1762   M
            'Magnificence'
        'Charles Ricardo' (*P. divaricata* x *P. pilosa*)
        'Chattahoochee' (*P. divaricata* ssp. *laphamii* x *P. pilosa*)
        condensata (A. Gray) E. Nelson 1899 (*P. caespitosa* ssp. *condensata*)   M-CA
        decussata Lyon ex Pursh 1814 = **P. paniculata**
        diffusa Bentham 1849 (*P. douglasii* var. *diffusa*)   M
        divaricata Linnaeus 1753 (*P. canadensis*)   M-**DGP**

'Dirigo Ice'
ssp. **laphamii** (Clute) Wherry 1955 (*P. laphamii*)

L   **douglasii** Hooker 1838   M-PGP-RD
'Apollo'   M-CA-DGP
'Boothman's Variety'   [S. Boothman]
'Concorde'   DGP-RD
'Crackerjack'
var. *diffusa* (Bentham) A. Gray 1870 = **C. diffusa**
'Eva'
'Galaxy'   RD
'Georg Arends'   [G. Arends]
'Holden Variety'   [R. Milne-Redhead]
'Iceberg'
'Ice Mountain'
'J. A. Hibberson'
'Kelly's Eye' = **P. 'Kelly's Eye'**
'Lilac Cloud'
'Lilac Queen' = **P. douglasii 'Lilakönigen'**
'Lilakönigen' ('Lilac Queen')
'Octopus'
'Pink Cushion'
'Purple Cushion'
'Red Admiral'
'Rosea'
'Rose Cushion'
'Rose Queen'
'Silver Rose'
'Star Dust'
'Supreme'
'Tycoon'   DGP
'Violet Queen'
'White Cushion'
'Waterloo'
'Frondosa' (*P. nivalis* x *P. subulata*)
hoodii Richardson 1823   M
'Kelly's Eye' (*P. douglasii* x *P. subulata*)
kelseyi Britton 1892   M
'Rosette'
laphamii Clute 1919 = **P. divaricata** ssp. **laphamii**
x *lilacina* hort. = **P. nana 'Lilacina'**
maculata Linnaeus 1753   M-PGP-RD
'Alba'
'Alpha'   [G. Arends 1918]   PGP-**DGP-RD**
'Miss Lingard'   [Pre-1933]   PGP-DGP-RD
L   'Omega'   [A. Bloom]   PGP
'Rosalinde'   [G. Arends 1918]
'Schneelawine'   [G. Arends 1918]
mesoleuca Greene 1905 = **P. nana** ssp. **ensifolia**
nana Nuttall 1848   M
'Arroya'
ssp. **ensifolia** Brand 1907(*P. mesoleuca*)   M
'G. F. Wilson'
'Lilacina'
'Manjana'
'Mary Maslin'
Mexican Hybrids
'Paul Maslin'
'Tangelo'
'Vanilla Cream'

nivalis Loddiges & Sweet 1823-27		M
'Camla' (*P. camlaensis* hort.)		
'Nivea'		
ovata Linnaeus 1753		M-PGP
'Bostonian' [via A. Bloom]		
NL **paniculata** Linnaeus 1753 (*P. decussata* hort.)		M-PGP-RD
'A E Amos'		
'Aida' [W. Pfitzer 1933]		
'Alba'		
'Albert Leo Schlageter' [G. Arends 1925]		
'Alison Jane'		
'Amarantriese'		
'Amethyst'		
'Ann'		
'Annie Laurie'		
'Balmoral'		
'Barnwell'		
'Bern'		
'Bill Green' [A. Bloom]		
'Blue Boy'		
'Blue Ice'		RD
'Blue Mist`		RD
'Blue Moon'		
'Border Gem'		RD
'Borgon-on-Dell'		
'Bornimer Nachsommer' [K. Foerster 1951]		
'Branklyn'		
'Brigadier' [Thos Carlile Ltd]		**DGP**
'Bright Eyes'		
'B. Symons-Jeune' [B. H. B. Symons-Jeune]		
'Buccaneer'		
'Caroline van den Berg'		
'Cecil Hanbury' [B. H. B. Symons-Jeune]		
'Charmaine'		
'Cherry Pink'		RD
'Chintz'		DGP
'Cinderella'		
'Cool of the Evening' [B. H. B. Symons-Jeune]		
'Daily Sketch'		
'Dauerbrand'		
'Dauerrot' [H. Hagemann]		
'Denny'		
'Dodo Hanbury Forbes'		
'Dorffreude' [K. Foerster 1939]		
'Dresden China' [B. H. B. Symons-Jeune]		
'Duchess of Gloucester'		
'Düsterlohe' [K. Foerster]		
'Early Gem'		
'Eclaireur'		
'Elizabeth Arden'		
'Endurance' [B. H. B. Symons-Jeune]		
'Europa'		
'Eurphorion'		
'Eva Cullum' [A. Bloom]		RD
'Eva Foerster' [K. Foerster]		
'Evangeline'		
'Eventide'		
'Excelsior'		
'Fairy's Petticoat' [B. H. B. Symons-Jeune]		
'Fesselballon' [K. Foerster]		

'Feuerfackel'   [zur Linden]
'Feuerpyramide'   [K. Foerster]
'Firefly'
'Flamingo'   [zur Linden]
'Flammenkuppel'
'Fort du France'
'Franz Schubert'   [A. Bloom]   RD
'Frau A Buchner'
'Frau A von Mauthner'   [Ruys 1927]('Spitfire')
'Frauenlob'   [K. Foerster 1949]
'Fujiyama' ('Mount Fuji')   PGP-RD
'Füllhorn'
'Gaiety'
'Geoffrey Goatcher'
'Glamis'
'Glow'
'Graf Zeppelin'
'Hampton Court'
'Harewood'
'Harlequin'   [A. Bloom]   PGP
'Herbstglut'
'Inspiration'
'Iris'
'Jacqueline Maille'
'Josephine Gerbeaux'
'Joy Marsh'
'Jules Sandeau'   [Pfitzer 1919] ('Württembergia')
'Juliglut'   [Bornimer Staudenkulture]('July Glow')
'Karminvorläufer'   [K. Foerster]
'Kelway's Cherub'
'Kirchenfürst'   [K. Foerster 1956]
'Kirmesländler'   [K. Foerster 1938]
'Landhochzeit'   [K. Foerster 1949]
'Le Mahdi'
'Leo Schlageter' = **P. paniculata** 'Albert Leo Schlageter'
'Lilac Time'   [B. H. B. Symons-Jeune]
'Little Lovely'
'Look Again'   [B. H. B. Symons-Jeune]
'Lord Lambourne'
'Marlborough'
'Mary Fox'   [A. Bloom]   RD
'Mia Ruys'   [Ruys]
'Mies Copijn'
'Mittsommer'   [H. Hagemann]
'Monte Cristallo'   [K. Foerster]
'Mother of Pearl'   [A. Bloom]   DGP
'Mount Fuji' = **P. paniculata** 'Fujiyama'
'Mrs A. E. Jeans'
'Mrs Ethel Prichard'
'Mrs Fincham'
'Newbird'
'Nora Leigh'   PGP-DGP
'Nymphenburg'   [Büchner 1954]
'Orange'   [A. Schöllhammer 1955]
'Orange Perfection'
'Orange Prince'
'Othello'
'Otley Choice'
'Otley Ideal'
'Pastorale'   [K. Foerster]

'Patsy Anne'
'Pax'   [A. Schöllhammer 1955]
'Pinafore Pink'
'Pink Chintz' = **P. paniculata 'Chintz'**
'Pink Glow'
'Pink Gown'
'Prince George'
'Prince of Orange'   DGP-RD
'Prospero'   [K. Foerster 1956]
'Purpurkuppel'   [H. Hagemann]
'Rapture'
'Red Indian'   RD
'Redivivus'   [K. Foerster]
'Rembrandt'
'Rheinländer'
'Rijnstroom'
'Rosa Pastell'   [K. Foerster 1958]
'Rosendom'
'Rotball'   [zur Linden 1972]
'Russian Violet'
'Sally'
'San Antonio'
'Sandringham'   RD
'Schaumkrone'   [Bornimer Staudenkulture 1975]
'Schneeferner'   [K. Foerster]
'Schneelavine'
'Schneerausch'
'Shenstone'   [B. H. B. Symons-Jeune]
'Silver Salmon'
'Sir John Falstaff'
'Sir Malcolm Campbell'
'Skylight'   RD
'Snowball'
'Snowdrift'
'Sommerfreude'   [A. Schöllhammer 1954]
'Sommerkleid'   [A. Schöllhammer]
'Spätlicht'   [Bornimer Staudenkulture]
'Spätrosa'   [K. Foerster]
'Spätrot'   [K. Foerster 1934]
'Spitfire' = **P. paniculata 'Frau A. von Mauthner'**
'Starfire'   [Ruys 1959]   DGP-RD
'Sternhimmel'   [A. Schöllhammer 1950]
'Tenor'
'The King'
'Toits de Paris'
'Vintage Wine'   RD
'Violetta Gloriosa'   [K. Foerster 1956]
'White Admiral'
'Widar'
'William Kesselring'   [Ruys 1923]
'William Ramsay'
'Windsor'
'Württembergia' = **P. paniculata 'Jules Sandeau'**
pilosa Linnaeus 1753   M-PGP
x procumbens Lehmann 1802 (*P. stolonifera* x *P. subulata*)   M
       'Millstream'   [H. L. Foster]
       'Rosea'   RD
       'Variegata'   RD
reptans Michaux 1803 = **P. stolonifera**
x rugellii Brand 1907 (*P. amoena* x *P. divaricata*)   M

stellaria A. Gray 1870 = **P. bifida** ssp. **stellaria**
'Stellaria' hort. non A. Gray (*P. bifida* x *P. subulata*)   M
stolonifera Sims 1802 (*P. reptans*)   M-RD
    'Ariane'   RD
    'Blue Ridge'   [Mrs N. Henry]   RD
    'Mary Belle Frey'
    'Pink Ridge'

NL **subulata** Linnaeus 1753
    'Alexander's Suprise'   M-RD
    'Amazing Grace'   RD
    'Apple Blossom'
    'Arlette'   RD
    'Atropurpurea'
    'Beauty of Ronsdorf' = **P. subulata 'Ronsdorfer Schöne'**
    'Bonita'
    'Betty'   RD
    'Blue Eyes' = **P. subulata 'Oakington Blue Eyes'**
    'Blue Saucer'
    'Bressingham Blue Eyes' = **P. subulata 'Oakington Blue Eyes'**
    'Brightness'
    'Brilliant'   DGP
    ssp. **brittonii** (Small) Wherry 1951 (*P. brittonii*)   M
    ssp. **brittonii 'Rosea'**
    'Chuckles'
    'Daisy Hill'   [T. Smith]
    'Daniel's Cushion' = **P. subulata 'MacDaniel's Cushion'**
    'Daphne'
    'Emerald Cushion Blue'
    'Emerald Pink'
    'Fairy'
    'G. F. Wilson' = **P. nana 'G. F. Wilson'**
    'Greencourt Purple'
    'Jill Alexander'
    'Kelly's Eye' = **P. 'Kelly's Eye'**
    'Lindental'   [Häus]
    'MacDaniel's Cushion'('Daniel's Cushion')
    'Marjorie'
    'Maischnee'   [G. Arends]('May Snow', 'Snow Queen')   DGP
    'May Snow' = **P. subulata 'Maischnee'**
    'Model'
    'Moerheimii'   [Ruys]
    'Mrs Balfour'
    'Mrs Chambers'
    ssp. *nivalis* Brand 1907 non Loddiges 1823 = **P. subulata** ssp. **brittonii**
    'Oakington Blue Eyes'   [A. Bloom]
    'Pink Delight'
    'Red Wings'
    'Ronsdorfer Schöne'   [G. Arends]('Beauty of Ronsdorf')   **DGP**
    'Rose Mabel'
    'Rotraud'
    'Samson'
    'Scarlet Flame'   RD
    'Schneewittchen'
    'Sensation'
    'Snow Queen' = **P. subulata 'Maischnee'**
    'Starglow'
    'Temiskaming'   DGP-RD
    'Vivid' = **P. 'Vivid'**
    'White Delight'
    'White Drift'

'Winifred'
'Woodside'
'Vivid' (*S. nivalis* x *S. subulata*)   DGP

PHORMIUM Forster & Forster f. 1776   [*Phormiaceae (Liliaceae)*]
   colensoi Hooker f. 1864 = **P. cookianum**
N **cookianum** Le Jolis 1848 (*P. colensoi*)   EGF.1-PGP-RD
'Cream Delight'
'Emerald Green'
'Tricolor'   PGP
N **tenax** Forster & Forster f. 1776   EGF.1-PGP-**DGP**-RD
'Alpinum Purpureum' = **P. tenax 'Nanum Purpureum'**
'Atropurpureum'
'Black Edge' ('Nigro-marginatum', 'Nigropictum')
'Burgundy'
'Dark Delight'
'Duet'
'Dusky Chief'
'Dwarf Red'
'Firebird'
'Glauca' = **P. tenax 'Goliath'**
'Gold Spike'
'Gold Sword'
'Goliath' ('Glauca')   PGP
'Guardsman'
'Jack Spratt'
'Maori Chief'
'Montana'
'Nanum'
'Nanum Purpureum' ('Alpinum Purpureum')
'Nigro-marginatum' = **P. tenax 'Black Edge'**
'Nigropictum' = **P. tenax 'Black Edge'**
'Powerscourtii'
'Purple Giant'   PGP
'Purpureum'   PGP-**RD**
'Radiance'   PGP
'Rubrum'
'Sundowner'
'Surfer'
'Tom Thumb'
'Tricolor'
'Variegatum'   **PGP-RD**
'Veitchii'   DGP
'Williamsii'
'Yellow Queen'   PGP

HYBRID CULTIVARS

'Apricot Queen'
'Aurora'   PGP
'Bronze Baby'   PGP
'Coffee'
'Dazzler'
'Maori Maiden'
'Maori Sunrise'
Rainbow Hybrids
'Smiling Morn'   PGP
'Sunset'
'Thumberlina'
'Yellow Wave'

PHRAGMITES Adanson 1763   [*Poaceae (Gramineae)*]
NL   **australis** (Cavanilles) Trinius1841 (*P. communis*)   EGF.2-PGP
       'Variegatus' (Mutel 1837) Weber   PGP
      communis (Linnaeus) Trinius 1820 = **P. australis**

PHUOPSIS (Grisebach) Hooker f 1873   [*Rubiaceae*]
N   **stylosa** (Trinius) B.D. Jackson (*Crucianella stylosa*)   PGP
       'Purpurea' ('Rubra')
      'Rubra' = **P. stylosa 'Purpurea'**

PHYGELIUS E. Meyer ex Bentham 1836   [*Scrophulariaceae*]
S   **aequalis** Harvey ex Hiern in Dyer 1904   PGP-**DGP**-RD
      'Aureus' = **P. aequalis 'Yellow Trumpet'**
      'Cream Trumpet' = **P. aequalis 'Yellow Trumpet'**
      'Yellow Trumpet'   [1973]   **RD**
SL   **capensis** E. Meyer ex Bentham 1836   PGP-**DGP-RD**
      'Albus'
      'Coccineus'   [pre-1926]   **DGP**-RD
      'Roseus'
   x rectus (*P. aequalis x P. capensis*) Coombes 1988
      'African Queen'   [J. May 1969]
      'Devil's Tears'   [P. Dummer via Hillier Nurseries 1985]
      'Indian Chief'
      'Moonraker'   [P. Dummer via Hillier Nurseries 1985]
      'Pink Elf'   [P. Dummer via Hillier Nurseries 1985]
      'Salmon Leap'   [P. Dummer via Hillier Nurseries 1985]
      'Winchester Fanfare'   [P. Dummer via Hillier Nurseries]
      'Winton Fanfare' = **P. x rectus 'Winchester Fanfare'**

PHYLA Loureiro 1790   [*Verbenaceae*]
   canescens (Kunth) Greene 1899 (*Lippia canescens, L. repens* hort.)
   nodiflora (Linnaeus) Greene 1899 (*Lippia nodiflora*)

PHYLLITIS Ludwig 1757   [*Aspleniaceae*]
   scolopendrium (Linnaeus) Newman 1844 = **Asplenium scolopendrium**

PHYSALIS Linnaeus 1753   [*Solanaceae*]
N   **alkekengi** Linnaeus 1753   PGP-**DGP-RD**
L   var. **franchetii** (Masters) Makino 1908 (*P. franchetii*)   PGP-**DGP-RD**
      franchetii Masters 1894 = **P. alkekengi** var. **franchetii**

PHYSARIA (Torrey & A. Gray) A. Gray 1848   [*Brassicaceae (Cruciferae)*]
   didymocarpa A. Gray 1848

PHYSOPLEXIS (Endlicher) Schur 1853   [*Campanulaceae*]
   comosa (Linnaeus) Schur 1853 (*Phyteuma comosum*)   **CA-DGP-RD**

PHYSOSTEGIA Bentham 1829   [*Lamiaceae (Labiatae)*]
   virginiana (Linnaeus) Bentham 1834 (*Dracocephalum virginianum*)   PGP-DGP-RD
      'Alba'   PGP
      'Bouquet Rose' ('Rose Bouquet')   PGP-RD
      'Rosea'
      'Rose Bouquet' = **P. virginiana 'Bouquet Rose'**
      'Rosy Spire'
      'Summer Snow'   PGP-**RD**
      'Summer Spire'   RD
      'Variegata'
      'Vivid'   PGP-**DGP**-RD

PHYTEUMA Linnaeus 1753   [*Campanulaceae*]
    betonicifolium Villars 1787
    comosum Linnaeus 1753 = **Physoplexis comosa**
    hemisphaericum Linnaeus 1753   CA-RD
    halleri Duby 1830 non Allioni 1773 = **P. ovatum**
    humile Schleicher ex Gaudin 1810
    nigrum F. W. Schmidt 1794
N‡   **orbiculare** Linnaeus 1753   RD
    ovatum F. W. Schmidt 1793 (*P. halleri* Duby)
    scheuchzeri Allioni 1773   RD
    sibiricum Vest ex Roemer & Schultes 1819
    sieberi Sprengel 1813
N‡   **spicatum** Linnaeus 1753   PGP

PHYTOLACCA Linnaeus 1753   [*Phytolaccaceae*]
    acinosa Roxburgh 1832
HN **americana** Linnaeus 1753 (*P. decandra*)   PGP-**RD**
    clavigera W. W. Smith 1918   PGP
    decandra Linnaeus 1762 = **P. americana**

PILULARIA Linnaeus 1753   [*Marsileaceae*]
N   **globulifera** Linnaeus 1753   EGF.1

PIMELEA Banks & Solander ex Gaertner 1788 nom. cons.   [*Thymelaeaceae*]
    coarctata hort. = **P. prostrata 'Coarctata'**
S   **prostrata** (Forster & Forster f.) Willdenow 1797   CA
    'Coarctata'   CA

PIMPINELLA Linnaeus 1753   [*Apiaceae (Umbelliferae)*]
AH **anisum** Linnaeus 1753
N‡   **major** Hudson 1762
       'Rosea'   PGP
       var. **rubra** (Hoppe) Fiori & Beguinot 1900
HN‡ **saxifraga** Linnaeus 1753

PINELLIA Tenore 1830 nom. cons.   [*Araceae*]
    cordata N. E. Brown   SB
    pedatisecta Schott 1857 (*P. tripartita*)   EGF.2-SB
    ternata (Thunberg) Tenore ex Breitenbach 1879 (*P. tuberifera*)   EGF.2-SB
    tripartita Schott 1856 = **P. pedatisecta**
    tuberifera Tenore 1839 = **P. ternata**

PISTIA Linnaeus 1753   [*Araceae*]
    stratiotes Linnaeus 1753   EGF.2

PLAGIORHEGMA Maximowicz 1859   [*Berberidaceae*]
    dubium Maximowicz 1859 = **Jeffersonia dubia**

PLANTAGO Linnaeus 1753   [*Plantaginaceae*]
    asiatica hort. non Linnaeus 1753 = **P. major**
N‡   **major** Linnaeus 1753 (*P. asiatica* hort.)
       'Purpura' = **P. major 'Rubrifolia'**
       'Rosularis'
       'Rubrifolia' ('Purpurea')
       'Variegata'
N‡   **media** Linnaeus 1753
    nivalis Boissier 1841   CA
    raoulii Decaisne 1852
    sempervirens Crantz 1766
    triandra Berggren 1877

PLATANTHERA L. C. M. Richard 1817 nom. cons.   [*Orchidaceae*]
N‡   **bifolia** (Linnaeus) L. C. M. Richard 1817 (*Habenaria bifolia*)   EGF.2

PLATYCODON A. de Candolle 1830   [*Campanulaceae*]
     grandiflorus (Jacquin) A. de Candolle 1830   PGP-DGP-RD
          'Albus' nom. dub.   RD
          'Apoyama'   DGP
L   'Mariesii'   PGP-**DGP**-RD
          'Mother of Pearl' = **P. grandiflorus 'Perlmutterschale'**
          'Perlmutterschale' ('Mother of Pearl')   PGP-RD
          'Snowflake'   RD

PLEIONE D. Don 1825   [*Orchidaceae*]

M - PHILLIP CRIBB & IAN BUTTERFIELD *'The Genus Pleione'*; A Kew Magazine Monograph 1988

     bulbocodioides (Franchet) Rolfe 1903   **M**-EGF.2
          'Lapwing'
          'Yunnan'(P. yunnanensis hort.)
     x confusa Cribb & C. Z. Tang 1983 (*P. albiflora* x *P. forrestii*)   **M**-EGF.2
     formosana Hayata 1911   **M**-EGF.2-CA-**DGP**-**RD**
          'Abingdon Feast'
          'Achievement'   M
          'Alba'
          'Arrington Queen'   CA-**DGP**-**RD**
          'Avalanche'
          'Blush of Dawn'   **M**
          'Cairngorm'   M
          'Clare'   M
          'Dainty Lady'
          'Emperor'   M
          'Iris'
          'Lilac Beauty'   M
          'Lilac Jubilee'
          'Oriental Grace'   **M**
          'Oriental Jewel'   M
          'Oriental Splendour'   **M**-DGP-**RD**
          'Orwell Glory'   M
          'Pink Rim'
          'Pitlochry'   M
          'Polar Star'   **M**
          'Polar Sun'
          'Serenity'   M
          'Silver Jubilee'
          'Snow White'   **M**
          'Taiwan'
          'White Swan'
          'Wimpole Beauty'
     forrestii Schlechter 1912   **M**-EGF.2-**CA**
     forrestii hort. non Schlechter = **P. x confusa**
     hookeriana (Lindley) B. S. Williams 1885   **M**-EGF.2-CA
     humilis (J. E. Smith) D. Don 1825   **M**-EGF.2-CA-**RD**
          'Frank Kingdon Ward'   M
     limprichtii Schlechter 1922   **M**-EGF.2-CA-**DGP**-**RD**
          'Primrose Peach'
     maculata (Lindley) Lindley in Paxton 1851   **M**-EGF.2-CA
     pogonioides hort. = **P. speciosa**
     praecox (J. E. Smith) D. Don 1825   **M**-EGF.2-CA-**RD**
     pricei hort. non Rolfe = **P. formosana 'Oriental Splendour'**
     scopulorum W. W. Smith 1921   **M**

speciosa Ames & Schlechter 1919   **M-CA**
yunnanensis (Rolfe) Rolfe 1903   M-EGF.2-CA
yunnanensis hort. non Rolfe = **P. bulbocodioides 'Yunnan'**

HYBRID CULTIVARS & GROUPS

    Alishan (grex) ®   [Hazelton 1979]   M
    Alishan 'Merlin'   **M**
    Barcena (grex) ®   [I. Butterfield 1982]   **M**
    Brigadoon (grex) ®   [I. Butterfield 1982]   **M**
    Cotopaxi (grex) ®   [I. Butterfield 1982]   M
    Danan (grex) ®   [I. Butterfield 1982]   M
    Eiger (grex) ®   [I. Butterfield 1979]   **M**
    El Pico (grex) ®   [I. Butterfield 1980]   M
    Erebus (grex) ®   [I. Butterfield 1982]   **M**
    Etna (grex) ®   [I. Butterfield 1979]   M
    Fuego (grex) ®   [I. Butterfield 1980]   **M**
    Hekla (grex) ®   [I. Butterfield 1982]   **M**
    Irazu (grex) ®   [I. Butterfield 1982]   M
    Jorullo (grex) ®   [I. Butterfield 1982]   M
    Katla (grex) ®   [B. Williams via I. Butterfield 1980]   M
    Matupi (grex) ®   [I. Butterfield 1983]   M
    Shantung (grex) ®   [Harberd 1972]   **M**
    Sorea (grex) ®   [I. Butterfield 1983]   M
    Soufriere (grex) ®   [B. Williams via I. Butterfield 1983]   **M**
    Stromboli (grex) ®   [I. Butterfield 1979]   M
    Stromboli 'Fireball'   **M**
    Stromboli 'Osprey'
    Tarawera (grex) ®   [I. Butterfield 1982]   M
    Tolima (grex) ®   [I. Butterfield 1979]   M
    Tongariro (grex) ®   [I. Butterfield 1981]   M
    Versailles (grex) ®   [Morel 1966]   M
    Versailles 'Bucklebury'   **M**
    Versailles 'Greenfinch'
    Versailles 'Heron'   M
    Vesuvius (grex) ®   [I. Butterfield 1978]   M

PLEUROSPERMUM Hoffmann 1814   *[Apiaceae (Umbelliferae)]*
    brunonis (de Candolle) C. B. Clarke 1879

PLUMBAGO Linnaeus 1753   *[Boraginaceae]*
    larpentae Lindley 1847 = **Ceratostigma plumbaginoides**

POA Linnaeus 1753   *[Poaceae (Gramineae)]*
    abbreviata R. Brown 1823
N‡ **alpina** Linnaeus 1753
    badensis Haenke ex Willdenow 1797
    caesia Smith 1800 = **P. glauca**
N   **chaixii** Villars 1785   EGF.2
    colensoi Hooker f. 1864
N   **glauca** Vahl 1790 (*P. caesia*)   EGF.2
N‡ **nemoralis** Linnaeus 1753

PODOPHYLLUM Linnaeus 1753   *[Berberidaceae]*
    diphyllum = **Jeffersonia diphylla**
    emodi Wallich 1824 nom. nudem. = **P. hexandrum**
H   **hexandrum** Royle 1834 (*P. emodi*)   **PGP-DGP-RD**
      'Majus' nom. dub.   RD

H   **peltatum** Linnaeus 1753   PGP
    pleianthum Hance 1883   PGP

POLEMONIUM Linnaeus 1753   [*Polemoniaceae*]
    boreale Adams 1817 (*P. lanatum* var. *humile* hort.)
    brandegei Greene 1887
HN‡L **caeruleum** Linnaeus 1753 (*P. yezoense*)   PGP-RD
        'Album'
    carneum A. Gray 1878   PGP-**RD**
    delicatum Rydberg 1901
        'Album'
    foliosissimum A. Gray 1878   PGP-DGP-RD
        'Album' = **P. foliosissimum** var. **alpinum**
        *var. **alpinum**
    heydenii Nelson 1899 = **P. pulcherrimum**
    lanatum Pallas ex Marshall von Bieberstein 1819
        var. *humile* hort. non Salisbury = **P. boreale**
    pauciflorum S. Watson 1888
    pulcherrimum Hooker 1830 (*P. heydenii*)
        'Tricolor'
H   **reptans** Linnaeus 1759   RD
        'Blue Pearl'   RD
        'Königsee'
        'Lambrook Manor'
        'Lymington'
        'Pink Beauty'
        'Sapphire'
    x richardsonii Graham 1827 (*P. caeruleum* x *P. reptans*)
        'Album'
        'Pallidum'
        'Superbum'
    yezoense (Miyabe & Kudo) Kitamura 1941 = **P. caeruleum**

POLIANTHES Linnaeus 1753   [*Amaryllidaceae*]
    tuberosa Linnaeus 1753   EGF.1-**DGP**-RD
        'The Pearl'   **RD**

POLYGONATUM Miller 1754   [*Convallariaceae (Liliaceae)*]
    biflorum (Walter) Elliott 1817   EGF.1-RD
    canaliculatum Pursh 1814 (*P. commutatum, P. giganteum*)   PGP-RD
    cirrhifolium (Wallich) Royle 1839
    commutatum (Schultes) Dietrich 1835 = **P. canaliculatum**
    falcatum A. Gray 1858 (*P. japonicum*)   EGF.1-PGP
        'Flore Pleno'
        'Variegatum'   PGP
    geminiflorum Decaisne 1844   PGP
    giganteum Dietrich 1835 = **P. canaliculatum**
    hirtum (Poiret) Pursh 1814 (*P. latifolium*)   EGF.1
    hookeri Baker 1875   EGF.1-**RD**
    humile Fischer & Maximowicz 1859   EGF.1-PGP
HNL   **x hybridum** Brügger 1886 (*P. multiflorum* x *P. odoratum*) (*P. multiflorum* hort.)
                                                           EGF.1-PGP-**DGP**-RD
        'Flore Pleno'   PGP
        'Nanum'nom. dub.
        'Striatum'
        'Variegatum'   PGP
    japonicum Morren & Decaisne 1834 = **P. falcatum**
    kingianum Collett & Hemsley 1890
    latifolium (Jacquin) Desfontaines 1807 = **P. hirtum**
    macranthum (Maximowicz) Koidzumi 1919 = **P. stenanthum**

miserum Satake 1942
HN‡ **multiflorum** (Linnaeus) Allioni 1785   EGF.1-PGP
H   *multiflorum* hort. non (Linnaeus) Allioni 1785 = **P. x hybridum**
N‡ **odoratum** (Miller) Druce 1906 (*P. officinale*)   EGF.1-PGP
        'Gilt Edge'
        'Grace Barker'
        'Flore Pleno'   PGP
        'Silver Wings'
        var. **thunbergii** (Morren & Decaisne) Hara (*P. thunbergii*)   EGF.1-RD
        'Variegatum'   EGF.1
    officinale Allioni 1785 = **P. odoratum**
    oppositifolium (Wallich) Royle 1839
    orientale Desfontaines 1807 (*P. polyanthemum*)
    polyanthemum (Marshall von Bieberstein) Link 1829 = **P. orientale**
    racemosum F. T. Wang & Tang 1937
    roseum (Ledebour) Kunth 1850   EGF.1-PGP
    sibiricum Delaroche 1811   EGF.1-PGP
    stenanthum Nakai 1913 (*P. macranthum*)   EGF.1
    stewartianum Diels 1912   EGF.1
    thunbergii Morren & Decaisne 1834 = **P. odoratum** var. **thunbergii**
N‡ **verticillatum** (Linnaeus) Allioni 1785   EGF.1-PGP
        'Rubrum'

POLYGONUM Linnaeus 1753   [*Polygonaceae*]
    affine D. Don 1825 = **Persicaria affinis**
    alatum D. Don 1825 non Buchanan-Hamilton ex Sprengel 1827 = **Persicaria alata**
    alpinum Allioni 1774 = **Persicaria alpina**
    alpinum hort, non Allioni = **Persicaria sericea**
    amphibium Linnaeus 1753 = **Persicaria amphibia**
    amplexicaule D. Don 1825 = **Persicaria amplexicaulis**
    bistorta Linnaeus 1753 = **Persicaria bistorta**
        ssp. *carneum* (C. Koch) Coode & Cullen 1967 = **Persicaria bistorta** ssp. **carneum**
    brunonis Wallich ex Meissner 1832 = **Persicaria affinis**
    campanulatum Hooker f. 1886 = **Persicaria campanulata**
        var. *lichiangense* (W. Smith) Steward 1930 = **Persicaria campanulata** var. **lichiangense**
    capitatum Buchanan-Hamilton ex D. Don 1825 = **Persicaria capitata**
    carneum C. Koch 1849 = **Persicaria bistorta** ssp. **carnea**
    cuspidatum Siebold & Zuccarini 1825 = **Fallopia japonica**
    emodi Meissner 1832 = **Persicaria emodi**
    equisetiforme hort., non Smith 1804 = **P. scoparium**
    filiforme Thunberg 1789 = **Persicaria filiformis**
    macrophyllum D. Don 1825 = **Persicaria macrophylla**
    milletii Leveille 1913 = **Persicaria milletii**
    molle D. Don 1825 = **Persicaria molle**
    oxyphyllum Wallich ex Meissner 1832 = **Persicaria amplexicaulis**
    polymorphum Ledebour 1850 = **Persicaria polymorpha**
    polystachyum Wallich ex Meissner 1832 = **Persicaria polystachya**
    regelianum Komarov 1936 = **Persicaria bistorta**
    reynoutria Makino 1901 = **Fallopia japonica**
    reynoutria hort., non Makino = **Fallopia japonica** var. **compacta**
    rude Meissner 1856 = **Persicaria mollis** var. **rude**
    runcinatum Buchanan-Hamilton ex D. Don 1825 = **Persicaria runcinata**
    sachalinense F. Schmidt ex Maximowicz 1859 = **Fallopia sachalinensis**
    scoparium Requien ex Loiseleur 1827 (*P. equisetiforme* hort., non Smith)
    sericeum Pallas 1776 = **Persicaria sericea**
    sericeum hort., non Pallas 1776 = **Persicaria alpina**
    sphaerostachyum Meissner 1826 = **Persicaria macrophylla**
    speciosum Meissner 1826 = **Persicaria amplexicaulis**

tenuicaule Bisset & Moore 1878 = **Persicaria tenuicaulis**
vacciniifolium Wallich ex Meissner 1832 = **Persicaria vacciniifolia**
virginianum Linnaeus 1753 = **Persicaria virginiana**
viviparum Linnaeus 1753 = **Persicaria vivipara**
weyrichii F. Schmidt 1859 = **Persicaria weyrichii**

POLYPODIUM Linnaeus 1753   [Polypodiaceae]
    australe Fee 1852 = **P. cambricum**
N   **cambricum** Linnaeus 1753 (P. australe)   EGF.1-PGP
    glycyrrhiza D. C. Eaton
    glycyrrhiza agg.
        'Longicaudatum'   PGP
N   **interjectum** Shivas 1961   EGF.1-PGP
    x mantonii Rothmaler 1962 (P. interjectum x P. vulgare)
    x shivasiae Rothmaler 1945 (P. cambricum x P. interjectum)
NL   **vulgare** Linnaeus 1753   EGF.1-PGP-RD
    vulgare agg.
        'Acutum'
        'Bifido-cristatum'
        'Bifido-grandiceps'
        'Cambricum Barrowii'
        'Cambricum Oakleyae'
        'Cambricum Wilharris'
        'Cornubiense'   PGP-RD
        'Cornubiense multifidum'
        'Crispum cristatum' ('Jean Taylor')
        'Cristatum Forster'
        'Jean Taylor' = **P. vulgare** agg. **'Crispum cristatum'**
        'Pulcherrimum'   RD
        'Pulcherrimum Barnes'
        Pulcherrimum Form 2
        'Semilacerum Jubilee'

POLYSTICHOPSIS (J. Smith) Holttum 1947   [Dryopteridaceae]
    nipponica (Rosenstock) Tagawa 1958 = **Arachniodes nipponica**

POLYSTICHUM Roth 1799   [Dryopteridaceae]
    acrostichoides (Michaux) Schott 1834   EGF.1-PGP-RD
NL   **aculeatum** (Linnaeus) Roth 1799   EGF.1-PGP-RD
        'Cristatum'
        'Grandiceps'
    andersonii Hopkins
    angulare (Willdenow) C. Presl 1836 = **P. setiferum**
    braunii (Spenner) Fee 1852
    californicum (D. C. Eaton) Diels 1899
    falcinellum (Swartz) C. Presl 1836
N   **lonchitis** (Linnaeus) Roth 1799   EGF.1-PGP
    munitum (Kaulfuss) C. Presl 1836   EGF.1-PGP-RD
    polyblepharum (Roemer ex Kunze) C. Presl 1836
    rigens Tagawa 1937
N   **setiferum** (Forsskal) Woynar 1913 (P. angulare)   EGF.1-**RD**
        'Acutilobum'   PGP-RD
        'Congestum'
        'Congestum Broughton Mills'
        'Cristato-gracile'
        'Cristato-gracile Moly'
        'Cristato-pinnulum'
        'Cristatum'
        'Dahlem'
L   **'Divisilobum'**   **PGP-RD**

'Divisilobum densum' = **P. setiferum 'Plumoso-densum'**
'Divisilobum grandiceps'
'Divisilobum Iveryanum' ('Iveryanum')
'Divisilobum Oakfield'
'Divisilobum Wollaston'
'Foliosum'
'Gracilis Moly' = **P. setiferum 'Cristato-gracile Moly'**
'Herrenhausen'
'Imbricatum'
'Iveryanum' = **P. setiferum 'Divisilobum Iveryanum'**
'Lineare'
'Manica-infantis'
'Percristatum'
'Perserratum'
'Plumosum'
'Plumosum Bevis' ('Pulcherrimum Bevis')
'Plumoso-densum' ('Plumoso-multilobum', 'Divisilobum densum', 'Plumoso-
divisilobum densum')

'Plumoso-densum Perry's Variety'
'Plumoso-divisilobum'   RD
'Plumoso-divisilobum densum' = **P. setiferum 'Plumoso-densum'**
'Plumoso-multilobum' = **P. setiferum 'Plumoso-densum'**
'Proliferum'   RD
'Proliferum Dahlem' = **P. setiferum 'Dahlem'**
'Profilerum Herrenhausen' = **P. setiferum 'Herrenhausen'**
'Proliferum Iveryanum'
= **P. 'Divisilobum Iveryanum'**
'Pulcherrimum Bevis' = **P. setiferum 'Plumosum Bevis'**
'Pulcherrimum Bornim' nom. dub.
'Pulcherrimum Dahlem' = **P. setiferum 'Dahlem'**
'Ramo-pinnum'
'Rotundatum'
'Tripinnatum'
'Wollastoni' = **P. setiferum 'Divisilobum Wollaston'**
tsus-simense (Hooker) J. Smith 1875   EGF.1-PGP

POLYXENA Kunth 1843   [*Hyacinthaceae (Liliaceae)*]
 corymbosa (Linnaeus) Jessop 1976
 ensifolia (Thunberg) Schoenland 1910 (*P. maughanii, P. odorata*)
 maughanii Barker 1931 = **P. ensifolia**
 odorata Nicholson 1886 = **P. ensifolia**

PONTEDERIA Linnaeus 1753   [*Pontederiaceae*]
NL **cordata** Linnaeus 1753   EGF.1-**DGP-RD**
  var. **lanceolata** (Muhlenberg) Torrey
 dilatata Buchanan-Hamilton in Symes

PORTULACA Linnaeus 1753   [*Portulacaceae*]
AHN **oleracea** Linnaeus 1753

POTAMOGETON Linnaeus 1753   [*Potamogetonaceae*]
N‡ **coloratus** Vahl 1813
N‡L **crispus** Linnaeus 1753   EGF.1
 densus Linnaeus 1753 = **Groelandia densa**
N‡ **lucens** Linnaeus 1753
N‡L **natans** Linnaeus 1753   EGF.1
N‡ **pectinatus** Linnaeus 1753
N‡ **perfoliatus** Linnaeus 1753

POTENTILLA Linnaeus 1753   [*Rosaceae*]

    alba Linnaeus 1753   CA

    alchemilloides Lapeyrous 1782

    alpestris Haller f. 1818 = **P. crantzii**

    ambigua Cambessedes 1844 = **P. cuneata**

N‡   **anglica** Laicharding 1790

N‡   **argentea** Linnaeus 1753

    argyrophylla Wallich ex Lehmann 1831 (*P. leucochroa*)   PGP

    atrosanguinea Loddiges ex D. Don 1825   PGP-DGP

          HYBRID CULTIVARS

          'Blazeaway'

          'Etna'

          'Fireflame'   PGP-DGP

          'Flamenco'

          'Flammea'   PGP-RD

L   **'Gibson's Scarlet'**   PGP-**DGP-RD**

          'Gloire de Nancy' ('Glory of Nancy')   PGP-**RD**

          'Glory of Nancy' = **P. 'Gloire de Nancy'**

          'Helen Jane'

          'Karneval'

          'Melton'

          'Monsieur Rouillard'   PGP-**DGP**

          'Roulette'

          'Versicolor Plena'

          'William Rollinson'   PGP-RD

L   **'Yellow Queen'**   PGP-RD

    aurea Linnaeus 1756   CA

        'Aurantiaca'

        ssp. **chrysocraspeda** (Lehmann) Nyman 1878 (*P. ternata*)   RD

        ssp. **chrysocraspeda** 'Nana' nom. dub.

        'Flore Pleno'

        'Goldklumpen'

        'Rathboneana'

    caulescens Linnaeus 1756

    cinerea Chaix ex Villars 1779

    collina Wibel 1799

N‡   **crantzii** (Crantz) G. Beck ex Fritsch 1897 (*P. alpestris*)   CA

        'Goldrausch'

    cuneata Wallich ex Lehmann 1831 (*P. ambigua*)

    delavayi Franchet 1890   PGP

HNL   **erecta** (Linnaeus) Raeuschel 1797 (*P. tormentilla*)

    eriocarpa Wallich ex Lehmann 1831

    fragiformis Willdenow ex Schlecht 1813 = **P. megalantha**

    gracilis Douglas ex Hooker 1830

    leucochroa Lindley 1828 nom. nud. = **P. argyrophylla**

    megalantha Takeda 1911 (*P. fragiformis*)

        'Majlands'

        'Perfecta Plena'

    nepalensis Hooker 1824   PGP-DGP

        'Flammenspiel'

L   **'Miss Willmott'**   PGP-DGP-RD

        'Roxana'   PGP-DGP-RD

    neumanniana Reichenbech 1832

    nevadensis Boissier 1838   CA

    nitida Linnaeus 1756   **CA**-DGP-**RD**

        'Alba'   CA

        'Compacta'

'Lissadell'
'Rubra'   DGP-RD
N‡   **palustris** (Linnaeus) Scopoli 1772 (*Comarum palustre*)
    pamirica T. Wolf 1915
    plattensis Nuttall 1838
N   **recta** Linnaeus 1753   PGP-DGP
      'Pallida' = **P. recta** var. **sulphurea**
      var. **sulphurea** Lamarck
      'Warrenii'   DGP-RD
    reuteri Boissier 1856
N‡   **rupestris** Linnaeus 1753
S   **salesoviana** Stephan 1809 (*Comarum salesovianum*)
    speciosa Willdenow 1800
N‡   **tabernaemontani** Ascherson 1891   RD
      'Aurea'
      'Nana'
    ternata C. Koch 1847 non (Maximowicz) Freyn = **P. aurea** ssp. **chrysocraspeda**
    thurberi A. Gray ex Lehmann 1854
    x tonguei Hort. ex W. Baxter 1850 (*P. anglica* x *P. nepalensis*)
      'Kirsten'
    tormentilla Neck 1770 = **P. erecta**
    tridentata Solander 1810 = **Sibbaldiopsis tridentata**
    verna Linnaeus 1753 nom. ambig. = **P. crantzii**
    villosa Pallas ex Pursh 1814 non (Crantz) Zimmeter   CA

POTERIUM Linnaeus 1753   [*Rosaceae*]
    canadense (Linnaeus) A. Gray 1867 = **Sanguisorba canadensis**
    officinale (Linnaeus) A. Gray 1868 = **Sanguisorba officinalis**
    sanguisorba Linnaeus 1753 = **Sanguisorba minor**
    tenuifolium Franchet & Savatier 1875 = **Sanguisorba tenuifolia**

PRATIA Gaudichard 1826   [*Campanulaceae*]
    angulata (Forster f.) Hooker f. 1844   RD
      'Messenger'
      'Ohau'
      'Tennyson'
      'Treadwellii' (P. treadwellii hort.)   CA-RD
      'Woodside'   [M.T. Feesey]
    arenaria Hooker f. 1844
    irrigua Bentham 1868
    macrodon Hooker f. 1864
    pedunculata (R. Brown) F. Mueller ex Bentham 1868 (*Isotoma fluviatilis*)   RD
      'Blue Stars'   [G. Hutchins]
      'Clear Skies'   [G. Hutchins]
      'County Park'   [G. Hutchins]
      'Jack's Pass'   [G. Hutchins]
      'Kinsey'   [G. Hutchins]
      'Stone'   [G. Hutchins]
      'Tunnack'   [G. Hutchins]
    perpusilla Hooker f. 1864
      'Fragrant Carpet'   [G. Hutchins]
      'Summer Meadows'   [G. Hutchins]
    physaloides (A. Cunningham) Hemsley 1886
    puberula Bentham 1868
    repens Gaudichard 1829
    treadwellii hort. = **P. angulata 'Treadwellii'**
    *villosa

PRESLIA Opiz 1824   [*Lamiaceae (Labiatae)*]
    cervina (Linnaeus) Fresenius 1828 = **Mentha cervina**

PRIMULA Linnaeus 1753   [*Primulaceae*]

Classification as per W. W. Smith & Forrest 1928
and W. W. Smith & Fletcher 1941-1949

SECTION

1	**Amethystina**
2	**Auricula**
3	**Bullatae**
4	**Candelabra**
5	**Capitatae**
6	**Carolinella**
7	**Cortusoides**
8	**Cuneifolia**
9	**Denticulata**
10	**Dryadifolia**
11	**Farinosae**
12	**Floribundae**
13	**Grandis**
14	**Malacoides**
15	**Malvacea**
16	**Minutissimae**
17	**Muscarioides**
18	**Nivales**
19	**Obconica**
20	**Parryi**
21	**Petiolares**
22	**Pinnatae**
23	**Pycnoloba**
24	**Reinii**
25	**Rotundifolia**
26	**Sikkimensis**
27	**Sinenses**
28	**Soldenelloideae**
29	**Souliei**
30	**Vernales**

30	*acaulis* (Linnaeus) Hill 1764 = **P. vulgaris**	
11	**algida** Adams ex F. Weber & Mohr 1805	
2	**allionii** Loiseleur 1801	**CA-DGP-RD**
	'Alba'	CA
	'Anna Griffith'	
	'Austen'	
	'Avalanche' [J. Elliott]	
	'Crowsley Variety' [R. Bevan]	CA
	'Elliott's Variety'	
	'Frank Barker'	
	'Marion'	
	'Martin'	
	'Mary Berry'	
	'Pennine Pink'	
	'Picton's Variety'	
	'Praecox'	CA
	'Snow Flake'	
	'Vicountess Byng'	CA
	'William Earle'	
26	**alpicola** (W. W. Smith) Stapf 1932	PGP
	var. **alba** W. W. Smith 1943	

	var. **luna** (Stapf) W. W. Smith 1943	PGP
	var. **violacea** (Stapf) W. W. Smith 1943	PGP
30	*altaica* Hort. ex Pax 1905 = **P. elatior** ssp. **meyeri**	
20	**angustifolia** Torrey 1823	
4	**anisodora** Balfour f. & Forrest 1916	
2	**x arctotis** A. Kerner 1875 *(P. auricula x P. hirsuta)*	
9	**atrodentata** W. W. Smith 1911	CA
	'Alba'	
4	**aurantiaca** W. W. Smith & Forrest 1923	PGP-**RD**
21	**aureata** Fletcher 1941	CA
	ssp. **fimbriata** A. Richards ex Gould 1982	
2	**auricula** Linnaeus 1753	CA-**DGP**-**RD**
	var. *albo-cincta* Widmer 1891 = **P. auricula** ssp. **bauhini**	
	ssp. **bauhini** (Beck) Lüdi	
	ssp. **ciliata** (Moretti) Lüdi	CA
	var. **serratifolia** (Rochebrune) Lüdi	

SHOW AURICULAS

'Alfred Niblett'	[H. A. Cohen 1963]
'Alice Haysom'	[C. G. Haysom 1935]
'Almondbury'	[J. Stant 1969]
'Amethyst'	
'Astolat'	
'Ballet'	
'Baupaume'	
'Beauty of Bath'	
'Beechen Green'	
'Ben Wyves'	
'Big Ben'	
'Bilton'	
'Blackcock'	
'Black Ice'	
'Bluebird'	
'Blue Gown'	
'Blue Jean'	[D. L. Telford 1972]
'Blue Lagoon'	
'Blue Nile'	[R. Newton 1962]
'Bramshill'	
'Brass Dog'	
'Brazil'	[D. L. Telford 1981]
'Broughton'	
'Carole'	
'Carolina Duck'	
'C G Haysom'	[R. Loake 1962]
'Chaffinch'	
'Cherry'	[P. A. Duthie 1968]
'Chirichua'	
'Chloe'	[F. Buckley 1967]
'Chloris'	
'Chorister'	[A. E. James 1967]
'Citron'	
'Clare'	[P. G. Ward 1980]
'Colonel Champney'	
'Consersative'	
'Consett'	[D. L. Telford 1973]
'Coppernob'	
'Coral'	
'Cortina'	
'Daftie Green'	

'Dakota'
'Daphnis'
'Douglas Black'
'Douglas Blue'
'Douglas Green'
'Douglas Rose'
'Douglas Salmon'
'Downlands'
'Dunlin'
'Durness'
'Elegance'
'Elsinore'   [P. G. Ward 1976]
'Embley'
'Emerald'   [F. Buckley 1962]
'Emery Down'
'Esso Blue'
'Ettrick'
'Everest Blue'   [H. D. Hall 1959]
'Fanciful'
'Fanny Meerbeck'   [B. Simonite 1898]
'Flamingo'   [D. L. Telford 1980]
'Fleminghouse'   [J. Stant 1967]
'Firecrest'
'Freda'
'Geronimo'
'Girlguide'
'Gizabroon'   [D. L. Telford1974]
'Gleam'
'Gold Blaze'
'Goldcrest'
'Golden Lilliput'
'Green Charmer'
'Greenfinger'
'Greenheart'
'Green Isle'
'Green Jacket'
'Green Mouse'   [S. Kos 1974]
'Green Shank'
'Greensleeves'
'Greenwood'
'Green Woodpecker'
'Greta'
'Grey Monarch'   [J. Douglas]
'Gueldersome Green'
'Guinea'   [D. A. Duthie 1981]
'Hardley'
'Hawkwood Fancy'
'Helena'   [F. Buckley 1959]
'Hew Dalrymple'   [C. G. Haysom 1947]
'Hurstwood Mayday'
'Hyacinth'
'Idmiston'
'James Arnot'
'King Cole'
'Kristen Stripe'
'Lady Croft'
'Lechistan'
'Light Sussex'
'Lilac Domino'
'Lindley'   [D. L. Telford 1976]

'Lisa's Red'
'Lisa's Smile'   [D. L. Telford 1982]
'Lovebird'   [J. Douglas 1932]
'Mandan'
'Manka'
'Margot'
'Marsco'
'Martin's Red'
'Matley'
'Midnight'
'Milk Chocolate'
'Minley'
'Minsmere'
'Mojave'
'Moonglow'   [D. G. Hadfield 1974]
'Moonlight'
'Neat and Tidy'   [R. Newton 1955]
'Night Heron'
'Nocturne'   [R. Newton 1955]
'N Telford'
'Oakes Blue'   [D. L. Telford]
'Old Gold'   [J. Douglas 1920]
'Orb'   [D. A. Duthie 1971]
'Pat'   [J. Ballard 1966]
'Patience'
'Pennant's Parakeet'
'Philip Green'
'Plush Royal'
'Pot of Gold'
'Prince Charming'
'Purple Heron'
'Purple Lake'
'Purple Velvet'
'Queen of Sheba'   [F. Buckley 1958]
'Rajah'   [J. Douglas]
'Red Beret'   [D. L. Telford 1980]
'Red Gauntlet'   [D. A. Duthie 1970]
'Red Rum'
'Remus'   [W. R. Hecker 1970]
'Rolts'
'Rosalie Edwards'   [A. J. Martin 1972]
'Rosanna'
'Royal Purple'   [J. W. Midgeley 1946]
'Royalty'
'Sailor Boy'
'Saint Boswells'
'Sandmartin'
'Scarlet Ibis'
'Scarlet Lancer'
'Serenity'
'Shaheen'
'Sheila'   [C. A. Hawkes 1961]
'Shere'   [K. J. Gould 1967]
'Slioch'
'Spring Meadows'   [J. F. Ballard]
'Stant's Blue'
'Stella'   [R. Newton 1966]
'Sunburst'
'Sungold'
'Sunny Boy'

'Superb'   [F. Buckley 1962]
'Super Para'
'Sweet Pastures'
'Tavistock'
'Teem'   [T. Meek 1957]
'Tenby Grey'
'The Baron'
'The Bishop'
'The Bride'   [F. Buckley 1959]
'The Mikado'   [W. Smith 1906]
'The Snods'   [D. L. Telford 1977]
'Tinkerbell'   [C. Cookson 1932]
'Trojan'
'Trudy'
'True Briton'
'Victoria'   [D. G. Hadfield 1981]
'Violet'
'Violetta'
'Vivien'   [S. Kos 1975]
'Walhampton'
'Wexland'
'White Ensign'
'White Wings'
'Woodpidgeon'
'Yellow Hammer'   [F. Buckley 1958]
'Yorkshire Grey'

ALPINE AURICULAS

'A Delbridge'
'Adrian'   [A. Delbridge 1970]
'Alison Jane'
'Alpine Violet'
'Andrea Julie'   [D. L. Telford]
'Applecross'   [D. Edwards 1968]
'Argus'   [J. J. Keen 1887]
'Aurora'
'Basuto'
'Beatrice'
'Blossom'   [S. Auker 1960]
'Blue Bonnet'
'Bookham Firefly'   [J. Douglas 1936]
'Brown Bess'
'Carole'   [K. Ellerton 1977]
'Coll'
'Commander'
'Craig Vaughn'
'C W Needham'   [P. Johnson 1934]
'Desert Dawn'
'Desert Magic'
'Desert Peach'
'Desert Queen'
'Desert Rose'
'Desert Sands'
'Desert Star'
'Diane'
'Donhead'
'Elizabeth Ann'
'Ellen Thompson'
'Elsie'   [J. Allen 1977]

'Elsie May'
'Fairy'
'Finchfield'
'Frank Crosland'
'Frank Faulkner'
'Galen'
'Gem'
'Gordon Douglas'
'Holne'
'Ida'
'Jeannie Telford'   [D. L. Telford 1977]
'Jenny'
'Joan Elliott'
'Joanne'
'Joy'   [P. Johnson 1931]
'Kathy'
'Kelso'
'Kercup'
'Kim'
'Kingcup'
'Kinloch'
'Lady Daresbury'   [C. F. Faulkner 1961]
'Lady Joyful'
'Lee'
'Lepton Jubilee'
'Lilian Hill'
'Ling'
'Lisa'   [D. L. Telford 1978]
'Margaret Faulkner'   [C. F. Faulkner 1961]
'Mark'   [D. L. Telford 1972]
'Maureen Millward'
'Merridale'
'Mink'
'Mrs L Hearne'
'Norah'
'Norma'
'Pathan'
'Paul'
'Peggy'
'Phyllis Douglas'   [J. Douglas 1908]
'Pink Lady'
'Pippin'
'Pixie'
'Prince John'
'Purple Emperor'
'Rabley Heath'   [C. A. Hawkes 1972]
'Robinson's Variety'
'Rodeo'
'Rowena'
'Roxburgh'
'Salome'
'Sandra'
'Sandwood Bay'
'Senorita'
'Shogun'
'Sirius'   [F. Jacques 1979]
'Sonya'
'Sphinx'
'Spinney Lane'
'Stonnal'

'Sue'
'Summer Sky'
'Swale'
'Tally-ho'
'Tarantula'
'Ted Roberts'   [J. Allen 1977]
'The Czar'
'Thetis'
'Tiphareth'
'Valerie'   [C. A. Hawkes 1972]
'Vee Too'   [C. A. Hawkes 1973]
'Verdi'
'Vulcan'
'Walton'
'Winifred'   [F. Faulkner 1970]

DOUBLE AURICULAS

'Albury'
Barnhaven Hybrids   [Barnhaven]
'Barnhill'
'Blakeney'
'Camelot'
'Catherine'   [K. J. Gould]
'Crackley Seashell'
'Crackley Tagetes'
'Delilah'
'Devon Cream'
'Doublet'
'Elizabeth Saunders'
'Kirklands'
'Maid Marion'
'Marigold'   [R. Newton]
'Mary'   [E. Lester-Smith]
'Sarah Lodge'   [R. Cole]
'Shalford'   [W. R. Hecker]
'Sir Robert Ewbank'   [E. Lester-Smith]
'Standish'
'Susannah'
'The Cardinal'
'Walton Heath'
'Watt's Purple'
'Zambia'

L

BORDER AURICULAS

'Aubergine'
'Balfouriana'
Barnhaven Hybrids   [Barnhaven]
'Betty Sheriff'
'Blue Velvet'
'Broadwell Gold'   [J. Elliott]
'County Park'   [G. Hutchins]
'County Park Cream'   [G. Hutchins]
'County Park Red'   [G. Hutchins]
'Dusky'
'Elizabeth Fry'
'George Edge'
'George Harrison'
'Jane Grey'

'Jezebel'
'Kolind'
'Old Dusty Miller'
'Old Gold Dusty Miller'
'Old Irish Blue'
'Old Red Dusty Miller'   RD
'Old Suffolk Bronze'
'Old Yellow Dusty Miller'   RD
'Paradise Yellow'
'Proctor's Yellow'
'Redstart'
'Queen Alexandra'   DGP
'St Gerrans' White'
Triumph Hybrids
'Velvet Knight'
'Windways Marilyn'
'Windways Mystery'

11	**auriculata** Lamarck 1792	
2	**'Beatrice Wooster'** *(P. allionii x P. marginata)*	
4	**beesiana** Forrest 1911	PGP-DGP-RD
2	**x berninae** A. Kerner 1875 *(P. hirsuta x P. latifolia)*	CA
	'Windrush'	CA
21	**bhutanica** Fletcher 1941 *(P. whitei* 'Sherriff's Variety'*)*	CA
2	**x biflora** Huter ex A. Kerner 1875 *(P. glutinosa x P. minima)*	CA
2	**x bileckii** Sündermann 1898 *(P. hirsuta x P. minima)*	CA-**RD**
2	**'Blairside Yellow'**	DGP
4	**'Bonfire'**	
21	**boothii** Craib 1917	C
	'Alba'	
	'Edrom'	
	'Schilling'	
21	**bracteosa** Craib 1917	CA
4	**Bressingham Hybrids** [A. Bloom]	
4	**x bulleesiana** Janson 1928 *(P. beesiana x P. bulleyana)*	
	Asthore Hybrids	PGP
4	**bulleyana** Forrest 1908	PGP-RD
4	**burmanica** Balfour f. & Kingdon-Ward 1920	PGP
21	**calderiana** Balfour f. & Cooper 1915	CA
	ssp. **strumosa** (Balfour f. & Cooper) A. J. Richards 1977 *(P. strumosa*	
5	**capitata** Hooker f. 1850	
	ssp. **crispata** (Balfour f. & W. W. Smith) W. W. Smith & Forrest 192	
	'Early Lilac'	
	ssp. **mooreana** (Balfour f. & W. W. Smith) W. W. Smith & Forrest 19.	
2	**carniolica** Jacquin 1778	CA
28	**cawdoriana** Kingdon-Ward 1926	
18	**chionantha** Balfour f. & Forrest 1915	
26	**chumbiensis** W. W. Smith 1912	
4	**chungensis** Balfour f. & Kingdon-Ward 1920	PGP
4	**x chunglenta** Mulligan 1930 *(P. chungensis x P. pulverulenta)*	PGP
11	**clarkei** Watt 1882	CA-RD
2	**clusiana** Tausch 1821	CA
4	**cockburniana** Hemsley 1892	
2	*commutata* Schott 1852 = **P. villosa**	
17	**concholoba** Stapf & Sealy 1932	
7	**cortusoides** Linnaeus 1753	
2	*cottica* Widmer 1889 = **P. villosa**	
5	*crispa* Balfour f. & W. W. Smith 1916 = **P. glomerata**	
8	**cuneifolia** Ledebour 1815	
	ssp. **hakusanensis** (Franchet) W. W. Smith & Forrest	

L appears at left margin beside **bulleyana**

	2	**daonensis** (Leybold) Leybold 1855 *(P. oenensis)*	
	11	**darialica** Ruprecht 1863	
L	9	**denticulata** J. E. Smith 1805	PGP-**DGP-RD**
		'Alba'	RD
		'Bressingham Beauty' [A. Bloom]	
		'Caleche'	
		'Cashmeriana'	
		'Cashmeriana Rubin' ('Rubin')	
		'Crimson Emperor'	
		'Glenroy Crimson'	
		'Inshriach Carmine'	
		Kelmscot Hybrids	
		Lavender and Mauve Hybrids	
		'Prichard's Ruby'	
		Purple Hybrids	
		Red Hybrids	
		'Rhonsdorfer Hybrid'	
		'Robinson's Red'	
		'Rosea'	
		'Rubin' = **'Cashmeriana Rubin'**	
		'Rubinball'	
		'Rubra'	
		'Variegata'	
	2	**deorum** Velenovsky 1896	CA
	2	**x deschmannii** Gusmus 1903 *(P. minima x P. wulfeniana)*	
	21	**deuteronana** Craib 1917	
	2	**'Dianne'** *(P. x forsteri x P. x pubescens)*	
	2	**x dinyana** Lagger 1839 *(P. integrifolia x P. latifolia)*	
	18	**duthieana** Balfour f. & W. W. Smith 1916	
	21	**edgeworthii** (Hooker f.) Pax 1905	CA-**DGP-RD**
		'Alba'	CA
		'Chrysops'= **P. aureata** ssp. **fimbriata**	
HN‡L	30	**elatior** (Linnaeus) Hill 1764	PGP
		hybrida hort. = **P. x polyantha**	
		ssp. **leucophylla** (Pax) J. Heslop-Harrison 1931 *(P. leucophylla)*	PGP
		ssp. **meyeri** (Ruprecht) Valentine & Lamond 1978 *(P. altaica* hort.*)*	
		ssp. **meyeri 'Grandiflora'**	
	21	**ellisiae** Pollard & Cockerell 1902	
	2	**'Ethel Barker'** *(P. allionii x P. hirsuta)*	
	9	**erosa** Wallich ex Regel 1852	
	26	**erythra** Fletcher 1943 *(P. rubra)*	
	2	**x facchinii** Schott 1852 *(P. minima x P. spectabilis)*	
N‡	11	**farinosa** Linnaeus 1753	CA-**DGP-RD**
	11	*fauriae* Franchet 1886 = **P. modesta** var. **fauriae**	
	26	**firmipes** Balfour f. & Forrest 1920	
	28	**flaccida** Balakrishnan 1972 *(P. nutans)*	RD
	2	**x floerkeana** Schrader 1811 *(P. glutinosa x P. minima)*	CA
		'Alba'	
		'Biflora'	
L	26	**florindae** Kingdon-Ward 1926	PGP-**DGP-RD**
		Keylor Hybrids	
		'Rubra'	
	3	**forrestii** Balfour f. 1908	CA-**DGP**
	2	**x forsteri** Stein 1879 *(P. hirsuta x P. minima)*	CA
	11	**frondosa** Janka 1873	CA-RD
	25	**gambeliana** Watt 1882	CA
	7	**geraniifolia** Hooker f. 1882	CA
	2	**glaucescens** Moretti 1822	
	5	**glomerata** Pax 1905 *(P. crispa)*	
	2	**glutinosa** Wulfen 1778	CA

2   **x goebelii** A. Kerner 1875 *(P. auricula x P. hirsuta)*
21   **gracilipes** Craib 1917   CA-**DGP**-**RD**
       'Linnet'
       'Minor' Hort. ex Richards 1977 = **P. petiolaris**
       'Winter Jewel'
21   **griffithii** (Watt) Pax 1889
11   **halleri** J. Gmelin 1775 *(P. longiflora)*   CA
2   **x heeri** Brügger 1880 *(P. hirsuta x P. integrifolia)*   CA
4   *helodoxa* Balfour f. 1916 = **P. prolifera**
7   **heucherifolia** Franchet 1886
24   **hidakana** Miyabe & Kudo ex Hara 1935
2   **hirsuta** Allioni 1773   RD
       'Alba'
       f. **excapa** (Hegetschweiler & Heer) Pax
26   *hopeana* Balfour f. & Cooper 1918 = **P. sikkimensis** var. **hopeana**
17   **hyacinthina** W. W. Smith 1936   CA
4   **ianthina** Balfour f. & Cave 1916
4   **Inshriach Hybrids**   [J. Drake]
2   **integrifolia** Linnaeus 1753
2   **x intermedia** Portenschlag 1814 *(P. clusiana x P. minima)*
4   **'Inverewe'**   RD
11   **involucrata** Wallach ex Duby 1844 *(P. wardii, P. yargonensis)*
26   **ioessa** W. W. Smith 1937
4   **japonica** A. Gray 1858   PGP-**DGP**-**RD**
       'Alba'
       'Carnea'
       'Fiery Red'
       'Fuji'
       'Glowing Embers'
L   **'Miller's Crimson'**   PGP-DGP-**RD**
       'Oriental Sunrise'
       Pagoda Hybrids
L   **'Postford White'**   PGP-**DGP**-**RD**
       'Red Hug'
       'Splendens'
       'Valley Red'
7   **jesoana** Miquel 1867
11   **'Johanna'** *(P. clarkei x P. warshenewskiana)*
30   **juliae** Kusnezov 1901   RD
30   **x juliana** Rosenheim ex May 1919 nom. nud. *(P. elatior x P. juliae)* RD
       Hybrids see under: **P. x pruhonicensis**
2   **x juribella** Sündermann 1889 *(P. minima x P. tyrolensis)*
24   ***kamanashi**
7   **kisoana** Miquel 1867
       'Alba'
       polyneura (Franchet) hort. = **P. polyneura**
30   *komarovii* Losina-Losinskaja 1933 = **P. vulgaris** ssp. **sibthorpii**
2   **latifolia** Lapeyrouse 1813 *(P. viscosa)*
       'Cream Form'
       'Crimson Velvet'
       'Sonya'
7   **latisecta** W. W. Smith 1926
11   *laurentiana* Fernald 1928 = **P. mistassinica** var. **macropoda**
30   *leucophylla* Pax 1897 = **P. elatior** ssp. **leucophylla**
17   *littoniana* Forrest 1908 = **P. vialii**
2   **x loiseleurii** Sündermann 1925 *(P. allionii x P. auricula)*
       'Lismore Yellow'   [J. A. Burrow]
11   *longiflora* Allioni = **P. halleri**
11   **luteola** Ruprecht 1863
18   **macrophylla** D. Don 1825

4	**poissonii** Franchet 1886	PGP-RD
30	**x polyantha** Miller 1768 *(P. veris x P. vulgaris)*	**DGP**

    Barnhaven Cowichan Hybrids   [Barnhaven]
    Barnhaven Juliana Hybrids   [Barnhaven]
    Barnhaven Silver Dollar Hybrids   [Barnhaven]
    Barnhaven Victorian Hybrids   [Barnhaven]
    'Casino'   [Zwaan-Pannevis]
    'Crescendo'   [E. Benary]
    Double Gold Lace Hybrids
    Double Jack-in-the-Green Hybrids
    Gold Lace Hybrids
    Gold Lace Hose-in-Hose Hybrids
    Gold Lace Jack-in-the-Green Hybrids
    'King Arthur'   [Zwaan-Pannevis]
    'Las Vegas'   [Walz-Samen]
    Les Kaye's Hybrids   [L. Kaye]
    Oaklea Hybrids
    Old Gold Hybrids
    Pacific Hybrids   DGP-**RD**
    'Titurel'   [Zwaan-Pannevis]

7	**polyneura** Franchet 1895	
16	**primulina** (Sprengel) Hara 1962 *(P. pusilla)*	CA
4	**prolifera** Wallich 1820 *(P. helodoxa, P. smithiana)*	PGP-**DGP-RD**
30	**x pruhonicensis** Zeman ex Bergmans 1924 *(P. elatior x P. juliae x P. vulgaris)*	

L

    'Alan Robb'
    'Alba Plena'
    'April Rose'
    Barnhaven Double Hybrids
    'Barrowby Gem'
    'Beamish Foam'
    'Betty Green'
    'Blue Horizon'
    'Blue Riband'
    'Blutenkissen'   [G. Arends]
    'Bon-Accord Cerise'   [Cocker Bros c1900]
    'Bon-Accord Gem'   [Cocker Bros c1900]
    'Bon-Accord Purple'   [Cocker Bros c1900]
    'Buckland Wine'
    'Buckland White'
    'Butter Yellow'
    'Captain Blood'
    'Cherry'
    'Chevithorne Pink'
    'Chocolate Soldier'
    'Corporal Baxter'
    'Craven Gem'
    'Crimson Beauty'
    'Crimson Queen'
    'Crimson Velvet'
    'Damson Queen'
    'David Green'
    'Doctor Borresen'
    'Doctor Molly'
    'Dorothy'
    'Double Sulphur'
    'Enchantress'
    'Ethel M Dell'
    'Eugenia'
    'Fliederstrahl'
    'Freckles'

'Frühlingszauber'
'Garnet'
'Garryarde Crimson'
'Garryarde Guinevere'   **DGP**-RD
'Gerard's White'
'Gloriosa'
'Granny Graham'
'Groeneken's Glory'
'Gruss an Konigslut'
'Guinevere' = 'Garryarde Guinevere'
'Helge'   [Krupp]
'Ingram's Blue'
'Iris Mainwaring'
'Jubilee'
'Ken Dearman'
'Kinlough Beauty'   [Johnson]
'Lady Greer'
'Lambrook Lilac'
'Lambrook Pink'
'Lambrook Peach'
'Lilacina Plena'
'Lilian Harvey'
'Lizzie Green'
'Lingwood Beauty'
'Lopen Red'
'Marianne Davey'
'Marie Crousse'   [Pre-1882]
'McWatt's Claret'
'McWatt's Cream'
'Miss Indigo'
'Mrs MacGillivary'
'Old Irish Sulphur'
'Oliver Wyatt'
'Osiered Amber'
'Ostergruss'   [Oheimb]
'Our Pat'
'Perle von Bottrop'   [Holtkötter]
'Primrose Yellow'
'Profile'
'Purpurkissen' ('Purple Cushion')   [G. Arends]
'Queen of Whites'
'Red Paddy'
'Red Velvet'
'Rhapsody'
'Romance'
'Romeo'
'Rose O'Day'
'Roy Cope'
'Schneekissen' ('Snow Cushion')   [G. Arends]
'Schneewittchen' = 'Sneuwwitje'
'Silver Laced Blue'
'Sneuwwitje' ('Schneewittchen', 'Snovit', 'Snow White')
'Snovit' = 'Sneuwwitje'
'Snow Cushion' = 'Schneekissen'
'Snow White' = 'Sneuwwitje'
'Springtime'
'Sue Jervis'
'Sunshine Susie'
'Tawny Port'
'Techley Red'

	'The Bride'	
	'Tipperary Purple'	
	'Tomato Red'	
	'Twilight'	
	'Vanity'	
	'Vic's Blue'	
	'Vic's White'	
L	'Wanda'	**RD**
	'Wanda Hose-in-Hose'	
	'Wanda Improved'	
	'White Wanda'	
	'William Chalmers'	
	'Wisley Red' ('Wisley Crimson')	
2	**x pseudoforsteri** Sündermann 1898 *(P. hirsuta x P. minima)*	
2	**x pubescens** Jacquin 1778 *(P. auricula x P. hirsuta)*	CA-DGP-RD
	'Bellunense'	
	'Bewerley White'	
	'Boothman's Variety'	
	'Carmine'	
	'Chamois'	
	'Christine'	DGP
	'Cream Viscosa'	
	'Elphenor'	
	'Faldonside'	CA-DGP-RD
	'Freedom'	
	'Harlow Car' [Harlow Car Gardens]	
	'Henry Hall'	
	'Holland'	
	'Joan Gibbs'	
	'Mrs J H Wilson'	CA-DGP-RD
	'Nivea'	
	'Old Rose'	
	'Pat Barwick'	
	'Peggy Fell'	
	'Pink Freedom'	
	'Rufus'	**DGP**
	'The Fawn'	
	'The General'	**CA**
	'White Pearl'	
	'Windrush' = **P. x berninae 'Windrush'**	
4	**pulverulenta** Duthie 1905	PGP-**DGP**-**RD**
L	**Bartley Hybrids** [G. H. Dalrymple c1920]	PGP-DGP-**RD**
	Pastel Shade Hybrids	
	Pink and Apricot Shade Hybrids	
16	*pusilla* Wallich 1824 = **P. primulina**	
4	**'Quarry Wood'**	
2	**'Ramona'** *(P. latifolia x P. marginata)*	
28	**reidii** Duthie 1885	CA-**DGP**-RD
	var. **williamsii** Ludlow 1955	CA-RD
	var. **williamsii 'Alba'**	
24	**reinii** Franchet & Savatier 1879	CA
16	**reptans** Hooker f. ex Watt 1882	CA
2	**'Rheniana'** *(P. auricula x P. marginata)*	
11	**rosea** Royle 1836	DHP-**RD**
	'Delight' = **P. rosea 'Micia Visser de Geer'**	
	var. **elegans** (Duby) Hooker f. 1882	
	'Gigas'	
	'Grandiflora'	**RD**
	'Micia Visser de Geer' *('Delight')*	**DGP**-RD
25	*rotundifolia* Wallich 1824 nom. nudem. = **R. roxburghii**	

4	**'Rowallane Rose'**	PGP
25	**roxburghii** Balakrishnan 1972	CA
2	*rubra* Gmelin 1775 = **P. hirsuta**	
26	*rubra* Kingdon-Ward 1936 = **P. erythra**	
20	**rusbyi** Greene 1881	
28	**sapphirina** Hooker f & Thomson ex Hooker f. 1882	
7	**saxatilis** Komarov 1901	
11	**scandinavica** Bruun 1938	
21	**x scapeosa** *(P. bracteosa x P. scapigera)*	
2	**x schottii** Sündermann 1907 *(P. minima x P. tyrolensis)*	

N‡ 11   **scotica** Hooker 1821   CA

26	**secundiflora** Franchet 1885	PGP-**RD**
2	**x seriana** Widmer 1891 *(P. daonensis x P. hirsuta)*	
2	**x serrata** Widmer 1891 *(P. minima x P. wulfeniana)*	
4	**serratifolia** Franchet 1885	
7	**sieboldii** E. Morren 1873	**DGP-RD**

        'Alba'
        'Carefree'
        'Cherokee'
        'Cherubim'
        'Chinese Mountain'
        'Dancing Ladies'
        'Deechin'
        'Hakutsuri'
        'Harunuyuki'
        'Galaxy'
        'Geisha Girl'
        'Joan Jervis'
        'Lilac Sunbonnet'
        'Manakoora'
        'Mikado'
        'Pago-Pago'
        'Ruriden'
        'Snowflakes'
        'Shironyi'
        'Shirowashi'
        'Tah-ni'
        'Sunrokumare'
        'Tsuruhotei'
        'Winter Dreams'
        'Ykiguruma'

26   **sikkimensis** Hooker f 1851   PGP-RD
        var. **hopeana**(Balfour f. & Cooper) W. W. Smith & Fletcher 1943
                                   (P. hopeana)   RD
        var. **pudibunda** (W. W. Smith) W. W. Smith & Fletcher 1943   **RD**
        'Tilman no 2'

18	**sinoplantaginea** Balfour f. 1920	CA
18	**sinopurpurea** Balfour f. ex Hutchinson 1918	
4	*smithiana* Craib 1913 = **P. prolifera**	
28	**soldanelloides** Watt 1882	
21	**sonchifolia** Franchet 1885	CA
11	**sorachiana** Miyabe & Tatewaki 1933	
21	**'Soup Plate'** *(P. sonchifolia x P. whitei)*	
2	**spectabilis** Trattinnick 1814	DGP
2	*x steinii* Obrist ex Stein 1879 = **P. x forsteri**	
16	**stirtoniana** Watt 1882	
21	*strumosa* Balfour f. & Cooper 1916 = **P. calderiana** ssp. **strumosa**	
8	**suffrutescens** A. Gray 1868	
24	**takedana** Tatewaki 1928	
21	**tanneri** King 1886	

		ssp. **nepalensis** (W. W. Smith) A. J. Richards 1977 *(P. nepalensis)*
	21	**'Tantallon'** *(P. edgeworthii x P. whitei)*
	2	**x thomasiana** Sündermann ex Widmer 1891 *(P. hirsuta x P. integrifolia)*
	30	*x tommasinii* Grenier & Godron 1853 = **P. x variabilis**
	2	**tyrolensis** Schott 1851
	30	*uralensis* hort. = **P. veris** ssp. **macrocalyx**
	30	**x variabilis** Goupil 1825 *(P. veris x P. vulgaris)* *(P. x tommasinii)*
		'Bois Sovin'
HN‡L	30	**veris** Linnaeus 1753
		ssp. **canescens**(Opiz) Hayek ex Lüdi 1927
		ssp. **columnae** (Tenore) Lüdi 1927
		ssp. **macrocalyx** (Bunge) Lüdi 1927 *(P. uralensis* hort.*)*
	17	**vialii** Delavay ex Franchet 1891 *(P. littoniana)*
	2	**villosa** Wulfen 1778 *(P. commutata, P. cottica)*
	2	*viscosa* Allioni 1785 = **P. latifolia**
	2	**x vochinensis** Gusmus 1890 *(P. minima x P. wulfeniana)*
HNL	30	**vulgaris** (Linnaeus) Hill 1762 *(P. acaulis)*
		'Alba'
		'Alba Plena'
		'Coerulea'
		'Lutea'
		ssp. **sibthorpii** (Hoffmansegg) W. W. Smith & Forrest 1928 *(P. komarovii, P. woronovii)*
		'Rubra'
	26	**waltoni** Watt ex Balfour f. 1915
	11	*wardii* Balfour f. 1915 = **P. involucrata**
	11	**warshenewskiana** B. Fedtschenko 1902
	2	**x wettsteinii** Wiemann 1886 nom. nud. *(P. clusiana x P. minima)*
	21	**whitei** W. W. Smith 1911
		'Arduaine'
		bhutanica (Fletcher) hort. = **P. bhutanica**
		'Sherriff's Variety' = **P. bhutanica**
		'Tinny's Appleblossom' [G. R. Mundey]
		'Tinny's Dairymaid' [G. R. Mundey]
	4	**wilsonii** Dunn 1902
	2	**'Wockei'** *(P. arctotis x P. marginata)*
	30	*woronovii* = **P. vulgaris** ssp. **sibthorpii**
	2	**wulfeniana** Schott 1852
	11	*yargonensis* Petitmengin 1908 = **P. involucrata**
	11	**yuparensis** Takeda 1913
		'Alba'

Column tags on far right of certain entries: CA, CA, RD, DGP-RD, CA, DGP-RD, PGP, RD, CA-DGP.

PRUNELLA Linnaeus 1753 *[Lamiaceae (Labiatae)]*

	incisa Link 1822 = **P. vulgaris**	
L	**grandiflora** (Linnaeus) Scholler 1775 *(P. 'Pink Loveliness')*	RD
	'Alba'	
	'Blue Loveliness'	
	'Little Red Riding-hood' = **P. grandiflora 'Rotkäppchen'**	
	'Loveliness' [J. Elliott]	DGP-RD
	'Pink Loveliness' = **P. grandiflora**	
	'Rosea' nom. dub.	
	'Rotkäppchen' ('Little Red Riding-hood')	
	'Rubra'	
	'White Loveliness'	
HN‡	**vulgaris** Linnaeus 1753 *(P. incisa)*	
	'Alba'	
	'Rubra'	
	x webbiana Hort. ex N. Taylor 1914 *(P. grandiflora x P. hastifolia)*	DGP
	'Alba'	DGP-RD
	'Rosea'	DGP-RD

PSEUDOMUSCARI Garbari & Greuter 1970   *[Hyacinthaceae (Liliaceae)]*
    azureum (Fenzl) Garbari & Greuter 1970 (*Muscari azureum*)   CA-DGP-RD-SB
        'Album'
    pallens (Marshall von Bieberstein) Garbari 1971 (*Muscari pallens*)   SB
    parviflorum (Desfontaines) ! (*Muscari parviflorum*)   SB

PTERANTHUS Forskaal 1775   *[Caryophyllaceae]*
    *urticifolius

PTERIDIUM Gleditsch ex Scopoli 1760   *[Dennstaedtiaceae]*
    aquilinum (Linnaeus) Kuhn 1879
        var. **esculentum** (Forster f.) Kuhn 1882
            'Grandiceps'
            'Percristatum'

PTERIDOPHYLLUM Siebold & Zuccarini 1843   *[Fumariaceae]*
    racemosum Siebold & Zuccarini 1843

PTEROCEPHALUS Adanson 1763   *[Dipsacaceae]*
    parnassii Sprengel 1824 = **P. perennis**
    perennis Coulter 1823 (*P. parnassii, Scabiosa parnassii, S. pterocephala*)   CA

PTEROSTYLIS R. Brown 1810   *[Orchidaceae]*
    coccinea Fitzgerald 1875
    curta R. Brown 1810   EGF.2
    pedunculata R. Brown 1810   EGF.2

PTILOSTEMON Cassini 1816   *[Asteraceae (Compositae)]*
    casabonae (Linnaeus) W. Greuter 1967 (*Cnicus casabonae*)

PTILOTRICHUM C. A. Meyer 1831   *[Brassicaceae (Cruciferae)]*
S   **pyrenaicum** Willkomm 1880 (*Alyssum pyrenaicum*)   CA
S   **spinosum** (Linnaeus) Boissier 1839 (*Alyssum spinosum*)   CA
        'Coccineum'
        'Roseum'   CA

PULMONARIA Linnaeus 1753   *[Boraginaceae]*
    angustifolia Linnaeus 1753   PGP-**DGP-RD**
L   ssp. **azurea** (Besser) Gams   PGP-RD
        'Blaues Meer'   [E. Pagels]
        'Mawson's Variety'
        'Munstead Blue'   PGP-RD
        'Lewis Palmer'   RD
N‡ **longifolia** (Bastard) Boreau 1857   PGP
        'Bertram Anderson'
    mollis Wulfen ex Horneman 1813   PGP
        'Royal Blue'
H‡L **officinalis** Linnaeus 1753   PGP-**RD**
        'Alba'
        'Cambridge Blue'
        'Marjorie Lawley'
        'White Wings'
L   **rubra** Schott 1851   PGP-RD
        'Bowles' Red'   RD
        'Redstart'   [The Plantsmen c1970]
    saccharata Miller 1768   PGP-**RD**
        'Alba'
        'Argentea' ('Argentifolia')   RD
        'Argentifolia' = **P. saccharata 'Argentea'**
        'Barfield Pink'

    'Blue Carpet'
    'Fiona'
    'Frühlingshimmel' ('Spring Beauty')   [H. Klose 1981]
    'Grout's Pink'
    'Highdown'   CA
    'Mrs Moon'   PGP
    'Nurnberg'
L   **'Pink Dawn'**   PGP-RD
    'Sam Gamgee'
    'Sissinghurst White'
    'Spring Beauty' = **P. saccharata 'Frülingshimmel'**
    'Wisley White'
villarsae A. Kerner 1878   PGP
    'Margery Fish'

PULSATILLA Miller 1754   [*Ranunculaceae*]
    alba hort. non Reichenbach 1832 = **P. vulgaris 'Alba'**
    albana (Steven) Berchtold & Presl 1823/35 (*Anemone albana*)
        'Lutea'
N   **alpina** (Linnaeus) Delarbre 1800   PGP-CA-**DGP**-RD
        ssp. **apiifolia** (Scopoli) Nyman 1878 (*P. alpina* ssp. *sulphurea*) PGP-CA-**DGP**-RD
        ssp. *sulphurea* (de Candolle) Ascherson & Graebner = **P. alpina** ssp.
                              apiifolia
    ambigua (Turczaninow ex G. Pritzel) Juzepczuk 1937
    grandis Wendelroth 1830 = **P. halleri** ssp. **grandis**
    halleri (Allioni) Willdenow 1809 (*Anemone halleri*)   PGP-CA-**DGP**
        ssp. **grandis** (Wendelroth) Meikle (*P. grandis, P. vulgaris* ssp. *grandis*)
        ssp. **slavica** (G. Reuss) Zamels 1926 (*P. slavica*)
        ssp. **styriaca** (G.A. Pritzel) Zamels 1926
        ssp. **taurica** (Juzepczuk) K. Krause 1958
    montana (Hoppe) Reichenbach 1832   PGP
        'Ambigua' = **P. ambigua**
    patens (Linnaeus) Miller 1768
    pratensis (Linnaeus) Miller 1768 (*Anemone pratensis*)
    slavica G. Reuss 1853 = **P. halleri** ssp. **slavica**
N   **vernalis** (Linnaeus) Miller 1768 (*Anemone vernalis*)   **CA**-DGP-RD
HN‡L   **vulgaris** Miller 1768 (*Anemone pulsatilla*)   PGP-CA-**DGP-RD**
    'Alba'   DGP
    'Barton's Pink'
    ssp. *grandis* (Wendelroth) Zamels 1926 = **P. halleri** ssp. **grandis**
    'Mrs van der Elst'   PGP-RD
    'Röde Klokke'
    'Rubra'   **CA**-DGP-RD
    'Weisser Schwan'

PUSCHKINIA Adams 1805   [*Hyacinthaceae (Liliaceae)*]
    libanotica Zuccarini 1837 = **P. scilloides**
    scilloides Adams 1805 (*P. libanotica*)   EGF.1-CA-**BB-SB**-DGP-RD
        'Alba' ®   [Van Tubergen]

PUYA Molina 1782   [*Bromeliaceae*]
    alpestris (Poeppig & Endlicher) Gay 1853   EGF.2-PGP-**DGP**
    alpestris hort. non (Poeppig & Endlicher) Gay 1853 = **P. berteroniana**
    berteroniana Mez 1896 (*P. alpestris* hort.)
    laxa L. B. Smith 1958

PYCNANTHEMUM Michaux 1803 nom. cons.   [*Lamiaceae (Labiatae)*]
H   **pilosum** Nuttall 1818

PYGMAEA B. D. Jackson 1864   [*Scrophulariaceae*]
   pulvinaris Hooker f. 1864 (*Veronica pulvinaris*)   CA

PYRETHRUM Zinn 1757   [*Asteraceae (Compositae)*]
   cinerariifolium Trevisan 1820 = **Tanacetum cinerariifolium**
   parthenium (Linnaeus) Smith 1802 = **Tanacetum parthenium**
   ptarmiciflorum (Ball) Webb = **Tanacetum ptarmiciflorum**
   roseum (Adams) Marshall von Bieberstein 1808 = **Tanacetum roseum**

RAMONDA Richard 1805 nom. cons.   [*Gesneriaceae*]
   myconi (Linnaeus) Reichenbach 1831   CA-**DGP**-RD
     '**Alba**'   CA-RD
     '**Albo-rosea**'
     '**Rosea**'   CA
   nathaliae Pancic & Petrovic 1882   CA-RD
     '**Alba**'   CA
   serbica Pancic 1874   CA-RD
     '**Alba**'

RANUNCULUS Linnaeus 1753   [*Ranunculaceae*]
   abnormis Cutanda & Willkinson 1859
   aconitifolius Linnaeus 1753   **PGP**-RD
L   '**Flore Pleno**' ('Pleniflorus')   PGP
N‡ **acris** Linnaeus 1753   PGP-**DGP**-RD
     '**Flore Pleno**' ('Multiplex')   **DGP**-RD
   alpestris Linnaeus 1753   CA
     '**Flore Pleno**'
     var. *traunfellneri* (Hoppe) hort. = **R. traunfellneri**
   amplexicaulis Linnaeus 1753   **DGP**
     '**Grandiflorus**'
N‡L **aquatilis** Linnaeus 1753   RD
     ssp. *circinatus* (Sibthorp) Holmboe 1914 = **R. circinatus**
     ssp. *fluitans* (Lamarck) hort. = **R. fluitans**
   asiaticus Linnaeus 1753   **BB-DGP**-RD
     var. **albus** Hayek
N‡ **bulbosus** Linnaeus 1753   RD
     'Flore Pleno' = **P. constantinopolitanus 'Flore Pleno'**
     '**F. M. Burton**'
     'Speciosus Plenus' = **R. constantinopolitanus 'Flore Pleno'**
   calandrinioides Oliver 1889   **CA-RD**
N‡ **circinatus** Sibthorp 1794 (*R. aquatilis* ssp. *circinatus*)
   clivalis Allan 1961 (*R. geraniifolius* Hooker f.)
   constantinopolitanus (de Candolle) Urville 1822
     '**Flore Pleno**' (*R. bulbosus* 'Speciosus Plenus', 'Flore Pleno')   PGP-**RD**
   crenatus Waldstein & Kitaibel 1799   CA
   creticus Linnaeus 1753
   eschsholtzii Schlecht 1820
HN‡L **ficaria** Linnaeus 1753   **BB**-DGP
     '**Albus**'
     'Anemonifolia' = **R. ficaria 'Collarette'**
     'Aurantiacus' = **R. ficaria 'Cuprea'**
     'Bowles' Double' = **R. ficaria 'E. A. Bowles'**
     '**Brazen Hussy**'
     '**Collarette**' ('Anemonifolia')
     '**Cuprea**' ('Aurantiacus')
     '**E. A. Bowles**' ('Bowles' Double')
     '**Flore Pleno**'
     '**Grandiflorus**'
     '**Greencourt Gold**'
     '**Green Petal**'

	'Lemon Queen'	
	'Major'	**DGP**
	'Picton's White'	
	'Primrose'	
	'Randall's White'	
	'Salmon's White'	
N‡L	**flammula** Linnaeus 1753	
N‡	**fluitans** Lamarck 1778	
	geraniifolius Pourret 1788 = **R. montanus**	
	geraniifolius Hooker f. 1852 = **R. clivalis**	
	glacialis Linnaeus 1753	CA-**DGP**
	grandiflorus hort. non Linnaeus 1753 = **R. amplexicaule 'Grandiflorus'**	
	gouanii Willdenow 1800 (*P. montana* var. *dentatus*)	RD
	gramineus Linnaeus 1753	**DGP-RD**
	insignis Hooker f. 1852	PGP
	japonicus Thunberg 1794	
	kochii Ledebour 1842	**BB**
	kotschyi Boissier 1846	
N‡	**lingua** Linnaeus 1753	PGP-**DGP**-RD
	'Grandiflorus'	
	lyallii Hooker f. 1864	PGP
	millefoliatus Vahl 1791	
	montanus Willdenow 1800 (*P. geraniifolius* Pourret)	
	var. *dentatus* Baumgarten = **R. gouanii**	
	'Molten Gold'	
	novus Leveille & Vaniot 1906	
	parnassifolius Linnaeus 1753	**CA**
	psilostachys Grisebach 1843	
N‡	**repens** Linnaeus 1753	PGP
	var. **pleniflorus** Fernald	PGP
	rupestris Gussone 1826	
	seguieri Villars 1779	CA
	traunfellneri Hoppe 1826	CA

RAOULIA Hooker f. 1846	[*Asteraceae (Compositae)*
australis Hooker f. in Raoul 1846 (*R. lutescens*)	CA-**DGP**-RD
glabra Hooker f. 1853	CA-RD
haastii Hooker f. 1853	
hookeri Allan 1961	RD
leontopodium (Hooker f.) hort. = **Leucogenes leontopodium**	
x loganii Cheeseman 1925 = **X Leucoraoulia loganii**	
lutescens Beauverd 1910 = **R. australis**	
monroi Hooker f. 1864	
subsericea Hooker f. 1853	CA
tenuicaulis Hooker f. 1853	

REHMANNIA Liboschitz ex Fischer & C. Meyer 1835 nom. cons.	[*Gesneriaceae*
glutinosa Liboschitz ex Fischer & C. Meyer 1835	

REINECKEA Kunth 1844 nom. cons.	[*Convallariaceae (Liliaceae)*
carnea (Andrews) Kunth 1844	EGF.1-PGP

RESEDA Linnaeus 1753	[*Resedaceae*
HN‡ **luteola** Linnaeus 1753	
N **odorata** Linnaeus 1759	DGP-RD

REYNOUTRIA Houttuyn 1777	[Polygonaceae
japonica Houttuyn 1777 = **Fallopia japonica**	
sachalinensis (F. Schmidt) Nakai 1919 = **Fallopia sachalinensis**	

RHAZYA Decaisne 1835   *[Apocynaceae]*
   orientalis (Decaisne) A. de Candolle 1844   PGP-**DGP**

RHEUM Linnaeus 1753   *[Polygonaceae]*
   'Ace of Hearts' (*R. kialense x R. palmatum*)   [The Plantsmen c1970]
   acuminatum Hooker f. & Thomson ex Hooker f. 1855
   alexandrae Batalin 1894
   kialense Franchet 1895   **PGP-DGP**
H   **officinale** Baillon 1871   PGP
   palmatum Linnaeus 1759   PGP-**DGP**-RD
      'Atrosanguineum' ('Atropurpureum')   **PGP-RD**
L   **'Bowles' Variety'** ('Bowles' Crimson')   PGP
      'Rubrum'
   tanguticum (Regel) Maximowicz 1879   PGP
   webbianum Royle 1836

RHODIOLA Linnaeus 1753   *[Crassulaceae]*
   fastigiata (Hooker f. & Thomson) Fu 1965 = **Sedum fastigiatum**
   himalensis (D.Don) Fu 1965 = **Sedum himalensis**
   kirilowii (Regel) Maximowicz 1859 = **Sedum kirilowii**
   linearifolia (Royle) Fu 1965 = **Sedum trifidum**
   primuloides (Franchet) Fu 1965 = **Sedum primuloides**
   rosea Linnaeus 1753 = **Sedum roseum**

RHODOCHITON Otto & A. Dietrich 1833   *[Scrophulariaceae]*
C   **atrosanguineum** (Zuccarini) Rothmaler 1943 (*R. volubile*)
   volubile Otto & A. Dietrich 1833 = **R. atrosanguineum**

RHODOHYPOXIS Nel 1914   *[Hypoxidaceae]*
   baurii (Baker) Nel 1914   EGF.1-CA-**BB**-SB-**DGP-RD**
      'Alba'
      'Albrighton'   [Garnett-Botfield]
      'Appleblossom'   [McConnel]   SB
      var. **baurii**   SB
      'Dawn'   [McConnel]   EGF.1
      'Douglas'   [McConnel]   SB
      'Dulcie'   [Garnett-Botfield]
      'Eva Kate'   [Garnett-Botfield]
      'Fred Broome'   [Garnett-Botfield]
      'Garnett'   [McConnel]
      'Great Scott'
      'Harlequin'   SB
      Hazelmere Hybrids
      'Knockdolian Red'   [McConnel]
      'Perle'   [McConnel]
      'Pictus'   [McConnel]
      var. **platypetala** (Baker) Nel 1914   EGF.1-CA-SB
      'Red King'
      'Red Queen'
      'Ruth'   [Garnett-Botfield]
      'Stella'   [Garnett-Botfield]   **CA**-SB
      'Susan Garnett-Botfield'   [Garnett-Botfield]
      'Tetraploid Pink' nom. dub.
      'Tetraploid Red' nom. dub.
      'Tetraploid White' nom. dub.
      'White Princess'

RHODOPHIALA C. Presl 1844   *[Amaryllidaceae]*
   bifida (Herbert) Traub 1953 = **Hippeastrum bifidum**

RIDAN Adanson 1763   [*Asteraceae (Compositae)*]
   alternifolius (Linnaeus) Britton 1913 = **Actinomeris alternifolia**

RODGERSIA A. Gray 1858   [*Saxifragaceae*]
L   **aesculifolia** Batalin 1893   PGP-RD
   pinnata (Franchet) Franchet 1888   PGP-DGP-**RD**
      'Elegans'
      'Irish Bronze'
L   'Superba'   **PGP-DGP**-RD
   podophylla A. Gray 1858   PGP-**DGP-RD**
      'Pagode'   [E. Pagels]
      'Rotlaub'   [E. Pagels]
      'Smaragd'   [E. Pagels]
      'Purdomii'
   sambucifolia Hemsley 1906   PGP
      'Rothaut'   [Götz 1970]
   tabularis (Forbes & Hemsley) Komarov = **Astilboides tabularis**

ROMANZOFFIA Chamisso 1820   [*Hydrophyllaceae*]
   californica Greene 1902 = **R. suksdorfii**
   sitchensis Bongard 1833
   suksdorfii Greene 1902 (*R. californica*)
   unalaschkensis Chamisso 1820

ROMNEYA Harvey 1845   [*Papaveraceae*]
S   **coulteri** Harvey 1845   PGP-**DGP-RD**
      var. **trichocalyx** (Eastwood) Jepson 1922 (*R. trichocalyx*)   PGP-DGP-**RD**
      'White Cloud'   [U.S.A.]   PGP-RD
   trichocalyx Eastwood 1898 = **R. coulteri** var. **trichocalyx**

ROMULEA Maratti 1772 nom. cons.   [*Iridaceae*]
   bulbocodium (Linnaeus) Sabastiani & Mauri 1818   EGF.1-CA-**BB**-SB-**DGP**
      'Album'
      var. **clusiana** (Lange) ! (*R. clusiana*)   SB
      var. **leichtliniana** (Heldreich) Beguinot 1908   EGF.1-SB
   campanuloides Harms 1894
   clusiana (Lange) Nyman 1865 = **R. bulbocodium** var. **clusiana**
N‡ **columnae** Sebastiani & Mauri 1818   EGF.1-CA-**BB**-SB-DGP
   duthieae L. Bolus 1928 = **R. tabularis**
   flava (Lamarck) de Vos 1970   EGF.1
   leichtliniana Heldreich 1896 = **R. bulbocodium** var. **leichtliniana**
   macowanii Baker 1876   EGF.1-SB
      var. **alticola** (Burtt) de Vos 1970   EGF.1-SB
   nivalis (Boissier & Kotschy) Klatt 1882   EGF.1-**BB**-SB
   ramiflora Tenore 1827   EGF.1-SB
      ssp. **gaditana** (Kunze) Marais 1975   EGF.1-SB
   sabulosa Schlechter ex Bequinot 1907   EGF.1-SB
   tabularis Ecklon ex Beguinot 1907 (*R. duthieae*)
   tempskyana Freyn 1897   EGF.1-**BB**-SB
   'Zahnii'

ROSCOEA J.E. Smith 1804   [*Zingiberaceae*]
   alpina Royle 1839   EGF.2-CA-**BB**-SB
   auriculata K. Schumann 1904   EGF.2-**SB**
   'Beesiana'   SB
   cautleoides Gagnepain 1902   EGF.2-PGP-**BB**-SB-**DGP-RD**
      'Grandiflora'   [G. Preston]
   humeana Balfour f. & W.W. Smith 1916   EGF.2-PGP-**BB**-SB-**DGP-RD**
   procera Wallich 1832 = **R. purpurea**
   purpurea J.E. Smith 1804 (*R. procura*)   EGF.2-PGP-CA-SB-RD
      'Superba'

ROSULARIA (de Candolle) Stapf 1923   [*Crassulaceae*]
    aizoon (Fenzl) A. Berger 1930
    alpestris (Karelin & Kirilow) A. Boriss 1939
        ex Zozila
    chrysantha (Boissier) Takhtadjan 1953 (*Cotyledon chrysantha, R. pallida*)   CA
    haussknechtii (Boissier ex Reuter) A. Berger 1930
    libanotica (Labillardiere) Muirhead 1972
        ex Kaypak
    pallida (Schott & Kotschy) Stapf 1923 = **R. chrysantha**
    persica (Boissier) A. Berger 1923
    pestalozzae (Boissier) Samuelson & Fröderström 1960 = **R. sempervivum**
    platyphylla (Schrank) A. Berger 1923
        ex Murat Dag
    radiciflora (Steudel) A. Boriss 1939
        ex Bitlis
        ssp. **glabra** (Boissier) Chamberlain & Muirhead 1972
        ssp. **glabra** ex Beyas Dag
    sedoides (Decaisne) H. Ohba 1977 (*Sempervivella sedoides*)
        var. **alba** (Edgeworth) P. J. Mitchell ex P. J. Mitchell 1979   CA
    sempervivum (Marshall von Bieberstein) A. Berger 1930 (*R. pestalozzae*)   CA
        ex Quachaghem Kuh
    serpentinica (Werdermann) Muirhead 1972
        ex Sandras Dag
    serrata (Linnaeus) A. Berger 1930
        ex Crete
    setosa M. Bywater 1979
        ex Yiftach
    spathulata hort. = **Cotyledon spathulatus**
    turkestanica (Regel & Winkler) A. Berger 1930

RUBIA Linnaeus 1753   [*Rubiaceae*]
HN   **tinctorum** Linnaeus 1753

RUDBECKIA Linnaeus 1753   [*Asteraceae (Compositae)*]
    deamii S.F. Blake 1917 = **R. fulgida** var. **deamii**
    fulgida Aiton 1789   PGP-**DGP**-RD
        var. **deamii** (S.F. Blake) Perdue 1958 (*R. deamii*)   PGP-RD
        var. **speciosa** (Wenderoth) Perdue 1958 (*R. newmanii*)   RD
        var. **sullivantii** (Boynton & Beadle) Cronquist 1945 (*R. sullivantii*)   PGP
L   var. **sullivantii 'Goldsturm'**   [K. Foerster via H. Hagemann 1937]   PG-**RD**
N   **laciniata** Linnaeus 1753   PGP-DGP-RD
        'Goldkugel'   [Pötschke via Walther 1963]
L   **'Goldquelle'**   [Benary via Walther 1951]   PGP-**DGP**-RD
    maxima Nuttall 1841   **PGP**
    newmanii Loudon 1830 = **R. fulgida** var. **speciosa**
    nitida Nuttall 1834   PGP-RD
        'Herbstsonne'   **RD**
        'Juligold'   [Weinreich c1960]
    purpurea Linnaeus 1753 = **Echinacea purpurea**
    subtomentosa Pursh 1814   PGP-RD
    sullivantii Boynton & Beadle 1901 = **R. fulgida** var. **sullivantii**
    triloba Linnaeus 1753

RUMEX Linnaeus 1753   [*Polygonaceae*]
HN‡   **acetosa** Linnaeus 1753
    acetosa hort., non Linnaeus = **R. rugosus**
HN   **alpinus** Linnaeus 1753
    britannicus Linnaeus 1753 nom. confus.
    flexuosus Solander & Hooker f. 1854
N‡   **hydrolapathum** Hudson 1778

luxurians Linnaeus 1769 (*R. sagittatus*)
N   **patientia** Linnaeus 1753
H   **rugosus** Campdera 1819
      sagittatus Thunberg 1794 = **R. luxurians**
N‡   **sanguineus** Linnaeus 1753
HN   **scutatus** Linnaeus 1753
      scutatus hort., non Linnaeus = **R. rugosus**

SACCHARUM Linnaeus 1753   [*Poaceae (Gramineae)*]
      ravennae (Linnaeus) Murray 1774 (*Erianthus ravennae*)   EGF.2-PGP

SAGINA Linnaeus 1753   [*Caryophyllaceae*]
N   **boydii** Buchanan-White 1887   CA
      decumbens (Ell.) Torrey & A. Gray 1831 (*S. subulata* Torrey & A. Gray)
      glabra (Willdenow) Fenzl 1833 (*Minuartia verna*)
      '**Aurea**'
N‡   **subulata** (Swartz) Presl 1826
      subulata Torrey & A. Gray 1838 = **S. decumbens**
      subulata Urville 1826 = **Colobanthus hookeri**

SAGITTARIA Linnaeus 1753   [*Alismataceae*]
      japonica hort. = **S. sagittifolia** var. **leucopetala**
      lancifolia Linnaeus 1753   EGF.1
      latifolia Willdenow 1805   EGF.1-**RD**
N‡L   **sagittifolia** Linnaeus 1753   EGF.1-DGP-RD
           var. **leucopetala** Miquel   RD
           var. **leucopetala** '**Flore Pleno**'   EGF.1-**DGP**-RD
N   **subulata** (Linnaeus) Buchenau 1871   EGF.1

SALVIA Linnaeus 1753   [*Lamiaceae (Labiatae)*]
      aethiopis Linnaeus 1753   PGP
      ambigens hort. non Briquet 1889 = **S. guaranitica** '**Blue Enigma**'
B   **argentea** Linnaeus 1753   **PGP**-RD
      arizonica A. Gray 1878
S   **aurea** Linnaeus 1762   PGP
      aurea Hort. ex Bentham 1833 = **S. lamiifolia**
      azurea Michaux ex Lamarck 1792   PGP
           var. *grandiflora* Bentham 1848 = **S. azurea** ssp. **pitcheri**
           ssp. **pitcheri** (Torrey ex Bentham) Epling 1939 (*S. azurea* var. *grandiflora*)
S   **blepharophylla** Brandegee ex Epling 1930   PGP
      buchananii Hedge 1963
      bulleyana Diels 1912   PGP
      cacaliifolia Bentham 1848
S   **caespitosa** Montbret & Aucher 1836
S   **candelabra** Boissier 1838
S   **chaemaedryoides** Cavanilles 1793-4
A   **coccinea** Jussieu ex Murray 1779
      coerulea Bentham 1833 = **S. guaranitica** '**Black and Blue**'
S   **concolor** Lambert ex Bentham 1833
S   **confertiflora** Pohl 1830   PGP
      discolor Humboldt, Bonpland & Kunth 1818
      dorisiana Standley 1950
S   **elegans** Vahl 1804   RD
      farinacea Bentham 1833   PGP-**RD**
           '**Porcelaine Blanche**'
           '**Victoria**'   RD
      forskohlei Linnaeus 1766
S   **fulgens** Cavanilles 1791   PGP
S   **gesneriiflora** Lindley & Paxton 1851
      glutinosa Linnaeus 1753   PGP

grahamii Bentham 1830 = **S. microphylla** var. **neurepia**

S **grandiflora** Etlinger 1777 (*S. officinalis* ssp. *major*)

S **greggii** A. Gray 1870

S **guaranitica** A. Saint-Hilaire ex Bentham 1833   PGP-DGP
    'Black and Blue' J. Compton 1987 (*S. coerulea* Bentham)   PGP
    'Blue England' J. Compton 1987 (*S. ambigens* hort.)

L **haematodes** Linnaeus 1753 (*S. pratensis* var. *haematodes*)   **PGP-DGP-RD**
    'Indigo'   [A. Bloom]   PGP
    'Mittsommer'   PGP

hians Royle ex Bentham 1833   PGP

A **hispanica** Linnaeus 1753

A **horminum** Linnaeus 1753   DGP-RD

S **interrupta** Schousboe 1880   PGP

S **involucrata** Cavanilles 1793   PGP
    'Bethellii'   **PGP**

jurisicii Kosanin 1926   PGP
    'Alba'

lamiifolia Jacquin 1798 (*S. aurea* Bentham)

S **lavandulifolia** Vahl 1804 (*S. officinalis* ssp. *lavandulifolia*)

lemmonii A. Gray 1885 = **S. microphylla** var. **wislizenii**

leptophylla Bentham 1833

S **leucantha** Cavanilles 1791

S **mellifera** Greene 1892   PGP

S **mexicana** Linnaeus 1753

S **microphylla** Humboldt, Bonpland & Kunth 1818   PGP
    var. **neurepia** (Fernald) Epling 1939 (*S. neurepia*)   PGP-**DGP-RD**
    var. **wislizenii** A. Gray 1886 (*S. lemmonii*)

S **multicaulis** Vahl 1804   PGP

N **nemorosa** Linnaeus 1762   PGP
    'East Friesland' = **S. nemorosa** 'Ostfriesland'

L   'Lubeca'   PGP-DGP

L   'Ostfriesland' ('East Friesland')   [E. Pagels 1955]   PGP
    'Superba' = **S. x superba**

neurepia Fernald 1900 = **S. microphylla** var. **neurepia**

nutans Linnaeus 1753   PGP

SH **officinalis** Linnaeus 1753   PGP-DGP
    'Albiflora' ('Alba')
    'Aurea' hort. = **S. officinalis** 'Icterina'
    'Berggarten'
    'Crispa'
    'Icterina'
    ssp. *lavendulifolia* (Vahl) Gams = **S. lavendulifolia**
    ssp. *major* Gams = **S. grandiflora**
    'Milleri'
    'Purpurascens' ('Purpurea')
    'Rubrifolia'
    'Salicifolia'
    'Sturnina'
    'Tenuior'
    'Tricolor'   **DGP**

patens Cavanilles 1799   PGP-**RD**
    'Cambridge Blue'   PGP

pitcheri Torrey ex Bentham 1833 = **S. azurea** ssp. **pitcheri**

N‡ **pratensis** Linnaeus 1753   PGP
    var. *haematodes* (Linnaeus) Briquet = **S. haematodes**

przewalskii Maximowicz 1881   PGP

recognita Fischer & C. A. Meyer 1854   PGP

S **ringens** & Smith 1806   PGP
    var. **romanica** Prodan

roemeriana Scheele 1849

SH	**rutilans** Carr 1873	PGP-RD
	scabiosifolia Lamarck 1792	
BH	**sclarea** Linnaeus 1753	**DGP-RD**
	'Turkestanica'	PGP
	x superba Stapf 1928 (*S. nemorosa x S. villicaulis*)	PGP-DGP
	x sylvestris Linnaeus 1753 (*S. nemorosa x S. pratensis*)	PGP
	'Blauhügel' [E. Pagels]	
	'Blaukönigin' ('Blue Queen) [E. Benary]	
	'Blue Queen' = **S. x sylvestris 'Blaukönigin'**	
	'Lye End'	PGP
	'Mainacht' ('May Night') [K. Foerster 1956]	PGP-**DGP**
	'May Night' = **S. x sylvestris 'Mainacht'**	
	'Negrito' [E. Pagels]	
	'Primevere' [E. Pagels]	
	'Rose Queen'	
	'Rügen' [E. Pagels]	
	'Viola Klose' [H. Klose 1975]	
	'Wesuwe' ('Vesuvius') [E. Pagels]	
A	**tiliifolia** Vahl 1794	
	transsylvanica(Schur & Grisebach) Schur 1853	
	turkestanica hort. = **S. sclarea 'Turkestanica'**	
	uliginosa Bentham 1833	PGP-**DGP**
L	**verticillata** Linnaeus 1753	PGP
	'Alba'	PGP
	viridis Linnaeus 1753	

SALVINIA Seguier 1754		[*Salviniaceae*]
	natans (Linnaeus) Allioni 1785	EGF.1

SANDERSONIA Hooker 1853		[*Colchicaceae (Liliaceae)*]
	aurantiaca Hooker 1853	EGF.1

SANGUINARIA Linnaeus 1753		[*Papaveraceae*]
	canadensis Linnaeus 1753	CA-DGP-RD
	'Peter Harrison'	
	'Flore Pleno' ('Multiplex')	**CA-DGP-RD**

SANGUISORBA Linnaeus 1753		[*Rosaceae*]
N	**canadensis** Linnaeus 1753 (*Poterium canadense*)	PGP-CA-**DGP-RD**
N	**minor** Scopoli 1772 (*Poterium sanguisorba*)	
	obtusa Maximowicz 1874	PGP-**RD**
	'Alba'	
N‡L	**officinalis** Linnaeus 1753 (*Poterium officinale*)	PGP
	sitchensis C.A. Meyer 1856 = **S. stipulata**	
	stipulata Rafinesque (*S. sitchensis*)	
	tenuifolia Fischer ex Link 1821 (*Poterium tenuifolium*)	RD
	var. **alba** Trautvetter & C. A. Meyer	

SANICULA Linnaeus 1753		[*Apiaceae (Umbelliferae)*]
HN‡	**europaea** Linnaeus 1753	

SAPONARIA Linnaeus 1753		[*Caryophyllaceae*]
	x boissieri Sündermann (*S. caespitosa x S. ocymoides*)	
	'Bressingham' (*S. ocymoides x S. x olivana*) [A. Bloom]	CA
	caespitosa de Candolle 1808	CA-RD
	haussknechtii Simmler 1910	
	x lempergii hort. (*S. cypria x S. haussknechtii*)	
	'Max Frei'	
	lutea Linnaeus 1762	
NL	**ocymoides** Linnaeus 1753	DGP-**RD**

       'Alba'
       'Foulis Frosty'
       'Rubra Compacta'
       'Splendens'   **DGP**-RD
HN‡ **officinalis** Linnaeus 1753   **RD**
       'Alba Plena'   PGP-**RD**
       'Fischbachau'   PGP-RD
       'Rosea Plena'
       'Rubra Plena'   PGP-RD
       'Variegata'   PGP
     x olivana Wocke (*S. caespitosa x S. pumilio*)
     pulvinaris Boissier 1849 = **S. pumilio**
     pumilio (Linnaeus) Fenzl ex A. Braun 1843   CA
     x weimannii Fritsch 1897 (*S. caespitosa x S. lutea*)
     zawadzkii (Herbich) hort. = **Silene zawadzkii**

SATUREJA Linnaeus 1753   *[Lamiaceae (Labiatae)]*
SH **coerulea** Janka 1891 (*S. montana* 'Coerulea')   **DGP**
AH **hortensis** Linnaeus 1753
HN **montana** Linnaeus 1753
      'Coerulea' = **S. coerulea**   PGP-DGP
     ssp. **illyrica** Nyman 1881 (*S. subspicata*)
     repanda hort. = **S. spicigera**
SH **spicigera** (C. Koch) Boisser 1879 (*S. repanda* hort.)
S   **spinosa** Linnaeus 1756
     subspicata Berthelot ex Visiani 1829 = **S. montana** ssp. **illyrica**

SAUROMATUM Schott 1832   *[Araceae]*
     guttatum (Wallich) Schott 1832 = **S. venosum**
     venosum (Aiton) Kunth 1841 (*Arum cornutum, S. guttatum*)   EGF.2-PGP

SAURURUS Linnaeus 1753   *[Saururaceae]*
     cernuus Linnaeus 1753
     cernuus Thunberg 1784 non Linnaeus 1753 = **S. chinensis**
     chinensis Hort. ex Loudon 1845 (*S. loureiri, S. cernuus* Thunberg)
     loureiri Decaisne 1845 = **S. chinensis**

SAXIFRAGA Linnaeus 1753   *[Saxifragaceae]*

Classification as per:
G. HEGI - *'Illustrierte Flora von Mitteleuropa'* Revised Edition 1975

SECTION
    1   **Micranthes**
    2   **Hirculus**
    3   **Gymnopera**
    4   **Diptera**
    5   **Trachyphyllum**
    6   **Xanthizoon**
    7   **Aizoonia** (*Silver or Encrused Saxifrages*)
    8   **Porophyllum** (*Kabschia Saxifrages*)
    9   **Porophyrion**
   10   **Miscopetalum**
   11   **Saxifraga**
   12   **Trachyphylloides** (*Mossy Saxifrages*)
   13   **Cymbalaria**
   14   **Discogyne**

    8   **afghanica** Aitchinson & Hemsley 1880
N‡ 6   **aizoides** Linnaeus 1753
          var. **atrorubens** (Bertolini) Sternberg 1832   DGP
                                       CA

aizoon Jacquin 1778 = **S. paniculata**

12   **'Amoena'**   CA

8   **andersonii** Engler & Irmscher 1912

12   **'Ane Kirstine'**

3-7   **x andrewsii** Harvey 1848 (*S. hirsuta* x *S. paniculata*)

8   **x anglica** Horny, Sojak & Webr 1974 (*S. aretioides* x *S. lilacina* x *S. media*)
     'Arthur'   [1934]
     'Beatrix Stanley'   [R. V. Prichard 1924]   CA
     'Christine'   [R. V. Prichard c1930]   CA
     'Cranbourne'   [R. V. Prichard 1925]   CA-RD
     'Felicity'   [R. V. Prichard 1929]
     'Grace Farwell'   [R. V. Prichard 1927]
     'Myra'   [R. Farrer c1918]
     'Valerie Keevil'   [R. V. Prichard 1923]
     'Winifred'   [G. W. Gould c1925]

7   **'Annot'**

12   **androsacea** Linnaeus 1753 (*S. pyrenaica*)

8   **x anormalis** Sündermann ex Horny. Sojak & Webr 1974 (*S. pseudolaevis* x
                                                  S. stribrnyi)
     'Gustav Hegi'   [F. Sündermann c1920] (*S. x anormalis*)

8   **x apiculata** Engler 1894 (*S. marginata* x *S. sancta*)
     'Alba'   [c1908]   RD
     'Gregor Mendel'   [c. 1890](*S. x apiculata*)   DGP-RD
     'Primrose Bee'   [c1920]
     'Pseudo-pungens'   [F. Sündermann c1920]
     'Pungens'   [F. Sündermann 1907]

12   **'Apple Blossom'**

12   **x arendsii** nom. non rite publ.
     'Alba'

8   **aretioides** Lapeyrouse 1801   CA

8   **x arco-valleyi** Sündermann 1919 (*S. lilacina* x *S. marginata*)
     'Alba' = **'Ophelia'**
     'Arco'   [F. Sündermann 1919] (*S. arco-valleyi*)   CA
     'Dainty Dame'
     'Hocker Edge'   [H. Edge 1937]
     'Ophelia'   [1954]
     'Sara Sinclair'   [H. L. Foster 1968]

5   **aspera** Linnaeus 1753   CA

12   **'Atrosanguinea'**

12   **'Backhousei'**
     baldensis (Farrer) hort. = **S. paniculata** var. **baldensis**

12   **'Ballawley Guardsman'**   [D. Shaw-Smith 1940s]   RD

11-12   **'Bathoniensis'**   RD

8   **x bertolonii** Sündermann 1906 (*S. sempervivum* x *S. stribrnyi*)
     'Antonio'   [F. Sündermann 1906] (*S. x bertolonii*)   CA

8   **x biasolettii** Sündermann 1915 (*S. federici-augusti* ssp. *grisebachii* x
                                             S. sempervivum)   CA
     'Crystalie'   [? G. P. Baker 1934]
     'Feuerkopf'   [J. Eschmann 1980]
     'Lohmuelleri'   [F. Sündermann]
     'Phoenix'   [F. Sündermann 1912] (*S. x biasolettii*)

12   **'Biedermeier'**

9   **biflora** Allioni 1773
     'Big Ben' = **S. x kellereri 'Kewensis'**

8   **x bilekii** Sündermann 1915 (*S. ferdinandi-coburgi* x *S. tombeanensis*)
     'Castor'   [F. Sündermann c1913] (*S. x bilekii*)   CA

12   **'Birch Baby'**
     'Birch Yellow' = **S. x borisii 'Pseudo-borisii'**

12   **'Blütenteppich'**

12 'Bob Hawkins'   [via W. Archer]
8   x boeckeleri Sündermann 1915 (*S. ferdinandi-coburgi* x *S. stribrnyi*)
        'Armida'   [F. Sündermann c1913] (*S. x boeckleri*)   CA
8   x borisii Kellerer ex Sündermann 1910 (*S. ferdinandi-coburgi* x *S. marginata*)
        'Aemula'   [F. Sündermann pre-1913]
        'Faust'   [F. Sündermann pre-1913]
        'Josef Manes'   [R. Horny 1965]   CA
        'Karlstejn'   [R. Horny 1965]
        'Kyrilli'   [J. Kellerer via F. Sündermann 1906]
        'Margarete'   [F. Sündermann c1920]
        'Marianna'   [K. Stivin c1960]
        'Mona Lisa'   [F. Sündermann]
        'Pseudo-borisii'   [F. Sündermann pre-1915]
        'Sofia'   [J. Kellerer pre-1906](*S. x borisii*)   CA-RD
        'Vesna'   [R. Horny 1965]
        'Vincent van Gogh'   [R. Horny 1965]
    boryi Boissier & Heldreich 1853 = **S. marginata**
    'Boughton Orange' = **S. 'Edgar Irmscher'**
8   x boydii Dewar 1890 (*S. aretioides* x *S. burseriana*)
        'Aretiastrum'   [F. Sündermann pre-1915]   RD
        'Cherrytrees'   [J. B. Boyd c1900]   CA
        'Cleo'   [H. L. Foster 1969]
        'Corona'   [H. L. Forster 1967]
        'Faldonside'   [J. B. Boyd c1900]   RD
        'Friar Tuck'   [H. L. Foster 1967]
        'Hindhead Seedling'   [1930s]
        'Klondike'   [H. L. Foster c1967]
        'Luteola'   [F. Sündermann pre-1915]   RD
        'Oriole'
        'Pilatus'   [J. Eschmann 1958]
        'Pollux'   [F. Sündermann pre-1915]
        'Sulphurea'   [G. M. Simpson Hayward pre-1918]   CA-**DGP**-RD
        'William Boyd'   [F. Sündermann pre-1915](*S. x boydii*)   CA
8   x boydilacina Horny, Sojak & Webr 1981 (*S. aretioides* x *S. burseriana* x
                                                                S. lilacina)
        'Penelope'   [R. Dunford c1972]
5   bronchialis Linnaeus 1753
        'Nana' nom. dub.
    brunoniana Wallich 1829 nom. nud. = **S. brunonis**
2   brunonis Wallich ex Seringe 1830 (*S. brunoniana*)
        'Nana' nom. dub.
5   bryoides Linnaeus 1753
    bucklandii hort. ex Stein 1886 = **S. cuneifolia**
7   x burnatii Sündermann 1906 (*S. paniculata* x *S. cochlearis*)   RD
8   burseriana Linnaeus 1753   CA-DGP-RD
        'Brookside'   [Brookside Nurseries 1930s]   RD
        var. burseriana (*S. burseriana* var. *minor*)   CA
        'Crenata'   [via F. Sündermann c1895]   CA
        'Falstaff'   [H. L. Foster 1970]
        'Ganymede'   [H. L. Foster 1964]
        'Gloria'   [c1900]   CA-**DGP**-RD
        'His Majesty' = **S. x irvingii 'His Majesty'**
        'Lutea' = **S. x boydii 'Pollux'**
        'Major Lutea' = **S. x boydii 'Luteola'**
        'Mars' = **S. elizabethae 'Mars'**
        var. *minor* Sündermann 1906 = **S. burseriana** var. **burseriana**
        'Prince Hal'   [H. L. Foster 1970]
        'Princess'   [H. L. Foster 1969]
        'Seissera'   [H. Simon 1975]

	'Speciosa'	
	'Sulphurea' = **S. boydii 'Sulphurea'**	
7	**caesia** Linnaeus 1753	CA
	'Saint John'	
	x *calabrica* nom. non rite publ. = **'Tumbling Waters'**	
7	**callosa** Smith in Dickson 1791 (S. lingulata)	CA-RD
	'Albertii'	
	'Albida'	
	var. **australis** (Moricand) D. A. Webb 1987	
	var. **australis 'Superba'**	
	var. *bellardii* hort. = **S. callosa**	
	ssp. **catalaunica** (Boissier) D. A. Webb 1963	CA
	var. *lantoscana* (Boissier & Reuter) Engler 1869 = **S. callosa** var. **australis**	
	*var. **latonica**	
	*var. **sancta-balmae**	
	'Winterfeuer'	
12	**'Cambria Jewel'**	
8	**'Cambridge Seedling'**	
12	**camposii** Boissier & Reuter 1872 (S. wallacei)	
8	**'Camyra'** [UK]	
12	**canaliculata** Boissier & Reuter ex Engler 1872	
7	**x canis-dalmatica** nom. non rite publ. (S. paniculata x S. cotyledon)	
12	**'Carnival'**	
	cartilaginea Willdenow ex Sternberg 1810 = **S. paniculata** ssp. **cartilaginea**	
8	**caucasica** Sommier & Levier 1894	
	var. *desoulavyi* (Oettingen) Engler & Irmscher = **S. desoulavyi**	
12	**cebennensis** Rouy & Camus 1901	CA
	'Cerise Queen' = **S. x anglica 'Christine'**	
N‡ 12	**cespitosa** Linnaeus 1753	
	'Chetwynd' = **S. marginata 'Chetwynd'**	
8	**cinerea** H. Smith 1958	
12	**'Clare Island'**	
8	**x clarkei** Sünderman 1915 (S. media x S. vandellii)	
	'Sidonia' [F. Sünderman pre-1915](S. x clarkei)	CA
5	**cherleroides** D. Don 1882	
7	**'Churchillii'** (S. hostii x S. paniculata)	CA
	'Cloth of Gold' = **S. moschata 'Cloth of Gold'**	
7	**cochlearis** Reichenbach 1832	CA-**RD**
	'Major'	CA
	'Minor'	CA-RD
	'Pseudo-valdensis'	
12	**conifera** Cosson & Durieu 1864	
12	**continentalis** (Engler & Irmscher) D. A. Webb 1950 (S. *hypnoides* ssp.	
		continentalis)
	corbariensis Timbal-Lagrave 1875 = **S. fragilis**	
	correvoniana hort. = **S. paniculata 'Correvoniana'**	
4	**cortusifolia** Siebold & Zuccarini 1846	PGP
L	var. *fortunei* (Hooker f.) Maximowicz = **S. fortunei**	
	*var. **yakusimensis**	
8	**corymbosa** Boissier 1843 (S. luteo-viridis)	CA
7	**cotyledon** Linnaeus 1753	CA-RD
	'Caterhamensis'	CA
	'Norvegica'	CA
	'Pyramidalis'	CA
	'Somerset Seedling'	
L	**'Southside Seedling'**	RD
8	**'Cream Seedling'** nom. dub.	
	'Crimson Diall' = **S. x irvingii 'His Majesty'**	
4	**crispa** nom. non rite publ.	
7	**crustata** Vest 1804 (S. incrustata)	

*var. **vochinensis**

12 **cuneata** Willdenow 1799
3 **cuneifolia** Linnaeus 1763
    'Aureo-maculata' nom. dub.
    var. *capillipes* Reichenbach 1832 = **S. cuneifolia**
    'Subintegra' nom. dub.
    'Variegata'
4 **cuscutiformis** Loddiges 1818

AN‡ 13 **cymbalaria** Linnaeus 1753
    dalmatica hort. = **S. obtusa**
12 **'Dartington Double'**
8 **'Dawn'**   [H. L. Foster]
12 **densa** Haworth 1803
8 **desoulavyi** Oettingen 1909 (*S. caucasica* var. *desoulavyi*)
12 **'Diana'**
8 **diapensioides** Bellardi 1792   CA-RD
    'Lutea' = **S. x malbyana 'Primulina'**
2 **diversifolia** Wallich ex Seringe 1830
7 **'Doctor Ramsay'** (*S. cochlearis* x *S. longifolia*)
8 **x doerfleri** Sünderman 1915 (*S. frederici-augusti* x *S. stribrnyi*)
    'Ignaz Dörfler'   [F. Sünderman pre-1915](*S. x doerfleri*)   CA
12 **'Dornröschen'**   [E. Benary]

L 12 **'Dubarry'**
8 **'Edgar Irmscher'**   [F. Sünderman c1960]
12 **'Edie Campbell'**
8 **x edithae** Sünderman 1915 (*S. marginata* x *S. stribrnyi*)
    'Bridget'   [c1930]
    'Edith'   [F. Sünderman pre-1915](*S. x edithae*)   CA
    'Jubilee'   [P. Barrow]
12 **'Elegantissima'**
12 **'Elf'**   DGP
8 **x elizabethae** Sünderman 1906 (*S. burseriana* x *S. sancta*)
    'Boston Spa'   [pre-1939]
    'Carmen'   [F. Sünderman 1898](*S. x elizabethae*)   RD
    'Galahad'   [H. L. Forster 1967]
    'Jason'   [H. L. Foster c1967]
    'Leo Gordon Godseff'   [UK pre-1911]
    'Mars'   [H. L. Forster 1960s]
    'Millstream Cream'   [H. L. Forster 1964]
    'Mrs Leng'   [1920s]
    'Ochroleuca'   [F. Sünderman pre-1913]
    'Primrose Dame'   [R. V. Prichard 1938]
    'Tulley'
7 **x engleri** Huter (*S. crustata* x *S. hostii*) (*S. x paradoxa* hort.)
12 **erioblasta** Boissier & Reuter 1856   CA
7 **'Esther'** (*S. cochlearis* x *S. paniculata* 'Lutea')   CA
8 **x eudoxiana** Kellerer ex Sündermann 1906 (*S. ferdinandi-coburgi* x *S. sancta*)
    'Eudoxia'   [J. Kellerer pre-1906](*S. x eudoxiana*)   CA
    'Gold Dust'   [via A. Bloom 1950s]
    'Haagii'   [F. Sündermann c1908]   RD
12 **exarata** Villiars 1779   CA
    ssp. **moschata** (Wulfen) Cavillier 1913 (*S. moschata*)   RD
    ssp. **moschata 'Cloth of Gold'**   RD
    ssp. **moschata 'Compacta'** nom. dub
    ssp. **moschata 'Variegata'**
12 **'Fairy'**
12 **'Farbenteppich'**
7 **x farreri** nom. non rite publ. (*S. callosa* x *S. cochlearis*)
8 **federici-augusti** Biasoletto 1841
    ssp. **grisebachii** (Degen & Dörfler) D. A. Webb 1987 (*S. grisebachii*)
                                       CA-DGP-RD

ssp. **grisebachii 'Wisley'** [W. E. Th. Ingwersen c1920] CA-DGP-RD
8 **ferdinandi-coburgi** Kellerer & Sündermann 1901 CA-**DGP**
    'Drakula' [K. Stivin c 1960]
    var. *radoslavoffii* Stojanov 1931 = **S. ferdinandi-coburgi** var. **rhodopea**
    var. **rhodopea** Kellerer & Stojanov 1929
    var. *pravislavia* hort. = **S. ferdinandi-coburgi** var. **rhodopea**
1 **ferruginea** Graham 1829
12 **'Feuerteppich'**
12 **'Feuerwerk'**
12 **'Findling'** ('Findling's White')
    'Findling's White' = **S. 'Findling'**
8-6 **x finnisae** Horny, Sojak & Webr 1974 (*S. aizoides* x *S. aretoides* x *S. lilacina* x
                                                        S. media)
    'Parcevalis' [1950s]
2 **flagellaris** Willdenow ex Sternberg 1810
8 **x fleischeri** Sündermann 1915 (*S. federici-augusti* x *S. luteo-viridis*)
    'Buchholzii' [via F. Sündermann 1960s]
    'Mephisto' [F. Sündermann pre-1915] (*S. x fleischeri*) CA
7 **florulenta** Moretti 1823 **CA**
    'Flowers of Sulphur' = **S. 'Schwefelblüte'**
L 4 **fortunei** Hooker f. 1863 (*S. cortusifolia* var. *fortunei*)
    'Blanda' nom. dub
    'Chinensis' nom. dub
    'Mount Awoba'
    'Mount Nachi'
    'Nana' nom. dub.
    'Obtusocuneata' nom. dub.
    'Rokujo'
    'Rosea' nom. dub.
    'Rubrifolia'
    'Wada's Variety' ('Wada')
12 **'Four Winds'**
12 **fragilis** Schrank 1821 (*S. corbariensis*)
7 **x fritschiana** Kellerer 1899 (*S. crustata* x *S. paniculata*)
12 **'Gaiety'**
7 **x gaudinii** Brügger 1868 (*S. cotyledon* 'Pyramidalis' x *S. paniculata*) CA
8 **georgei** Anthony 1933
8 **x geuderi** Heinrich ex Sündermann 1915 (*S. x boydii* x *S. ferdinandi-coburgi*)
    'Eulenspiegel' [E. Heinrich pre-1915](*S. x geuderi*)
3 **x geum** Linnaeus 1753 (*S. hirsuta* x *S. umbrosa*)
    'Dentata' PGP
    'Hirsuta' = **S. x geum**
    'Major'
8 **x gloriana** Hort. ex Horny, Sojak & Webr 1974 (*S. lilacina* x *S. obtusa*)
    'Amitie' [R. V. Prichard c1925] CA
    'Amitie' hort. p.p. = **S. x gloriana 'Godiva'**
    'Godiva' [R. V. Prichard 1925]
12 **'Gloriosa'**
8 **'Goeblii'**
12 **'Gnome'**
12 **'Golden Falls'**
12 **'Grandiflora Alba'**
N‡L 11 **granulata** Linnaeus 1753 RD
    'Flore Pleno' RD
8 **x grata** Engler & Irmscher 1919 (*S. arietioides* x *S. ferdinandii-coburgi*)
    'Annemarie' [F. Sündermann c1915]
    'Loeflingii' [F. Sündermann c1915]
    grisebachii Degen & Dörfler 1897 = **S. federici-augusti** ssp. **grisebachii**
    'Guardsman' = **S. 'Ballawley Guardsman'**
8 **x gusmusii** Sündermann ex Irving & Malby 1914 (*S. luteo-viridis* x *S.*
                                            sempervivum) CA

'Subluteiviridis'   [F. Sündermann pre-1912]
x haagii Sündermann 1915 = **S. x eudoxiana 'Haagii'**
'Harder Zwerg' = **S. 'Luschtinez'**

8   **x hardingii** Horny, Sojak & Webr 1974 (*S. aretioides* x *S. burseriana* x *S. media*)
     'Buster'   [via V. Finnis 1960s]
     'Iris Prichard'   [R. V. Prichard c1930]   CA-RD
     'Harlow Car' = **S. x anglica 'Winifred'**
     hartii D. A. Webb = **S. rosacea** ssp. **hartii**

12   'Hartswood White'
7-6   **x hausmannii** Kerner 1863 (S. aizoides x S. mutata)
8   **x heinrichii** Sündermann 1915 (*S. aretioides* x *S. stribrnyi*)
     'Ernst Heinrich'   [E. Heinrich c1915]   (*S. x heinrichii*)
8   'Herbert Cuerdon'nom. inval.
7   'Highdownensis'
12   'Hi-Ace'
N‡ 2   **hirculus** Linnaeus 1753
     *var. **hirculoides**
N‡ 3   **hirsuta** Linnaeus 1759
     'Hocker Edge Seedling' = **S. x arco-valleyi 'Hocker Edge'**
8   **x hoerhammeri** Sündermann ex Engler & Irmscher 1919 (*S. federici-augusti*
                      ssp. *grisebachii* x *S. marginata*)
     'Lohengrin'   [Hörhammer c1915](*S. x hoerhammeri*)
8   **x hofmannii** Sündermann 1915 (*S. burseriana* x *S. sempervivum*)
     'Bodensee'   [F. Sündermann pre-1915](*S. x hofmannii*)   CA
     'Ferdinand'   [F. Sündermann]
12   'Holden Seedling'
2   **hookeri** Engler & Irmscher 1912
8   **x hornibrookii** Horny, Sojak & Webr 1974] (*S. lilacina* x *S. stribrnyi*) CA
     'Ariel'   [H. L. Forster 1960s]
     'Bellisant'   [R. V. Prichard 1925]
     'Coningsby Queen'   [G. W. Gould 1930s]
     'Lydia'
     'Riverslea'   [R. V. Prichard 1925]   **DGP-RD**
7   **hostii** Tausch 1828   CA
     var. *altissima* (Kerner) Engler & Irmscher 1919 = **S. hostii** ssp. **hostii**
     *var. **bartiae**
     ssp. **rhaetica** (Kerner) Braun-Blanquet 1922   CA
N‡ 12 **hypnoides** Linnaeus 1753
     ssp. *continentalis* Engler & Irmscher 1916 = **S. continentalis**
     var. **egemmulosa** Engler & Irmscher 1919 (*S. kingii* hort.)
     'Rosea' nom. dub.
8   **hypostoma** H. Smith 1958
     incrustata Vest 1804 nom. nud. = **S. crustata**
12   'Ingeborg'   [H. K. Marx]
8   **iranica** Bornmüller 1906
11   **irrigua** Marshall von Bieberstein 1808
8   **x irvingii** Hort. ex May 1915 (*S. burseriana* x *S. lilacina*)
     'Gem'   [R. V. Prichard c1920]   CA
     'Harry Marshall'   [R. V. Prichard pre-1920]
     'His Majesty'   [R. V. Prichard 1927]   CA
     'Jenkinsiae'   [E. H. Jenkins pre-1921]   **CA-DGP-RD**
     'Mother of Pearl'   [R. V. Prichard c1930]
     'Mother Queen'   [1930s]
     'Rubella'   [R. V. Prichard 1920s]
     'Walter Irving'   [W. Irving 1909](*S. x irvingii*)   **CA-RD**
12   'James Bremner'
     'Jendini' = **S. x geuderi**
     'Jenkinsae' = **S. x irvingii 'Jenkinsiae'**
     'Jewel' = **S. 'Juwel'**
     'Joy' = **S. x petraschii 'Kaspar Maria Sternberg'**

'Juliet' = **S. x hornibrookii 'Riverslea'**

8 **juniperifolia** Adams 1806 (*S. macedonia*)   CA
    var. *macedonica* (Degen) Engler & Irmscher 1919 = **S. juniperifolia**
    ssp. *sancta* (Grisebach) D. A. Webb 1963 = **S. sancta**

12 **'Juwel'** (S. 'Jewel')

12 **'Kardinal'**

8 **'Kath Dryden'**   [H. L. Foster c1974]

7 **'Kathleen Pinsent'** (*S. callosa* x *S. paniculata* ssp. *kolenatiana*)   [C. Elliott]
                                                                                     CA

8 **x kayei** Horny, Sojak & Webr 1974 (*S.x aretioides* x *S. burseriana* x *S. ferdinandi-coburgi* x *S. sancta*)
    'Buttercup'   [R. V. Prichard 1930s]   CA

8 **x kellereri** Sündermann 1908 (*S. burseriana* x *S. stribrnyi*)
    'Johann Kellerer'   [J. Kellerer 1906](*S. x kellereri*)   CA-RD
    'Kewensis'   [W. Irving 1909]   CA-RD
    'Landaueri' = **S. x landaueri 'Leonore'**
    'Schleicheri' = **S. x landaueri 'Schleicheri'**
    'Suendermannii'   [F. Sündermann 1915]
    'Suendermannii Major'   [F. Sündermann 1920]
    kestonensis hort. = **S. x salmonica 'Kestoniensis'**
    kewensis hort. = **S. x kellereri 'Kewensis'**
    kingii hort. = **S. hypnoides** var. **egemmulosa**

12 **'Kingstone White'**

12 **'Knapton Pink'**   [M. Hornibrook]

12 **'Knapton White'**
    kolenatiana Regel 1865 = **S. paniculata** ssp. **cartilaginea**

8 **kotschyi** Boissier 1856
    'Lady Beatrix Stanley' = **S. x anglica 'Beatrix Stanley'**

8 **x laeviformis** Sündermann ex Horny, Sojak & Webr 1981 (*S. marginata* x *S. pseudolaevis*)
    'Egmont'   [F. Sündermann c1920](*S. x laeviformis*)
    laevis hort. = **S. pseudolaevis**

12 **'Lammefjord'**

8 **x landaueri** Sündermann ex Horny, Sojak & Webr 1981 (*S. x kellereri* x *S. marginata*)
    'Leonore'   [F. Sündermann c1920](*S. x landaueri*)   CA
    'Schleicheri'   [F. Sündermann c1920]
    latina (N. Terracciano) Hayek 1905 = **S. oppositifolia** ssp. **latina**

11 **latepetiolata** Willkomen 1874

12 **'Leuchtkäfer'**   [E. Benary]

8 **x leyboldii** Sündermann 1915 (*S. marginata* x *S. vandellii*)
    'August Heyek'   [F. Sündermann 1915] (*S. x leyboldii*)   CA

8 **lilacina** Duthie 1904   CA-RD
    lingulata Bellardi 1793 = **S. callosa**

8 **'Lomieri'**   [J. Eschmann 1980]

7 **longifolia** Lapeyrouse 1801   CA-DGP-RD
    'Knebworth'
    'Tumbling Waters' = **S. 'Tumbling Waters'**
    'Walpole's Variety'   CA

12 **'Luschtintez'** (S. 'Harder Zwerg')
    luteola hort. = **S. x boydii 'Luteola'**

8 **x luteo-purpurea** Lapeyrouse 1801 (*S. aretiodes* x *S. media*)
    nm. **aurantiaca** (Sündermann) Horny, Sojak & Webr
    luteo-viridis Schott & Kotschy 1851 = **S. corymbosa**

1 **lyallii** Engler 1869
    macedonica Degen = **S. juniperifolia**

7 **x macnabiana** Lindsay (*S. callosa* x *S. cotyledon*)

8 **x malbyana** Horny, Sojak & Webr 1974 (*S. aretioides* x *S. diaspensioides*)
    'Primulina'   [J. Atkins c1894]   RD-RD

1 **mandschuriensis** (Engler) Komarov

8 **marginata** Sternberg 1822 (*S. boryi*)   CA

'Balkan' = **S. marginata** var. **rocheliana**
'Chetwynd' nom. dub.
var. **coriophylla** (Grisebach) Engler 1872   CA
var. *coriophylla* 'Lutea' = **S. x borisii 'Margarete'**
var. **karadzicensis** (Degen & Kosanin) Engler & Irmscher 1919   CA
'Major'   [F. Sündermann 1970]
var. **marginata**
'Minor'   [F. Sündermann 1920s]
'Purpurea'   [F. Sündermann 1920s]
var. **rocheliana** (Sternberg) Engler & Irmscher 1919   CA
var. *rocheliana* 'Lutea' = **S. x borisii 'Faust'**

8   **x mariae-theresiae** Sündermann 1915 (*S. burseriana* x *S. federici-augusti*
ssp. *grisebachii*)
'Theresia'   [F. Sündermann pre-1915] (*S. x marie-theresiae*)
12   **'Marshall Joffre'**
8   **media** Gouan 1773   CA
8   **x megaseaflora** Hort. ex May & Musgrave 1931 (*S. aretioides* x *S. burseriana* x
S. lilacina x *S. media*)   CA
'Mrs Gertie Prichard'   [R. V. Prichard 1928]
'Robin Hood'   [R. V. Prichard 1931]
1   **michauxii** Britton ex Small & Vail 1894
8   **x millstreamiana** Horny, Sojak & Webr 1981 (*S. burseriana* x *S. ferdinandi-*
coburgi x *S. tombeanensis*)
'Eliot Hodgkin'   [H. L. Forster c1974]
'Luna'   [H. L. Forster c1975]
12   **'Mrs E. Piper'**
12   *moschata* Wulfen 1781 = **S. exarata** ssp. **moschata**
2   **mucronulata** Royle 1833
7   **mutata** Linnaeus 1762
1   **nelsoniana** D. Don 1822
4   **nipponica** Makino
x obristii hort. = **S. x salmonica 'Obristii'**
8   **obtusa** (Sprague) Horny & Webr 1985 (*S. dalmatica* hort., *S. scardica* var.
obtusa)   CA

N‡ 9   **oppositifolia** Linnaeus 1753   CA-DGP-RD
'Alba'
'Florrissa'   CA-RD
ssp. **latina** N. Terracciano (*S. latina*)   CA
ssp. **rudolphiana** (Hornschurch ex Koch) Engler & Irmscher 1919
(*S. rudolphiana*)   CA
'Ruth Draper'   [V. Finnis]
'Splendens'
'Theoden'   DGP-RD
'W. A. Clark'   [Backhouse]   CA
'Vaccarina' (*S. vaccarina* hort.)   CA
'Wetterhorn'   CA

orientalis hort. non Jacquin = **S. paniculata** var. **orientalis**
7   **paniculata** Miller 1768 (*S. aizoon*)   DGP-RD
'Archdale'   [G. Osmond]
'Balcana' = **S. paniculata** var. **orientalis**
var. **baldensis** Farrer 1911 (*S. baldensis*)   CA-DGP-RD
*var. **brevifolia** (*S. paniculata* 'Minor')   CA
var. **brevifolia** 'Glauca'
'Carinthiaca'
ssp. **cartilaginea** (Willdenow ex Sternberg) D. A. Webb 1963
(*S. kolenatiana*)   CA
ssp. **cartilaginea** 'Major'
'Carniolica'
'Correvoniana'
'Crimson Rose'
'Eriophylla'

438   SAXIFRAGA

'Glauca' = **S. paniculata** var. **brevifolia 'Glauca'**
'Hartside'
'Hirtella'   CA
'Koprvnik'
'Labridorica'
'Lagraveana'
'Lutea'   RD
'Minor' = **S. paniculata** var. **brevifolia**
'Minutifolia'   CA
'Nutans' = **S. paniculata** var. **prorepens**
var. **orientalis** (Engler 1872) ! (*S. orientalis* hort.)
var. **orientalis 'Dormitor'**
var. **orientalis 'Orjen'**
var. **orientalis 'Rhodope'**
'Portae'   CA
*var. **prorepens** (*S. paniculata* 'Nutans')
*var. **punctata** (*S. punctissima*)
'Purpurascens'
'Rex'
'Rosea'   CA-RD
'Rosularis'
'Stabiana'
'Sturmiana'
'Venetia'   CA

14 **paradoxa** Sternberg 1810
    x paradoxa hort. non Sternberg 1810 = **S. x engleri**
6-7 **x patens** Gaudin 1818 (*S. aizoides* x *S. caesia*)   CA
8   **x paulinae** Sündermann 1906 (*S. burseriana* x *S. ferdinandi-coburgi*)
    'Franzii'   [F. Sündermann pre-1920]
    'Kolbiana'   [F. Sündermann 1918]
    'Paula'   [F. Sündermann 1905] (*S. x paulinae*)
8   **'Peach Blossom'**   [H. L. Forster]
7   **x pectinata** nom. non rite publ. (*S. cristata* x *S. paniculata*)   CA
    'Alba'
    'Rosea'
    'Perle Rose' = **S. x anglica 'Pearl Rose'**
L 12 **'Pearly King'**
12 **pedemontana** Allioni 1795 non Engler 1869
12 **'Peter Pan'**   DGP-RD
8   **'Petra'**   [F. Sündermann 1960s]
8   **x petraschii** Sündermann ex Irving 1908 (*S. burseriana* x *S. tombeanensis*)
                                                                       CA
    'Affinis'   [F. Sündermann 1910]
    'Assimilis'   [F. Sündermann 1910]
    'Dulcimer'   [H. L. Forster 1965]
    'Kaspar Maria Sternberg'   [F. Sündermann 1900]
    'Prospero'   [H. L. Forster 1969]
    'Schelleri'   [F. Sündermann 1920s]
12 **'Pike's Primrose'**
12 **'Pike's White'**
    'Pink Pearl' = **S. x irvingii 'Walter Irving'**
12 **'Pixie'**   DGP-RD
8   **poluniniana** H. Smith 1958
12 **'Pompadour'**
8   **porophylla** Bertoloni 1814   CA
    var. *sibthorpiana* (Grisebach) Engler & Irmscher 1919 = **S. sempervivum**
8   **x pragensis** Horny, Sojak & Webr 1974 (*S. ferdinandi-coburgi* x *S. marginata* x
                                                                    S. stribryni)
    'Golden Prague'   [F. Holenka 1961]
    prichardii hort. = **S. x megasaeflora 'Mrs Gertie Prichard'**
12 **'Priestwood White'**

6-3   **x primulaize** nom. non rite publ. (*S. aizoides* x *S. x umbrosa* var. *pimuloides*)
'Orange'
'Salmon'
primuloides hort. = **S. x urbium** var. **primuloides**

8   **x prossenii** (Sündermann) Ingwersen 1930 (*S. sancta* x *S. stribrnyi*)

'Regina'   [F. Sündermann pre-1920]   CA
pseudo-borisii hort. = **S. x borisii** 'Pseudo-borisii'

8   **x pseudo-kotschyi** Sündermann 1906 (*S. kotschyi* x *S. marginata*)
'Denisa'   [F. Sündermann 1906](*S. x pseudo-kotschyi*)

7-3   **x pseudo-forsteri** nom. non rite publ. (*S. crustata* x *S. cuneifolia*)
8   **pseudolaevis** Oettingen 1909 (*S. laevis* hort.)
12   **pubescens** Pourret 1788
ssp. **delphinensis** (Ravaud 1889) !
ssp. **iratiana** (F. W. Schultz) Engler & Irmscher 1916

8   **pulvinaria** H. Smith 1958
punctata Sternberg non Linnaeus 1753 = **S. nelsoniana**

12   'Purpurea'
12   'Purpurmantel'
12   'Purpurteppich'
pyrenaica Scopoli 1771 = **S. androsacea**

8   **quadrifaria** Engler & Irmscher 1919
7   'Rainsley Seedling'
12   'Red Admiral'   DGP
9   **retusa** Gouan 1773   CA-RD
12   'Riedels Farbenkissen'
12   **rosacea** Moench 1794
ssp. **hartii** (D. A. Webb) D. A. Webb 1987 (*S. hartii*)

12   'Rosakönigin'
8   'Rosemarie'   [F. Sündermann 1960s]
12   'Rosenschaum'
12   'Rosenzwerg'
12   'Roseum Elegans'
8   **x rosinae** Sündermann ex Horny, Sojak & Webr 1974 (*S. diapensioides* x *S. marginata*)

'Rosina Sündermann'   [F. Sündermann 1936](*S. x rosinae*)
10   **rotundifolia** Linnaeus 1753
rudolphiana Hornschurch ex Koch 1835 = **S. oppositifolia** ssp. **rudolphiana**

12   'Ruffles'
12   'Ruth McConnell'
12   'R. W. Hosin'
x salomonii hort. = **S. x salmonica** 'Salomonii'

8   **x salmonica** Jenkins 1900 (*S. burseriana* x *S. marginata*)
'Assimilis' = **S. x petraschii** 'Assimilis'
'Friesei'   [F. Sündermann c1920]
'Kestoniensis'   [G. Reuthe pre-1910]
'Maria Luisa'   [J. Kellerer]
'Mrs Helen Terry'   [via V. Finnis 1960s]
'Obristii'   [F. Sündermann c1905]   CA
'Salomonii'   [F. Sündermann 1894]
'Schreineri'   [F. Sündermann c1920s]

8   **sancta** Grisebach 1843 (*S. juniperifolia* ssp. *sancta*)
ssp. *pseudosancta* (Janka) Kuzmanov 1970 = **S. juniperifolia**

8   'Sandpiper'
12   'Sanguinea Superba'   DGP
sarmentosa Linnaeus f. 1782 = **S. stolonifera**
sartori hort. non Heldreich & Boissier = **S. x webrii** 'Pygmalion'

8   **scardica** Grisebach 1843   CA
var. *obtusa* Sprague 1909 = **S. obtusa**
'Schmulleri' = **S. x biasolettoi** 'Lohmeulleri'

12   'Schneeteppich'

12	**'Schöne von Ronsdorf'**	
12	**'Schwefelblüte'** (*S.* 'Flowers of Sulphur')	
8	**x semmleri** Sündermann ex Horny, Sojak & Webr 1974 (*S. ferdanandi-coburgi* x *S. pseudolaevis* x *S. sancta*)	

8   **x semmleri** Sündermann ex Horny, Sojak & Webr 1974 (*S. ferdanandi-coburgi* x *S. pseudolaevis* x *S. sancta*)
    'Martha'   [F. Sündermann pre-1920](*S. x semmleri*)

8   **sempervivum** C. Koch 1846 (*S. porophyllum* var. *sibthorpiana*)   CA
    f. **alpina** (A. Terraciano) Engler & Irmscher 1919
    f. **sempervivum**
    *f. **stenophylla**
    'Waterperry'   [V. Finnis 1960s]

11   **sibirica** Linnaeus 1759
12   **'Sir Douglas Haig'**
8   **x smithii** Horny, Sojak & Webr 1974 (*S. marginata* x *S. tombeanensis*)
    'Vahlii'   [F. Sündermann pre-1920]

7   **'Snowflake'**
N 3   **spathularis** Brotero 1804
12   **'Spätlese'**
12   **'Sprite'**   DGP
8   **spruneri** Boissier 1843   CA
7   **squarrosa** Sieber 1821   CA
12   **'Standsfieldii'**
12   **'Standsfieldii Rosea'**
8   **stolitzkae** Duthie ex Engler & Irmscher 1919
4   **stolonifera** Meerburgh 1775 (*S. sarmentosa*)   RD
    'Cuscutiformis'
    'Tricolor'   **RD**
8   **x stormonthii** Sündermann ex Horny, Sojak & Webr 1974 (*S. desoulavyi* x *S. sancta*)
    'Stella'   [F. Sündermann 1920]
8   **stribrnyi** (Velenovsky) Podpera 1902   CA
    'Isolde'   [F. Sündermann 1960s]
    'Tristan'   [F. Sündermann 1960s]
8   **x stuartii** Sündermann 1915 (*S. aretioides* x *S. media* x *S. stribrnyi*)
    'Lutea'   [F. Sündermann 1913]
    'Rosea'   [F. Sündermann 1913]
10-3   **x tazetta** nom. non rite publ., stat. dub. (*S. cuneifolia* x *S. taygetea*)
7   **'Teckles'**
12   **tenella** Wulfen 1790
8   **'Thorpi'**   [?R. V. Prichard 1931]
7   **'Timballii'**
8   **tombeanensis** Boissier ex Engler 1872   CA
12   **'Tom's Red'**
12   **'Tom Thumb'**
12   **trifurcata** Schrader 1809
12   **'Triumph'**   RD
7   **'Tumbling Waters'** (*S. callosa* x *S. longifolia*) (*S.* x *calabrica*) 1913 CA-DGP-RD
N 3   **umbrosa** Linnaeus 1762   PGP-RD
    var. **primuloides** nom. non rite publ.   **DGP-RD**
    var. **primuloides 'Clarence Elliott'** ('Elliott's Variety')   RD
    var. **primuloides 'Walter Ingwersen'** ('Ingwersen's Variety')
NL 3   **x urbium** D. A. Webb 1963 (*S. spathularis* x *S. umbrosa*)   PGP-RD
    'Aureo-punctata' ('Variegata Aurea')
    'Chelsea Pink'
    'Colvillei'
    'Letchworth Gem'
    'Miss Chambers'
    'Morrisonii'
    'Picta Aurea' nom. dub.
    'Variegata'   RD
    'Variegata Aurea' = S. x urbium **'Aureo-punctata'**
8   **x urumoffii** Sündermann ex Horny, Sojak & Webr 1974 (*S. ferdinandi-coburgi* x *S. luteo-viridis*)

'Ivan Uromov'   [F. Sündermann c1920](*S. x urumoffii*)
vaccarina hort. = **S. oppositifolia** var. **vaccarina**
'Valborg' = **S. x anglica 'Cranbourne'**
7   **valdensis** de Candolle 1815   CA
'Valentine' = **S. x anglica 'Cranbourne'**
'Valerie Finnis' = **S. x boydii 'Aretiastrum'**
8   **vandellii** Sternberg 1810
12   **vayredana** Luizet 1913
4   **veitchiana** Balfour 1916
1   **virginiensis** Michaux 1803
7   **'Waithman's Variety'**
wallacei MacNab 1883 = **S. camposii**
8   **'Walpolei'** nom. dub.
12   **'Wargrave Rose'**
8   **x webrii** Horny, Sojak & Webr 1981 (*S. sancta* x *S. scardica*)
         'Pymalion'   [c1930s]
8   **x wendelacina** Horny & Webr 1977 (*S. lilacina* x *S. wendelboi*)
         'Wendrush'   [H. L. Forster 1974]
         'Wendy'   [H. L. Forster 1974]
8   **wendelboi** Schönbeck-Temesy 1967
8   **'Wheatley Rose'**   [Mr. Paris 1950s]
8   **'White Imp'**   [H. L. Forster c1972]
7   **'Whitehill'** (*S. cochlearis* x *S. paniculata* ?)
12   **'White Pixie'**
12   **'White Spire'**
'White Star' = **S. x petraschii 'Schelleri'**
whitlavei hort. = **S. continentalis**
'Wisley Primrose' = **S. x paulinae 'Kolbiana'**
7-3   **'Winifred Bevington'** (*S. paniculata* x *S. umbrosa*)
12   **'Winston Churchill'**
7-3   **x zimmeteri** Kerner 1870 (*S. cuneifolia* x *S. paniculata*)   CA

SCABIOSA Linnaeus 1753   [*Dipsacaceae*]
alpina Linnaeus 1753 = **Cephalaria alpina**
N   **caucasica** Marshall von Bieberstein 1808   PGP-DGP-**RD**
         'Alba'
         'Ballerina'
         'Blauer Atlas'   [Grunert]
         'Blue Mountain'   [A. Bloom]
         'Bressingham White'   [A. Bloom]   DGP-RD
         'Challenger'
L   **'Clive Greaves'**   PGP-**DGP**-RD
         'Fama'
         'Floral Queen'
         'Goldingensis'
         House's Hybrids
         'Kompliment'
         'Miss Willmott'   PGP-RD
         'Moerheim Blue'   PGP-RD
         'Moonstone'
         'Mount Cook'
         'Nachtfalter'   [Kayser & Siebert]
         'Perfecta'
         'Perfecta Alba'
         'Prachtkerl'   [Kayser & Siebert]
         'Rhinsburg Glory'
         'Stäfa'   [Frikart]
    cinerea Lapeyrouse ex Lamarck 1792
N‡   **columbaria** Linnaeus 1753   PGP
         'Butterfly Blue'   [Pride of Place Plants]

'Nana'   RD
    var. **ochroleuca** (Linnaeus) Coulter 1823 (*S. ochroleuca*)   **PGP**
    var. **webbiana** (Don) Matthews 1972 (*S. ochroleuca* var. *webbiana*)
gigantea Ledebour 1841 = **Cephalaria gigantea**
graminifolia Linnaeus 1753   PGP
    'Pinkushion'   PGP
japonica Miquel 1867
    var. **alpina** Takeda
lucida Villars 1779
ochroleuca Linnaeus 1753 = **S. columbaria** var. **ochroleuca**
    var. *webbiana* (Don) Boissier 1875 = **S. columbaria** var. **webbiana**
parnassi (Sprengel) hort. = **Pterocephalus perennis**
S   **pseudograminifolia** Huber-Morath 1963
pterocephala Linnaeus 1753 = **Pterocephalus parnassi**
rumelica hort. = **Knautia macedonica**
succisa Linnaeus 1753 = **Succisa pratensis**
tatarica Marshall von Bieberstein 1808 = **Cephalaria gigantea**
vestita Facchini ex Koch 1843

SCADOXUS Rafinesque 1836   [*Amaryllidaceae*]
   multiflorus (Martyn) Rafinesque 1836 (*Haemanthus coccineus, H. multiflorus*)
                                                 EGF.1-DGP
   puniceus (Linnaeus) Friis & Nordal 1976   EGF.1
      'König Albert'   EGF.1

SCHIVERECKIA Andrzejowski ex de Candolle 1821   [*Brassicaceae (Cruciferae)*]
bornmuelleri Prantl ex Bornmueller = **S. doerfleri**
doerfleri (Wettstein) Bornmueller 1921 (*S. bornmuelleri*)
podolica (Besser) Andrzejowski 1821

SCHIZOCODON Siebold & Zuccarini 1843   [*Diapensiaceae*]
ilicifolius Maximowicz 1868 = **Shortia ilicifolia**
rotundifolius Maximowicz 1888 = **Shortia rotundifolia**
soldanelloides Siebold & Zuccarini 1843 = **Shortia soldanelloides**
uniflorus Maximowicz 1868 = **Shortia uniflora**

SCHIZOSTYLIS Backhouse & Harvey 1864   [*Iridaceae*]
L   **coccinea** Backhouse & Harvey ex Hooker f. 1864   EGF.1-PGP-**BB-DGP-RD**
     'Alba'
     'Cardinal'   [J. C. Archibald c.1976]
     'Gigantea' = **S. coccinea 'Major'**
     'Grandiflora' = **S. coccinea 'Major'**
     'Major' ('Gigantea', 'Grandiflora')   PGP-DGP-RD
     'Mrs Hegarty'   EGF.1-PGP-**DGP-RD**
     'November Charm'
     'November Cheer'   PGP-RD
     'Pallida'
     'Professor Barnard'   PGP
     'Rosalie'   PGP
     'Rose Glow'
     'Salmon Charm'   RD
     'Sunrise'   [The Plantsmen c1970]   PGP-RD
     'Viscountess Byng'   EGF.1-PGP-DGP-RD
     'Zeal Salmon'

SCHOENUS Linnaeus 1753   [*Cyperaceae*]
pauciflorus (Hooker f.) Hooker f 1864

SCILLA Linnaeus 1753   [*Hyacinthaceae (Liliaceae)*]
adlamii Baker 1891 = **Ledebouria cooperi**

amethystina Visiani 1829 = **S. litardieri**
amoena Linnaeus 1753
armena Grossheim 1927 = **S. sibirica** ssp. **armena**   EGF.1-SB
N‡   **autumnalis** Linnaeus 1753   EGF.1-**BB**-SB
bifolia Linnaeus 1753   EGF.1-CA-**BB**-SB-**DGP**-**RD**
    'Alba'   ®   [c1590]   EGF.1-CA
    ssp. **danubialis** F. Speta 1974
    'Rosea'   ®   [c1601]   EGF.1-CA-**BB**
bithynica Boissier 1846   SB
    'Rosea'
campanulata Aiton 1810 = **Hyacinthoides hispanica**
chinensis Bentham 1861 = **S. scilloides**
cilicica Siehe 1908   **BB**-SB
greilhuberi F. Speta 1975   SB
hispanica Miller 1768 = **Hyacinthoides hispanica**
hohenackeri Fischer & C. A. Meyer 1846   EGF.1-SB
hohenackeri hort. non Fischer & C.A. Meyer = **S. greilhuberi**
ingridae Speta 1977   **BB**-SB
japonica Thunberg 1784 = **Heloniopsis orientalis**
lilio-hyacinthus Linnaeus 1753   **BB**-SB
    'Alba'
litardierei Breitroffer 1954 (*S. amethystina, S. pratensis*)   CA-**BB**-SB-**DGP**
mischtshenkoana Grossheim 1927 (*S. tubergeniana*)   CA-**BB**-SB-**DGP**-**RD**
    'Zwanenburg'   ®   [Van Tubergen 1945]   DGP
monophyllos Link 1800   **BB**-SB
nivalis Boissier 1844   **BB**-SB
non-scripta (Linnaeus) Hoffmannsegg & Link 1803 = **Hyacinthoides non-scripta**
nutans Smith 1797 = **Hyacinthoides non-scripta**
peruviana Linnaeus 1753   PGP-**BB**-SB-**DGP**-**RD**
    'Alba'   [c1817]
pratensis Waldstein & Kitaibel 1804 non Bergeret = **S. litardierei**
puschkinioides Regel 1875   **BB**-SB
ramburei Boissier 1838   **BB**-SB
reverchonii Degen & Hervier 1906   SB
rosenii C. Koch 1849   SB
scilloides (Lindley) Druce 1917 (*S. chinensis*)   CA-**SB**
siberica Haworth 1804   CA-**BB**-SB-**DGP**-RD
    'Alba'   ®   [A. C. van Eeden 1880]   CA-RD
    ssp. **armena** (Grossheim) Mordak (*S. armena*)   **BB**-SB
    'Spring Beauty'   ®   [W. J. Eldering pre-1939]   **BB**-DGP-**RD**
    'Taurica'   ®   [E. Whittall via Barr & Sons 1890]   CA-RD
    *trifolia
tubergeniana Stearn 1950 = **S. mischtschenkoana**
N‡   **verna** Hudson 1778   CA-**BB**-SB

SCIRPUS Linnaeus 1753   [*Cyperaceae*]
N‡   **angustifolius** (Honckeny) T. Koyama 1958 (*Eriophorum angustifolium, E. polystachion*)
        ssp. **latifolius** (Hoppe) T. Koyama 1958 (*Eriophorum latifolium*)
    atrovirens Willdenow 1809 (*S. georgianus*)
A   **cernuus** Vahl 1806   EGF.2
    fauriei (Camus) T. Koyama 1958
N‡   ssp. **vaginatus** (Linnaeus) T. Koyama 1958 (*Eriophorum vaginatum*)
        ssp. **vaginatus** 'Heidelicht'   [Zillmer c1967]
    georgianus Harper 1900 = **S. atrovirens**
L   **lacustris** Linnaeus 1753   EGF.2
        ssp. **tabernaemontani** (C.G. Gmelin) A. & D. Löve 1975   EGF.2
        ssp. **tabernaemontani** 'Albescens'   RD
        ssp. **tabernaemontani** 'Zebrinus'   DGP-**RD**

SCLERANTHUS Linnaeus 1753   [*Caryophyllaceae*]
    biflorus (Forster & Forster f.) Hooker f. 1852
    brockiei P.A.Williamson 1956
    uniflorus P.A. Williamson 1956

SCOLIOPUS Torrey 1856   [*Trilliaceae (Liliaceae)*]
    bigelovii Torrey 1856   EGF.1

SCOPOLIA Jacquin 1764 nom. cons.   [*Solanaceae*]
    carniolica Jacquin 1764   PGP
        ssp. **hladnikiana** (Freyer ex Koch) Nymans   PGP

SCROPHULARIA Linnaeus 1753   [*Scrophulariaceae*]
    aquatica Linnaeus 1753 nom. ambig. = **S. auriculata**
HN‡ **auriculata** Linnaeus 1753 (*S. aquatica*)   PGP
H   'Variegata'   PGP-**DGP-RD**
    calycina Bentham 1846
H   **nodosa** Linnaeus 1753   PGP
      'Variegata' = **S. auriculata 'Variegata'**

SCUTELLARIA Linnaeus 1753   [*Lamiaceae (Labiatae)*]
    alpina Linnaeus 1753
      'Alba'
      'Greencourt'
N   **altissima** Linnaeus 1753
    austinae Eastwood 1903
    baicalensis Georgi
HN‡L **galericulata** Linnaeus 1753
N   **hastifolia** Linnaeus 1753 (*S. hastata* hort.)
    hastata hort. = **S. hastifolia**
    incana Sprengel 1807
    indica Linnaeus 1753
      var. *japonica* hort. = **S. indica** var. **parvifolia**
      var. **parvifolia** (Makino) Makino
H   **lateriflora** Linnaeus 1753
    novae-zealandiae Hooker f. 1855
S   **orientalis** Linnaeus 1753
      ssp. **pinnatifida** (Boissier) Edmonson 1980
    scordiifolia Fischer ex Schrank 1822

SEDUM Linnaeus 1753   [*Crassulaceae*]

M - EVANS, RONALD L., *'Handbook of Cultivated Sedums'* 1983

HN‡ **acre** Linnaeus 1753   **M-DGP**-RD
      var. **aureum** Masters 1878   RD
      'Cristatum'
      var. **elegans** Masters 1878   **M**
      krajinae (K. Domin) hort. = **S. krajinae**
      var. **majus** Masters 1878 (*S.* 'Maweanum')   **M**
      'Minus' ('Minor')   M
S   **adolphi** Hamet
    adolphi hort. non Hamet = **S. nussbaumerianum**
    aizoon Linnaeus 1753   **M-PGP-DGP-RD**
      'Aurantiacum'   PGP-RD
    albescens Haworth = **S. reflexum** var. **albescens**
    alboroseum Baker   **M**-PGP
      'Medio-variegatus' Regel   **M**-PGP

N‡   **album** Linnaeus 1753 (*S. athoum*)   M-RD
    'Purpureum'
    var. **chloroticum** Lamotte
    var. *laconicum* (Boissier) hort.= **S. laconicum**   M
    var. **micranthum** Bastard
    var. **micranthum 'Coral Carpet'**   **M**
    *var. **murale**   **M**
  amplexicaule de Candolle 1808 = **S. tenuifolium**
  anacampseros Linnaeus 1753   **M**
N‡   **anglicum** Hudson 1778   **M**
    var. **minus** Praeger 1921   CA
  anopetalum de Candolle = **S. ochroleucum**
  athoum de Candolle = **S. album**
  atlanticum Maire   **M**
  'Autumn Joy' = **S. 'Herbstfreude'**
  'Bertram Anderson'
  brevifolium de Candolle   **M**
    var. **quinquefarium** Praeger 1921   **M**
  bithynicum Boissier 1849 = **S. hispanicum** var. **bithynicum**
    'Aureum' = **S. hispanicum** var. **minus 'Aureum'**
  borissovae Balkovsky 1953   **M**
  capablanca hort. = **S. spathulifolium 'Cape Blanco'**
  caucasicumGrossheim   M
  cauticola Praeger 1921   M-CA-**DGP**-RD
    'Lidakense'   M
    'Robustum' = **S. 'Ruby Glow'**
S   **confusum** Hemsley   **M**
  corsicum hort. = **S. dasyphyllum** var. **glanduliferum**
  crassipes Wallich (*Rhodiola crassipes*)   **M**
  cyaneum Rudolph   **M**
  cyaneum hort. non Rudolph = **S. ewersii** var. **homophyllum**
N‡   **dasyphyllum** Linnaeus 1753 (*S. glaucum* Lamarck)   **M**-CA-RD
    var. **glanduliferum** Moris (*S. corsicum* hort.)   M-CA
    'Riffense'
    'Rubrum'
    'Suendermannii'
  divergens S. Watson   **M**
  douglasii hort. = **S. stenopetalum 'Douglasii'**
  elegans hort. non Lejeune = **S. ochroleucum** ssp. **montanum 'Elegantissimum'**
  ellacombianum Praeger 1917   **M**-CA
  ewersii Ledebour 1829   **M**-CA-RD
    'Hayesii'
    var. **homophyllum** Praeger 1921 (*S. cyaneum* hort.)   **M**
    'Nanum'
N‡   **fabaria** Koch 1853 (*S. telephium* ssp. *fabaria*)   M
    var. **borderi** Rouy & Camus   **M**-PGP
  farinosum Lowe   M
  fastigiatum Hooker f. & Thompson (*Rhodiola fastigiata*)   **M**
  *floriferum*hort. = **S. kamtschaticum** var. **floriferum**
N‡   **forsterianum** J. E. Smith 1802 (*S. rupestre* 'Minor')   M
  glaucum Lamarck = **S. dasyphyllum**
  glaucum Waldstein & Kitaibel = **S. hispanicum** var. **minus**
  gracile C. A. Meyer 1831   **M**
  guatemalayense hort. = **S. rubrotinctum**
  gypsicola Boissier & Reuter   **M**
L   **'Herbstfreude'** (*S. telephium* x *S. spectabile*)   [G. Arends]   PGP-**DGP**-RD
  heterodontum Hooker f. & Thompson   **M**
  'Hidakense' (*S. spectabile* x *S. sieboldii* ?)
  himalensis D. Don (*Rhodiola himalense*)   **M**
  hispanicum Linnaeus 1759 non Poiret   **M**

	'Albescens' Hort. non Haworth	M
	var. **bithynicum** (Boissier) Boissier (*S. bithynicum*)	M
	var. **minus** Praeger 1921 (*S. glaucum* hort.)	M
	var. **minus 'Aureum'**	M
	humifusum Rose	M-CA
	hybridum Linnaeus 1753	M
	'Immergrünchen'	
	kamtschaticum Fischer & C. A. Meyer	M
	var. *ellacombianum* (Praeger) R. T. Clausen = **S. ellacombianum**	
	var. **floriferum** Praeger 1921	M-RD
L	var. **floriferum 'Weihenstephaner Gold'**	
	var. *middendorfianum* (Maximowicz) R. T. Clausen = **S. middendorfianum**	
	'Variegatum'	M
	kirilowii Regel ex Maximowicz (*Rhodiola kirilowii*)	M
	var. **rubrum** (*Rhodiola linifolia*)	M
	krajinae K. Domin	
	laconicum Boissier 1845 (*S. album* var. *laconicum*)	
	lidakense hort. = **S. cauticolum 'Lidakense'**	
	lineare Thunberg	M
	'Variegatum'	M
N	**lydium** Boissier	M-CA
	'Aureum'	
	'Glaucum'	
	makinoi Maximowicz	M
	'Variegatum'	M
	'Maweanum' = **S. acre** var. **majus**	
	maximum (Linnaeus) Suter 1802 = **S. telephium** ssp. **maximum**	
	micranthum Bastard 1809 = **S. album** var. **micranthum**	
	middendorfianum Maximowicz 1859 (*S. kamtschaticum* var. *middendorfianum*)	
		M
	var. **diffusum** Praeger 1921	M
	montanum Songeon & Perrault = **S. ochroleucum** ssp. **montanum**	
	moranense Humboldt, Bonpland & Kunth	M
	multiceps Cosson & Durieu	M-CA
	murale hort. = **S. album** var. **murale**	
	nevii A. Gray	M
	nicaeense Allioni 1785 = **S. sediforme**	
S	**nussbaumerianum** Bitter (*S. adolphi* hort.)	M
	obtusatum hort. non A. Gray = **S. oreganum**	
	ochroleucum Chaix 1786 (*S. anopetalum*)	M
	'Centaurium'	
	'Forsterianum' Hort. non J. E. Smith	M
	Green Form	
	ssp. **montanum** (Songeon & Perrault) D. A. Webb 1961	M
	ssp. **monatnum 'Elegantissimum'** (*S. elegans* hort.)	
	oppositifolium Sims 1816 (*S. spurium* 'Album')	M
	'Superbum' [G. Arends]	
	oreganum Nuttall (*S. obtusatum* hort.)	M
	'Procumbens'	M
	oregonense (S. Watson) M. E. Peck	M
	***pachyclados**	
S	**pachyphyllum** Rose	M
	'Rubrum'	
S	**palmeri** S. Watson	M
	'Philip Houlbrook'	
B	**pilosum** Marschall von Bieberstein	M-CA
	pluricaule (Maximowicz) Kudo 1923	M-RD
	'Rosenteppich' ('Rose Carpet')	
	'Sachalin'	
	populifolium Pallas	M-CA

S   **praealtum** A. de Candolle 1847   **M**
       primuloides Franchet (*Rhodiola primuloides*)   M-CA
       pruinatum Link ex Brotero 1804   **M**
       pruinosum Britton = **S. spathulifolium** var. **pruinosum**
       pulchellum Michaux
       purdyi Jepson   **M**
                          M
       quinquefarium (Praeger) hort. = **S. brevifolium** var. **quinquefarium**
N‡   **reflexum** Linnaeus 1762   **M**-RD
           var. **albescens** Haworth (*S. albescens*)   M
           'Chameleon'
           'Cristatum' = **S. reflexum 'Mostrosum Cristatum'**
           'Elegant'
           'Monstrosum Cristatum' ('Cristatum')   **M**
       rhodiola de Candolle = **S. rosea**
N‡   **rosea** (Linnaeus) Scopoli (*Rhodiola rosea, Sedum rhodiola*)   **M**-PGP-RD
           ssp. **atropurpureum** Turcaninow   **M**
           var. *heterodontum* (Hooker & Thompson) hort. = **S. heterodontum**
       rubroglaucum Praeger 1921
S   **rubrotinctum** Clauson   **M**-RD
       'Ruby Glow' (*S. cauticolum* x *S. telephium*)   **DGP**-RD
       rupestre Linnaeus   **M**
           var. *forsterianum* (J. E. Smith) hort. = **S. forsterianum**
           'Minor' hort. =**S.forsterianum**
       sarmentosum Bunge   **M**
       sartorianum Boissier 1856   **M**
           ssp. **stribrnyi** (Velenosky) D. A. Webb 1963 (*S. stribrnyi*)   **M**
       sediforme (Jacquin) Pau 1917 non Hamet 1909 (*S. nicaeense*)   **M**
       selskianum Regel & Maack 1861   **M**
B   **sempervivoides** Marshall von Bieberstein   M-CA
       serpentini Janchen 1920
N   **sexangulare** Linnaeus 1753   **M**
       'Weisse Tatra'
       sichotense Voroschilov 1961   **M**
       sieboldii Sweet   **M-DGP**-RD
           'Medio-variegatis   **M-RD**
       'Silvermoon' (*S. laxum* ssp. *heckneri* x *S. spathulifolium*)   M
       spathulifolium Hooker   M-CA-DGP-**RD**
           'Aureum'   M
           'Cape Blanco' (*S. capablanca* hort.)   **M**-CA-**DGP**-RD
           'Majus'
           ssp. **pruinosum** (Britton) R. T. Clausen   M
           ssp. **pruinosum** var. **purpureum** Praeger   M-CA
           'Roseum'   M
           'William Pascoe'   M
       spectabile Boreau   **M**-PGP-DGP-**RD**
           'Atropurpureum'   PGP
           'Aureo-variegatum' = **S. alboroseum 'Medio-variegatum'**
L   **'Brilliant'**
           'Carmen'   PGP-RD
           'Humile'   RD
           'Iceberg'
           'Indian Chief'
           'Meteor'   PGP-**DGP**-RD
           'Rosenteller'
           'Septemberglut' ('September Glow')   PGP
           'Variegatum' = **S. alboroseum 'Medio-variegatus'**
N   **spurium** Marshall von Bieberstein 1808   **M**-DGP-**RD**
           'Album' = **S. oppositifolium**
           'Coccineum'   M
           'Dragon's Blood' = **S. spurium 'Schorbuser Blut'**

    'Erdblut'
    'Fuldaglut'   [H. Klose 1975]
L   'Green Mantle'
    'Purpureum'
    'Purpurteppich' ('Purple Carpet')   [E. Benary]
    'Roseum'
L   'Ruby Mantle'
    'Schorbuser Blut' ('Dragon's Blood')   **DGP**-RD
    'Tricolor'
    'Variegatum'
stenopetalum Pursh   **M**
    'Douglasii' Hort. non Hooker   **M**
stoloniferum S. T. Gmelin   **M**
stribrnyi Velenovsky = **S. sartorianum** ssp. **stribrnyi**
'Sunset Cloud' (*S. telephium maximum* 'Atropurpureum' x *S.* 'Ruby Glow')
                  [The Plantsmen c1970]   PGP
tatarinowii Maximowicz   **M**
telephium Linnaeus 1753   M-PGP-RD
    var. *borderi* (Rouy & Camus) hort. = **S. fabaria** var. **borderi**
    ssp. *fabaria*(Koch) Kirschleger 1852 = **S. fabaria**
    ssp. **maximum** (Linnaeus) Krocker 1760 (*S. maximum*)   **M**-PGP-DGP
L   ssp. **maximum** 'Atropurpureum'   M-PGP-**DGP**-RD
    'Arthur Branch'
    'Munstead Red'   M-PGP-RD
    'Roseo-variegatum' = **S. alboroseum** 'Medio=variegatus'
tenuifolium (Smith) Strobl 1884 non Franchet 1896 (*S. amplexicaule*)   **M**
    ssp. **ibericum** t'Hart 1974   **M**
ternatum Michaux   **M**
'Vera Jameson' (*S. telephium maximum* 'Atropurpureum' x *S.* 'Ruby Glow')
                  [via J. Elliott]   M-PGP-RD

SELAGINELLA Palisot de Beavois 1805 nom. cons.   [*Selaginellaceae*]
    caulescens (Wallich) Spring 1843 = **S. involvens**
    helvetica (Linnaeus) Spring 1838
    involvens (Swartz) Spring 1843 non Baker 1887 (*S. caulescens*)
N   **kraussiana** (Kunze) A. Braun 1860   EGF.1
    tamariscina (Palisot de Beauvois) Spring 1843

SELINUM Linnaeus 1753 nom. cons.   [*Apiaceae (Umbelliferae)*]
L   **tenuifolium** Wallich ex C.B. Clarke 1879   **PGP**

SELLIERA Cavanilles 1799   [*Goodeniaceae*]
    radicans Cavanilles 1799 (*Goodenia repens*)

SEMIAQUILEGIA Makino 1902   [*Ranunculaceae*]
    adoxoides (de Candolle) Makino 1902
    ecalcarata (Maximowicz) Sprague & Hutchinson 1921 (*S. simulatrix*)
    simulatrix J. R. Drummond & Hutchinson 1920 = **S. ecalcarata**

SEMPERVIVELLA Stapf 1923   [*Crassulaceae*]
    acuminata (Schott) A. Berger 1930
    alba (Edgeworth) Stapf 1923 = **Rosularia sedoides** var. **alba**
    sedoides (Decaisne) Stapf 1923 = **Rosularia sedoides**

SEMPERVIVUM Linnaeus 1753   [*Crassulaceae*]
    allionii (Jordan & Fourreau) Nyman 1879 = **Jovibarba allionii**
    alpinum Grisebach & Schrank 1852 = **S. tectorum** ssp. **alpinum**
    altum Turrill 1936   CA
    andreanum Wale 1941   CA
    arachnoideum Linnaeus 1753 (*S. doellianum*)   **CA-DGP-RD**

'**Album**'
var. **bryoides** Schnittspahn
var. **glabrescens** Willkomm 1882
var. **glabrescens** '**Album**'
*****gnaphalium
var. *hookeri* hort. = **S. x barbulatum** '**Hookeri**'
var. *laggeri* hort. = **S. arachnoideum** ssp. **tomentosum**
'**Minor**'
ex Opitz
'**Rubrum**'
'**Sultan**'   ®   [Ford 1973]
ssp. **tomentosum** (C. B. Lehmann & Schittspahn) Schinz & Thellung 1923
                                                                  CA-RD
ssp. **tomentosum** '**Major**'
ssp. **tomentosum** '**Minor**'
ssp. **tomentosum** '**Stansfieldii**'   ®
'Webbianum' = **S. arachnoideum** ssp. **tomentosum**
arachnoideum x **S. calcareum**
arachnoideum x **S. nevadense**
arachnoideum x **S. pittonii**
arenarium Koch 1837 = **Jovibarba arenaria**
armenum Boissier & Huet 1856   CA
ex Gumush Hane
avernense Lecocq & Lamotee 1847 non Coste = **S. tectorum**
atlanticum Ball 1878
'**Edward Balls**'   ®('Balls' Variety')
ex Oukaimaden
balcanicum Stojanov 1951
ballsii Wale 1940   CA
ex Hampechio
ex Tchumba Petzi
ex Skrutsch
ex Smolika
x **barbulatum** Schott 1853 (*S. arachnoideum* x *S. montanum*)
'**Hookeri**'
borissovae Wale 1942
braunii Funk 1835 = **S. montanum** ssp. **stiriacum**
x **calcaratum** Baker 1847 (*S. tectorum* x ?)
calcareum Jordan 1849 (*S. tectorum* var. *calcareum*)
'**Atropurpureum**'
'**Greenii**'   ®
'**Griggs Surprise**'   ®
'**Limelight**'   ®   CA
'Monstrosum' = **S. calcareum** '**Griggs Surprise**'
'**Mrs Giuseppi**'   ®
'**Nigricans**'
'**Sir William Lawrence**'   ®
'**Spinulifolium**'
cantabricum Praeger ex J. A Huber 1934   CA
ssp. **guadarramense** A. C. Smith 1981
ssp. **guadarramense** ex Lobo, No 1
ssp. **guadarramense** ex Lobo, No 2
ssp. **guadarramense** ex Morcuera, No 1
ssp. **guadarramense** ex Morcuera, No 3
ssp. **guadarramense** ex Navafria, No 1
ex Lago de Enol
ex Leitariegos
ex Piedrafita
ex Someido
ssp. **urbionense** A. C. Smith 1981

ssp. **urbionense** ex Valvanera
cantabricum x **S. montanum** ssp. **stiriacum**
cantalicum Jordan & Fourreau 1868 = **S. tectorum** ssp. **cantalicum**
caucasicum Ruprecht ex Boissier 1872   CA
charadzeae Gurgenidze ex Gurgenidze 1984
x **christii** Wolf 1889 non Praeger (*S. grandiflorum x S. montanum*)
ciliosum Craib 1914
    ex Ali Botusch   CA
    var. **borisii** (Degen & Urumov 1915) P. J. Mitchell ex P. J. Mitchell 1979
                                                          CA
    ex Corni di Canzo
    var. **galicicum** A. C. Smith 1978
    var. **galicicum** ex Mali Hat   CA
    var. **galicicum** ex Ochrid
ciliosum x **S. leucanthum**
ciliosum x **S. marmoreum**
ciliosum x **S. marmoreum** ex Sveta Peta
*****cistaceum**
x comolli hort. = **S. x calcaratum**
davisii Muirhead 1969
x **degenianum** Domokos 1936 (*S. banaticum x S. ruthenicum*)
doellianum C. B. Lehmann 1850 = **S. arachnoideum** var. **glabrescens**
dolomiticum Facchini 1855   CA-RD
dolomiticum x **S. montanum**
dzhavachischvilii Gurgenidze 1969
*****elianum**
erythraeum Velenovsky 1898   CA-RD
    'Major'
    ex Pirin   CA
    'Red Velvet'   ®
    ex Rila   RD
*****excelsum**
x **fauconetti** Reuter 1832 (*S. arachnoideum x S. tectorum*)
    *****thompsonii** (Linsdsay 1900) ?
x fimbriatum hort.= **S. x roseum fimbriatum**
flagelliforme Fischer ex Link 1822 = **S. montanum**
flavipilum Hausmann ex Sauter 1857 = **S. x fauconetti**
'Frigidum' non Lamotte 1864
x **funckii** F. Braun ex Koch 1832 (*(S. arachnoides x S. montanum) x S. tectorum*)
                                                          RD
    *****aqualiense**
giuseppii Wale 1941   CA
    ex Pena Espigueta
    ex Pena Prieta
glabrifolium A. Boriss 1939
globiferum Wulfen non Linnaeus 1753 = **S. wulfenii**
grandiflorum Haworth 1821   CA
    'Fasciatum'
    'Keston'   ®
    'Matterhornchen'
grandiflorum x **S. montanum**
grandiflorum x **S. tectorum**
heuffelii Schott 1852 = **Jovibarba heuffelii**
hirtum Linnaeus 1753 = **Jovibarba hirta**
hookeri hort. = **S. barbulatum** 'Hookeri'
x huteri Hausmann ex Seboth 1876 non Kerner = **S. x rupicolum**
ingwersenii Wale 1942   CA
italicum Ricci 1961
kindingeri Adamovic 1904   CA
kosaninii Praeger 1930   CA

  ex Koprivnik
  ex Visitor
leucanthum Pancic 1813
macedonicum Praeger 1930   CA
  ex Ljubotin   CA
marmoreum Grisebach 1843
  var. **angustissimum** S. Priszter 1980
  var. *blandum* (Schott) K. Konapova & R. Konapova 1983
  'Brunneifolium' ® [Praeger 1932]
  'Chocolate' = **S. 'Chocolate'**
  var. **dinaricum** Becker
  var. **dinaricum** ex Karawanken
  'Edinburgh'
  ex Kanzan Gorge
  ex Monte Tirone
  ex Okol
  'Ornatum' ® [Durez 1930s]
  'Rubicundum' = **S. marmoreum 'Rubrifolium'**
  'Rubrifolium' ® [1858]
  ex Sveta Peta
minus Turrill 1940
montanum Linnaeus 1753   CA
  var. *blandum* (Schott) hort. = **S. marmoreum** var. **blandum** DGP-RD
  ssp. **burnatii** Wettstein ex Hayek 1921
  ssp. **stiriacum** Wettstein & Hayek 1921
  ssp. **stiriacum 'Lloyd Praeger'** ®
  ssp. **stiriacum** ex Mauterndorf
nevadense Wale 1941
  'Hirtellum'   CA
  ex Puerto de San Francisco
octopodes Turrill 1937
  var. **apetalum** Turrill 1937   CA
ornatum hort. = **S. marmoreum 'Ornatum'**
ossetiense Wale 1942
patens Grisebach & Schrank 1852 = **Jovibarba heuffelii** CA
pittonii Schott, Nyman & Kotschy 1854   CA
x praegeri Rowley 1972 (*S. ciliosum x S. erythraeum*)
pumilum Marshall von Bieberstein 1808   CA
  ex Adyl Su, No 1
  ex Adyl Su, No 2
  ex Armchi
  ex Armchi x **S. ingwersenii**
  ex Elbruz, No 1
  ex Elbruz, No 2
reginae-amaliae Heldreich & Guicciardi ex Halascy 1901 CA
  ex Kambeecho, No 1
  ex Kambeecho, No 2
  ex Kiona
  ex Marvi Petri
  ex Peristeria
  ex Sarpun
  ex Vardusa
x rupicolum Chenevard & Schmidely 1898 (*S. grandiflorum x S. montanum*)
x roseum Huter & Nyman 1878 (*S. arachniodeum x S. wulfenii*)
  * **fimbriatum** (Schott ex Hegi 1921 non Schnittspahn & Lehmann) ?
ruthenicum Koch 1846 (*S. zeleborii*)
schlehanii Schott 1853 = **S. marmoreum**
x schottii C. B. Lehmann & Schnittspahn 1860 non Baker 1874 (*S. montanum x S. tectorum*)

soboliferum Sims 1812 = **Jovibarba sobilifera**

sosnowskyi Ter-Chatschatorova 1947
stansfieldii hort. = **S. arachniodeum 'Standsfieldii'**
HN   **tectorum** Linnaeus 1753   RD
    ssp. **alpinum** Wettstein ex Hayek 1921
    ssp. **alpinum** ex Gasson
    ex Andorra
    'Atropurpureum'   ®
    'Atroviolaceum'   ®
    'Boissieri'   ®   [Baker 1879]
    var. *calcareum* (Jordan) Cariot & St. Leger 1854 = **S. calcareum**
    * ssp. **cantalicum** (Jordan & Fourreau 1868) ? (*S. cantalicum*)
    'Elegans'
    'Giganteum'
    var. **glaucum** (Tenore) Praeger 1932
    'Monstrosum'
    ex Mount Ventoux
    'Nigrum'   ®   [1920s]
    'Noir'   ®   [Moore 1950s]
    'Red Flush'   ®   [1970]
    'Robustum'
    'Royanum'   ®   [1914]
    ex Sierra del Cadi
    'Sunset'   ®
    'Triste'   ®   [1879]
    'Val Minera' = **S. tectorum 'Sunset'**
    'Violaceum'
thomayeri Correvon 1891 = **S. x fauconetti**
thompsonianum Wale 1940   CA
thompsonii Lindsay 1900 = **S. x fauconetti thompsonii**
transcaucasicum Muirhead 1965
x vaccarii (Wilczek) Wilczek 1905 (*S. arachniodeum x S. grandiflorum*)
x versicolor Velenovsky 1903 (*S. marmoreum x S. zeleborii*)
vincentei Pau 1925
x widderi Lehmann & Schnittspahn 1860 (*S. tectorum x S. wulfenii*)
    'Peter Davis'
wulfenii Hoppe ex Mertens & Koch 1831 (*S. globiferum* Wulfen)   CA
zeleborii Schott 1857 = **S. ruthenicum**

NAMED HYBRID CULTIVARS

    'Abba'   ®   [Ford 1980]
    'Abernelli'
    'Adlerhorst'   ®   [Kayser & Siebert 1972]
    'Alaric'   ®   [Payne 1974]
    'Aldo Moro'   ®   [van der Steen 1977]
    'Alluring'   ®   [Skrocki 1977]
    'Alpha'   ®   [Arends 1929]
    'Amanda'   ®   [Ingram 1976]
    'Ambergreen'   ®
    'Amtmann Fischer'   ®
    'Apache'   ®   [Haberer 1980]
    'Apollo'   ®   [Haberer 1980]
    'Apple Blossom'
    'Arrowheads Red'   ®
    'Ashes of Roses'   ®   [Payne 1976]
    'Athen'   ®
    'Aymon Correvon'   ® ('Correvon's Hybrid')
    'Bedivere'   ®   [Skrocki 1973]
    'Belladonna'   ®   [MacPherson 1970]
    'Bella Meade'   ®   [Ford 1978]

'**Bellotts Pourpre**'   ®   [van der Steen 1979]
'**Berggeist**'   ®   [Kayer & Siebert 1972]
'**Bernstein**'   ®
'**Beta**'   ®   [Arends 1929]
'**Bicolor**'   ®
'**Big Red**'   ®
'**Black Prince**'   ®   [Earl 1962]
'**Blood Tip**'   ®   [MacPherson]
'**Blue Moon**'   ®   [Payne 1975]
'**Booths Red**'   ®   [Colvin]
'**Boromir**'   ®   [Bronow]
'Boissieri' = **S. tectorum 'Boissieri'**
'**Braun Kugel**'   ®   [Haberer]
'**Brock**'   ®   [Earl 1961]
'**Bronco**'   ®   [Haberer 1980]
'**Bronze Pastel**'   ®   [Moore]
'**Bronze Tower**'   ®   [Moore 1950s]
'**Brownii**'   ®
'**Burgundy Velvet**'   ®   [Drown 1974]
'**Cafe**'
'**Caliphs Hat**'   ®   [Moore]
'**Camelot**'   ®   [Skrocki 1974]
'**Canada Kate**'   ®
'**Cancer**'   ®   [Haberer]
'**Candy Floss**'   ®   [Ford 1976]
'**Carluke**'   ®   [Moore]
'**Carmen**'   ®   [Payne]
'**Carnival**'   ®   [Skrocki]
'**Cavo Doro**'   ®   [Ford 1975]
'**Ceylon**'   ®   [MacPherson]
'**Cherry Frost**'   ®   [1970]
'**Cherry Tart**'   ®   [Ford 1977]
'**Chivalry**'   ®   [Vaughn 1976]
'**Chocolate**'   ®
'Christii' = **S. x christii**
'**Christmas Time**'   ®   [Vaughn 1969]
'**Clara Noyes**'   ®   [MacPherson]
'**Clare**'   ®
'**Cleveland Morgan**'   ®   [1972]
'**Climax**'   ®   [Ford 1969]
'**Clipper**'   ®   [Skrocki]
'**Collage**'   ®   [Skrocki 1972]
'**Collecteur Anchisi**'
'**Commander Hay**'   ®
'**Compte de Congae**'   ®
'**Congo**'   ®   [Ford 1976]
'**Cordeurs Memory**'
'**Cornstone**'   ®   [Ford]
'**Coronet**'   ®   [Skrocki 1974]
'Correvons Hybrid' = **S. 'Aymon Correvon'**
'**Corsair**'
'**Cresta**'   ®   [Haberer 1980]
'**Crimson Velvet**'
'**Crispyn**'   ®   [van der Steen 1974]
'**Cupream**'   [1890s]
'**Dallas**'   ®   [Ford 1981]
'**Damokles**'
'**Dark Beauty**'   ®   [Lewis]
'**Dark Cloud**'   ®   [Bishop 1976]
'**Darkie**'   ®   [Ford 1979]

DGP-RD

'Dark Point' ®   [Moore]
'Director Jacobs' ®   [van der Steen 1975]
'Disco Dancer' ®   [Ford 1981]
'Donarrose' ®   [Kayser & Siebert 1965]
'Downland Queen' ®   [1978]
'Duke of Windsor' ®   [Hansen]
'Dunstan' ®   [Earl 1961]
'Dusky' ®   [Vaughn 1972]
'Elgar' ®   [Adams]
'El Greco' ®   [Ford 1973]
'El Toro' ®   [Ford]
'Elvis' ®   [Zelina 1979]
'Emerald Giant' ®   [Wood 1971]
'Engles Rubrum' ®   [Engle]
'Engles 13-2' ®   [Engle]
'Excalibur' ®   [Skrocki 1972]
'Exclesior'
'Exhibitor' ®   [Skrocki 1976]
'Exhorna' ®   [Earl 1976]
'Fame' ®   [Moore]
'Feldmaier' ®   [Kayser & Siebert]
'Festival'   [Cmiral]
'Finerpointe' ®   [Skrocki 1976]
'Firebird' ®   [Nixon 1971]
'Flaming Heart' ®   [Drown 1974]
'Flasher' ®   [Vaughn]
'Floriade'
'Fords Amability' ®   [van der Steen]
'Fords Giant' ®   [van der Steen]
'Fords Spring' ®   [van der Steen]
'Frosty'
'Galahad' ®   [Skrocki 1973]
'Gamma' ®   [Arends 1929]
'Garnet' ®   [Ford 1971]
'Gay Jester'
'Gazelle' ®   [Ford 1971]
'Georgette' ®   [Ford 1972]
'Giant Red' = S. 'Red Giant'
'Ginnies Delight' ®
'Gipsy' ®   [Ford 1973]
'Gizmo' ®   [Skrocki 1980]
'Gloriosum' ®   [Malby]
'Glowing Embers' ®   [Skrocki 73]
'Gollum' ®   [Bronow 1975]
'Granada' ®   [Payne 1972]
'Granat' ®   [Kayser & Siebert 1965]
'Granby' ®   [Earl 1967]
'Grapetone' ®   [Skrocki 1971]
'Gray Dawn' ®   [Skrocki 1974]
'Green Apple' ®   [Ford 1977]
'Green Gables' ®   [Skrocki 1974]
'Greenii' = S. calcareum 'Greenii'
'Greyfriars' ®   [Earl 1968]
'Grey Ghost' ®   [Ford]
'Gruard Larose' ®   [Moore]
'Grunrand'
'Grune Rose' ®
'Grunschnabel' ®   [Kayser & Siebert 1965]
'Halls Hybrid'
'Hart'

'Hatra'   ®   [Haberer]
'Haullaurs Seedling'   ®   [Haullauer 1969]
'Hayling'   ®   [Ford 1966]
'Heigham Red'   ®   [Braun]
'Hekla'   ®   [Haberer]
'Hester'   ®   [Skrocki 1980]
'Hey Hey'   ®   [Moore 1950s]
'Hidde'   ®   [van der Steen 1979]
'Hortulanus Smit'   ®   [van der Steen]
'Hot Peppermint'   ®   [Adams]
'Icicle'   ®
'Imperial'   ®   [Skrocki]
'Inca'   ®   [Payne 1972]
'Irazu'
'Jack Frost'   ®   [Adams]
'Jewel Case'   ®   [Skrocki 1976]
'Jolly Green Giant'   ®   [Nixon 1969]
'Jubilation'   ®   [Earl 1961]
'Jubilee'   ®   [Hansen]
'Jubilee Tricolor'   ®
'Jungle Shadows'   ®   [Vaughn 1973]
'Jupiter'   ®   [Haberer]
'Just Plain Crazy'   ®   [Vaughn 1973]
'Kalinda'   ®   [Skrocki 1976]
'Kansas Gorge' = S. marmoreum ex Kansas Gorge
'Kappa'   ®   [Ford 1969]
'Kelly Jo'   ®   [Skrocki 1970]
'Kermit'
'King George'   ®   [Hansen]
'King Lear'   ®
'Kip'   ®   [Skrocki 1976]
'Kismet'   ®   [Nixon 1970]
'Kolagas Mayfair'   ®
'Kolibri'
'Kramers Spinrad'   ®   [van der Steen]
'Kristina'   ®   [van der Steen]
'Kubi'   ®   [Ford 1972]
'Lady Kelly'   ®
'Launcelot'   ®   [Skrocki 1976]
'Laura Lee'   ®   [MacPherson]
'Lavender And Old Lace'   ®   [Payne]
'Le Clairs Hybrid No 4'
'Leneca'   ®   [van der Steen]
'Lenniks Glory' = S. 'Crispyn'
'Lenniks Time'   ®   [van der Steen 1979]
'Leocadias Nephew'   ®   [Moore]
'Lilac Time'   ®   [Milton]
'Liliane'
'Limelight'   ®
'Lipari'
'Lipstick'   ®   [Vaughn 1970]
'Lively Bug'   ®   [Skrocki 1980]
'Lou Bastidou'   ®
'Lynns Choice'   ®   [Payne]
'Madame Arsac'
'Magnificum'   ®   [1920s]
'Mahogony'   ®
'Maigret'   ®   [Ford 1972]
'Majestic'
'Malarbron'   ®   [Moore]

'Malbys Hybrid, No 1' = **S. 'Reginald Malby'**
'Malbys Hybrid, No 2' = **S. 'Gloriosum'**
'Marijntje' ®
'Mauvine' ®
'Mayfair Hybrid' = **S. 'Kolagas Mayfair'**
'Medallion' ®   [Skrocki 1976]
'Melanie'
'Mercury' ®   [Skrocki 1973]
'Metallicum Giganteum'
'Michael' ®   [Vaughn 1972]
'Mila' ®
'Mini Frost' ®   [Adams]
'Missouri Rose' ®   [Drown 1969]
'Moerkerks Merit' ®   [van der Steen 1979]
'Mondstein' ®   [Kayser & Siebert]
'Monstrosum' = **S. tectorum 'Griggs Surprise'**
'Mors' ®
'Mount Hood' ®   [Haberer]
'Mount Usher' ®   [Moore]
'Mystic' ®   [Ford 1981]
'Nico'
'Night Raven' ®   [Skrocki]
'Nightwood' ®   [Moore 1960]
'Nigrum' = **S. tectorum 'Nigrum'**
'Nocturn' ®
'Noir' = **S. tectorum 'Noir'**
'Norne' ®   [Kayser & Siebert 1972]
'Nortofts Beauty' ®
'Nouveau Pastel' ®   [Moore]
'Ockerwurz' ®   [Kohlein 1962]
'Oddity' ®   [MacPherson]
'Ohio Burgundy' ®   [Skrocki 1972]
'Olivette' ®   [Skrocki 1973]
'Omega'   [Ford]
'Ordensstern'
'Ornatum' = **S. marmoreum 'Ornatum'**
'Othello' ®   [Sponnier c1959]
'Packardian' ®   [Skrocki 1972]
'Palissander'
'Pastel' ®   [Moore]
'Patrician' ®   [Skrocki 1973]
'Pekinese' ®   [Payne 1975]
'Peppermint'
'Petersen's Ornatum' ®   [Petersen 1920s]
'Pilatus'
'Pink Puff'
'Pippin' ®   [Bronow]
'Pixie'
'Plumb Rose' ®   [Bishop 1977]
'Pluto' ®   [Skrocki 1972]
'Poke Eat' ®   [Moore]
'Polaris'
'Pompeon'
'Pottsii'
'President Arsac' ®   [van der Steen 1976]
'Pruhonice' ®
'Pseudo-ornatum' ®
'Purdys 50-6' ®   [Purdy]
'Purdys 90-1' ®   [Purdy]
'Purple Beauty' ®

RD

'Purple King' ®   [Earl 1967]
'Purple Passion' ®   [Nixon 1972]
'Purpuriese' ®   [Kayser & Siebert 1965]
'Queen Amealia' ®   [MacPherson]
'Raspberry Ice' ®   [Colvin 1973]
'Rauhreif' ®
'Red Ace'
'Red Beam' ®   [Ford 1980]
'Red Chief'
'Red Delta'
'Red Devil' ®   [Ford]
'Red Flush' = **S. tectorum 'Red Flush'**
'Red Giant' ®
'Red Mountain' ®
'Red Planet' ®   [Ford]
'Red Rum' ®   [Ford]
'Red Velvet' = **S. erythraeum 'Red Velvet'**
'Red Wings' ®   [Ford]
'Reginald Malby' ®
'Rheinkiesel' ®   [Goos & Koenemann 1937]
'Rhone' ®   [Eschmann 1965]
'Rita Jane' ®   [MacPherson 1971]
'Robin' ®   [Ford 1976]
'Ronny' ®   [van der Steen]
'Roosemaryn' ®   [van der Steen]
'Rosie' ®   [Smith 1970]
'Rosty' ®   [Haberer 1979]
'Roter Kristall'
'Rotkopf' ®   [Kohlein 1962]
'Rotmantel' ®   [Kayser & Siebert 1972]
'Rotsandsteinriese' ®   [Kayser & Siebert]
'Rotund'
'Rouge' ®   [Ford 1968]
'Royal Flush' ®   [Vaughn]
'Royal Opera' ®   [Skrocki 1980]
'Royal Ruby' ®   [Skrocki 1971]
'Royanum' = **S. tectorum 'Royanum'**
'Rubellum'
'Rubicon' ®   [Skrocki 1970]
'Rubicon Improved' ®   [Skrocki 1970]
'Rubin' ®   [Goos & Koenemann 1937]   RD
'Rubra Ash' ®   [Macpherson]
'Rubra Ray' ®   [MacPherson]
'Ruby' ®   [Ford 1975]
'Ruby Heart' ®   [Vaughn 1969]
'Rusty' ®   [Ford 1976]
'Saga' ®   [Ford 1969]
'Samba' ®   [Ford]
'Santis' ®   [Eschmann 1969]
'Saturn' ®   [Skrocki 1974]
'Seerosenstern' ®   [Kayser & Siebert]
'Serena' ®   [Skrocki 1974]
'Shirleys Joy' ®   [Moore]
'Silberkarneol' ®
'Silberknopf'
'Silverine' ®   [MacPherson]   RD
'Silver Spring' ®   [Vaughn 1974]
'Silver Thaw' ®
'Simplonstern' ®
'Sioux' ®   [Haberer]

'Sir William Lawrence' = **S. calcareum 'Sir William Lawrence'**
'Skovtroldens Triumf'   ®   [Johansen]
'Skrockis Bronze'   ®   [van der Steen 1978]
'Smaragd'   ®   [Goos & Koenemann 1937]
'Smokey Jet'   ®   [Skrocki 1981]
'Snowberger'   ®
'Spanish Dancer'   ®   [Skrocki 1973]
'Spherette'   ®   [Skrocki 1977]
'Spinell'   ®   [Kayser & Siebert]
'Spode'
'Sponnier'
'Springmist'   ®   [Drown 1976]
'Sprite'   ®   [Ford 1979]
'Stansfieldii' = **S. arachnoideum 'Stansfieldii'**
'Starshine'   ®   [Skrocki 1980]
'State Fair'   ®   [Ford 1981]
'Strider'   ®   [Bronow]
'Sunkist'   ®   [Skrocki 1975]
'Sultan' = **S. arachnoideum 'Sultan'**
'Sunset' = **S. tectorum 'Sunset'**
'Sun Waves'   ®   [Skrocki 1980]
'Syston Flame'   ®
'Thayne'   ®   [Payne 1970]
'Thera'   ®   [Haberer]
'Titania'   ®   [Skrocki 1980]
'Topaz'   ®   [Goos & Koenemann 1937]
'Tordeurs Memory'   ®   [van der Steen 1975]
'Traci Sue'   ®   [Skrocki 1971]
'Triste' = **S. tectorum 'Triste'**
'Truva'   ®   [Earl 1968]
'Turmalin'   ®   [Kayser & Siebert]
'Twilight Blues'   ®   [Nixon 1972]
'Uralturmalin'   ®
'Val Minera' = **S. tectorum 'Sunset'**
'Vanbaelen'   ®   [van der Steen]
'Video'
'Violetta'
'Virgil'   ®   [Skrocki 1980]
'Virginus'   ®   [Payne]
'Vulcano'
'Webbianum' = **S. arachniodeum** ssp. **tomentosum**
'Webby Flame'   ®   [Skrocki 1972]
'Wega'   ®   [Haberer]
'Weirdo'   ®   [Vaughn]
'Wendy'   ®   [Earl 1960]
'Westerlin'   ®
'Whitening'
'Witchery'   ®
'Woolcotts Variety'
'Wunderhold'   ®   [Kayser & Siebert 1972]
'Zackenkrone   ®
'Zenobia'   ®   [Payne]
'Zenocrate'   ®   [Moore]
'Zeppelin'
'Zinaler Rothorn'   ®
'Zircon'   ®   [Ford]
'Zone'   ®   [Ford 1970]
'Zuzu'   ®   [Haberer]
'Zwielicht'   ®   [Kayser & Siebert 1972]

SENECIO Linnaeus 1753   *[Asteraceae (Compositae)]*
     abrotanifolius Linnaeus 1753
     adonidifolius Loiseleur 1807
     candicans de Candolle 1838
S   **bicolor** Willdenow 1859
N‡   ssp. **cineraria** (de Candolle) Chater 1974 (*S. cineraria, S. maritima*)
                                                      PGP-DGP
          'Alice'
          'Cirrus'
          'Ramparts'
          'Silver Filigree'
          'White Diamond'   PGP-**DGP**
     cineraria de Candolle 1838 = **S. bicolor** ssp. **cineraria**
     clivorum Maximowicz 1871 = **Ligularia dentata**
N   **doria** Linnaeus 1759
S   **heritieri** de Candolle 1838
     ledebourii Schultz-Bip 1845 = **Ligularia macrophylla**
S   **leucostachys** Baker 1877   PGP
     littoralis Gaudich 1825
     maritimus Reichenbach 1833 = **S. bicolor** ssp. **cineraria**
     przewaldskii Maximowicz 1880 = **Ligularia przewaldskii**
     pulcher Hooker & Arnott 1841   **PGP**
N   **smithii** de Candolle 1838 (*Ligularia smithii*)   PGP
     stenocephalus Maximowicz 1871 non Boissier = **Ligularia stenocephala**
N   **tanguticus** Maximowicz 1881 (*Ligularia tangutica*)   PGP-DGP
     veitchianus Hemsley 1905 = **Ligularia veitchiana**
     wilsonianus Hemsley 1905 = **Ligularia veitchiana**

SERAPIAS Linnaeus 1753 nom. cons.   *[Orchidaceae]*
     lingua Linnaeus 1753
     parviflora Parlatore 1837

SERIPHIDIUM (Besser) Poljakov 1961   *[Asteraceae (Compositae)]*
     maritimum (Linnaeus) Poljakov 1961 (*Artemisia maritima*)   PGP-DGP
     nutans (Willdenow) Bremer & Humphries in press (*Artemisia nutans*)   PGP
     palmeri (A. Gray) Bremer & Humphries in press
     rothrockii (A. Gray) Bremer & Humphries in press (*Artemisia rothrockii*)
     tridentatum (Nuttall) Bremer & Humphries in press (*Artemisia tridentata*)

SERRATULA Linnaeus 1753   *[Asteraceae (Compositae)]*
     seoanei Willkomm 1889 (*S. shawii* hort.)   **DGP**
     shawii hort. = **S. seoanei**

SESELI Linnaeus 1753   *[Apiaceae (Umbelliferae)]*
     gracile Waldstein & Kitaibel 1802

SESLERIA Scopoli 1760   *[Poaceae (Gramineae)]*
N‡   **albicans** Kitaibel 1814
     argentea (Savi) Savi 1808
     autumnalis (Scopoli) F. W. Schultes 1855
     caerulea (Linnaeus) Arduino 1764
     heufleriana Schur 1853
     nitida Tenore 1815
     rigida Heuffel ex Reichenbach 1830

SHORTIA Torrey & A. Gray 1842 nom. cons.   *[Diapensiaceae]*
     x interdexta Marchant 1951 (*S. galacifolia x S. uniflora*)
          'Wimborne'   [J. Marchant]
     galacifolia Torrey & A. Gray 1842   RD
        var. **brevistyla** Davies 1952

soldanelloides (Siebold & Zuccarini) Makino 1907 (*Schizocodon soldanelloides*)
CA-DGP-RD

'**Alba**' nom. dub.
f. **alpina** (Maxomowicz) Makino 1907   CA
'**Askival**'   [M. A. Stone]
var. **ilicifolia** (Maximowicz) Makino 1907 (*Schizocodon ilicifolium*)   CA
var. **ilicifolia** '**Alba**'
var. **intercedens** Ohwi
var. **magna** Makino   CA-**DGP**
var. **minima** (Makino) Masamura
'Nana' = **S. soldanelloides** var. **minima**
uniflora (Maximowicz) Maximowicz 1871   **DGP**-RD
'**Grandiflora**'   **RD**
var. **kantoensis** Yamazaki

SIBBALDIA Linnaeus 1753   [*Rosaceae*]
cuneata Hornemann ex Kuntze 1847 (*S. maxima*)
maxima Kesselring ex Muravjera 1936 = **S. cuneata**

SIBBALDIOPSIS Rydberg 189   [*Rosaceae*]
tridentata (Solander) Rydberg 1898 (*Potentilla tridentata*)

SIDALCEA A. Gray ex Bentham 1848   [*Malvaceae*]
candida A. Gray 1849
malviflora (de Candolle) A. Gray ex Bentham 1848

HYBRIDS

'**Brilliant**'
'**Crimson Beauty**'
'**Crimson King**'
'**Croftway Red**'   RD
'**Elsie Heugh**'   PGP
'**Loveliness**'   PGP-RD
'**Mr Lindbergh**'
'**Mrs Borrodaile**'
'**Mrs Cadman**'
'**Mrs Galloway**'
'**Mrs Lindberg**'
'**Mrs T Anderson**   PGP
'**Nimmerdor**'   RD
'**Oberon**'   PGP-RD
'**Progress**'
'**Rev Page Roberts**'   PGP
'**Rose Beauty**'
'**Rose Bouquet**'
'**Rose Queen**'   **RD**
'**Rosy Gem**'
'**Stark's Hybrid**'
L   '**Sussex Beauty**'   PGP
'**The Duchess**'
'**William Smith**'   RD

SILENE Linnaeus 1753   [*Caryophyllaceae*]
N‡   **acaulis** (Linnaeus) Jacquemonti 1762   CA-**RD**
'**Alba**'   CA
'**Correvon's Variety**'
*ssp. **elongata** ('Pedunculata')   CA
ssp. **exscapa** (Allioni) J. Brown 1913   CA
'**Floribunda**'

ssp. **longiscapa** (Kerner ex Vierhapper) Hayek 1903
'Pedunculata' = **S. acaulis** ssp. **elongata**
saxatilis (Sims) hort. = **S. saxatilis**
alpestris Jacquemonti 1773 (*Heliosperma alpestre*)
   'Flore Pleno' ('Pleniformum')
   'Heidi'
   'Pleniflorum' = **S. alpestris 'Flore Pleno'**
bryoides Jordan 1852 = **S. acaulis**
caroliniana Walter 1788
caryophylloides (Poiret) Otth 1824
   ssp. **echinus** (Boissier & Heldreich) Coode & Cullen 1967
ciliata Pourret 1788

N   **coeli-rosa** (Linnaeus) Godron 1847 (*Lychnis oculata*)   **RD**
N‡L **dioica** (Linnaeus) Clairville 1811 (*Lychnis dioica, Melandrium rubrum*)   **PGP**
   'Flore Pleno'
   'Rosea Plena'
   'Rubra' = **S. dioica**
   'Rubra Plena' = **S. dioica 'Flore Pleno'**
elisabethae Jan ex Reichenbach 1832 (*Melandrium elisabethae*)   **CA**
hookeri Nuttall 1838   **CA**
ingramii Tidestrom & Dayton 1929   **CA**
N   **italica** (Linnaeus) Persoon 1805
keiskei Miquel 1865 (*Melandrium keiskei*)   **CA**
   *apetalum
   var. **minor** (Takeda) Ohwi & Ohashi 1974   **CA**
maritima Witherinng 1792 = **S. vulgaris** ssp. **maritima**
moorcroftiana Wallich ex Bentham 1834
N‡ **nutans** Linnaeus 1753
petersonii Maguire 1941
pseudovelutina Rothmaler 1943
pusilla Waldstein & Kitaibel 1812 (*Heliosperma pusilla*)
pygmaea Adam 1805
saxatilis Sims 1803
saxifraga Linnaeus 1753
N   **schafta** S. G. Gmelin ex Hohenacker 1838   **RD**
   'Abbotswood Rose' = **Lychnis x walkeri 'Abbotswood Rose'**
   'Robusta'
   'Splendens'
sibirica (Linnaeus) Persoon 1805 (*Lychnis sibirica*)
tenuis Willdenow 1809
vallesia Linnaeus 1759
viridiflora Linnaeus 1762
N‡ **vulgaris** (Moench) Garcke 1869
   ssp. **maritima** (Witherinng) A.&D. Löve 1961 (*S. maritima*)   **RD**
   ssp. **maritima 'Flore Pleno'**
   ssp. **maritima 'Rosea'**
   ssp. **maritima 'Weisskehlchen'**   [Berggarten-Herrenhausen]
   ssp. **maritima 'White Bells'**
   ssp. **prostrata** (Gaudin) Chater & Walters 1964
   'Robin Whitebreast' = **S. vulgaris** ssp. **maritima 'Weisskehlchen'**
zawadzkii Herbich 1835 (*Melandrium zawadzkii*)

SILPHIUM Linnaeus 1753   [*Asteraceae (Compositae)*]
   laciniatum Linnaeus 1753   **PGP**
   perfoliatum Linnaeus 1759   **PGP**

SILYBUM Adanson 1763 nom. cons.   [*Asteraceae (Compositae)*]
BN **marianum** (Linnaeus) Gaertner 1791   **DGP-RD**

SINNINGIA Nees 1825   *[Gesneriaceae]*
    hirsuta (Decaisne ex Hanstein) Nicholson 1886 (*Gloxinia hirsuta*)
    speciosa (Loddiges) Hiern 1877 (*Gloxinia speciosa*)   DGP-RD
    velutina (Martius) Lindley 1827
    x youngeana Marnock ex Paxton 1840 (*S. speciosa x S. velutina*)

SISYRINCHIUM Miller 1754   *[Iridaceae]*
    angustifolium Miller 1768   RD
    angustifolium hort. non Miller 1768 = **S. douglasii**
    arenarium Poeppig 1833 (*S. cuspidatum*)   EGF.1
    bellum hort. non S. Watson 1877 = **S. idahoense**
    bermudianum Linnaeus p.p. non Coste = **S. graminoides**
    birameum hort. non Piper 1900 = **S. graminoides**
    'Biscutellum'
    boreale (Bicknell) J. K. Henry 1915 = **S. californicum**
    brachypus (Bicknell) J. K. Henry 1915 = **S. californicum**
N   **californicum** (Ker-Gawler) Dryander 1812 (*S. boreale, S. brachypus, S. convolutum*
                                         Klatt)   EGF.1-**RD**
    chilense Hooker 1827 (*S. scabrum*)   EGF.1
    coeruleum Vellozo c1827 = **Gelasine coerulea**
    convolutum Nocca 1800   EGF.1
    convolutum Klatt 1866 non Nocca 1800 = **C. californicum**
    cuspidatum Poeppig 1833 = **S. arenarium**
    douglasii A. Dietrich 1833 (*S. grandiflorum* Douglas)   EGF.1-CA-**RD**
        'Album'   CA
    'E. K. Balls' ('Balls' Mauve')
    filifolium Gaudichaud-Beaupre 1825   EGF.1-CA
        ssp. **junceum** (Presl) Parent (*S. juncifolium*)   EGF.1
    graminoides Bicknell 1899 (*S. bermudianum* Linnaeus p.p.)   EGF.1-**DGP**
        'Album'
        'Bermuda Blue'
        'Kiel'
    grandiflorum Douglas 1830 non Cavanilles 1790 = **S. douglasii**
    idahoense Bicknell 1899 (*S. bellum* hort., *S. birameum* Piper, *S. macounii*)
                                                   EGF.1-CA
        'Album'
    iridifolium Humboldt, Bonpland & Kunth 1816   EGF.1
    juncifolium Herbert 1843 = **S. filifolium** ssp. **junceum**
    littorale Greene 1899
    macounii Bicknell 1900 = **S. idahoense**
    * **macrocarpon** Bicknell 1901 ? or Hieron 1881 ?
    'Mrs Spivey'
N   **montanum** Greene 1899   EGF.1
        ssp. **crebum** (Fernald) Böcher   EGF.1
    'North Star' ('Pole Star')
    nudicaule Philippi 1895
    patagonicum Philippi ex Baker 1877
    pulchellum R. Brown 1810 (*Libertia pulchella*)
    'Quaint & Queer'
    scabrum Chamisso & Schlecht 1831 non Philippi 1857 = **S. chilense**
L   **striatum** Smith 1792   EGF.1-**DGP-RD**
        'Aunt May' ('Variegatum')   PGP-RD
        'Variegatum' = **S. striatum 'Aunt May'**
    tenuifolium Humboldt & Bonpland ex Willdenow 1809   EGF.1

SIUM Linnaeus 1753   *[Apiaceae (Umbelliferae)]*
H   **sisarum** Linnaeus 1753

SMELOWSKIA C.A. Meyer 1831   *[Brassicaceae (Cruciferae)]*
    calycina C.A. Meyer 1831

SMILACINA Desfontaines 1807 nom. cons.   [*Convallariaceae (Liliaceae)*]
   japonica Perry 1857 = **Maianthemum nipponicum**
   racemosa (Linnaeus) Desfontaines 1807 = **Maianthemum racemosum**
   stellata (Linnaeus) Desfontaines 1807 = **Maianthemum stellatum**

SMYRNIUM Linnaeus 1753   [*Apiaceae (Umbelliferae)*]
BHN **olusatrum** Linnaeus 1753
BN   **perfoliatum** Linnaeus 1753
                                       PGP

SOLDANELLA Linnaeus 1753
   alpina Linnaeus 1753   [*Primulaceae*]
                             CA-**DGP-RD**
   austriaca Vierhapper 1904
   carpatica Vierhapper 1904
     'Alba'
   cyanaster Schwarz 1975 nom. nud.
   dimoniei Vierhapper 1904 = **S. pindicola** var. **dimoniei**
   hungarica Simonkai 1887
   minima Hoppe 1806   CA-RD
     'Alba'   CA
   montana Willdenow 1809   CA-**DGP-RD**
     'Alba'
     'Tinkerbell'
   pindicola Haussknecht 1886   CA-RD
     var. **dimoniei** (Vierhapper) Markgraf 1931 (*S. dimoniei*)
   pusilla Baumgarten 1816   **CA**-DGP-RD
   villosa Darracq 1850   DGP-RD

SOLEIROLIA Gaudich 1826   [*Urticaceae*]
N **solierolii** (Regel) Dandy 1965 (*Helxine solierolii*)   **RD**
     'Argentea' = **S. solierolii 'Variegata'**
     'Aurea' ('Golden Queen')   RD
     'Golden Queen' = **S. solierolii 'Aurea'**
     'Silver Queen' = **S. solierolii 'Variegata'**
     'Variegata' ('Argentea', 'Silver Queen')   RD

SOLENOMELUS Miers 1841   [*Iridaceae*]
   chilensis Miers 1841 = **S. pedunctulatus**
   pedunculatus (Hooker) Hochreutiner 1910 (*S. chilensis, Libertia chinense*) EGF.1

SOLIDAGO Linnaeus 1753   [*Asteraceae (Compositae)*]
   algida Piper 1915 = **S. multiradiata**
   alpestris Waldstein & Kitaibel ex Willdenow 1803 = **S. virgaurea** ssp. **alpestris**
   altissima Linnaeus 1753 = **S. canadensis** var. **scabra**
   aurea Sprengel 1826 (*Aster aureus*)
   bicolor Linnaeus 1767
   brachystachys hort. = **S. cutleri**
   caesia Linnaeus 1753   RD
N **canadensis** Linnaeus 1753   DGP-RD
     var. **scabra** (Muhlenberg ex Willdenow) Torrey & A. Gray 1842
   cutleri Fernald 1908 (*S. brachystachys* hort., *S. virgaurea* var. *alpina*) PGP-RD
     'Pyramidalis'
     'Robusta'
N **graminifolia** (Linnaeus) Salisbury 1796
   x hybridus hort. = **X Solidaster luteus**
   linoides Torrey & A. Gray 1841 = **S. uniligulata**
   minutissima (Makino) Kitamura 1934 (*S. virgaurea* var. *minutissima*)
   missouriensis Nuttall 1834
   multiradiata Aiton 1789 (*S. algida*)
   rigida Linnaeus 1753
   shortii Torrey & A. Gray 1841

spathulata de Candolle 1836
uniligulata (de Candolle) Porter 1894 (*S. linoides*)
HN‡ **virgaurea** Linnaeus 1753   PGP
    ssp. **alpestris** (Waldstein & Kitaibel ex Willdenow) Gaudin 1829 (*S. alpestris*)
    var. *alpina* Bigel 1824 = **S. cutleri**
    ssp. **minuta** (Linnaeus) Arcangeli 1882
    var. *minutissima* Makino = **S. minutissima**

HYBRID CULTIVARS

    'Baby Gold'
    'Cloth of Gold'
    'Crown of Rays'   **DGP**
    'Goldchild'
    'Goldelfe'
    'Golden Dwarf' = **S. 'Goldzwerg'**
    'Golden Falls'
    'Goldengate'   [Burleydam 1948]   RD
L   **'Goldenmosa'**   [Burleydam]   **PGP-DGP**-RD
    'Goldenplume'   [Walkden 1949]
    'Golden Shower'   [Walkden]
    'Golden Thumb' = **S. 'Queenie'**
    'Golden Wings'   PGP-DGP-RD
    'Gold Radiance'
    'Goldschleier'
    'Goldstrahl' ('Peter Pan')   RD
    'Goldwedel'
    'Goldzwerg' ('Golden Dwarf')
    'Laurin'
    'Leda'   [Walkden 1949]
    'Ledsham'   [Walkden 1956]
    'Lemore' = **X Solidaster luteus 'Lemore'**
    'Leraft'   RD
    'Lesden'
    'Loddon'
    'Mimosa'   RD
    'Perkeo'
    'Peter Pan' = **S. 'Goldstrahl'**
    'Praecox'
    'Queenie' ('Golden Thumb')   **DGP**-RD
    'Strahlenkrone'   [K. Foerster]
    'Tom Thumb'

X SOLIDASTER Wehrahn 1932   [*Asteraceae (Compositae)*]
  hybridus hort. = **S. luteus**
  luteus (Everett) M. L. Green ex Dress 1937 (*Aster ptarmicoides* x *Solidago canadensis*)
                                                            PGP-**DGP**
    'Lemore'   [Thos. Carlisle Ltd. 1948]   PGP-**DGP**-RD

SORGHASTRUM Nash 1901   [*Poaceae (Gramineae)*]
  nutans (Linnaeus) Nash 1903 (*Chrysopogon nutans*)   EGF.2

SPARAXIS Ker-Gawler 1804   [*Iridaceae*]
  bulbifera (Linnaeus) Ker-Gawler 1804   EGF.1
  elegans (Sweet) Goldblatt 1969   EGF.1
    'Coccinea'
  grandiflora (Delaroche) Ker-Gawler 1804   EGF.1
    ***acutiloba**
  pendula (Linnaeus f.) Ker-Gawler 1812 = **Dierama pendulum**
  pulcherrima Hooker f. 1866 = **Dierama pulcherrimum**
  tricolor (Schneevogt) Ker-Gawler 1804   **RD**

SPARGANIUM Linnaeus 1753   *[Sparganiaceae]*
N‡   **angustifolium** Michaux 1803
N‡   **erectum** Linnaeus 1753 (*S. ramosum*)   EGF.2
N‡   **minimum** Wallroth 1840   EGF.2
    ramosum Hudson 1770 = **S. erectum**

SPARTINA Schreber 1789   *[Poaceae (Gramineae)]*
    michauxiana C. L. Hitchcock 1908 = **S. pectinata**
    pectinata Link 1820 (*S. michauxiana*)   EGF.2-PGP
        'Aureo-marginata' = **S. pectinata 'Variegata'**
        'Variegata' Marie-Victorin 1944   PGP

SPATHIPAPPUS Tzvelev 1961   *[Asteraceae (Compositae)]*
    griffithii (Clarke) Tzvelev 1961 = **Tanacetum griffithii**

SPATHIPHYLLUM Schott 1832   *[Araceae]*
    wallisii Hort. ex Gardener's Chronicle 1875   EGF.2-**DGP-RD**

SPATHYEMA Rafinesque 1808   *[Araceae]*
    foetida (Linnaeus) Rafinesque 1808 (*Symplocarpus foetidus*)   EGF.2-PGP

SPEIRANTHA Baker 1875   *[Convallariaceae (Liliaceae)]*
    convallarioides Baker 1875 (*S. gardenii*)   EGF.1-PGP
    gardenii Baillion 1894 = **S. convallarioides**

SPHACELE Bentham 1829 nom. cons.   *[Lamiaceae (Labiatae)]*
S   **caerulea** Hort. ex Gardener's Chronicle 1865

SPHAERALCEA A. Saint-Hilaire 1825   *[Malvaceae]*
S   **fendleri** A. Gray 1852   PGP
    munroana (Douglas) Spach 1834   PGP

SPIRAEA Linnaeus 1753   *[Rosaceae]*
    digitata Willldenow 1799 = **Filipendula palmata**
    filipendula Linnaeus 1753 = **Filipendula hexapetala**
    gigantea hort. = **Filipendula palmata**
    palmata Thunberg 1784 = **Filipendula purpurea**

SPIRANTHES Richard 1817 nom. cons.   *[Orchidaceae]*
    cernua (Linnaeus) Richard 1817   EGF.2
    sinensis (Persoon) Ames 1908   EGF.2
N‡   **spiralis** (Linnaeus) Chevallier 1828   EGF.2

SPIRODELA Schleiden 1839   *[Lemnaceae]*
N‡   **polyrhiza** (Linnaeus) Schleiden 1839 (*Lemna polyrhiza*)

SPODIOPOGON Trinius 1822   *[Poaceae (Gramineae)]*
    sibiricus Trinius 1822   EGF.2

SPRAGUEA Torrey 1854   *[Portulacaceae]*
    umbellata Torrey 1854 = **Calyptridium umbellatum**

SPREKELIA Heister 1748   *[Amaryllidaceae]*
    formosissima (Linnaeus) Herbert 1821   EGF.1-**DGP-RD**

STACHYS Linnaeus 1753   *[Lamiaceae (Labiatae)]*
H   **affinis** Bunge 1831 non Fresenius 1833 (*S.* 'Tubifera')
    betonica Bentham 1834 non Crantz 1769 = **S. officinalis**
L   **byzantina** K. Koch 1848 (*S. lanata* Jacquin, *S. olympica*)   **DGP**-RD
    'Cotton Boll' ('Sheila Macqueen')   PGP

'Primrose Heron'
'Sheila Macqueen' = **S. byzantina** 'Cotton Boll'
L   'Silver Carpet'   PGP-DGP-**RD**
'Variegata' nom. dub.
candida Bory & Chaubard
S   **citrina** Boissier & Heldreich
corsica Persoon 1806
S   **discolor** Bentham 1834 (*S. nivea*)
floribunda Montbret & Aucher ex Bentham 1836 = **S. pumila**
N‡   **germanica** Linnaeus 1753   PGP
grandiflora (Steven ex Willdenow) Bentham 1834 non Host 1831 = **S. macrantha**
lanata Jacquemonti 1751 non Crantz 1769 = **S. byzantina**
S   **lavandulifolia** Vahl 1790
macrantha (C. Koch) Stearn 1951 (*Betonica grandiflora, S. grandiflora, S.* 'Spicata')
                                                   PGP-**DGP-RD**
'Alba'
L   'Robusta'   PGP-**DGP**
'Rosea'   RD
'Superba' = **S. macrantha** 'Robusta'
monieri (Gouan) P.W. Ball
nivea Bentham 1848 = **S. discolor**
HN‡   **officinalis** (Linnaeus) Trevisan 1842 (*Betonica officinalis, S. betonica*)   PGP-RD
'Alba'   PGP
'Rosea'   PGP
olympica Briquet 1893 non C. Koch = **S. byzantina**
S   **pumila** Banks & Solander 1794 (*S. floribunda*)
saxicola Cosson & Balsana 1873
'Spicata' = **S. macrantha**
'Tubifera' = **S. affinis**

STATICE Linnaeus 1753 = **LIMONIUM** p.p. & **GONIOLIMON** p.p.

STENANTHIUM (A. Gray) Kunth 1843 nom. cons.   [*Melanthiaceae (Liliaceae)*]
    robustum S. Watson 1879   EGF.1-PGP

STERNBERGIA Waldstein & Kitaibel 1803   [*Amaryllidaceae*]

M - **MATHEW, B.**: *'A Review of the Genus Sternbergia'* The Plantsman Vol 5:1, 1-16 (1983)

candida Mathew & T. Baytop 1979   M-EFG.1-**BB-SB**
clusiana (Ker-Gawler) Sprengel 1825 (*S. macrantha*)   M-EFG.1-**BB**-SB-RD
colchiciflora Waldstein & Kitaibel 1803   M-EFG.1-**BB**-SB
fischeriana (Herbert) Ruprecht 1868   M-EFG.1-CA-**BB**-RD
N   **lutea** (Linnaeus) Ker-Gawler ex Sprengel 1825   M-EFG.1-CA-**BB**-SB-**DGP-RD**
    'Angustifolia'   SB-DGP
    ssp. *sicula* (Tineo ex Gussone) D. A. Webb 1978 = **S. sicula**
macrantha Gay ex Baker 1888 = **S. clusiana**
sicula Tineo ex Gussone 1844-5 (*S. lutea* ssp. *sicula*)   M-EFG.1-CA-**BB-SB**-RD

STIPA Linnaeus 1753   [*Poaceae (Gramineae)*]
    arundinacea (Hooker f.) Bentham 1881   PGP
      'Autumn Tints'   [G. Hutchins]
      'Gold Hue'   [G. Hutchins]
    barbata Desfontaines 1798 non Michaux 1803   RD
    calamagrostis (Linnaeus) Wahlenberg 1813 (*Achnatherum calamagrostris,*
                          Lasiagrostis calamagrostis)   EGF.2-PGP-**DGP-RD**
      'Algäu'
    capillaris Lamarck 1791 = **Muhlenbergia capillaris**
    capillata Linnaeus 1762   PGP

      'Brautschleier'
L   **gigantea** Link 1816   EGF.2-PGP-RD
      lagascae Roemer & Schultes 1817 non Gussone 1826
      pennata Linnaeus 1753   EGF.2-**PGP-DGP**-RD
      pulcherrima K. Koch 1848
      splendens Trinius 1821 (*Achnatherum splendens, Lasiagrostis splendens*)   EGF.2
      tenuifolia Steudel 1854
      ucrainica P. Smirnov 1926
      zaleskii Wilensky 1921

STOKESIA L'Heritier 1788   [*Asteraceae (Compositae)*]
      laevis (Hill) E. Greene 1893   PGP-**DGP-RD**
          'Alba'   PGP-DGP
          'Blue Cloud'
L   'Blue Star'   PGP-DGP-RD
          'Wyoming'

STRATIOTES Linnaeus 1753   [*Hydrocharitaceae*]
N‡L **aloides** Linnaeus 1753   EGF.1

STREPTOPUS Michaux 1803   [*Convallariaceae (Liliaceae)*]
      amplexifolius (Linnaeus) de Candolle 1805   EGF.1-PGP

STROBILANTHES Blume 1826   [*Acanthaceae*]
      atropurpureus Nees 1832   PGP
      violaceus Beddome 1868

STRUTHIOPTERIS Scopoli 1754 = **MATTEUCCIA**

STYLIDIUM Sweet ex Willdenow 1805 nom. cons.   [*Stylidiaceae*]
      graminifolium Sweet ex Willdenow 1805   CA

STYLOPHORUM Nuttall 1818   [*Papaveraceae*]
      diphyllum (Michaux) Nuttall 1818   PGP-**DGP**

SUCCISA Haller 1768   [*Dipsacaceae*]
N‡L **pratensis** Moench 1794 (*Scabiosa succisa*)
          'Nana' nom. dub.

SWERTIA Linnaeus 1753   [*Gentianaceae*]
      iberica Fischer & C. A. Meyer 1849
      kingii Hooker f. 1883
      longifolia Boissier 1844
      petiolata D. Don 1836   PGP

SYMPHYANDRA A. de Candolle 1830   [*Campanulaceae*]
      armena (Steven) A. de Candolle 1830
B   **hofmannii** Pantocsek 1881
      ossetica (Marshall von Bieberstein) A. de Candolle 1830 (*Campanula ossetica*)
      pendula (Marshall von Bieberstein) A. de Candolle 1830
      wanneri (Rochel) Heuffel   CA

SYMPHYTUM Linnaeus 1753   [*Boraginaceae*]
H   **caucasicum** Marshall von Bieberstein   PGP-**RD**
      grandiflorum hort. non de Candolle = **S. ibericum**
      'Hidcote Blue' (*S. ibericum* x *S. x uplandicum*)
      'Hidcote Pink'
      'Hidcote Variegated'
HNL **ibericum** Steven ex Marshall von Bieberstein 1819   RD
        'Goldsmith'   [E. Smith]

        'Jubilee'
        'Rosea' = **S. 'Hidcote Pink'**
        'Variegatum'   PGP
        'Wisley' nom. dub.
HN   **officinale** Linnaeus 1753   DGP
        ssp. **bohemicum** (F.W. Schmidt) Celak
        'Coccineum'
N   **orientale** Linnaeus 1753 (*S. tauricum*)   RD
        peregrinum hort. non Ledebour = **S. x uplandicum**
        'Rubrum' (*S. ibericum* x *S. officinale* 'Coccineum')   PGP-**RD**
        tauricum Willdenow 1799 = **S. orientale**
N‡   **tuberosum** Linnaeus 1753
HN‡L **x uplandicum** Nyman 1854 (*S. peregrinum* hort.) (*S. asperum* x *S. officinale*)
                                         PGP-RD
L   **'Variegatum'**   PGP-RD

SYMPLOCARPUS Salisbury ex Nuttall 1818 nom. cons.   [*Araceae*]
      foetidus (Linnaeus) Salisbury ex Nuttall 1818 = **Spathyema foetida**

SYNNOTIA Sweet 1826   [*Iridaceae*]
      variegata Sweet 1826   EGF.1
           var. **meterlerkampiae** (L. Bolus) L. Bolus

SYNTHYRIS Bentham 1846   [*Scrophulariaceae*]
      reniformis (Douglas) Bentham 1846   CA
      reniformis hort. non (Douglas) Bentham 1846 = **S. stellata**
      stellata Pennell 1933 (*S. reniformis* hort.)   CA

TACCA Forster & Forster f. 1776 nom. cons.   [*Taccaceae*]
      chantrieri Andre 1901   EGF.1

TALINUM Adanson 1753 nom. cons.   [*Portulacaceae*]
      okanoganense English 1934   CA
S   **spinescens** Torrey 1874   CA

TANACETUM Linnaeus 1753   [*Asteraceae (Compositae)*]
   abrotanifolium (Linnaeus) Druce 1914 (*Chrysanthemum millefoliatum, T.*
                                           millefoliatum)
   argenteum (Lamarck) Willdenow 1789 (*Achillea argentea, Chrysanthemum argenteum*)
H **balsamita** Linnaeus 1753 (*Balsamita major, B. vulgaris, Chrysanthemum balsamita*)
   bipinnatum (Linnaeus) Schultz-Bip 1844
HN **cinerariifolium** (Trevisan) Schultz-Bip 1844 (*Chrysanthemum cinerariifolium,*
                                Pyrethrum cinerariifolium)
HN **coccineum** (Willdenow) Grierson 1974 (*Chrysanthemum coccineum, C. roseum,*
                           Pyrethrum roseum)   DGP

    HYBRID CULTIVARS (*"GARDEN PYRETHRUMS"*)

        'Abendröte'
        'Alfred'
        'Amethyst'
        'Avalanche'   RD
        'Bees' Pink Delight'
        'Brenda'   PGP-**DGP-RD**
        'Bressingham Red'   RD
        'Duro'
L   **'Eileen May Robinson'**   PGP-**DGP-RD**
        'Evenglow'   PGP-RD
        'Figaro'
        'Galway'

'Gartenschatz'
'James Kelway'
'J. N. Twerdy'
'King Size'   RD
'Marjorie Robinson'
'Mont Blanc'
'Pfingstgruss'   RD
'Queen Mary'
'Red King'
'Regent'
'Robinson's Pink'
'Robinson's Red'
'Salmon Beauty'
'Sam Robinson'
'Scarlet Glow'
'Silver Challenger'   RD
'Strahlenkrone'

corymbosum (Linnaeus) Schultz-Bip 1844 (*Chrysanthemum corymbosum*)
                                                              PGP-RD
   ssp. **clusii** (Fischer ex Reichenbach) Heywood 1976 (*Chrysanthemum clusii*)
*dahurica (*Chrysanthemum dahuricum*)
densum (Labilliardiere) Schultz-Bip 1844 (*Chrysanthemum densum*)
   ssp. **amani** Heywood 1952   DGP
griffithii (Clarke) Muradyan 1970 (*Spathipappus griffithii*)
haradjanii (Reichenbach f.) Grierson 1975 (*Chrysanthemum haradjanii*) **DGP-RD**
haradjanii hort, non (Reichenbach f.) Grierson = **T. densum**
herderi Regel & Schmalhausen 1877   PGP
macrophyllum (Waldstein & Kitaibel) Schultz-Bip 1844 (*Chrysanthemum*
                               macrophyllum)   PGP
millefoliatum Fischer & C.A.Meyer 1838 = **T. abrotanifolium**
pallidum (Miller) Maire 1929 = **Leucanthemopsis pallida**
HN **parthenium** (Linnaeus) Schultz-Bip 1844 (*Chrysanthemum parthenium, Pyrethrum*
                                 parthenium)   PGP-DGP
   'Aureum'   PGP-RD
   'Flore Pleno'   PGP
   'Golden Ball'   **DGP**-RD
   'Snowball'
   'White Bonnet'   PGP-**DGP**-RD
   'White Stars'   DGP
praeteritum (Horwood) Heywood 1952
   ssp. **massicyticum** Heywood 1952
ptarmiciflorum (Webb & Berthelot) Schultz-Bip 1844 (*Pyrethrum ptarmiciflorum*)
HN‡ **vulgare** Linnaeus 1753 (*Chrysanthemum tanacetum*)
   var. **crispum** de Candolle 1837

TANAKAEA Franchet & Savatier 1875   [*Saxifragaceae*]
   radicans Franchet & Savatier 1875   CA

TAPEINANTHUS Herbert 1837 nom. rejic. = **NARCISSUS**   [*Amaryllidaceae*]

TARAXACUM Weber in Wiggers 1780 nom. cons.   [*Asteraceae (Compositae)*]
HN‡ **officinale** Weber 1780

TECOPHILAEA Bertero ex Colla 1836   [*Amaryllidaceae*]
   cyanocrocus Leybold 1862   EGF.1-CA-**BB**-**SB**-**DGP**-RD
   'Leichtlinii'   EGF.1-CA-**BB**-SB-DGP-RD
   'Violacea'   EGF.1-CA-SB

TELEKA Baumgarten 1816   [*Asteraceae (Compositae)*]
    speciosissima (Linnaeus) Lessing 1832 (*Buphthalmum speciosissimum*)   PGP
NL   **speciosa** (Schreber) Baumgarten 1816 (*Buphthalmum speciosum*)   PGP

TELESONIX Rafinesque 1837   [*Saxifragaceae*]
    jamesii (Torrey) Rafinesque 1837 (*Boykinia jamesii*)   **CA-DGP**
    var. **heucheriformis** (Rydberg) Bacigalupi 1947

TELLIMA R. Brown 1823   [*Saxifragaceae*]
NL   **grandiflora** (Pursh) Douglas ex Lindley 1828   PGP-**RD**
    '**Alba**'
L   '**Purpurea**' ('Rubra')   PGP-RD
    '**Purpurteppich**'   [H. Klose 1985]
    Scented Form

TEUCRIUM Linnaeus 1753   [*Lamiaceae (Labiatae)*]
    '**Ackermanii**'
S   **arduini** Linnaeus 1767
S   **aroanium** Orphanides 1859   RD
SHN‡   **chamaedrys** Linnaeus 1753   PGP-CA-**RD**
    '**Nanum**' nom. dub.
    '**Variegatum**'
    cinereum Boissier 1838 = **T. rotundifolium**
S   **compactum** Clemente ex Lagasca 1816
S   **creticum** Linnaeus 1753 (*T. rosmarinifolium*)   RD
S   **flavum** Linnaeus 1753
    hircanicum Linnaeus 1759   PGP
S   **x lucidrys** Boom 1957 (*T. chamaedrys* x *T. lucidum*)
S   **marum** Linnaeus 1753
S   **musimonum** Humbert ex Maire 1924
S   **polium** Linnaeus 1753   CA
    ssp. **aureum** (Schreber) Arcangeli 1882
    pyrenaicum Linnaeus 1753   CA-RD
    rosmarinifolium Lamarck 1788 = **T. creticum**
S   **rotundifolium** Schreber 1773 (*T. cinereum*)
N‡   **scordium** Linnaeus 1753
    '**Crispum**'
    '**Crispum Marginatum**'
SHN‡   **scorodonia** Linnaeus 1753
S   **subspinosum** Pourret ex Willdenow 1809   CA
    '**Roseum**'

THALICTRUM Linnaeus 1753   [*Ranunculaceae*]
    adiantifolium hort. = **T. minus 'Adiantifolium'**
N‡   **alpinum** Linnaeus 1753   CA
L   **aquilegifolium** Linnaeus 1753   PGP-**DGP-RD**
    '**Album**'   PGP-DGP-RD
    '**Thundercloud**'   RD
    chelidonii de Candolle 1824   PGP
    coreanum Leveille 1902
L   **delavayi** Franchet 1886 (*T. dipterocarpum* hort.)   PGP-DGP-**RD**
    '**Album**'   [1920]   PGP-RD
L   '**Hewitt's Double**'   PGP-**DGP-RD**
    diffusiflorum Marquand & Airy Shaw   PGP
    dipterocarpum hort. non Franchet 1866 = **T. delavayi**
N‡   **flavum** Linnaeus 1753   PGP-RD
L   ssp. **glaucum** (Desfontaines) Batt. (*T. speciosissimum*)   PGP-**RD**
    foetidum Linnaeus 1753   PGP
    isopyroides C. A. Meyer 1830

kiusianum Nakai 1928   CA-RD
koreanum hort. = **T. coreanum**
N‡   **minus** Linnaeus 1753   PGP
        'Adiantifolium'   RD
      orientale Boissier 1841   CA
      rochebrunianum Franchet & Savatier 1875   PGP-DGP-RD
        speciosissimum hort. = **T. flavum** ssp. **glaucum**

THELYPTERIS Schmidel 1763 nom. cons.   [*Thelypteridaceae*]
      dryopteris (Linnaeus) Slosson 1917 = **Gymnocarpium dryopteris**
      limbosperma (Bellardi ex Allioni) H. P. Fuchs 1959 = **Oreopteris limbosperma**
N   **palustris** Schott 1834   EGF.1-PGP
      phegopteris (Linnaeus) Slosson 1918 = **Phegopteris connectilis**
      robertiana (Hoffmann) Slosson 1917 = **Gymnocarpium robertianum**

THEMEDA Forsskal 1775   [*Poaceae (Gramineae)*]
      japonica (Willdenow) C. Tanaka 1925 = **T. triandra** var. **japonica**
      triandra Forsskal 1775
          var. **japonica** (Willdenow) Makino 1912 (*T. japonica*)

THERMOPSIS R. Brown 1811   [*Fabaceae (Leguminosae)*]
      caroliniana M. A. Curtis 1843
      fabacea (Pallas) de Candolle 1825 = **T. lupinoides**
      lanceolata R. Brown ex Aiton 1811   PGP-RD
      lupinoides (Linnaeus) Link (*T. fabacea*)
      montana Nuttall 1840   PGP-**RD**

THLASPI Linnaeus 1753   [*Brassicaceae (Cruciferae)*]
      bellidifolium Grisebach 1845 non Tineo
      bulbosum Sprunnier ex Boissier 1844
      rotundifolium (Linnaeus) Gaudin 1829   CA-**DGP**
      stylosum (Tenore) Mutel 1834

THYMUS Linnaeus 1753   [*Lamiaceae (Labiatae)*]
      azoricus Loddiges 1830 = **T. cilicicus**
S   **caespititius** Brotero 1804 (*T. micans*)   CA
        'Aureus'
S   **carnosus** Boissier 1841 (*T. erectus, T. nitidus* hort.)   CA-RD
        'Argenteus'
      chamaedrys Fries 1824 = **T. pulegioides**
      ciliatus Lamarck 1779
          *****pubescens**
      cilicicus Boissier & Balansa 1859 (*T. azoricus*)   CA-RD
SH   **x citriodorus** (Persoon) Schreber in Schweigger & Korte 1811 (*T. pulegioides* x *T.
                                                      vulgaris*)   RD
            'Annot'
            'Archer's Gold'
            'Argenteus'
            'Aureus'   RD
            'Bertram Anderson' ('Anderson's Gold', 'E. B. Anderson')   [E.B. Anderson
                                                                        via J. Elliott]
            'Compactus'
            'Fragrantissimus'
            'Golden Dwarf'
            'Golden King'
            'Golden Lemon'
            'Golden Queen'
            'Nyewoods'
            'Silver King'
            'Silver Posie' = **T. x citriodorus 'Variegatus'**

	'Silver Queen'	RD
	'Variegatus' ('Silver Posie')	
	coccineus hort. = **T. serpyllum 'Coccineus'**	
S	**comosus** Heuffel ex Grisebach & Schenk 1852	CA
S	**doerfleri** Ronniger 1924 (*T. hirsutus* var. *doerfleri*)	RD
	'Bressingham Pink' [A. Bloom]	
	drucei Ronniger 1924 = **T. praecox** ssp. **arcticus**	
	erectus hort. = **T. vulgaris 'Erectus'**	
	***epiroticus**	
	ericifolius Roth 1800 = **Micromeria varia**	
	fragrans hort. = **T. x citriodorus**	
	fragrantissimus hort. = **T. x citriodorus 'Fragrantissimus'**	
SH	**herba-barona** Loiseleur 1807	CA-RD
	hirsutus Marshall von Bieberstein 1808	
	var. *doerfleri* (Ronniger) Ronniger = **T. doerfleri**	
	'Hispanicus' hort. non Poiret	
	lanuginosus hort. non Miller = **T. pseudolanuginosus**	
S	**leucotrichus** Halascy 1902	
S	**mastichina** Linnaeus 1763	
S	**membranaceus** Boissier 1838	CA-RD
	micans Lowe 1831 = **T. caespitosus**	
	neiceffii Degen & Urumoff 1922	
	nitidus Gussone 1844 = **T. richardii** ssp. **nitidus**	
	nitidus hort. non Gussone 1844 = **T. carnosus**	
	odoratissimus Marshall von Bieberstein 1819 = **T. pallisianus**	
	pallisianus H. Braun 1892 (*T. odoratissimus*)	
	pannonicus Allioni 1773	
SN	**praecox** Opiz 1824	
L	ssp. **arcticus** (E. Durand) Jalas 1970 (*T. drucei*)	RD
	ssp. **arcticus 'Albus'**	RD
	ssp. **arcticus 'Minus'**	
	ssp. **polytrichus** (A. Kerner ex Borbas) Jalas 1970	
S	**pseudolanuginosus** Ronniger 1926	
	'Hall's Variety'	
SN‡	**pulegioides** Linnaeus 1753 (*T. chamaedrys*)	
S	**richardii** Persoon 1806	
	ssp. **nitidus** (Gussone) Jalas 1971 (*T. nitidus*)	CA
	ssp. **nitidus 'Albus'**	
	ssp. **nitidus 'Peter Davis'**	
	rotundifolius Schur 1850	
	'Purpurteppich'	
HN‡	**serpyllum** Linnaeus 1753	DGP
	'Albus'	
	'Annie Hall'	
	'Aureus'	
	'Carol Ann'	
	'Citriodorus'	
	'Coccineus'	DGP-RD
	'Coccineus Majus'	
	'Coccineus Minor'	
	'Dartmoor' [Southcombe Garden Nursery]	
	'East Lodge'	
	'Elfin' [W. Archer]	
	'Fermanagh'	
	'Flossy'	
	'Goldstream'	
	'Lanuginosus' = **T. pseudolanuginosus**	
	'Little Heath'	
	'Lemon Curd'	
	'Minimus'	

'Minor' ('Minus')
'Nosegay'
'Pink Chintz'
'Pinkushion'   DGP
'Pink Ripple'
'Pygmaeus'
'Rainbow Falls'
'Roseus'
'Russettings'
'September'
'Snowdrift'
'Vey'
'Waterperry'
'Winter Beauty'

S   **villosus** Linnaeus 1753
SH   **vulgaris** Linnaeus 1753   CA
'Aureus'
S   **zygis** Linnaeus 1753

HYBRID CULTIVARS

'Desboro'
'Doone Valley'   [W. Archer]
'Neigrand'
'Neif'
'Onyx'
'Porlock'   [N. Hadden]
'Southcombe Spreader'   [Southcombe Garden Nursery]
'Valerie Finnis'
'Widecombe'   [Southcombe Garden Nursery]
'Wintergold'
'Westmoor'

TIARELLA Linnaeus 1753   [*Saxifragaceae*]
L   **cordifolia** Linnaeus 1753   RD
ssp. **collina** Wherry 1940   **DGP-RD**
ssp. **colina** 'Rosalie'
'Moorgrun'
'Purpurea'
polyphylla D. Don 1825   **DGP**-RD
trifoliata Linnaeus 1753   RD
wherryi Lakela 1937   RD
wherryi hort. non Lakela = **T. cordifolia** ssp. **collina**

TIGRIDIA Jussieu 1789   [*Iridaceae*]
dugesii S. Watson 1885
durangense Molseed ex Cruden 1968
pavonia (Linnaeus f.) de Candolle 1802 (*T. pringlei*)   EGF.1-PGP-**DGP**-RD
pringlei S. Watson 1888 = **T. pavonia**

TILLAEA Linnaeus 1753   [*Crassulaceae*]
recurva Hooker f. 1856 = **Crassula helmsii**

TOLMIEA Torrey & A. Gray 1840 nom. cons.   [*Saxifragaceae*]
N   **menziesii** Torrey & A. Gray 1840   RD
'Maculata' = **T. menziesii 'Taff's Gold'**
'Taff's Gold' ('Maculata', 'Variegata')
'Variegata' = **T. menziesii 'Taff's Gold'**

TOLPIS Adanson 1763   *[Asteraceae (Compositae)]*
    staticifolia (Allioni) Schultes-Bip 1861

TOVARA Adanson 1763 nom. rejic. = **PERSICARIA**   *[Polygonaceae]*

TOWNSENDIA Hooker 1853   *[Asteraceae (Compositae)]*
    eximia A. Gray 1853
    excapa (Richard) Porter 1894 (*T. wilcoxiana* Wood)   CA
    florifer (Hooker) A. Gray 1881
    formosa Greene 1906
    hookeri Beaman 1857
    parryi D. Eaton 1874
    rothrockii A. Gray ex Rothrock 1878 (*T. wilcoxiana* hort.)
    wilcoxiana Wood 1875 = **T. excapa**
    wilcoxiana hort., non Wood = **T. rothrockii**

TRACHELIUM Linnaeus 1753   *[Campanulaceae]*
    asperuloides Boissier & Orphanides 1856   **CA**
S   **caeruleum** Linnaeus 1753
    jacquinii (Sieber) Boissier 1875
        ssp. **rumelianum** (Hampe) Tutin 1976

TRACHYSTEMON D. Don 1832   *[Boraginaceae]*
N   **orientalis** (Linnaeus) G. Don f. 1837   PGP

TRADESCANTIA Linnaeus 1753   *[Commelinaceae]*
L   **x andersoniana** W. Ludwig & Rohweder 1954 (*T. virginiana* x *T. species*)
                                EGF.2-PGP-**DGP**-RD
       'Alba'
       'Alba Major' nom. dub.
       'Atroviolacea'
       'Bärbel'   [K. Foerster]
       'Blue Stone'   [Prichard]   RD
       'Brevicaulis' = **T. brevicaulis**
       'Caerulea'
       'Caerulea Plena'   RD
       'Carmine Glow' = **T. x andersoniana 'Karminglut'**
       'Eva'   [K. Foerster]
       'Flore Pleno'
       'Gisela'
       'Innocence'
L   **'Iris Prichard'**   DGP
L   **'Isis'**   **DGP-RD**
       'J. C. Weguelin'   [Prichard]   PGP-RD
       'Karminglut' ('Carmine Glow')   [K. Foerster]
       'Karminenspiegel'
       'Leonora'
       'Lilac Time'
       'Osprey'   PGP-DGP-RD
       'Pauline'
       'Purewell Giant'   [Prichard]   PGP
       'Purple Dome'   PGP-RD
       'Purple Glow'
       'Rosi'   [K. Foerster]
       'Rubra'
       'Taplow Crimson'
       'Valour'
       'Zwanenburg Blue'
    bracteata Small 1898
       'Alba'

brevicaulis Rafinesque 1832
virginiana Linnaeus 1753   EGF.2
x virginiana hort. non Linnaeus = **T. x andersoniana**

TRAGOPOGON Linnaeus 1753   [*Asteraceae (Compositae)*]
N‡   **pratensis** Linnaeus 1753

TRAPA Linnaeus 1753   [*Trapaceae*]
A   **natans** Linnaeus 1753

TRICHOPETALUM Lindley 1832   [*Anthericaceae (Liliaceae)*]
    plumosum (Ruiz & Pavon) Macbride 1918 (*Anthericum plumosum, Bottionea plumosa*)

TRICYRTIS Wallich 1826 nom. cons.   [*Convallariaceae (Liliaceae)*]

M - MATHEW, B., *'A Review of the Genus Tricyrtis'* The Plantsman: 6: 4 193-224

affinis Makino 1903   M-EFG.1
bakeri Koidzumi 1924 = **T. latifolia**
flava Maximowicz 1867   M-EFG.1
formosana Baker 1879 (*T. stolonifera*)   M-PGP-**DGP-RD**
    'Variegata'
hirta (Thunberg) Hooker 1863   M-EFG.1-PGP-RD
    'Alba'   M-PGP-RD
    'Nana' nom. dub.
    'Rubra'
    'Variegata'
    'White Towers'
ishiiana (Kitagawa & T. Koyama) Ohwi 1965   **M**
latifolia Maximowicz 1867 (*T. bakeri*)   M-EFG.1-PGP-RD
macrantha Maximowicz 1888   M-EFG.1
macranthopsis Masamune 1935   M-EFG.1-PGP
macropoda Miquel 1867   M-EFG.1-PGP
    'Striata'
maculata (D. Don) MacBride 1918 (*T. pilosa*)   M-EFG.1
nana Yatabe 1893   M-EFG.1
    'Yakushimensis'   **M**
ohsumiensis Masamume 1930   M-EFG.1
perfoliata Masamune 1935   M-EFG.1
pilosa Wallich 1826 = **T. maculata**
stolonifera Matsumura 1887 = **T. formosana**

TRIFOLIUM Linnaeus 1753   [*Fabaceae (Leguminosae)*]
    alpinum Linnaeus 1753
AN‡   **incarnatum** Linnaeus 1753
HN‡   **pratense** Linnaeus 1753
N‡   **repens** Linnaeus 1753
        'Aureum'
        'Pentaphyllum' = **T. repens 'Quinquefolium'**
        'Purpurascens'
        'Purpurascens Quadrifolium' = **T. repens 'Purpurascens'**
        'Quinquefolium'
        'Susan Smith'

TRILLIUM Linnaeus 1753   [*Trilliaceae (Liliaceae)*]
    albidum J. D. Freeman 1975   EGF.1
    amabile Miyabe & Tatewaki 1938   EGF.1
    angustipetalum (Torrey) J. D. Freeman 1975   EGF.1
    apetalon Makino 1910 = **T. smallii**
    californicum Kellogg 1860 = **T. ovatum**

catesbaei Elliott 1821 (*T. nervosum, T. stylosum*)   EGF.1-PGP-SB
cernuum Linnaeus 1753   EGF.1-PGP-SB
chloropetalum (Torrey) Howell 1902   EGF.1-PGP-SB-**DGP**
   'Aureum'
   var. **giganteum** (Hooker & Arnott) Munz 1958   EGF.1-SB
cuneatum Rafinesque 1840 (*T. sessile* hort.)   EGF.1-SB
   Bronze Form
decumbens Harbison 1902   EGF.1-SB
discolor Wray ex Hooker 1834   EGF.1
erectum Linnaeus 1753   EGF.1-PGP-**BB**-SB-**RD**
   var. **album** (Michaux) Pursh 1814   EGF.1-PGP-**BB**
   f. **luteum** Louis-Marie 1940   EGF.1
   'Roseum'
erythrocarpum Michaux 1803 = **T. undulatum**
flexipes Rafinesque 1840   EGF.1-SB
   f. **walpolei** (Farwell) Fernald 1944
govanianum Wallich ex Royle 1836   EGF.1-SB
L   **grandiflorum** (Michaux) Salisbury 1805   EGF.1-PGP-**BB**-SB-**DGP**-**RD**
   'Flore Pleno'   EGF.1-PGP
   'Roseum'   EGF.1-**PGP**
   'Rubrum'
hibbersonii Wiley nom. illegit. = **T. ovatum** f. **hibbersonii**
kamschaticum Ledebour 1852   EGF.1-PGP-SB
kurabayashii J. D. Freeman 1975
lancifolium Rafinesque 1840
luteum (Muhlenberg) Harbison 1901 (*T. viride* var. *luteum*)   EGF.1-PGP-**BB**-SB
nervosum Elliott 1821 = **T. catesbaei**
nivale Riddell 1835   EGF.1-CA-**BB**-SB
ovatum Pursh 1814 (*T. californicum*)   EGF.1-PGP-**BB**-**SB**-**RD**
   var. **hibbersonii** Taylor & Szczawinski 1975   EGF.1-SB
petiolatum Pursh 1814   EGF.1
pusillum Michaux 1803
   var. **ozarkanum** (Palmer & Steyermark) Steyermark 1960
   var. **virginianum** Fernald 1943
recurvatum Beck 1826   EGF.1-SB
rivale S. Watson 1885   EGF.1-**SB**
rugelii Rendle 1901
sessile Linnaeus 1753   EGF.1-PGP-**BB**-SB-**DGP**-**RD**
   Eastern Form
   var. *luteum* Muhlenberg 1813 = **T. luteum**
sessile hort. non Linnaeus = **T. cuneatum**
smallii Maximowicz 1883 (*T. apetalon*)   EGF.1-SB
stylosum Nuttall 1818 = **T. catesbaei**
tschonoskii Maximowicz 1883   EGF.1-**BB**
undulatum Willdenow 1801 (*T. erythrocarpum*)   EGF.1-PGP-CA-**BB**-SB-RD
vaseyi Harbison 1901   EGF.1-SB
viride Beck 1826   EGF.1
   var. *luteum* (Muhlenberg) Gleason 1952 = **T. luteum**

TRIOSTEUM Linnaeus 1753   [*Caprifoliaceae*]
  aurantiacum Bicknell 1901

TRIPLEUROSPERMUM Schultz-Bip 1844   [*Asteraceae (Compositae)*]
  caucasicum (Willdenow) Hayek 1924 (*Matricaria caucasica*)

TRITELEIA Douglas ex Lindley 1830   [*Alliaceae (Liliaceae)*]
  ixioides (Aiton) Greene 1886 (*Brodiaea ixioides, Ipheion ixioides*)   EGF.1-**BB**-**SB**
  laxa Bentham 1835 (*Brodiaea laxa, Ipheion laxa*)   EGF.1-**BB**-SB-**DGP**
  peduncularis Lindley 1835 (*Brodiaea peduncularis*)   EGF.1-SB
  sellowiana Kunth 1843 = **Ipheion sellowianum**

x tubergenii Lenz 1970 (*T. laxa* x *T. peduncularis*)   EGF.1-SB
    '**Konigin Fabiola**'   ® ('Queen Fabiola')   [A. Twaalfhoven 1956]   SB

TRITOMA Ker-Gawler 1814 = **KNIPHOFIA** Moench 1794

TRITONIA Ker-Gawler 1802   [*Iridaceae*]
    crocata (Linnaeus) Ker-Gawler 1802   EGF.1-**RD**
    disticha Baker 1892
        ssp. **rubrolucens** (R. C. Forster) de Vos 1983 (*T. rosea*)   EGF.1-**PGP**-RD
    rosea Klatt 1863 = **T. disticha** ssp. **rubrolucens**
    pottsii (Baker) Baker 1883 = **Crocosmia pottsii**
    securigera (Aiton) Ker-Gawler 1883

TROLLIUS Linnaeus 1753   [*Ranunculaceae*]
    acaulis Lindley 1842
N **asiaticus** Linnaeus 1753   PGP-RD
    chinensis Bunge 1835 (*T. ledebourii* hort.)   PGP-DGP-RD
        '**Golden Queen**'   PGP-**DGP**-RD
        '**Imperial Orange**'   PGP-RD
    x cultorum Bergman 1924 (*T. asiaticus* x *T. chinensis* x *T. europaeus*)   PGP
        '**Alabaster**'   [G. Arends]   PGP-RD
        '**Baudirecktor Linne**'
        '**Bressingham Hybrids**'   [A. Bloom]
        '**Byrne's Giant**'   PGP
        '**Canary Bird**'   PGP-RD
        '**Commander-in-Chief**'
L   '**Earliest of All**'   [van Veen]   PGP-DGP-RD
        '**Empire Day**'
        '**Etna**'
        '**Feuertroll**' ('Fire Globe')
        'Fire Globe' = **T. x cultorum 'Feuertroll'**
        '**Frülingsbote**' ('Spring Beauty')
        '**Fuldmane**'
        '**Gold Cup**'
        '**Golden Monarch**'
L   '**Goldquelle**'   **DGP**
        '**Goliath**'
        '**Golden Wonder**'   RD
        '**Helios**'
        '**Höhes Licht**'
        'Ledebourii' = **T. chinensis**
        '**Lemon Queen**'   [Schoot]
        '**Maigold**'   [zur Linden]
        '**Meteor**'   [Lubbe]
        '**Miss Mary Russell**'   [Russell]
        '**Orange Globe**' ('Orangekugel')
        '**Orange Princess**'   PGP-**DGP**-RD
        '**Prichard's Giant**'   [Prichard]   PGP-RD
        '**Salamander**'   RD
        '**Yellow Beauty**'
N‡L **europaeus** Linnaeus 1753   PGP-DGP
        '**Superbus**'   PGP-**DGP**
    ledebourii hort. non Reichenbech 1825 = **T. chinensis**
    patulus Salisbury 1807 = **T. ranunculinus**
    pumilus D. Don 1825   PGP-**RD**
        '**Albus**'
        '**Wargrave**'
        var. *yunnanensis* Franchet = **T. yunnanensis**
    ranunculinus (Smith) Stearn 1941 (*T. patulus*)   PGP
    stenopetalus (Regel) Egor & Siplivinsky 1970   PGP
    yunnanensis (Franchet) Ulbrich 1922   **PGP**

TROPAEOLUM Linnaeus 1753   [*Tropaeolaceae*]
L   **polyphyllum** Cavanilles 1798   PGP-**BB**-DGP-RD
L   **speciosum** Poeppig & Endlichter   PGP-**BB**-DGP-RD
     tricolor Sweet 1829   DGP-RD
     tuberosum Ruiz & Pavon 1802   PGP-**BB**-DGP-RD
     'Ken Aslet'   RD

TROXIMON Nuttall 1813   [*Asteraceae (Compositae)*]
     cuspidatum Pursh 1816 = **Agoseris cuspidata**
     glaucum Pursh 1814 = **Agoseris glauca**

TUBERARIA (Dunal) Spach 1836   [*Cistaceae*]
S   **globularifolia** (Persoon) Willkomen 1859 (*Helianthemum globularifolium*)
S   **lignosa** (Sweet) Sampaio 1922 (*Helianthemum tubararia*)

TULBAGHIA Linnaeus 1771 non. cons.   [*Alliaceae (Liliaceae)*]
     alliacea Linnaeus f. 1781   EGF.1
     capensis Linnaeus 1771 (*T. pulchella* Ave-Lallemant)   EGF.1
     cepacea Linnaeus f. 1781
     fragrans Verdoorn 1931 (*T. pulchella* Barnes)   EGF.1
     pulchella Ave-Lallemant 1844 = **T. capensis**
     pulchella Barnes 1930 = **T. fragrans**
     violacea Harvey 1837   EGF.1-PGP
          'Maritima'
          'Pallida'

TULIPA Linnaeus 1753   [*Liliaceae*]
     acuminata Hornemann   EGF.1-SB-RD
     aitchisonii A. D. Hall = **T. clusiana**
          ssp. *cashmiriana* A. D. Hall = **T. clusiana** var. **chrysantha**
     albertii Regel   EGF.1-SB
     aleppensis Boissier ex Regel 1873   EGF.1-SB
     altaica Pallas ex Sprengel   EGF.1-SB
     armena Boissier 1859   EGF.1-**BB**-SB
          var. **lycica** (Baker) Marais 1980   SB
     aucheriana Baker   EGF.1-CA-**BB**-SB
     aucheriana hort. non Baker = **T. humilis** (form)
     australis (*T. sylvestris* ssp. *australis*)   EGF.1-CA-**BB**-SB-DGP-RD
     bakeri A. D. Hall = **T. saxatilis**
     batalinii Baker (*T. linifolia* var. *batalinii*)   EFG.1-CA-**BB**-SB-DGP-RD
          'Apricot Jewel' ®   [G H Hageman & Sons 1961]   EGF.1-SB
          'Bright Gem' ®   [Jan Roes 1952]   EGF.1-SB
          'Bronze Charm' ®   [van Tubergen Ltd 1952]   EGF.1-SB
          'Yellow Jewel' ®   [G H Hageman & Sons 1961]
     biflora Pallas 1776 (*T. polychroma*)   EGF.1-CA-**BB**-SB-RD
          'Major'
     bifloriformis Vvedensky   **BB**-SB
     butkovii Z. Botschantzeva 1961   EGF.1-SB
     carinata Vvedensky   EGF.1-SB
     celsiana de Candolle   EGF.1-CA-SB
     chrysantha hort. = **T. clusiana** var. **chrysantha**
     clusiana de Candolle 1802   EGF.1-CA-**BB**-SB-RD
          var. **chrysantha** (A. D. Hall) Sealy (*T. chrysantha* hort.)   EGF.1-CA-**SB**-**DGP**-RD
          var. **chrysantha 'Tubergen's Gem'** ®   [van Tubergen 1969]
          'Cynthia' ®   [van Tubergen Ltd 1959]
          'Cashmiriana' nom. dub.
          var. **stellata** (Hooker) Regel (*T. stellata*)   EGF.1-CA-SB-DGP-RD
     cretica Boissier & Heldreich 1853   EGF.1-**BB**-SB
     dasystemon (Regel) Regel 1880   EGF.1-CA-**BB**-SB
     dasystemon hort. non (Regel) Regel = **T. tarda**

didieri Jordan = **T. gesneriana**
doerfleri Gandoger = **T. orphanidea**
dubia Vvedensky EGF.1-**BB**-SB
edulis (Miquel) Baker EGF.1-**BB**
eichleri Regel EGF.1-**BB**-SB-**DGP**-RD
ferganica Vvedensky EGF.1-**BB**-SB
fosteriana Irving 1906 EGF.1-CA-**BB**-SB-DGP-RD
fulgens Baker EGF.1-SB
galatica hort. non Freyn SB
gesneriana Linnaeus 1753 (*T. didieri*) EGF.1-SB
goulimyi Sealy & Turrill EGF.1-SB
greigii Regel EGF.1-CA-SB-**DGP**-RD
    'Aurea' ®
grengiolensis Thommsen EGF.1-SB
hageri Heldreich 1877 EGF.1-CA-**BB**-SB
    'Splendens' ®   [van Tubergen Ltd 1945]
heterophylla (Regel) Baker EGF.1-**BB**-SB
hissarica Popov & Vvedensky SB
humilis Herbert 1844 EGF.1-CA-**BB**-**SB**
    *var. **pulchella** EGF.1-SB-DGP-RD
    'Eastern Star' ®   [P Visser Czn 1975]
    'Magenta Queen' ®   [W Kooiman 1975]
    'Odalisque' ®   [P Visser Czn 1976]
    'Persian Pearl' ®   [P Visser Czn 1975]
    'Violacea' Black Base Form EGF.1
    'Violacea Pallida' EGF.1-CA
    'Violacea' Yellow Base Form
ingens T. Hoog 1902 EGF.1-CA-SB
julia C. Koch 1849 EGF.1-**BB**-SB
kaufmanniana Regel EGF.1-**CA**-**BB**-SB-**DGP**-RD
kolpakowskiana Regel 1877 EGF.1-CA-**BB**-SB-**DGP**
lanata Regel EGF.1
linifolia Regel EGF.1-CA-**BB**-SB-**DGP**-RD
    var. *batalinii* hort. = **T. batalinii**
    var. *maximowiczii* hort. = **T. maximowiczii**
marjolettii Perrier & Songeon
mauritiana Jordan EGF.1-SB-RD
    'Cindy' ®   [P Visser Czn] EGF.1-SB
maximowiczii Regel(*T. linifolia* var. *maximowiczii*) EGF.1-**BB**-SB
montana Lindley (*T. wilsoniana*) EGF.1-CA-**SB**-RD
neustrueviae Pobedimova 1949 SB
orphanidea Boissier ex Heldreich 1862 (*T. doerfleri, T. whittallii*) EGF.1-CA-**BB**-SB-**DGP**
    'Flava'
ostrowskiana Regel 1884 EGF.1-CA-**BB**-SB
persica hort. = **T. sylvestris** ssp. **australis**
planifolia Jordan
platystigma Jordan SB
polychroma Stapf = **T. biflora**
praecox Tenore 1811 EGF.1-CA-SB-**DGP**-RD
praestans T. Hoog 1903 EGF.1-CA-**BB**-SB-**DGP**-RD
    'Fusilier' ®   [Jac B Roozen] EGF.1-**BB**-RD
    'Van Tubergen's Variety' ®   [T. Hoog] EGF.1-**BB**-RD
    'Unicum' ®   [C A Verdegaal 1975]
pulchella (Fenzl ex Regel) Baker 1974 = **T. humilis** var. **pulchella**
    'Alba Coerulea Oculata' = **T. humilis**
rhodopea (Velenovsky) Velenovsky = **T. urumoffii**
saxatilis Sieber ex Sprengel 1825 (*T. bakeri*) EGF.1-**BB**-SB
    'Lilac Wonder' ®   [P Visser Czn 1971]
schrenkii Regel 1881 EGF.1-SB

sosnowskyi Achverdov & Mirzoeva 1950   **BB**
sprengeri Baker 1894   EGF.1-PGP-CA-**BB**-SB
    'Trotter's Form'
stellata Hooker = **T. clusiana** var. **stellata**
subpraestans Vvedensky   EGF.1-SB
N‡ **sylvestris** Linnaeus 1753   EGF.1-SB-**RD**
    ssp. *australis* (Link) Pampanini 1914 = **T. australis**
    ssp. *celsiana* (de Candolle) Hayek = **T. celsiana**
tarda Stapf 1933 (*T. dasystemon* hort.)   EGF.1-**CA**-**BB**-SB-**DGP**-**RD**
tetraphylla Regel   SB
tschimganica Z. Botschantzeva 1961   EGF.1-**BB**-SB
tubergeniana T. Hoog 1904   EGF.1-CA-**BB**-SB-**DGP**-**RD**
    'Kerkenhof' ®   [Jan Roes 1952]
turkestanica (Regel) Regel 1875   EGF.1-CA-**BB**-SB-**DGP**-**RD**
undulatifolia Boissier 1844   EGF.1-SB
urumiensis Stapf   EGF.1-CA-**BB**-**SB**-RD
urumoffii Hayek 1911 (*T. rhodopea*)   EGF.1-SB
violacea Boissier & Buhse = **T. humilis** 'Violacea'
vvedenskyi Z. Botschantzeva 1953   EGF.1-**BB**-**SB**
    'Chatkal'
    'Josef Marks'
    'Nana' nom. dub.
    'Tangerine Beauty' ®   [P Visser Czn 1980]
whittallii A. D. Hall = **T. orphanidea**
wilsoniana T. Hoog 1902 = **T. montana**
zenaidae Vvedensky   SB

TULIP CULTIVARS

Classification in accord with:
'Revised Classification of Tulips'
Koninklijke Algemeene Vereeniging voor Bloembollenculture 1981

EARLY FLOWERING
1   Single Early Tulips
2   Double Early Tulips

MID-SEASON
3   Triumph Tulips
4   Darwin Hybrid Tulips

LATE FLOWERING
5   Single Late Tulips
6   Lily-Flowered Tulips
7   Fringed Tulips
8   Viridiflora Tulips
9   Rembrandt Tulips
10   Parrot Tulips
11   Double Late Tulips

SPECIES TULIPS & THEIR HYBRIDS
12   Kaufmanniana Tulips
13   Fosteriana Tulips
14   Greigii Tulips

3   **'Abra'** ®   [C V Hybrida 1959]
3   **'Abu Hassan'** ®   [J F van den Berg & Sons Ltd 1976]
4   **'Ad Rem'** ®   [Konijnenburg & Mark Ltd 1966]
3   **'African Queen'** ®   [J Ligthart 1983]

3   'Ajax'   ®   [J Jonkheer Gzn 1975]
6   'Aladdin'   ®   [De Mol-Nieuwenhuis 1942]   DGP-**RD**
3   'Albury'   ®   [D W Lefeber & Co 1959]
12 'Alfred Cortot'   ®   [C G van Tubergen Ltd 1942]   DGP
14 'Ali Baba'   [C V Hybrida 1955]
11 'Allegretto'   ®   [J F van den Berg & Sons Ltd 1963]
12 'Ancilla'   ®   [C G van Tubergen Ltd 1955]
8   'Angel'   [D W Lefeber & Co 1956]   **RD**
11 'Angelique'   ®   [D W Lefeber & Co 1959]   RD
3   'Annie Schilder'   ®   [P Visser Czn 1982]
4   'Apeldoorn'   ®   [D W Lefeber & Co 1951]   **BB**-DGP-RD
4   'Apeldoorn Elite'   ®   [J S Verdegaal 1968]
1   'Apricot Beauty'   ®   [C van der Vlugt van Kimmenade 1953]   **RD**
10 'Apricot Parrot'   ®   [H G Huyg 1961]
2   'Arie Alkemade's Memory'   ®   [C P Alkemade Cz 1959]
5   'Aristocrat'   ®   [Segers Bros Ltd 1935]   **BB**
7   'Arma'   ®   [Knijn Bros 1962]   RD
8   'Artist'   ®   [Captein Bros 1947]   **BB**-DGP-RD
5   'Asta Nielsen'   ®   [Segers Bros Ltd 1950]
3   'Astarte'   ®   [P Visser Czn 1983]
6   'Astor'   ®   [van Tubergen Ltd 1936]
3   'Athleet'   ®   [E Kooi Ltd 1942]   **RD**
3   'Attila'   ®   [G van der May's Sons 1945]   **RD**
5   'Avignon'   ®   [W Dekker 1966]
5   'Balalaika'   ®   [Konijnenburg & Mark Ltd 1952]
6   'Ballade'   ®   [Nieuwenhuis Bros 1953]   RD
4   'Beauty of Apeldoorn'   ®   [Q M Bentvelzen 1960]   **RD**
4   'Beauty of Oxford'   ®   [A Overdevest Gz & Sons 1961]
7   'Bellflower'   ®   [Segers Bros Ltd 1970]
1   'Bellona'   ®   [H de Graaff & Sons Ltd 1944]   **BB**-RD
12 'Berlioz'   ®   [C G van Tubergen Ltd 1942]   RD
4   'Big Chief'   ®   [A Frijlink & Sons Ltd 1959]   **BB**
3   'Bing Crosby'   ®   [B P Heemkerk 1947]
5   'Bingham'   ®   [Segers Bros Ltd 1950]
10 'Bird of Paradise'   ®   [J de Goede Sz 1962]
10 'Black Parrot'   ®   [C Keur & Sons 1937]   **BB**-DGP-RD
5   'Black Swan'   ®   [F Rijnveld & Sons Ltd 1963]
3   'Blenda'   ®   [L A Hoek 1947]
5   'Bleu Aimable'   ®   [E H Krelage & Son pre-1916]   RD
7   'Blue Heron'   ®   [Segers Bros Ltd 1970]
10 'Blue Parrot'   ®   [J F Ch Dix pre-1935]   DGP-**RD**
    'Blue Suprise' = T. 'Lotty van Beuningen'
5   'Blushing Bride'   ®   [P H Beelen 1959]   **DGP**
11 'Bonanza'   ®   [1943]
2   'Bravissimo'   ®   [P Nijssen & Sons Ltd 1955]
1   'Brilliant Star'   ®   [1906]   RD
6   'Burgundy'   ®   [J J Grullemans & Sons Ltd 1957]
7   'Burgundy Lace'   ®   [Segers Bros Ltd 1961]   **RD**
13 'Candela'   ®   [K van Egmond & Sons 1961]
13 'Cantata'   ®   [C G van Tubergen Ltd pre-1942]   **BB**-RD
5   'Cantor'   ®   [C Colijn & Sons Ltd 1960]   RD
14 'Cape Cod'   ®   [C V Hybrida 1955]
3   'Capri'   ®   [F C Bik 1974]
2   'Carlton'   ®   [C P Alkemade Cz 1950]
11 'Carnival de Nice'   ®   [C G van Tubergen Ltd 1953]
3   'Carrara'   ®   [E H Krelage & Son pre-1912]
5   'Cashmir'   ®   [Segers Bros Ltd 1969]
12 'Cesar Franck'   ®   [F Rijnveld & Sons Ltd 1940]   DGP
1   'Charles'   ®   [C P Alkemade Cz 1954]
5   'Charlotte'   ®   [J Groot-Vriend 1985]

5   **'Chatham'** ®   [P Visser Cz 1967]
6   **'China Pink'** ®   [De Mol-Nieuwenhuis 1944]   **BB-RD**
12 **'Chopin'** ®   [C G van Tubergen Ltd 1942]
1   **'Christmas Gold'** ®   [1948]
1   **'Christmas Marvel'** ®   [L Schoorl 1954]
5   **'Clara Butt'** ®   [E H Krelage & Son 1889]   **BB-DGP-RD**
10 **'Comet'** ®   [C A Verdegaal 1952]
14 **'Compostella'** ®   [C V Hybrida 1955]
13 **'Concerto'** ®   [C V Hybrida]
14 **'Corsage'** ®   [C V Hybrida 1960]
1   **'Couleur Cardinal'** ®   [1845]   **BB-DGP-RD**
3   **'Danton'** ®   [Konijnenburg & Mark Ltd 1952]
4   **'Dawnglow'** ®   [J J A Kendall 1965]
4   **'Daydream'** ®   [J N M van Eeden 1980]
12 **'Daylight'** ®   [M H M Thoolen Ltd 1955]
5   **'Demeter'** ®   [C G van Tubergen Ltd pre-1932]   **RD**
1   **'Diana'** ®   [A van den Berg Gz 1909]   **BB-RD**
5   **'Dillenburg'** ®   [C G van Tubergen Ltd pre-1916]   **DGP-RD**
4   **'Diplomate'** ®   [D W Lefeber & Co 1950]
5   **'Dix' Favourite'** ®   [J C Kavelaars 1952]
1   **'Doctor Plesman'** ®   [Van Graven Bros 1955]
14 **'Donna Bella'** ®   [C V Hybrida 1955]
3   **'Don Quichotte'** ®   [Konijnenburg & Mark Ltd 1952]
    'Doorman' = **T. 'Karel Doorman'**
14 **'Dreamboat'** ®   [C V Hybrida 1953]
3   **'Dreaming Maid'** ®   [J J Kerbert 1934]   **BB**
5   **'Dreamland'** ®   [H G Huyg 1969]
12 **'Duplosa'** ®   [P Bijvoet & Co Ltd 1955]
3   **'Dutch Princess'** ®   [Jac Tol Jr 1959]   RD
3   **'Edith Eddy'** ®   [Zocher & Co]
2   **'Electra'** ®   [1905]   **RD**
6   **'Elegant Lady'** ®   [Nieuwenhuis Bros 1953]
4   **'Elizabeth Arden'** ®   [De Mol-Nieuwenhuis 1957]   RD
12 **'Elliott'** ®   [M H M Thoolen Ltd]
3   **'Elmus'** ®   [J F van den Berg & Sons Ltd 1933]
3   **'Elsie Eloff'** ®   [Segers Bros Ltd 1949]
3   **'Emmy Peeck'** ®   [C V Hybrida 1949]
4   **'Empire State'** ®   [D W Lefeber & Co 1956]
11 **'Eros'** ®   [Zocher & Co 1937]   **BB-DGP-RD**
8   **'Esperanto'** ®   [J Pranger 1968]
10 **'Estella Rijnveld'** ('Gay Presto') ®   [Segers Bros Ltd 1954]   **RD**
5   **'Esther'** ®   [C J Keppel 1967]
12 **'Fair Lady'** ®   [C G van Tubergen Ltd pre-1939]
7   **'Fancy Frills'** ®   [Segers Bros Ltd 1972]
10 **'Fantasy'** ®   [1910]   **BB-DGP-RD**
12 **'Fashion'** ®   [Tenhagen Bros 1962]
3   **'Feyenoord'** ®   [F Roozen 1970]
3   **'Fidelio'** ®   [G R Tromp 1952]
    'Fireside' = **T. 'Vlammenspel'**
3   **'First Lady'** ®   [C V Hybrida 1951]
4   **'Flaming Gold'** ®   [A Overdevest Gz & Sons 1965]
10 **'Flaming Parrot'** ®   [B P Heemskerk 1968]
8   **'Formosa'** ®   [Polman Mooy 1926]
12 **'Franz Lehar'** ®   [J C van der Meer 1955]
14 **'Fresco'** ®   [C V Hybrida 1959]
7   **'Fringed Apeldoorn'** ®   [L P Looijestein & Sons 1971]
12 **'Fritz Kriesler'** ®   [C G van Tubergen Ltd 1942]   DGP-RD
12 **'Gaiety'** ®   [C G van Tubergen Ltd]
13 **'Galata'** ®   [D W Lefeber & Co 1942]
5   **'Galaxy'** ®   [F Rijnveld & Sons Ltd 1960]

1	**'Galway'** ®	[C P Alkemade Cz 1956]	
2	**'Garanza'** ®	[Segers Bros Ltd 1944]	
3	**'Garden Party'** ®	[P Hopman & Sons Ltd 1944]	**BB**-RD
	'Gay Presto' = **T. 'Estella Rijnveld'**		
1	**'Generaal de Wet'** ®	[1904]	DGP-RD
5	**'Georgette'** ®	[C V Hybrida 1952]	
12	**'Giuseppe Verdi'** ®	[J C van der Meer 1955]	
12	**'Glück'** ®	[C G van Tubergen Ltd 1940]	DGP
5	**'Golden Age'** ®	[C G van Tubergen Ltd pre-1930]	
4	**'Golden Apeldoorn'** ®	[C Gorter Sz & A Overdevest Gz & Sons pre-1960]	
8	**'Golden Artist'** ®	[Captein Bros 1959]	
6	**'Golden Duchess'** ®	[C G van Tubergen Ltd pre-1938]	
13	**'Golden Eagle'** ®	[C V Hybrida 1955]	DGP-RD
5	**'Golden Harvest'** ®	[Nicolaas Dames 1928]	DGP-RD
3	**'Golden Melody'** ®	[P Hermans 1961]	RD
3	**'Golden Mirjoran'** ®	[Jac Tol Jr 1964]	
11	**'Golden Nizza'** ®	[P Visser Cz 1951]	
4	**'Golden Oxford'** ®	[A Overdevest Gz & Sons 1959]	**RD**
4	**'Golden Parade'** ®	[A Overdevest Gz & Sons 1963]	
4	**'Golden Springtime'** ®	[D W Lefeber & Co 1957]	
11	**'Gold Medal'** ®	[C P Alkemade Cz 1946]	RD
4	**'Gordon Cooper'** ®	[Konijnenburg & Mark Ltd 1963]	
12	**'Goudstuk'** ®	[C G van Tubergen Ltd 1952]	
	'Grand Duc' = **T. 'Kiezerskroon'**		
13	**'Grand Prix'** ®	[C G van Tubergen Ltd 1949]	
	'Greenland' = **T. 'Groenland'**		
5	**'Greuze'** ®	[E H Krelage & Son 1891]	
3	**'Grevel'** ®	[Chr van den Outenaar 1969]	
8	**'Groenland'** ('Greenland') ®	[J F van den Berg & Sons Ltd 1955]	
			DGP-RD
4	**'Gudishnik'** ®	[D W Lefeber & Co 1952]	**BB-DGP**-RD
5	**'Halcro'** ®	[Segers Bros Ltd pre-1949]	
12	**'Heart's Delight'** ®	[C G van Tubergen Ltd 1952]	RD
7	**'Hellas'** ®	[Segers Bros Ltd 1973]	
3	**'Henry Dunant'** ®	[Konijnenburg & Mark Ltd 1959]	
5	**'Henry Ford'** ®	[J F van den Berg & Sons Ltd 1953]	
11	**'Hermoine'** ®	[P Dames Nz 1943]	
3	**'High Noon'** ®	[K Wiedijk 1953]	
3	**'High Society'** ®	[Jac Tol Jr 1958]	RD
13	**'Hit Parade'** ®	[W Lemmers 1979]	
4	**'Hollands Glorie'** ®	[D W Lefeber & Co 1942]	DGP-RD
8	**'Hollywood'** ®	[Captein Bros 1956]	RD
8	**'Humming Bird'** ®	[D W Lefeber & Co 1961]	
2	**'Hytuna'** ®	[J F van den Berg & Sons Ltd 1959]	
1	**'Ibis'** ®	[1910]	BB
5	**'Ile de France'** ®	[Blom & Padding 1968]	
9	**'Insulinde'** ®	[E H Krelage & Son]	
5	**'Insurpassable'** ®	[J J Grullemans & Sons Ltd 1932]	RD
3	**'Invasion'** ®	[C V Hybrida 1944]	
9	**'Jack Laan'** ®	[C Colijn & Sons Ltd 1951]	
6	**'Jacqueline'** ®	[Segers Bros Ltd 1958]	
	'Jewel Dance'		
4	**'Jewel of Spring'** ®	[A Overdevest Gz & Sons 1956]	DGP-RD
3	**'Johanna'** ®	[Zocher & Co]	
7	**'Johann Gutenberg'** ®	[Segers Bros Ltd 1970]	
12	**'Johann Strauss'** ®	[C G van Tubergen Ltd pre-1966]	DGP-RD
13	**'Juan'** ®	[C G van Tubergen Ltd 1961]	
5	**'Kaj Munk'** ®	[H 't Mannetje 1954]	
3	**'Kansas'** ®	[Zocher & Co]	BB
10	**'Karel Doorman'** ('Doorman') ®	[John B Meskers & Sons 1946]	

3   **'Kees Nelis'** ('Ringo')   ®   [H 't Mannetje 1951]   **DGP**-RD
1   **'Kiezerskroon'** ('Grand Duc')   ®   [1756]   **BB-DGP-RD**
5   **'Kingsblood'**   ®   [Konijnenburg & Mark Ltd 1952]
4   **'Koningin Wilhelmina'** ('Queen Wilhelmina')   ®   [C Nieuwenhuis 1965]
5   **'Kryptos'**   ®   [P Visser Cz 1965]
     'Lady Diana'
5   **'La Fayette'**   ®   [D W Lefeber & Co 1943]
14   **'Large Copper'**   ®   [L Stassen Jr Ltd 1963]
5   **'Landseadel's Supreme'**   ®   [D W Lefeber & Co 1958]
5   **'La Tulipe Noire'**   ®   [E H Krelage & Son 1891]   **BB-DGP-RD**
4   **'Lefeber's Favourite'**   ®   [D W Lefeber & Co 1942]   **BB**
11   **'Lilac Perfection'**   ®   [C V Hybrida 1951]
4   **'London'**   ®   [D W Lefeber & Co 1950]
3   **'Los Angeles'**   ®   [J F van den Berg & Sons Ltd 1965]
9   **'Lotty van Beuningen'**   ®('Blue Suprise')
3   **'Lucky Strike'**   ®   [P & J W Mantel 1954]
3   **'Lustige Witwe'** ('Merry Widow')   ®   [G van der Mey's Sons Ltd 1942]
10   **'Lutea Major'**   ®   [1665]
13   **'Madame Lefeber'** ('Red Emperor')   ®   [C G van Tubergen Ltd pre-1931
                                                                      DGP-RD

3   **'Madam Spoor'**   ®   [N Zandbergen Wzn 1951]
7   **'Maja'**   ®   [Segers Bros Ltd 1968]
5   **'Mamasa'**   ®   [De Mol-Nieuwenhuis 1942]   **DGP**
14   **'March of Time'**   ®   [Captein Bros 1970]
2   **'Marechal Niel'**   ®   [1930]   **BB**-DGP-**RD**
14   **'Margaret Herbst'** ('Royal Splendour')   ®   [D W Lefeber & Co 1949]
                                                                      DGP
6   **'Mariette'**   ®   [Segers Bros Ltd 1942]   **DGP**-RD
6   **'Marilyn'**   ®   [C N Verbruggen 1976]
6   **'Marjolein'**   ®   [P Visser Cz 1962]
     'Marshal Joffre'
14   **'Mary Ann'**   ®   [C V Hybrida 1955]
5   **'Maureen'**   ®   [Segers Bros Ltd 1950]   **BB**
6   **'Maytime'**   ®   [De Mol-Nieuwenhuis 1942]   **RD**
11   **'Maywonder'**   ®   [C V Hybrida 1951]   **BB**
3   **'Meissner Porzellen'**   ®   [Konijnenburg & Mark Ltd 1952]
1   **'Merry Christmas'**   ®   [Th & W B Reus 1972]
     'Merry Widow' = **T. 'Lustige Witwe'**
3   **'Midway'**   ®   [L B Kaptein's Sons 1985]
5   **'Mirella'**   ®   [P Bijvoet & Co Ltd 1953]   DGP-RD
2   **'Monte Carlo'**   ®   [Anton Nijssen & Sons Ltd 1955]
5   **'Montgomery'**   ®   [E J van der Zaal 1945]
11   **'Mount Tacoma'**   ®   [Polman Mooy pre-1926]   **BB**-RD
2   **'Mr Van der Hoef'**   ®   [1911]   **BB**-RD
5   **'Mrs John T Scheepers'**   ®   [C G van Tubergen Ltd pre-1930]
                                                                      BB-DGP-RD

3   **'Musical'**   ®   [F C Bik 1972]
3   **'Negrita'**   ®   [F C Bik 1970]
5   **'Niphetos'**   ®   [J J Grullemana & Sons Ltd 1933]   **DGP**-RD
4   **'Olympic Flame'**   ®   [A Verschoor Jr 1971]
4   **'Olympic Gold'**   ®   [Eugene van der Schoot 1962]
5   **'Orange Bouquet'**   ®   [Konijnenburg & Mark Ltd 1964]
12   **'Orange Boy'**   ®   [C G van Tubergen Ltd 1957]
14   **'Orange Elite'**   ®   [C V Hybrida 1952]
13   **'Orange Emperor'**   ®   [K van Egmond & Sons 1962]
10   **'Orange Favourite'**   ®   [K C Vooren & Sons 1930]
4   **'Orange Goblet'**   ®   [A Frijlink & Sons Ltd 1959]
3   **'Orange Monarch'**   ®   [G Lamboo 1962]
     'Orange Sun' = **T. 'Oranjezon'**
11   **'Orange Triumph'**   ®   [C Nieuwenhuis 1944]   RD

3	'Orange Wonder' ®	[A Sabelis 1940]	**BB**
2	'Oranje Nassau' ®	[1930]	RD
4	'Oranjezon' ('Orange Sun') ®	[C V Hybrida 1947]	**BB**
14	'Oratorio' ®	[C V Hybrida 1952]	
14	'Oriental Beauty' ®	[C V Hybrida 1952]	RD
14	'Oriental Splendour' ®	[D W Lefeber & Co 1961]	DGP
3	'Ornament' ®	[L van Berkel Sr 1944]	
5	'Ossi Oswalda' ®	[J J Grullemans & Sons Ltd 1939]	**BB**
4	'Oxford' ®	[D W Lefeber & Co 1945]	DGP
4	'Oxford's Elite' ®	[G G Kol 1968]	
5	'Palestrina' ®	[Captein Bros 1944]	RD
5	'Pandion' ®	[Segers Bros Ltd pre-1951]	
14	'Pandour' ®	[C V Hybrida 1952]	
4	'Parade' ®	[D W Lefeber & Co 1951]	
3	'Paul Richter' ®	[F Rijnveld & Sons Ltd 1943]	
3	'Pax' ®	[P van Kooten 1942]	RD
2	'Peach Blossom' ®	[1890]	
14-12	**Peacock Hybrids** ®		
3	'Peerless Pink' ®	[H Carlee 1930]	
10	'Perfecta' ®	[1750]	
14	'Perlina' ®	[C V Hybrida 1960]	
5	'Phillipe de Comines' ®	[E H Krelage & Son 1891]	
5	'Picture' ®	[G Baltus Sinnige & Sons 1949]	
5	'Pilgrim' ®	[F Rijnveld & Sons Ltd pre-1960]	
8	'Pimpernel' ®	[D W Lefeber & Co 1956]	
1	'Pink Beauty' ®	[Baars & Dibbits 1889]	**BB-RD**
5	'Pink Supreme' ®	[Captein Bros 1947]	RD
1	'Pink Trophy' ®	[B P Heemskerk 1939]	
14	'Plaisir' ®	[C V Hybrida 1953]	
3	'Preludium' ®	[P van Kooten 1945]	
4	'President Kennedy' ®	[P J de Groot 1961]	
	'Prince Carnival' = **T. 'Prins Carnaval'**		
3	'Prince Charles' ®	[P Hopman & Sons Ltd 1952]	
1	'Prince of Austria' ®	[1860]	**BB**-DGP-RD
13	'Princeps' ®	[Jan Roes]	RD
5	'Princess Elizabeth' ®	[E H Krelage & Son 1898]	
	'Princess Irene' = T. **'Prinses Irene'**		
5	'Princess Margaret Rose' ®	[J Bankert 1944]	RD
1	'Prins Carnaval' ('Prince Carnival') ®	[1930]	**BB**
1	'Prinses Irene' ('Princess Irene') ®	[P van Reisen & Sons 1949]	
3	'Prominence' ®	[P van Kooten 1943]	
13	'Purissima' ('White Emperor') ®	[C G van Tubergen Ltd 1943]	DGP-RD
	'Purity' = **T. 'Schoonoord'**		
3	'Purple Star' ®	[S J Zandvoort 1952]	**BB**
4	'Queen' ®	[D W Lefeber & Co 1968]	
5	'Queen of Bartigons' ®	[P Bakker Mz Ltd 1944]	DGP-RD
5	'Queen of Night' ®	[J J Grullemans & Sons Ltd pre-1944]	RD
6	'Queen of Sheba' ®	[De Mol-Nieuwenhuis 1944]	DGP-RD
	'Queen Wilhelmina' = **T. 'Koningin Wilhelmina'**		
10	'Red Champion' ®	[H M Ruysenaars 1930]	
	'Red Emperor' = **T. 'Madame Lefeber'**		
5	'Red Georgette' ®	[P Visser Cz 1983]	
4	'Red Matador' ®	[C G van Tubergen Ltd 1942]	DGP
10	'Red Parrot' ®	[J C Evers 1940]	RD
14	'Red Reflection' ®	[C V Hybrida 1955]	
14	'Red Riding Hood' ®	[C V Hybrida 1953]	**BB-RD**
6	'Red Shine' ®	[C V Hybrida 1955]	RD
7	'Redwing' ®	[Segers Bros Ltd 1972]	
3	'Reforma' ®	[1946]	

5	**'Renown'** ® [Segers Bros Ltd 1949]		
2	**'Rheingold'** ® [P van Reisen & Sons 1942]		
	'Ringo' = **T. 'Kees Nelis'**		
13	**'Rockery Beauty'** ® [Ant Lefeber 1942]		
10	**'Rococo'** ® [H Slegtkamp & Co 1942]		
13	**'Rondo'** ® [C V Hybrida 1952]		
5	**'Rosa van Lima'** ® [D W Lefeber & Co 1943]		
5	**'Rose Copland'** ® [J W Mantel 1918]		RD
5	**'Rosy Wings'** ® [C G van Tubergen Ltd 1944]		**BB**-DGP
	'Royal Splendour' = **T. 'Margaret Herbst'**		
1	**'Ruby Red'** ® [B P Heemskerk 1944]		
10	**'Salmon Parrot'** ® [De Mol & C A Verdegaal 1956]		
5	**'San Marino'** ® [F Rijnveld & Sons Ltd 1961]		
2	**'Scarlet Cardinal'** ® [J de Ruyter 1914]		RD
12	**'Scarlet Elegance'** ® [Jac B Roozen 1942]		
2	**'Schoonoord'** ('Purity') ® [1909]		RD
5	**'Schotte de Vries'** ® [P & J W Mantel 1952]		
12	**'Shakespeare'** ® [C G van Tubergen Ltd 1942]		**DGP-RD**
5	**'Shirley'** ® [F C Bik 1968]		
9	**'Show Girl'** ® [F Rijnveld & Sons Ltd 1957]		
12	**'Showwinner'** ® [F Rijnveld & Sons Ltd 1966]		
5	**'Smiling Queen'** ® [N L A Roozen pre-1938]		**RD**
5	**'Snowpeak'** ® [Konijnenburg & Mark Ltd 1952]		RD
	'Snow Queen'		
	'Snowstorm'		
5	**'Sorbet'** ® [J J van den Eijken 1959]		
14	**'Sparkling Fire'** ® [C V Hybrida 1955]		
8	**'Spring Green'** ® [P Liefting 1969]		
13	**'Spring Pearl'** ® [F Rijnveld & Sons Ltd 1955]		
4	**'Spring Song'** ® [J H Veldhuizen van Zanten Axn 1946]		
6	**'Stanislaus'** ® [C G van Tubergen Ltd pre-1936]		
2	**'Stockholm'** ® [Anton Nijssen & Sons Ltd 1952]		RD
12	**'Stressa'** ® [C G van Tubergen Ltd 1942]		**RD**
4	**'Striped Apeldoorn'** ® [A Overdevest Gz & Sons 1963]		
3	**'Sucess'** ® [K C Vooren & Sons 1971]		
13	**'Summit'** ® [K van Egmond & Sons 1962]		
7	**'Sundew'** ® [1930]		
5	**'Sunkist'** ® [C G van Tubergen Ltd pre-1933]		
5	**'Sussex'** ® [P Visser Cz 1971]		
5	**'Sweet Harmony'** ® [Jac B Roozen 1944]		**RD**
13	**'Sweetheart'** ® [C Nieuwenhuis 1976]		RD
14	**'Sweet Lady'** ® [J C van der Meer 1955]		
3	**'Tambour Maitre'** ® [C Colijn & Sons Ltd 1956]		
14	**'Tango'** ® [C V Hybrida 1952]		
14	**'Tarafa'** ® [A Overdevest Gz & Sons 1955]		
5	**'Tarakan'** ® [Nieuwenhuis Bros 1957]		
5	**'Temple of Beauty'** ® [D W Lefeber & Co 1959]		
10	**'Texas Flame'** ® [J J de Wit Cz 1958]		
10	**'Texas Gold'** ® [G van der Mey's Sons Ltd 1944]		
12	**'The First'** ® [F Roozen 1946]		**DGP-RD**
3	**'Thule'** ® [Anton Nijssen & Sons Ltd 1954]		
14	**'Toronto'** ® [Jac Uittenbogaard & Sons 1963]		
14	**'Trinket'** ® [Captein Bros 1963]		
5	**'Twinkle'** ® [Segers Bros Ltd 1968]		
11	**'Uncle Tom'** ® [Zocher & Co pre-1939]		RD
5	**'Union Jack'** ® [P Bakker Mz Ltd 1958]		**RD**
3	**'Valentine'** ® [F C Bik 1970]		RD
3	**'Van der Eerden'** ® [E H Krelage & Son pre-1933]		RD
	'Vermeer'		
12	**'Vivaldi'** ® [C G van Tubergen Ltd pre-1942]		

5   **'Vlammenspel'** ('Fireside')   ®   [P Groot Nz 1941]
6   **'West Point'**   ®   [De Mol-Nieuwenhuis 1943]   **BB**-RD
3   **'White Dream'**   ®   [J F van den Berg & Sons Ltd 1972]
    'White Emperor' = **T. 'Purissima'**
10 **'White Parrot'**   ®   [J Valkering & Sons Ltd 1943]   RD
6   **'White Triumphator'**   ®   [C G van Tubergen Ltd 1942]   **BB**-DGP-RD
3   **'White Virgin'**   ®   [E H Krelage & Son 1932]
2   **'Willemsoord'**   ®   [Paul Roozen 1930]
5   **'Wim van Est'**   ®   [Segers Bros Ltd 1952]
14 **'Yellow Dawn'**   ®   [C V Hybrida 1953]   RD
4   **'Yellow Dover'**   ®   [A Overdevest Gz & Sons 1963]
    'Yolanda'
14 **'Zampa'**   ®   [C V Hybrida 1952]
13 **'Zombie'**   ®   [C V Hybrida pre-1954]
5   **'Zomerschoon'**   ®   [1620]

TUNICA Scopoli 1772   *[Caryophyllaceae]*
   saxifraga Scopoli 1772 = **Petrorhagia saxifraga**

TUSSILAGO Linnaeus 1753   *[Asteraceae (Compositae)]*
HN‡   **farfara** Linnaeus 1753

TWEEDIA Hooker & Arnott 1834   *[Asclepiadaceae]*
   caerulea D. Don ex Sweet 1837 (*Oxypetalum caeruleum*)

TYPHA Linnaeus 1753   *[Typhaceae]*
N‡   **angustifolia** Linnaeus 1753   EGF.2
N‡L   **latifolia** Linnaeus 1753   EGF.2-**RD**
      laxmannii Lepachin 1801 (*T. stenophylla*)
N   **minima** Funck ex Hoppe 1794   EGF.2-RD
      shuttleworthii W. Kock & Sonder 1844   EGF.2
      stenophylla Fischer &C. A. Meyer 1845 = **T. laxmannii**

UMBILICUS de Candolle 1801   *[Crassulaceae]*
N‡   **rupestris** (Salisbury) Dandy 1948

UNCINIA Persoon 1807   *[Cyperaceae]*
   egmontiana Hamlin 1959 (U. rubra hort., p.p.)
   divaricata Boott 1853
   rura Boott 1853
   rubra hort. non Boot = **U. egmontiana** p.p., **U. unciniata** p.p.
   unciniata (Linnaeus f.) Kükenthal 1909 (*U. rubra* hort. p.p.)
   'Rubra' = **U. unciniata**

UNIOLA Linnaeus 1753   *[Poaceae (Gramineae)]*
   latifolia Michaux 1803 = **Chasmanthium latifolium**

URGINEA Steinheil 1834   *[Hyacinthaceae (Liliaceae)]*
   maritima (Linnaeus) Baker 1873   EGF.1-**BB**

UROSPERMUM Scopoli 177   *[Asteraceae (Compositae)]*
   dalechampii (Linnaeus) Boissier 1875   PGP

UVULARIA Linnaeus 1753   *[Convallariaceae (Liliaceae)]*
   caroliniana (Gmelin) Wilbur 1961 (*U. pudica*)   EGF.1
   cirrhosa Thunberg 1784
   grandiflora J. E. Smith 1804   EGF.1-PGP-CA
   perfoliata Linnaeus 1753   EGF.1-PGP
   pudica (Walker) Fernald 1939 = **U. caroliniana**
   sessilifolia Linnaeus 1753 (*Oakesiella sessilifolia*)   EGF.1-PGP

VALERIANA Linnaeus 1753   [*Valerianaceae*]
    arizonica A. Gray 1883
N‡   **dioica** Linnaeus 1753
    montana Linnaeus 1753
HN‡L **officinalis** Linnaeus 1753   PGP
    phu Linnaeus 1753
       'Aurea'   PGP-**RD**
    rotundifolia Villars 1787
    supina Arduino 1763   CA

VALERIANELLA Miller 1754   [*Valerianaceae*]
AHN‡ **locusta** (Linnaeus) Laterrade 1821 (*V. olitoria*)
    olitoria (Linnaeus) Pollich 1776 = **V. locusta**

VALLOTA Herbert 1821 nom. cons.   [*Amaryllidaceae*]
    purpurea (Aiton) Herbert 1821 = **Cyrtanthus purpureus**
    speciosa (Linnaeus f.) Durand & Schinz 1895 = **Cyrtanthus purpureus**

VANCOUVERIA Morren & Decaisne 1834   [*Berberidaceae*]

M - STEARN, W.T.: '*Epimedium and Vancouveria*' Journ. Linn. Soc. (Botany) v 51, no 340 (1938)

    chrysantha Greene 1885   M
    hexandra (Hooker) Morren & Decaisne 1834   M-PGP
    planipetala Calloni 1887   M-PGP

VELTHEIMIA Gleditsch 1771   [*Hyacinthaceae (Liliaceae)*]
    bracteata Harvey ex Baker 1871   EGF.1-PGP-RD
       'Rosalba' ®   [van Tubergen pre-1958]   EGF.1-RD
    capensis (Linnaeus) de Candolle 1808 (V. viridifolia)   EGF.1-PGP-**RD**
    viridifolia Hort. ex Vilmorin 1875 = **V. capensis**

X VENIDIO-ARCTOTIS Hort.   [*Asteraceae (Compositae)*]
    hybridum hort. (*Arctotis grandis & A. breviscapa* x *Venidium fastuosum*)   RD
       'Flame'
       'Wine'

VERATRUM Linnaeus 1753   [*Melanthiaceae (Liliaceae)*]
    album Linnaeus 1753   EGF.1-PGP
    californicum Durand 1855   EGF.1-PGP
    maackii Regel 1861 = **V. nigrum** ssp. **maackii**
L   **nigrum** Linnaeus 1753   EGF.1-**PGP**-RD
       ssp. **maackii** (Regel) Kitamura 1966 (*V. maackii*)   EGF.1
    viride Aiton 1789   EGF.1-**PGP**-RD
    wilsonii O. Loesener ex C. H. Wright 1938   PGP

VERBASCUM Linnaeus 1753   [*Scrophulariaceae*]
    acaule Kuntze 1891 (*Celsia acaulis*)   CA-**DGP**
BN **blattaria** Linnaeus 1753
       'Albiflorum'
B   **bombyciferum** Boissier 1844 (V. *broussa* hort.)   PGP-RD
       'Polarsommer' ('Arctic Summer')
    brousa hort. = **V. bombyciferum**
    chaixii Villars 1779   PGP-**DGP**-RD
       'Album'
BN **densiflorum** Bertoloni 1810 (*V. thapsiforme*)   RD
    'Densiflorum' (*V. densiflorum* x *V. nigrum*) (*V. vernale* hort.)   PGP
    dumulosum P. H. Davis & Huber-Morath 1952   CA-**DGP**-RD
    'Golden Bush' (*V. nigrum* x *V. spinosum*)   [E. Smith via Hillier 1963]   PGP
    'Letitia' (*V. dumulosum* x *V. spinosum*)   [Wisley Gardens 1960]   DGP-**RD**

N‡	**nigrum** Linnaeus 1753	
B	**olympicum** Boissier 1844	PGP-RD
B	**phlomoides** Linnaeus 1753	RD
N	**phoeniceum** Linnaeus 1753	PGP-RD
N	**pulverulentum** Villars 1779	
	roripifolium (Halacsy) I. K. Ferguson 1971 (*Celsia roripifolia*)	
	'Silberkandelaber' (*V. bombyciferum* x *V. olympicum*)	
	thapsiforme Schrader 1813 = **V. densiflorum**	
BHN‡L	**thapsus** Linnaeus 1753	RD
	undulatum Lamarck 1797 non Marshall von Bieberstein	
	vernale hort. = **V. 'Densiflorum'**	

HYBRID CULTIVARS

	'Boadicea'	
	'Bridal Bouquet'	PGP
	'C. L. Adams'	**RD**
	'Cotswold Beauty'	RD
	'Cotswold Gem'	RD
	'Cotswold Queen'	**DGP**-RD
L	**'Gainsborough'**	PGP-**DGP**-RD
	'Hartleyi'	
	'Les Clements'	
	'Mont Blanc'	RD
L	**'Pink Domino'**	PGP-**DGP**-**RD**
	'Roger Watson'	
	'Royal Highland'	
	'Yellow Princess'	

VERBENA Linnaeus 1753		[*Verbenaceae*]
bonariensis Linnaeus 1753		PGP-RD
canadensis (Linnaeus) Britton 1894		
chamaedrifolia Jussieu 1806 = **V. peruviana**		
corymbosa Ruiz & Pavon 1798		PGP
x hybrida Hort. ex Vilmorin 1884		DGP
	'Elizabeth'	
	'Foxhunter'	
	'Gravetye'	
	'Hidcote Purple'	
	'Lawrence Johnston'	
	'Loveliness'	
	Perfecta Hybrids	
	'Pink Bouquet'	
	'Rose Queen'	
	'Silver Ann'	
	'Sissinghurst' ('Sissinghurst Pink')	
	'Tenerife' = **V. x hybrida 'Sissinghurst'**	
	'Wisley Pink' = **V. x hybrida 'Sissinghurst'**	

	mahonetii Vilmorin 1863 = **V. tenera 'Mahonetii'**	
HN	**officinalis** Linnaeus 1753	
	peruviana (Linnaeus) Druce 1914 (*V. chamaedrifolia*)	**DGP-RD**
	'Alba'	
	phlogiflora Chamisso 1832	
	pulchella Sweet 1829 = **V. tenera**	
	rigida Sprengel 1827 (*V. venosa*)	PGP-**DGP**-RD
	tenera Sprengel 1827 (*V. pulchella*)	DGP
	'Alba'	
	'Mahonetii'	**DGP**
	tenuisecta Briquet	
	venosa Gillies & Hooker 1830 = **V. rigida**	

VERBESINA Linnaeus 1753   [*Asteraceae (Compositae)*]
   alternifolia (Linnaeus) Britton 1893 = **Actinomeris alternifolia**

VERNONIA Schreber 1791 nom. cons.   [*Asteraceae (Compositae)*]
   arkansana de Candolle 1838 = **V. crinita**
   crinita Rafinesque 1836 (*V. arkansana*)   PGP
   noveboracensis (Linnaeus) Willdenow 1804

VERONICA Linnaeus 1753   [*Scrophulariaceae*]
N‡   **alpina** Linnaeus 1753
    aphylla Linnaeus 1753
    armena Boissier & Huet 1856   CA
      'Rosea'
    austriaca Linnaeus 1759
      ssp. **teucrium** (Linnaeus) D. A. Webb 1972 (*V. teucrium*)   **RD**
      ssp. **teucrium** 'Blue Fountain'   PGP-**DGP**
      ssp. **teucrium** 'Blue Tit'
L   ssp. **teucrium** 'Crater Lake Blue'   PGP-**DGP**
      ssp. **teucrium** 'Kapitän'   [K. Foerster]
      ssp. **teucrium** 'Knallblau'
      ssp. **teucrium** 'Rosea'   RD
      ssp. **teucrium** 'Royal Blue'   PGP
L   ssp. **teucrium** 'Shirley Blue'   RD
      *ssp. **vahlii** (*V. teucrium* ssp. *dubia*)
HN‡L **beccabunga** Linnaeus 1753
    bellidioides Linnaeus 1753
    bombycina Boissier & Kotschy 1856   CA
    bonarota Linnaeus 1753 = **Paederota bonarota**
    caespitosa Boissier 1844   CA
    catarractae Forster f. 1786 = **Parahebe catarractae**
    cinerea Boissier & Balansa 1859   CA-RD
    crassifolia Nyman = **V. spicata** ssp. **crassifolia**
    cuneifolia D. Don 1841
    dabneyi Hochstetter 1844
    derwentiana Andrews 1808 = **Parahebe derwentiana**
    exaltata Maunders 1834   PGP-**DGP-RD**
N‡   **filiformis** Smith 1791   **RD**
N‡   **fruticans** Jacquemont 1762 (*V. saxatilis*)
L   **gentianoides** Vahl 1790   PGP-**DGP**-RD
      'Alba'
      'Robusta'   [K. Foerster]
      'Variegata'   PGP-RD
      *'guthrieana'
    x hendersonii hort. = **V. subsessilis**
    incana Linnaeus 1753 = **V. spicata** ssp. **incana**
    kellereri Degen & Urumov 1911
    kotschyana Bentham 1846
    liwanensis C. Koch 1849
N   **longifolia** Linnaeus 1753   PGP-DGP-**RD**
      'Alba'
      'Blaubart'   [H. Hagemann]
      'Blaubündel'   [K. Foerster]
      'Blaue Sommer'   [E. Benary]
      'Blauriesen'   [K. Foerster]
      'Foerster's Blue'
      'Schneeriesen'   [K. Foerster]
    nivea Hooker f. 1844 = **Parahebe hookeriana**
S   **nummularia** Gouan 1773
N‡L **officinalis** Linnaeus 1753
      'Rosea'

orchidea Crantz 1769 = **V. spicata** ssp. **orchidea**
S **orientalis** Miller 1768
pectinata Linnaeus 1767
    'Rosea'   RD
perfoliata R. Brown 1810 = **Parahebe perfoliata**   RD
petraea Steven 1812
    'Mme Mercier'
pinnata Linnaeus 1767
    'Blue Eyes'
prostrata Linnaeus 1762 (*V. rupestris* hort.)   DGP-RD
    'Alba'   [K. Foerster]
    'Blue Ice'
    'Blue Sheen'
    'Loddon Blue'
    'Miss Willmott'
L   'Mrs Holt'
    'Nana'
    'Rosea'
    'Royal Blue'   RD
    'Silver Queen'
    'Spode Blue'   RD
    'Trehane'   [W. S. C. Pinwill]   DGP
                                               DGP-RD
pulvinaris (Hooker f.) Bentham & Hooker f. 1876 = **Pygmea pulvinaris**
N **repens** Clarion ex de Candolle 1805
rupestris hort. = **V. prostrata**
S **saturejoides** Visiani 1847   RD
saxatilis Scopoli 1771 = **V. fruticans**
schmidtiana Regel 1864
    'Nana'
    'Rosea'
selleri hort. = **V. wǒrmskjoldii**
N‡ **spicata** Linnaeus 1753   PGP-DGP-RD
    'Alba'   **RD**
    'Baccarole'   PGP-RD
    'Blaufuchs' ('Blue Fox')   [E. Benary]
    'Blue Fox' = **V. spicata 'Blaufuchs'**
    'Coerulea'
    ssp. **crassifolia** (Nyman) Hayek 1926 (*V. crassifolia*)
    'Erika'
    'Heidekind'
    ssp. **incana** (Linnaeus) Walters 1972 (*V. incana*)   PGP-**DGP**-RD
    ssp. **incana** 'Candidissima'
    ssp. **incana** 'Nana'
    ssp. **incana** 'Rosea'
L   ssp. **incana** 'Saraband'   DGP
    ssp. **incana** 'Silver Carpet'   PGP-DGP
L   ssp. **incana** 'Wendy'   PGP-RD
    'Minuet'   PGP
    ssp. **orchidea** (Crantz) Hayek 1913 (*V. orchidea*)
    'Pavane'
    'Pointed Finger'   RD
    'Red Fox' = **V. spicata 'Rotfuchs'**
    'Rotfuchs' ('Red Fox')   [E. Benary]
    'Romiley Purple'
    'Spitzentraum'   [VEB Bornim]   PGP
stelleri Pallas ex Link 1820 = **V. wormskjoldii**
subsessilis Furumi 1916 (*V. x hendersonii* hort.)
surculosa Boissier & Balansa 1856
telephiifolia Vahl 1805
teucrium Linnaeus 1753 = **V. austriaca** ssp. **teucrium**   CA

ssp. *dubia* (Chaix) Nyman = **V. austriaca** ssp. **vahlii**
S   **turrilliana** Stojanov & Stefaner 1923
virginica Linnaeus 1753 = **Veronicastrum virginicum**
***whitleyi**
wormskjoldii Roemer & Schultes 1817 (*V. stelleri*)

VERONICASTRUM Heister ex Fabricius 1759   *[Scrophulariaceae]*
virginicum (Linnaeus) Farwell 1917 (*Veronica virginica*)   **PGP-RD**
L   **'Album'**   RD
      'Roseum'

VESICARIA Adanson 1763   *[Brassicaceae (Cruciferae)]*
utriculata (Linnaeus) Lamarck 1805 = **Alyssoides utriculata**

VICIA Linnaeus 1753   *[Fabaceae (Leguminosae)]*
crocea (Desfontaines) Fritsch 1895 (*Lathyrus aurantius*)

VILLARSIA Ventenat 1803 nom. cons.   *[Menyanthaceae]*
crista-galli Hooker in 1837 = **Menyanthes crista-galli**
nymphoides Ventenat 1803 = **Nymphoides peltata**

VINCA Linnaeus 1753   *[Apocynaceae]*
L   **difformis** Pourret 1788   PGP-DGP
N   **major** Linnaeus 1753   **DGP**-RD
      'Elegantissima' = **V. major 'Variegata'**
      ssp. **hirsuta** (Boissier) Stearn 1932
      'Maculata' (*V. major* 'Reticulata')
      'Oxyloba'
      'Reticulata' = **V. major 'Maculata'**
L   **'Variegata'** ('Elegantissima')   **RD**
N‡   **minor** Linnaeus 1753   DGP-**RD**
      'Alba'   RD
      'Albo-variegata'
      'Argenteo-variegata'
L   **'Atropurpurea'**   RD
L   **'Aureo-variegata'**   RD
      'Aureo-variegata Alba'
      'Azurea Flore Pleno'   RD
      'Bowles' Variety' = **V. minor 'La Grave'**
      'Burgundy'   RD
      'Coerulea' nom. dub.
      'Coerulea Plena' = **V. minor 'Azurea Flore Pleno'**
      'Dartington Star'
      'Flore Pleno'
      'Gertrude Jekyll'
      'Grüner Teppich'   [Kayser & Siebert]
      'Halstenbek'
L   **'La Grave'** ('Bowles' Variety')   RD
      'Multiplex'   RD
      'Purpurea' = **V. minor 'Atropurpurea'**
      'Rubra' = **V. minor 'Atropurpurea'**
      'Variegata' = **V. minor 'Aureo-variegata'**
      'Violacea Plena' = **V. minor 'Azurea Flore Pleno'**

VIOLA Linnaeus 1753   *[Violaceae]*
alata hort. = **V. elatior**
albanica Halacsy 1900
arenaria de Candolle 1805 = **V. rupestris**
AN‡ **arvensis** Murray 1770
     athois W. Becker 1902

bertolonii Pio 1813 (*V. heterophylla* Bertoloni)
bertolonii Salisbury 1836 non Pio 1813 = **V. corsica**
betonicifolia Smith 1817
biflora Linnaeus 1753   CA-**RD**
blanda Willdenow 1806   CA
bosniaca Formanek 1887 = **V. elegantula**
bubanii Timbal-Lagrave 1882
calcarata Linnaeus 1753   CA
   'Alba'
   ssp. **zoysii** (Wulfen) Merxmüller 1967 (*V. zoysii*)
californica M. S. Baker 1953
N‡ **canina** Linnaeus 1753 non Walter 1788
canina Walter 1788 non Linnaeus 1753 = **V. walteri**
cenisia Linnaeus 1763   **CA**
HNL **cornuta** Linnaeus 1763   PGP-DGP-**RD**
   'Alba'   PGP-RD
   'Alba Minor'
   'Altona'
   'Amethyst'
   'Belmont Blue'
   'Belmont Blue Variegated'
   'Blaue Schönheit'
   'Blauwunder'
   'Blue Loveliness'
   'Boughton Blue'
   'Boughton Dome'
   'Boullion' = **V. cornuta 'Bullion'**
   'Bridal Morn'
   'Bullion'
   'Claes'
   'Caerulea'
   'Dr. Smart'
   'Germanica'
   'Grovemount Blue'
   'Gustav Wermig'
   'Hansa'
   'Hextable'
   'Ilona'
   'Laura'
   'Lilacina'   PGP
   'Lord Nelson'
   'Martin'   [J. Elliott]
   'Minor'   [J. Elliott]   RD
   'Minor-alba' = **P. cornuta 'Alba Minor'**
   'Moonlight'
   'Morso'
   'Norah Leigh'
   'Paganini'
   'Perle von Aalsmeer'
   'Primrose Dame'
   'Rosea'
   'Rubra'
   'Silver Cloud'
   'Velvet Beauty'
   'Victoria Cawthorne'
   'White Superior'
   'W. H. Woodgate'
corsica Nyman 1854 (*V. bertolonii* Salisbury)
crassa Makino 1905
cucullata Aiton 1789 = **V. obliqua**

delphinifolia Nuttall 1838 = **V. pedatifida**
doerfleri Degen 1897
elatior Fries 1828   PGP-RD
elegantula Schott 1857 non Greene 1899 (*V. bosniaca*)
eximia Formanek 1900
flettii Piper 1898   CA
glabella Nuttall 1838
gracilis Smith 1806   DGP-RD
    'Blue Carpet'
    'Lutea'
    'Major'   **DGP**-RD
    'Mauve Haze'
    'Midnight'
    'Roem van Aalsmeer'
hederacea Labillardiere 1805   CA
heterophylla Poiret 1808
heterophylla Bertoloni 1810 = **V. bertolonii** Pio
N‡ **hirta** Linnaeus 1753
hispida Lamarck 1778
jooi Janka 1857
jordanii Hanry 1853
koraiensis Nakai 1916
L **labradorica** Schrank 1818   RD
    'Purpurea' = **V. labradorica**
N‡ **lutea** Hudson 1762
    ssp. **elegans** W. Becker
    ssp. **sudetica** W. Becker
magellensis Porta & Rigo ex Strobl 1877
mandshurica W. Becker 1917
niger hort. = **V. tricolor ' E. A. Bowles'**
nuttallii Pursh 1814
    ssp. **praemorsa** (Douglas ex Lindley) Piper 1906 (*V. praemorsa*)
L **obliqua** Hill 1768 (*V. cucullata*)   RD
    'Alba'
    'Rosea'
HN‡L **odorata** Linnaeus 1753   **RD**
    'Admiral Avellan'
    'Alba'
    'Alassio' = **V. odorata 'Mrs. R. Barton'**
    'Aurea'
    'Baronne Alice de Rothschild'
    'Blue Bournemouth Gem'
    'Bournemouth Gem'
    'Brunear'
    'California'
    'Cendrillon'
    'Coeur d'Alsace'   RD
    'Czar'   RD
    'Elsie Coombs'
    'Governor Herrick'
    'Jean Arnot'
    'John Raddenbury'
    'Königin Charlotte' = **V. odorata 'Queen Charlotte'**
    'Lianne'
    'Lutea'
    'Luxonne'
    'Madame Armandine Pages'
    'Mrs. R. Barton' ('Alassio')
    'Nora Church'

        'Opera'
        'Perle Rose'
        'Princess Alexandra'
        'Princess de Galles' ('Princess of Wales')   RD
        'Purple Czar'
        'Queen Charlotte' ('Königin Charlotte')
        'Rawson's White'
        'Red Charm'
        'Red Queen'
        'Reine des Blanches'
        'Rosina'
        'Rubrifolia'
        'Russian Superb'
        'St Helena'
        'Sulphurea'   RD
        'Triumph'
        'Windward'
    orphanidis Boissier 1867
    palmata Linnaeus 1753
N‡ **palustris** Linnaeus 1753
    papilionacea Pursh 1814 = **V. sororia**
    pedata Linnaeus 1753   CA
        var. **bicolor** Pursh 1824
        var. **concolor** Brainerd 1921
    pedatifida D. Don 1831 (*V. delphinifolia*)   RD
    praemorsa Douglas ex Lindley 1829 = **V. nuttallii** ssp. **praemorsa**
    pubescens Aiton 1789
N‡ **reichenbachiana** Jordan ex Bor 1857 (*V. silvestris*)
        'Purpurea'
    rhodopeia W. Becker 1910
    rhodopeia hort. non W. Becker 1910 = **V. stojanowii**
N‡L **riviniana** Reichenbach 1823
        'Alba'
        'Autumn White'
    rotundifolia Michaux 1803
N‡ **rupestris** Schmidt 1791 (*V. arenaria*)
        'Rosea'
    selkirkii Pursh ex Goldie 1822
    septentrionalis Greene 1898   RD
        'Alba'
        'Rubra'
    sororia Willdenow 1809 (*V. papilionacea*)   RD
        'Albiflora' ('Immaculata')
        'Freckles'
        'Immaculata' = **V. sororia 'Albiflora'**
        'Priceana'   RD
    stojanowii W. Becker 1924 (*V. rhodopeia* hort.)
    suavis Marshall von Bieberstein 1819
    silvestris Lamarck 1778 nom. illegit. = **V. reichenbachiana**
HN‡L **tricolor** Linnaeus 1753   RD
        'E. A. Bowles' ('Bowles' Black')
        ssp. **macedonica** (Boissier & Heldreich) A. Schmidt 1907
    verecunda A. Gray 1858
        'Yakusimana'
    velutina Formanek 1892
    walteri House 1906 (*V. canina* Walter)
N   **x wittrockiana** Hort. ex Kappert 1932
    zoysii Wulfen 1790 = **V. calcarata** ssp. **zoysii**

HYBRID VIOLET CULTIVARS

'Achilles'
'Adams' Gold'
'Adelina'
'Admiration'   RD
'Agneta'
'Alma'
'Alys'
'Anna'
'Alanta'
'Alcea'
'Alice Woodall'
'Amelia'
'Annabelle'
'Anne Mott'
'Annette Ross'
'Ann Robb'
'Anthea'
'Aphrodite'
'Arabella'
'Ardross Gem'   **DGP**
'Arkwright's Ruby'   DGP
'Aspasia'
'Athena'
'Aurelia'
'Aurora'
'Azurella'
'Bambino'
'Barbara'
'Barbara Swan'
'Benjie'
'Beshlie'
'Beth'
'Bettina'
'Betty'
'Blue Butterfly'
'Blue Cloud'
'Blue Heaven'
'Blue Lace'
'Bonna Cawthorne'
'Bronwen'
'Bullion' = **V. cornuta 'Bullion'**
'Buxton Blue'
'Callia'
'Calypso'
'Campanula Blue'   DGP
'Caroline'
'Chandler's Glory'
'Chantryland'   **DGP**
'Charlotte Mott'
'Chelsea Girl'
'Cindy'
'Clementina'
'Cleo'
'Clodagh'
'Compte Brazzi' = **V. 'Swanley White'**
'Connie'   [J. Elliott]
'Cordelia'
'Cox's Moseley'

'Cream Sensation'
'Cyril Bell'
'Dartington'
'David Wheldon'
'Daisy Smith'
'Davina'
'Delia'
'Delmonden'
'Delphine'
'Demeter'
'Desmonda'
'Dobbies' Bronze'
'Dobbies' Red'
'Dominy'
'Duchess de Parme'
'Elizabeth'
'Emily Mott'
'Emma'
'Eris'
'Eros'
'Etain'
'Ethena'
'Evelyn Jackson'
'Fairy Tails'
'Felicity'
'Fiona'
'Florence'
'Foxbrook Cream'
'Gatina'
'Gazania'
'Gemma'
'Gladys Finlay'
'Glenroyd Fancy'
'Grey Owl'
'Haslemere' (V. 'Nellie Britton')   [N. Britton]
'Haze'
'Helen'
'Helena'
'Helen W Cochrane'
'Hespera'
'Hesperis'
'Honey'
'Horrie'
'Hugh Campbell'
'Huntercombe Purple'
'Hyperion'
'Iden Gem'
'Inverewe Beauty'
'Inverewe Mauve'
'Iona'
'Irina'
'Irish Molly'
'Iver Grove'
'Ivory Queen'
'Ivory White'
'Jackanapes'
'James Pilling'
'Jamie'
'Jane Askew'
'Jane Mott'

RD

A

'Janet'
'Janna'
'Jeannie'
'Jeannie Bellew'
'Jemma'
'Jenny Wren'
'Jersey Gem'
'Jesse East'
'Jimmie's Dark'
'Johnny-Jump-Up'
'John Yelmark'
'Juno'
'Jupiter'
'Katinka'
'Karen'
'Kathleen Hoyle'
'Kathleen Williams'
'Kilruna'
'King of the Blues'
'Kitty White'
'Kizzy'
'Lady Tennyson'
'Larissa'
'Laverna'
'Lavinia'
'Leda'
'Lee'
'Letitia'
'Liliana'
'Little Liz'
'Lizzie's Favourite'
'Lola'
'Lord Plunket'
'Lorna'
'Lorna Moakes'
'Louisa'
'Louise Gemmel'
'Luca'
'Ludy May'
'Lulu'
'Lydia'
'Madelaine'
'Maggie'
'Maggie Mott'
'Mandy Miller'
'Margaret'
'Marie Louise'
'Mark Talbot'
'Mars'
'Martin' = V. cornuta 'Martin'
'Mary Dawson'
'Mattie'
'Mauve Beauty'
'Mauve Radiance'
'May Roberts'
'Megumi'
'Mercury'
'Midnight Turk'
'Milkmaid'
'Mina Walker'

RD

'Minerva'
'Miss Brookes'
'Mistral'
'Molly Sanderson'
'Monica'
'Moonlight' = **V. cornuta 'Moonlight'**
'Moseley Ideal'
'Moseley Perfection'
'Mrs Alex Forrest'
'Mrs Chichester'
'Mrs Lancaster'
'Myfawny'
'Mylene'
'Mysie'
'Nadia'
'Natasha'
'Nell'
'Nellie Britton' = **V. 'Haslemere'**
'Neptune'
'Nina'
'Olive Edmonds'
'Oriana'
'Palmer's White'
'Pamela'
'Pandora'
'Pat Creasy'
'Patricia Brookes'
'Penny Black'
'Pickering Blue'
'Piper'
'Pixie'
'Priam'
'Primrose Cream'
'Primrose Dame'
'Prince Henry'
'Prince John'
'Ravenna'
'Rhoda'
'Richard Vivian'
'Richard's Yellow'
'Romilly'
'Rowena'
'Roxholm'
'Royal Picotee'
'Ruth Blackall'
'Ruth Elkins'
'Quink'
'Sammy Jo'
'Saughton Blue'
'Serena'
'Sheila'
'Sissinghurst'
'Sky Blue'
'Sophie'
'Steyning'
'Susie'
'Swanley White'
'Talitha'
'Thea'
'Thelma'

RD

'Thetis'
'Tina'
'Titania'
'Tom Tit'
'Toyland'
'Venetia'
'Vignette'
'Virginia'
'Virgo'
'Vita'
'Wheatley Violet'
'White Swan'   RD
'William Fife'
'William Wallace'
'Winifred Jones'
'Winifred Wargent'
'Woodlands Cream'
'Woodlands Gold'
'Woodlands Lilac'
'Woodlands White'
'Xantha'
'Yo-Yo'
'Zara'
'Ziglana'
'Zona'

VIOLETTA CULTIVARS

'Atalanta'
'Bianca'
'Boy Blue'
'Buttercup'
'Bryony'
'Calantha'
'Calliandra'
'Candida'
'Carina'
'Cassandra'
'Chlöe
'Colleen'
'Daena'
'Dawn'
'Dione'
'Dominy'
'Fabiola'
'Gazelle'
'Gina'
'Hebe'
'Iantha'
'Janine'
'Jenny'
'John Zanini'
'Kadishca'
'Kathy'
'Lamorna'
'Leora'
'Lerosa'
'Little David'
'Livia'
'Luna'

'Malvena'
'Marslands Yellow'
'Meena'
'Melinda'
'Myntha'
'Nerena'
'Nesta'
'Petra'
'Pippa'
'Princess Mab'
'Purity'
'Queen Disa'
'Rebecca'
'Remora'
'Sally'
'Samantha'
'Soula'
'Susannah'
'Thalia'
'Tullia'
'Velleda'
'White Gem'
'Winona'
'Yellow Gem'
'Zalea'
'Zöe'

VISCARIA Bernhardt 1800   [*Caryophyllaceae*]
   alpina (Linnaeus) G. Don f. 1831 = **Lychnis alpina**
   viscosa Ascherson 1859 = **Lychnis viscaria**

VITALIANA Bertoloni 1835   [*Primulaceae*]
   primuliflora Bertoloni 1835 (*Androsace vitaliana, Douglasia vitaliana*)   CA-DGP
      ssp. **cinerea** (Sündermann) I. K. Ferguson 1969
      *ssp. **gaudinii**
      ssp. **praetutiana** (Buser ex Sündermann) I. K. Ferguson 1969
      Silver Leaf Form
      *ssp. **tridentata**

WACHENDORFIA Burman 1757   [*Haemodoraceae*]
   paniculata Linnaeus 1758
   thyrsiflora Linnaeus 1758   PGP

WAHLENBERGIA Schrader 1814 nom. cons.   [*Campanulaceae*]
   albomarginata Hooker 1852
      'Blue Mist'
      'Harkness'
   cartilaginea Hooker 1864
   ceracea Lothian 1956
   consimilis Lothian 1947 (*W. stricta*)
   dinarica (A. Kerner) hort. = **Edraianthus dinaricus**
   gloriosa Lothian 1947
   gymnoclada Lothian 1947
   matthewsii Cockayne 1915   CA
   pumilio (Portensch) hort. = **Edraianthus pumilio**
   saxicola de Candolle 1830 (*W. tasmanica* hort.)   CA
   serpyllifolia (Visiani) hort. = **Edraianthus serpyllifolius**
   simpsonii J. A. Hay 1961
   stricta Sweet 1830 nom. illegit. = **W. consimilis**
   tasmanica hort. = **W. saxicola**
   trichogyna Stearn 1951

WALDHEIMIA Karelin & Kirilow 1842   [*Asteraceae (Compositae)*]
   tomentosa (Decaisne) Regel 1880 = **Allardia tomentosa**

WALDSTEINIA Willdenow 1799   [*Rosaceae*]
   geoides Willdenow 1799
   sibirica Trattinick 1823 = **W. ternata**
L   **ternata** (Stephan) Fritsch 1889 (*W. sibirica*)   **DGP**

WATSONIA Miller 1759 nom. cons.   [*Iridaceae*]
   albo-rosea hort. = **W. meriana 'Ardernei'**
   aletroides (Burman f.) Ker-Gawler 1801
   angusta Ker-Gawler 1804 = **W. fulgens**
   ardernei Sander 1899 = **W. meriana 'Ardernei'**
   beatricis Mathews & L. Bolus 1926   EGF.1-**PGP-DGP**
   fourcadei Mathews & L. Bolus 1925   EGF.1
   fulgens (Andrews) Persoon 1805 (*W. angusta*)   EGF.1
   marginata (Ecklon) Ker-Gawler 1802   EGF.1
   meriana (Linnaeus) Miller 1768   EGF.1
      'Ardernei' (*W. ardernei, W. albo-rosea* hort.)   EGF.1-PGP
      'Rosea'
   pyramidata (Andrews) Stapf 1932 (*W. rosea*)   EGF.1-DGP
   rosea Ker-Gawler 1804 = **W. pyramidata**
   'Stanford Scarlet'
   'Starspike'

WOODSIA R. Brown 1810   [*Woodsiaceae*]
N   **ilvensis** (Linnaeus) R. Brown 1815
   obtusa (Sprengel) Torrey 1840
   polystichoides D. C. Eaton 1858

WOODWARDIA Smith 1793   [*Blechnaceae*]
   radicans (Linnaeus) Smith 1793   EGF.1-PGP
   virginica (Linnaeus) Smith 1793   PGP

WULFENIA Jacquin 1781   [*Scrophulariaceae*]
   amherstiana Bentham 1835
   baldaccii Degen 1897   CA
   carinthiaca Jacquin 1781
   orientalis Boissier 1844   CA

XANTHOSOMA Schott 1832   [*Araceae*]
   nigrum (C. Vellozo) Mansfeld 1959 (*X. violaceum*)   EGF.2
   violaceum Schott ex Schott 1856 = **X. nigrum**

XERONEMA Brongniart & Gris 1864   [*Phormiaceae (Liliaceae)*]
   callistemon W. R. B. Oliver 1926

XEROPHYLLUM Michaux 1803   [*Melanthiaceae (Liliaceae)*]
   tenax (Pursh) Nuttall 1818   EGF.1-PGP

YUCCA Linnaeus 1753   [*Agavaceae*]
S   **aloifolia** Linnaeus 1753   EGF.1-RD
      'Marginata'
      'Purpurea'   RD
      'Variegata' = **Y. aloifolia 'Marginata'**
   angustifolia Pursh 1814 = **Y. glauca**
   angustifolia hort., non Pursh = **Y. filamentosa**
S   **arizonica** MacKelvey 1935   EGF.1
   australis (Engelmann) Trelease 1892 = **Y. filifera**
S   **baccata** Torrey 1859   EGF.1

S	**constricta** Buckley 1863 (*Y. louisiananensis*)	
S	**elata** Englemann 1882	EGF.1-PGP
S	**filamentosa** Linnaeus 1753	EGF.1-PGP-**DGP-RD**
	'Aureo-variegata'	
	'Bright Edge'	
	'Eisbär'	
	'Elegantissima' [L. Lindner]	PGP
	'Fontäne'	
	'Glockenriese' [K. Foerster]	
	'Golden Sword'	
	'Rosenglocke'	PGP
	'Schellenbaum' [K. Foerster]	
	'Schneefichte' [K. Foerster]	PGP
	'Schneetanne' [K. Foerster]	
	'Variegata'	PGP-RD
S	**filifera** Chabaud 1876 (*Y. australis*)	EGF.1
S	**flaccida** Haworth 1819	EGF.1-**PGP**-DGP-RD
	'Ivory' [Jackman]	PGP
S	**glauca** Nuttall 1813 (*Y. angustifolia*)	EGF.1-DGP
S	**gloriosa** Linnaeus 1753 (*Y. recurvifolia*)	EGF.1-PGP-DGP-**RD**
	'Variegata'	PGP
S	**harrimaniae** Trelease 1902 (*Y. neomexicana*)	
	louisiananensis Trelease 1902 = **Y. constricta**	
	neomexicana Wooton & Standley 1913 = **Y. harrimaniae**	
	parviflora Torrey 1859 = **Hesperaloe parviflora**	
S	**recurvifolia** Salisbury 1806	EGF.1-PGP-DGP-RD
S	**whipplei** Torrey 1859	EGF.1-PGP-DGP

	ZANTEDESCHIA Sprengel 1826 nom. cons.	[*Araceae*]
	aethiopica (Linnaeus) Sprengel 1826	EGF.2-PGP-**BB**-DGP-**RD**
	'Aztec Gold'	
	'Billy Langdon'	
	'Black Magic'	
L	'Crowborough'	**PGP-DGP-**RD
	'Dusky Pink'	
	'Golden Affair'	
	'Green Goddess' [via C. Morris]	PGP
	'Little Gem' [H. Elliott pre-1890]	PGP
	'Majestic Red'	
	'Peter's Pygmy'	
	'Perle von Stuttgart' [W. Pfitzer 1898]	PGP
	'White Sail'	PGP
	albo-maculata (Hooker) Baillon ex Engler 1883	
	angustiloba Engler 1883 (*Z. pentlandii*)	EGF.2-RD
	elliottiana (W. Watson) Engler 1915	EGF.2-PGP-**RD**
	pentlandii (R. Whyte ex W. Watson) Wittmack 1898 = **Z. angustiloba**	
	rehmannii Engler 1883	EGF.2-**RD**
	'Carminea' [van Tubergen 1915]	
	'Solfatare' (*Z. adlamii* x *Z. elliottiana*) [M. Leichtlin 1902]	

	ZAUSCHNERIA C. Presl 1841	[*Onagraceae*]
	arizonica Davidson 1902 = **Z. californica** ssp. **latifolia**	
L	**californica** C. Presl 1831 (*Z. mexicana*)	PGP-DGP-**RD**
	'Albiflora' Tralau 1958	
	'Benton End' = **Z. californica** 'Sir Cedric Morris'	
	'Dublin'	RD
	'Glasnevin' = **Z. californica** 'Dublin'	
	ssp. **latifolia** (Hooker) Keck 1940 (*Z. arizonica, Z. latifolia*)	RD
	ssp. **mexicana** (C. Presl) Raven 1962	
	var. *microphylla* A. Gray = **Z. cana**	

'Sir Cedric Morris' ('Benton End')
  var. **villosa** (Greene) Jepson 1925 (*Z. villosa*)
cana Greene 1887 (*Z. californica* var. *microphylla*)   PGP-**DGP**-RD
latifolia (Hooker) Greene 1887 = **Z. californica** ssp. **latifolia**
mexicana C. Presl 1841 = **Z. californica** ssp. **mexicana**
villosa Greene 1887 = **Z. californica** var. **villosa**

ZEPHYRANTHES Herbert 1821 nom. cons.   [*Amaryllidaceae*]
  candida (Lindley) Herbert 1826   EGF.1-**BB**-SB-**DGP**
  carinata (Sprengel) Herbert 1825 (*Z. grandiflora*)   EGF.1-DGP
  citrina Baker 1882   SB
  grandiflora Lindley 1825 = **Z. carinata**
  robusta (Herbert) Baker 1888 = **Habranthus robustus**
  rosea Lindley 1821   EGF.1
  texana Herbert 1836 = **Habranthus texanus**

ZIGADENUS Michaux 1803   [*Melanthiaceae (Liliaceae)*]
  elegans Pursh 1814   EGF.1-PGP
    ssp. **glaucus** (Nuttall) Hulten 1973 (*Z. glaucus*)   EGF.1-PGP
  fremontii (Torrey) S. Watson 1871   EGF.1-**BB**
    var. **minor** (Hooker & Arnott) Jepson 1923
  glaucus Nuttall 1834 = **Z. elegans** ssp. **glaucus**
  nuttallii S. Watson 1879   EGF.1

ZINGIBER Boehmer ex Adanson 1763 nom. cons.   [*Zingiberaceae*]
H   **officinale** (Willdenow) Roscoe 1807   EGF.2

ZIZANIA Linnaeus 1753   [*Poaceae (Gramineae)*]
A   **aquatica** Linnaeus 1753
  caducifolia Nakai 1952 = **Z. latifolia**
  latifolia (Grisebach) Turczaninow ex Stapf 1909 (*Z. caducifolia*)